America's Religions

America's Religions
Traditions and Cultures

PETER W. WILLIAMS

University of Illinois Press

Urbana and Chicago

For Jeremy Adams
teacher extraordinary
firm friend

Illini Books edition, 1998
© 1990, 1998 by Peter W. Williams
Manufactured in the United States of America
P 5 4 3 2 1

This book is printed on acid-free paper.

Library of Congress Cataloging-in-Publication Data

Williams, Peter W.
America's religions : traditions and cultures / Peter W. Williams.
p.   cm.
Originally published: New York : Macmillan ; London : Collier
Macmillan, c1990.
Includes bibliographical references and index.
ISBN 0-252-06697-9 (pbk. : alk. paper)
1. United States—Religion.
I. Title.
[BL2525.W485   1995]
200'.973—dc21

A Note on the 1998 Paperback Edition

This is an interim version of the 1990 edition originally published by Macmillan. The text is identical to the earlier edition except for the bibliography, which has been substantially updated and expanded to include much new scholarship. A thoroughly revised and expanded edition of the entire text is in progress and should be available to greet the millennial year of 2000. My thanks to Liz Dulany and her editorial colleagues at the University of Illinois Press for making these new editions available to future generations of students of the ever-changing but always fascinating world of American religion.

—P.W.W.

Preface

The past is never complete. Each generation must rewrite the story of how its own present emerged out of the lengthening stretch of years and events that preceded it. This necessity holds as true for the history of religion as it does for any other history. In 1970, few would have guessed that an upsurge of evangelical Protestantism would not only swell the ranks of the Southern Baptists and other conservative denominations, but also have profound consequences for American society and politics as well. Similarly, Vatican II and its revolutionary consequences could hardly have been anticipated by the most acute observers of the religious scene in 1950, when Catholic-Protestant tensions still ran high. The gift of prophecy is granted to very few; the task of retrospective interpretation, however, is an ongoing challenge that must be addressed on a regular basis to see, paradoxically, how the past—or at least our own assessment of the past—continues to change with the present.

The recent and often startling events in the American religious scene have also been accompanied by a proliferation of scholarship bringing more and more of America's religious past into focus—often through new interpretive points of view. Directly or obliquely, the notion that the United States is a genuinely pluralistic society has emerged as a fundamental assumption as scholars from a growing variety of ethnic and religious backgrounds have uncovered the neglected stories of the Native American, African-American, Roman Catholic, and evangelical Protestant communities. In doing so, they have not only rejected the normative character of Protestantism as an interpretive starting point, but have also brought new approaches such as those of cultural anthropology, oral and social history, the history of religions, and material culture studies to illuminate religious traditions that have not manifested themselves primarily through written verbal evidence.

America's Religions: Traditions and Cultures seeks to tell the story of the religious experience of the people of the United States in a unified way while also taking into account our growing awareness of the genuinely plural character of our cultural, social, and religious heritage. Key to its character are the assumptions that religion does not exist in a compartment by itself and that it cannot be reduced to social, economic, or other sorts of phenomena that are supposedly more central to human life. Without making judgments as to the ultimate validity of particular religious claims, I have tried to take religion seriously as a vital part of American culture. America's religions, while existing in continual interaction with other dimensions of that culture, nevertheless possess an irreducible identity and integrity of their own.

The book begins with an extensive survey of the roots of those aspects of Western religious life which have been particularly formative of the American experience. Since many Americans today do not automatically acquire a deep knowledge of Hebrew and Christian scripture or of the histories of the various traditions based on them, I have tried to explain succinctly the essentials of Judaism and the principal branches of historic Christianity—Eastern Orthodox, Roman Catholic, and the several branches of the Reformation—as they have emerged over the centuries in the Mediterranean basin and in Europe. I have also tried to introduce non-Western religious traditions—Native American, Afro-American, and, to a lesser degree, Asian—into the story as well in order to take seriously the genuine pluralism of the American experience.

The largest part of this work is a chronological survey of the development of religion in the United States, from colonial beginnings to the present day. In telling this story, I have tried to adhere as closely as possible to individual religious traditions as the point of focus, as they have developed together in the context of one another and the broader American culture. Their collective stories overlap considerably as each group has come to terms with the common American experiences of cultural pluralism, independence, war, slavery, the frontier, urbanization, and the like. The theme of Americanization—by no means a simple one—is a major emphasis of this book, and the internal dynamics that have often profoundly changed many religious traditions in America receive considerable emphasis. On the other hand, these stories, though sharing many similarities, are by no means interchangeable. Each religious tradition, whether originating in prehistory, in the Old World, or in the modern United States itself, possesses an irreducible uniqueness which I have tried to convey.

This uniqueness expresses itself in part in the core of phenomena central to any religion: symbols, myths (or historical narratives with the same function), and rituals, together with the intellectual and social structures needed to give them coherence and continued existence. Religions, however, do not live in voids, but are maintained by specific groups of people. Whether ethnically homogeneous or socially mixed, the people who constitute a particular religious community interact with that tradition's heritage to generate a distinctive religious culture, which exists in the matrix of the broader American society and its subcommunities.

A major emphasis of *America's Religions* is the description and analysis of the varied religious cultures that have existed in America's past and present. Such cultural experience has been the theme of much American popular expression in recent years: nostalgic reminiscences of Jewish life on Manhattan's Lower East Side; bittersweet reflections on ethnic Catholic childhoods; recollections of the role of song and preaching in sustaining the spirits of southern blacks through innumerable adversities; and Black Elk's memoirs of Little Big Horn and the Wounded Knee massacre. Perhaps, before long, Fundamentalists, Mormons, and Muslims will be creating similar accounts of their own collective pasts. Whatever their popular expression, though, all of these communities have experienced common lives in America in which religion has played a significant role in sustaining their identities and helping them through troubles while distancing them from other American subcommunities. Religion has, in short, helped to shape and sustain many distinctive cultures, or subcultures, within the broader American society. "Culture," of course, is a protean word and can point to any number of dimensions of collective social experience. Most broadly, it denotes the patterns of thought, feeling, and action guiding people through their everyday lives. Religion has helped shape such patterns in many ways, ranging from overall stresses on law or liberty to the regulation of diet, hair, and clothing styles and other mundane realities. Culture also includes the expressive dimensions of human life, from the learned treatises of Puritan divines to the gospel music of urban black choirs which helped lay the musicological bases for the "Motown sound." I have tried to take into account this whole range of reference in delineating America's varied religious cultures in this volume as they have evolved in time and space.

America's Religions is designed to accommodate a variety of approaches to the teaching of religion in America, either as a course's central text or as a supplement to other works. For those who choose to emphasize the historical development in America, the first and final units can be omitted or used as recommended supplements. For those who prefer—as I do—to deal with each tradition in its entirety from its beginnings and beliefs through its current manifestations, the chapters can be rearranged topically with little violence; the Topical Guide to Chapters following the Contents indicates which chapters form such logical sequences. For those emphasizing particular periods or topics, various sections can be used selectively—for example, Part IV for courses in history or American studies on Victorian American culture. The bibliography is also arranged topically, largely following individual traditions and clusters of traditions, and includes a wide variety of materials, including some recordings, indicative of the focus of this work on religious traditions and cultures. It is keyed especially to the *Encyclopedia of the American Religious Experience*, which includes lengthier topical articles and further bibliographical suggestions.

Finally, a word on this book's origins: Its contents and approaches have emerged from some twenty years of teaching this subject matter, primarily at Miami University, but at several other institutions—Albertus Magnus, Bowdoin, Stanford, and Yale—in earlier years as well. Much of its contents began as detailed lecture outlines. I began several years ago to duplicate and distribute these for my students to spare them the bother of having to scribble down all the information I was conveying so that they could concentrate more on the core ideas in each lecture. This book's genesis, then, is in the actual *praxis* of pedagogy. Its sequences of materials and ideas grew out of years of experimenting with what worked—and what didn't—in a classroom of bright but not always well-prepared undergraduates, most of them taking the course for distribution credit toward general education requirements. The first section especially grew out of this experimentation. After all my historical explanations, students would come back and say plaintively, "But I still don't know what Baptists believe." (Or ask, more problematically, "Do Jews believe in the Virgin Mary?") For me, the main questions teachers have to ask themselves continuously are "What have I presupposed? Is it too much?" The answer to the latter is almost always "Yes." The mission of this book is to convey the fruit of that continual questioning and provide the information that is too often presupposed so that these basics can then be built upon creatively in the classroom.

In putting together a work of this scope, acknowledgments of those whose work I have drawn upon in the process are potentially endless. I trust that textual references and bibliographical citations *passim* indicate sufficiently my debt to the company of scholars whose labors have made this attempt at a provisional synthesis possible. Especially worthy of note is the diverse group I had the pleasure of working with while helping edit the *Encyclopedia of the American Religious Experience,* whose essays have been extremely useful in the task of writing this text. More particularly, though, I am delighted to acknowledge the more immediate circle of friends, acquaintances, and colleagues who have reviewed portions of the manuscript or made themselves available as "resource persons" on particular traditions.

First, a number of colleagues at Miami University in Oxford, Ohio, deserve mention: Newell S. Booth, Jr.; Mary Kupiec Cayton; Curtis W. Ellison; Harold O. Forshey; Elliott J. Gorn; Jack Temple Kirby; Carl Jantzen; Alan L. Miller; Roy Bowen Ward; Ann and Robert Wicks; and Greg Anderson, a graduate student. Second, a number of parish clergy and campus ministers in the Oxford area have lent their expertise: Dr. Michael Beatty, St. Mary's Catholic Church; Fred Cook, Faith Lutheran Church; William Duffy, United Campus Ministry; John Nicholas Gill, Holy Trinity Episcopal Church; Dr. Robert Goldy, Arthur Beerman Center Hillel Foundation; R. John Harris, now of Miami Shores (Florida) Presbyterian Church; and Prudence Zimmerman, Oxford Presbyterian Church.

Beyond the vicinity of Oxford, several academics in other areas of religious studies have provided valuable information on their own traditions: Harry Baker Adams, Chaplain, Yale University; David L. Bartlett, Union Theological Seminary (Richmond); and Abraham Malherbe, Yale Divinity School. The Reverends William Hobbs of Spring Glen Church (UCC), Hamden, Connecticut, and Leonard R. Klein, Trinity Lutheran Church, York, Pennsylvania have been most obliging with their time as well.

Finally, numerous colleagues in the field of American religious history and what the American Academy of Religion now aptly calls "North American Religions" have provided a great deal of assistance: Randall Balmer, Columbia University; James D. Bratt, Calvin College; John Corrigan, University of Virginia; John H. Erickson, St. Vladimir's Orthodox Theological Seminary; Eldon G. Ernst, Graduate Theological Union; David L. Holmes, College of William and Mary; Charles H. Lippy, Clemson University; Christa R. Klein, the Lilly Foundation; Albert J. Raboteau, Princeton University; Leonard Sweet, United Theological Seminary; Grant Wacker, University of North Carolina at Chapel Hill; Charles I. Wallace, Jr., Willamette University; Mary Jo Weaver, Indiana University; and John F. Wilson, Princeton University. Of these worthies, Professors Bratt and Wacker deserve special note for having waded through nearly the entire manuscript in its final versions. In addition, Martin E. Marty, John F. Wilson, and the late Sydney E. Ahlstrom all richly deserve thanks for their unfailing aid and encouragement over the years. Needless to say, I bear final responsibility for errors of fact and judgment that may have escaped the collective scrutiny this work has received, and hope that readers who detect such mistakes or misjudgments will let me know for the sake of possible future editions.

The College Division at Macmillan, especially Jennifer Crewe and Helen McInnis, have also been instrumental in this work's conception and execution. Kathleen Marie Grondin and her office staff at the Miami Department of Religion relentlessly churned out typescript for many days over the past several years. The inspiration and college term bills generated by my stepchildren, Dana (Bowdoin '92) and Jonathan (Miami '91) Schneider, have been powerful incentives for the expeditious completion of this work. My mother, Harriet Williams, proved herself a dedicated and effective reader of proof. Finally, there has always been my wife Ruth Ann, without whom. . . .

Peter W. Williams

Contents

PART IV

The End of the Frontier and the Rise of the City   227

PART V

The Twentieth Century: Further Encounters with Modernity and Pluralism   321

Topical Guide to Chapters

America's Religions follows the organizational scheme outlined in the preface, which is a modified chronological approach. For those wishing to organize courses or reading in other ways, this book can be utilized more topically as well, with little violence done to the narrative flow. The following indicates which chapters deal with the principal religious traditions covered here. Chapters in parentheses are relevant as background to the tradition indicated, but can be safely omitted.

Native American Religions (American Indians) 1, 21, 39

Afro-American Religions (Black) 2, 27, 35, 40, 49

Judaism 3, 4, 20, 38, 45, 46

Eastern Christianity (Eastern Orthodoxy) 5, 37

Roman Catholicism 6, 7, 20, 36, 47, 48

Lutheranism (The Evangelical Church) 8, 26, 42, 43

Anglicanism (The Episcopal Church) 9, 12, (23–25), 26, (31), 32, 33, (42), 43

The Reformed Tradition (Calvinism, Puritanism, Congregationalism, Presbyterianism, Dutch & German Reformed Churches) 10, 13, 14, 17, (18, 22), 23–25, 31, 32, (34), 35, 42–44

The Free Church Tradition (Anabaptism, Baptists) 11, 17, 19, (22), 23–25, 27, 31, 32, 34, 35, (42), 43, 44

The Peace Churches (Amish, Brethren, Mennonites, Friends/Quakers) 11, 15, 19

Methodism (The Wesleyan Tradition) 16, 17, 23–25, 27, 31, 32, (34), 35, 42, 43

Liberalism (Unitarian-Universalism) 18, (22), 28, 32, 51

Restorationism (Churches of Christ, Disciples of Christ) (23–25), 29, 34, 35, 42–44

America's Religions

PART I

The Traditions

A. Oral Traditions

INTRODUCTION

According to conservative estimates by archaeologists, writing on tablets dates back to roughly the middle of the fourth millennium B.C. (3300–3500), while the earliest alphabets used in the Ancient Near East appeared less than four thousand years ago. The use of writing to record religious lore became important in the Western world quite early in the human experience, but even the Hebrew Bible (Old Testament) began as a collection of oral traditions. For centuries after scripture began to be codified in written form, the vast majority of people even in the West were unable to read, and its preservation and interpretation were entrusted to a small elite of rabbis and priests. It was not until the Reformation era that literacy began to spread widely, abetted by the invention of printing with movable type. The radical notion that all people should be able to read and write did not gain great currency until the settlement of North America by English-speaking Protestants in the seventeenth century.

In the areas of the world that remained isolated from the forces of modernization, oral culture predominated until recent times. This was very much the case among Native American, African, and Afro-American cultures until at least the nineteenth century. The transmission of religious traditions through memory and word of mouth, often in astounding quantity and complexity, has certain features that differentiate it from the written lore to which most Americans are accustomed. Changes and borrowings occur frequently but with little notice, so that the process in oral culture is more fluid and more protean than that which takes place with a set of fixed sacred texts. The role of the few "religious specialists"—priests, shamans, and medicine men—who constitute a people's collective memory also takes on a very special character. It is they who determine what is to be remembered and what discarded.

This is not to say that oral traditions have disappeared in our own day. Folk preachers, both black and white, continue to cultivate their art, which is ostensibly based on written scripture but often takes on a life of its own. Radio and television have opened up entirely new avenues for oral religious expression. Some very ancient motifs of traditional religion, such as healing and the warding off of evil, manifest themselves throughout the spectrum of traditional, folk, and popular cultures. The texture of the religious life of a people who have lived for centuries without contact with the technology and values of modernity, though, differs substantially from the world of Jimmy Swaggart and Oral Roberts. In order to evoke this texture, the first two chapters of this survey of the American religious experience begin by exploring the religious cultures of the aboriginal inhabitants of North America and Africa. This can be done only in a very general way, given both the multiplicity and complexity of these traditions. Also, as soon as these traditions entered the consciousness of Europeans and Euro-Americans, they immediately began to change through the inevitable and often forced cultural contacts that also began immediately. In later chapters, the metamorphoses of these traditions—as they encountered, embraced, adapted, or resisted the Christianity of Euro-America—will unfold in all their own complexity.

CHAPTER 1

The Varieties of Native American Religious Life

Focusing on the American Indian, or Native American, peoples to begin a survey of the religions of what is now the United States has a number of advantages. First, it helps to overcome a historic blindness induced by preoccupation with America's European cultural heritage, to the detriment of religious impulses that do not fit readily into Euro-American categories. Second, it raises a number of issues about the basic character of religion that are not as readily apparent in the exclusive study of the traditions of the modern West. Third, it obeys strictly the logic of history—a "chrono-logic"—in beginning at the beginning, with the aboriginal inhabitants of a very old continent. Fourth, it opens up an array of highly diverse yet in some ways curiously similar religious experience and expression that are easily written off by most contemporary Americans as exotically "other" or that become so romantically idealized that they bear little resemblance to reality.

The notions of "Americanness" and "Indianness" in themselves have always been problematic. The American "Indians," of course, were not what Columbus thought them to be—that is, residents of Southern Asia. On the other hand, as Sam Gill has pointed out, the term *Indios* in Columbus's day referred generically to any of the inhabitants of the part of the world that lay east of the Indus River. Since the ancestors of the American Indians most probably originated in Siberia and crossed what was then a land bridge across the Bering Strait to Alaska at some remote time in prehistory, Columbus may have not been so far off in his identifying these "new" people as Asians. The notion of "America," as distinct from the sought-after Asia, came hard and slowly to the cognitively bewildered European newcomers. The subsequent development of the "United States" out of a contiguous collection of European colonies and areas inhabited by aboriginal peoples was also a process that took time and required active feats of imagination to rationalize. Two recent works of scholarship, Edmundo O'Gorman's *The Invention of America* and Garry Wills's *Inventing America,* indicate in their convergent titles the intellectual difficulties involved in making sense first out of an entire hemisphere and, much later, of the new political creation of a group of transplanted English colonists wanting to become an independent nation.

Although the idea of "America" today carries with it features and values of a modernized, technologically sophisticated society very remote from the life of the continent's aboriginal peoples, there exist some intriguing arguments for these people having been archetypically American. In the first place, like all subsequent inhabitants of North America, the Indians were immigrants. As we have already noted, their ancestors most probably arrived from Siberia, in pursuit of big game. Second, like later immigrants and more settled Americans as well, they were a mobile people, ultimately fanning out from the Bering Strait through two continents, all the way south to Tierra del Fuego. For some, mobility was more or less continuous as they adopted nomadic patterns in pursuit of game. Others, such as the agriculturists of the south, became more settled but never escaped from the periodic need to readjust to new circumstances often engendered by intercultural encounters or changes in the natural environment. Third, as Americans of today are proud to claim about themselves, these Native Americans were an infinitely adaptable people. Even though they lacked sophisticated technology, they adjusted their life patterns to environmental conditions ranging from the arctic to the tropical, and learned to extract a living from the most varied of circumstances. The ultimate encounter with Europeans was no exception: The animals and firearms of the Spanish were rapidly adopted by the Plains Indians, for example, and the latter's myths began to incorporate the previously unknown horse as an archetypal symbol.

Finally, like Americans of later times, the earliest Americans were extraordinarily varied in the cultures they developed. Just as the diet, language, religions, and other components of the American culture of our own day have been enriched from the endless comingling of almost infinitely varied national stocks living together, so did the aboriginal peoples continually diversify, lend, and borrow in response to changing circumstances. This diversity was maintained over the years through the lack of continual interaction made possible by today's means of cultural homogenization—widespread literacy, mass media, and centralized educational and political institutions.

Native American cultures were by no means static. Ecological changes or social dynamics continually prompted these peoples to migrate and come into contact with others, whether peaceably or otherwise, and cultural borrowing and assimilation were ongoing factors in the evolution of Native American culture. The Aztec civilization that Cortés and his followers beheld on their arrival in Mexico was an imperial creation, and many peoples had been forced by the powerful Aztecs to submit to a yoke that was not always very welcome. Myth and ritual changed their contents to embrace new circumstances, a process that continued through the fusions of Indian and Christian themes of the Peyote Cult starting in the late nineteenth century.

Because of this remarkable cultural and religious diversity stretched over both space and time, it is difficult to be both general *and* meaningful in discussing Native American religions: One runs the risks of generating either a series of abstractions in need of endless qualification and counterexamples, or else an equally endless chain of anecdotes and descriptions having little to do with one another. Still, there are some ways of approaching the topic that illuminate the general patterns of Native American religious expression and its underlying characteristics, especially insofar as it differs significantly from the characteristics of religion in the modernized society to which most of us have become accustomed.

First, there are a number of ways of perceiving the world that are characteristic of traditional cultures in general and Native American peoples in particular. Religion itself, for example, is a concept for which most such cultures lack specific words. In our own society, religious activity tends to become compartmentalized and relegated to a specific time and place—for instance, Sunday morning at church. In traditional cultures the religious or symbolic life of a people is instead frequently integrated into the fabric of daily activity, so that any act connected with what the culture identifies as significant takes on a religious meaning. For premodern cultures especially, the production or acquisition of food is of central importance—in contrast with our own society, in which only a small percentage of the population is directly engaged in agricultural work. Therefore, killing an animal or harvesting the year's supply of maize is not just a routine, "secular" event but rather one surrounded with ritual or ceremony developed as a constant reminder of the cosmic significance of the particular act. Perhaps saying grace before meals, now largely abandoned in homes where parents and children keep wildly different schedules and communicate through notes on the refrigerator door, is an example of the way in which such practices linger and eventually dissolve in the solvent of modernity.

Another aspect of Native American religious life that differentiates it from our own experience is its relationship to the social order. In the pluralistic America of today, religion is seen both generally and by law as a matter of individual choice among any number of conceivable alternatives. In fact, our choice may be constrained by our own situation in society more than may be readily apparent, but the theoretical range of options remains open. In traditional societies, however, the religious life of a people is coextensive with the people itself and seldom extends beyond a coherent social group. For example, a Navajo would be as unlikely to adopt the religion of the Apache as to begin speaking the Apache language, even though cross-fertilizations may occur among religions or languages.

A system of religious practices therefore develops within the context of the experience of a particular people, remains confined among that people, and is virtually the only option open to any of the members of the people, although change is always possible through commonly accepted visionary experience. This relationship of religion to society is reflected in tribal naming, where the word a people use to describe themselves frequently means "the people" or "human beings." For an individual group, its own experience of the world is normative and exclusive, and is regarded as universal only in the sense that the religions of other peoples are irrelevant to its own situation. Other peoples, as well as their religions, are basically not "really real." Society, culture, religion, and cosmos are coincident, and together constitute the sum of reality for a particular people as long as they manage to cohere as a self-sufficient group.

Two other basic cultural categories that have direct implications for religion are the ways in which a given people perceive and experience time and space. For contemporary Americans, both time and space are usually experienced as linear, divisible, and subject to precise measurement and manipulation. The theory of relativity may have modified these notions at a high level of scientific abstraction, but the logic of modern life dictates otherwise in our everyday round. Clocks and watches are everywhere, on our walls and desks and wrists. Complex organizations such as businesses, hospitals, and universities depend on a precise synchronization of activity, and woe be to those who are habitually late. Space is similarly compartmentalized: Parking spaces, apartments, house lots, and offices all represent the division and privatization of the space in which we daily live and work.

Among traditional peoples, however, time and space are generally experienced in other ways. Verb tenses in Native American languages frequently lack the clear-cut distinction of past, present, and future that characterize the linear interpretation of time implicit in English and other Indo-European tongues. In the modern West, time progresses in a straight line, from an origin through the present into a future that will be distinct, and hopefully better, than what has preceded it. Implicit in this schematization of time is the notion of progress, which reached its apogee in the optimism of the Victorian era when technology and democracy promised to bring about a secular millennium of peace and prosperity here on earth.

This sense of time is by no means universal, and in fact is quite recent in the course of human history. Far more typical of the world's peoples is an experience of time as an endless repetition of the same events, with humans striving eternally to emulate the patterns handed down by the gods or other superhuman beings in the mythical time of beginnings. Left to themselves, humans tend to muddy the proverbial waters and are in need at regular intervals of returning to this "strong time" of origins—*illud tempus,* in Mircea Eliade's phrase—in order to bring the course of the world back into line with the original divinely given paradigms for human action. Instead of inevitable progress, regress is the normal course of things, and must be regularly compensated for if life is to continue.

Similarly, space in the sense of clearly delineated land belonging to a particular person is alien to the sensibilities of most traditional peoples. For nomadic hunting peoples especially, the notion of fixed space as in any way significant is virtually nonsensical. Land is provided in the order of things for human habitation and use, but it can be said to "belong" to an individual or groups only insofar as they are actually inhabiting or otherwise utilizing it. On the other hand, almost all peoples engage in making certain aspects of space symbolically significant, thus creating *order,* or *cosmos,* out of what is otherwise undifferentiated *chaos* unfit for human habitation. For the Navajo, for example, the world (in the sense of cosmos) is delineated by four sacred mountains at its corners. Whether these are actual, physical mountains is of secondary importance. What is ultimately important, rather, is the sense of orientation, of living in a space that is organized spiritually for human existence.

In some cases, actual topographic features, especially mountains, take on this orienting function. For the Dakota Sioux of the Great Plains, nomadic hunters in the nineteenth century, the renowned Sun Dance ceremony could be performed anywhere. The coming together of scattered people for the ceremony was a symbolic affirmation of their unity, which was not always visually apparent. In the Sun Dance, as in the rituals of many other peoples, a tree was set into the ground to constitute a pole representing the center of the cosmos—an *axis mundi,* or world axis, in the phrase of Eliade. This center was none the less real because its location was arbitrary—in the Indian world view, it was *more* real than any naturally rooted tree since its ultimate reality was bestowed by the ceremonies performed around it.

Just as Native Americans' experience of time and space was significantly different from that of members of modernized societies, so was their interpretation of and relationship with the complex of forces and entities we call nature. Just as modernized peoples distinguish sharply among past, present, and future, so do we experience nature as being sharply different from ourselves. Human beings hold a special place in the universe, a distinctiveness supported by the early chapters of Genesis. Domestic animals occupy an intermediate role, but the rest of nature, the realm of plant and animal life, is frequently perceived as so different from our own realm that it is subject to dominance and manipulation for our own purposes with impunity.

It is interesting that one of the ways in which the traditional cosmos of the Native American peoples has reentered our own world views has been through the ecological crisis that was first perceived by Rachel Carson and other environmentalists in the 1960s. Although much sentimentalization and distortion of American Indian modes of perception has occurred in the process, the essential insight that has been recently appropriated by many contemporary Americans is valid—namely, the idea that the American Indians regarded humans as one among a number of animate forces in the world that had to live in harmony with one another if life was to continue in a tolerable fashion.

For example, a hunter propitiating a bear before killing it illustrates this relationship. The Indians were not vegetarians who shuddered at the idea of taking life. Rather, they recognized the claims of all life to a place in the cosmos and the proper respect that different life forms owed one another in the divine ecology. The logic of that ecology dictated that humans were to use bears as a source of nutrition, but that did not reduce the bear to the status of an object of sport or casual violence. Human and bear each had a proper role to play in the cosmic round, but the significance of that round had to be repeatedly and carefully reasserted each time an act of potential disruptiveness was anticipated.

The same sense of participating in a cosmos in which all beings formed an interrelated continuum also shaped Native American conceptions of the supernatural realm. In the Christian world view, God and humanity are radically distinct from one another, even though the latter may have been made in the image of the former. Calvinistic Protestantism, which helped to shape the modern world-picture even more than other varieties of Christianity, carried this contrast to an extreme, and insisted that the Divine Word was the only possible point of contact between the two realms.

For American Indians, however, the monotheism characteristic of the principal Western religions—Judaism, Christianity, and Islam—is simply absent. In some cases a particularly powerful creator god may be ultimately responsible for the world's coming into existence, but such a god usually then takes on the characteristics of what Eliade calls a *deus otiosus*—an "otiose" or inactive god who takes little interest in the subsequent fate of that creation. More usually, Native American creation stories, which vary greatly in their precise content, are narratives of the activities of different kinds of supernatural beings who help humanity emerge from nothingness or some primordial condition of existence into the mundane world. For both the Navajo and the Zuni, for example, the original inhabitants of the world emerged from underground. In other versions, the Earth Diver—a diving bird or animal—brought soil up from beneath the primordial water that had covered the world and set in motion the process of creation. This latter motif, incidentally, was widespread among peoples of Eastern Asia, the probable ancestral home of the natives of the New World.

Many other sorts of supernatural beings inhabit the Native American cosmos. In the Seneca creation account, which is shared by many other peoples as well, a good twin brother brings a perfect world into being, after which his bad twin proceeds to foul it up. Supernatural forces in animal or bird form, as in the case of Earth Diver, also can play roles in world creation. Another sort of figure related to the Seneca creator-twins is generically known as the Culture

Hero. This being plays a role in many myths, such as those of the Algonkians, as the source of human life-patterns. The Culture Hero is not really a god, but nevertheless lives in a realm of mythic beginnings rather than in the here-and-now of the everyday world.

Still another widely known *theriomorph*—a human-like character in the form of an animal—is the Trickster, who frequently appears as a raccoon, coyote, or other proverbially mischievous creature. Many stories chronicle Trickster's exploits in playing jokes on other characters and frequently, in the end, on himself. A number of these have to do with sexual adventures, often of the most grotesque sort, or with excrement, illustrating the fact that the Native American religious outlook can accommodate many things that the Westerner of average piety would view with shock or at least extreme distress.

The typical Native American spiritual world, then, is highly pluralistic. Humans do not possess the powers of divine beings, but can avail themselves of this power, and avoid its ill effects, through maintaining a proper relationship with all aspects of the cosmos in which this power inheres. Again, our example of the bear and bear-killer is pertinent: The bear itself is not necessarily divine, but one's interaction with the bear can be the occasion in which supernatural power is unleashed for better or worse. Such power may also inhere in certain natural features such as mountains, but only those that for some reason are singled out as specially significant for a particular people or individual.

The most specifically religious dimension of Native American life consists of the means employed by native people to align themselves with benevolent supernatural power and to avoid or rid themselves of harmful forces. Here, again, there are not sharp dichotomies between good and evil as in most Western religious systems. As illustrated in the story of the twin brothers who bring humanity into being, power for good or evil is situational; the power itself seems to be undifferentiated in its essence, and can be put by different personalities to different purposes. The general Native American attitude toward the dead similarly illustrates this theme. In the first place, there is no sharp differentiation between the existence led by the living and that of the dead; the two realms of existence are more in continuity than disjunction, and their relationship is not seen as particularly problematic. Few cults of the dead, such as are common among traditional African peoples, existed in North America. Second, Christian missionaries were often frustrated in trying to persuade their Indian audience that it needed to be afraid of punishment in the world to come for sins committed in this life. Such ideas were simply unintelligible to them: The notions of radical sin meriting radical punishment and that punishment being visited on the dead were utterly alien to their patterns of thought.

The principal means of assuring harmony between humans and the spiritual powers of the universe lay in retelling myths in the context of the performance of ritual. As Eliade repeatedly points out, "myth" in this sense lacks the connotation of falsity that it has taken on in ordinary discourse. A myth in the context of Native American religion should rather be understood as a story told to explain the way in which the cosmos and its various significant components came into being. The beginning of the book of Genesis is a good example of a creation myth: "In the beginning God created the heavens and the earth." Whether and how this statement may be literally, historically true is still the subject of heated controversy among American Christians today. We can define it as "myth" not on the basis of such criteria but rather because of what it does—that is, it explains how the cosmos came into being. We have already referred to several Native American creation myths, of which the variety is almost inexhaustible. What all have in common, regardless of their particulars, is the emergence of cosmos—purposeful order—out of chaos.

A myth is basically a story, an example of the fondness for narrative form typical of societies in which the transmission of culture takes place orally rather than in writing. Such a story, however, does not exist in isolation to be enjoyed simply for its literary and aesthetic qualities. Rather, it becomes operative in the context of ritual, usually with the accompaniment of music and dance. Even here, the complex of activity is not simply a "multimedia" event, but is aimed at bringing the participants into effective contact with the spiritual world. What we have, in short, is worship or liturgy, the end of which is to establish—or, more properly reestablish—an efficacious relationship between two realms of being.

The content and function of myth and ritual can best be understood in the context of "the eternal return" we discussed earlier—the return from the limitations of earthly life and time to the "strong time," *illud tempus*. The idea of worship is not simply to recall fondly the way things were in the beginning, but to restore the pattern of everyday life to harmony with the cosmic patterns revealed to humanity in the beginning, *in illo tempore*. Such an attitude is by no means confined to oral cultures. For example, the Jewish *seder* meal at Passover or the Christian celebration of the Eucharist are both rituals that aim at a return to a time or event that established a basic pattern for the proper relationship between the human and the divine. Before anything more specific can be accomplished, the general pattern of harmony between the two spheres, which does not last forever but must be renewed at periodic intervals, has to be reestablished.

The performance of myth and ritual is not always connected with the achievement of specific goals, but that benefits of some kind will ultimately result is a safe assumption. At the deepest level of significance, they might be viewed as an integral part of a common quest for "ontological security"—a sense that life has ultimate meaning and purpose, that the transient lives of humans are anchored in a deeper, more enduring reality. Since an individual's sense of reality is profoundly rooted in participation in the collective life of a people, the reenactment of the beginnings of the world also has the function of reaffirming that sense of peoplehood—of existing not simply as isolated individuals but as a social unit. This becomes particularly important for nomadic peoples, such as the Sioux of the Plains, whose renowned Sun Dance was the occasion for their reassembling as a group and reasserting their collective sense of community.

Specific rituals might also be performed at crucial times in the life of a people, such as the onset of a war or a hunt. Among agricultural peoples, such as the Creeks' Green Corn ceremony, a festival celebrating the first fruits of the annual maize planting was held near midsummer, with the earliest ears of corn being offered in thanksgiving for this indication that another year's sustenance was in prospect. Presumably, some of the ceremony's significance was a collective desire to ensure the continuation of the earth's bounty in years to come. Whatever role such intentions may have played, however, the broader context of the ceremony was that of an annual rite of collective and cosmic renewal. A *bosquito*, or "busk," was an integral part of the ceremony, which extended for several days, in which both individuals and houses were purified of the real and symbolic "dirt" that had accumulated over the previous year. (Thoreau praised this practice in *Walden* as an admirable means of simplifying one's life.) Old fires were extinguished and a new one kindled, offenses were forgiven, and the new crops could be eaten after extended fasting. The levels of parallel symbolic activity should be evident: At once the individual, the society, the village, nature, and by extension the entire cosmos were joining in a round of purification and renewal.

Ritual played an important role at crucial stages in the life of the individual as well as in society as a whole. Emergence into adulthood, often at the onset of puberty, was the most frequent occasion for the observation of these "rites of passage." Young women usually went through a ritual involving temporary isolation at the onset of menstruation. The vision quest for males in the hunting cultures of the North, such as the Massachuset of New England or the Ojibwa of the Great Lakes, tended to be more dramatic. A boy would be conditioned over the years to expect to undertake the quest for a uniquely personal vision, putting him into contact with the supernatural world and thereby authenticating his entry into the adult world. After appropriate ritual preparation, a vision might be achieved after days spent in the wilderness with no food or water; in the case of the Sun Dance, intense pain brought about through suspension on ropes fastened to needles inserted in the dancer's flesh induced a trance state conducive to visionary experience. In some societies narcotic drugs or tobacco-smoking were utilized to help induce an appropriately altered state of consciousness as well.

As for other critical stages of life, births were not usually celebrated in public, although the mother and child might later be presented to the group in a ceremony. Most peoples did not seem to have elaborate ceremonies focusing on marriage, except for puberty rites that prepared young people to be eligible for matrimony. At the termination of life, funeral customs vary considerably, although many Northern peoples practiced burial on elevated platforms. In the case of the Hurons, this was a temporary resting place; every fifteen years, the remains would be collected and interred in a great Feast of the Dead, after which the entire village would change its location.

Other problematic aspects of life requiring ritual mediation were illness and witchcraft, the first sometimes resulting from the practice of the second. It is interesting to note that, although native peoples lacked the sophisticated medical technology of today, many aspects of their approach to the issue of healing are finding increasing favor in an age when *holistic* medicine—dealing with all aspects of a person and not simply physical condition—is becoming a watchword. Again, Indians did not draw the sharp distinctions among body, mind, and spirit that have been characteristic of the modern western world-picture. Rather, disease was the result of a lack of harmony between the afflicted individual and broader spiritual forces. This disharmony might be induced by natural causes, in which case treatment with herbal medicines might be efficacious. However, illness might also be the result of taboo violation, contact with ghosts, witchcraft, or "soul loss," so that a supernatural remedy must be invoked to reestablish proper harmony between the sufferer and the cosmos.

The close relationship between curing and the supernatural is indicated in the fact that what we might call religious specialists or "professionals" in Native American cultures have the remedy of disease as one of their primary functions. In settled agricultural tribes, such as the Pueblo, this function may be institutionalized in the form of one of voluntary societies of men concerned with the crucial affairs of the people. Even where the "medicine man" operates as an individual rather than a member of a group of religious specialists, he derives his power more from the possession of traditional ritual lore thought to be efficacious in bringing about cures than from any special personal gifts. Disease is often thought to result from the presence in the body of a foreign object that has entered through supernatural means, such as witchcraft. In such a situation the medicine man brings about a cure through sucking it out and displaying the object—often a feather—to the afflicted person. To the skeptical Westerner, this may appear as a sort of sleight-of-hand, which it probably is in a literal sense. From the native point of view, however, the point is that the source of affliction has been localized in something tangible, and the literal origins of the offending object are not particularly interesting or relevant.

Another sort of religious specialist found more frequently in Northern, hunting cultures is the *shaman*, a name derived from the particularly intense version of this practitioner originally found in Siberia. The shaman is characterized not so much by the possession of traditional knowledge as by his (or sometimes her) personal ability to engage in trance-voyages in the supernatural realm. Such individuals are often psychologically marginal—perhaps even border line psychotic, in modern parlance—but are valued by their fellows as rarely gifted individuals with direct access to other realms of being. Those with such abilities are valued much in the broader religious realm as bringing the visions that are the ultimate source of myth and ritual, and more specifically as being possessed of healing powers. For someone who has "lost his soul"—one possible cause of disease—recovery is possible only if the shaman undertakes a journey into the supernatural realm to recover and restore it.

The roles of shaman and medicine man were by no means mutually exclusive, and the combination of factors giving them authority varied from people to people. Similarly, shamans may not be at all the only people with access to visions. Among the Massachusets, for example, the shaman, or "powwow," was recognized as having supernatural authority only as long as he could continue to "produce" accounts of communication with the spirit world, interpret dreams, and cure illnesses. His powers were different from those of others not so much in kind but in degree, and private visions could be obtained by many people in appropriate circumstances. The status of "powwow," then, had to be continually reaffirmed, and such a person had continually to reassert his claim to power if he was to retain respect in a highly individualistic society.

As we have seen, witchcraft was regarded by many peoples as an important cause of illness, and the power of shamans or medicine men was frequently exercised to counteract its effects. Witchcraft, or the intentional use of spiritual power by an individual to do harm to others, is by no means confined to Amerind societies; its emergence in Salem in 1692 and as a part of much Afro-American lore in the antebellum South indicates European and African antecedents as well. Among the Navajo especially, belief in witchcraft is pervasive, and has given rise to a complex lore distinguishing among different sorts of witchcraft and prescribing means of avoiding its effects or curing them once they have been worked. Even among contemporary Navajo who have become thoroughly assimilated into Euro-American culture, such beliefs still surface at times of stress especially, and witchcraft accusations and occasional killings have taken place well into the twentieth century. Among some peoples, medicine men or shamans who had a suspiciously low rate of success in saving people from various afflictions might well be accused of witchcraft themselves, since the power manipulated by healers and sorcerers was essentially the same. Although witchcraft beliefs are common in many cultures, a particular preoccupation with witchcraft often indicates that a community is undergoing severe stress and change, and that someone must be found to blame for it and thereby reverse the ill effects.

In this survey of what we might broadly identify as "religious life" among the native peoples of North America, we have already come across instances of the effects of cultural change, particularly that induced by contacts with Euro-American society. As this contact became widespread and it became apparent that the old ways could not be continued indefinitely, Native peoples reacted in a number of ways. A substantial number simply died, killed by the epidemic diseases introduced by Europeans, against which they had no immunity. Others converted to Christianity, a response especially common when a traditional culture was faced with nearly total collapse in the face of white incursions. Finally, a number of "pan-Indian" movements, usually incorporating distinct religious dimensions, began to emerge during the late eighteenth century. Some of these, such as the Ghost Dance, ultimately failed, while others, such as the Peyote religion, endure to the present. These stories will be taken up in later chapters.

CHAPTER 2

The African Background of New World Religions

In many ways, the traditional religions of Africa were similar to those of the aboriginal peoples of North America. In both cases, knowledge and lore were transmitted orally rather than in written form. Religious and mythological systems varied considerably from region to region and people to people, although a number of themes were common to most. Supernatural beings were plural rather than singular, as in monotheistic religions, and the line between this world and the supernatural was not sharply drawn. Religion was not identifiable with an organizational structure and a statement of beliefs in propositional forms, but rather with the myths and rituals that were periodically retold and enacted in the course of a people's common life. These are all characteristics of other traditional peoples' religious experience as well, and such similarities should come as no great surprise.

Similar also are the changes that arose in both cases through the shock of cultural contacts, often unsought and unwelcome, between these traditional peoples and the aggressive newcomers from Europe who sought to extend their hegemony overseas. Both the overtures of Christian missionaries and the responses of native peoples resulted in adaptation and innovation within the old frameworks. What distinguished the Afro-American experience from the Native American was not the shock of Euro-American imperialism or the emergence of new religious forms, or even the widespread suffering and death that resulted from these hostile contacts. Rather, the most significant differences resulted directly from the way in which the African peoples came to the New World. This migration took place not through free choice, as had been the case with most other immigrant groups, but rather through a forcible, involuntary massive population movement in the context of the slave trade and the institution of slavery. This context dominated Afro-American life until the American Civil War, and its consequences have been inescapable to the present day.

A further distinction can be made in the two hemispheres of the Americas as to patterns of black settlement and subsequent life. Slavery itself was an institution that had pervaded colonial society—English, French, Portuguese, and Spanish—from Maryland through the West Indies and deep into South America, and that had reached even as far north as New England for a time. Its character varied considerably over these two continents. The tendency of the British was to plant permanent colonies of settlers in the New World, while the

Iberians regarded their vast lands more as arenas from which valuable goods could be extracted to enrich those who had remained at home in Europe. All of the colonizing powers agreed that Africans were not the human equivalent of Europeans, and therefore could be enslaved with impunity. Although the work of Bartolomé de las Casas on behalf of the aboriginal peoples of the Americas may have had some marginal effect in alleviating the condition of the Africans, these people consistently were regarded as the lowest estate of humanity, and thus susceptible to the greatest forms of exploitation.

In South America and the West Indies, African slaves vastly outnumbered the European population, and were also less likely to be systematically separated from their fellow tribespeople than was the case in what would become the United States. Conditions were thus far more propitious in Ibero-America and the Caribbean for the continuation of the traditional cultures of Africa, especially those of the western Guinea coast from Gambia to the Congo, the source of the largest percentage of the possibly twelve million slaves who reached New World shores alive. Although the living and working conditions of those few who had survived the arduous, forcible crossing of the Atlantic from Africa to the New World—the "Middle Passage"—were oppressive, the bitterness of these people was partially offset by the possibility of keeping alive the old ways, including religion. The Catholic Church's missionaries attempted to spread the Christian Gospel among the slaves, but their numbers were too few and many of the plantations were too isolated to make a great deal of difference.

As was the case with many Native Americans, who in North America were occasionally enslaved but without lasting success, the more usual response of traditional peoples to new and powerful cultural forces was not a rigid maintenance of the old but a blending of old and new. The religions of west Africa varied in detail, but generally involved belief in a creator god, or *deus otiosus*, who was not actively involved in the subsequent course of earthly affairs. More relevant to everyday matters were a host of lesser divinities who were immanent within the natural realm and who served as the tutelary deities of local villages and other social units. These supernatural beings reflected the most important concerns of a particular people, and priests conducted sacrifices on altars to propitiate these beings and ensure that life continued smoothly. The priests could also acquire considerable political power and reputation.

Just as these divinities represented practical concerns in the midst of everyday life, so were the ancestors of a particular people regarded as continuing as relevant presences in the here and now. They served as guardians of their descendants' laws and customs, and could play an intermediary role between humans and supernatural beings. Consequently, burial rites were of considerable importance, and it was incumbent on the living to make sure that the dead were content. Further, just as divinities could enter into the bodies of their devotees and manifest themselves in spirit-trances, so did the ancestors continue to live on in their progeny. A firm division, in short, did not exist between the natural and the supernatural, or the living and the dead. These different realms of being instead coexisted in an ongoing mutual interaction, so that human well-being was intimately involved in a broader, ecological pattern of relationships.

This active, pluralistic cosmos was brought to New World shores by the African emigrants, where it came into active contact with the Roman Catholicism of the French, Spanish, and Portuguese masters. For the most part, the Africans regarded this new faith not as something completely alien, to be accepted or rejected as a whole, but rather as a source for creative borrowings and adaptations. Where the radical monotheism of North American Protestantism was uncongenial, the panoply of ceremonies and saints that Catholicism offered presented numerous correspondences, at least on the surface, with the rituals and divinities of African practice. The result was the development of a variety of *syncretistic* cults—that is, incorporating elements from more than one religion—blending elements of African and Catholic practice into new wholes. These included Candomblé in Brazil, Shango in Trinidad, Obeah in Jamaica, and, most familiar in the United States, Haitian *Vodun* and Cuban *Santería*.

Vodun is the syncretistic cult (i.e., pattern of worship) that emerged in French colonial Haiti and that has subsequently coexisted with Catholicism as the dominant religion of that nation to the present day. Its career in Haiti, where it had been an illicit folk religion for most of its existence, took on a sinister turn in the twentieth century when it was utilized by President "Papa Doc" Duvalier as an instrument of political terror. Vodun came to North America early with Haitian blacks who began to arrive in Louisiana, also a center of French creole (i.e., colonial) culture, after the Haitian revolution around 1800. In New Orleans, where it became known as *Voodoo*, it flourished during slavery days especially under two priestesses, mother and daughter, both named Marie Laveau, and focused on the cult of a snake god known as "Li Grand Zombi"—a practice probably derived ultimately from Dahomey in Africa. During its heyday, New Orleans voodoo was an organized system, characterized by practices of African origins such as ritual dancing, trance possessions, and sacrifices. However, as its influence spread beyond into the rural South, it began to lose coherence and disintegrated into a collection of magical practices known as "hoodoo" or "rootwork," best regarded less as religion than as folklore. (*Magic* is usually distinguished from *religion* in that the former is aimed at immediate, specific, this-worldly results attained through the manipulation of occult forces, without regard to any larger metaphysical or moral system.)

More recently, the influx of Cuban refugees in the Miami and New York metropolitan areas brought with them another Afro-Caribbean cult known as *Santería*—the "way of the saints." Santería is derived from the traditional religion of the Yoruba, the dominant African people in Cuba, who continue to live in and around present-day Nigeria. The religion of the Yoruba and its transformation into Afro-American Santería is exemplary of traditional African religion and both its Old and New World metamorphoses.

The first important thing to note about the Yoruba and their religion is that neither people nor religion is uniform or unchanging. The Yoruba, who today are estimated to number anywhere from five to ten million, are divided into a number of groups that maintain independent traditions of religion and culture. They are united, however, by a common language and an agreement on the centrality of the sacred city of Ife—the Yoruba's *axis mundi*, or center of the cosmos, and the continuing locus of religious power. According to Benjamin Ray, their creation myth reflects the conquest during the fifteenth century of the Ibo, who had been the first to live in the vicinity of Ife.

Whatever its special political and historical purposes, this creation myth is typical of those of many African peoples. Its first character is Olorun, the "owner of the sky," who is the Yoruba's "high god." (The meaning of his older name, Olodumare, is not as clear. Newell Booth suggests that the clarity of "Olorun" may indicate the more recent influence of monotheistic Christianity and Islam in the area.) He is also associated with the cosmic serpent, manifested in the rainbow. Olorun resides in the sky (*Orun*) as a *deus otiosus*, an ultimate source of power who has little direct relation to life in the other half of the cosmos—that is, the earth (*Aiye*). Humans living in the latter realm can relate directly not to Olorun himself, but rather with *oris[h]as*—which can be loosely translated as "gods" or "divinities"—and human ancestors now residing in *Orun*.

Since Yoruba religious practice is not highly centralized, there is no definitive creation account, but rather a number of variants on a theme. In one typical version, Orishanla (a.k.a. Obatala), the first-created and principal orisha, was charged by Olodumare with creating the world from some earth and a five-toed chicken, who set to work spreading the earth about. In the version of the story told at Ife, Orishanla became drunk on palm wine before finishing the job, which was completed by his brother Oduduwa. Upon awaking, Orishanla got into a fight with his brother, which may echo the long-past struggle between the Yoruba and the Ibo. The result was the victory of Oduduwa, who established the divine kingship of Ife, and thus legitimated the ongoing rule of the Yoruba. Orishanla, however, was not vanquished, but given the task of creating the first humans. His presence is manifested especially in dwarfs and others of abnormal shape, who are regarded as sacred beings and reminders of Orishanla's power.

Many other gods—who are not always clearly differentiated from one another, and whose identities may overlap—also make up the Yoruba pantheon, and are associated with particular locales, peoples, and aspects of nature. Ogun, for instance, is associated with metals and war, and is invoked in situations where these phenomena are involved. Ogun is supposed to have been an early king of Ife. When the earliest humans, newly created by the gods, did not respect him, he went off to kill himself. A similar story is associated in some traditions with Shango, the god of thunder and lightning. Shango was a bad king who was so hated by his subjects that he hanged himself. When he heard someone say that he had done so, though, he became angry and destroyed the tale-bearer with lightning. As a result, he has always been known as "the king who did not hang himself."

Ogun is particularly interesting in his dual role as god and human. Now a god, he began on earth as a human, and thus is also identified as a dead ancestor residing in the world beyond. As such, he is one of many intermediaries between the realms of *Orun* and *Aiye*. Ancestors are particularly important for the Yoruba in this mediating function. Not all the dead are regarded as "ancestors" in the strong sense; those who have led an unworthy life are relegated to a hot and dry land of broken potsherds. The good, however, ascend to the "good heaven" of Olorun and the orishas, and are venerated by their descendants. Some remain important simply for their families, while others—the "deified ancestors"—have shrines maintained for them by whole towns. Gods and ancestors alike are regarded as important conduits of supernatural power.

A final aspect of Yoruba belief and practice that deserves mention is their attitude toward individual destiny. All people are made up of a physical and a spiritual component. Before birth, they choose a destiny, which is identified with an ancestor but is forgotten upon birth. This destiny is somewhat malleable for better or worse, but cannot be affected without a recovered knowledge of its character. This knowledge can be acquired only through the activity of a diviner (*babalawo*). The babalawao establishes contact with the supernatural world through a process involving the transfer of palm nuts rapidly from hand to hand and the working out of a set of traditional parables that correspond to the results of this process. These parables point to specific advice about one's destiny and life-course, and are accompanied by sacrifices.

These traditional practices are still very much alive among the Yoruba, though their character is continuously subject to change along both geographical and temporal lines. The importation of Christianity and Islam to West Africa has affected the nature of the traditional religion, and has also resulted in the emergence of new, syncretistic religions. As Joseph Murphy has demonstrated, this adaptability is clearly illustrated in the religious life of the Yoruba after their forcible transplantation to the New World. In Cuba, where Roman Catholicism was officially established and traditional religions outlawed, the Yoruba adapted their ancestral practices to the symbolism of the Catholic pantheon of saints, who became identified with various orishas. Santería shrines thus ostensibly honor Catholic saints, but in their deeper meaning actually are dedicated to Yoruba orishas. Saint Barbara, for example, is depicted in Western iconography as mounted on horseback; in Santería, she becomes equated with Shango, who is similarly represented in Yoruba tradition. In contemporary America, Santería is usually practiced in the home, where shrines are assembled consisting of Catholic devotional objects, such as saints' statues and pictures, combined with traditional African elements, such as stones consecrated by priests or priestesses in ceremonies involving blood from animal sacrifices.

The *botánicas,* or religious goods stores, that are familiar features in Caribbean neighborhoods in America's large cities are exotic reminders that the African heritage is very much alive and well in America today. Their appeal, however, is not so much to blacks with deep roots in America as to more recent immigrants from the West Indies whose ancestors were better able to preserve over the decades a direct line of continuity with their African origins. The story of the emergence of Afro-American religion in the United States is much more closely involved with Christianity, but in a subtle and often controversial way that only recently has begun to be systematically explored.

B. The Mediterranean Matrix

INTRODUCTION

The origins of the religions and cultures we call "Western" lie in the eastern reaches of the Mediterranean basin, and date back at least four millennia. The roots of the culture that has flourished in Europe and North America and by the late twentieth century had extended its reach around the entire globe are complex. Most of its languages are of the Indo-European family, which most likely originated in the Indian subcontinent. Much of the Western heritage of thought, education, law, and politics can be traced to ancient Greece and Rome, which successively dominated their environs for many centuries.

The religions of classical antiquity, however, survive mainly in the names of gods and goddesses now affixed to intercontinental missiles. The religious tradition that now dominates the West and is well represented throughout the rest of the world had its origins among a Semitic people who only briefly enjoyed a rather limited political dominance in part of the Middle East, and were soon conquered and scattered. Their sacred writings—the Hebrew Bible, or Old Testament—had their origin in oral traditions, and incorporated preliterate and even "Oriental" elements as they expanded and were gradually codified. Their bearers, who became known as the Jewish people, eventually dispersed throughout the world, and never greatly expanded their numbers. Their very survival as a people over the centuries has been radically problematic, and constitutes one of the most gripping stories of the twentieth as well as earlier centuries.

It was only through the spread of a messianic movement that had originated among the Jews of the later Roman Empire that this Hebrew tradition became the basis of a powerful and aggressive world religion. After the first Christians accepted the premise that their converts did not first have to become Jews, the way became clear for universal evangelization. In the twilight of imperial Rome, a persecuted Jewish sect with apocalyptic expectations eventually became the official religion of the entirety of Europe, and still later of Europe's overseas empires. Even as both Judaism and Christianity began to lose ground to secularism, it became obligatory in public pronouncements to invoke the (somewhat nebulous) "Judaeo-Christian tradition" as the groundwork of our society and culture.

For all of these transformations, there is no doubt that the religion of the large majority of Americans has some sort of historical connection with the religious heritage of the Mediterranean basin that took shape between two and four millennia ago. To understand Judaism and Christianity, then, we have to survey those origins, and see how three distinct traditions—the Jewish, and the Eastern and Western Christian—arose in a political and social context that was hardly favorable to their growth, but in which, despite all odds, they eventually flourished and dominated.

1. JUDAISM AND THE EMERGENCE OF HISTORICAL RELIGION

Chapter 3

The Jewish Tradition

Even more than most religions, Judaism is intended to be *lived* rather than simply believed or accepted. Certainly most religions teach that their precepts must be translated into everyday practice rather than remain at the level of nominal belief. The Jewish tradition, however, has more explicitly than most maintained that to be a good Jew is not primarily to *believe* the correct ideas, but to *do* the correct things. Such deeds are known as *mitzvoth* (MITZ-vahs), or, in the singular, *mitzvah* (MITZ-vah).* A mitzvah is literally a divine commandment or, more broadly, a good deed or work performed for God's glory. In Jewish tradition, there are 613 specific mitzvoth, 365 of which are negative and the remaining 248 positive injunctions relating to ritual observance and also to just and proper relations among people. Even among Jews who do not regard such detailed tradition as binding, the notion of mitzvah as a general obligation to live justly in the world is still powerful.

Judaism has thus always emphasized *orthopraxis*—correct action or living—

* Spellings and pronunciations of Hebrew words in transliteration vary somewhat.

over *orthodoxy*—correct belief—and has never been given to drawing up creeds containing specific propositions about God that have to be accepted by believers. On the other hand, as in most modern religions, there is a cluster of symbols, rituals, texts, and roles that forms the core around which the varieties of Jewish practice have unfolded themselves. The traditional triad of foci has been *God, Torah,* and *Israel.*

The relationship of the Jewish people with their God is summarized in the central prayer of their tradition, the *Shema* (sh'MAH) (Deuteronomy 6:4–7):

> Hear, O Israel: The Lord our God, the Lord is One!—And thou shalt love the Lord thy God with all thy heart, and with all thy soul, and with all thy might. And these words, which I command thee this day, shall be upon thy heart, and thou shalt teach them diligently unto thy children, and thou shalt talk of them when thou sittest in thy house, and when thou walkest by the way, and when thou liest down, and when thou risest up. And thou shalt bind them for a sign upon thy hand, and they shall be for frontlets between thine eyes. And thou shalt write them upon the door-posts of thy house and thy gates.

In addition to mandating certain practices of worship, the *Shema* conveys a vivid sense of the God of the people of Israel—one God, who enters into a personal, covenantal relationship with his chosen people and in return demands their undivided allegiance. Although the nature of God has subsequently been debated and questioned by Jewish thinkers, the centrality to historic Judaism of the notion of a single, personal god is clear.

The second term in the central triad is *Torah*—the Pentateuch, or first five books of the Hebrew scripture traditionally attributed to Moses. These five books are regarded as the holiest part of scripture, and are kept in scroll form in the Ark of the Covenant at the heart of the synagogue. *Torah* may also refer in an extended sense to the remainder of Hebrew scripture—or, even more broadly, to the "sacred wisdom" of the tradition.

In addition to Torah and the rest of scripture, Jewish tradition is based on a related collection of lore known as the *Talmud* (or simply *Talmud.*) The Talmud is the collective body of interpretations of scripture that developed as a central part of Jewish life since the fifth century B.C. It is sometimes called "oral Torah," following the tradition that it was delivered by God in oral form to Moses at the same time that he received the written Torah. The Talmud is lengthy and complex, and consists of *Mishnah*—a collection of ritual laws—and *Gemara*—records of rabbinical discussions of Mishnah. Basically, it represents the application of deductive logic to scripture in order to develop an ethic—*[H]aggadah*—and a code of law—*Halakah*—for the guidance of the Jewish people. During the ages when Jewish communities were semiautonomous, the Talmud formed the legal system and body of precedents on which their governance was based. Rabbis functioned in such contexts as governors and judges, and continued to apply Talmudic principles and precedents to everyday situations. Even though a *Beth Din,* or rabbinic court, is unusual among assimilated American Jews, such judgments are still preferred by some traditionalists to those of the civil courts. Still another body of extrabiblical lore is *Midrash,* numerous collections of rabbinical interpretations of or sermons based on scripture.

The third member of this triad is *Israel,* the name of both a holy land and its holy people. Although the physical relationship of the Jewish people to the land of Israel has been problematic over the centuries, the restoration of independence in recent years has revived Israel as a powerful emotional, religious, and political symbol for American Jews regardless of their specific theological propensities. Similarly, the Holocaust forcibly reminded Jews throughout the world of their collective identity and relationship as a people, despite periodic efforts to reinterpret that identity in more universalistic religious terms—that is, by stressing the commonality of Judaism with other religions rather than its uniqueness.

Although all Jews are traditionally expected to participate actively in religious observance, a number of specialized religious roles have emerged over the centuries. After the temple disappeared as the focus of Jewish worship, the role of the priest, who conducted cultic sacrifices therein, became obsolete. In place of the priest emerged the *rabbi,* or "teacher," who has persisted to the present as the Jewish religious leader in diaspora. Traditionally, the rabbi—a title and function dating back to the sixth century B.C.—served as a scholar of Torah and Talmud who could apply that knowledge practically to the needs of the Jewish community. In the American context, however, where no rabbis even existed until the 1840s, and where the model of the Protestant minister has been widely influential, the role of the rabbi has changed significantly. For example, many American rabbis now preach regularly—a function unknown in earlier years in Europe—as well as counseling, administering, and performing the myriad organizational tasks familiar to most American clergy. In addition, women are now ordained by the Conservative, Reform, and Reconstructionist branches of American Judaism in what is certainly a distinctive departure from tradition.

Among many traditional Jews even today, one of the primary functions of the rabbi is the supervision of the laws of *kashrut,* or dietary code derived from the book of Leviticus. The original motivations for this code have been the subject of considerable speculation, but over the centuries its maintenance has emerged as a primary sign of holiness of life for the observant Jew. The operative everyday word here is *kosher,* which means ritually clean and fit to eat. (In its broader contemporary sense, it is used informally by Jews and gentiles alike to mean "okay" or legitimate.) The following are some of its more important features:

1. Pork and shellfish, together with a long list of foods from animals seldom encountered today, are *trayf,* that is, not fit to eat. *Trayf* animals are those whose features do not conform to certain criteria—for example, mammals should both chew their cud and have cloven hoofs, and fish should possess both scales and fins.
2. Meat and milk products are not to be mixed. A kosher kitchen will have two sets of dishes, one for milk and one for meat. Even an accidental mixing

renders such dishes unclean, so that they have to be either ritually purified or destroyed.
3. Even animals such as cattle that are potentially fit to eat must be slaughtered in a kosher manner, so that the blood is drained from the brain immediately. A *shochet*, or special functionary trained in the laws of kashrut, must perform such butchering under rabbinic supervision.

Keeping kosher is one of the most visible ways in which traditional Jews manifest their piety. From a secular viewpoint, kosher food has the virtue of being free of many controversial chemical additives widely used today, and is also obtained through a humane method of slaughtering animals.

Another traditional Jewish role is that of *chazzen*, or cantor. Prior to the advent of the first rabbis in America in the 1840s, congregations employed *chazzonim* to lead them in prayer. Although the voices of the *Chazzonim* were their leading feature, many other aspects of synagogue life also devolved upon them in earlier days in the absence of a rabbi.*

Although worship for Jews is manifested in private prayers, in study, and in the round of daily life, it is also carried out, as with most organized religions, at specific times and places in public. The physical setting for public worship bears several names:

• *Shul*—"school" or "house of study"—is a traditional Yiddish term.
• *Synagogue* is probably most familiar, originally signifying the congregation meeting in diaspora for worship, and later coming to mean primarily the building used for worship.
• *Temple,* which no longer exists in its ancient sense as a place for conducting sacrifices, was revived by Reform Jews as a synonym for synagogue, with the implication that the temple of old was permanently superseded by this new institution.

Since Jewish life in diaspora has been conducted in so many different host cultures, no authoritative styles of synagogue design have ever emerged, and American synagogues have undergone a variety of phases of architectural development. Synagogue arrangements always include an Ark of the Covenant for the Torah scrolls and one or more *bemas,* or reading platforms. In traditional synagogues, women are sequestered from and invisible to men; in more contemporary arrangements, families usually sit together in pews. Although God may not be represented in pictorial form, other religious themes are frequently depicted in synagogue art.

For public prayer to be valid, Jewish tradition dictates that a *minyan,* or group of ten adult male Jews, be present. (A rabbi, however, is not essential.)

---

* *Chazzen* is one of a number of Yiddish words beginning with the "ch" sound that is articulated as a strong guttural emerging from deep in the throat. It is also used in German, but not in English. In many cases, such as "Hasidism" or "Hanukkah," the initial "c" is often dropped in transliteration.

Daily and Sabbath prayer are conducted according to a fixed ritual in one of several versions of the *Siddur* or prayer book—an English version for Reform, Hebrew for most others. The sequence of prayer varies at different times of the day—morning, afternoon, and evening—and may include praises of and petitions to God, readings from the Torah, and the recitation of the Shema. As an adjunct to public worship, traditionally inclined men wear a *yarmulke* (YOM-muk-kah), or skullcap; a *tallit*, or tasselled prayer shawl; and *tefillin*, or phylacteries, which are leather containers, attached to the left arm and head by leather straps, in which scrolls with scripture verses are kept. A similar practice on the domestic side is the affixing of *mezuzahs*, or prayer scrolls, to the doorposts of Jewish homes.

The core of Jewish worship, however, is the weekly observance of the Sabbath—*Shabbes* in Yiddish, or *Shabbat* (shah-BOTT) in Hebrew. Sabbath begins at sundown on Friday, and continues until the corresponding time on Saturday. (The Christian Sabbath, or Sunday observance, is derived from the Jewish custom, but uses a different reckoning of time, as Reform Jews have occasionally attempted.) On the Sabbath all work ceases. Meals and other necessities are provided for beforehand, so that the entire day may be consecrated to rest and worship—"re-creation" in the root sense. Public worship is held on Friday evening and, most especially, on Saturday morning, and domestic rituals, such as the mother's lighting the candles before the Friday evening meal, extend the observance into the home as well. Contemporary Jews adhere to these rites with varying degrees of strictness, but the weekly Sabbath is without question the core of Jewish religious life.

In addition to the weekly Sabbath observance, Jewish worship focuses on a yearly cycle of holidays, the occurrence of which is governed by a traditional lunar calendar utilized today almost solely for such ceremonial purposes. Two holiday sequences are observed almost universally by American Jews: Passover, in the spring, and the High Holy Days (or "Days of Awe"), which begin early in the fall with Rosh Hashanah, the New Year, and end with Yom Kippur, the Day of Atonement. Others, such as Sukkoth and Purim, are folk festivals rather than solemn religious observances, and are not usually the occasion of remaining home from school or work. Yet another, Hanukkah, has come to occupy a distinct place in the interaction of Jewish tradition with American culture.

Passover, or *Pesach* (PAY-sock), usually occurs in the spring fairly close to the Christian Easter, and was the occasion of Jesus' "Last Supper." Passover commemorates the archetypal event in the sacred history of Israel, the deliverance by Yahweh of the Hebrew people out of Egyptian bondage. Its celebration extends over eight days (seven in Israel), which are preceded by a ritual cleansing to ensure that not even the slightest trace of leavened bread or other foods with leavening remains in the house. The highlight of Passover is the *seder* (SAY-durr), at which all of the family gather for a ritual meal.

The seder meal consists of two primary components: a specific array of foods and wine, and a special liturgy called *Haggadah*. The foods include the following:

- *Karpas*—parsley or another green vegetable symbolizing spring and re-birth.
- *(C)haroset(h)*—a mixture that usually includes chopped apples, nuts, wine, and spices, signifying the materials from which the Hebrews made bricks while serving as Egyptian slaves.
- *Maror*—bitter herbs (usually horseradish), reminiscent of the bitterness of Egyptian bondage.
- *Beitzah* and *Zeroa*—a roasted egg and bone, symbols of the sacrifices once brought to the Temple.
- *Matzo(h)*—unleavened bread, recalling that made in haste once the depar-ture from Egypt was to begin.

Sweet kosher wine is also served to all, including children. The *Haggadah* (Hah-GAH-dah) service is led by the father or oldest male family member present, and consists of prayers and readings from the Talmud and from the book of Exodus. A favorite part of the family-oriented service is the posing of the traditional question "Why is this night different from all other nights?" by the youngest son, with four similar ritual questions and answers following.

Rosh Hashanah (roshe ha-SHO-nah), the Jewish new year that celebrates the creation of the world, inaugurates the ten-day cycle of High Holy Days (Days of Awe). Services are held in the synagogue, and are marked by the periodic blowing of the *shofar*, or ram's horn. The cycle ends with *Yom Kippur* (yahm KIP-pur), or the Day of Atonement, which is also observed at the synagogue rather than in the home. The theme of this holy day and its special chanted liturgy, the *Kol Nidre*, is repentance and forgiveness for offenses committed during the past year—a ritual of individual and collective spiritual renewal.

Other festivals that are not quite of the same stature but are still frequently observed include *Succot(h)* (or *Sukkot*, pronounced SOOK-ess or SOOK-ote), the Feast of Booths (or Tabernacles), which begins the fifth day after Yom Kippur. This is a thanksgiving holiday in which the booths set up by observant families recall the transient character of the forty years spent in the wilderness after the Exodus. *Purim* (POOR-im), the Feast of Lots, commemorates the deliverance of the Jews of Persia from mass extermination by the wicked royal minister Haman, as narrated in the book of Esther. Its celebration is festive, and includes the booing of the name of Haman by children during the syna-gogue service.

Another holiday commemorating a specific historical event is *(C)Hanukka(h)* (HAHN-ah-kah, beginning with the gutteral "ch" sound), or the "Feast of Lights." Although the holiday commemorates the successful rebellion of Ju-dah "the Hammer" and his followers, the Maccabees, against Syrian oppres-sion in the second century B.C., its celebration has taken on a very different significance in the American context. As Christmas came to assume a larger and larger role in American secular as well as religious life, Jewish children felt excluded from the gentile world that seemed to explode yearly in caroling, gift-buying and -giving, and the rest of the interwoven commercial, festive, and sacred observances that the holiday acquired. As a response, Hanukkah was elevated from the status of a relatively minor holiday into a seasonal alternative to Christmas. This is very much a home-centered observance, with one of eight candles on the *menorah*, or candleholder, lit daily with a ninth. This is symbolic of an oil lamp that burnt for eight days on one day's supply of fuel during the Maccabean revolt. Popular customs include making *latkes*, or potato pancakes; games played with a *draydl*, or spinning top traditionally made from clay; and giving *Hanukkah gelt*, gilt-wrapped chocolate coins representing those of the Maccabean era. Some Jews eager to approximate Gentile customs even further—and with tongues often firmly in cheek—add a "Hanukkah bush," or Christmas tree substitute, and even have visits from "Uncle Max the Hanukkah Man," a clear counterpart to a well-known Christmas figure.

These and other holidays (described by Michael Strassfeld in *The Jewish Holidays*) correspond to the yearly round of observances that characterize many religions. Individual Jews and Jewish communities observe them with different degrees of intensity, though a great many Jews observe Passover and the High Holy Days with special reverence. In addition to the Sabbath observance and the yearly round of holidays, the Jewish tradition also acknowledges in symbol and ritual special times in the individual life cycle. The first of these is the *bris*, or circumcision performed on male infants eight days after birth. The infant's foreskin is surgically removed by a *mohel* (MOY-ull), who is not a rabbi but rather a man specially trained in this craft.

The next stage of life that is ritually mediated comes at age 13—on or about the onset of puberty—in the ceremony of *Bar Mitzva(h)*. At this time, a Jewish boy becomes a "son of the commandment" (the meaning of the phrase) by reading a prayer and a passage from the Torah in Hebrew. The ceremony, in which the boy announces "Today I am a man," is preceded by instruction in Hebrew school and is immediately followed by a great celebration of family and friends. Its immediate origins lie in late Medieval Europe, although the symbolic recognition of coming of age has much deeper historical roots. A *Bas* or *Bat Mitzvah* ceremony for girls is of considerably more recent origin, practiced mainly in Reform and Conservative congregations. The latter traditions also may add, or substitute, a confirmation ceremony later in one's teens.

Early marriage and the bearing of children was traditionally encouraged among Jews, although contemporary Jewish demographics in America have tended in the opposite direction so greatly that some leaders fear that the community may eventually die out from attrition. The Jewish wedding, however, has taken its place in the American array of ethnic celebrations as a particularly lavish and joyful event, much like the Bar Mitzvah. A traditional wedding is performed with the couple standing under a *(c)huppa(h)*, or canopy. At the end of the ceremony, the groom breaks a glass under his foot, which is usually (but not definitively) explained as a reminder of the destruction of the Temple and the sufferings of the Jewish people. Although many Jews now simply obtain secular divorces when necessary, Jewish law allows for religious divorce, or *get*, under certain circumstances.

Although funeral practices differ among contemporary Jews, tradition calls for a simple burial in white linen garments in a plain wooden coffin. Cremation has never been permitted in traditional Judaism. The funeral service is equally simple, and features the recital of the *Kaddish* (KOD-dish). On each anniversary of a death, the family of the deceased may light a *Yahrzeit* (or *Yortzeit*) candle in their memory.

The cycle of Jewish observances, then, is a complex one that has developed over the centuries from the time of ancient Israel, with many additions and adaptations in the intervening centuries. Rituals are celebrated in both the home and the synagogue, depending on the character of the observance. Some themes that intertwine among the many observances are the sanctity of daily life and the ongoing need to fulfill the demands of the covenant. In their combination of traditional practices and everyday concreteness, these observances demonstrate vividly much about the character of the Jewish religion.

CHAPTER 4

From the Religion of the Hebrews to the Restoration of Israel

It has become a commonplace in discussing American Judaism to begin with "the problem of Jewish identity": what does it mean to be Jewish? It is also proverbial among Jews that where you have two Jews, you'll find three opinions. Jews as well as Gentiles (non-Jews) find this question both centrally important and vexingly difficult to answer. What follows will contribute, if not to an answer, at least to an exploration of the question's dimensions.

The question asserts itself from the beginning of Jewish history, and is manifest in the multiplicity of names for the Jewish people that have to be sorted out at the outset. What, for instance, is the difference between "Jewish" and "Hebrew" when used as adjectives to identify a people and their religion, tradition, and scripture? And, when those who attack Jews are called "anti-Semites" or "anti-Semitic," how does this multiplication of terms further expand, or confuse, the question of who the Jewish people may be?

To begin at the end, *Semitic* is a generic term that designates a family of languages spoken primarily in the Middle East. This Semitic language family is not part of the Indo-European group that includes English, Yiddish (the vernacular language of many Jews in the past), and most other modern European languages. Other Semitic languages are Arabic, spoken by many Muslim peoples; Ethiopic, which is still in use in northeastern Africa; Aramaic, the vernacular of the Middle East at the time of Jesus; and a variety of long-extinct tongues spoken by contemporaries of the ancient Hebrew people such as Akkadian, Moabite, and Phoenician. The use of the term *Semitic* to refer specifically to the Jewish people—usually in the construct "anti-Semitic" and its variants—is relatively recent. Many Jews take exception to the term since it implies a racial categorization.

The related words *Jewish* and *Jew* originate in the later biblical period, and will be introduced and explained a bit later. The word *Hebrew*, the original meaning of which is not clear, can be used to designate a specific Semitic language—namely, that utilized by a particular group of Ancient Near Eastern people. The linguistic name became attached also to the people among whom it was spoken. These "Hebrews" differed from their neighbors in their seminomadic character and their supporting themselves not through settled agriculture but rather as herders. Their identity as a distinct people with an even more distinctive religion is attributed in the book of Genesis to the calling of the patriarch (paternal ruler) Abraham. The god who thus called Abraham would from now on be regarded as the god of the Hebrews and from the time of Moses be known as Yahweh.* Similarly, the Hebrew people would now no longer be defined simply by language or kinship, but by their allegiance to this, their god.

At Yahweh's instructions, Abraham moved from Mesopotamia into the land of Canaan, later known as Palestine. The story of Abraham and his descendants—the *patriarchs* of Israel—is legendary in character, but may be rooted in historical events taking place around the first quarter of the second millennium B.C.—that is, 2000–1750 B.C.[†]

It is with Abraham and his covenant with Yahweh that the history of the Hebrews as a chosen people properly begins. Abraham's willingness to sacrifice his son Isaac demonstrated his devotion to Yahweh, and Isaac's son Jacob founded the twelve tribes that constituted the people of *Israel*—the name that

---

* The meaning of the name Yahweh remains uncertain, although some scholars have argued that it is an invocation of God's role as creator. Although *Yahweh* is the form that is widely accepted as closest to the biblical YHWH (spelled in Hebrew consonants only, without vowel points, and now usually pronounced YAH-way), it is not that which is commonly used by Jews. *Adonai* (ah-doh-NOI, "lord") and *Elohim* (ell-oh-EEM, meaning uncertain) are Hebrew forms used as substitutes, and even these are altered slightly when uttered by many Jews.

† The question of indicating dates illustrates the profound influence that Christianity has had on the entire course of Western history, including the calendar. The calendar introduced by Julius Caesar in 46 B.C. was adopted by Christians, and the convention of fixing dates with reference to the supposed year of the birth of Jesus gradually spread throughout the West during the early Middle Ages. The calendar used almost universally today is based on a reform of this Christianized Julian calendar, introduced by Pope Gregory XIII during the sixteenth century. Although most American Jews use the Gregorian calendar for everyday reckoning, some depart from it in two ways. When using it, they substitute C.E. and B.C.E. ("Common Era" or "Before the Common Era") for A.D. (*Anno Domini*, "in the year of [our] Lord,") and B.C. ("Before Christ"), respectively. For ceremonial purposes—e.g., in dating the cornerstone of a synagogue—the Jewish calendar devised by Hillel II (ca. 360 A.D.) is sometimes utilized. This system reckons years by adding 3761, based on a traditional reckoning of the date of creation, to the Gregorian date. For convenience, however, the usual forms of B.C. and A.D. will be retained throughout this work.

Jacob received after successfully wrestling with God himself (Genesis 32:22 ff). One of Jacob's sons, Joseph—he of the many-colored coat—was forced by his brothers into Egypt, where he prospered as Pharaoh's prime minister. Later, the rest of Jacob's family were forced by famine into Egypt as well, where they benefited from Joseph's position. This privileged status was later lost under "a new king over Egypt, who did not know Joseph," and the Hebrews were reduced to the status of slaves. It was this unpleasant situation that provided the context for the most dramatic event in the history of the Hebrew people, the memory of which is crucial for their identity to the present day.

The book of Exodus retells the story of the emergence of Moses, who was rescued by Pharaoh's daughter from the bulrushes, raised in the royal court, and forced to flee into the land of Midian after killing a brutal Egyptian overseer who had been beating Hebrew slaves. While living as a herdsman, Moses experienced a *theophany*, or appearance of the divine: he encountered Yahweh, the god of the Hebrew people, in the form of a burning bush. Moses then returned to Egypt at Yahweh's command, presented himself as a champion of the Hebrews against Pharaoh, brought down a series of plagues upon the Egyptians when Pharaoh proved unyielding, and ultimately led his people safely through the parted waters of the Red (or, more accurately, "reed") Sea. From here Moses and his people journeyed to Mount Sinai, which Moses ascended to receive the Decalogue, or Ten Commandments, on two stone tablets. After years of wandering in the wilderness, the people finally entered into the promised land of Canaan—without Moses, who died after only glimpsing it.

It is this story of deliverance that has remained normative—the "root experience"—for the Hebrew (or Jewish) people ever since; in it are contained and developed the major themes that define the character of the Hebrew people and their covenantal relationship with their god, Yahweh. These themes are not restricted to the Hebrew religion; they are also the basis for the central theological conceptions and beliefs that would later inform the two other religions that have dominated the Western world in the course of its history—Christianity and Islam. It is worth pausing here to develop briefly some of these themes.

1. In contrast with the religious systems of the other Ancient Near Eastern peoples among whom the Hebrews arose and lived, the god of the Hebrew people was *the only god* with which they were permitted to have a relationship. This religion eventually developed into a full-fledged *monotheism*, or belief in one god to the exclusion of all other deities. This was the first such religion of any consequence ever to arise in human history.
2. In addition to his singularity, another characteristic of this god of the Hebrews was his concern with human history itself. The deities of the neighboring peoples, not unlike those of prehistoric Africa and the Americas, were primarily representations of natural forces, and had to be appeased in order to ensure the continuing fertility of the soil. On the contrary, the Hebrew god Yahweh took a direct interest and role in the course of specific human events. In particular, he was concerned with the fortunes

and misfortunes of his chosen people, the Hebrews. On occasion he appeared to their representatives—as in the cases of Abraham, Jacob, and Moses—and actively interfered in the historical realm—for example, in his deliverance of the Hebrew people out of bondage in Egypt. As his name *Yahweh* may be construed, he is a *god who acts* in human affairs.

3. As should by now be apparent, this god Yahweh is a personal god, not simply a personified force of nature. He has a name—actually, several, of which Yahweh (sometimes mistranslated as "Jehovah") is the most central and sacred. He enters into direct relationships with individuals, at times in quite dramatic forms as when he wrestled with Jacob. Nor is he eternally unchanging, at least in appearance, as shown in the different ways and circumstances in which he manifests himself to the Hebrews.

4. The basic form in which Yahweh's successive relationships with his people Israel take place is through the form of the *covenant.* A covenant is a relationship between two parties, and in a sense is a sort of contract. Unlike a simple contract entered into for the straightforward exchange of goods, services, and/or money, however, a covenant is personal and open-ended, without specific stipulations as to who owes what. In the present day, when impersonal contracts predominate, marriage might be an apt illustration of a covenant relationship. The covenant into which Yahweh entered with Moses at Sinai was most likely based on suzerainty or vassalage treaties employed by other Ancient Near Eastern peoples, in which personal, open-ended allegiance would be pledged by the weaker party in return for protection by the stronger. This theme of a stronger and weaker party was incorporated into this biblical covenant. Yahweh, of course, was the stronger one, who offers deliverance and prosperity to his people if they keep his covenant with him, and punishment should they transgress its terms.

The record of these covenants between Yahweh and his chosen people is the major theme and connecting thread through the religious annals of the Hebrews—the *Bible.* (Christians refer to these Hebrew scriptures as the *Old Testament,* while Jews generally prefer the terms *Hebrew Bible* or *Tanak,* an abbreviation of the Hebrew words for the three divisions of scripture: Torah, the Prophets, and Writings.) "Bible" is derived from the Greek *ta biblia,* or "books." Although the Bible is sometimes bound as and referred to as a single book—for example, "the Good Book"—it is in fact a collection of writings of various kinds, compiled over several hundred years, often derived from earlier oral traditions, and reflecting the collective religious experience of the Hebrew people in a wide variety of circumstances expressed in many different literary genres. Very briefly, the books of the Hebrew Bible can be summarized as follows:

1. The first group is known as the *Torah,* or *Pentateuch,* sometimes called "the five books of Moses," to whose authorship they were traditionally attributed. These are regarded by Jews as the most sacred core of scripture, and, inscribed on scrolls, are central to Jewish worship. The first, *Genesis,* begins

with an account of the creation of the cosmos and the world by Yahweh; proceeds with the story of the introduction of evil and death into the world in its account of Adam and Eve; retells other legendary stories such as those of the Tower of Babel, and Noah and the Flood; and then emerges into early historical times in its accounts of the Patriarchs Abraham, Isaac, Jacob, and Joseph. *Exodus* narrates the story of Moses and the deliverance of the Hebrew people from bondage in Egypt, a story continued in *Numbers* and *Deuteronomy*. *Leviticus* is composed primarily of detailed cultic regulations concerning ritual purity.*

2. A second group of books narrate the history of the Hebrew people in Canaan, the era of the Judges, the establishment of the monarchy under Saul and his successors, the division of the land into the two nations Israel and Judah, their conquest by their enemies, and the destruction of the Temple (586 B.C.) and its rebuilding (520–515 B.C.) These books include *Joshua, Judges, Ruth,* 1 and 2 *Samuel,* 1 and 2 *Kings,* 1 and 2 *Chronicles, Ezra, Nehemiah,* and *Esther*.

3. A third major category of biblical literature is the *prophetic books,* of which the "major"—that is, longer—prophets, Isaiah and Jeremiah, are among the best known. The Hebrew prophets, who flourished during the eighth through the sixth centuries B.C., did not set out to foretell the future in a literal way, but rather announced judgments by Yahweh that would follow if the Hebrew people did not observe the terms of the covenant. These "prophecies" were denunciations of ethical transgressions, such as the exploitation of the weak by the powerful. The force of their message can be summarized in the words of Micah (6:8): "What does the Lord require of you, but to do justice and to love kindness and to walk humbly with your God?" The ethical thrust of biblical prophecy and the call to social justice rather than simply cultic purity as the proper fulfillment of the covenant has been a major motif through the subsequent history not only of Judaism but of Christianity as well.

4. The final grouping of books in Hebrew scriptures consists of "Wisdom literature" and other poetic works, such as Job, the Psalms, Proverbs, and Ecclesiastes, and the Song of Songs. Some of these works, such as Job, are profoundly steeped in the Hebrew sense of the relationship between the divine and the human; others, such as Ecclesiastes and Proverbs, reflect a notion of "wisdom" that was international in character and somewhat at odds with traditional Hebrew sensibilities in its individualism and lack of a historical perspective.

Over many centuries and with much editing, this collection of highly diverse literature coalesced into a *canon,* or list of works commonly acknowledged as divinely inspired. A number of respected but not fully accepted books, such as

---

* Greek names for a number of books of Hebrew scripture derive from the *Septuagint,* a Greek translation prepared during the Hellenistic period during the second and third centuries B.C. Roman Catholics until recently employed forms of the names of some Old Testament books derived from the Septuagint, which differed from other usage. There is now general agreement among the major religious traditions on English usage, however.

Maccabees and Tobit, were relegated to the periphery and known as *apocrypha*. This canon of Hebrew scripture was probably closed, or regarded as complete and definitive, around the end of the first century A.D.

At the core of the collection of scripture, again, is the history of the Hebrew people in successive covenants with Yahweh. The earlier books celebrate the deliverance of Yahweh's people out of bondage and into a spectacular hegemony in the days of the kingship of David and Solomon in their glory. The preceding description of some of the later books, though, makes it clear that the subsequent epochs were less than triumphant. With the death of Solomon in 922 B.C., the kingdom split into two separate entities, Israel in the north and Judah in the south. Israel then fell to the Assyrians in 721 B.C. Later, during the days of Jeremiah the Prophet (ca. 600 B.C.), the kingdom of Judah began to succumb to internal disarray and the superiority of external forces, culminating in the Babylonian king Nebuchadnezzar's destruction of Jerusalem in 586 B.C. Although the Jerusalem temple was rebuilt in 520–515 B.C. and lasted till its final destruction by the Romans in A.D. 70, the days of the Hebrew people as independent in their own land were clearly over. From this time onward, their normative state was not one of territorial hegemony but rather of *Diaspora*—a scattering, eventually throughout the entire world, in which they had to make the best peace they could with the various "host" cultures among whom they dwelt.

One of the most significant of these host cultures for the subsequent development of Jewish religion and culture was the Hellenistic, so called because of the dominance of Greek language and civilization spread through the eastern Mediterranean basin and beyond by Alexander the Great, who conquered Palestine in 332 B.C. It was the displacement of Hebrew by Greek as the language of learned discourse that eventually led to the production of the Septuagint, or Greek translation of Hebrew scripture, as well as to a shift in philosophical and theological attitude reflected in the "Wisdom" tradition and the later writings of the great Philo of Alexandria, alien to the mainstream of Hebrew thought. It is also during these years that a metamorphosis was taking place in the vocabulary utilized to characterize the Hebrew people. The word *Jew* is ultimately derived from the Hebrew name for the kingdom of Judah. After the Exile (from Judah and Jerusalem to Babylonia, ca. 600 B.C.), it began to gain currency as a designaton for any of what we now refer to as the "Jewish" people (as distinct from "Gentiles" or *goyim*, i.e., non-Jews; *goy* or, in its plural form, *goyim*, is a Yiddish word derived originally from Hebrew). The transition from *Hebrew* to *Jew*, witnessed in Greek, Latin, and modern European forms of the latter word, is indicative of a major change in self-identification by a Jewish community for whom Hebrew was no longer the language of everyday discourse.

The Diaspora remained the normative condition of what were now known as the *Jewish* people until only recently, with the reestablishment of the state of Israel as a Jewish homeland following World War II. Jews continued to live in the eastern Mediterranean area under a variety of rulers, but an abortive revolt against the Romans in A.D. 66 resulted in the ultimate destruction of the Temple four years later and the death of perhaps a million of the rebels. After continued suppression and revolts during the ensuing decades, a measure of stability was finally attained after the death of the Emperor Hadrian in A.D. 138. The ancient Jewish land of Judaea, now renamed Palestine by the Romans, continued to serve as a center for the ancient faith until even more drastic restrictions on Jewish life were imposed by Christian dominance in the fifth century. Babylonia became the center of Jewish life in the Middle East, while more and more Jews began to fan out along the frontiers of empire.

Two major groups of Jews, who would ultimately have a major impact on American Jewish history, emerged in the course of this process of dispersion. One of these was the *Sephardim,* or Sephardic Jews, who fanned out through northern Africa and into the Iberian Peninsula (Spain and Portugal). Muhammed, (570–632), the founder of the new religion of Islam, was hostile toward Jews as well as Christians for their refusal to accept him as the prophet of Allah, but his successors tempered their positions. The end of Christian hegemony in Iberia at the hands of the Muslims in the eighth century ultimately proved beneficial to the Sephardim, who developed a flourishing culture there and proved invaluable to their "hosts" in a variety of ways. Sephardic Jewish civilization was in turn stimulated by the growth of Muslim philosophy.

This generally happy relationship of cooperation and interaction came to an end in the late fifteenth century with the defeat of the Muslims and the "reconquest" and unification of Spain by the "Christian monarchs," Ferdinand of Aragon and Isabella of Castille. Catholicism of the most militant sort then became equated with Spanish nationalism, and Jews were given the unpleasant choices of exile, conversion to Christianity, or death. It is ironic that in 1492, the year of Columbus's first encounter with the New World—a voyage in which he was accompanied by Spanish Jews—the Sephardim were again forced into yet another painful exile. Many of the participants in this new diaspora found refuge eventually in the anti-Spanish Netherlands and their New World colonies, and later established the first Jewish presence in what would become the United States. Jews who converted to Christianity became known as Marranos, and spread throughout the Spanish Empire in the New World as well as remaining in Iberia. Recently, a number of families in New Mexico have made public the surreptitious observance of Jewish customs, many of them only in vestigial and dimly remembered form, that has continued among them to the present day.

The other Jewish group of major significance for our story is the *Ashkenazim,* or Ashkenazic Jews. (The name comes from a descendant of Noah who was thought to have settled in the general area of Germany.) The Ashkenazim followed the routes of the Roman legions during the later days of the Roman Empire and the early Middle Ages to settle across northern and central Europe. The focus of Ashkenazic life was in the German-speaking area, although some were dispersed in France and England, and large and influential communities developed in Poland and Russia. The tension in which they lived with the dominant Christians set many of the themes for Gentile-Jewish relations in later times, by no means always for the better. Although not in the same category with heretics—Christians who deviated from the orthodoxy of the Roman church and who were therefore always outlawed—the Jews occupied an ambiguous position in medieval Christian thought. By law, they were barred from owning agricultural land and were generally compelled to live in special areas. In the more urbanized reaches of the west, these were called *ghettoes,* or districts of a city solely reserved for Jewish habitation. Here Jews were accorded some autonomy and their rabbis enjoyed considerable prestige and power. (The word "ghetto," pronounced GETT-oe, is of Italian origin and uncertain meaning.) In the less rapidly modernizing eastern part of Europe, Jews lived instead in villages called *shtetls* (SHTET-uls or SHTATE-uls; i.e., "little cities").

Thus isolated geographically, Jews were unique in their status in other ways as well. The prohibition of the medieval church on usury—lending money at interest—did not apply to Jews, who at times served as moneylenders to popes and bishops. This special advantage served on the one hand to permit the accumulation of considerable fortunes, as in the case of the fabled house of Rothschild. On the other hand, it helped reinforce the negative stereotype of the Jew as Shylock, Shakespeare's grasping moneylender who showed no mercy toward Gentiles. Another dimension of this negative image was the Jew as Christ-killer, which was perpetuated at higher levels of discourse through a reading of the Gospels as placing on the Jews the responsibility for the death of Jesus. More popularly, the image of the Jew as murderer was reinforced by the folkloric belief that Jews kidnapped Gentile children to use as sacrifices in secret rituals. Folklore depicted the Jew alternately as one in league with Satan and also as the perpetual exile—"the wandering Jew"—doomed to live forever without a fixed abode as punishment for the crime of deicide (i.e., "god-killing"). This attitude resulted, not surprisingly, in periodic outbreaks of violent anti-Semitism, particularly in times of crisis or popular excitement such as the Crusades, when mobs invaded the ghettoes and slaughtered Jews. Although, needless to say, this folklore had no factual basis, it legitimated Christians' using Jews as scapegoats and objects for the fulfillment of deep and perverse fantasies.

The situation of medieval Jewry, though continually precarious, was conducive to perpetuating a very traditional religious culture in which rabbis enjoyed great influence and prestige as teachers, judges, and arbiters with the Gentile world. By a combination of choice and necessity, most Ashkenazic Jews lived in an entirely Jewish world. Their worship, life-styles, and world views were shaped by the traditional lore of the Talmud, and their religious practice was highly conservative. This is not to say that a rich religious culture did not develop and flourish; however, its direction lacked the stimulus provided the Sephardim by Islamic civilization, since positive interaction with the Christian world was unusual. Innovations that did emerge in some quarters were Hasidism, a mystical movement with antiintellectual implications and the rationalism of Baruch Spinoza, the seventeenth-century philosopher who was disowned by his fellow Amsterdam Jews and forced into exile by them for his radicalism.

It has been said with some justice that the Middle Ages in Europe lasted much longer for Jews than for Christians, since the isolation of the former outlived the era of the Renaissance by several centuries. It was the eighteenth century—"the Age of Enlightenment"—that saw the first major confrontation between the Jewish community and what we have come to regard as "the culture of modernity." On the one hand, the Enlightenment and the French Revolution, which was inspired partly by Enlightenment ideals of rationality and universalism, led to the emancipation of Jews in France and elsewhere from the legal constraints that had traditionally been imposed upon them. Jews were free to leave the ghettoes and to live as Gentiles if they chose, enjoying the full privileges of citizenship.

On the other hand, an intellectual and religious response from within the Jewish community was already in the making. Moses Mendelssohn (1729–1786), a learned German Jew, set about to bring what he saw as the essence of Judaism into conformity with the principles of the Enlightenment. Mendelssohn argued that Judaism as a religion could be both theoretically and practically separated from the baggage of traditional Jewish culture that had accumulated over the centuries, and that stood in the way of the Jewish people's adaptation to modern civilization. Essentially Judaism, when properly understood, was an eminently rational faith and embodied those tenets—the existence of an omnipotent god, freedom of the human will, immortality of the soul—that Enlightened thinkers generally agreed were deducible from reason and observation without the dubious benefit of revelation, tradition, and authority. Jews, then, could participate readily in the broader life of the Gentile community. They would no longer be distinguishable by dress, dietary habits, or other superficial customs, but solely by their embracing a system of religious belief that was at once distinct from Christianity while conforming with the avant-garde intellectual trends of the time. Paradoxically, however, Mendelssohn himself fully observed the customs of traditional Judaism, and believed that they had been revealed directly by God to Moses.

Mendelssohn's thought laid the foundations both for enthusiastic participation in Emancipation in Europe and the New World, and for a new religious strain that would become known as Reform. Unfortunately, the problems of being a Jew in a predominantly Gentile society did not disappear in the aura of the Enlightenment. In Russia, which throughout the nineteenth century remained one of the most retrograde sections of Europe, traditional anti-Jewish sentiment vented itself in the form of *pogroms* [poh-GROHMZ], or raids by armed cossack soldiers on Jewish settlements—the *shtetls* that dotted the broad agricultural belt stretching between the Black and Baltic Seas, in which relations between Jewish artisans and merchants and their Gentile peasant neighbors were never entirely amicable. (The comments of Polish peasants in the film *Shoah* demonstrate the abiding suspicion and dislike of mercantile Jewish "outsiders" that has been part and parcel of peasant culture for centuries.)

Anti-Jewish sentiment was seldom as virulent in the more modernized western parts of Europe during the nineteenth century as it was farther east. In the twentieth century, however, it was the very Germany that had been a seedbed of Enlightenment thought and modern scientific development that erupted in violence against the Jewish people on a scale unprecedented in human history. In other parts of the Euro-American world, including the United States and Italy, Jews received some blame for the devastating Depression of the 1930s, but in most cases these mutterings had little important result without the further catalyst of Nazism. It was in Germany that the devastation of World War I; its subsequent settlement, resulting in ongoing political and economic chaos and bitter resentments; and the further blow of worldwide economic collapse came together to mobilize ancient folklore and modern ideology and fantasy into a violent program of genocide. Germany's very real problems were blamed by Hitler and his National Socialists on the Jewish community, who were depicted as part of the international conspiracy of financial manipulators who had brought on the Depression and who served Jews at the expense of any national loyalties.

Although it resurrected some of the charges against Jews that had been common in medieval Christian lore, Nazism also repudiated Christianity as a "slave morality" unworthy of a master race. It appealed to a primordial, mythic Teutonic spirit that had been emasculated by the Christian exaltation of weakness, and set out to destroy all—especially the Jews—who stood in the way of its triumphant path to world dominion. It is worth remembering that the majority of the victims of the Nazi program of death and terror were not Jews, but a variety of people deemed inferior by the Nazis—Poles and other Slavs, German Catholics, gypsies, and homosexuals. However, the campaign against none of these was as systematic, determined, and hate-filled as that against the Jews, who were singled out for total eradication. What has since come to be called the *Holocaust*—a word of Greek origin used to indicate a burnt offering such as that of the ancient Hebrews (*Shoah*)—was intended by the Nazis to be the "final solution" to the "Jewish question." It came frighteningly close to achieving its goals, at least in continental Europe. Between five and six million Jews died under the most hideous circumstances in the gas ovens of Auschwitz, Buchenwald, Bergen-Belsen, Treblinka, Ravensbrück, and other concentration camps. After World War II, the once multitudinous Jewish communities of Germany, Poland, and the rest of central Europe had been decimated, and many of the survivors chose to emigrate to the United States, Israel, or elsewhere rather than attempt to continue life in such a grim context.

Needless to say, the Holocaust was one of the most definitive events of Jewish history in the twentieth century, and an enormous literature has been generated attempting to understand and express its anguish, sources, and meaning. At almost exactly the same time that the victorious Allied armies were liberating the concentration camps, however, another movement of extraordinary consequence for all of the Jewish people was beginning to achieve fulfillment. During the nineteenth century many Jews, especially those under the influence of Mendelssohn and the Reform movement, had accepted the Diaspora as the normative condition of the Jewish people. They thought it not only necessary but desirable that Jews should continue to live scattered among various Gentile societies, from which they should be distinguishable only in religion. For other Jews of a wide variety of intellectual backgrounds, however, a very different movement was beginning to coalesce under the name of *Zionism*.

Some supporters of the restoration of an independent Jewish homeland—

preferably in Palestine, the historical land of Israel—were motivated by a deeply religious drive for the restoration of traditional Judaism. (Most religious Jews, however, were opposed to the movement in its early, more secular forms.) Others saw Zionism as a pragmatic, secular campaign to free Jews from the threat of persecution that was manifest even in such "enlightened" nations as France, in which the Jewish army officer Alfred Dreyfus was framed for treason and sent off to Devil's Island before his ultimate exoneration. The central catalytic figure in modern Zionism was Theodor Herzl (1860–1904), an Austrian Jew who promoted the idea through his book *Der Judenstaat* ("the Jewish State") of 1896 and his organization the next year of the World Zionist Congress. The cause was furthered by the Balfour Declaration of 1917, in which the British pledged the restoration of Palestine as a Jewish homeland in the context of their wresting the territory from Turkey at the end of World War I. After a series of advances and retreats, the Zionist cause prevailed in 1948, when the newly founded United Nations proclaimed the independence of the State of Israel. After several decades of precarious, sometimes violent, and always controversial existence surrounded by Arab neighbors, Israel continues to provide a focus of identity for Jews throughout the world.

The story of the Jewish people is the oldest continuous such narrative in the Western world. Jewish history has oscillated among a number of poles: Diaspora and homeland, reason and tradition, prosperity and suffering. Lacking a central organization, the Jews have been free to adapt their beliefs and practices within a wide variety of cultural and intellectual circumstances. However varied the understandings of Jewish identity that have emerged, there has always remained a deep sense of shared history, of constituting a people whose collective experience has been, though troubled, still infinitely rich and meaningful. However much they may differ on its meaning, Jews can hardly help but continue to regard themselves as a "chosen people."

CHAPTER 5

The Eastern Orthodox Tradition

The Jewish community in the Roman Empire was by no means unified at the time of the life of Jesus of Nazareth. It can be described as consisting of a number of sects or factions—Pharisees, Sadducees, Essenes, and Zealots, to name some of the best known. It was in this context that a new sect arose that believed the Jewish God was acting through Jesus of Nazareth to transform the whole created realm. One of the first major disputes among these early "Christians" was whether they were required to continue to practice all of the dictates of the traditional Jewish law, and therefore should require that male Gentile converts be circumcised. The answer provided by Peter, Paul, and other disciples assembled at the Council of Jerusalem (Acts 15) was in the negative. Christianity—as this new religion came to be known—was to be universal, welcoming all, rather than restricted to the people of Israel. Paul especially was instrumental in spreading the Gospel—the "Good News"—of Jesus throughout the Roman Empire. According to tradition, both he and Peter were martyred and buried in Rome, the imperial capital.

Although Christianity was thus from the beginning destined to be a "universalistic" rather than a "particularistic" faith, its rapid spread was not at all to the liking of the Roman authorities. The first three centuries of its existence were spent in a twilight world of dubious legal standing in which violent persecution might break out at any time, as it did under the Emperors Nero, Decius, and Diocletian. Although the Jews had negotiated with the Romans a right to continue their traditions, the Christians were unwilling to do so. The loyalty of the Christians was always to a higher power, and they were willing to suffer torture and death rather than seek earthly permission for worshiping the one true god. Their early gatherings for worship were of necessity covert, taking place in private homes or sometimes literally underground in catacombs.

Another characteristic of early Christianity was what has been called its "eschatological world picture." *Eschatology* is the branch of theology that deals with the "last things"—in Christian tradition, death, judgment, Heaven, and Hell. For these earliest Christians, eschatology dominated their entire religious view. Given the precarious situation in which they found themselves, and their belief that Jesus would return again to earth soon, these Christians placed little hope or confidence in earthly life. They regarded it as a holding action against the forces of evil; it could at any moment give way to a radical transformation of the whole created realm. Revelation, or the Apocalypse—the final book of Christian scripture, or "New Testament"—is a document reflecting a specifically eschatological world view. It relates in symbolic form this final consummation of things, for which Christians waited eagerly and in anticipation of which they were prepared to make the most drastic sacrifices.

This situation changed dramatically early in the fourth century with the triumph of Constantine in a struggle for leadership of a divided and declining Empire. According to legend Constantine, who was the son of the Christian (later Saint) Helena, was preparing for the Battle of the Milvian Bridge with his rival Maxentius in 312. He beheld in the sky the sign of the cross and the words *In hoc signo vinces*—"by this sign you shall conquer." Conquer he did, and upon accession to the imperial throne set about making Christianity not only a legal religion but the favored religion of the Empire. Although he did not himself receive baptism till the end of his life, a common practice at the time, his reign stands as the most critical turning point in the fortunes of Christianity from the time of Jesus and his followers at least till that of Charlemagne's crowning as Holy Roman Emperor nearly five centuries later.

Constantine not only favored Christianity but as emperor actively intervened in its internal affairs. Christians had established communities throughout the Mediterranean world by this time, but they had become torn by one of a series of controversies over the precise nature of the man Jesus whom they acknowledged as the Son of God. A party led by a priest named Arius held that Jesus had not himself been God, but rather had been created by God and entrusted with a special mission to humanity. Another party rejected this "subordinationist" Christology (i.e., interpretation of the nature of Christ), and maintained that the Son was truly divine and the equal of God the Father.

To settle this controversy, Constantine convened the bishops, or local leaders, of the Christian world in 325 at the town of Nicea as the first ecumenical, or worldwide, council in the history of Christianity. The principal work of the Council of Nicea was settling the Arian controversy in a document still widely regarded as authoritative in many churches—the Nicene Creed. This creed, or brief statement of the essentials of the faith, begins "We believe in one God, the Father Almighty [or All-Governing], creator of all things visible and invisible." It rapidly proceeds to settle the issue in dispute with the words "And in one Lord Jesus Christ, the Son of God, begotten of the Father as only begotten, that is, from the essence of the Father . . . begotten not created. . . ."*

* Source of text: John H. Leith, ed., *Creeds of the Churches* (Garden City, NY: Doubleday Anchor, 1963), p. 30. The more familiar form used in many churches today was the work of the later Council of Constantinople.

Arius and his followers were thus confounded and relegated to the status of heretics. Although they gained converts among some of the barbarian tribes then encroaching on Roman dominion and perpetuated their influence for a while, they clearly had lost the contest to the "Orthodox"—that is, the "correct believers"—as the victors became known.

Although the creed and its contents are themselves extremely significant turning points in Christian development, the active role of the Emperor in convening and supervising the Council was also of the utmost importance for the subsequent relationship between the Christian church and the civil order. Instead of living a precarious existence as at best a suspect community, Christians from now on were to enjoy a privileged status that would last through the Middle Ages—an epoch in which the term *Christendom* would describe the dominance of Christianity throughout most of Europe. On the other hand, the price of this new status was the constant danger of civil encroachment into the church's affairs, as Constantine's own benevolent intercession into the Arian dispute demonstrated.

Still another action of Constantine with decisive consequences for the future was his abandonment of the ancient capital of Rome in favor of the city of Byzantium in Asia Minor, later renamed "Constantinople" (the *polis*, or city, of Constantine.) An imperial representative remained behind in Italy at the city of Ravenna, but as the post-Constantinian empire in the West began to crumble, his presence was ineffective. The power vacuum that thus developed was filled instead by the head of the church in the West—namely, the Bishop of Rome. This latter figure, who was gradually acquiring exclusive rights to the title of "Pope" (i.e., "Papa" or "Father"), had emerged as the most influential of the leaders of Christianity in the West, and by virtue of his location was heir to much of the administrative talent and the broader cultural, legal, and political tradition of the Roman Empire. In the longer run, the Pope began to make claims of supremacy over all of the other leaders of the church in the East—claims that were almost universally accepted in the West, where Latin and its derivatives remained dominant, but rejected in the East, where Greek held sway. This issue of papal supremacy continues to the present day as a major source of division between the Eastern Orthodox and Roman Catholic churches.

Although no formal break was to occur for centuries, the geographical isolation and cultural and linguistic diversity that characterized Rome and Constantinople gradually gave rise to the division of Christianity into two separate spheres, Western and Eastern. The story of the West is continued in later chapters on "Western Catholicism." In the East, the firm hold of the Emperor established by Constantine set a tone that would impress itself for centuries on what became known as the Byzantine Empire and its church. The church was clearly subordinate politically to the state, and enjoyed little of the independence that characterized its counterpart in the West. Rather, a new culture emerged that focused on the imperial court (which has given rise to the use of "Byzantine" to describe extremely convoluted internal politics), the Greek language, and a version of Christianity preoccupied more with mystic symbolism than with law and logic.

During the period that has come to be known as the Middle Ages, East and West grew apart as much from inertia as active hostility. Six more ecumenical councils took place in the years between Nicea and Nicea II in 787. Probably the most significant of these was Chalcedon (451), at which the question of whether Jesus was fully human as well as fully divine was settled in the affirmative. This made heretical the teachings of the *Monophysites* (from the Greek words for "one nature"), whose refusal to speak of Jesus as being "in two natures" appeared to question his full humanity or to make it different from our own. Monophysitism, however, did not disappear, but continues to the present day in such groups as the Armenian Apostolic Church and various Coptic and Syrian Jacobite groups. As a result of this dispute, those Eastern churches that accept the Council's decree favor the term *Chalcedonian* as a self-designation. These seven councils, however, were accepted as fully authoritative by both Eastern Orthodox and Roman Catholics, while subsequent councils through Vatican II have been acknowledged as authoritative only by the latter.

Estrangement between East and West continued to grow during these and succeeding centuries, focusing at times on what may seem minor theological controversies such as the insertion of the *filioque* clause into the Nicene Creed in the West. (*Filioque* means "and from the Son," indicating that the Holy Spirit did not proceed from God the Father alone.) The Pope and the "Ecumenical Patriarch," as the Archbishop of Constantinople had come to be known, mutually excommunicated one another in 1054, again over issues that in retrospect seem too unimportant to have been the real cause of the estrangement. The most serious blow to these steadily deteriorating relations came in 1204 with the sacking of Constantinople during the Fourth Crusade. This holy war was ostensibly being waged against the Muslims, but Eastern Christians felt the wrath of the West as well. From then until the good will that Vatican II generated with the invitation of Eastern observers by Pope John XXIII, the two camps stood in mutual enmity despite their profound underlying similarities. Although no longer hostile, the state of the relationship between the Roman Catholic and Eastern Orthodox churches is characterized by the term *schism*—that is, a political split not involving *heresy*, or formal religious error.

The Byzantine Empire eventually began to lose its hegemony to the powerful forces of Islam that during the Middle Ages had overwhelmed most of the Middle East and North Africa. The final blow came with the fall of Constantinople in 1453, but by this time Eastern Christianity was no longer confined to the Mediterranean basin. Where missionaries had fanned out from Rome to spread its version of Christianity among the peoples of France, Germany, and the British Isles, envoys from the East were performing similar work in the areas of Europe to their north. Saints Cyril and Methodius are celebrated in tradition as the original apostles to the Slavic tribes in the ninth century, and the name of the former is perpetuated in the "Cyrillic" alphabet for transcribing Slavic languages that he is credited with having devised. In the long run, these early efforts were eminently successful: in 988 the Kievan Rus, the forerunner of modern Russia and the Ukraine, was converted to the Eastern version of Christianity, and in 1448 the Russian church based at Moscow declared itself to be *autocephalous*—that is, an autonomous national or ethnic church within the Orthodox "family." In 1721, Czar Peter the Great made the Russian church in effect into a department of state, thus constricting its autonomy in a way that lasted until the 1917 revolution—after which the church experienced even greater restrictions under Communist antireligious policies.

By the time of significant migration of Orthodox Christians to the New World in the late nineteenth and early twentieth centuries, the world of Orthodoxy stood apart from both Roman Catholicism and the various Protestant traditions in the West. It zealously guarded its traditions and adherence to the teachings of the seven ecumenical councils, but remained geographically and politically limited by the circumstances of its history. Its historical core was located in the great ancient patriarchates—the seats of the oldest and most prestigious Christian communities and their bishops—of Alexandria, Antioch, Jerusalem, and Constantinople. (Rome was the fifth, but had gone its own way.) Muslim conquests, a long tradition of subordination of church to state, the Russian Revolution of 1917, and the political fragmentation of southeastern Europe, where Orthodoxy was strongest, all combined to produce a problematic fragmentation as much as the healthy decentralization on which the Orthodox have always prided themselves. At the time the great emigration began, Orthodox Christians could be found in significant numbers in what are now Greece, Rumania, Bulgaria, Albania, Yugoslavia, and the eastern reaches of the Soviet Union, as well as in the Middle East. The specific story of Orthodoxy's coming to America begins in Russia—although, as we shall see later, its ways of passage were intriguingly circuitous.

In the Eastern Orthodox tradition that has thus taken shape over the centuries, stress has always been placed on the act of *worship*. This is not to say that belief is unimportant: the very term *orthodoxy* is indicative of a commitment to "correct belief." Orthodoxy shares with the other liturgical traditions a foundation in the creedal statements of the early church and the first seven ecumenical councils. These established particularly the doctrines of the Trinity and the dual nature of Jesus Christ being both divine and human as the firm dogmatic basis of Christian belief. Conformity to the teachings of these councils is the hallmark of orthodoxy, and any faith statements that are not in harmony with them are by definition *heterodox*—that is, "other" or false belief.

Given a shared commitment to these early creeds, however, there has still been room for significant divergences in interpretation and emphasis between East and West. One of the most influential of the "Church Fathers" of the West was Cyprian (d. 258), the bishop of Carthage in North Africa, whose writings dealt primarily with the nature of the church. Of even greater importance in the long run was Augustine (354–430), bishop of Hippo (also in North Africa), whose *Confessions* detailed the story of his personal conversion, and whose *City of God* developed a theology of God's awful power and the corresponding finite and sinful character of humanity. Together, Cyprian and Augustine represent characteristic Western emphases respectively on the importance of the institutional church and on a pessimistic view of human nature, stressing the radical gulf between the human and the divine. Although later Western theology, such as that especially of Thomas Aquinas in the thirteenth century, was rather more hopeful in its appraisal of human possibilities, Augustine remained in the background as the most powerful and original exponent of a distinctively Western standpoint.

The theological writings of the Eastern church fathers, written in Greek rather than Latin, represent a very different point of view. Prominent among their number were Athanasius, Gregory of Nyssa, Gregory Nazianzen, Basil the Great, and John Chrysostom, all of whom flourished during the fourth century. (The study of the thought of the Eastern and Western church fathers together is known as *patristics*.) As opposed to Augustine's doctrine of predestination, which is based on God's power and goodness and on human depravity and helplessness, the theology that emerged in the East was instead grounded in a much more optimistic appraisal of the human condition. Central to Orthodox thought is the term *theosis*, or "divinization," which refers to the human capacity for being transformed into the divine likeness. The emphasis is therefore not on a divine remission of the penalties for human sin, but rather on putting off the constraints of mortality while still on earth and participating in the divine nature instead.

This transformation has its locus in the *liturgy*—that is, the collective and public worship of God. The emphasis here is not on thought but on being, or rather, the gradual transformation of one's being through participation in divine worship. Eastern Orthodox liturgy is in its basic outlines similar to that of the Roman Catholic Church: The structure of the eucharistic service is not radically different; the cycle of the liturgical year is followed through its various seasons; and seven sacraments, known as *mysteries*, are recognized, together with a number of other rites that have a sacramental or grace-mediating quality. The differences lie more in nuances, emphases, and interpretations that make the liturgy of supreme importance in the Orthodox tradition and that differentiate it in significant ways from the practices of the other liturgical traditions.

Upon entering an Orthodox church, one is struck at first by the physical differences that set it off from those of other Christian communities. Greek churches usually are laid out in the form of a "Greek cross"—that is, with all four arms of equal length, and capped with a rounded dome in the Byzantine tradition. Russian Orthodox churches differ in having one or more "onion domes," in which the crest rises to a sharp point. The interiors of these churches are even more distinctive. In almost every direction, including the vertical, one beholds scores of *icons*, one of the most singular aspects of Orthodox belief and worship. In Orthodox usage, an icon is a stylized, two-dimensional depiction of a sacred subject, usually on a wooden background. The themes may include Jesus or the Trinity; the saints recognized by Orthodoxy, especially the Virgin Mary, known as *Theotokos* or "God-bearer"; or important events in the history of the church. The image depicted on each icon was not the product of an individual artist's imagination, but rather an objective revelation of an aspect of the Incarnation. It is, in short, an *epiphany*—a manifestation of the divine in the midst of this world. As opposed to the Western artistic tradition, where originality has been prized, icons are not supposed to be original, but rather to be copied, often by monks, in a manner as faithful as possible to the divinely revealed prototype.

Icons are thus an essential key to understanding the importance that Orthodoxy places on worship. They are physical vehicles through which the human and the divine come into contact—windows between two worlds—and thus are means through which the human can take on a progressively more divine character. Their arrangement in a church is prescribed by tradition. In the ceiling or dome is the icon of *Christos Pantocrator*—Christ, the Ruler of the Universe. The *Theotokos* with the Christ child can be found above the sanctuary in the apse (the projection at the rear of the area where the altar is located.) The majority of icons are arranged on the *iconstasis* (or *iconostasion*). This is a large screen that divides the sanctuary, which is reserved for the priest and his assistants, from the nave, where the congregation sits (or, in Old World manner, stands) during the lengthy service. The iconostasis emphasizes the mysterious character of the eucharistic celebration, while the icons upon it represent Jesus and other figures important in the Christian experience. Through the mediating function of the icons and the sacramental mysteries performed in their presence, the believer comes into the presence of the divine, and in the eucharist receives a foretaste of the heavenly realm.

The liturgy itself usually follows one of two traditional rites, those identified with St. John Chrysostom and St. Basil the Great. In addition, there is a Liturgy of the Pre-Sanctified Gifts, where a previously consecrated Communion is distributed at specific times during Lent and Holy Week. Although the liturgy was traditionally celebrated in Greek, Old Church Slavonic, and other languages of the Old World, it has in recent times been translated into English to accommodate the large majority of American Orthodox no longer familiar with these ancestral tongues. Practical considerations have also led most to abandon the traditional Julian calendar for everyday purposes, although it is still utilized for determining parts of the liturgical cycle. Other differences from Western practice include the use of the term *Epiphany* to designate the commemoration of the baptism of Jesus, rather than the appearance of Jesus to the Magi; the use of bread mixed with wine in the distribution of the Eucharist; and the practice of *chrismation,* an anointing administered immediately after baptism, rather than in a separate, later rite such as the West's sacrament of confirmation.

In addition to the seven sacraments or mysteries shared with the Roman church, Orthodoxy recognizes a number of other rituals as sacramental in character. Among these is the administration of the *tonsure*—a symbolic clipping of hair—to those taking monastic vows. Monasticism has played an important role in Orthodoxy from early on, and Mount Athos on the Greek coast has been a major center of Orthodox spirituality. Monasticism also plays an important role in Orthodox polity, since bishops are usually elevated from the ranks of celibate monks. (Widowers are also eligible.) Other clergy may marry before they receive ordination, but are thereafter barred from the episcopate. Clergy, laity, and bishops all participate in councils that set policy for the entire communion. In America, the scarcity of bishops and clergy in the early years led to a stronger role for the laity in governance. The exact character of polity varies according to the size, needs, and traditions of the several branches of Orthodoxy represented in North America, but continuity within the Apostolic Succession of Bishops is a constant.

In the Christian spectrum today, especially in the United States, Eastern Christianity remains something of an anomaly. In terms of Will Herberg's classic typology of "Protestant, Catholic, Jew," Eastern Christians fall through the cracks (together with Anglicans, many of whom reject such easy classification). Although Eastern ways of belief and worship closely resemble those of the more familiar Roman Catholic tradition in many ways, the issue of papal supremacy has placed the Orthodox churches in closer alliance with the Protestant churches on such matters as participating in the National and World Councils of Churches. Although their ethnic identities remain distinct and in many ways restrictive, their continued vitality on the American scene is a caution against too facile a reduction of America's religious communities into generic categories that are easy to think but poor reflections of a complex reality.

CHAPTER 6

The Roman Catholic Tradition

The Roman Catholic Church is the largest single religious organization in the United States today. Like those of many religious groups, its name, which had been bestowed upon it after the English Reformation by Anglicans hostile to the Papacy in Rome, originally had derogatory connotations. In recent times, however, the name has been widely accepted in English-speaking countries as proper and official. Until the Reformation era, the modifier "Roman" was unnecessary, since the Catholic Church, with its center in the Roman Papacy, was officially the only representative of Christianity in Western Europe. Despite the challenges that began in earnest with Luther's protests in the early sixteenth century, the Roman Catholic Church represents to this day the largest single tradition within the Christian religion, as well as the most universally dispersed.

Roman Catholicism affirms the traditional teachings of the early church as expressed in the creeds of Nicea and Chalcedon, the decrees of subsequent ecumenical councils (worldwide assemblages of bishops, held periodically, such as the most recent Vatican II), and the dogmatic pronouncements of the Popes. It shares with virtually all other Christian groups a belief in the inspired and authoritative character of the Hebrew and Christian scriptures (the Old and New Testaments) together with the so-called Apocrypha.

However, it also maintains that Scripture can be interpreted properly only through the *magisterium,* or teaching authority, of the institutional church. The fullness of this authority resides in the Papacy, which is the custodian of the body of teaching known as *Tradition.* Tradition is based on revelation as contained in Scripture, but also includes doctrines, such as the bodily assumption of the Virgin Mary into heaven. These are not explicit in Scripture but have been developed within the Catholic community over the centuries from implicit scriptural evidence. The Pope is further able to make infallible pronouncements on matters of faith and morals when he speaks *ex cathedra*—that is, officially from his "chair," which is a symbol of his office.

A major key to understanding the Catholic theological perspective is through its approach to the relationship of the realms of "Nature" and "Grace." The Catholic Church has traditionally taught that the realm of Nature is God's creation. Although finite and flawed, nature, including humanity, is fundamentally good. Human nature has been corrupted by Original Sin; still, it is capable of redemption through divine grace, which is potentially available to all of humanity.

The usual channel of such grace is the sacraments. These rituals, seven in number, are said to have been instituted by Jesus Christ. They are ordinarily administered by the clergy, who are thus empowered by ordination to the priesthood (itself a sacrament) or, in some cases, by a bishop (e.g., confirmation and ordination). Sacraments employ both verbal and material elements, and are examples of the Catholic belief that grace, or divine saving power, does not repudiate but rather builds upon and perfects a natural substratum.

As should be evident by now, the Catholic Church has always placed great emphasis on the institutional church as an intermediary between the divine and the human. From the time of the Council of Trent (1545–1563), the church was identified primarily with the clergy, or priests, and the hierarchy, or bishops headed by the Pope. The Second Vatican Council (1962–1965), however, redefined the character of the church through a much greater emphasis on the role of the laity (a category including nuns and sisters, who, though "religious professionals," cannot receive ordination because of their sex).

Traditional Catholic ethics, which is frequently called moral theology, is based on the notion of *natural law,* an idea that correlates with the theology of nature and grace. This fundamental approach in both theology and ethics is derived from the thought of the thirteenth-century philosopher St. Thomas Aquinas (1225–1274), who adapted the categories of the Greek philosopher Aristotle for Christian purposes. According to natural law theory, all important human activities have a proper goal that is defined by nature and knowable by reason unaided by grace. For example, sexual intercourse has as its natural goal procreation, and the use of artificial contraceptives to thwart the fulfillment of this goal is unnatural and therefore immoral.

Needless to say, this particular application of natural law theory has been extremely controversial. Since Vatican II, a diversity of teachings on a wide variety of ethical matters, including the morality of nuclear warfare and capital punishment as well as sexuality in its various forms, has arisen within the American Catholic community. (The difficulties of the American ethicist Charles Curran and the German theologian Hans Küng with the Vatican over their teachings on a variety of matters, from contraception to papal infallibility, are illustrative of the ferment and tensions within the international Catholic community.) Similarly, new theological approaches influenced by contemporary philosophical movements such as existentialism and phenomenology have arisen to challenge traditional scholastic philosophy and theology based on Aquinas's teachings. Central to this reconceptualization of theology has been a movement away from a focus on objective, external processes, goals, and criteria toward an emphasis on the individual self in personal relationship with God and the Christian community. Continental European theologians such as Bernard Häring, Karl Rahner, Hans Küng, Bernard Lonergan, Pierre Teilhard de Chardin, and Edward Schillebeeckx—some of them still controversial—have all exercised an important influence on contemporary American Catholic thought.

One way of understanding both the centrality to Catholicism of sacramental worship and the ways in which thought and practice have changed significantly in the wake of Vatican II is to look more carefully at each of the seven sacraments, a number fixed during the later Middle Ages after long debate. These seven can be separated analytically into two categories: those that are usually received once (at most) during the course of the life cycle, and those that are received on a regular basis.

To begin with the latter, the rite that has traditionally been known as *penance* has undergone some of the most dramatic reinterpretation in recent years. For centuries penance had been administered on a very individualistic basis in which penitents would confess their sins to the priest, usually while kneeling in a confessional (a wooden box designed for the purpose with screens between priest and penitents to provide an atmosphere of anonymity). After confessing their sins, penitents would receive absolution, or a declaration of divine forgiveness, from the priest, and be assigned a set of prayers or other pious acts to be performed as a condition of this forgiveness. Criticism of this approach arose on the grounds that the process had become too mechanical and impersonal, with excessive emphasis on the legalistic and objective recitation of particular deeds. As a result of post-Vatican II shifts in perspective, the sacrament, now known as *reconciliation,* more frequently takes place with the priest and penitent facing one another. Emphasis is placed on a subjective transformation of one's priorities and relations with others. The practice of a more generalized absolution of whole groups has come into practice in some parts of America, but does not enjoy official institutional sanction as an ordinary practice.

The other sacrament that is intended to be received on a regular basis is the *Eucharist*—also known as "Holy Communion"—which is the core of the church's central ritual, the Mass. The Mass, which is closely paralleled by the Eucharistic rites used by Anglicans and Lutherans, developed gradually over many centuries, and still uses Latin and Greek forms to indicate sections that originated in early Christian usage but are now rendered solely in English. The following is an outline of the Mass as it is now usually celebrated by American Catholics:

A. Introductory Rites
    1. Entrance hymn
    2. Greeting by celebrant and response by people
    3. Rite of blessing and sprinkling with holy water
    4. Penitential rite: general confession of sin and absolution including the *Kyrie Eleison:* a Greek form, "Lord have mercy"
    5. The *Gloria,* retaining its Latin name: "Glory to God in the highest . . ."
    6. The opening prayer

B. The Liturgy of the Word
    1. Old Testament reading
    2. A psalm, recited alternately by the reader and the congregation
    3. New Testament reading
    4. Gospel reading
    5. The homily (i.e., sermon)
    6. The profession of faith (the Nicene Creed)
    7. General intercessions: prayers for specific categories of intentions

C. The Liturgy of the Eucharist
    1. The Preface
    2. The *Sanctus:* "Holy, holy, holy . . ."
    3. The memorial acclamation (one of several forms)
    4. The final doxology
    5. The Lord's Prayer
    6. The Sign of Peace: the congregation greets one another
    7. The breaking of bread, with recitation of the *Agnus Dei:* "Lamb of God, you take away the sins of the world, have mercy on us."
    8. Administration of Communion (bread and wine)
    9. Silent prayer after Communion

D. Concluding Rite: greeting, blessing, and dismissal

The Mass takes its name from its concluding words in Latin, *Ite, missa est:* "Go, you are sent forth." Its exact form has varied over the centuries; the present-day English version is based on the Latin form dating to the time of the Council of Trent, which led to the standardization of a great deal of Catholic practice. In addition to the use of the vernacular, the reforms of Vatican II have brought about several other noteworthy changes. Instead of being turned toward a marble altar, the celebrant (i.e., the priest) now faces the congregation over a wooden table. The congregation takes a more active role in responding to the priest, and participates in bringing forward the elements (bread and wine) and in exchanging the sign of peace (usually a handshake). Scripture is read by lay people, including women. The priest is free to improvise some of the prayers, which formerly had set forms, and is also encouraged to present a well-crafted homily or sermon, an art form frequently neglected in earlier American Catholic practice.

Music during worship is another area in which considerable change has taken place since Vatican II. During the nineteenth and earlier twentieth centuries, Catholic liturgical music was rather eclectic, and tended toward the operatic or sentimental when used at all. The Liturgical Movement led in America by the Benedictine monks at St. John's Abbey in Collegeville, Minnesota, emphasized the revival of Gregorian Chant as part of a new stress on a dignified, participatory liturgy. Since Vatican II, chant has yielded to congregational singing, an experience to which many Catholics had never been accustomed. Current collections used in Catholic worship reflect the general broad range of sources found in the hymnals used by Episcopalians, Lutherans, and Presbyterians, though some hymns with specific Catholic themes—for instance, devotion to Mary—provide small notes of distinctiveness. "Folk Masses" with guitars and folk songs became popular during the late 1960s, and are still celebrated in some parishes.

The other five sacraments can be arranged in the order of the progress of the individual human life cycle. Parallels with these rituals in many other religious cultures present no problem theologically; the Catholic idea of grace building on and completing what has already been anticipated in nature legitimates these correspondences or, in some cases, appropriations. The same argument holds for the divisions of the liturgical year, which are betokened by the changing colors of the vestments of the priest and the cloths draped over the altar. This annual cycle begins with Advent, a period of waiting and preparation, which is marked by the four Sundays preceding Christmas. Christmas Day, which is not fixed on the (unknown) actual birthdate of Jesus but rather on the Roman festival of the unconquered sun, is another good example of the appropriation of religious symbols from other cultures with a Christian reinterpretation. The year continues through other major holy days commemorating major events in the life of Jesus (his Epiphany and Circumcision); of Mary (her Immaculate Conception—i.e., conception free from original sin—and bodily Assumption into heaven); and those of other saints, especially All Saints's Day on November 1. Easter, preceded by the forty penitential days of Lent and coming usually in the early spring, is another good example of the coincidence of an event of the utmost significance for Christians—the Resurrection of Jesus—with both the Jewish Passover and the more general celebration of the annual renewal of nature.

The first of what might be called the sacraments of the life cycle is that of Baptism, or Christian Initiation. Baptism was available in the early church only to adults and only after a considerable period of instruction. After Christianity had become the official religion of the Empire, it was routinely administered to newborn infants by sprinkling (aspersion) rather than immersion. Although infant baptism is still the norm, a new emphasis since Vatican II has also revived the importance of the symbolism of the adult initiation in the early Christian manner. Since infant baptism is a vicarious process, with the parents and godparents providing the witness, the sacrament of *confirmation* provides for a conscious completion of the initiatory process by the "candidate" at a later age. In traditional American Catholic practice this took place around the age of eight or nine, but more recently it is carried out in early adolescence. Baptism is performed by a priest, although lay people may confer it in unusual circumstances; confirmation is ordinarily administered by a bishop.

The onset of adulthood traditionally involved a choice between marriage or the religious life, each of which was acknowledged sacramentally. Holy orders, or ordination, is the ritual of entry into the priesthood, and is also administered by a bishop. Women entering religious orders as nuns or sisters participate in elaborate ceremonies in which they take solemn vows, but these are not technically sacraments. Matrimony, or marriage, does have a sacramental character, and is technically dissoluble only through an annulment, or declaration that a proper marriage has never taken place because of nonconsummation, lack of free consent on the part of both parties, or other technical reasons. In practice, the binding character of both of these sacraments has come into question in recent years. Diocesan marriage tribunals have extended the grounds of annulment to psychological as well as physical and legal criteria, and many Catholics simply obtain civil divorces. The status of divorced Catholics, who are technically unable to receive Communion, is thus a sensitive point, and many support groups have arisen to help them deal with the situation. Similarly, the reappraisals of the priesthood brought about by Vatican II have resulted in many priests seeking and obtaining dispensation from their vows, while others have simply left the priesthood.

The last of the "life-cycle" sacraments was formerly known as extreme unction—the anointing with oil of the gravely ill and dying. Its revised name, "the anointing of the sick," has given it a less dire character; it is no longer administered solely to those close to death, but rather in cases of reasonably serious illness, with an emphasis on its life-affirming character. Cremation of the dead had long been banned because it had at one time been practiced as a denial of Catholic teaching on the resurrection of the body. More recently, though, it has reemerged as a permissible option under some circumstances. Burial in consecrated ground—that is, a Catholic cemetery—is still the preferred means for disposing of the earthly remains of the dead.

A final topic of distinctively Catholic belief and practice is the complex of devotions focusing on Jesus, the Virgin Mary, and the saints. Many of these practices originated in the "Baroque" era of piety that flourished in France and Italy during the seventeenth and eighteenth centuries. Prior to Vatican II, "para-liturgical" practices such as the recitation of the Rosary and other prayers and pious acts focusing on the Virgin Mary and the saints had become central to the religious life of many Catholics, and were promoted actively by many religious orders. The Liturgical Movement helped undermine these practices by its focus on the Mass as an event in which the laity were to participate actively, rather than attend to their own devotions while the priest conducted the liturgy unilaterally. The emphasis on the dialogic character of worship promoted by the Council has resulted in a deemphasis on devotional practices, though many older Catholics still find them rewarding. On the other hand, the new interest in female religious symbolism promoted by the feminist movement in theology has focused attention on the significance of the Virgin Mary, though from a very nontraditional perspective.

As should be clear from the discussion of the development and general character of Roman Catholicism, the tradition's stress on the importance of the institutional church as a channel for divine grace, together with its Roman heritage, combine to create an elaborate and intricate structure of organization and governance. The basic structure of the Catholic Church is hierarchical; that is, it resembles a pyramid in which power is concentrated at the top and is diffused downward through increasingly broad layers.

At the very top of this pyramid of authority is the Bishop of Rome—the *Pope*—who as Supreme Pontiff holds ultimate authority over the entire church. The Pope is assisted in his duties by the *Curia*, or cabinet, which consists primarily of *Cardinals* (on which more later) and other bishops residing in Rome who preside over the various divisions of papal government, with corresponding titles such as "Secretary of State." The Pope and his advisors reside in the Vatican City, a small area of only a few acres within the city of Rome but entirely independent politically and possessing all of the agencies of government. These include a diplomatic corps with representatives throughout the world's capitals, and even a small army of sorts, the famous and colorful Swiss Guards. The Vatican is all that remains of the Papal States, a belt of territory that bisected the Italian peninsula and over which the Pope presided as political ruler until the achievement of Italian unification in 1870.

The *College of Cardinals,* which supplies the highest level of staffing for much of the Vatican's activities, is a group of men, of late about 130 in number, whose sole official duty is the election of a new Pope when the office falls vacant by death or, rarely, by abdication. (The Pope traditionally serves for the remainder of his lifetime after election.) Almost all of the Cardinals are bishops, usually archbishops of major cities, appointed by the Pope. Until recently, the College (and the Papacy) were dominated by Italians, but since the reign of John XXIII it has become more cosmopolitan in membership, with a number of Third World Cardinals appointed in the last few decades. (The election of John Paul II, Archbishop of Cracow, Poland, as Pope in 1978 also put an end to the longtime hold on the Papacy by Italians.) Although any Roman Catholic male can theoretically be named a Cardinal, in practice the College's ranks have been filled by prominent archbishops.

The rank of Cardinal is largely honorific, with the election of the Pope as its only distinctive function. More central to the church's structure is the office of *Bishop.* Bishops are said to be direct successors of the Apostles, and the doctrine of the Apostolic Succession is crucial to the church's notion of authority. (This idea is also accepted by a number of other religious groups, such as the Eastern Orthodox and Anglican Churches, but the Roman Catholic Church does not recognize all of these claims as valid.) Administratively, bishops preside over territories called *dioceses,* geographical units into which virtually the entire earth is divided. Each bishop has full power over the ecclesiastical life of his diocese, including finances, property, personnel matters (especially the assignment of priests), and teaching and worship. A bishop answers directly only to the Pope, although the notion of collegial sharing of authority with clergy and laity has become more important since the Second Vatican Council. In terms of worship, two of the seven sacraments of the Church—ordination to the priesthood and confirmation—can ordinarily be administered only by bishops.

Although all bishops are considered to be successors to the Apostles, not all bishops have equal prestige and authority. Bishops of large and important cities in the Catholic world are often given the title of *Archbishop*, a designation that goes with responsibility for a particular territory known as an Archdiocese. Bishops of other cities are officially known as *suffragan* bishops; however, they enjoy the same fullness of power as an Archbishop, whose only real additional function is the right to convene the bishops of his *province*—that is, the territory composed of the dioceses of which his, the Archdiocese, is first among equals. Archbishops or bishops of large dioceses may also be assisted by *auxiliary* bishops. Finally, a *bishop coadjutor* is sometimes appointed when a bishop is old or infirm. Such a bishop functions as an assistant until the senior bishop's death or retirement, at which time the coadjutor automatically becomes bishop in his own right.

Bishops, Cardinals, and Popes are all chosen ultimately from the ranks of the *priesthood*, the basic group of "professional religious" men in the church whose professions are given spiritual legitimation through the sacrament of ordination. Priests are distinguished from the laity primarily through their power to administer the sacraments. However, priests have many other duties and functions, including the administration of a parish, or basic geographical division of the church, usually a town or urban neighborhood, all of the Catholic inhabitants of which are expected to attend the church designated for that parish; pastoral counseling; preaching; and the various other activities usually associated with the Christian ministry. A priest who is in charge of a parish is known as a *rector;* any assistants he might have are called *curates.* *Monsignor* is an honorary title sometimes bestowed on senior priests as a special recognition of their services.

Not all priests, however, are assigned to parishes, especially those belonging to religious orders. The major division of the priesthood is usually given as that between the *secular* clergy, who are part of the diocesan hierarchy and who answer directly to a bishop, and the *regular* clergy, who belong to religious orders such as the Jesuits or Dominicans and who answer to their order's superior. The term *secular* does not indicate a lack of religious zeal, but rather refers to this sort of priest's residence in the world (Latin *saeculum*), usually in a parish. "Regular clergy," on the other hand, are those who live according to a rule (Latin *regula*), frequently in communities by themselves apart from the secular world. Regular clergy were originally monks, such as the Trappists, who continue to live in monasteries and have little contact with the outside world. Others, such as Jesuits, Dominicans, and Franciscans—orders of priests, brothers, or *friars* originating in the later Middle Ages or Catholic Reformation eras—are active in the world, and may function as missionaries, teachers, or at times as parish priests. Members of religious orders also take vows of poverty, chastity, and obedience as part of their commitment, while secular clergy may own private property. The latter, however, are supposed to be obedient to their bishops, and rarely marry under the prevailing code of church discipline.

Ordination to the priesthood is the culmination of a series of ordinations to lesser ecclesiastical ranks, or orders, including those of lector, acolyte, exorcist, and subdeacon—all known as *minor orders.* In the early Christian church, these were functions exercised by separate individuals. In modern times, however, these and another major order, that of *deacon,* became conflated into preliminaries to the priesthood itself. In the past two decades, the order of the *diaconate* (i.e., of deacons) has been reinterpreted to give new importance to the role of *permanent deacon.* Married men may be ordained to the permanent diaconate, and carry out an extension of the ancient roles of the order— administration of the sacraments (without being able to celebrate the Eucharist), caring for the needy, and other important ministries. Many American parishes are now assigned permanent deacons who usually follow secular careers at the same time.

In addition to the clergy, other members of the church dedicate their lives totally to religion without being ordained. Men in this category are usually known as brothers, who perform menial tasks in some religious orders, or who sometimes, as in the case of the Christian Brothers, belong to orders composed primarily of unordained men who engage in teaching and other distinctive tasks (including wine-making). Women, on the other hand, are not able to receive the sacrament of ordination under any circumstances, but are able to enter into religious orders and take vows similar to those of their male counterparts and likewise live in community. Although such religious women are usually referred to generically as *nuns,* this term is more properly reserved for those who live in communities secluded from the secular world and dedicated to a purely contemplative life. Religious women who engage in such tasks as teaching and nursing, such as the Sisters of Mercy and the Sisters of Charity, are technically referred to as *sisters.* (In the United States, though, this distinction has never been much observed.) Since religious women cannot be ordained, their status is technically that of *laity* (as opposed to *clergy*).

Finally, the large majority of the world's Roman Catholics are not ordained and do not belong to any religious order, but live their lives in the secular world in the pursuit of any number of occupations while presumably attending church and receiving the sacraments with some regularity. These are the laity, or laymen and laywomen. In the years before the Second Vatican Council, these laity were generally regarded as rather passive in their role in the church compared with the clergy and other religious functionaries, and did not ordinarily play a major role in the decision-making and teaching roles of the church. In more recent times, however, the role of the laity has been redefined in more positive and active terms. This activity has taken such forms as participation in parish councils, which help in the planning and execution of parish activities, and in teaching at a variety of levels, from parochial elementary schools, which can no longer rely on large numbers of teaching sisters, to seminary theological faculties.

This lengthy account of the belief, worship, and organizational structure of

Roman Catholicism indicates the importance placed by this tradition on the objective, formal aspects of the religious life. This has been in large part an outgrowth of its distinctively Roman cultural heritage, with an analysis of which the following chapter begins. The development of the Western, Roman tradition of Christianity over nearly two millennia can be read as an ongoing interplay or dialectic between these powerful forces of order and other impulses in revolt against a centralization, uniformity, and traditionalism perceived as overly rigid and spiritually deadening. In some cases—most dramatically in the era of the Reformation—that tension has resulted in a revolutionary sundering of the unity that Roman Christianity has so prized. In others, it has led to the flourishing of internal diversity. That dialectic has received new impetus in the later twentieth century as a result of Vatican II, and any ultimate resolution of those tensions remains doubtful. This is perhaps for the best: were resolution to be achieved, it might be a sign that the tradition's centuries-old vitality was finally nearing a close.

CHAPTER 7

Western Catholicism from the Time of Constantine

Each of the three words that make up its modern name reveals some important aspects of the character of the Roman Catholic Church. Its association with the city of Rome dates to the earliest days of the Christian religion and the residence there of the apostles Peter and Paul. Peter, the chief of the apostles, gradually came to be regarded as the first of an unbroken line of bishops of the city. The text of Matthew 16:18 ff. ("And I say unto thee, thou art Peter, and on this rock I shall build my church") is regarded by Catholics as evidence that Jesus himself was the source of the original authority of the Roman bishop's office.

In a monumental shift in the history of Christianity, the Roman Emperor Constantine (d. 337) elevated Christianity from the status of a suspect and potentially treasonable "underground" religion to the official creed of the Empire. In another epoch-making act, he removed the imperial capital to Byzantium (which was subsequently renamed "Constantinople") early in the fourth century A.D. The Roman bishop, who had acquired the title of "Pope" ("father"), thus found himself the leader not only of the official religion of the West but in many regards the civil ruler as well. He was faced with the problem of serving as not just spiritual but also temporal administrator for Italy, the western reaches of northern Africa, and other territories not directly under the aegis of Constantinople. The Pope and his staff therefore found themselves becoming diplomats, distributors of relief, and even on occasion military figures in dealing with civil disorganization and the ravages both of nature and the ever-encroaching barbarian hordes from the north. As a result, a complicated bureaucratic apparatus began to emerge at the papal court that formed the basis for today's *curia*—that is, the bureaus, often headed by a cardinal, that make up the papal government.

Part of the distinctively *Roman* character of the Catholic Church, then, is its elaborate administrative apparatus, which it developed out of temporal necessity and also as the heir to the legacy of the Roman Empire. In the era of close church-state relations known as the *Middle Ages*, a *Holy Roman Empire* and other Christianized secular powers emerged to reclaim the civic functions that the Papacy had foisted upon it willy-nilly. Still, the church retained and even continued to expand its internal administrative apparatus and develop its code of *canon* (i.e., church) *law*, another heritage from the Roman Empire.

The emergence of a Christian secular power during the so-called Middle Ages, however, did not mark an end to the church's claim to temporal authority. The titles of Bishop, Abbott, and especially Pope carried with them control of wealth and power that, when challenged, was seldom readily relinquished. It was not until the unification of the modern Italian nation in 1870 that papal control over the "Papal States," which ran through the central part of the Italian peninsula, came to a definitive end, and with it the Pope's role as a secular prince. This situation was not normalized until the signing of a concordat, or papal treaty, with Mussolini in 1929. The bitterness of this struggle contributed to the suspicion and sometimes outright hostility with which the papal government viewed the secular order during the nineteenth and early twentieth century.

Taken together, these elements of a conscious heritage from the Roman Empire—bureaucratic complexity, an elaborate legal code, and an interweaving of religious and political authority—have all contributed to the development of the quality of *Romanità*, a term often invoked to characterize the distinctive ethos of the Vatican and the Papacy. Another way of characterizing this quality is as the possession of a sense of history that views with suspicion rapid change and looks at matters *sub specie aeternitatis*—from the perspective of the ages rather than the present moment. This attitude, needless to say, is very different from the present- and future-mindedness of many Americans, Catholics included. This difference in perspective has often led to conflict between Vatican authority and the American branch of the church.

The second feature of Roman Catholicism worth noting is its claim to *catholicity*—universality and inclusiveness. The Catholic Church has for centuries claimed that it possesses the fullness of saving truth in its structures, sacraments, and tradition, and that all of humanity should rightfully find a place within it as the surest guide to salvation. Some of the church's claims to exclusive possession of such truth have been modified by Vatican II, but the church still regards its goal as universal membership. To this end, it maintains a worldwide missionary effort, conducted principally by members of religious orders, and coordinated by the Congregation for the Propagation of the Faith in Rome.

In many ways, the claim of the Roman Catholic Church to be universal is borne out in reality. It is the largest single organized religious body both in the United States and in the world, with well over a half-billion adherents world-wide. Its members are spread through every inhabited continent, with the heaviest concentrations in Europe and the Americas. Much of this geographical spread was achieved during the period of exploration and colonization of the Renaissance, when the Catholic nations of France, Spain, and Portugal established hegemony throughout virtually all of Latin American and substantial portions of North America and Africa. Even after the age of colonization and the onset of Third World independence, the Catholic Church continues to enjoy wide adherence in former colonial areas, though it has been aggressively challenged by Marxism on the one hand and by Pentecostal and other evangelical Protestant missionary efforts on the other. In recent years, the acute problems of economic inequality and political oppression especially in Latin America have led to the emergence of a new movement in Catholic thought and action called Liberation Theology. Articulated in the work of thinkers such as Leonardo Boff and Gustavo Gutierrez, this school of thought focuses on the relevance of the teachings of the Gospel to present-day human need in situations of want and oppression and has been extremely controversial in both religious and political circles.

The third element in Catholicism's name is *church*, a term that carries with it a variety of levels of meaning. "Church" may refer to a building in which worship is conducted, the congregation that assembles for worship, or the organizational structures that unite a number of local congregations into a larger denomination. In the vocabulary of such founders of the sociology of religion as Max Weber and Ernst Troeltsch, however, the term *church* took on another, more technical meaning that is particularly useful in understanding the significance of the term in this context.

The primary models of religious structure that presented themselves to this generation of thinkers came from the classic pattern of the Middle Ages, which was rapidly breaking up in the Europe of the later nineteenth century. Until the era of the Reformation, one universal church—at least in theory—included the entirety of the population of western Europe within its scope. The only exceptions to this all-encompassing Christendom ruled spiritually by the Pope and temporally by the Holy Roman Emperor were the Jews, who enjoyed an exempt status when times were favorable, and various groups of Christian dissidents labeled by the church as heretics. These later people, such as the Waldenses of twelfth-century northern Italy or the Hussites of fifteenth-century Bohemia (Czechoslovakia), regarded themselves as reformers who rejected on various grounds the claims to authority of institutional Catholicism. The term later given by sociologists to these groups was *sect*, and their adherents were *sectarians*.

The idea of a sect in practical terms presupposes that of a church, since sectarians receive their warrant for existence in their rejection of what they regard as the inevitable compromises of any church that attempts inclusiveness of membership. This ideal of inclusiveness, which is manifest in the term *catholic* itself, has always been a characteristic of Catholicism. Even after the Reformation had effectively divided Europe into a number of separate and frequently hostile religious spheres, this idea of the "church" as including by definition all of the people in a given political unit remained dominant throughout most of Europe, whether in the form of Anglicanism in England, Lutheranism in many of the German states, or Catholicism, which continued to prevail primarily in the southern parts of the Continent. Even though its actual scope was curtailed, however, the Catholic Church continued to assert its claims to universal inclusiveness, and directed its energies at once to missionary expansion overseas as well as to the reestablishment of its influence in Protestant Europe through such arms of the "Catholic (or Counter) Reformation" as the Jesuit order founded by Ignatius Loyola in 1540.

Even though the idea of a "church" in this context carries with it strong political overtones, it also has an important religious dimension. The earliest Christian communities had been more sectarian than "churchly" in the rigor of their requirements for membership and the ever-present danger of martyrdom that confronted them. The Constantinian Revolution then resulted in a radically transformed organization that found itself responsible for the welfare of the entire community. From that time on, the Catholic Church began to regard itself as the institutional means through which God's redeeming grace was mediated, potentially to the entirety of humanity. This was not to say that everyone would ultimately achieve salvation; it was, however, to affirm that all people should at least be exposed to the means of saving grace, and it provided a warrant for the church's campaign through missionary work and institutional expansion throughout what was then regarded by Europeans as virtually the entire world.

Another aspect of the "catholicity" of Roman Catholicism has been its provision of a wide variety of religious life-styles to accommodate the wide variety of spiritual types it takes in. The most totally committed men and women have from early on had the option of being called to the monastic life. Many of the most spectacular "spiritual athletes" of the early Christian centuries chose the life of *anchorites,* or hermits living in isolation. St. Benedict of Nursia provided an alternative, and ultimately more viable, model in the community he organized at Monte Cassino in Italy around A.D. 540. Monks who followed this communal style, in which they lived together in work and prayer organized according to a rule, were known as *coenobites* (SEN-oh-bites). This coenobitic monasticism soon displaced the anchoritic style as normative in western Christendom. Religious orders for women as well as men also emerged at an early date.

Monasticism flourished during the Middle Ages, undergoing various high and low periods and frequent reforms, and continues to the present day in a variety of communities with differing traditions. Benedictines, for example, are involved in the world through the maintenance of colleges, such as St. John's in Minnesota, and other educational endeavors, while Trappists live a life of silent contemplation in almost complete withdrawal from the secular realm. Monasticism is now comparatively unusual in late twentieth-century

America; however, its popularity received a major boost through the life and writings of Thomas Merton (1915–1968), whose autobiographical *Seven Storey Mountain* (1948) presented the contemplative life as an intellectually respectable and spiritually compelling alternative to what Merton represented as the arid secularity of contemporary American life. Merton's later antiwar activism and death while participating in a conference at a Buddhist monastery further demonstrated that even the most rigorous monastic life-style was not incompatible with an engaged participation in the broader concerns of humanity.

In addition to the monastic life, a number of alternative models for living in community developed with the changing conditions of later centuries. The urbanization of late medieval Europe brought about the most eminent preaching orders of the Franciscans and Dominicans. Members of these orders were not remote from the world, but rather engaged to spread the Gospel among the urban dwellers who seemed to be falling through the cracks of the new social order. Later, in the Reformation era, the Society of Jesus was founded by the Spanish former soldier Ignatius Loyola in 1540. The Jesuits came into existence to try to halt the spread of Protestant ideas, particularly through the rigorous education of the sons of influential families. In later centuries, all three of these orders turned their attention to overseas missions, education, scholarship, and a wide variety of other tasks. Religious orders of women—known in America more or less interchangeably as "nuns" or "sisters"—had existed from the time of the early church, but began to come into prominence especially during the post-Reformation era. Like their male counterparts, some of these women retreated from the world into cloistered lives of prayer. The majority, though, turned their attention, especially in nineteenth- and early twentieth-century America, to the practical tasks of teaching, nursing, and various forms of social work.

Although lay people have always been thought capable of lofty spiritual attainments, the bias of the institutional church until the changes of direction brought about by Vatican II had been toward the special recognition of those men who had been ordained to the priesthood or women and lay brothers who had entered a religious order. A major category used by the Catholic Church to recognize lives of heroic piety, whether led by clergy or laity, is that of *sainthood*. The term *saint* was used in the early church to designate followers of Jesus, but gradually began to take on other associations. During the decades of persecution that took place periodically prior to the Constantinian settlement, Christians who remained faithful even unto death were acclaimed as *martyrs*, and thus achieved, albeit posthumously, a heroic status in the eyes of the Christian community. After the age of martyrdom had passed, a new preoccupation with the ability of martyrs and other witnesses to the faith—*ascetics*, for example, who lived lives of rigorous self-denial and punishment—to work miracles began to arise. *Cults* devoted to the preservation and veneration of the memories and relics of such miracle-workers grew up spontaneously throughout Christendom, and the spiritual heroes who were thought to be so divinely favored as to perform miraculous healings and other events of a supernatural character were acclaimed as *saints*. Eventually, the recognition of saints was routinized by the institutional church, and an elaborate process of collection and evaluation of evidence must now be undergone prior to an individual's being declared—always posthumously—to be among the ranks of the saints.

Such spiritual heroes, however, were not the only Christians who made up the church. Most individuals, though not capable of such heroic piety, nevertheless could expect salvation through the more ordinary means to that goal provided by the institutional church through the sacraments. Particularly directed toward this expectation of human failings was *penance*—more recently renamed *reconciliation*—which provided a regular means for the confession of and atonement for the lapses into sinfulness into which all humans periodically strayed. After confessing one's sins to a priest, receiving absolution, and performing prescribed acts of penance, one could regularly enter (or reenter) into a state of *grace,* or reconciliation with God, and therefore be fit to enter into Heaven upon one's death if one had died in the appropriate state. For the ordinary run of mortals, however, one would ordinarily expect to undergo some experience of *Purgatory,* a state of otherworldly atonement for the effects of one's sins prior to admission into Paradise itself.

This world view, which evolved gradually during those centuries collectively designated the Middle Ages and received definitive expression during the time of Dante and St. Thomas Aquinas (ca. 1200–1300), received a revivification and also a rigidification in the wake of the Reformation of the sixteenth century. The challenge to papal authority begun by Martin Luther in 1517 and carried further by Calvin, Zwingli, and the other Reformers generated a Counter-, or Catholic, Reformation as a response to the questions of belief and practice that these harbingers of a new era raised. On the one hand, most Catholics were prepared to admit that there was considerable failure within the church to live up to its own ideals. Abuses among clergy and hierarchy were rife. On the other hand, the institutional church was *not* prepared to acknowledge the validity of the claims of Luther and his followers to theological revisionism, for example, the rejection of the Catholic idea of *tradition* as a valid source of religious authority.

The means through which both an internal house-cleaning and a vigorous counterattack against the inroads of the Reformers were carried on was the convening of an ecumenical council at Trent, in northern Italy, in 1545. The Council of Trent, which was in session on and off for the next eighteen years, made great strides in establishing a disciplined, educated, and moral clergy that would be impervious to the accusations of both external and internal critics of the previous decades. In addition, a number of new religious orders, especially Ignatius Loyola's Jesuits, helped to wage a vigorous effort to combat the inroads of the Reformation wherever possible.

The three centuries that elapsed between Trent and the Second Vatican Council coincided almost exactly with that period in England and America that Sydney Ahlstrom has characterized as "the Great Puritan Epoch." For the Roman Catholic Church and the areas in which it remained dominant, this same period might well be called "the Great Tridentine Epoch." According to the sociologist Max Weber, Puritanism and other forms of Protestantism helped to provide the ideological basis for the transformation of Western society often described as "modernization": the displacement of country by city, agriculture by industry, oral culture by literacy, monarchy by democracy, provincialism by cosmopolitanism, the hold of tradition by the idea of progress. Although the parts of southern and central Europe that remained Catholic following the Reformation were not immune to the solvents of modernity, the coming of its inexorable components was certainly slower than in the Protestant climes of the Netherlands, the British Isles, and those colonies that would become the United States. During these centuries, Catholic hegemony was maintained, often through uneasy compromises, with the forces of tradition in European life that continued to dominate especially in Spain, Italy, Austria, and France. When change came, as it inevitably did in all of those regions, the consequences were frequently cataclysmic.

The post-Tridentine Catholic Church may be characterized as authoritarian, traditionalistic, clerical, legalistic, and devotionally oriented. The papacy strove continually to regain its hegemony and enhance its eminence, in which effort it was only periodically successful. With a few major exceptions, such as the work of that convert from Anglicanism John Henry Cardinal Newman (1801–1890), the Catholic theology that emerged in this era was derivative, consisting primarily of extensive commentaries on the work of Thomas Aquinas and other Medieval and Counter-Reformation era theologians. The Vatican viewed theological innovation with suspicion, and intellectual venturesomeness was not encouraged by the centralized clerical education mandated by Trent.

The administration of the church grew even more bureaucratic. A legalistic outlook prevailed both in the realms of administration and in moral theology, where highly detailed guidelines for individual conduct provided norms for behavior. Creative religious energies were focused on the founding of new religious orders, especially in seventeenth- and eighteenth-century France, which in turn provided the seedbeds for an efflorescence of piety inspired by appearances of the Virgin Mary to members, usually female, of those orders. These devotions consisted of saying prayers; wearing scapulars; venerating statues of Jesus, Mary, and other saints; undertaking pilgrimages to holy sites such as Lourdes (where a particularly important appearance of the Virgin was reported in 1858); and membership in societies founded to promote these activities.

Although these tendencies were characteristic of most of the Tridentine epoch, their apogee came in the nineteenth century with the pontificate of Pius IX ("Pio Nono") from 1846 to 1878. By the time Pius had ascended to the papal throne, the relationship of the Catholic church with the parts of Europe that had remained loyal since the Reformation had been undergoing an upheaval as traumatic as the revolt of Luther and his successors. Although the underpinnings of the new revolt against traditional Catholicism lay in the broad intellectual movement known as the Enlightenment and the economic and demographic transformations that were slowly changing the infrastructure of European life, the decisive historical turning point was the French Revolution. In the minds of the insurgents, the institutional church had been intimately complicit in the political order that had weighed so oppressively on the French people for so long, and that now had to be overturned—if necessary, by violence. The result was the wholesale execution at the guillotine of priests and bishops as well as nobles, and the driving into exile of many more.

Not surprisingly, the new ideologies of the eighteenth and nineteenth centuries—Freemasonry, socialism, anarchism, communism, and "liberalism" of various sorts—did not find ready acceptance by the Catholic Church. Pius IX himself had been regarded as something of a liberal at the beginning of his reign, but the anticlerical character that the movement for the unification of Italy assumed soon soured him on all things modern. One result was the "Syllabus of Errors" of 1864, a series of eighty theses that Pius condemned as erroneous. The last of these was the proposition that "the Roman pontiff can and ought to reconcile and harmonize himself with progress, with liberalism, and with modern civilization." Even allowing for a somewhat different sense of the key terms, especially *liberalism,* in the context of the time from that to which we are now accustomed, it is clear that this is not a statement of enthusiasm for rapid change.

The other major event associated with the pontificate of Pius IX that has had major ramifications for Catholic life and thought up to the present was his convening an ecumenical council at Rome in 1869, known in retrospect as "Vatican I." The major agenda item at this coming together of all the bishops of the Roman Catholic world was the formal definition of the infallibility of the Pope when speaking on matters of faith and morals *ex cathedra* ("from the chair")—that is, in his capacity as the intentional and ultimate arbiter of orthodox belief. This absolutizing of papal authority, even under clearly and rather narrowly delimited circumstances, was intended to bolster the Pope's prestige at a time when it was under attack from a variety of quarters. In the longer run, it came to be a symbol of the propensity of the institutional Catholic Church to draw rigid boundaries between itself and other Christian communions, and continues to prove an obstacle in ecumenical conversations. It is worth noting that only two doctrines have been formally declared in an infallible manner in recent times: the immaculate conception of the Virgin Mary (Pius IX, 1854), and her bodily assumption into heaven (Pius XII, 1950). These too have proven problematic in ecumenical discussions with Protestant groups that have never endowed the Virgin with such supernatural attributes.

Pius and his successors continued on this defensive course for the next several decades. When the Vatican Council was disrupted in 1870 by the Italian occupation of Rome, Pius was faced with the loss of temporal control of the Papal States. He declared himself a "prisoner of the Vatican," a status maintained by his successors until a concordat, or treaty, was negotiated between Pius XI and Mussolini in 1929. Leo XIII (reigned 1878–1903) showed signs of a new appreciation of the unique problems of the modern industrial age in his encyclical letter *Rerum Novarum* ("Of New Things," 1891), but later demonstrated a more traditionalist side in *Testem Benevolentiae* (1899), a response to disputes within the American church. Leo's successor, Pius X, issued a far-reaching condemnation of theological accommodation with contemporary biblical criticism in his encyclical *Pascendi Dominici Gregis* ("Feeding the Lord's Flock," 1907), a move that had a profound impact on the American scene as well. Papal intransigence against modern "isms" was further reinforced by the attacks on the church, its personnel, and its property by both the Right, in the form of Nazism and Italian Fascism, and the Left, as manifested in the virulent anticlericalism of the Mexican and Russian Revolutions as well as the Spanish Civil War.

Signs of change gradually appeared, for instance, in Pius XII's endorsement of modern biblical criticism in his encyclical *Divino Afflante Spiritu* ("Inspired by the Divine Spirit," 1943). However, the general posture of the institutional Catholic Church remained firmly conservative until the end of this latter Pius's pontificate in 1958. Upon his death, the College of Cardinals elected a dark horse, Angelo Giuseppe Roncalli, the elderly Cardinal Patriarch of Venice, for what many assumed would be a brief, "caretaking" pontificate. Roncalli, who took the name John XXIII, surprised almost everyone by convening a second ecumenical council at the Vatican to complete the agenda of the first council and to bring about, in John's word, an *aggiornamento*, an "up-to-dateness" of the church within the world around it.

The Council, which soon became known as Vatican II, began its deliberations in 1962 and concluded its work under John's successor, Paul VI (ruled 1963–1978), three years later. Vatican II was an instant success as a media event, in part because of the enormous personal charm and warmth of its convenor. Its mission was primarily "pastoral" rather than dogma-defining, and its ecumenical character was emphasized by the inclusion of Eastern Orthodox and Protestant representatives as nonvoting participants. Its impact was extraordinary, since the Council's documents, or "constitutions," provided often dramatically new approaches to a wide variety of issues on which the institutional church had previously taken an uncompromisingly traditionalist stand.

For Catholics themselves, the most visible result of the work of the Council was liturgical change and reform, described in the preceding chapter. There were many other results of the Council, conspicuous or subtle, that represented major changes in the life and thinking of Catholics throughout the world. Priests and religious women were now encouraged to enter more fully into worldly life rather than trying to emphasize their separation from it. Clerical dress and sisters' habits were duly, and sometimes radically, modified, so that it became difficult to distinguish their wearers from "secular" men and women. This deemphasis on boundaries between the church and the world contributed to the reappraisals that many priests and sisters brought to their "vocations," and large numbers began to apply for dispensations to leave the priesthood or convent to take up a new life in the secular world, including marriage. Although such permission was at first much easier to obtain than it had been, many omitted the formalities and simply left.

This deemphasis on the boundaries between the Catholic Church and the rest of the world also set in motion a chain of new developments. The presence of non-Roman Catholic observers at the Council betokened a new receptivity to positive relations with other religions, including the Jewish and Eastern traditions, and even with Marxism and other nontheistic ideologies. The *ecclesiology*, or doctrine of the church, promulgated in the Council's documents helped make this possible. The Council shifted the governing metaphor from the "Church Militant," or the church as a perfect society, to the idea of the "pilgrim people of God" engaged in collectively seeking truth and salvation here on earth.

By admitting that the Catholic Church was not perfect, a way of acknowledging the positive elements in other religions became available. "Dialogue" groups from the parish to the formal international level began to take place, and Catholic clergy and laity were no longer barred from participating in non-Catholic or interdenominational worship. Discussions with other "liturgical" churches such as the Lutheran, Anglican, and Eastern Orthodox have proven particularly fruitful in bringing about agreement by theologians on long-disputed questions such as the nature of justification (salvation), and close relationships between individual local parishes—for instance, Roman Catholic and Episcopal or Lutheran—have resulted in "covenants" bringing the congregations together in ways stopping only at intercommunion. However, more "political" issues such as papal infallibility and the ordination of women continue to impede major progress toward full intercommunion or organic union.

An ambiguous consequence of Vatican II was the new perspectives that it brought to bear on the question of *authority* within the Roman Catholic Church. Since the days of Trent, the church had become accustomed to an authoritative, hierarchical, and monarchical system of governance reinforced by the definition of papal infallibility at Vatican I and legitimating itself on the basis of tradition as well as Scripture. Vatican II began to change this. First, Scripture was accorded a renewed importance, and was now interpreted through sophisticated historical criticism rather than in the static, propositional categories that Catholic exegetes had shared with their conservative Protestant counterparts. This new historical-critical awareness undermined the ahistorical self-image that the church had for many centuries promoted, in which contemporary systems of belief and practice were projected back into New Testament times. Awareness of the reality of change in the past thus reinforced the idea of the possibility, and even the desirability, of change in the present. As in the Reformation, change was not necessarily seen as innovation, but rather as the *restoration* of the practices of biblical times—for example, in authority-sharing and lay participation in the liturgy.

Another challenge to traditional authority was the concept of *collegiality*, or the sharing of power within the church among its various constituents. Pope John convened the Council ostensibly to complete the work left unfinished at Vatican I, where papal authority had been definitively addressed but that of the bishops had not been dealt with. According to this idea, all of the components of the church—the papacy, the episcopate, the clergy, and the laity—had an essential and responsible part to play in the church's life, and a model in which authority simply flowed downward from the top was no longer adequate. The Council itself, in which bishops, advised by theologians, shared authority with the Pope, was a model at one level of this new collegial outlook. Sharing of authority also was implemented at the diocesan level, where priests met in regular assemblies to advise the bishop, and in parish councils, where lay delegates played a similar role for the priest. In practice, these structures did not always work well when a reluctance to share power manifested itself on the part of the bishop or priest, but the idea of absolute and unquestionable authority now was clearly on the defensive.

The major crisis of authority in the post-Vatican church took place when Pope John's successor, Paul VI, issued his encyclical *Humanae Vitae* ("Of Human Life," 1968) condemning artificial contraception against the advice of the majority of the commission he had assembled to assist him on the issue. Reaction among Catholics of child-bearing age, especially in the developed nations of the West, was overwhelmingly negative, and the papal judgment on the matter was simply ignored by many lay people and their clerical advisors. Dissent at the theological level also continued, with prominent thinkers such as Germany's Hans Küng calling the doctrine of papal infallibility into serious question in his 1971 work, *Infallible?*

Challenges to traditional authority emerged from the right as well as from the left. Political conservatives, especially in America, have taken exception to a whole series of encyclicals by recent popes that made a strong case for peace and social justice, particularly in the context of the emergent nations of the Third World. These began with Pope John's *Mater et Magistra* ("Mother and Teacher," 1961) and have continued through John Paul II's *Sollicitudo Rei Socialis* ("The Social Concern of the Church," 1988), which attacked exploitation of developing nations by both "liberal capitalism and Marxist collectivism." Also, a "traditionalist" reaction to the substitution of the vernacular for the Latin Mass was led by Marcel Lefebvre. This ultraconservative French Archbishop challenged the authority of the church to change, and in 1988 led his followers into a *schism*—or political split not involving doctrine—following years of unsuccessful negotiations with Rome. Lefebvre's movement was a manifestation of the position known as "Integralism" formulated by conservatives early in the century, which affords all papal teachings the same level of authority accorded the Bible by Protestant fundamentalists. (Integralism has been called "Catholic fundamentalism" by some writers.) The dilemmas arising from papal condemnation of Integralist activities are obvious, as manifested in the abandonment of Lefebvre by many of his followers following his condemnation by the Pope. This reaction, however, was an indication that the reforms issuing from Vatican II were not without their cost in terms of Catholic unity.

The death of Paul VI in 1978 ushered in the "year of the three popes" when his successor, who took the name John Paul I, died within a few weeks of his election. A second assemblage of the College of Cardinals chose the first non-Italian to the papacy since the Dutchman Adrian VI in the 1520s—Karol Wojtyla, the Cardinal Archbishop of Crakow in the Communist-dominated but overwhelmingly Catholic nation of Poland. Wojtyla, who took the name John Paul II, was both a scholar and an activist, whose career was shaped by the twin hostile forces of Nazism and Communism, and whose interpretation of the role of the institutional church was correspondingly much more aggressive than that of his three immediate predecessors. John Paul gained wide exposure through his extensive worldwide travels, including more than one visit to the United States, in which he gained much good will through his engaging personality. However, his doctrinal conservatism, his willingness to assert his office's traditional authority vigorously, and his unreceptivity to dissent have rendered his pontificate an extremely strong, albeit controversial one.

C. The Reformation Era: The Sundering of Western Christendom and the Emergence of the Protestant Traditions

INTRODUCTION

The term *Protestant* is venerable and resonant, but its meaning in practice is so diffuse that it is difficult to pin down very precisely. Negatively, it describes those traditions in Western Christianity that reject the authority of the Pope, thus reflecting its origins in Martin Luther's refusal to acknowledge Roman claims to obedience. More positively, it can be interpreted through its roots as meaning a "witness for" something—that something often defined as Luther's doctrine of salvation by faith through grace and the ultimate authority of Scripture.

The term *Protestant* made its first appearance in the *Protestatio* of the Diet of Speyer in 1529. However, even during that seedtime of Protestantism—the Reformation of the sixteenth century—the varieties of non-Roman Christianity that rapidly took shape during the early and middle 1500s were so diverse that it is difficult to speak meaningfully of them in specifics. John Calvin, for example, accepted many of Luther's basic insights, but developed them in such a way that his theology forms the basis for a distinctive tradition within Christianity. On the other hand, the Lutheran and Anglican traditions are often treated as manifestations of "Liturgical Christianity," with a stress on their affinities with their Roman Catholic origins rather than the distinctly "Protestant" character of, for example, "Low Church" Episcopalianism and "Eastern" Lutheranism in nineteenth-century America.

For all its difficulties, though, the term *Protestant* remains with us. What is less ambiguous is the fact that, during the sixteenth century, Europe was torn apart by theological ferment, ecclesiastical reform,

and political upheaval bent on bringing that reform to life. The following chapters discuss some of the major features of this seminal era
and the enduring traditions that took shape during those years.

CHAPTER 8

The Lutheran Tradition

Martin Luther was arguably the most significant single individual in the history of Christianity between the time of Constantine and the present. The
complex of ideas that exploded in the Reformation of the sixteenth century
did not all originate with him. It was his genius, though, that combined them
into a coherent system of theology as well as a program for action that was able
to channel the impulses of his time into a colossal upheaval with consequences
that are very much with us to the present day. He ranks with very few other
figures in Western history—Alexander the Great, Napoleon, Lincoln—as having "world-historical" stature, however controversial his achievements may
have proven.

That the person as well as the work and thought of Luther was a significant
aspect of his achievement was evident even to his contemporaries. After his
career as a reformer had been firmly established, his friends and followers
began to record even his dinner-table conversation, which was subsequently
published as the *Tischreden* or "table-talk." Although he himself strongly preferred that the branch of Christianity that he brought into being be known as
the *evangelische Kirche*—that is, "Evangelical Church" or "Church of the
Gospel"—his own name ultimately displaced that which he had preferred, and
his spiritual descendants now proudly call themselves Lutherans. Even the
nomenclature of American Lutheranism—in which names associated with his
careers, such as Augsburg, Wartburg, and Wittenberg are attached to colleges
and publishing houses—demonstrates the deep impact his personality left
upon the movement to which he gave rise.

Perhaps not surprisingly, the details of Luther's life are still sources of
controversy. In recent years, as arguments between Catholics and Protestants
over the significance of Luther have moved toward an ecumenical convergence, scholars are still attempting to separate the biographical facts from the
pious and heroic legends that early became part of his followers' account of his
life. For example, Luther is said to have decided to enter a monastery as a
result of making a vow to Saint Anne when he became terrified during a
thunderstorm. Recent research casts doubt on the literal authenticity of this
and similar stories. However, their status as folklore rather than history is

significant in what it reveals about the power of Luther to inspire this kind of reverential invention. Such stories are characteristic in Christianity and other religious traditions as a form of *hagiography*—saints' lives as a literary genre— and therefore indicate the awe he was capable of arousing.

Martin Luther was born in Saxony in 1483. After receiving a thorough philosophical education, he entered the Augustinian monastery at Erfurt in 1505, whether as a result of his terror in the storm or for more complicated reasons. Although he proved a brilliant student and teacher of theology and Scripture, he was never fully comfortable as a monk because he was unable to assure himself of the certainty of his salvation. Luther's psychology was complex; it has been the subject of speculation from the time of his concerned confessor Staupitz to the theorizing of the eminent contemporary psychologist Erik H. Erikson in his groundbreaking and controversial work of psychobiography, *Young Man Luther* (1955). It seems likely, though, that many of Luther's problems stemmed from his problematic relationship with his overbearing father Hans, a Saxon miner who was displeased with his precocious son's forsaking a lucrative secular career as a lawyer for that of a monk. Whatever the reasons, Luther was a clear example of what the psychologist William James called a "twice-born" person: someone to whom life did not come easily, and who needed to undergo a dramatic resolution of his internal tensions before he could experience peace.

Such a resolution did indeed come to Luther—in a tower, according to tradition—but its details are again shrouded in uncertainty. The occasion of this resolution was Luther's perusal of Paul's letter to the Romans, particularly the phrase "the just shall live by faith." What Luther came of a sudden to realize was that his previous attempts to achieve assurance through the rigorous monastic routine of prayer, study, and sacramental observance were destined to fail in the absence of what he now understood to be the true significance of God's grace and corresponding human faith. In reflecting on his own insight and personal transformation, Luther developed the ideas of *sola gratia* and *sola fide*—salvation by "grace alone" and "by faith alone"—as expressions of this experience. "Salvation by grace through faith alone" has subsequently come to be one of the bywords of the Lutheran tradition and, more broadly, of Protestant Christianity ever since.

Basically, Luther was now maintaining that the traditional Catholic interpretation of the process of salvation had begun at the wrong end. In late medieval Catholicism, emphasis had been placed on the centrality of the church and its clergy as custodians of the sacraments, the faithful reception of which was the key to individual salvation. Although Luther never rejected the sacraments as such, he did come to repudiate them as a means of *achieving* salvation. The general problem, which Luther identified as the heresy of "works-righteousness," lay in the notion that salvation could somehow be *achieved* through human effort. To rely on pleasing God and thereby attaining righteousness in his sight through "good works"—which included sacraments, prayers, charitable deeds, and anything else that was the result of human striving—was to miss the fundamental point that nothing solely of human origin could appease God and thereby win salvation. Human nature in Luther's view was so far fallen that only God himself could counteract the effects of original sin. To speak meaningfully of salvation, then, one had to begin not with human effort but with divine initiative.

Luther's new account of the dynamics of salvation thus began with the phrase *sola gratia*—by God's grace, or saving power, alone, was salvation made possible. The corollary of this offer of grace was the human recipient's response in faith—"by faith alone," *sola fide*, was the transaction of salvation completed. This response was not the result of free choice, however, but the work of the Holy Spirit. It was the only way in which one could respond once grace had been proffered. All of this did not mean that the person who had experienced justification had entered into any state of purity or guiltlessness. Rather, Luther used the formula *simul justus et peccator*—"at the same time justified and sinful"—to stress that the impact of original sin itself had not been removed, but rather that the divinely imposed penalty for it had been taken away. To complete this description, Luther added a complementary third term, *sola Scriptura,* to emphasize the centrality of Scripture as the only source of saving knowledge. It was in the Bible, God's Word, that the true account of the relationship of God and humanity could be found. Although the church still had its place in Luther's scheme, as the place where grace was experienced, he radically deflated the claims of the Roman Catholic Church as an institution to play an indispensable role in the administration of the sacraments and thereby in bringing about salvation. The implications of this line of thought were, to say the least, subversive of the status quo.

The roots of the transformation of this personal experience and theological insight into a program of institutional reform lay in Luther's earlier visit to Rome in 1510. Instead of being edified by his pilgrimage to the center of Christendom, Luther, like many of his contemporaries, was instead shocked by the secularism and corruption that he now witnessed at first hand. A whole catalog of terms had arisen to describe the abuses that characterized the Renaissance papacy: *nepotism,* or the appointment of relatives (sometimes illegitimate) to high ecclesiastical office; *simony,* or the sale of church offices for profit; *pluralism,* or the holding of several profitable church offices simultaneously, usually in an absentee relationship; and *nicolaitism,* or clerical concubinage. Faithful Catholics such as Erasmus of Rotterdam were outraged by such abuses, and the Council of Trent ultimately put a stop to most of them. However, Luther was not content to settle for internal change, since he was becoming convinced that the whole structure of Catholic belief and practice was based on the fundamental errors as to the character of salvation that he was engaged in refuting.

The specific occasion that launched Luther as a reformer was the coming to Germany of the Dominican preacher Johann Tetzel in 1517. Tetzel had been sent to raise funds for building the new St. Peter's basilica in Rome under the sponsorship of Pope Leo X, a scion of the Medici family. His fund-raising focused on the sale of *indulgences*. An indulgence was a reduction of the penalties imposed by the church for sins, which had its origins in the time of the Crusades. By the time of Tetzel, indulgences had come to be interpreted by the Catholic Church not only as a means of escaping the penalties imposed by the church itself in this world, but also as a release from sufferings in Purgatory in the hereafter. To make indulgences even more attractive, they were presented as efficacious not only for the purchasers, but for their departed friends and family as well. To obtain an indulgence, one needed, according to Tetzel, only to make a contribution to the Pope's architectural enterprises. When this was done, the "Treasury of Merits" built up by the overflowing good works of Jesus and the saints could be drawn upon by the church for the supernatural benefit of contributors and their kindred.

Luther, needless to say, was outraged by the commercialism of this enterprise as well as by what he saw as the dubious theological foundations on which the whole notion of indulgences was based. For indulgences to be effective, the church on earth had to have some control or at least influence over the supernatural realm. For Luther, this was presumptuous nonsense. The indulgence question was therefore one against which Luther could muster the whole theological arsenal that he had been accumulating since the resolution of his personal religious questions some years earlier. In response to Tetzel's slogan that "each time a coin in the coffer rings, another soul from Purgatory springs," Luther responded in Wittenberg on October 31, 1517, by publicly posting ninety-five theses—that is, brief controversial assertions directed against Tetzel's claims.

Luther's theses aroused the wrath of the Catholic authorities, who summoned him to a judgment at Augsburg in 1518. Had luck not been with him, he most likely would have met the same fate as his spiritual predecessor, the Bohemian reformer Jan Hus (or John Huss), who had been burned at the stake in 1415 after he had raised many of the same objections to Catholic belief and practice. History, however, now proved to be on Luther's side. Many of the rulers of the German states of the era were annoyed with papal interference in their affairs as well as the outflow of cash that resulted from the hawking of indulgences. Luther found in particular a protector in the Elector Frederick of Saxony. After Luther and his teachings had been condemned at the Diet of Worms in 1521, Frederick arranged for Luther to be taken into protective custody at his castle, the Wartburg, until the situation could be resolved.

By the early 1530s it had become clear that no reconciliation was likely to take place between Luther and Rome, and that Western Christianity was to be split irrevocably into mutually exclusive camps. Luther himself, it should be noted, had never seen himself as the founder of a new church; rather, he wanted to reform the church in which he had lived his entire life, but that now seemed to offer him no choice except leaving. He later coined the phrase *ecclesia semper reformanda*—"the church always reforming itself"—as an expression of the continuing need for an imperfect, earthly institution to be continually on the alert for the corruption into which it would inevitably fall. The Roman church was clearly unwilling to adopt this attitude. Luther and his followers, especially Philip Melanchthon, now entered into a long period of negotiation with secular rulers and other religious dissidents to translate his theology into an actual program of reform.

One significant event in this process was the Diet of Speyer in 1529, which confirmed the German rulers' right to regulate religion in their own realms. The Diet of Augsburg the following year resulted in the *Augsburg Confession,* one of the first definitive summaries of Luther's positions. Luther also during these years engaged in relentless pamphlet warfare with his Catholic and other opponents, and developed and disseminated his religious and political ideas in such important works as his *Open Letter to the Christian Nobility, The Babylonian Captivity of the Church,* and *The Freedom of a Christian,* all written in 1520. Luther was an enormously prolific writer during his entire career, and the definitive edition of his collected works fills over fifty volumes of sermons, lectures, tracts, and other religious genres. The development of movable-type printing only a few decades earlier and a rapid rise in the rate of popular literacy facilitated the spread of his writings and those of his opponents, and the Reformation rapidly developed into a continental war of words.

Luther's program of reform was not piecemeal, but followed from the central theological principles that had impressed themselves on him through personal experience. Following from the premise that God alone brought about justification (i.e., salvation made possible through divine remission of the consequences of human sin), he argued that the church should no longer be considered the instrument through which salvation takes place mechanically; rather, it was the fellowship of those united in God's saving love who assemble for the preaching of God's Word and the reception of the sacraments, as well as "a mother in which faith is begotten." The sacraments were reduced by Luther from the seven recognized by medieval Catholicism to the two that Luther believed were directly instituted and commanded by Jesus himself: the Eucharist, of which the Last Supper was the prototype, and Baptism, based on Jesus's own immersion in the Jordan by John the Baptist. Luther also spent much time on the question of the meaning of the Eucharist, which he felt had been reduced to too mechanical a level in late medieval teaching. Although his own interpretation varied during his career, he continued to maintain that Jesus was genuinely present in the sacrament. In doing so, however, he rejected Thomas Aquinas's concept of *transubstantiation*—that is, the idea that after consecration the bread and wine ceased to be bread and wine, but were completely transformed into the body and blood of Christ while only retaining the appearance of their old natures. Luther thought that this explanation, derived from Aristotelean metaphysics, was too easily reduced to a kind of magical transformation. Throughout his career, he continually affirmed the Real Presence—that the body and blood of Jesus Christ were actually present in the Eucharist.

Luther's enforced leisure at the Wartburg provided him with the opportunity to carry out one of his major campaigns in implementing his new ideas. Drawing on the results of his years spent in the monastery as a teacher of Scripture, he prepared German translations of first the New and then the Old Testament from the original Greek and Hebrew. This task would not have been easy for the most learned scholar, since there did not exist at the time any standard German language but rather a collection of dialects. It was a significant part of Luther's achievement that he was able to choose skillfully among these linguistic variants to devise a new idiom that transcended regional particularities and was thus suitable for the communication of the word of God in intelligible, even elegant form to all German-speakers. In the longer run, the availability of this new German language forged in the *Luther Bibel* contributed to a sense of German cultural unity that saw fruition only centuries later in the unification of the German states under Bismarck.

A vernacular Bible provided a major part of the equipment that Luther needed to carry out a more thorough-going reform of Christian life and worship for his followers. Luther rejected the medieval notion that the clergy were the sole guardians of God's word and worship, which hitherto had been available exclusively in Latin. Luther now set about adapting the Eucharistic service, or Mass, into German, which was now to be performed with the celebrant facing the congregation. (Lutherans continued to use Latin as well for the next two centuries, however.) To enhance this program of liturgical democratization, Luther also began to compose hymns in the vernacular which were set to popular melodies of the time, and which could thus be sung by the congregation. Previously, such liturgical music as existed was in the form of Gregorian chant, or plainsong, which could be executed only by trained monks or choristers. Now the entire congregation could participate in lusty renditions of such hymns as *Ein' Feste Burg*—"A Mighty Fortress Is Our God," a roar of defiance against those who dared to deny the rightness of Luther's teachings.

A further course of democratization was articulated in his formula "the priesthood of all believers." Luther continued to maintain, as did his Catholic opponents, that a specially educated clergy was necessary as the mark of a true church, along with the preaching of the Word, and the administration of the sacraments. However, Luther did not regard the clergy as acquiring any specially elevated spiritual status by virtue of their ordination. Since Jesus's sacrifice had been effective once and for all in making salvation possible, there was no need to believe that priests repeated this unique sacrificial act in the Mass. This reinterpretation thus went far in depriving their office of much of its mystique. Real priesthood for Luther meant serving as a mediator between God and one's neighbor, a service that any Christian could and should perform. Therefore, the priesthood encompassed all believers, who by virtue of divine grace would be expected spontaneously to perform the good works of Christian witness that flowed from "justification by grace through faith alone."

A corollary to this notion was Luther's reinterpretation of the idea of *vocation*. In traditional Catholic usage, only a small number of Christians received from God a special vocation (from the Latin *vocare*, to call) or calling to the higher religious life as a priest, monk, or nun. Other Christians might well be saved through the faithful reception of the sacraments and perseverance in good works, but their status was somewhat inferior to the specially called. Luther argued instead that all Christians were equal in God's sight in both intrinsic sinfulness and in divinely offered grace, and that spiritual distinctions therefore did not apply. Rather, all Christians had equally valid callings to honorable earthly occupations, whether as preachers, teachers, farmers, princes, or whatever profession met their special skills and circumstances.

Luther therefore abolished the institution of monasticism, rejecting what the sociologist Max Weber has called its "other-worldly asceticism" in favor of a responsible and faithful life in this world led for God's honor and glory. Luther followed this counsel not only by leaving the monastery himself but by marrying Katharina von Bora, a former nun with whom he lived happily and who bore him six children. He died in 1546.

From the German states where it first took hold, Luther's "Evangelical Church" spread rapidly northward into the Scandinavian countries, where it has been dominant to the present day. Although specifically "Lutheran" Christianity was confined in Europe primarily to these areas—and a significant part of Germany remained Catholic—the influence of Luther's ideas reached far beyond. Subsequent reformers such as John Calvin built on Luther's beginnings, and no aspect of Protestant thought was unaffected by the basic premises he had established as the starting point for any critique of Roman Catholic orthodoxy. Western Christianity was now irretrievably divided into those loyal to Rome and those who rejected the claims of papal supremacy in favor of the principle of *sola Scriptura*—the authority of the Bible alone.

Despite the radical impact of Luther's movement on the Christianity of his age, the Lutheran tradition today seems more similar to Roman Catholicism, especially in its liturgical focus, than to later manifestations of Protestantism. One significant way in which it differs from other "liturgical" traditions such as Anglicanism and Roman Catholicism is in its lack of a centralized or even a common polity. Luther himself had a functional or instrumental view of church government, and did not care a great deal how churches were administered as long as conditions were proper for the achievement of the hallmarks of a truly Christian church: the preaching of the Word and the proper administration of the sacraments. In the early years, Luther was forced to depend on the good will of the German princes for the survival of his evangelical church, and those very princes often served as heads of the church in their realms, sometimes using the title of "emergency bishop."

Although the title of bishop has been retained in most branches of Lutheranism, it is primarily in the Swedish church that the older Catholic notion of the office as validated by the Apostolic Succession has been retained. In other countries the office is primarily functional, and does not have a sacramental mystique attached to it. The title is employed by the Evangelical Lutheran Church in America, with a bishop, vice-president, and national secretary as its three national officers, and a division into regional *synods*, each presided over by a bishop. In addition, it has a number of divisions and commissions, based in Chicago, to serve the denomination as a whole. The other major American group, the Missouri Synod, uses the term *synod* to refer to the denomination as a whole. A president is elected by a national convention as head of the entire Synod, which is subdivided into "districts," each of which is also supervised by a president (rather than a bishop). Traditionally, however, considerable power resides in individual congregations.

Polity has therefore never been a means through which Lutherans could preserve their unique traditions, either in the Old World or the New. No pope or archbishop, no canon law, and not even a commonly agreed-upon form of organization could be resorted to by all. A different route to continuity, however, lay in doctrine. Personal religious experience has sometimes been valued by Lutherans, but the more dominant concern has been with the *objectivity* of religious truth. One of the hallmarks of the Lutheran tradition from its beginnings has been an emphasis on correct belief—"orthodoxy" in its strictest sense. The traditional "symbol" of Lutheran orthodoxy has been the *Book of Concord*, compiled in 1580 by Luther's followers to provide a standard of reference for ascertaining correctness of belief. The *Book of Concord* contains the three creeds of the early Christian church (Nicene, Apostolic, and Athanasian); several of Luther's own writings, including his Small and Large Catechisms; and a number of documents drawn up by his followers to set forth the Lutheran position in negotiations with other reformers and among Lutherans themselves. Of these, the most influential has been the "Augsburg Confession," drafted by Luther's lieutenant Philip Melanchthon in 1530 and held by Lutherans over the centuries as a definitive statement of their faith. Lutherans have not always been in accord as to the exact interpretation or authority of these documents, but altogether the *Book of Concord* has served as a revered symbol of the beliefs that transcend the forces dividing Lutherans one from another.

Liturgy is another force that, though productive at times of division or at least diversity, is also a common bond uniting a people that have traditionally followed a formal ritual for its communal worship. Luther himself did not create a new liturgy, but rather adapted the late medieval Catholic Mass to fit his reinterpretation of such issues as the character of the sacraments and the relationship of the celebrant and the congregation. During the period of ferment among American Lutherans in the nineteenth century, a wide variety of liturgical practices arose. "Eastern" Lutherans, particularly members of Samuel Simon Schmucker's General Synod, tended to follow the lead of their evangelical neighbors: grape juice was substituted for wine, services were conducted in English, the Eucharist was celebrated as seldom as twice yearly, and the liturgical year—even Christmas—was not observed. The opposite course was typical of the ethnic synods of the Midwest, where doctrinal sermons were preached in the old languages from side (rather than central) pulpits; wine was used in a communion taken first by men and then women; and the traditional liturgical year was the basis of the cycle of worship.

With the erosion of regional and ethnic particularity in the twentieth century, American Lutherans of all sorts began to converge on a common liturgy. A variety of cooperative endeavors culminated in the formation of an Inter-Lutheran Commission on Worship in 1966 by several American Lutheran denominations. The result, first issued in 1978, was the *Lutheran Book of Worship*, which is now standard in slightly different versions for the two major Lutheran bodies (Evangelical Lutheran Church in America and Missouri Synod.) It reflects the liturgical revival that swept over a number of Christian churches during the mid-twentieth century, and the basic eucharistic service differs only in detail from the Roman Catholic and Episcopal versions. Weekly celebration of the Eucharist is the recommended norm, but individual congregations exert considerable latitude in deciding how far they want to accommodate their often diverse practices, rooted in a variety of ethnic traditions, to those outlined in the *Book of Worship*.

The *Book of Worship* contains not only liturgical texts but musical settings as well, including both chants and hymns. One of the richest aspects of the Lutheran tradition from the time of Luther himself has been a delight in choral music, perhaps reflective of the German ethos from which the *evangelische Kirche* arose. In addition to Luther's own hymnody, of which "A Mighty Fortress" remains the most famous among Christians of all stripes, the choral works of Johann Sebastian Bach and George Frederick Handel have been outstanding in their beauty and universal appeal. Bach wrote much of his work in his capacity as *Kantor* (church musical director): His cantatas were composed to be performed according to the cycle of the liturgical year, and the congregation was expected to participate during Lent in his *Passions*—those according to St. Matthew and St. John. Handel's *Messiah* has, of course, become part of the common musical heritage of the Western world, and is still frequently performed at Christmas and Easter by many religious and even secular groups. Hymns in the *Book of Worship* are drawn from a variety of sources, both Lutheran and other; the former range from the work of German Pietist composers such as Paul Gerhardt and Nicholas von Zinzendorf to Swedish folk melodies.

Despite the divisions that still persist among American Lutherans, bonds that transcend the institutional and even the narrowly theological provide a sense of commonality to the American Lutheran community; surveys have indicated that Lutheran loyalty is more to the tradition as a whole than to any particular branch of it. Part of this loyalty springs from the powerful symbols of Luther's personality, life, and work, and the mystique that the very word *Reformation* still evokes for many. As Jaroslav Pelikan has pointed out, the Lutheran parsonage has served as a potent means of preserving and transmitting the tradition as well through the remarkably talented families that it has nurtured. The tradition of communal worship and especially of music that dates back to Luther himself has also provided a major vehicle of continuity. Perhaps the concluding verse of *Ein' Feste Burg* expresses best the deep sense of conviction and loyalty that has characterized Lutherans to this day:

> That word above all earthly powers,
> No thanks to them, abideth;
> The Spirit and the gifts are ours
> Through him who with us sideth:
> Let goods and kindred go,
> This mortal life also;
> The body they may kill:
> God's truth abideth still,
> His kingdom is forever.*

* Martin Luther, 1529; transl. Frederick Henry Hedge, 1852.

CHAPTER 9

The Anglican Tradition

Until the sixteenth century, western Europe was nominally united under the Pope and the Holy Roman Emperor as "Christendom." This supposed unity was gradually being undermined by the emergence of distinctively national varieties of Catholic Christianity in those areas of Europe that were beginning to emerge as consolidated nation-states rather than loose feudal social and cultural aggregates. Spain, which would later be regarded as one of the most politically backward parts of the Continent, took the lead in this process with the marriage of Ferdinand of Aragon and Isabella of Castille—"the Catholic Monarchs"—in 1469. This dynastic union made possible the political consolidation of the nation, which was furthered by the expulsion of the Muslims and Jews from the Iberian Peninsula during the 1490s and the aggressive development of the Spanish Empire in the following decades. The Spanish crown, which usually controlled the Holy Roman Empire as well, received extensive privileges from the papacy in the appointment of bishops and other areas that came close to political independence in the ecclesiastical realm. A similar process was taking place in France at about the same time, where "Gallicanism"—the claim that the French Church was virtually independent of the Pope—had attracted adherents since the fourteenth century. In neither case did these jealous guardings of national traditions and control lead to a break with Rome. However, both are evidence that the more radical course of events that was to occur in England had important parallels on the Continent.

Christianity had existed in the British Isles since early Roman times, and its history of relations with Rome was not that unusual in the context of almost perpetual struggles for power between church and state. By the time of Luther, however, many English people had become disenchanted with the role that international church politics had come to play in their national life. Although ideas of reform were beginning to enter academic circles, the real impetus for the decisive break that would begin to take shape in 1531 lay even higher. Independence for English Christianity from Roman control was not the work either of scholarly reformers or an upswell of popular sentiment. Rather, it had its source squarely in the will of King Henry VIII (1491–1547), the second of the Tudor dynasty and one of the most extraordinarily effective sovereigns of his time and country or any other. In this sense, the emergence of an independent Church of England was a chapter in the story of what has been called the "Magisterial Reformation"—reform by action of the magistrate, or civil ruler. Therefore, the English Reformation had much more in common politically with that of Luther in Germany and Calvin in Geneva than it did with the disorganized, decentralized, popular movements—the "Radical Reformation"—that began to sweep the Rhine Valley in the 1520s.

The occasion of Henry's break with the papacy was the refusal of Pope Clement VII to annul the marriage Henry had entered into with his brother's widow, Catharine of Aragon. Henry, who was desperate for a male heir that his union with Catharine proved unable to give him, now claimed that his union was incestuous, even though he had previously received papal dispensation to enter into it. Henry's case was actually quite strong in terms of the marriage laws of the time. The Pope might well have acceded to Henry's request had Henry's wife been cooperative, and had she not been the aunt of Charles V, the Holy Roman Emperor, who exerted powerful control over the papacy. When the declaration of nullity was not forthcoming, Henry, who had earlier been awarded the papal title of "Defender of the Faith" for a refutation of Luther's teachings, took matters into his own hands and secured from the English Parliament in 1534 an Act of Supremacy declaring that he, as King, was "Supreme Head" of the English Church. Although a few influential persons, such as the Lord Chancellor Thomas More, who had earlier supported Henry's request for an annulment, refused to accept this new state of affairs, the passage of English Christianity from papal to regal leadership occurred with remarkably little protest or resistance. (More, who was beheaded for his obstinacy, was later recognized as a saint by the Roman Catholic Church.)

Until Henry's death in 1547, the English Reformation remained primarily a political rather than a theological event. Mass continued to be said in Latin, bishops and priests presided over the spiritual life of the church much as before, and the effect of the new regime on the religious life of the average person was scarcely noticeable. The one major change in church life was Henry's suppression of England's numerous monasteries, which created a bounty of wealth that could be used to reward the King's supporters. The existence and magnitude of this very wealth, however, was indicative of the material abundance that had proliferated in late medieval times among the religious orders, and that presumably did little to enhance the spiritual qualities of the monastic life. Most of the monks accepted Henry's secularization of their life-style with little protest, although a few who resisted came to very unpleasant ends. Henry's motives in suppressing monasticism were probably not deeply theological, but his actions did bring English practice closer to that of the former Augustinian Martin Luther, whose Evangelical Church existed without benefit of monastic institutions.

Henry was succeeded by his one son, Edward VI, who had been born of a later marriage and ruled under the tutelage of Calvinist noble "regents" until his death at the age of 16 in 1553. It was during Edward's brief reign that impulses toward liturgical and theological reform that had not been able to emerge into the open under Henry now found a more receptive atmosphere. In particular Thomas Cranmer, whom Henry had made Archbishop of Canterbury in 1532, brought his genius to bear on the revision of the church's order of worship. Until now, worship in England had continued to be conducted in Latin, a language that was unintelligible not only to the laity but most likely to many of the ill-trained clergy as well. In the two editions of the

Book of Common Prayer that appeared in 1549 and 1552, Cranmer set about following Luther's example in creating an order of worship that all could understand. In these superb examples of English prose, Cranmer not only adapted the medieval Mass into English; he also substantially altered its character to reflect a new concern for the centrality of Scripture and the importance of the liturgies of the early church, as well as a desire to disown a popular and highly literal notion of the nature of the presence of Jesus Christ that was said to take place in the Eucharistic sacrifice. Although the wordings of these rites changed somewhat from the earlier edition to the later, and the precise character of Cranmer's theology was never entirely clear, there is little doubt that the ideas of the Continental Reformation were beginning to have an impact on English thought and practice.

Cranmer came to a martyr's end after Edward's death, when Edward's successor and half-sister, Mary I, attempted to restore England to Roman control. Although Mary (reigned 1553–1558) had the former Archbishop and numerous others who refused to acknowledge the restoration of papal authority consigned to the "fires of Smithfield," her own reign was cut short by her death after six years and the accession of her half-sister, Elizabeth I.

Elizabeth, who had been educated by Protestant tutors, had little use for religious controversy, and attempted to separate the political and theological dimensions of religious observance. Her main concern was that all the people of England acknowledge the royal supremacy over the governance of the church, and renounce any loyalty to Roman dominion, which Elizabeth regarded as the equivalent of treason. This policy of "comprehensiveness" aimed at the creation of political uniformity and stability, with little concern for theological disagreements, which would be allowed to flourish as long as they carried no political implications with them. Her aim, in short, was the achievement of common prayer in public rather than common belief.

This spirit of inclusiveness did generate a theological corollary, however. During Elizabeth's reign a party began to develop in the Church of England at Cambridge University, which acquired the nickname "Puritan" for its adherents' concern with the moral, liturgical, and theological purification of the church. For the Puritans, Scripture was to be the sole source of religious authority, and all church practices had to be based on Scripture in order to be licit. This desire to make the entire English church conform to one rather rigid interpretation of Scripture drew not only political suppression from the government of Elizabeth and her Stuart successors, but also evoked an eloquent response on theoretical lines from Richard Hooker, an Oxford-educated country clergyman who composed the *Treatise on the Laws of Ecclesiastical Polity* in response to the Puritan challenge. (The first five books were published in 1594–1597; the complete work not until the mid-seventeenth century.) Against the Puritan claim that there must be explicit scriptural warrant for every belief and practice of the church, including its governance or "polity," Hooker argued instead that human reason is also God-given, and capable of knowing a "natural law" that complements the revelations of Scripture. Therefore, reason and tradition are also valid grounds for particular church practices—such as "episcopal polity," or government by bishops—in cases where Scripture does not explicitly contradict the church's practice. This articulation of a threefold groundwork for religious authority—Scripture, reason, and tradition—has come to be the philosophical basis of that distinctively Anglican conception of the Church of England and its daughter churches as a *via media*—a "middle way" between the extremes of Roman Catholicism on the one hand and Protestantism, especially in its Calvinistic form, on the other.

The final major component of a distinctly Anglican form of religious expression took place in stages during the sixteenth century. It culminated during the reign of the first of the Stuart monarchs, James I (reigned 1603–1625), in the publication of the Authorized or "King James" translation of the Bible into English in 1611. One of the few good things ever to come out of a committee, the King James Bible represented not only the most advanced biblical scholarship of the era but also one of the masterworks of English prose in an age noted for the flourishing of the written word. This translation built on the work of a series of predecessors, including William Tyndale and Miles Coverdale, who in turn had drawn on the direct access to Greek and Hebrew texts that had been the fruit of the Humanist movement of the Renaissance. Although the "KJV" is no longer regarded by scholars as reliable, it has in turn formed the basis for subsequent revisions, and has exerted an effect on the rhythms of the English language exceeded only perhaps by Shakespeare. A good example is found in some of the opening verses of the book of Ecclesiastes, which Ernest Hemingway used as an epigraph for the novel whose title can roughly be found therein:

> One generation passeth away, and another generation cometh: but the earth abideth forever. The sun also ariseth, and the sun goeth down, and hasteth to his place where he arose. The wind goeth toward the south, and turneth about unto the north; it whirleth about continually, and the wind returneth again according to its circuits. All the rivers run into the sea; yet the sea is not full; unto the place from whence the rivers come, thither they return again. (I:4–7)

The primary motivation, however, was not aesthetic. From the time of Cranmer and before, the religious shapers of the Church of England had been concerned with the centrality of Scripture in worship, a centrality that had been obscured by the inaccessibility of the Latin Vulgate to all but a handful of appropriately trained clergy. Although Anglican eloquence at times had an elitist slant, as in the sermons of John Donne, Lancelot Andrews, and others of the great preachers at the Stuart court, that eloquence could also be put to democratic uses. The Authorized Version, for example, utilizes only some 8,000 words, and was therefore presumably comprehensible to the greater number of readers and auditors. (Shakespeare, in contrast, used over 50,000.)

As the English from the time of James I began to colonize the New World, a transcontinental Anglicanism began to develop, first in North America and then throughout virtually the entire world in the wake of the British Empire. With it, a new relationship began to emerge between the Church of England, which was inextricably intertwined with the British monarchy and nation, and the developing religious tradition known as Anglicanism. When the Protestant Episcopal Church was created in the newly formed United States in the aftermath of the American Revolution, the political structure known as the Church of England was no longer adequate to encompass those who considered themselves Anglican but could not maintain allegiance to the English monarchy that headed that church. As other former colonies attained independence and other autonomous national churches developed as a result, these several churches began gradually to regard themselves as a Worldwide Anglican Communion, sharing a common understanding of worship and theology and regarding one another as fully legitimate heirs of a common tradition, but not exerting any authority over one another other than that of mutual respect.

The principal institutional expression of this Communion is the Lambeth Conference. Beginning in 1867, bishops of the various Anglican churches began to assemble at roughly ten-year intervals at Lambeth Palace, the residence of the Archbishop of Canterbury. (The latter is the spiritual head of the Church of England and one of its two archbishops, the other residing at York.) Although these conferences were originally conceived as a means of resolving doctrinal disputes in the manner of the early ecumenical councils, they soon evolved into a less authoritative vehicle for bishops of common heritage to gather from around the world and issue statements that were on matters of common concern and that had no binding character. In some ways, the Communion is similar to the relationships among the Eastern Orthodox churches, who acknowledge one another's validity while maintaining political independence and traditions that vary according to individual patterns of cultural development. On the same analogy, the Archbishop of Canterbury enjoys a role more similar to that of the Patriarch of Constantinople than to that of the Pope: a primacy accorded respect and serving as a symbol of unity, but not carrying with it any actual power.

Contemporary Anglicans, including the Episcopal Church in the United States, shy away both from highly centralized political control and mandatory statements of belief which go beyond Scripture and the creeds of the early church, finding unity instead in an order of common public worship. The major document that has united Anglicans since the days of Cranmer has been *The Book of Common Prayer*, which is best defined as a collection of liturgical texts. An examination of the contents of the present American edition, which dates from 1977, gives a useful overview of the Episcopal attitude toward the relationship between worship and belief.

At the core of the *Prayer Book*, as it is usually known, are two alternate versions of the Eucharistic liturgy. In earlier versions—the next most recent dated from 1928—only one rite existed, which was not radically dissimilar from the 1559 edition of Queen Elizabeth I's reign. The 1977 version was intended to make the liturgy as accessible as possible to the contemporary worshipper, a concern anticipated by Roman Catholics in Vatican II. Rite I is modeled on the more traditional usage, employing only slightly modernized diction and eliminating phraseology reflecting a Calvinistic interpretation of the human condition (e.g., "miserable offenders"). Rite II, on the other hand, strives vigorously to be contemporary, and includes a version of the Lord's

Prayer recast in less formal English. (The *Lutheran Book of Worship* contains a similar alternative.) These attempts at contemporaneity have been the occasion of heated protest, and have been in part the grounds for some of the formal divisions in the Episcopal Church in the 1970s and beyond.

In addition to the Eucharistic services, which have become the standard for Sunday worship in most Episcopal churches, the *Prayer Book* also provides the texts of Morning and Evening Prayer. Morning Prayer was often utilized in the "Low Church" tradition on most Sundays, but this is less often the case today. Both services were originally adapted by Cranmer from the daily monastic offices—that is, orders of worship recited by monks at seven specified intervals in the course of each day. In Anglican usage, these have been reduced to two, and are now used as supplementary public devotions, primarily on weekdays, for the ordinary worshipper. The order of Evening Prayer is especially notable for its two readings from the Gospel of Luke, the lyrical *Magnificat* ("My soul doth magnify the Lord . . . ") and the haunting *Nunc dimittis* ("Lord, now lettest thou thy servant depart in peace . . . ").

Another major component of the *Prayer Book* is a set of rituals for sacramental worship other than the Eucharist. This arrangement reflects a particular ambiguity in Anglicanism. On the one hand, traditional Anglican/Episcopal teaching follows Luther and other Continental reformers in maintaining that there are only two "dominically" (i.e., by the Lord Jesus himself) instituted sacraments, baptism and the Eucharist. On the other hand, the *Prayer Book* provides liturgical texts for the other five sacraments recognized by the Roman Catholic Church and Eastern Orthodoxy as well—confirmation, marriage, penance, clerical ordination, and services for the sick and dying. Still other "rites of passage," such as adoption of a child and the burial of the dead, are included. There thus may be only two officially recognized sacraments, but the ordinary cycle of liturgical observance goes far beyond those two occasions.

Still another section of the *Prayer Book* is entitled "Historical Documents of the Church," a phrasing studiously chosen to indicate a respect for tradition on the one hand and a reticence to promulgate binding creedal positions on the other. These documents include the creeds of the early Church, especially the Nicene, which is recited weekly during the Eucharistic service; the "Articles of Religion," an American version of the Elizabethan 39 Articles containing controversial theological statements now probably foreign to most Episcopalians; and finally, a document of considerable interest, the Chicago-Lambeth Quadrilateral of 1886–1888.

The latter document received its name from its four principal parts, and from its adoption first by the bishops of the American church, meeting in Chicago in 1886, and then by their English counterparts in session at Lambeth Palace two years later. The operative part of this "Quadrilateral" is so brief as to merit quotation in full:

> As inherent parts of this sacred deposit, and therefore as essential to the restoration of unity among the divided branches of Christendom, we account the following, to wit:

1. The Holy Scriptures of Old and New Testament as the revealed Word of God.
2. The Nicene Creed as the sufficient statement of the Christian faith.
3. The two Sacraments,—Baptism and the Supper of the Lord,—ministered with unfailing use of Christ's words of institution and of the elements ordained by Him.
4. The Historic Episcopate, locally adapted in the methods of its administration to the varying needs of the nations and peoples called of God into the unity of His Church.

There are a number of interesting emphases, as well as omissions, in this statement of the essentials of the Christian faith and life from the Anglican perspective. First, the emphasis on Scripture is presumably acceptable to all Christians, although such an emphasis is traditionally more Protestant than Catholic. Second, the focus on the Nicene Creed, though held in common with Roman Catholics, may actually indicate more of a sympathy with Eastern Orthodoxy, which emphasizes the creeds and councils of the early Church as alone authoritative (in contrast with later ecumenical councils and papal decrees acceptable to Western, or Roman, Christendom alone). The addition of any early creed to Scriptures, however, is indicative of a distancing from classical Protestantism. The definition of two (and only two) sacraments is, however, a Protestant characteristic, although the inclusion of rituals in the *Prayer Book* corresponding to the other five Roman Catholic sacraments provides a balance in the opposite direction.

Finally, the concept of the "historic episcopate" is a firm departure from Protestantism in favor of both Roman Catholic and Eastern Orthodox theory in the realm of polity. What this phrase refers to is the idea of the apostolic succession of bishops, held by Anglicans in common with those two traditions as well as with Swedish and Baltic Lutherans, "Old Catholics," and a few other small groups that Anglicans recognize as fully valid communions. Basically, this is a theological-historical rationale for the "episcopal" form of governance— that is, by bishops, who are thought to derive their authority by virtue of their standing in an unbroken succession from the apostles themselves. The apostles, who were in this theory the original bishops chosen by Jesus himself, laid hands on their chosen successors, who did the same with *their* successors, and so on without interruption until the present.

Although the *Prayer Book*, which also contains the Psalms in their entirety and a set of weekly Scripture readings for liturgical use on a three-year cycle, can be used for private devotions, it is primarily a collection of texts intended for *public* worship. Anglicans tend to shy away from dogmatic statements on various articles of faith, and prefer to allow a wide latitude to individual interpretation and judgment on such questions as what really takes place during the celebration of the Eucharist. Where Anglicans *do* converge is in their weekly public coming together for common worship, in which mutual participation in the proclamation of the divine Word, its interpretation in the sermon, and the reception of the sacrament of the Eucharist are primary. Individual congregations and even dioceses still vary somewhat on the emphasis placed on "High" (sacramental) versus "Low" (Scripture- and preaching-oriented) liturgical practice, but these differences have eroded considerably in the twentieth century.

Two other aspects of Episcopal/Anglican worship link it to the liturgical practices of the other "liturgical churches"—Roman Catholic, Eastern Orthodox, and Lutheran—and are worthy of comment. First, Episcopalian worship is visual and tactile as well as verbal, especially where a leaning to "High Church" (or, more accurately, "Anglo-Catholic") practice is present. Clergy wear appropriate and sometimes rather elaborate vestments during the celebration of the sacraments, and others participating in the worship in specific auxiliary roles—acolytes, choir members, and "lay readers" (lectors)—usually wear robes or simple vestments as well. Services usually begin and end with a vested procession, and in "high" services are often accompanied by incense. All of the senses, in short, are engaged, in consonance with a sacramental theology in which all aspects of creation can become means for the transmission of divine grace.

Second, worship is attuned to the cycle of the seasons. As with the other liturgical churches, the year begins with Advent prior to Christmas, and each season dictates appropriately colored vestments and coverings for the altar. Special hymns are appropriate for specific seasons, and Christmas, as in most Christian churches, evokes a very particular set of music and ritual. A distinctively Anglican event is the "Service of Lessons and Carols," which has its rather recent origins at Cambridge University and is now popular with many other Christian communities during the Christmas season. In this service, Scripture passages beginning with Genesis I are read in alternation with the singing of traditional Christmas carols, culminating in a brief prayer service. Other seasonal liturgies, such as the Easter Vigil can be dramatic and poignant as well.

Although Anglicanism had its origins in the power politics of the Tudor monarchy, it gradually underwent a transformation from a purely national church into a worldwide religious community united by a common tradition. That tradition, which informs the Episcopal Church in the United States as well as the other members of the Worldwide Anglican Communion, balances an emphasis on continuity with the church of the apostles with a decentralized approach to contemporary governance. Although it affirms the traditional symbols of Christianity—Bible, creeds, and sacraments—its followers are united not so much by a common theological interpretation of these symbols as by sharing in the use of these symbols in common worship. Anglicanism's distinctiveness thus cannot be summarized in one specific teaching—for instance, the Lutheran "justification by faith" or the Reformed "sovereignty of God"—but rather in balance of approaches to ultimate saving truth: scripture, tradition, and reason.

CHAPTER 10

Calvinism and the Reformed Tradition

Martin Luther's successor as the major leader of Reformation thought and action was Jean Cauvin (1509–1564), better known as John Calvin. Born in Noyon in the Picardy region of France, he was intended for a career in the church, and studied both theology and law. After a conversion to the Protestant understanding of Christianity, he was called to Geneva in 1536 as an assistant to the reformer Guillaume Farel. Ousted two years later, he took up work as a minister and teacher in the French city of Strasbourg, only to be recalled by his former Genevan patrons in 1541. For the remainder of his life, he served his French-speaking Swiss constituency as a religious and moral reformer so determined and so effective that he has often been characterized as a theocratic dictator. Under his leadership, Geneva became a model of reforming ideas and ideals that went far beyond Luther's—which seemed, in comparison, highly conservative.

A comparison between the two reformers is instructive in a variety of ways. Where Luther was outgoing and gregarious, and the details of his life became objects of fascination and even legend to his disciples. Calvin's personality had little to do with the appeal of his ideas. Not a great deal has been recorded about his personal life, which seems to have been exemplary if rather lacking in anecdotal incident. Where Luther's conversion had a momentous impact on his life and character, little is known of Calvin's. Where Luther's collected works consist primarily of *ad hoc* writings such as lectures, sermons, and pamphlets, Calvin's more usually take the form of systematic treatises. His best-known work, the *Institutes of the Christian Religion,* which was published in several editions between 1536 and 1560, has an architectonic character, dealing with the entirety of Christian theology in tightly logical form and buttressed throughout with biblical proof-texts. Where Luther seemed always on the brink of overflowing, Calvin rather presented an image of constraint verging on constriction.

To an even greater degree than Luther's, Calvin's thought was firmly rooted in the writings of Augustine of Hippo, especially his *De Civitate Dei* ("The City of God," 413–426.) Where later medieval Catholic theology, such as that of Thomas Aquinas, had emphasized the continuities between the realms of God and his creation, both Augustine and Calvin stressed rather the infinite discontinuity between "nature" and "grace." His message focused on what the twentieth-century theologian H. Richard Niebuhr has called "radical monotheism": the singularity of God as opposed to all other beings, and a fierce opposition to any religious beliefs or practices that compromised that uniqueness and awesome power.

The major symbol of divine power that Calvin found in Augustine was that of predestination. Predestination was rooted in the belief that human nature had from the beginning of time been radically compromised and estranged from God through the Fall—that is, the primordial transgression of Adam and Eve. Original sin, then, was the operative principle in human nature. However, human beings, whether the "first parents" or their innumerable generations of offspring, did not freely decide either to defy or obey God. Rather, their spiritual characters had been decided in God's mind at least since the time of the Fall, when he had for his own inscrutable reasons decreed that some should be spared from the eternal consequences of inevitable sin and that others—and by far the larger part—should be damned for ever.

This doctrine of predestination is certainly one of the least palatable ideas of the reformers to the twentieth-century sensibility, and few hard-core Calvinists remain in America today. Luther himself had accepted the idea, but had not emphasized it since he thought it might discourage his followers and lead them to fatalism. For Calvin, though, "the sweet and pleasant doctrine of damnation" was not intended as an expression of despair in humanity. Rather, he saw it as an acknowledgment of the depravity that seemed to characterize so much of the human condition as well, and even more, of the unutterable and unfathomable majesty of God. "Where were you when I created the whirlwind?" asked God of Job, and Calvin might have echoed this same marvel that humans should dare to question the wisdom of God's decrees. God was by definition the measure of all things, and all that he had ordained was by definition good. To suggest otherwise was to cast serious doubts on one's own spiritual state.

The nature of the doctrine of predestination was succinctly articulated in 1618–1619 by the Synod of Dort, an assembly of Calvinist divines held in the heavily Reformed Netherlands. These worthies had gathered to refute what they saw as the errors of their colleague, Jacobus Arminius, who taught that humans could play some positive role in their salvation. The canons, or decrees, of Dort in response to the teachings of Arminius are easily remembered through the mnemonic device of the TULIP formula, invoking the flower of their land of origin:

- *Total Depravity*, the complete lack or absence of any merit in the unregenerate human condition unaided by divine grace, and the all-pervasive effects of original sin on the human character;
- *Unconditional Election*, the calling by God of some to salvation without regard to any merits they themselves might possess;
- *Limited Atonement*, the sacrificial death of Jesus on behalf only of those whom God had chosen for salvation rather than potentially for the whole of humanity;
- *Irresistible Grace*, the inability of those whom God had elected to salvation to refuse the divine gift of saving power;
- *Perseverance of the Saints*, the inevitable salvation of God's elect even after doubts and lapses during their earthly lives.

Calvin, like Luther, taught that human nature was hopelessly estranged from God by original sin and unable to fulfill the demands of God's law. Further, both agreed that salvation took place through divine action, or grace, to which the chosen believer inevitably responded in faith. Unlike Luther, however, Calvin made no bones about the reality and significance of predestination. He believed that it would provide comfort and courage to the elect while reminding the reprobate and unregenerate of the hopelessness of their condition, thereby frightening them into obedience if not salvation. Further, where Luther had taught simply that God had predestined his chosen to salvation and left the rest to their own devices, Calvin affirmed the notion of "double predestination"—that is, God's active consignment of the reprobate to damnation as well.

Although God and humanity were radically estranged from one another through Original Sin, there was nevertheless one means through which the gap between them could be bridged and salvation for the elect accomplished. This was God's Word, the theme of the Fourth Gospel: "In the beginning was the Word, and the Word was with God, and the Word was God" (John 1:1). "The Word became flesh and dwelt among us" (1:14). For Calvin, the Word of God was preeminently to be found in Scripture, in which God reveals to humanity that which he wishes to be known. Where Luther had doubts about the credibility of some parts of Scripture, such as the letter of James, and believed that the Hebrew Scriptures had been displaced by the New Testament, Calvin recognized the authority of both. The proclamation of Scripture in preaching thus became central to his notion of worship, and the Law of God as found especially in the Old Testament assumed a positive centrality in his thought and practice that was completely absent for Luther.

Even though Luther had reduced the number of sacraments to the two he had found specifically instituted by Jesus, he did not object to any number of other religious practices that were without explicit scriptural basis, as long as they did not contradict the Word of God. For Calvin, however, all Christian practice had to be based firmly on positive scriptural mandate. Worship, therefore, was to be a manifestation of the Word of God alone. To implement this, he and his followers gutted the churches of Geneva, such as Calvin's own St. Pierre, and destroyed all altars, statues, paintings, and any other sensual compromises with biblical rigor. Music was similarly confined to songs found in Scripture itself—that is, the Psalms. The complex and formal liturgy that Luther had adapted from Latin into German was abandoned in favor of a simple order of prayer, Psalm-singing, and especially preaching, in which the Word was proclaimed and expounded. A more elaborate Reformed aesthetic of worship did not emerge until considerably later.

The sacraments, which all of the Reformers had followed Luther in reducing to two, had a somewhat problematic place in Calvin's scheme. Like Luther, he never articulated a very clear and systematic interpretation of the Eucharist (or Lord's Supper). Like Luther also, he rejected the radical interpretation of Huldreich (or Ulrich) Zwingli, the religious leader of Zurich, who taught that Jesus Christ is present only in the minds of believers when the Lord's Supper is celebrated. Calvin instead maintained that, for the believer, Jesus really became present, although the exact nature of that presence remained somewhat hazy. Similarly, Calvin's retention of the baptism of infants presented some problems in the light of his doctrine of predestination, but he refused to follow the lead of the radical Anabaptists in the Rhine Valley in permitting the baptism of only adult believers.

One area in which Calvin's reforms were decisive and systematic, going far beyond those of Luther, was in his teaching and practice on the nature of the church. Like Luther, he maintained that the church was present where the Word of God was preached and the sacraments properly administered. Unlike Luther, however, he thought that it was possible and necessary to make some provisional judgments on who should be regarded as full and proper members of the church on earth, that is, as "saints." In redefining this latter term, Calvin applied his policy of basing all usage on Scriptural precedent with manifest rigor. In medieval and subsequent Roman Catholic usage, the term *saint* has been reserved for those believers who had led lives of heroic piety while on earth. These had then died and gone directly to Heaven, where they enjoyed a special closeness to God, as demonstrated in their ability to work miracles on behalf of those still on earth who invoked their aid in interceding with God. Calvin, however, employed the term with greater fidelity to early Christian usage, and regarded as "saints" all those who appeared to be followers of God's Word here on earth, and were thus presumably among God's elect.

A major problem for Calvin, and later for many of his disciples, was that of how to know for certain who these saints might be. This question was vital not only to determining who might be admitted to full membership in the church here on earth, but also to anticipating one's eternal destiny. Calvin perhaps wisely disclaimed the ability to answer such questions with any certainty, but did maintain that for practical purposes some guesses might be made. As a result, those who professed a belief in Calvin's interpretation of Christianity, who were willing to partake of the sacraments, and who lived upright lives in conformity with God's Law might be accepted as full members of the church. Hypocrisy might triumph in this world, but God would not be deceived in the next. The larger question of knowing with certainty whether one was in fact among the elect was never fully answered by Calvin, and became the subject of greater attention among subsequent generations of his followers, especially in the Anglo-American world.

The question of church structure, or polity, also evoked from Calvin a thoroughly biblical response. Where Luther was largely indifferent to the question of how the church should be organized and governed, Calvin believed that the New Testament, especially the Book of Acts, provided a workable model for the present that had the force of prescription. Calvin saw the church administered by four kinds of officials: pastors, who preached the Word and most nearly approximated what today would be regarded as a minister; elders, or laymen charged with maintaining strict moral discipline; doctors, who were the equivalent of seminary professors and were to instruct the clergy; and deacons, who supervised church finances and cared for the poor.

The two former offices were the most important, and involved clergy and laity together in church governance through the participation of the two orders in the *consistory*. Although this body had control of church matters, it also advised the *council*, that is, the civil government of the city of Geneva. The two bodies thus worked together in different spheres at the common task of the proclamation and enforcement of God's law. This latter was a major emphasis of Calvin's, who saw the Law as serving several functions: a rule for civil government; a means of impressing sinners with the depravity of their condition; and a guide for the elect, who despite their favored status were still not exempt from the effects of original sin.

This emphasis on God's Law gave Calvin's Geneva a distinctive tone in the annals of the early Reformation. Although other states had rigorous moral codes as well, none was as thoroughgoing in its enforcement as the civil and religious elite of Geneva, working hand in glove under Calvin's direction. Neither sinful behavior nor dissent was tolerated, and the heretic Michael Servetus was burned at the stake in 1553. Such intolerance was hardly unknown in both Roman Catholic and other Protestant states—Servetus had previously been imprisoned by the Inquisition—in the bloody era of religious strife that was now beginning. Geneva, however, became a byword internationally for either admirable rigor or fanatical intolerance.

Geneva also served as a point of dispersal for that set of ideas advocated by Calvin and kindred spirits that collectively became known as the "Reformed Tradition." As had been the case with Luther, "Calvinism" originally had a pejorative cast to it. "Reformed" was the preferred designation for the movement that originally had its focus in several of the Swiss city-states and other cities in the Rhine Valley such as Strasbourg. Geneva and other Reformed outposts also became places of refuge for those of kindred views seeking asylum from persecution, especially during the reign of Queen Mary in England. Rapidly, the Reformed version of Protestant Christianity took on an international character, linked together by scholars and churchmen in continual communication with one another. By the end of the sixteenth century, it had acquired considerable influence in the English universities, where it formed the basis for the movement known as Puritanism within and outside the Church of England; in Scotland, led by John Knox and leading to the formation of the Presbyterian movement; in the German Palatinate; in France, where its followers were known as Huguenots; and in the Netherlands, where it provided an ideological rallying point in the quest for freedom from Catholic Spain. It is from several of these European bases that the Reformed movement found its way to the American colonies.

The legacy of Calvinism has been a lively topic among historians. For earlier generations, Calvin's theocratic rule over Geneva served as a cautionary example of tyranny and intolerance. More recently, many influenced by Max Weber's thought—especially his *Protestant Ethic and the Spirit of Capitalism*—have seen Geneva and its Puritan offspring in old and New England not so much as bulwarks of latter-day medieval repressiveness but rather as the vanguard of modernity. In this light, Calvin's notions of predestination have been interpreted as the forerunners of modern political ideology, endowing believers not with a fatalistic resignation to God's will but rather with a disciplined confidence in the rightness of their cause and the inevitability of its triumph. Calvin's systematic reordering of Geneva's civic life has also been viewed as a forerunner of modern society, in which all aspects of human life are subordinated to the needs of a rationalized, capitalistic economy. These interpretations, needless to say, are controversial and are by no means accepted uncritically and universally. Nevertheless, the rapid advance of Calvinism on the Continent and beyond during the sixteenth and seventeenth centuries was certainly one of the most dramatic religious transformations in Western history.

CHAPTER 11

The Radical Reformation and the Anabaptist Tradition

Many Americans regard "Pennsylvania Dutch Country" as a bastion of quaintness, patronized by the tour bus trade and romanticized in films such as "Witness." Few of these "Dutch," however, have ancestors from the Netherlands; rather, the term originated as a mispronunciation of *Deutsch*, or German. Not all Pennsylvania Germans, moreover, are bearded or bonneted Amish. Only about a quarter of the German-descended population of the area belong to sectarian groups such as the Amish and Mennonites; the majority belong to "churchly" traditions, for instance, Lutherans and Reformed. There is no doubt, though, that the ethos of the area has been profoundly shaped by the overwhelmingly German origins of the population, as manifested in the culture from its dietary customs to the German dialects still spoken by many.

The original German emigration to the American colonies began in the late seventeenth century and took southeastern Pennsylvania as its focus. Among its major sources were two loosely constituted religious communities that had arisen in German-speaking areas of the Rhine Valley and the Low Countries, beginning with the coming of the Reformation. The first of these movements was the Radical Reformation, the followers of which were known as Anabaptists. From this religious upheaval came today's Amish and Mennonites. Toward the end of the seventeenth century, a new ferment arose among the now well-established Lutheran and Reformed state churches of the same parts of Europe. This movement of religious renewal became known as Pietism, and had profound repercussions within English-speaking Protestantism as well. Anabaptism especially attracted persecution, and both movements induced a restlessness that found an outlet in William Penn's eagerness for new settlers in his peaceable kingdom in the New World.

The Radical Reformation was a very loosely allied series of movements that began to appear in Switzerland, the Netherlands, and parts of Germany almost immediately following Luther's break with Rome. The Rhine Valley was a primary channel of communication, and served as an effective conduit for the rapid spread of all manner of new ideas. Many of these movements came to rapid ends; notable among these was the millennial kingdom declared at Muenster in Westphalia in 1534, which was destroyed by the magistrates "with fire and sword."

The Reformation era was hardly one of widespread religious tolerance, and the challenge of the Anabaptists to the dominant principles of church and state was equally nettlesome to Catholic and Reformed. Luther, Calvin, and the Pope were all in agreement with the time-honored principle that each political unit should support, and be supported by, one church, however much they might differ as to which church should hold that position. Opposed to this principle, which underlay the "Magisterial Reformation"—as noted, religious change through the action of the civil ruler—was the "Radical" principle that church and state were fundamentally incompatible, and that Christians therefore should have as little as possible to do with the government. For Catholic and Protestant alike, this amounted not only to heresy but to anarchy, and their fury knew no bounds in putting such dissenters into prison and to torture and death.

"Anabaptism" was the name that arose to describe these radical reformers. It characterizes one of their distinctive practices, that is "rebaptism" or "believer's baptism." Virtually all other Christians were united in their adherence to the baptism of infants, usually by sprinkling, as an affirmation of their potential growth in faith through membership in a Christian family. Scriptural precedent, however, was on the side of the radicals, who were literalists in their recognition that infant baptism simply could not be found in Scripture and was therefore illegitimate. From this position, they saw Luther and Calvin as inconsistent in their adherence to what had become a long-standing churchly tradition.

For the Anabaptists, the baptism of adults seemed mandatory in the first place because Jesus himself had been baptized by immersion in the Jordan as an adult. Second, believer's baptism made sense as a symbol of the nature of the true church, which the Anabaptists conceived of in good sectarian fashion as a "conventicle"—a voluntarily assembled group of the like-minded—rather than as an aspect of the broader society in which membership was compulsory, and entered into in the unknowing state of infancy. To belong to the church was thus to repudiate rather than to reaffirm one's allegiance to the world, and "worldliness" became a major offense to the sectarian way of life.

A literal reading of the Bible, especially the New Testament, and an attempt to recreate the early Christian community characterized Anabaptist practice. Luther, Calvin, and other Reformers might have affirmed similar purposes, but only the sectarians were prepared to follow out to the end what they saw to be the consequences of such a path, come what may. Worship was the closest point of resemblance to the Reformed tradition developed by their Swiss neighbors, Calvin and Zwingli, though even here the Anabaptists were more venturesome. The Lord's Supper was an act of remembrance rather than a sacrament (i.e., a physical conduit for divine grace), and worship was conducted in barns, houses, or other secular buildings. Foot-washing was a biblical ordinance—an action mandated by Jesus—that had been virtually abandoned by other Christians but was revived by the Anabaptists. And, of course, baptism itself—usually conducted by immersion in running water, although this practice varied among different groups—was a key symbolic act.

In carrying out their program of a literal following of the teachings of Jesus, the Anabaptists also focused on a few texts—"Go the second mile," "Turn the other cheek"—that they interpreted as repudiations of all force and violence and a call to pacifism. They extended this policy of noncompliance to a refusal to cooperate in any way with a civil government whose legitimacy rested on actual or potential force—which included every known government. Therefore, most sectarians refused to pay taxes, swear oaths, or, of course, perform military duty. Needless to say, this made them extremely unpopular with every government they encountered, and many joined the ranks of martyrs when they were imprisoned, tortured, and executed for such civil disobedience. Lists and stories of these early martyrs, usually recorded in German, make up a considerable part of the literary heritage of Anabaptism, and are still read by the Amish and their other descendants today.

Although many of the wide variety of sectarian groups that arose in the Rhine Valley during the middle decades of the sixteenth century disappeared or were exterminated, some did survive, often by seeking refuge further to the east. Most present-day Anabaptists can trace their spiritual descent to the followers of Menno Simons (1496–1551), a Dutch Catholic priest who renounced his former faith in 1536 and became a leader of the new movement. Simons helped articulate a theology and life-style that incorporated the major themes of the movement, and became the rallying-point for many Swiss "brethren" (as they preferred to be called) who shared these ideals. The Mennonites of the present day take their name and most of their beliefs and practices from Simons and his group.

The major break within the movement after its early, anarchic days took place over the issue of discipline. Simons himself imposed strict norms on his followers, and insisted that those who persisted in breaking the rules should come under a ban and be shunned by their fellows, especially through a refusal to share meals with offenders. Toward the end of the century, in the midst of a growing laxity of communal discipline, Jacob Amman, a Swiss Mennonite leader, came into conflict with others over his similar insistence on a rigorous application of the *Bann und Meidung* ("banning and shunning"). Reconciliation never came, and Amman's followers, who were committed to a strict repudiation of "worldliness" in all ways, came to be called the "Amish."

The Anabaptist tradition was transmitted to the New World chiefly through the migrations of some of its surviving groups—Amish, Hutterites, and Mennonites—first to Pennsylvania, the colony noted for religious liberty, and later to the Midwest and the prairie provinces of Canada. Its fundamental practice of adult or believer's baptism, though, has been taken up by the far more numerous Baptist churches, whose more immediate origin lay in the left wing of English Puritanism. The broader legacy of the Radical Reformation lay in its witness to a rigorous and highly idealistic reading of Scripture, which placed a radical call to perfection above all considerations of earthly comfort and even survival. However much one might agree with these premises, one can still appreciate the role that these and other "peace churches" have played in America's ongoing debate between the demands of patriotism and the dictates of a standard of conduct higher than that demanded by any earthly power.

PART II

Colonial America: Europeans, Colonials, and Traditional Peoples Before the Revolution

INTRODUCTION

The American colonies were from their beginnings one of the most elaborate laboratories ever devised for the intermixing of peoples, cultures, religions, and social patterns. Native Americans were themselves a highly complex blend of peoples who had already changed and developed over the centuries through continual interaction. Their exposure to hostile colonists and (more or less) benevolent missionaries forced their adjustment to yet another set of cultures—English Protestant and French and Spanish Catholic—which resulted in a wide variety of responses, few if any of which were very successful in the long run. African slaves, who were also the bearers of traditional oral cultures, underwent even more forcible contact with European traditions. These slaves and their free descendants, however, eventually developed a highly creative and long-lasting synthesis of old and new, the story of which will be dealt with as a whole in the next section.

The original European settlers of what would eventually become the United States reflected every possible variation of relationship between religion and society, or church and state, that had emerged in the Old World during the Reformation era. English Anglicans, French and Spanish Catholics, Dutch Reformed and Swedish Lutherans all represented state-supported, "established" churches, usually involved in their governments' imperial ambitions. British Puritans and Quakers and Scotch-Irish Presbyterians were highly vocal English-speaking minorities who attained considerable power once transplanted to American shores. The fragmented nature of the colonies and the weak hold that England and its established church maintained during the seventeenth century made it possible for a wide variety of patterns of relationship between religion and society to emerge. This would provide an important context for the ultimate settlement that had to be forged after independence. Also, it worked subtle, or not-so-subtle, changes in the character of the colonial religious communities. New England Puritanism, for example, changed, in Perry Miller's memorable phrase, from a reformation into an administration.

Although it seemed for a while that the fate of North America was up for grabs among the major imperial powers—England, France, and Spain—it was only the first that would prevail in the longer run. Roman Catholics, therefore, had no real chance for hegemony, and had to learn to live as a minority community in both the United States and Canada. Finally, the Dutch and Swedes were so small in number that any hopes they may have entertained for the acquisition of power rapidly came to naught.

Still other groups came to the New World seeking not power but refuge. Sephardic Jews had been forced to flee their ancestral homes in Spain and Portugal in fear of their very lives, and settled into a comfortable and prosperous though somewhat isolated existence in the seaports of the Atlantic coast. The variety of groups that are frequently, and mistakenly, lumped together as "Pennsylvania Dutch" represent still another experience. Some, such as German-speaking Lutherans and Reformed, were accustomed to establishment status in the Old World. Mennonites, Amish, and other sectarian groups, however, wanted no part of worldly power. Rather, they shared the pacific ideals of the Friends (Quakers), who welcomed and even recruited them to share life in the Pennsylvania colony.

This is not to say that all of these wildly diverse communities lived together in warmth and harmony. The Puritans, it is said, fell first upon their knees, and then upon the aborigines. Puritans hung Quakers, and Maryland Anglicans overthrew their Catholic rulers. Aspirations to hegemony and fears of persecution died hard. By 1700, though, no one church exercised complete dominion even at the regional level. The competing claims of the various churches and the changing policies of the British government eventually resulted in a standoff, where ultimate English domination was becoming assured but in which no one religious community would either reign supreme or be hounded into extinction. Old World attitudes thus of necessity became modified over time, and with them the character of each community. The Great Awakening and then the struggle for independence further involved these peoples with one another in events that transcended religious particularism. Sometimes enthusiastically, sometimes reluctantly, and often unknowingly, all of these peoples were learning how to be Americans.

CHAPTER 12

Colonial Anglicans

In the beginning, Anglicanism was the established and dominant religion of the English colonies of North America, which extended along the eastern coast of the continent from what are now known as the maritime provinces of Canada to the Caribbean islands of Barbados, Bermuda, and Jamaica. Inroads of dissent gradually became established in Plymouth, Rhode Island, Pennsylvania, and other colonies, but even those Puritans led by John Winthrop who founded the formidable Massachusetts Bay Colony in 1630 still maintained that they were at least technically part of the Church of England. During the entirety of the colonial period, the Bishop of London was theoretically responsible for the spiritual welfare of the entirety of the Anglican colonists, and the establishment of a bishop on American shores was a possibility dreaded by those concerned with English encroachments on colonial rights. Church and empire marched together, and an uneasiness about the appropriateness of both reached a crescendo as the Revolution began to loom.

The first Anglican service on American soil was held under makeshift circumstances in 1607 in Captain John Smith's Jamestown. During the seventeenth century, the Church of England became the established church of all of the southern colonies and several counties in New York. However, its actual position—as opposed to its nominal dominance—was one of weakness and disorganization. Major problems included the absence of a resident bishop; the low number and quality of clergy; the scattered population; and competition from both Puritan and Presbyterian Calvinists, on the one hand, and the popular Methodists and Baptists on the other, especially following the Great Awakening of the 1740s. In Virginia, which was the strongest bastion of colonial Anglicanism, parishes were organized and churches established around a plantation society, in which wealthy planters served as wardens and vestrymen (lay officials) dominating a weak and scattered clergy. The tone of Virginia Anglicanism was from the beginning heavily tinged with Puritanism, which yielded to a tolerant "Latitudinarian" spirit in the eighteenth century and then to a "Low Church" or evangelical ethos in later times.

During the eighteenth century, a number of developments bolstered Anglican fortunes to a degree. The founding of the Society for the Propagation of the Gospel in Foreign Parts (SPG) by Thomas Bray in 1701 improved the number and quality of clergy somewhat, and its sister organization, the Society for Promoting Christian Knowledge (1698), also helped firm up the tenor of colonial religious life. The rechartering of the Massachusetts Bay colony in

1691 following the Glorious Revolution in England was part of a series of events that brought a royal governor for the first time to New England shores, and the establishment of King's Chapel in Boston in 1688 represented a modest Anglican inroad into Puritan hegemony. The ordination of Pennsylvania Quaker George Keith to the Anglican ministry in 1700 and the conversion of several Yale tutors and Connecticut Congregationalist clergy in 1722 laid the seeds for the extension of Anglicanism among the influential classes in those areas as well.

Any potentially widespread popularity of the established church, however, was undermined on both religious and political grounds. The Great Awakening—America's first religious revival—began in the late 1730s, and a new approach to Christianity based on emotional conversion spread in its wake. This Awakening, however, had virtually no positive impact on colonial Anglicanism. George Whitefield, the "Grand Itinerant" who turned the Awakening into an event that involved most of the Atlantic seaboard, was a priest of the Church of England. Despite his Anglican orders and Calvinist theology, though, he was much more closely aligned with his friend John Wesley in his approach to religion as something to be experienced intensely and personally. Wesley himself remained an Anglican priest to his dying day, but many of both his official and informal representatives in the colonies (following his own dismal experiences as a missionary in Georgia in 1736–1737) worked to spread Methodism as a virtually independent brand of Christianity rather than as a reform movement within Anglicanism. Therefore, although the Church of England had an institutional base already established throughout the whole of the colonies and especially in the south by the time of the Awakening, it was the Methodists, Baptists, and "New Light" Congregationalists and Presbyterians (i.e., supporters of the revival) who attracted countless followers among the many unchurched people scattered along the frontier.

On the political side, fear of the establishment of an Anglican bishop on American shores was one of the complex of actual and potential grievances that began to unite the colonists after the Awakening had started to instill among them a sense of their commonality. The Calvinist Puritans of New England and their middle-colony counterparts were opposed to further inroads on religious as well as political grounds, and helped create a rhetoric of revolution that pictured the whole English apparatus of church and state as part and parcel of an oppressive design that was set on doing the will of the Antichrist. On the other hand, Anglicans such as George Washington, who served as a vestryman in Alexandria, and the more theoretically minded Thomas Jefferson and James Madison opposed religious establishment on "enlightened" grounds that equated it with tyranny and obscurantism. When the Revolution did come, Anglican clergy were divided in their loyalties, and a majority of laity favored the colonial cause. Some half of the clergy, however, were Tory in sympathy, and fled to the more congenial Nova Scotia and to England itself.

Anglicanism in the colonial and early national periods thus occupied an oddly ambiguous status. On the one hand, it was the established church in the southern half of the Atlantic seaboard, and commanded significant prestige in the northern colonies as well through its association with both the English government and many families of wealth and power. Historians have demonstrated that its constituency was not entirely "genteel," and that the "all sorts and conditions of men" invoked in its *Book of Common Prayer* were represented within its ranks. Nevertheless, such monuments as Boston's King's Chapel, Christ Church in Philadelphia, and Bruton Parish Church in Williamsburg remain as material evidence of the wealth, taste and prestige the church could muster.

On the other hand, its associations with the higher levels of society did not always serve it well. Although Thomas Jefferson, for example, was nurtured in the established faith of the Mother Country, the depth of his ongoing religious attachment to that faith can most charitably be described as questionable. The rationalism that dominated much of eighteenth-century Anglican thought and was reflected in its Neoclassical architecture coincided well with the spirit that informed the framers of the Consitution, but also eroded their allegiance to formal belief. However, the close association with all things English that had been the source of much of the church's prestige in the colonial era also aroused resentments, at first from those who were excluded from the power elite—as in, especially, Virginia—and later from those patriots exasperated with what they saw as British oppression. The result by the time of independence was a church cut off from new currents at both popular and elite levels; the task of rebuilding that awaited it was formidable indeed.

CHAPTER 13

New England Puritans

Like the names of many religious groups, *Puritan* originated as a term of abuse in Elizabethan England for those who advocated what their enemies saw as an excess of rigor in religious observance. During the reign of Queen Mary (1553–1558), many leaders of the Church of England fled to the European continent to avoid either execution or a forcible conversion to Roman Catholic allegiance, and became imbued with the ideas of Calvin and his contemporaries while in exile. After the independence of the English church had been reestablished with the accession of Elizabeth I to the throne in 1558, these exiles began to return to their homeland, and Continental scholars with decidedly untraditional ideas began to teach at Oxford and Cambridge. It was these latter seedbeds of theological ferment that became the nurseries of a movement for religious reform, often along the lines of Calvin's Geneva, that went beyond the earlier English political break with Rome that had left worship, theology, and morals largely unaffected.

Scholars continue to argue as to exactly which and how many English people during Elizabeth's reign could be deemed radical enough to deserve the term *Puritan,* and whether these really saw themselves as a distinctive movement. Elizabeth's drive for a loose uniformity of religious behavior made open attacks on the Episcopal structure of the Church of England difficult, and not many went as far as calling for the abolition of bishops. Most of the reform-minded, whether clergy, laity, or even bishops, were more concerned with bringing the actual religious practice of the English people into conformity with the lofty standards that they regarded as mandated by Scripture, as interpreted by John Calvin. Their complaints about the status quo were numerous: Clergy were insufficiently rigorous in piety and morals, and doctrinally lax; the liturgy as it was celebrated was encumbered with too much of the ceremonial of medieval Catholic practice; and the laity lacked discipline and seriousness, preferring to spend the Sabbath in profane recreations rather than in scriptural study and spiritual contemplation.

As the Tudor dynasty yielded to the Stuart with the accession of James VI of Scotland as James I of England in 1603, the party that its opponents had been deriding as "Puritans" began to become more publicly assertive. James would have none of it, denied their petitions, and on occasion had their more vocal advocates imprisoned and mutilated. Some dissenters left in despair for the Calvinist Netherlands or, with longer-run consequences, the nearly uninhabited shores of New England. Those who remained experienced even greater frustration in the early years of James's successor, Charles I (reigned 1625–1649). Under the leadership of William Laud, whom Charles appointed Archbishop of Canterbury in 1633, the Church of England polarized still further. Laud carried the banner for the "Arminian" party—that is, those who rejected Calvinist theology in favor of that latter-day Dutch opponent of the Calvinists, Arminius. Closer to the Catholic than the Reformed tradition in his views on liturgy as well as theology and polity, he worked vigorously to suppress the Puritan party and earned their lasting enmity in return.

The Puritans had the last laugh, at least in the short run. Parliament was coming under the control of the newer mercantile social and economic interests who were transforming English life during the seventeenth century, and these entrepreneurs were strongly attracted by the Puritan call to the disciplined life. Charles governed ineptly, angering many English people by his marriage to the Roman Catholic Henrietta Maria of France. When tensions became too strong, he dissolved Parliament in 1629 and attempted to rule without it. War with the Scots and financial difficulties forced him to reconvene it in 1640, with consequences not to his liking. Civil War broke out between King and Parliament in 1642, with Charles and his Archbishop Laud ultimately suffering defeat, arrest, and execution. The "Interregnum" that followed under the leadership of Oliver Cromwell and, briefly, his son Richard was marked by radical experiments in church reorganization and the rise of a bewildering variety of sects, of which only the Society of Friends (Quakers) survived. After years of confusion ranging from dictatorship to anarchy, the English recalled the Stuart dynasty to the throne in the person of Charles II in 1660. From that time, the various forces of religious dissent that included

Puritanism were relegated, with Roman Catholics, to a limited role in English life, and the Church of England with its bishops returned to its established status.

While this momentous and sometimes violent drama was playing itself out in England, a number of Puritans began to think that the future of their vision of Christianity lay across the sea in the colonies that the English were beginning to plant along the North Atlantic coast. The first of these groups was among the more radical of the English Puritans in their refusal to acknowledge the legitimacy of the Church of England itself. These "Pilgrims," or "separating Puritans," were committed to a model of church order in which each congregation constituted an independent church with no need of bishops. They had earlier left English soil to try their luck in the congenially Calvinist society of the Netherlands. After a few years of life in Leyden, they grew restless in this religiously appropriate but still alien culture, and returned briefly to England to ready themselves for a more permanent venture into the unknown.

The subsequent story of these "Pilgrims" has become an inextricable part of American mythology, even though their role in the actual establishment of the "New England way" was minor in comparison with their larger and more influential neighbor, the Massachusets Bay Colony. Being first, however, has always been paramount in the popular vision of history, and the Pilgrims were indeed the first to organize a substantive colony on New England shores. Actually, their arrival there was something of a mistake, since they were supposed to sail to Virginia. The *Mayflower,* for whatever reasons, touched land instead at the tip of Cape Cod (now Provincetown) in November of 1620. After some weeks of reconnoitering, they finally alighted at Plymouth, on the mainland to the south of what is now Boston, and named it after their point of departure in England. Even before debarking, however, they entered into the famed "Mayflower Compact," banding themselves together "for the glory of God, and advancement of the Christian faith, and honor of our king and country."*

Governed for decades and immortalized by William Bradford (1590–1657) in his *History Of Plymouth Plantation* (pub. 1908), the "Pilgrim Colony" never grew beyond a few thousand in population, chronically lacked clergy, and ultimately was absorbed by the Massachusetts Bay Colony in 1684. This latter venture was led by the prosperous lawyer John Winthrop (1588–1649), who even before the arrival of his party of "non-separating" Puritans in 1630 set forth on board their ship the *Arbella* his vision of their enterprise in resounding biblical cadences:

> The Lord will be our God and delight to dwell among us as His own people and will command a blessing upon us in all our ways, so that we shall see much more of His wisdom, power, goodness, and truth than formerly we have been acquainted with. We shall find that the God of Israel is among us when ten of us shall be able to resist a thousand of our enemies: when He shall make us a praise

* Spelling and punctuation here and in later quotations is modernized.

and glory, that men shall say of succeeding plantations: the Lord make it like that of New England. For we must consider that we shall be as a city upon a hill, the eyes of all people are upon us; so that if we shall deal falsely with our God in this work we have undertaken and so cause Him to withdraw His present help from us, we shall be made a story and byword through the world.

The Massachusetts Bay venture, with its capital at Boston, differed from its predecessor and neighbor at Plymouth in refusing to repudiate completely the legitimacy of the Church of England (hence their label, "non-separating"). Geographical isolation from the mother country, however, made this difference moot. Eventually four "Holy Commonwealths," differing in detail of organization but united in common purpose, arose in New England. By the mid-1630s, the Connecticut colony arose out of a migration from Newtown (now Cambridge) led by Thomas Hooker. This venture eventually merged in 1662 with a settlement at Saye-Brook (Saybrook) on Long Island Sound and the nearby colony founded at New Haven in 1643 by Theophilus Eaton and John Davenport. These original colonial establishments, by the end of the century combined into two, were counterpointed by neighboring Rhode Island—the "sewer" of New England in the minds of the Puritans. "Rhode Island and Providence Plantations" was founded by and accommodated dissidents such as Roger Williams, who objected to what they saw as overly close ties between church and state in the original colonies.

As Winthrop's lay sermon on the *Arbella* proclaimed, the Puritan "errand into the wilderness" of New England was no ordinary commerical overseas venture. Rather, it was a systematic attempt with only minor variations among these "Holy Commonwealths" to emulate the example of Calvin's Geneva in a setting virtually free of the constraints of the English religious-political establishment and even of the fabric of medieval churches. Although the New England Puritans made some sporadic attempts to evangelize the Algonkians and other aboriginal settlers, little that was permanent came of these efforts, and most of the Indians either died of European-borne diseases or were pushed inexorably westward. The Atlantic colonial economy linked New England with Britain, the West Indies, and even Africa in a system of reciprocal trade, and lavish natural resources, especially of timber, offset the barrenness of the ground and the harshness of the climate. Although the earliest English settlers faced stern adversities, such as those chronicled in Bradford's account of Plymouth, the longer-range future was filled with opportunities for both religious experimentation and commerical prosperity.

The genius of Calvin's Geneva had lain in an attempt to order simultaneously all aspects of life—the individual, the church, the political and social orders—according to biblical dictates and prototypes. The New England Puritans took this plan as their starting point, and worked very consciously from the theology of Calvin as interpreted through his Dutch and English followers, preeminently the Cambridge divines William Ames and William Perkins. Calvin, again, believed that he could find in Scripture clear precedents for the organization of both church and state, respectively in the description of the earliest Christian community in the Book of Acts and other New Testament texts, and in the history of Israel in the Old Testament. Not all aspects of the latter, such as the cultic and dietary prescriptions of Leviticus, were to be accepted literally, but the general idea of a civil and ecclesiastical polity working in tandem according to God's ordinances and for God's greater glory was common to both Geneva and New England.

What was specifically added to the ideological framework of the New England attempt to establish a series of Holy Commonwealths was the notion of *covenant*. This "federal theology" (from Latin *foedus*, or "covenant") had roots in European and British Calvinist thought, as well as in medieval contract theory. It was in New England that the notion, which itself was derived from the Hebrew scriptures, was systematically applied to virtually all areas of life. Through the Covenant of Redemption, the saving act of Jesus had made possible the release of the saints from the eternal penalty for original sin. Through the Covenant of Grace, originally established by God with Abraham, the individual saint entered into a personal relationship with God through which his or her salvation was brought about. Similarly, various social relationships were interpreted in the convenantal framework. New churches were established through a covenanting between God and a select group of saints; marriage was no longer regarded as a sacrament but a covenant; and, at the more complex levels of social organization, each of the Holy Commonwealths was regarded as gaining its legitimacy through a collective covenanting with God.

At the individual level, these Puritans were intensely preoccupied with their spiritual state. One of the conundrums of Calvinism was the question of how to know whether one was in fact among the elect, and the New England "saints" pursued the question relentlessly. The topic was a common one in the sermons of the day, and countless diaries were kept that recorded minutely the daily interior religious experiences of the devout. Gradually, in Edmund Morgan's phrase, a "morphology of conversion" developed, a description of the distinct phases that characterized the religious development of many believers, which could then be used as a guide for those concerned with their own condition. Much of the voluminous theological literature of early New England dealt with the question of "preparation"—in other words, could individuals not yet sure of election do anything actively to prepare the way for God's saving work, or should they rather simply wait for God to take the initiative as he chose?

The question of knowing whether one was among God's elect had social as well as personal dimensions, since the New England Puritans determined to go a step beyond Geneva in tightening the requirements for full church membership. As opposed to the episcopal polity of the Church of England and the presbyterian system that had developed in Scotland on the Genevan plan, the churches of New England were relentlessly congregational, acknowledging no authority beyond the individual congregation other than God and Scripture. As colonization expanded beyond the original Boston area, one of the first acts undertaken by the founders of a new settlement would be the establishment of a church for which seven adult "saints" who had persuaded one another of their probable election were necessary as a nucleus. These then covenanted with one another and with God to establish a church, and could then proceed to call a minister, admit other members, and get on with their appointed tasks. This and other salient details of church governance were spelled out in the "Cambridge Platform," drawn up by a synod, or gathering, of colonial clergy in 1648 for the purpose of articulating authoritatively the "New England way."

Where in Geneva, however, the primary criteria for recognition as a probable saint were external, a new and more profound requirement for full membership rapidly developed in New England. When candidates desired this status, they presented themselves to the minister and a select group of church members and delivered an account of their internal spiritual development. If they satisfied their examiners that their experience was in conformity with the Puritan "morphology of conversion," and that they were neither hypocrites nor simply misinformed, they could assume the privileges reserved for "visible saints." These included the taking of communion, voting on congregational affairs, and ordinarily, if male, receiving enfranchisement in civic matters as well. However, this examination was not conducted with excessive rigor, and a "judgment of charity" was supposed to be rendered in the favor of the candidate when the evidence was not conclusive.

At the broader level of civil government, the New England commonwealths were conceived, as in Geneva, as dedicated to God's glory through the enforcement of his Law. Although the commonwealths have frequently been characterized as "theocracies" (i.e., governed by God through his human agents), the clergy were excluded from the ranks of the civil authorities. John Winthrop, who served as governor of the Bay Colony for most of the years between his arrival and death, was never ordained to the clergy, despite his eloquent sermon aboard the *Arbella*. Similarly, prominent clergy such as Cotton Mather, the third generation of his family in New England, exercised influence through advice and example but not through the holding of any civil office. Church and state worked together for a common goal, but did not employ the same personnel.

This unity of purpose that underlay the church-state alliance was central to the "New England way," and was manifested in a variety of other social and cultural forms as well. The role of education, for example, was eloquently evoked in *New England's First Fruits*, a promotional pamphlet published in 1643 to create a favorable impression of the New England experiment in the mother country:

> After God had carried us safe to New England, and we had built our houses, provided necessaries for our livelihood, reared convenient places for God's worship, and settled the civil government, one of the next things we longed for and looked after was to advance Learning and perpetuate it to posterity, dreading to leave an illiterate ministry to the churches when our present ministers shall lie in the dust. And as we were thinking and consulting how to effect this great work, it pleased God to stir up the heart of one Mr. Harvard (a godly gentleman, and a lover of learning, there living amongst us) to give the one half of his estate (it being in all about 1700 Ł.) towards the erecting of a college, and all his library. After him another gave 300 Ł., others after them cast in more, and the public

hand of the state added the rest. The college was, by common consent, appointed to be at Cambridge (a place very pleasant and accommodate) and is called (according to the name of the first founder) Harvard College.

Harvard was originally founded for the training both of a learned ministry, with an ongoing emphasis in the Reformed tradition, as well as a literate corps of civil leaders, nurtured on the traditional classical curriculum of the English universities with a good dose of Puritan divinity. The New England colonies also took the lead in promoting nearly universal literacy for the citizenry at large, on the premise that God's saints needed to be able to read if they were to encounter God's Word directly in Scripture. The *New England Primer* was a widely used text that, in such verses as the following, at once taught the alphabet and elementary moral, theological, and biblical lore:

In Adam's Fall,
We sinned all.

Job feels the rod
Yet blesses God.

Zaccheus he
Did climb a tree
His Lord to see.

During the nineteenth century, this Puritan drive for education was continued by more liberal spokesmen such as Horace Mann, the Massachusetts Education Secretary who crusaded successfully for free and universal secondary education. Education at all levels seemed to follow naturally from the Reformed impulse, and the plethora of colleges founded throughout the entire northern half of the nation from colonial days to the Civil War era was a tangible legacy of the Puritans and their Calvinist allies.

Two areas of Puritan practice that have embroiled subsequent historians in ongoing controversy have been politics and economics. The New England towns of the colonial era, though by no means permitting universal suffrage, did enfranchise considerably more adult males than had been the case in England. Town meetings through which local government was conducted by direct citizen participation were authentic examples of the affinities between Puritanism and democracy. On the other hand, the Puritans looked backward to a medieval world view in their political philosophy. This was based on the premise, as articulated early on in John Winthrop's *Arbella* sermon, that God had assigned different estates to men and women in this life, designating some to govern and others to serve. Wealth and social rank helped determine status in a variety of aspects of New England life, from the allocation of land in new settlements to the arrangement of pews at meeting houses.

Economics was another realm of cultural life in which the Janus-faced quality of Puritanism was apparent. On the one hand, the Puritan commonwealths exercised a careful control over prices, and perpetuated the medieval distrust of usury, or lending money at interest. On the other, economic success of a distinctively modern sort was hardly a rarity in colonial New England. One of the most stimulating and controversial documents of modern social science is Max Weber's *The Protestant Ethic and the Spirit of Capitalism* (1904–1905), in which the German sociologist argued that an "elective affinity" existed between Puritanism and the "spirit" of the nascent economy of capitalism that was emerging in northern Europe and its American extensions from the sixteenth through the eighteenth centuries. Weber argued that Puritanism fostered capitalism indirectly by encouraging the development of a personality type especially suited to this novel form of economic life, where self-discipline, indefinitely delayed gratification, rational calculation, and systematic reinvestment of surplus funds were the virtues most conducive to success. In addition to self-discipline and Luther's idea of labor for God's glory in a this-worldly vocation or calling, the preoccupation with one's ultimate destiny that Calvinism fostered but never satisfactorily answered gave capitalism yet another religious legitimation. According to Weber, the desire for assurance that one was indeed among God's elect could receive an indirect satisfaction from external evidences of worldly success, which could be interpreted as signs of divine favor. This syndrome, known variously as the "Puritan ethic," "Protestant ethic," and "work ethic," has certainly continued in secularized form over the centuries as an intrinsic part of American culture—as manifested, for example, in the "Yuppie" drive for success in business and the professions during the 1980s. Although social historians continue to dispute the accuracy of Weber's argument, it remains a richly suggestive insight into the role that Puritan culture played in shaping a latter-day American character and society.

In the realm of literary and artistic culture, the religious core of Puritan society was everywhere apparent, and is best illustrated in the character of worship itself. Its setting was not the church, a form of building consciously rejected by the Puritans as implying that God could somehow be confined in earthly space. Rather, they devised a new architectural form, the meeting-house, based on the model of medieval English market halls rather than on the Gothic churches of the Anglican heritage. These buildings looked rather like large private houses, forts, or other secular buildings. They were used initially for any number of civil as well as religious functions, since they were by definition not sacred in themselves. Seating was allocated according to social rank, with the most prominent families in box pews near the pulpit, and servants and occasional slaves in the galleries.

The interior of the meetinghouse was dominated by the pulpit, from which the minister proclaimed and expounded the Word of God in lengthy sermons on the Sabbath—the Hebrew term the Puritans substituted for the traditional "Sunday"—and occasional days of fast or thanksgiving. The sermon was supposed to be clear exposition and application of Scripture, without the elaborate literary embellishment characteristic of much contemporary fashionable English preaching. Similarly, the meetinghouse itself was austerely furnished, with no pictorial representations of religious themes (again in the Hebrew tradition of iconoclasm) or other ornament besides perhaps some skillful pulpit carving. Both sermon and meetinghouse thus reflected the Puritan aesthetic ideal known as the "plain style," that is, having an emphasis on a functional simplicity that would promote the execution of a task without sensual distraction from the glory of God himself. Church music was similarly austere: It was restricted to biblical Psalms translated into simple, often jangling English verse and sung to equally simple tunes. Most literature other than sermons was in the form of theological discourse, and occasionally gifted poetry such as that by Anne Bradstreet and Edward Taylor also followed the dictates of this "plain style."

Although the phrase *Puritan synthesis* has frequently been used to evoke this cultural unity that followed from a powerfully articulated set of religious goals, the Puritans were not very successful in maintaining this culture in very pure form for too long. From the beginning, dissent jarred their attempts at a harmonious uniformity. Such challengers of the established order as Roger Williams, Anne Hutchinson, and various parties of Quaker evangelists were either exiled to Rhode Island, as was the fate of the first two, or variously imprisoned, whipped, or even hanged upon repeated offenses, as happened to some of the Friends' representatives.

Anne Hutchinson (1591–1643?) presents an especially interesting study in dissent, since a major part of her offense was her being a powerfully articulate woman in a patriarchal society. However, her teaching itself, which atttracted a considerable following among both sexes, was corrosive enough in its own implications. Against the Puritan claim that only a probable knowledge of divine election of an individual was possible, and that only within the context of the church, Hutchinson instead maintained that God's chosen knew their own status certainly when God enlightened them, and were able to discern their fellow saints through intuitive knowledge as well. If this *antinomian* (i.e., "against law") heresy had prevailed, the role of the institutional church and its male clergy would have been drastically undermined, and the notion of a godly commonwealth would have collapsed. Hutchinson, who remained unrepentant and defiant through her trial, was not surprisingly consigned to exile.

The first generation was able to deal forcefully and, from its own viewpoint, effectively with such dissidence, which could be blamed on a handful of troublemakers. Before long, though, the clergy were beginning to deliver ritual denunciations of their fellow saints for systematic breaches of the covenant, which, it was argued, led to God's punishment of his "New Israel" through epidemics, Indian attacks, droughts and famines, and various other manifestations of divine displeasure. These denunciations soon took on a predictable, generic form that came to be known as the "jeremiad," after the prophet Jeremiah, whose condemnations of the earlier Israel provided their prototype. Typically they were delivered by prominent clergy who had been appointed to deliver the "election sermon" on the day that the lower house of the General Court (legislature) met to elect the upper. In such a public setting, these preachers provided an official interpretation of New England's mission, in which the bad news of collective transgressions underscored the underlying good news that God still cared for New England sufficiently to carry on his controversy with it. This theme of collective mission, even when expressed negatively, remained a powerful motif in the self-understanding not only of New England but of the subsequent American nation as well, an ongoing interpretation of Winthrop's image of the "city set on a hill."

Other problems, which in retrospect seem almost inevitable in a society based on such lofty ideals, made these jeremiads and their idealization of the earlier, founding generation seem plausible. One problem that began to chafe after some decades had passed was the question of admitting the children and then the grandchildren of the original saints to church membership if they had not passed the mandatory test of successfully narrating an account of their religious awakening. The second generation of New Englanders, perhaps because of the relaxation of the pressures and excitements that had inspired their parents, were experiencing fewer and fewer conversions, even though they by and large remained loyal to the New England way. They were thus relegated to second-class status, and could not receive communion or otherwise exercise the rights of full members.

The question became acute when this second generation began to increase and multiply, and to present their children for baptism. As had been the case in Geneva, infant baptism had been retained as an affirmation of the workings of divine grace through the family, even though the theological arguments for it were rather shaky when viewed from the standpoint of predestination. In the early years of New England, the privilege of baptism had been reserved for the children of saints, on the premise that their offspring were more likely than most to be elected as well. Clearly, a major dilemma was at hand, since the formally unconverted now wanted their children to be brought within the familial covenant that baptism symbolized.

The result was a compromise brought about at a 1662 assembly of divines, which acquired the name of "the Half-Way Synod" because of its results. Here it was proposed that the children of unconverted churchgoers who were otherwise in good standing might be baptized as well. This clearly was a relaxing of the rigor that had characterized the earlier New England conception of church membership. Edmund Morgan has interpreted it as an acknowledgment of the social force of what he has aptly called "Puritan tribalism"—that is, the triumph of family loyalty over religious principle. However, since Puritan polity was rigorously congregational, the Synod's decision was merely advisory and many congregations never adopted it.

By the end of the seventeenth century, a wide variety of events contributed to and reflected the breakdown of the "New England way" as other than a lofty but unrealizable ideal. Economic prosperity was widespread though not universal, and many latter-day emigrants were attracted less by the vision of the city on a hill than the economic main chance. (A *New Yorker* cartoon has one Puritan on shipboard saying to another, "In the short run, my goal is religious freedom, but in the long run I'd like to get into real estate.") More directly corrosive of Puritan dominance was the revocation of the Massachusetts Bay charter in 1684 and its rechartering in 1691 according to imperial rather than religious considerations. A royal governor brought with him a retinue loyal to the Church of England, and Anglican houses of worship such as Christ

Church and King's Chapel began to introduce liturgical, theological, and architectural variety into the Boston religious scene. In part as a result, the old meetinghouse form was soon abandoned, and eighteenth-century Puritan houses of worship began to boast steeples and spires. The franchise was now openly granted on the basis of property ownership rather than sainthood. Although Puritan leaders such as Cotton Mather remained influential, their power was seriously diluted. The witchcraft craze and subsequent executions that swept Salem Village in 1692, involving Mather among many others of all ranks, were at least as much an expression, on the one hand, of rapid social, economic, and political change and its resulting confusion as, on the other, the work of Satan in the colonists' midst.

The events of the Great Awakening beginning in the 1730s further eroded what still remained of the New England "synthesis" of church and state working together for the honor and glory of God, as did increasing religious pluralism and secularism. Three New England states retained an established church, now called "Congregational" rather than "Puritan," for some time after Independence: Connecticut (1818), New Hampshire (1819), and Massachusetts (1833). By this time, other churches, especially the liturgical Episcopal and the liberal Unitarian, vied with the Congregationalists for the allegiance of the wealthy and educated, while Jeffersonian democracy and a host of popular denominations undercut the prestige of the Federalists as the political expression of the older Puritan "oligarchy." The term *Puritan* had disappeared as anything but a historical reference by the early nineteenth century, and was more beloved by genealogists than theologians.

Puritanism, however, was by no means spent as a cultural force. Many of the issues raised by latter-day Puritans such as Jonathan Edwards preoccupied later theologians, and exerted a particular fascination for intellectuals again in the mid-twentieth century. The broader impulse toward education at all levels continued to be manifest in the burgeoning of schools and colleges of all descriptions in subsequent decades, although the rationale had shifted after Independence to the preparation of citizens for an active role in a democratic society. The Puritan concern with moral government also helped shape the political cultures of the northern tier of states to which New Englanders migrated in the nineteenth century. The Puritan ideal of the disciplined individual striving for evidence of election through hard work in a vocation can still be seen in secularized form in the ongoing American "dream of success." The notion of New Englanders as a people specially chosen by God, as with Israel of old, similarly became part of a later American rhetoric of nationalism, as exhibited in presidential inaugural addresses to the present day. Even Puritan aesthetics continue to manifest themselves in periodic protests against excessive ornament and ostentatious display, in favor of a simple, utilitarian "plain style" expressed in later years in the slogan that "form follows function."

Puritanism, in short, died long ago as an organized religious impulse, and the New England churches and congregations that had once espoused it are now usually affiliated either with the liberal United Church of Christ or the ultraliberal Unitarian-Universalist Association. The earliest Puritans had considered themselves to be protesters within the Church of England, seeking a restoration of biblical Christianity. After going into colonial exile, they began to interpret themselves as a New Israel, temporarily on an "errand" into the "waste and howling wilderness" that was New England. Gradually, however, they came to identify with that land that had once seemed so hostile and forbidding, and ceased to think of themselves simply as English saints in exile. Judge Samuel Sewall, a contemporary of Increase Mather, expressed this sentiment vividly when writing of Plum Island off the coast of Massachusetts in his *Phaenomena* of 1697:

> As long as Plum Island shall faithfully keep the commanded post, notwithstanding all the hectoring words and hard blows of the proud and boisterous ocean; as long as any salmon or sturgeon shall swim in the streams of Merrimac, or any perch or pickerel in Crane Pond; as long as the seafowl shall know the time of their coming, and not neglect seasonably to visit the places of their acquaintance; as long as any cattle shall be fed with the grass growing in the meadows, which do humbly bow down themselves before Turkey Hill; as long as any sheep shall walk upon Old Town Hills, and shall from thence pleasantly look down upon the River Parker, and the fruitful marshes lying beneath; and long as any free and harmless doves shall find a white oak, or other tree within the township, to perch, or feed, or build a careless nest upon, and shall voluntarily present themselves to perform the office of gleaners after barley harvest; as long as nature shall not grow old and dote, but shall constantly remember to give the rows of Indian corn their education, by pairs; so long shall Christians be born there, and being made first meet, shall from thence be translated, to be made partakers of the inheritance of the saints in light.

From these lyrical cadences, it is not far to

> I love thy rocks and rills,
> Thy woods and templed hills

in "My Country, 'tis of Thee" (Samuel Francis Smith, Baptist student at Andover Theological Seminary, 1832), and then to

> O beautiful for spacious skies, for amber waves of grain,
> For purple mountain majesties, above the fruited plain

by Katherine Lee Bates (Congregationalist), a professor of English at Wellesley College, in 1893.

As would Irish Catholics, Russian Jews, and Swedish Lutherans in subsequent generations, the Puritans were becoming Americans.

Presbyterians and Other Reformed Churches

The term *presbyterian* describes one of several types of polity, or church organization and governance, associated with the Reformed tradition. The term *presbyter* itself is derived from a Greek word for the officials of the earliest Christian churches in Palestine, and has been variously translated as "priest" or "elder." In Calvin's attempt to use the New Testament as a specific model for the church at Geneva, he devised a fourfold ministry: pastors, elders, teachers, and deacons. Of these four offices, the most important were pastors and elders, who periodically met with their counterparts from other congregations as a *consistory.* This sharing of authority between what were essentially clergy (pastors) and laity (elders), both within each separate church and in groups that constituted higher levels of authority, was the nucleus of the presbyterian system as it would be implemented in Scotland and later in America.

It is with Scotland especially that the origins of Presbyterianism as a distinctive strain within the Calvinist or Reformed tradition lie. Here, presbyterian polity took shape in the sixteenth-century reform movements led by John Knox, and has lasted to the present in virtually unchanged form and terminology. The grassroots unit here is the *session,* consisting of the clergy and lay elders of an individual congregation. These officials meet at appointed times with similar representatives of other congregations within a specific geographical area to constitute a *presbytery,* which ordains clergy, deals with disciplinary matters, and generally performs collectively those duties that a bishop would carry out in an episcopal system. A group of presbyteries similarly sends elected delegates to a *synod,* that is, a judicial body with authority over a larger region. Finally, a Presbyterian church as a whole—that is, the religious unit that includes an entire nation or similar large political unit—is governed by a *General Assembly* of clerical and lay delegates similarly elected by the groups below it. These terms may vary somewhat from place to place—for example, Dutch Reformed churches use *coetus* or *classis* instead of "presbytery"—but the idea remains constant of a succession of clerical and lay delegates forming hierarchically arranged groups with increasing degrees of authority.

Although Presbyterianism in the longer run has become a distinctively American denomination on this side of the Atlantic, its heritage has always been as firmly rooted in Scotland as that of Lutherans is inseparable from Germany and Scandinavia. Although its founder, John Knox (1513?–1572), is remembered as heroic in his almost single-handed transformation of the Scottish nation during his lifetime, he seems to have shared in his mentor Calvin's lack of personal charisma. The satiric poet Dorothy Parker once observed that "those whose love is thin and wise/May view John Knox in Paradise."

Where pre-Reformation Scotland has been described as something of a Celtic backwater, still torn apart by warring clans, Knox's work in naturalizing the ideals of Geneva on its soil produced a sternly disciplined nation that for a century would be at odds with neighboring England over the future of its religious establishment. A Church of Scotland organized on presbyterian principles was first constituted in 1560, but its success in resisting the attempt of the English to impose an episcopal system varied greatly over the years. When James VI of Scotland became King of England as well in 1603, he and the later Stuart dynasty had little sympathy with the party of Knox's successors and their English Puritan allies. The obstinacy of both parties was an important contributing factor to the outbreak of the English Civil War and the ultimate defeat and execution of Charles I in the 1640s. The principal mode of Scottish organization against what they perceived as English tyranny was the promulgation of successive *covenants,* or pacts, of which the most significant was the "Solemn League and Covenant" entered into with the antiroyalist English "Long" Parliament in 1643. It was not until after the final overthrow of the House of Stuart in the "Glorious Revolution" of 1688 that the Kirk (Church) of Scotland became permanently organized on presbyterian lines.

During this tumultuous century, the Scottish Kirk was also active in defining its doctrines, which were firmly based on the predestinarian teachings of Calvin. Most notable among these documents, which subsequent generations of Presbyterians on both sides of the Atlantic have looked to as a source of religious authority over the decades, has been the Westminster Confession of 1646. Prepared by order of Parliament during the Civil War after the adoption of the Solemn League and Covenant, it consisted of thirty-three chapters that dealt with the entirety of Christian belief from a Calvinist perspective. In addition to affirming predestination, it especially stressed the identity of the Christian Sunday with the Jewish Sabbath, and called for the strictest observance of that institution.

The New England Puritans of the seventeenth century were clearly very similar to the Scottish Presbyterians in their general approach to religion, and by the early eighteenth century the churches of the Connecticut colonies had developed a "consociational" system of governance, affirmed in the Saybrook Platform of 1708, that differed from the presbyterian pattern only in detail. As Scots began to emigrate to the Middle Colonies around that time, their contact with Puritans in Long Island and northern New Jersey was generally congenial, since they scarcely differed at all on matters of doctrine and polity. It was this contact that was to form the nucleus of one of the major factions within the American Presbyterianism that began to emerge during the early eighteenth century.

The first organizer of the scattered congregations that endorsed a presbyterian system of polity was Francis Makemie (1658–1708), who served as a missionary in Virginia, North Carolina, and Barbados before settling into a ministry at Rehoboth, Maryland, in 1698. In 1706, he brought together six other similarly inclined ministers to form the first American presbytery at Philadelphia. The following year he was imprisoned briefly in New York for preaching without a license, but won both acquittal for himself and a victory for religious noncomformity in the trial that ensued.

Although of Scottish extraction, Makemie, like many of his compatriots, was born not in Scotland but rather in northern Ireland, or Ulster. This Scottish presence in Ireland was the result of a colonization policy undertaken by James I to resettle Protestants, mainly from the lowlands of Scotland, on lands confiscated from rebellious Irish leaders. Later British policy, however, worked against the economic and religious interests of Presbyterian as well as Catholic Celts, and a mass migration of "Scotch-Irish," as they came to be known, began shortly after the turn of the eighteenth century. Most of these emigrants were poor but fiercely independent, and provided much of the stock that would produce the typical American frontiersman of later years. Before the move across the Cumberland Gap into Tennessee and Kentucky following Independence, the first generations of Scotch-Irish typically arrived in Pennsylvania and rapidly fanned out into that colony's western regions, as well as southward into what are now Virginia, West Virginia, and North Carolina. Although many were only loosely schooled in what by now had become their traditional faith and many would become eager converts to the Baptist, Methodist, and other aggressive new frontier denominations, they nevertheless provided one of the major ethnic components of the colonial Presbyterian presence.

It was in fact the loose division of early colonial Presbyterians into a primarily English area in the north and a Scottish-Scotch-Irish zone further south that set the scene for the conflicts that were to divide that community, often bitterly, during the pre-Revolutionary decades. The issues were versions of those that have over the years plagued almost every religious group that has achieved a critical mass of membership and with it a reasonable diversity of background and outlook. The "Scottish" party to the south was generally inclined toward a rigorous traditionalism, and looked upon the Westminster Confession as the ultimate test of doctrinal purity. The "English" party, as those from New England and New York might be loosely called, was less attached to this and similar creeds, and instead regarded the Bible itself as the final standard of orthodoxy. The mutual acceptance of an "Adopting Act" of 1729 marked a temporary peace, with the victory going to the latter, but the underlying issues of rigor and authority still festered.

The second phase of this conflict focused on a new movement that provided much of the impetus for the religious revival that would sweep the entire Atlantic seaboard: the Great Awakening of the 1730s and 1740s. Like other branches of the Reformed tradition, Presbyterian preaching traditionally had focused on the exposition of doctrine, that is, on theological teaching. In the Middle Colonies, however, a remarkable family named Tennent arose that led the way in that region in promoting a new form of preaching, aimed at the emotions rather than the intellect and designed not to instruct but to bring about an emotional awakening or conversion. William Tennent, Sr. (1673?– 1746) was the patriarch of this line of evangelical preachers, and he prepared his sons and other followers for their calling at a makeshift seminary in Neshaminy, Pennsylvania, that became known as the "Log College." His son Gilbert (1703–1764) especially gained a reputation as a firebrand of the later Awakening, and alienated many "Old Side" clergy with his attack on their alleged lack of vital faith in his notorious sermon "The Danger of an Unconverted Ministry." The Tennents and their partisans emerged as the "New Side" of the colonial Presbyterians as the Awakening led to polarization. In 1741 they organized the dissident New Brunswick Presbytery, which in 1745 joined with other prorevival groups to form the Synod of New York. As in earlier disputes, the question of whether Scottish (Old Side) or New England (New Side) influence would prevail was a major issue in this family quarrel.

A reconciliation took place in 1758 after revival fires had cooled somewhat, and the dissident groups united to form the Synod of New York and Philadelphia. The issue of doctrinal rigor versus revival preaching was by no means resolved, but it had retreated into a state of dormancy until frontier expansion began again in earnest in the decades following Independence. Two major events now drew attention from the reunited Presbyterians. First, the question of higher education had always loomed large in this tradition, as it did for their New England counterparts. The Reformed ministry was predicated on an educated clergy who could study Scripture in the original languages, and a vehicle for their training in the New World was highly desired. The result, largely the work of New Side initiative, was the chartering under public auspices in 1746 of the College of New Jersey, later to be known as Princeton. Although its earliest presidents, including the renowned New England theologian Jonathan Edwards, seemed to fall under some sort of curse and die shortly after taking office, stability came finally with the arrival of the Scotsman John Witherspoon (1723–1794) in 1768, the beginning of a 26-year administration.

Witherspoon served as a reconciling influence among the factions in this tradition, although he himself was of rather conservative bent. His espousal of the Scottish Common Sense philosophy made Princeton a major force in the development of Reformed theology in America during the nineteenth century, and underscored the emphasis in the Presbyterian tradition on the importance of the intellect. At least as important, however, was Witherspoon's role as a delegate to the Continental Congress, where he became the only clergyman to sign the Declaration of Independence. It is something of a paradox in the Reformed tradition that it contained on the one hand a stress on the legitimacy of civil government as a God-given means of enforcing the divine Law, while at the same time providing an ongoing support for rebellion against what its advocates perceived as usurpations of that Law by established governments. Witherspoon was therefore typical of American Presbyterians, as well as other Reformed churches such as the Puritan Congregationalists in New England, in taking the lead in the ideological battle that ultimately erupted into revolution—a pattern already familiar in Scotland, where resistance to English tyranny had become virtually a way of life.

A related characteristic of Scottish-American Presbyterianism was its contentiousness, and the willingness of its members to split and form new groupings on matters of principle. At the time of Independence, Presbyterians were outnumbered only by Congregationalists. Most were organized into four synods consisting of sixteen presbyteries, which combined in 1788 to form the General Assembly of the Presbyterian Church in the United States of America (PCUSA). However, two groups of Scottish derivation demonstrated their traditional principled resistance in refusing to join this new national church. One group was known as Covenanters, who in 1733 had emerged among Scots who had earlier refused to acknowledge the legitimacy of the restored Stuart monarchy. Their American adherents formed the Reformed Presbytery of America (later, the Reformed Presbyterian Church) in 1773.

A second group of dissidents were the Seceders, who came together in Scotland in 1743 to resist the practice of clergy being appointed and supported by lay patrons. In the colonies they formed the Associate Presbytery (later Associate Presbyterian Church) in 1753. Many of these American Covenanters and Seceders recognized their commonality and united in 1782 to form the Associate Reformed Presbyterian Synod (later Church). As might be expected, however, this union split in 1822 into northern and southern factions. That in the South, the ARPC (General Synod), remains independent to this day, with headquarters in South Carolina and a membership of about 35,000. The northern branch later combined with those Seceders (the Associate Presbyterian Church) who had never entered the union in the first place, and merged in 1958 with the "mainstream" PCUSA to form the United Presbyterian Church in the United States of America.

The colonial Presbyterian culture of the eighteenth century contained within itself two seeds for future development. On the one hand, Presbyterianism, with its leadership and educational centers based along the eastern seaboard, would emerge as one of the most elite of the new nation's denominations. Although Presbyterians shared many theological emphases with other evangelical groups such as the Baptists and Methodists, they were closer to the Episcopalians in social status, and were characterized especially by the old Reformed emphasis on divine and human law and on social and religious order. On the other hand, though, much of the most fertile soil for recruitment by popular movements and new denominations from the time of the Great Awakening on were the Scotch-Irish, inexorably moving southward and westward, away from the colonial centers of religious culture and authority. Here was a people fiercely committed to individual liberty of choice—of lifestyle and of belief. It was they who provided the matrix for much of the popular religious enthusiasm that characterized American development during much of the nineteenth century, especially in the south and west, a story that continues later with that of the Second Great Awakening.

The religious impulse unleashed in the Swiss city-states of the sixteenth century had a profound impact in the English-speaking world, but was by no means confined to that world. Calvinism spread rapidly into the Netherlands, where it became the dominant faith; to France, where it underwent both popularity and persecution until the latter finally prevailed; and throughout central Europe, especially in what are now Germany and Hungary, where it became entrenched in various states as a local majority or national minority of some consequence. Immigrants from all of these areas came to America and brought with them their own variants upon the common theme. In most cases, assimilation into the English-speaking Protestant community was more or less rapid and thorough, with one significant exception: the Dutch.

In the British Isles, another Celtic people, the Welsh, became converted during the eighteenth century in large numbers to the latter-day variant of the Reformed faith known as Calvinistic Methodism. Welsh-speakers who came to the farming and mining centers of Pennsylvania and Ohio in the nineteenth century established their own churches, but subsequent generations who spoke mainly English were usually absorbed into the Presbyterian fold. In 1920, most of the congregations of the Welsh Calvinistic Methodist Church formally merged with the Presbyterian Church in the United States of America, another casualty (or beneficiary) of the Americanization process.

In France, Calvin's native land, his followers became known for obscure reasons as Huguenots (HEW-geh-notts or UE-gay-nose). First organized formally in 1559, they rapidly gained powerful adherents and enemies, and several thousand were murdered in the St. Bartholomew's Day Massacre of 1572. Granted toleration under the Edict of Nantes in 1598, their situation was reversed in 1685 by Louis XIV. Some hundred and sixty thousand were forced into exile, many of whom found refuge in the vicinities of Boston, New York, and Charleston. Although many were commercially successful, few managed to maintain any coherent sense of community for long, and most were rapidly absorbed into Anglican, Dutch Reformed, or other congregations.

Among German-speakers, the Reformed impulse was most successful in the Palatinate in the Rhineland, from which many emigrants began to arrive in Pennsylvania in the 1720s and 1730s. Here they mingled with other Germans of any number of other varieties of Christianity, who collectively became known, erroneously, as "Pennsylvania Dutch" (a mispronunciation of *Deutsch*, i.e., German). In general, the German Reformed in America were more conscious of being German than Reformed; lacking a strong central organization, they were inclined toward cooperative arrangements with other German-speaking churches, especially the Lutheran Church. The first synod of the German Reformed Church was formally organized in Lancaster, Pennsylvania, in 1793, and dropped the "German" from the official name in 1869. The denomination increased about tenfold from its original 15,000 during the nineteenth century. In the twentieth century, the erosion of older ethnic and even theological divisions resulted in a series of ecumenical unions. The Reformed Church absorbed most of what had previously been the Hungarian Reformed Church in 1924, and in 1934 united with the Evangelical Synod of North America, a German Lutheran-Reformed body on the Prussian model in which doctrinal differences were subordinated to political unity. The resultant merged group was known as the Evangelical and Reformed Church. This new denomination then united in 1957 with the Congregational Christian Churches—the direct descendants of many of the old New England Puritan congregations—to form the United Church of Christ.

German Reformed churches in America never grew very large. Throughout their history they failed to develop a clear identity, and eventually lost their distinctiveness completely as the German language lost its place in American life. However, this community was influential beyond its numbers in its impact on American religious thought. During the middle and later nineteenth century, the tiny seminary at Mercersburg in central Pennsylvania (since removed to Lancaster) attracted two extraordinary professors, John Williamson Nevin (1803–1866) and Swiss-born Philip Schaff (1819–1893), whose work became known collectively as the "Mercersburg Theology." This school of thought (with two exponents) constituted a "high-church" movement within the Evangelical Protestantism of the nineteenth century, and stressed the role of the historical church and its sacraments over and against the dominant revivalism of the era. Later, in the twentieth century, the brothers Reinhold and H. Richard Niebuhr, nurtured at Eden Theological Seminary in St. Louis, became two of the most important voices within the "Neo-Orthodox" movement in American religious thought.

The one community among the American Reformed that most strenuously and successfully resisted complete Americanization has been the Dutch. These sturdy entrepreneurs first came to the Atlantic seaboard in the 1610s, with settlements in the New York City and Albany areas that early came under the control of the Dutch West India Company. The first Dutch Reformed Church was established in New Amsterdam (New York City) in 1628, and others were soon founded in the Hudson and Mohawk Valleys, Long Island, and northern New Jersey. These early Dutch settlers were intolerant of other religious groups, and managed to retain their privileged status, with an accompanying right to tax support, on an equal basis with the Church of England even after the English acquired the New York colony in 1664. The most notable personage in the colonial Dutch Reformed community was Theodore Jacob Frelinghuysen (1692–1748?), who helped lay the foundations for the Great Awakening through his preaching in New Jersey's Raritan Valley.

Until 1747, the year in which Frelinghuysen and his followers obtained permission to establish a semiindependent *coetus* (i.e., presbytery), both Dutch and German Reformed churches in America were largely under the control of the *classis* of Amsterdam. The subsequent development of the Dutch community followed the pattern of the Presbyterians and other groups. A charter was obtained in 1766 for Queen's College in New Jersey (later known, under secular auspices, as Rutgers); a seminary, still very much extant, was founded in New Brunswick, New Jersey, in 1784; and in 1792, the Reformed Protestant Dutch Church took its formal place in the roster of independent American denominations. (The name was changed to its present form, the Reformed Church of America, in 1867.)

The New York/New Jersey area has remained to the present day as a major geographical center of the Dutch Reformed community in America, and the Reformed Church in America (RCA) still maintains its denominational headquarters in Manhattan. Later immigration during the nineteenth century resulted in sizable concentrations of Dutch settlement in central Iowa, where Central College is located at Pella; parts of California; and the upper Midwest, especially the western part of Michigan's lower peninsula. In the latter region, Hope College and Western Theological Seminary, both sponsored by the

RCA, are located in the town of Holland, and Calvin College, maintained by the Christian Reformed Church, is in nearby Grand Rapids, which is also that denomination's headquarters. The heavily Dutch heritage of the local culture is evident in the proliferation of churches of both denominations, the annual tulip festival in Holland, and bumper stickers informing the outsider that "If You're Not Dutch, You're Not Much."

The coexistence of two Dutch Reformed denominations, with corresponding educational institutions, in western Michigan is the result of a schism in the Netherlands that had important repercussions in the United States. In 1834, a group that objected to the Dutch government's taking control of the church organized a rival protest movement that was brought to the United States shortly thereafter by emigrants leaving the Netherlands for economic as well as religious reasons. These schismatics attracted native Dutch-Americans who had become discontent with the RCA, and led to the formation, beginning in 1856, of what would eventually be known as the Christian Reformed Church (CRC).

Although both groups share a common heritage of Reformed belief and worship and Dutch culture, their division reflects more than anything a differential rate of Americanization. By the twentieth century, the RCA was not distinguishable in most ways from the mainstream of American Presbyterianism. The CRC, however, continued to use the Dutch language well into the present century, and objected to what its adherents regarded as the excessive liberalism of RCA practice. Many traditions in America, such as the Campbellites, have experienced similar divisions; probably the most direct analogue in this case, however, is with the Lutheran community, now divided between the more mainstream Evangelical Lutheran Church in America and the extremely conservative Missouri Synod. Like the latter, the CRC insists on purity of doctrine; the importance of creeds or confessions as adequate embodiments of scriptural truths; an emphasis on propositional theology, that is, a scholastic approach to religious truth as capable of being embodied in doctrinal statements; a strict moral code; and a separate school system to socialize the young into a community firmly committed to maintaining its distance from the larger society. Despite these differences, the two groups share many features of their common tradition, including a presbyterian form of polity, and are not radically disparate in size. (In 1983, RCA membership stood at 350,000, and CRC 300,000.)

The character and fortunes of these various Reformed communities are somewhat puzzling to the outsider, in part because of their low visibility on the American scene. The contrast here is noticeable with other non-English-speaking Protestant groups, such as the Lutherans and Amish/Mennonites, which have been considerably, and usually deliberately, slower in their capitulation to the forces of Americanization. One factor at work here was the prior presence of English-speaking religious groups with a similar theological outlook—for instance, the Congregationalists and Presbyterians—who provided a ready model for imitation or vehicle for merger for Continental newcomers.

Another, less tangible factor might lie in the "elective affinities" between the

Reformed tradition and the modernization process noted by Max Weber in his *Protestant Ethic and the Spirit of Capitalism* and the work of his followers. For many non-English-speaking groups, assimilation into America was retarded, for better or worse, by a world view and value system that were at odds with many aspects of American culture. (The Old Order Amish, of course, are among the most radical examples of this.) With the exception of the conservative wing of the Dutch, however, most adherents of Reformed theology were comfortable enough with the modern world, including its American version, to lack interest in maintaining the old ways in the New World. In the case of the Christian Reformed Church, the motives seem to have been a combination of religious and cultural, analogous in different ways to German Catholics on one hand and fundamentalists on the other. In order to preserve a theology and corresponding world view significantly at odds with that of the dominant culture, the distance provided by the maintenance of a foreign language was most useful. As a result, the cultural pluralism of the nation was enhanced for several generations by a community that still took Europe rather than America as the point of reference for its own identity. On the whole, however, the cultural transition from the Old World to the New seems to have been fostered more often than impeded by the presence of the Reformed tradition.

CHAPTER 15

The Society of Friends (Quakers)

New religious movements are most likely to arise during periods of social and cultural unrest, and mid-seventeeth-century England had unrest aplenty. Much of the tension that led to the outbreak of civil war and the defeat and execution of Charles I lay in the squaring off between Anglican supporters of the Stuarts—the older landed aristocracy—and the Puritan reformers and their Parliamentary allies, who predominated among the newly wealthy London merchants. Social and economic change thus combined with religious conflict to the point of outright revolution. From 1640, when war finally broke out between King and Parliament; through the beheading of Charles I; the government of England by the redoubtable Puritan, Oliver Cromwell; to the overthrow of Cromwell's ineffectual son Richard, and the restoration of the Stuart Charles II to the throne, the people of England were caught in the middle of the most bewildering variety of religious options ever to be thrown at them.

Out of this ferment grew any number of usually short-lived movements that can best be called *sects*—intensely fervent small groups of dedicated believers who have fastened on some unusual set of beliefs and practices that distinguish them from the ordinary run of Christians. Among those that arose in England at midcentury were the Ranters, a group of pantheists who rejected clergy, church, and Bible; the Diggers, who advocated communal ownership of land on religious grounds; the Muggletonians, whose founders claimed to be the "two witnesses" of the Book of Revelation; and the Fifth Monarchy Men, who believed the Millennium was about to be inaugurated. Just as all bets were off as to who was actually in charge of England, so were traditional sources of religious authority—Bible and Church—cast into radical doubt by so many contradictory contending claimants to truth.

In the midst of this confusion arose many "seekers." A seeker was a person who did not claim to know the truth, but was actively engaged in its pursuit. George Fox (1624–1691), the son of a weaver, was such a seeker whose spiritual quest attracted a great deal more interest than most. Beginning in 1643, Fox grew impatient with external forms of religion and began to teach that the truth could be found most purely within each individual. He soon attracted followers, who in their early days together in the movement shared the "enthusiasm"—as highly demonstrative, unconventional religious behavior was then called—apparent in Fox's own journal account for 1651:

> And as I was one time walking in a close with several Friends I lifted up my head and I espied three steeple-house spires. They struck at my life and I asked Friends what they were, and they said, Lichfield. The word of the Lord came to me thither I might go, so, being come to the house we were going to I bid friends that were with me walk into the house from me; and they did and as soon as they were gone (for I said nothing to them whither I would go) I went over hedge and ditch till I came within a mile of Lichfield. When I came into a great field where there were shepherds keeping their sheep, I was commanded of the Lord to pull off my shoes of a sudden; and I stood still, and the word of the Lord was like a fire in me; and being winter, I untied my shoes and put them off; and when I had done I was commanded to give them to the shepherds and was to charge them to let no one have them except they paid for them. And the poor shepherds trembled and were astonished.
>
> And I went about a mile till I came into the town, and as soon as I came within the town the word of the Lord came unto me again to cry, "Woe unto the bloody city of Lichfield!"; so I went up and down the streets crying, "Woe unto the bloody city of Lichfield!" Being market day I went into the market place and went up and down in several places of it and made stands, crying, "Woe unto the bloody city of Lichfield!", and no one touched me nor laid hands on me. As I went down the town there ran like a channel of blood down the streets, and the market place was like a pool of blood. [From Jessmyn West, ed., *The Quaker Reader*, pp. 63–64.]

The rhetoric and actions here are clearly those of a prophet, and Fox and his followers—known as "Friends"—became notorious for such extravagant behavior as disrupting church services by running through them naked. Many Friends were imprisoned, and not a few died in England's fetid jails.

The core belief of the "Friendly Persuasion" was that within each human being dwells an "inward" or "inner light." This light, which is the Holy Spirit or spirit of Christ, is the ultimate authority in matters of religious truth, and is to be cultivated and followed by all Friends in the context of their meetings for worship. These meetings were starkly different from ordinary church services. In traditional form, a Quaker meeting for worship—the "first-day meeting"—was conducted in an austere meetinghouse in an unornamented room, with men and women seated separately. (Early Friends rejected the usual weekday names, such as Sunday, as pagan.) Although there was no ordained ministry, officers known as "elders," "overseers," and "recorded ministers" developed to provide administrative continuity. Silence prevailed at meetings until a member felt the promptings of the Inner Light, which would be expressed in a ritualized sort of chanting. Business meetings were held monthly and were also conducted in silence, with no leader as such. Various members would speak according to the promptings of the Light until a consensus was reached; this would be recorded by a clerk. As the movement spread, regional, quarterly, and yearly meetings, attended by delegates from the monthly meetings within their purviews, eventually developed at London and then in the American colonies.

Similar, for instance, to many Anabaptist groups on the Continent, the Friends followed the sectarian pattern in distancing themselves from what they regarded as the ungodly ways of secular society. They were—and many still are—firm pacifists, and refuse to engage in any activity involving violence. In the early days in England, their refusal to recognize distinctions among different classes of people manifested itself in a variety of ways. A familiar example was their use of the familiar "thou" and "thee" to all, even those toward whom convention dictated that the more formal and respectful "you" be employed. (This usage continued even after "thou" and "thee" had become archaic.) This refusal to make distinctions resulted in frequent problems with the authorities. Friends refused to remove their hats in court, nor would they swear oaths. When told to tremble before the majesty of the law, as the story has it, they replied that the judge himself ought to tremble before God. This kind of exchange allegedly gave rise to the nickname of "Quakers," which, like many such derogatory nicknames, eventually came to be accepted by the group itself as an informal alternative to its more proper designation, "the Society of Friends."

Because of their refusal to conform not only with religious but civil norms, the early Quakers who escaped overt persecution were nevertheless reduced to a second-class state of citizenship in England. The military and the church, of course, could not be options, nor were university educations or the professions, which required religious conformity. The main avenue of worldly endeavor that remained was business. To this the Friends took naturally, and their reputation for complete reliability, together with a strenuous work ethic and a disciplined, frugal life-style, resulted in considerable financial success. Much of their gains was redirected into the group for the relief of the suffering of those who were persecuted, and for other philanthropic efforts for which the Friends became well known.

One convert to the Friendly cause was William Penn (1644–1718), the son of a prominent naval officer to whom the Stuart government owed considerable money. After Penn became a convert to the Quaker persuasion, he prevailed upon Charles II to settle his debts with the family by a large land grant in the Middle Atlantic colonies in the New World. This colony was called Pennsylvania—"Penn's woods"—and its capital Philadelphia—"the city of brotherly love." It was here in the freedom of the New World that Fox, Penn, and their followers had their main chance to create, in true American fashion, their own version of a Christian utopia quite literally from the ground up. Even in its physical arrangements, Philadelphia still reflects this attempt, with a grid of broad tree-lined avenues at its center designed to provide a spacious setting in which a society based on peace and harmony might take root and blossom.

In its founder's own words, Pennsylvania was intended from the beginning as "an example and standard . . . set up to the nations." Its instrument of government included such untraditional provisions as legal marriage without clergy, arbitrators or peacemakers attached to the courts, affirmations instead of oaths, and no militia. Although the franchise was restricted to Christians— among the broadest in the colonies—freedom of worship was extended to all. In keeping with the Quaker view that the Inner Light dwelt potentially in everyone, Penn's dealings with the Indians were notable for their probity, as efforts not only to avoid conflict but to avoid the exploitation and misunderstanding from which conflict arises. Although various domestic and foreign upheavals came in the way of Pennsylvania's immediate achievement of a utopian condition, the plans of the founder did achieve for several decades a genuine alternative to the "establishments of religion" and accompanying intolerance that were the norm for most of the colonies.

Penn did not intend that his foundation be restricted only to Friends, but actively sought other colonists of similar inclination through recruiting trips into the areas of the Rhine Valley where sectarians abounded. This resulted in the beginning of the emigration of the "Pennsylvania Dutch" (i.e., Germans) into the counties near Philadelphia soon after the colony was launched. The Friends, however, achieved rapid prosperity for reasons similar to those that prevailed in England, and they also kept a benevolent but firm hold upon the Assembly, which endeavored to reach decisions by general consent. Problems arose when the British government began to assess taxes to finance the French and Indian wars that erupted periodically through the early and middle eighteenth century. Although the Friends were for some time willing to equivocate and assign moneys "for the King's use," they eventually had to come to terms with the compromises imposed on their principles, and in 1756 finally yielded control of the colonial government to others. (Similar dilemmas were faced by Quakers in Rhode Island, where they constituted a significant segment of the population and frequently held high office, including the governorship.) In Philadelphia, however, their social and financial power remained strong for generations, and some colonial Quaker families continue to enjoy eminence to the present day.

The decades surrounding Independence brought about numerous changes within the Quaker community. The outbreak of the Revolution posed a severe challenge to their pacifist ways, and many suffered considerably at the hands of patriots who suspected their loyalty when they refused to take up arms. Another test of principle was raised in the work of the New Jersey Friend John Woolman (1720–1772), who argued widely and effectively that slave-holding was contrary to basic Quaker beliefs. Woolman was instrumental in persuading many slave-holding Friends to grant freedom to their human "property," and also played a role in Pennsylvania's early abolition of the "peculiar institution." Many Quakers played active roles in the formation of the first antislavery societies in the new nation, and Benjamin Lundy, the Quaker editor of *The Genius of Universal Emancipation,* helped shape the consciousness of his sometime assistant William Lloyd Garrison, the future editor of *The Liberator.*

Ferment and change were also affecting deeply the very core of American Quakerdom at Philadelphia in the realm of religious practice. Although they had renounced direct political power, many Philadelphia Quaker families had become very prosperous, and had established an interlocking set of dynasties through intermarriage. As Frederick Tolles points out in his classic study, *Meeting House and Counting House,* these great families remained faithful to the old customs of plain dress, but the quality of the material that went into that dress grew progessively finer as their fortunes accumulated.

As the distinction between these well-to-do urban Friends and their poorer rural counterparts increased, the kind of split occurred that frequently affects sectarian groups that have become established on a permanent basis. Elias Hicks (1748–1830) arose as a spokesman for the rural group, but his protest was couched in theological rather than socioeconomic terms. Hicks regarded himself as a restorationist, determined to bring Quaker practice back into line with what prevailed in the age of Fox and Penn. Hicks thus emphasized the "Inner Light" tradition, which he believed was being compromised by the "churchly" emphasis of the Philadelphia elite on more traditional Christian symbols such as the Bible and Jesus. These latter had been affirmed in 1806 by the Philadelphia Yearly Meeting, whose leadership had come into a cooperative relationship with the evangelical Protestant community in many benevolent as well as business activities.

This disagreement resulted in 1827 in an overt split of the Quaker community into "Orthodox" and "Hicksite" factions. This was only the beginning, however. Quakers, like most other Americans, were following the frontier westward, and many Friends who had settled in North Carolina and other parts of the South were beginning to head toward the Midwest as they became alienated from slave-holding society. Richmond, Indiana, near the Ohio border, emerged as a focus for these frontier Quakers, and their contact with the Methodists in particular made them receptive to the evangelical style that their Philadelphia counterparts had already absorbed to a degree too great for the likings of the Hicksites. Before long, Quakers in Indiana and the surrounding region could scarcely be distinguished from their Protestant neighbors in their use of revival preaching, hymns, churchlike buildings, and the equivalent of a professional ministry.

As the issues became more clearly defined, two more leaders arose whose names became eponymous for the emergent factions. Joseph John Gurney (1788–1847) became identified with the evangelical cause, stressing the authority of the Bible and the doctrine of Jesus's sacrificial atonement for the sins of humanity. It was Gurney's teachings that were adopted most eagerly by the Richmond group. Opposed to Gurney were the followers of John Wilbur (1774–1856), who, though "Orthodox" in their emphasis on the divinity of Jesus, also stressed the traditions of the Inner Light and plain speech and dress that they thought the Gurneyites were abandoning. These Wilburites were strongest in New England, and broke off to establish the Conservative Friends in 1847, as well as in the Philadelphia Yearly Meeting, which broke relations with the New England Meeting that had expelled Wilbur. The issue for many was thus becoming whether the distinguishing slogan for the Friends was to be the "Inner Light" or the "Blood of Jesus."

Despite these schisms, American Friends found plenty on which to unite during the turbulent decades of the nineteenth century. Their traditional witness for peace was tested especially during the Civil War and, together with other "peace churches" such as the Mennonites and the Brethren, they gradually won recognition for the status of conscientious objector. They were hardly isolated from the events leading up to the war, though, since many Friends, such as Cincinnati's Levi Coffin, played an active role in the antislavery movement and the Underground Railroad. (Coffin was a prototype for the Quaker abolitionist in *Uncle Tom's Cabin*.) Following the Civil War, Friends were also active in philanthropic work among the freedmen in the South. Quaker attempts at penal reform resulted in the first "penitentiary," Philadelphia's Walnut Street Jail of 1796. This involved a building designed not so much to punish but to reform malefactors through providing an opportunity to reflect on and repent of their misdoings. Quakers were also active throughout the century in any number of other philanthropic activities, all based on the premise of universal human goodness and equality that could be actualized through a drawing-out of the Inner Light in every individual. (Another consequence of this belief was the active role played in the movement by women, who from its beginnings served as preachers and missionaries. Special meetings for women also assured them an active role in communal religious life.)

During the twentieth century, the role of the Friends in American society has undergone some significant transformations, with corresponding realignments within the Quaker community itself. Representative of more recent emphases is the American Friends Service Committee (AFSC), which was founded in 1917 to help conscientious objectors find suitable deployment during World War I. Its work eventually broadened into postwar relief and a wide variety of other humanitarian endeavors, which have attracted support and good will from many non-Quakers. A prominent American Friend, Herbert Hoover, gained considerable recognition through his extensive contributions to postwar European relief, although his reputation as a humanitarian was later overshadowed by his unfortunate term as president. (Another president of California origins, Richard Nixon, also came from a Quaker background.) The Wider Quaker Fellowship, founded in 1936 by the influential theologian Rufus Jones, was another vehicle through which non-Friends who were sympathetic with Quaker ideals but not ready to enter into full membership could attain "fellow-traveler" status within the Quaker community. Colleges of Quaker origin, such as Earlham, Haverford, and Swarthmore, also perpetuate Quaker emphases and traditions in many of their practices, even though large numbers of their students have other or no religious affiliation.

At the present, American Friends are divided organizationally into three major groupings and some smaller ones, reflecting both the schisms of the nineteenth century and the circumstances of the twentieth. Largest is the Friends United Meeting, with about 60,000 members distributed among more than 500 local meetings. The FUM's organizational focus is the Earlham School of Religion in Richmond, Indiana, whose faculty reflects a diversity of theological standpoints but tends toward the evangelical end of the Quaker spectrum. FUM Quakers employ a professional ministry and frown on the use of alcohol and tobacco.

Where the FUM represents the continuation of the Gurneyite tradition into the present, the General Conference of the Society of Friends carries on the original Hicksite strain. General Conference Friends are often members by conversion or "convincement" rather than "birthright," and represent the social activist emphasis within the broader tradition. The General Conference does not utilize professional clergy, creeds, or sacraments, and downplays biblical authority. Its roughly 33,000 members and 350 meetings are divided into four yearly meetings, of which the Philadelphia Meeting, organized in 1681, represents a direct continuity with the beginnings of the tradition in America.

The third branch of present-day Friends with a fairly substantial membership is the Evangelical Friends Alliance, with about 27,000 members, which is based in the Midwest and West. EFA Quakers are the closest to conservative Protestantism, and have particular links with the Holiness tradition that emerged from Methodism in the late nineteenth century. The Wilburite tradition is perpetuated in the very small Religious Society of Friends, and a few thousand other Quakers belong to meetings that are not affiliated with any larger organization.

Like the Amish, the Quakers have acquired a stereotyped image, perpetuated through such media as the smiling visage on the fronts of oatmeal cartons, that obscures their ongoing witness to their traditional beliefs. With a few exceptions, contemporary Friends live much like their evangelical or "mainstream" neighbors, depending on the branch of the tradition with which they identify. The most distinctive feature of liberal Quakers is their commitment to peacemaking, which manifests itself not in language or dress but rather in social involvements. Like the Amish and Mennonites, Friends have had to accommodate themselves to the dilemmas of trying to follow idealistic principles in a pluralistic, modernized society that is no longer so much hostile as indifferent to their goals. For those who have taken on an evangelical Protestant identity, the task is perhaps easier. More difficult is the maintenance of the traditional witness of peacemaking and reconciliation in a world in which they are otherwise indistinguishable in their external lifestyle, and in which they are seldom hopeful of growing greatly in number. They remain as a leaven, hopeful that the light they kindle will radiate beyond their own small community.

John Wesley and the Rise of Methodism

Like most popular religious movements, Methodism arose in the midst of an age of social ferment. When John Wesley, a priest of the Church of England, began to preach out of doors to the coal miners of Kingswood in 1739, he was acknowledging by his deeds that "new occasions teach new duties." England was no longer the "green and pleasant land" lamented by the prophetic poet William Blake in his poem/hymn, "Jerusalem." Rather, it was turning into a nation of "dark Satanic mills," dependent on coal power and child labor to keep their steam turbines fueled. The Industrial Revolution was leading England into the vanguard of the modernization process, and the relevance of a Church of England that still was oriented toward an earlier, agrarian social order was no longer very clear.

In the midst of this disorienting change emerged a sensitive young clergyman who at first did not seem a very promising candidate for rewinning the hearts of England's emergent proletariat to Christianity. John Wesley (1703–1791) did, to be sure, come from an environment saturated with religion. His father Samuel was the rector of the Anglican parish at Epworth, while his mother Susanna played a critical role in imbuing her large brood of offspring with an evangelical-leaning piety. John and his younger brother Charles both attended Oxford, where they became involved with a group of earnest students, sometimes dubbed the "Holy Club," that met regularly in Pietist fashion for scriptural study and the pursuit of the devout life. Another member of this circle was George Whitefield, who would later become the focus of the dramatic colonial revival known as the Great Awakening.

After leaving Oxford, the Wesley brothers tried their own hands as missionaries for the Society for the Propagation of the Gospel in Georgia in 1735. John became involved in an unhappy romance while on his colonial "errand," handled it badly, and generally went through a low period of ineptness and lack of self-confidence. Once while crossing the Atlantic during this seemingly ill-fated adventure, though, he came into contact with a band of Moravians who were on their way to join the communities that their movement was founding in the New World. During a violent storm at sea—in those days, a life-threatening event—Wesley became profoundly impressed with their hymn-singing and calm acceptance of God's will. Here was yet another sign that the Pietist path of devotion was the way to achieve the inner peace he sought, and could not yet successfully impress upon others.

John Wesley was a good example of the sort of person that the philosopher William James characterized as "twice-born." Although the resolution of his inner doubts was probably not as dramatic as later legend would have it, he nevertheless did not come easily by the sense of spiritual security that his later teaching projected. And, like his fellow "twice-born" reformer Martin Luther, Wesley's dramatic presence and effectiveness as a mature religious leader gave him a charismatic aura typical of the most dynamic of such men and women. In particular, later Methodists have focused on the experience that Wesley recorded in his journal for May 14, 1738:

> In the evening I went very unwillingly to a society in Aldersgate Street, where one was reading Luther's preface to the Epistle to the Romans. About a quarter before nine, while he was describing the change which God works in the heart through faith in Christ, I felt my heart strangely warmed. I felt I did trust in Christ, Christ alone, for salvation: and an assurance was given me, that He had taken away my sins, even mine, and saved me from the law of sin and death.

It no longer seems clear that this "Aldersgate experience" was *the* decisive turning point in Wesley's spiritual journey; however, several aspects of the event are worth noting. First, the meeting on Aldersgate Street was conducted by Moravians, the German Pietists whose serenity of faith had already made such a positive impression on Wesley. Second, the impact on Wesley of Luther's reflections on Romans, which were the occasion of his own conversion experience, establishes a continuity of evangelical orientation between the two. Third, "Aldersgate" in later times became a watchword among Methodists—together with the phrase "my heart strangely warmed"—and Wesley's experience was thus treated as a norm for his later followers. Although recent scholarship has interpreted "Aldersgate" as one of an extended series of important developments in Wesley's inner life rather than as conclusive in its own right, it proved to be the stuff out of which traditions—like Luther's "tower experience"—are made.

Whatever the importance of Aldersgate, Wesley did overcome his early uncertainties to the point that he could direct his formidable energies and abilities toward the task of introducing a vital religion to what he saw as a spiritually starved England. Like his Continental Pietist predecessors, Wesley was not concerned with founding a new church; rather, he worked within the framework of the established Church of England to enrich its overly formal, impersonal round of worship and obsolete structure that failed to reach the multitudes of laborers and miners who no longer fit conveniently within the medieval parish system. To this end, Wesley began to organize small groups of lay people to meet for biblical study, prayer, and mutual improvement at times besides those for ordinary worship.

There were several noteworthy features to this "connexional" system that Wesley and his followers thus brought to life. First, although it was aimed at making religion accessible to the uneducated masses of workers, control remained firmly in the hands of the Oxford-educated Wesley. Second, although Wesley himself was an ordained priest of the Church of England, the people who made it work—including his "assistants," the preachers—were drawn from the ranks of the laity. Third, the system did work because of Wesley's genius for organization and the firm control he exercised throughout his lifetime on the activities of his followers. Fourth, although Wesley's evangelical approach to Christianity stressed the emotional dimensions of the religious life, these "affections" were never allowed to dominate those who experienced them, but were rather drawn under tight rein by the regimen of spiritual discipline that had given rise to the movement's name of "Methodism."

What distinguished Wesleyan Methodism from the ordinary worship of the Church of England was its emphasis on personal spiritual growth in the context of a small group of like-minded folk under the supervision of a layman specially designated for the task. The basic unit was the "society," which met for prayer, Scripture study, hymn-singing, and the like at a time other than regular Anglican church services. Smaller groups known as "bands" and "classes" also developed for more intensive group life. All of these groups were carefully supervised by traveling lay preachers who followed a regular circuit, and who met annually at the "conference" presided over by Wesley himself. Methodism was therefore highly "methodical"—rather than "enthusiastic"—both in this tightly coordinated national system of organization, and in the rigorous spiritual discipline that the societies imposed upon their members.

Although Wesley is best remembered as a preacher and organizer, he was also a theologian of no mean ability, and in his many writings sought to give an informed rationale for his plan of spiritual growth that had attracted so many followers. As opposed to his friend and colleague George Whitefield, Wesley rejected the Calvinism that was still influential in many evangelical circles and taught instead what was then called "Arminianism." Basically, this meant that while Wesley accepted the Reformed doctrine of the enslavement of the human will by the power of sin, he rejected the notion that salvation was confined to God's "elect." Instead, he stressed the cooperative role that the individual plays with God in attaining salvation when choosing to take advantage of God's "prevenient" (literally, "coming before") grace.

Salvation, or "justification," was not the end of the individual's spiritual journey on earth, however. For Wesley, a second religious experience was possible that he termed "entire sanctification." This experience—later known also as the "second blessing"—marked the attainment of a state of "holiness," that is, a transformation of consciousness characterized by a state of freedom from voluntary sin. This state would not necessarily last forever, but had to be continually maintained by the following of the disciplined spiritual and moral life that Wesley prescribed for his followers.

The Methodist way was not as somber as all this talk of "discipline" might make it seem, however. Rather, it stressed very much the cultivation of the emotions, or "affections," so that the ultimate goal of self-control was the attainment of a new and highly pleasant state of consciousness characterized by a personal relationship with Jesus. This "affective" dimension of Methodism can be seen most clearly in the hymns written by Charles Wesley, John's brother and collaborator. Charles was the author of over five thousand such hymns, including such perennial favorites as "Hark! The Herald Angels Sing" and "Love Divine, All Loves Excelling." Particularly popular within the Methodist tradition, though, have been those such as "Jesus, Lover of My Soul," which stress the personal dimension of the religious experience. Together with Isaac Watts, a near-contemporary English evangelical whose best-selling collections of hymns included "When I Survey The Wondrous Cross" and others that have endured as classics, Charles Wesley helped inaugurate a virtual revolution in Protestant religious music that would have far-reaching consequences for later American practice.

Although John Wesley lived out his long life as a priest of the Church of England, it was hardly conceivable that such an extensive and well-organized movement as his would not generate tension with the parent church. This was in fact the case, and English Methodism finally separated from the Established Church in 1795 after Wesley's death. In America, however, the path to independence took some distinctive turnings. Methodist societies began to form in the Middle Colonies during the 1760s, particularly in the neighborhoods of Baltimore, New York, and Philadelphia. Wesley himself started to send preachers from his own cadres in 1769. The following year Francis Asbury, who might well qualify as American Methodism's patron saint, made his way to these shores. Asbury would eventually log over a quarter-million miles on horseback, thus setting the example for subsequent "circuit riders"—mounted itinerant preachers—on the American frontier.

The establishment of a distinctively American Methodist church was not entirely smooth. Wesley, for example, was hostile to the American Revolution, and advised his followers here to remain neutral. The presence of a connection of Methodist societies on this side of the Atlantic also raised organizational problems. Wesley addressed these with increasingly bold measures, especially after American independence had been won. In 1784, he and two of his associates, who were also Anglican priests, ordained two lay preachers, Richard Whatcoat and Thomas Vasey, to the offices of both deacon and elder—titles that would endure in American Methodism as the official designations of clergy. Wesley then "set apart" Thomas Coke, one of his colleagues in the previous ordination procedure, to the office of "superintendent" of the American operation, and sent the three men—all elevated to ecclesiastical office outside of the ordinary channels of the Church of England—to America to help organize the ongoing work.

The culmination of this process took place at Lovely Lane in Baltimore in December of 1784. At this memorable "Christmas Conference," the Methodist Episcopal Church was established by Asbury, Coke, and about sixty other American Methodist preachers who had assembled for the purpose of creating an American Methodism. Unlike the parent movement, this New World Methodism was from its beginnings independent both of the Church of England and its offspring, the Protestant Episcopal Church, which saw its first bishop consecrated that very same year. Although Coke had been commissioned by Wesley to ordain Asbury as superintendent, his American colleagues balked at this violation of the democratic spirit, and both were elected to that office by the assembled preachers. In 1787, Asbury and Coke exchanged the functional title of "superintendent" for the more traditional "bishop," a move that annoyed Wesley greatly. The role of the two as founders of American Methodism has subsequently been honored in the word "Cokesbury," a conflation of their names still used by Methodist book outlets.

The combinations of tradition and innovative adaptation, discipline and emotion, structure and flexibility, democracy and strong leadership that characterized early Methodism both in England and America were powerful sources of appeal in the new nation. Here was an emergent Christian tradition that could easily adapt to the exigencies of frontier life, yet stood in direct continuity with the Anglo-American evangelical experience. Some scholars have attempted to interpret Methodism's rise as a response to a new industrializing, capitalist economic order's need for a work force that had internalized a rigorous self-discipline, such as Wesley had promoted. This is probably too reductionist a view of the matter, especially in the context of the American experience. However, it is certainly arguable that self-discipline enhanced one's "life chances" on the frontier as well as in the mill towns, and that most early American Methodists came from the ranks of farmers and laborers rather than the upper middle classes. In the nineteenth century, for whatever reasons, the spread and growth of Methodism would become one of the great success stories of American religion.

CHAPTER 17

The Great Awakening and the Baptist Tradition

The rise and spread of Pietism and Methodism along both sides of the Atlantic during the eighteenth century were closely related signs of a restlessness within Protestantism that was determined to express itself in new, more vital kind of religious life. Particularly interesting are the interrelationships among the various aspects of this movement, from Germany and the Netherlands through the British Isles to the North American colonies. German Pietism was a major inspiration for British evangelicals, and the impact of the Moravians on John Wesley was an impressively concrete example of a direct line of influence. The Calvinist George Whitefield was a friend of the Arminian Wesleys at Oxford, and went on to become the catalyst of the Great Awakening in the American colonies. The primary native mover of that Awakening, Jonathan Edwards, wrote an account of what he thought to be God's miraculous work in generating the revival. When published in England by the evangelical hymn-writer Isaac Watts, this account came into Wesley's hands and made a due impression. A German-speaking woman who knew no English was profoundly moved by Whitefield's preaching, of which she could not understand a word. This new spiritual force knew bounds of neither theology, tradition, geography, nor even language. As such, it was the most powerful—and diffuse—religious movement since the Reformation itself.

The culmination of this intercontinental movement toward a "religion of the heart" was the Great Awakening. Its sources can be located fairly precisely in smaller, earlier revivals in the colonies, but its ultimate causes remain obscure. The Revival's adherents included men and women of every region, social class, and branch of Protestant Christianity in the colonies, so that attempts to impose a simple economic or political interpretation are ill-advised. The most plausible correlation is geographical. The Awakening seems to have been strongest in its immediate appeal and its long-run effects along such inland waterways as the Connecticut River Valley; conversely, its greatest opposition arose in more cosmopolitan seaboard regions such as Boston. But this is a correlation, not a causal explanation. Perhaps the most plausible approach is to regard such a general outburst of religious "enthusiasm" as a manifestation of the unease brought about by rapid social change. This took the form, for example, of British challenges to various colonial privileges, such as the Puritan religious establishment, and a hardening of fluid socioeconomic patterns of an earlier, looser society into a more stratified "provincial" order. Even here, though, correlations are general and direct causality hard to pinpoint.

The Great Awakening was a massive religious revival that swept the entire English-speaking Atlantic seaboard beginning in the late 1730s. It elevated the personal, intense religious experience of emotional conversion—the "New Birth"—to a central role in the process of salvation. Such conversions, of course, were not new in themselves: Augustine and Luther both experienced them, and their accounts inspired later generations immensely. Such experiences, however, were seldom regarded as normative by their followers, but rather looked on as the unique stories of spiritual giants. New England Puritanism had encouraged a minute introspective attention to the workings of grace within the individual heart, so that a "morphology of conversion" emerged as a guide to the assessment of the spiritual condition of would-be church members. Here, though, the process was more likely to be gradual than sudden, and firmly located in the context of a patterned, disciplined social nurture.

The forerunners of the Awakening had two primary loci in the earlier decades of the eighteenth century. One was in the Middle Colonies—New Jersey and Pennsylvania—which were rapidly becoming a Presbyterian stronghold with large-scale migrations from Scotland and Northern Ireland beginning around 1700. It was in this context that there arose the redoubtable

Tennent family—William, Sr., (1673?–1746), the *paterfamilias*, and his three sons, who followed in his footsteps as evangelical awakeners of this barbaric domain. William Tennent institutionalized this impulse through his founding at Neshaminy, Pennsylvania, of the "Log College"—a roughhewn frontier school for the training of evangelical Presbyterian preachers. His son Gilbert (1703–1764) especially became active in the later Awakening as one of George Whitefield's chief lieutenants, and helped form the nucleus of the "New Side" Presbyterianism that resulted. A sign of the many-branched roots of the Awakening was the role played in Gilbert's development by Theodore Jacob Frelinghuysen, a Dutch Reformed evangelical minister educated among Pietists who presided over a series of small revivals in New Jersey's Raritan Valley in the 1720s.

The more immediate forerunner of the Awakening was Jonathan Edwards (1703–1758), the successor to his grandfather Solomon Stoddard as pastor of the Congregational church in Northampton, Massachusetts. Stoddard had been something of a maverick in the Puritan fold, a reputation gained through his willingness to admit all but the openly scandalous to communion in the hope that the reception of such "ordinances" would be a spur to conversion. In doing so, he repudiated openly the traditional New England notion that the core of the church consisted only of the "saints" who had been able to narrate a persuasive account of their experience of grace. Stoddard also was effective as a revival preacher, and counted five "seasons" of revival among his many accomplishments.

It was within this context that Jonathan Edwards carried on his grandfather's pastorate, initially as the latter's assistant and then on his own. In 1734–1735, Edwards began to notice a restlessness within his congregation, and emphasized increasingly in his sermons the theme of justification by faith. Conversions soon followed, and Edwards began to think that the results were not simply ephemeral, but rather a remarkable—even miraculous—manifestation of God's grace. From then on, his pulpit, and those he exchanged with his colleagues throughout the Connecticut Valley, became bases for the preaching of a revival that soon swept the entire region. When Whitefield later came to tour New England, a visit with Edwards for several days was an important part of his itinerary.

Edwards's role in the revival was crucial in several ways. In the first place, he was one of its most effective preachers. Edwards was steeped not only in traditional Puritan divinity but also in the early writings of the English Enlightenment—those of John Locke and Isaac Newton in particular. Through a combination of theory and practice, Edwards developed a new kind of preaching. His intent was not so much to proclaim Scripture and interpret it in the form of doctrine, but rather to bring about a change of consciousness in his listeners. This he attempted to do by appealing not primarily to their reason but rather to their "affections"—that is, emotions—through the evocation of vivid sensual images. His most famous—or, as it has been presented for generations, notorious—work in this line was "Sinners in the Hands of an Angry God," first delivered during a pulpit exchange at Enfield, Connecticut, in 1741. In this now-classic piece of rhetoric, Edwards compared the individual to a spider dangled by God over a fiery pit, whose immediate consumption by the flames was prevented only by God's inscrutable but deliberate act. The underlying message was traditionally Calvinist: God was in absolute control of every aspect of the universe, and all humans were incorrigible sinners who were spared, if at all, from the eternal punishment they deserved only by God's mysterious act of forbearance. Edwards's means, however, were novel, and reflected his understanding of the workings both of physical nature and human psychology, gleaned from his new learning.

Edwards was more than one of the Awakening's foremost preachers: He was also one of its most influential promoters, publicists, defenders, and interpreters. In his classic account, *A Faithful Narrative of the Surprising Work of God* (1737), Edwards undertook to describe the remarkable stirrings that had taken place among his congregation and to maintain their divine origin. In later works, he would defend the revival against such powerful critics as Boston's Charles Chauncy by attempting to demonstrate that its true fruits were a new life and consciousness in harmony with Christian teaching. Edwards also speculated that these massive stirrings of divine grace among the colonists were signs that America might have a special destiny in God's plan—as the site of the beginning of the millennial kingdom. In his later writings, such as the *Treatise Concerning Religious Affections* (1746) and the *Freedom of the Will* (1754), he developed in classic form a restatement of the essentials of Calvinism in a new philosophical framework that reflected both his thought and experience and that helped set the agenda of generations of American religious thinkers yet to come.

One consequence of Edwards's reformulation of traditional Puritanism was his rejecting the innovations of his grandfather, and his insistence that only the converted should be admitted to communion. More broadly, he brought an end to an important phase of the long New England tradition of covenant theology. Edwards now focused on the relationship between God and the individual, rather than the broader networks of church and society, as the center of Christian concern. These stern new teachings were far from agreeable to many in his congregation, who had grown comfortable in the easier ways of Stoddard's open communion. Push finally came to shove in 1750 when Edwards attempted to discipline some young people who had been circulating what passed as a naughty book—a manual for midwives. Edwards was dismissed from his long-time pastorate, and took up position as missionary to the Indians in Stockbridge in the far western reaches of the colony. In 1758, he was called to be president of the College of New Jersey, which had some of its roots in Tennent's "Log College," and which later grew into Princeton. Shortly after his arrival, Edwards developed complications from a smallpox inoculation and died.

Where Jonathan Edwards had been the greatest thinker of the Awakening, there is little doubt that George Whitefield (1714–1770) was its greatest preacher. Whitefield, who had been a friend and contemporary of John Wesley at Oxford, illustrated in his own person the multifaceted and even contradictory religious streams that fed into the Awakening. Whitefield (pronounced WHIT-field) was an ordained priest of the Church of England and a

Calvinist theologically; through his affinity with the evangelical piety of the Wesleys, he has frequently been identified as a Methodist. But the primary import of his career lay in neither his institutional affiliations nor his particular brand of theology.

Whitefield gained fame and influence as a traveling preacher throughout the American colonies during his several visits here, the most dramatic of which began in 1739. He soon acquired the nickname of "the Grand Itinerant"—a preacher who is not confined to one particular church and pulpit, but who proclaims the Word wherever he can find listeners. Listeners abounded for Whitefield. First they came to the churches of various traditions to which he was invited, and then assembled in the open air or in the vast tabernacle erected by his admirers in Philadelphia when his audiences grew enormous and the settled clergy became cooler to his presence. Even the eminently rational Benjamin Franklin was moved to the point of emptying his pockets after hearing Whitefield preach on behalf of the orphanage he was sponsoring in Georgia. It was said that he could reduce an audience to tears simply by pronouncing the word "Mesopotamia."

Whitefield thus served as the catalyst that built upon the local revivals kindled by Edwards and the Tennents and transformed them into an intercolonial phenomenon. Virtually everyone in the colonies from Nova Scotia to Georgia either had heard Whitefield personally or knew someone who could deliver a first-hand account. This being the case, Whitefield might be regarded as America's first celebrity—someone well known, if for nothing else than for the fact of being so well known. (Today he would undoubtedly appear on the cover of *People* magazine and on many late-night talk shows.) Whitefield's fame rested on more than such empty renown, however, and his presence gave the scattered colonists a sense of having something profoundly in common with one another: having been participants in, or at least witnesses of, America's finest massive revival.

Although Whitefield was not universally welcomed by the colonial clergy, his power and probity won him a respect and influence that brought him invitations from Puritan and Anglican alike. The Awakening began to become a matter of serious controversy only when its cause was taken up by less temperate domestic disciples of the Grand Itinerant. Gilbert Tennent, for example, aroused much ire through his polemical "The Danger of an Unconverted Ministry" of 1739. Here he laid out the common revivalist theme that many of the colonial clergy did not deserve their accustomed authority since they themselves had never been converted. When such accusations continued to come from even less "established" figures than Tennent, they became fighting words.

Tennent's attack on unconverted ministers was an example of *censorious* preaching, which was soon singled out by the established clergy as an intolerable affront. Out of the Awakening there soon emerged an entire vocabulary of such abuse. Three other innovations stood out especially as signs of either vital renewal or inexcusable perversion, depending on the observer's viewpoint. The first of these was *itinerant* preaching, represented most dramatically by Whitefield himself. Most of the older religious groups of the colonies—

Puritan Congregationalists, Presbyterians, Anglicans, Roman Catholics—were organized according to the timeless geographical order we might call the "parochial principle." This meant that believers were expected to belong to the congregation that served the geographical unit, or parish, in which they resided. These parishes frequently coincided with political units, such as the New England town, and reflected the traditional relationship of church and state as mutually supportive. Itinerancy undermined this principle at its heart, since it dissolved the bonds among residence, worship, and political allegiance. Some itinerancy was permissible when a guest preacher was specifically invited by a "settled" clergyman, since the latter's authority was thus respected. Those clergy especially who derived their support from the state, as in both Virginia and New England, were not surprisingly alarmed at what they saw as a challenge to their privileged status when itinerants began to invade their turf unbidden and unwelcomed.

Whitefield may have been the grandest of itinerants, but he was, after all, an ordained clergyman with the proper educational credentials and a reasonable amount of discretion. This was not so, however, with all his imitators. In addition to being on the move physically, they frequently were not ordained, but rather were responding to their sense of a personal divine calling. *Lay* preaching was thus the second offense of this new breed. Revival preachers also breached traditional clerical decorum by imitating Whitefield's custom of *extempore* preaching. The Puritan/Reformed tradition especially had prescribed that a sermon should be delivered at length by an ordained minister in a church from a prepared manuscript. Not only was it to be formal but also learned, reflecting the biblical and theological preparation ordinarily available only to the clergy. Extempore preaching violated many of these canons; when performed by a layman, all of the rules went by the boards.

The culmination of this growing ferment was the career of James Davenport (1716–1757), a minister of good New England stock and Yale training. Davenport claimed special prophetic gifts, and gained a following through his extravagantly emotional and censorious diatribes. An amusing account of the climax of Davenport's fevered career is included in the journal of Dr. Alexander Hamilton, an Englishman touring the colonies at the time:

Sunday, August 16 [New London, Conn.] I went home at 6 o'clock, and Dean Green's son came to see me. He entertained me with the history of the behavior of one Davenport, a fanatic preacher there who told his flock in one of his enthusiastic rhapsodies that in order to be saved they ought to burn all their idols. They began this conflagration with a pile of books in the public street; among them were Tillotson's Sermons, Beveridge's Thoughts, Drillincourt on Death, Sherlock, and many other excellent authors, and sung psalms and hymns over the pile while it was a-burning. They did not stop here, but the women made up a lofty pile of hoop petticoats, silk gowns, short cloaks, cambric caps, red heeled shoes, fans, necklaces, gloves, and other such apparel, and what was merry enough, Davenport's own idol with which he topped the pile, was a pair of old, worn out plush breeches. But this bonfire was happily prevented by one more moderate than the rest, who found means to persuade them that making such a sacrifice was not necessary for their salvation, and so everyone carried off their idols again, which was lucky for Davenport who, had fire been put to the pile, would have been obliged to strut about bare-arsed, for the devil another pair of breeches had he but these same old plush ones which were going to be offered up as an expiatory sacrifice.

By this time, the climate of opinion on the Awakening had begun to polarize, and parties emerged among both New England Congregationalists and Middle Colony Presbyterians. Among the latter, the breach between "Old Side" and "New Side" was temporary, and the resultant schism was patched up a few years later. In New England, the situation was complex. Davenport's tactics resulted in his arrest and exile after being declared insane. When Whitefield returned to New England in 1744 after his earlier triumphs, he was condemned by the faculties of both Harvard and Yale. What had once been an almost unanimous welcome for the message of the "new birth" now split into a welter of contention.

The most articulate spokesmen for the "Old Lights" and "New Lights" who respectively attacked and defended the Awakening were Charles Chauncy, minister at Boston's First Church, and Jonathan Edwards. Chauncy was the author of the influential tract *Seasonable Thoughts on the State of Religion in New England* (1743), which denounced the revival for its exaltation of emotion at the expense of reason. Edwards, who had earlier defended the revival in a number of occasional pieces, responded in 1746 with one of his systematic masterpieces, *A Treatise Concerning Religious Affections.* Here he argued that "true religion, in great part, consists in holy affections" rather than simply correct belief. From that time, New England began to divide up into spheres of theological influence. In the more cosmopolitan Boston area, Chauncy and his colleagues Ebenezer Gay and Jonathan Mayhew began to develop the rationalistic emphases that would culminate in Unitarianism, with Harvard as their intellectual center. In the more conservative Connecticut Valley, Edwards and his disciples held the allegiance of most of the clergy, and Yale became the focus for further evangelical development.

Old and New Light Congregationalists managed to remain in fellowship for many decades, however deep the disagreements among them ran. Another faction, however, was determined that the principles of the Awakening were too radical for a facile reconciliation, and insisted on separating from the established churches entirely. These sectarian "Separate" Congregationalists rejected governmental influence on their religious lives and insisted on the strictest standards for church membership. Many congregations split over these issues, though the institutional obstacles in the way of founding permanent new congregations were too great in most cases to achieve lasting results. To this day, however, two Congregational churches stand side by side on the New Haven Green across from the Yale campus. Although today their differences are minimal and both belong to the United Church of Christ, they still exist as a mute, material testimony to the powerful disharmony that the revival could leave in its wake.

A more lasting consequence of the separatist spirit was the rejuvenation of the Baptist, or Free Church, community, which had lain rather dormant in

Rhode Island since the early days of the New England experiment. The Baptist movement, which had its origins among early seventeenth-century English Puritans, added to the Calvinist tradition the Anabaptist premise that baptism should be restricted to believers. This was certainly a logical deduction from the premise that the true church is a small company of predestined saints who should gather themselves out from the world. However, it was not acceptable to most Puritans in either Old or New England, who believed that infant baptism should be retained as a symbol of God's working his grace in a broader social context. In most ways, however, early Anglo-American Baptists represented a variation on the broader Puritan theme in their congregational polity and (often) Calvinist creed; their ties to the Anabaptist tradition on the Continent were somewhat tenuous except for their one distinctive shared practice.

In New England, Roger Williams (1603?–1683), the minister of the church at Salem, was exiled to the wilds of Rhode Island for rejecting the Puritan alliance between church and state on the grounds that the power of the latter would inevitably corrupt the purity of the former. After founding a new settlement that provided a safe haven for dissent, Williams espoused the Baptist position and was immersed in 1639. He soon moved from this to the status of "seeker"—like the young George Fox, whom in his later life Williams personally engaged in vigorous debate—but is honored as the founder of the Baptist faith in America. More broadly, the Baptists are the principal descendants of what became known in England as the "Free Church" movement—those Puritans who refused to accept the established church's authority. Ironically, the tables were turned in the New World where Puritan Congregationalists themselves became established, and the Baptists were left to carry on the tradition of nonconformity against their sometime allies.

Baptist life for the next century was rather sleepy, confined to the two venerable churches in Providence and Newport and a few scattered congregations elsewhere in New England. The Awakening brought it back to a sometimes reluctant vivacity, when many Separate Congregationalists began to declare themselves to be Baptists. Older Baptists were not uniformly enthusiastic about the revival; still, they had to respond to their abrupt shift in status from an isolated sect to a rapidly growing denomination as individuals and entire congregations began to join their ranks. One of the most remarkable of these Separate Baptist converts was Isaac Backus (1724–1806). As a minister for these dissenters in Massachusetts, Backus became a major spokesman for the rights they felt had long been denied them in New England especially, and later helped lead the fight for official recognition of such rights in the Constitution of the new nation.

Voices of the Awakening and the Baptist cause alike began to be heard in the Southern colonies as well. Samuel Davies (1723–1761) was sent by the Presbyterians to evangelize Anglican Virginia, and eventually won a decree from London that granted toleration to religious dissenters in that colony. The growth of the Baptists in the South was more complicated, since that tradition has always been notable for its resistance to centralization. In 1707, the Philadelphia Baptist Association had brought together several early congregations, and provided a focus for the subsequent expansion of Particular (Calvinist) Baptists throughout Virginia and North Carolina. Some General (Arminian) Baptist congregations had earlier been founded in this part of the country, but were eventually converted to Particular principles through the superior organization and zeal of the latter party. Separate Baptists, led by New Englander Shubal Stearns, provided another path for an emergent Baptist presence. In 1755, Stearns and his extended family founded a Baptist church at Sandy Creek in North Carolina. Within five years the congregation had become the nucleus for the Sandy Creek Association, the first such organization in the region, which was soon paralleled by similar groups in Virginia. Although the Separates represented a more rough-and-ready, "enthusiastic" approach to the tradition than the more genteel Philadelphia group, the two were fundamentally united in theology. By the end of the century, the two factions had virtually merged, with Philadelphia as the organizational focus.

Although the Awakening had run its course as a visible movement by the end of the 1740s, it by no means disappeared as a factor in American religious life. Whitefield, for example, made several subsequent visits to the colonies in 1764 and 1770. The "New Light Stir" that swept rural northern New England during the Revolutionary era launched a new round of sectarian formation—Free Will Baptists, Shakers, and Universalists, all of whom combined enthusiastic religion with a non-Calvinist theology. It has even been argued that the Awakening never really ended at all, but continued here and there on a small scale until it melded into the "Second Great Awakening" that swept New England in the 1790s and continued westward along the frontier in newer, more dramatic form. However one might want to categorize such movements, there is no doubt that revivalism was from the time of Edwards and Whitefield established as a mainstay of evangelical Protestantism in America.

Other results were abundant, though some were more subtle than others. On the political scene, religious pluralism and agitation for the legal recognition of minority rights became more and more visible. Similarly, in social terms, the notion of a homogeneous order based on traditional patterns of deference was clearly anachronistic, since religious disagreement both reflected and fostered social division. The various Protestant churches were split into factions, with those favoring a religion of the "heart" squaring off against those who were partisans of the "head." Higher education was stimulated by the new demands for clergy who met the specifications of newly expanding groups. Princeton emerged from the early Presbyterian beginnings at Neshaminy, and Brown arose in Providence to serve the rejuvenated Baptists. Dartmouth in New Hampshire had similar origins in a new sense of mission among New England Congregationalists to spread the New Light message to Native Americans. The latter attempt was unsuccessful, but another brick had been laid in the Ivy League wall.

Division and pluralism were an obvious fruit of the Awakening, but so was a centripetal movement toward a new sort of unity that upset and transcended long-standing barriers of geography and tradition. Although its basic assumptions were Calvinist, the thrust of the revival had been away from an emphasis on theological particulars in favor of an awakening of the affections—in short, conversion. Further, a compelling need was generated by these conversions to spread the good news as widely as possible—a missionary imperative. New Light and Separate Congregationalists, New Side Presbyterians, General Baptists, emergent Methodists, and sympathizers from various other denominations from a handful of Anglicans to numerous German-speaking Pietists could unite on this program. American religious life would now be characterized for generations by the dominance of a new phenomenon that subsumed all of these communities in the broader religious culture known as Evangelical Protestantism.

CHAPTER **18**

The Origins of Modern Religious Liberalism

Liberal—like *conservative, orthodox, romantic, puritan,* and any number of other terms—is a word that may have a very specific or a very general meaning depending on the context. *Liberalism* is defined by historical and social setting; one generation's liberal may seem distressingly conservative to the next. Unlike radicals, liberals prefer to work within already established structures, softening rigidities and boundaries that structures impose when they go unquestioned for too long. In its broadest sense, liberalism implies a spirit of openness to change and novelty, and of pluralism—tolerance, respect, and even enthusiasm for the opinions of others.

In religion, liberalism implies a concern with ethics rather than metaphysics; a focus on this world rather than the supernatural; an impatience with rigid barriers separating different groups of people, realms of thought, or categories of being; a confidence in the powers of the individual to discern the ultimate truth, without excessive reliance on revelation, tradition, or other external authority; and a predisposition to stress the positive, the fundamentally benevolent character of humanity, the divinity, and the cosmos in its broadest sense.

The sources of modern religious liberalism, as well as many other aspects of contemporary culture, can be found in the era known as the *Renaissance*. This "rebirth"—of classical culture, in its original form—had its roots in fifteenth-century Italy, but rapidly spread throughout Europe to become a genuinely cosmopolitan movement. At the core of the Renaissance was a group of classical scholars who called themselves "humanists." By *humanism* they meant a disenchantment with the scholastic philosophy and the "decadent" Latin of the later Middle Ages. These they rejected in favor of a return to the purer sources of Western culture in ancient Greece and Rome. Although most were Christian, their interpretation of Christianity was strongly influenced by the neo-Platonic philosophy that many of them favored over medieval Aristotelianism. Humanists also tended to be sharply critical of tradition when it could not be defended by the new methods of historical investigation they practiced. An example of the latter was the humanist Lorenzo Valla's exposure as fraudulent of the "Donation of Constantine"—a document that was long believed to be the Emperor Constantine's will, in which he allegedly charged the Bishop of Rome with the secular custody of that part of Italy that had come to be known as the Papal States. Although this had nothing to do with church doctrine as such, the spirit of skeptical inquiry that underlay such investigations could hardly help but promote a more broadly critical spirit.

Some of that spirit found its way into the work of Martin Luther, who launched the thoroughgoing attack on Roman belief, practice, and structure that resulted in the Reformation and the irreversible sundering of Christendom into mutually hostile spheres. More representative of the spirit of Renaissance humanism, though, was Desiderius Erasmus of Rotterdam (ca. 1466–1536), who freshly translated the New Testament from the original Greek and also wrote scathing satires on corruption within the Catholic hierarchy. Although critical of the church, Erasmus wished to remain an insider; he accepted the basic premises of the Roman faith while bringing his critical powers to bear on its abuses. This role as a critic from within became harder to maintain as Europe polarized on religious lines, and institutions of the Counter-Reformation such as the Inquisition turned their attention to anyone suspected of the slightest disloyalty to the Roman establishment.

It was not a theologian but a scientist, Galileo Galilei (1564–1642), who is best remembered as the object of this campaign to suppress religious dissent. Using actual observations of heavenly bodies through his telescope as evidence, Galileo argued that the traditional system of astronomy taught by Ptolemy was obsolete, and that the Polish astronomer Nicholas Copernicus had been correct in maintaining that the earth and other planets revolved around the sun. Although Galileo's theories were condemned by the Inquisition as subversive of doctrine and authority and he was forced to recant, Galileo has been since remembered for his simple but eloquent appeal to empirical observation: "And yet it moves." (In recent years the Catholic Church has acknowledged that its treatment of Galileo was inappropriate.) This commitment to empiricism was given formal philosophical expression by Francis Bacon (1561–1626), whose *The Advancement of Learning* (1605) had a great long-range impact on the subsequent development of Anglo-American thought.

Another "heretic" who has often since been cited as an exemplar of religious liberalism was Michael Servetus (1511–1563), a Spanish scholar who denied the divinity of Christ and the doctrine of the Trinity. Servetus was one of an informal company of mystics and rationalists that the historian Roland Bainton has characterized as "the free spirits" of the Reformation era. These stout nonconformists lived in a twilight zone between Catholic and Protestant camps, usually detested by both. Servetus fled from the Roman Inquisition to Geneva, where he was charged by Calvin with heresy and burnt at the stake. A more successful proponent of similar ideas was Faustus Socinus (1539–1604), an Italian who found refuge in Transylvania and Poland. It was in these remote outposts that there thus arose the first organized forerunners of unitarian Christianity—that is, a Christianity that affirmed the oneness of God and thus denied the deity of Jesus.

These scattered appeals to unfettered scholarship, rationalism, empirical investigation, toleration, and free inquiry began to emerge into a new status by the end of the seventeenth century, after the dust had settled on the long and bloody warfare that had been the legacy of Europe's religious polarization. An international movement, consciously cosmopolitan in outlook, began to take shape on the European continent, in Britain, and ultimately in the New World, that took for itself the evocative name of "the Enlightenment." The cluster of ideas and emphases that dominated the intellectual life of the eighteenth century was propagated by a loose alliance of university scholars, clergy, and freelance thinkers who saw themselves as the avant-garde of a new era of liberation from the mental and institutional baggage of the past. Taking as their point of departure the scientific and philosophical issues of the Renaissance, the advocates of Enlightenment broadened this range of concern; gave it a new and aggressive cast in the freer, more secular air of the eighteenth century; and expanded its scope to include a critique of the whole range of contemporary thought and institutions.

The core of Enlightenment thought was epistemological: How do we know things to be true? In place of appeals to tradition, authority, and revelation, the leading thinkers of the Enlightenment instead argued that human reason, working with materials provided by the senses through empirical observation, was the surest path to reliable knowledge. The most important spokesmen for this viewpoint in the Anglo-American world were Sir Isaac Newton (1642–1727), who attempted to reduce the workings of nature to an orderly system of physical laws, and John Locke (1632–1704), who argued in his *Essay Concerning Human Understanding* (1690) that the human mind was a blank slate—*tabula rasa*—to which all contents came through the senses. Both Newton and Locke regarded themselves as Christians; both, however, helped to formulate a systematic approach to the investigation of the physical and mental worlds that made both Protestant and Catholic attitudes toward authority and revelation in religion problematic.

The impact of the Enlightenment on religion in the American colonies and the new nation took a number of forms, ranging from the fostering of avowed skepticism to an intellectual reinforcement of orthodoxy. Few went so far as to take the radical position of the Scottish philosopher David Hume (1711–1776), who in his *Dialogues Concerning Natural Religion* (pub. 1779) attempted to demonstrate the futility of trying to prove the existence of God through reason and observation. More representative of the religious "left" was the stance known as *Deism* (from the Latin *deus,* god), which took exactly the position that Hume had tried to refute: that all that could and needed to be known about God was knowable through the use of human reason.

In the American colonies, Benjamin Franklin (1706–1790) and Thomas Jefferson (1743–1826) were both Deists in their religious positions. They were also the closest American counterparts of the French *philosophes*—intellectuals of broad-ranging interests who turned their attention to practical as well as speculative matters. Franklin's development from provincial Boston Puritan to cosmopolitan man of affairs is narrated in his *Autobiography* (begun 1771), which has been described as a secular version of John Bunyan's *Pilgrim's Progress*. Franklin attributed his astonishing success not to God's favor or election, but rather to his disciplined cultivation of the kind of personality that could prove useful in achieving wealth and fame. One well-known passage describes, with more than a hint of self-mockery, Franklin's effort to perfect himself through the systematic cultivation of one virtue after another—for instance, "temperance" and "frugality"—by the use of a daily checklist. His thirteenth and final virtue is "humility"; to achieve this, one should "imitate Jesus and Socrates." The *Autobiography* also contains some amusing descriptions of Franklin's encounters with the great itinerant evangelist George White-field. During one of Whitefield's visits to Philadelphia, thousands came to hear his message and be moved to conversion; Franklin, in the meantime, occupied himself with estimating the size of the crowd.

Thomas Jefferson, America's third president and a polymath equal in virtuosity to Franklin, was also skeptical of traditional Christian conceptions of religion. As the author of the "Declaration of Independence," Jefferson exhibited the philosophical vocabulary of his day in appealing to "truths" held to be "self-evident" to the common run of humanity, who were "created equal" and "endowed by their Creator with certain unalienable rights." Jefferson was here invoking not the judgmental divine Father of the Puritans, but rather a more benevolent deity whose existence, character, and wishes could be known through human reason and observation. Jefferson, who had been raised as an Anglican but in his adult life had no formal affiliation, regarded Jesus as a fine ethical teacher but denied that he had any divine status. Along these lines, Jefferson prepared a work variously entitled "The Morals of Jesus" or *The Jefferson Bible*, in which he presented Jesus's words of moral instruction with all supernaturalistic references—for example, to miracles—carefully edited out. In addition to the "Declaration," Jefferson stated in later life that his finest accomplishments had been his founding of the University of Virginia, of which a library rather than a chapel was the focus, and his authorship of the "Virginia Statute of Religious Liberty" (1786), which provided for what would elsewhere be described as a "wall of separation" between church and state.

The larger impact of Enlightenment thought on religion, however, was in more "mainstream" channels. Broad Enlightenment ideals of toleration and church-state separation were widely popular among members of a variety of religious groups, from the small Jewish community to America's first Roman Catholic bishop, John Carroll of Baltimore. Many decades before, however, Protestant thought in the colonies had begun to come under the influence of the movement's emphasis on reason and observation. Jonathan Edwards (1703–1758), perhaps the greatest theologian in American history, early came under the spell cast by the writings of Locke and Newton. Instead of becoming a Deist, though, Edwards went on to utilize their ideas to reinterpret the traditional Calvinist doctrines of original sin and divine sovereignty. He also found

Locke's emphasis on direct experience useful in preaching the sermons—such as the well-known but not entirely typical "Sinners in the Hands of an Angry God" of 1741—that helped evoke the dramatic conversions characteristic of the Great Awakening revivals.

More characteristic of the intersection of Enlightenment principles with Christian tradition were a long series of British works such as John Locke's *The Reasonableness of Christianity* (1695); John Toland's *Christianity Not Mysterious* (1696); Bishop Joseph Butler's *Analogy of Religion, Natural and Revealed* (1736); and William Paley's *View of the Evidences of Christianity* (1794) and *Natural Theology* (1802). Although these writers were not uniform in their points of view, the commonality indicated in this series of popular titles is clear. Christianity depended for its credibility not on supernatural revelation but rather on its conformability with the evidence of the senses and the dictates of reason. God himself was no longer an awesomely transcendent mystery but rather the epitome of rationality, rather like a watchmaker who has skillfully crafted his product and now, with amiable detachment, contemplates his handiwork as it runs. Many of these writers were Anglicans, a tradition noted for its emphasis on rationality and toleration, but their influence extended far beyond that community.

The form of Enlightened Christianity that was to have the broadest impact on the American scene was imported not from England but rather its northern neighbor, Scotland. The "Common Sense" philosophy that emerged from the "Scottish renaissance" of the mid-eighteenth century took as its starting point the Enlightenment postulate that the evidences of the senses were reliable. Instead of limiting all knowledge to the physical senses, however, exponents of this position such as Dugald Stewart and Thomas Reid argued that all humans possess an innate moral sense that enables them to make responsible choices in their lives. Here was a combination of themes from Bacon, Locke, and many others of the more moderate stream of Enlightenment thought that could readily be reconciled with any number of varieties of Christianity by undergirding the reliability of our everyday knowledge of the external world. John Witherspoon (1723–1794), the Scotsman who became president of the College of New Jersey (Princeton) in 1768, was the foremost American exponent of this philosophy.

In the colonial era, liberalism had not yet become institutionalized. Although pervasive mainly among intellectuals, it helped shape the popular movement of Universalism, which rejected the idea of damnation, and was spread in more radical, skeptical form by such popular writers as Ethan Allen and, most powerfully, "Citizen" Tom Paine, the revolutionary propagandist. At the elite level, Enlightened thought helped shape the intellectual milieu of a number of highly disparate groups: "Old Light" New England Congregationalists who were turning away from the emotionalism of the Great Awakening to the beginnings of what would later emerge as Unitarianism; Virginia Anglicans, some of whom, like Jefferson, would abandon organized religion altogether; and Presbyterians such as Princeton's Witherspoon, who were molding the intellectual foundations for the transdenominational evangelicalism that would dominate American Protestantism during the coming century.

CHAPTER 19

Anabaptists and Pietists in Pennsylvania

The first Anabaptist settlement in the Atlantic colonies took place at Germantown, Pennsylvania, in 1683. This early migration of Mennonites and Amish to Pennsylvania resulted in part from Penn's recruitment along the Rhine and in the Palatinate, and later, from older immigrants urging their families and friends abroad to follow them to freer climes. More Amish from various German states arrived in the early nineteenth century during the heyday of German immigration, while Mennonites who had found refuge in Catherine the Great's Russia began to flee the Czar's draft in the 1870s for the American and Canadian prairies.

As with the Quakers and other sectarian groups, the American Anabaptist communities began to lapse into arguments and schism once they had become established in the United States (and Canada). The major theme of contention was the degree of accommodation to rapidly modernizing American society permissible within the bounds of their traditional values and practices. Most held firm to their pacifist commitments, and often cooperated with Quakers and other "peace churches" to secure legal recognition for their position. Some of the most conservative Amish, however, refused to have anything to do with the legal and political system, and urged their draft-eligible young men to accept jail terms rather than seek conscientious objector status.

Contemporary Amish and Mennonites are divided into at least nineteen distinct organized communities, ranging from the ultraconservative Old Order Amish to highly assimilated Mennonites who differ only in a few obvious particulars from other evangelical Protestants. The distinctiveness of the Amish, and the source of their "picturesque" character, is their having given religious significance to the preservation of the traditional agrarian ways their ancestors brought with them from Reformation-era Switzerland. They consequently avoid the use of modern technology, including automobiles, telephones, and electrical appliances, wherever possible, although modifications occasionally take place. Schisms and court cases, however, have arisen over issues such as the permissibility of brightly colored reflecting tape on horse-drawn wagons when required by state law. Other court tests have taken place on the constitutionality of state laws requiring Amish children to attend secondary school (*Wisconsin* v. *Yoder,* 1972; an Amish victory) and the legality of a family's enforcing a community ban (*Bann und Meidung*) on association with one of its own members (a defeat.) Other distinguishing features are an adherence to old-fashioned peasant-style dress, with men wearing beards and plain black clothing, and bonnets and aprons for women. Even buttons are looked on as worldly, and hook-and-eye fasteners are used instead. Curiously, modern medicine is accepted.

Estimates in the late 1980s suggest that the Old Order Amish may number about 100,000, with three-quarters in Ohio, Pennsylvania, and Indiana. Three other dissenting Amish groups number only a few thousand members each. At the Mennonite end of the continuum, the Mennonite Church is the largest and one of the most assimilated of the Mennonite bodies. Even it, however, still maintains a few distinctive practices such as its pacifist witness, the practice of excommunication, and, among a diminishing number of communities, head covering for women. Unlike most of the smaller sectarian groups of this tradition, for whom the extended family and local community provide most of the organizational structure, the Mennonite Church has developed a denominational apparatus, including national boards (for missions and education), periodicals, a publishing house, a seminary, and two colleges (Bethel in Kansas and Goshen in Indiana.) Other Mennonite denominations are very small, and are usually stricter on various matters of traditional observance. In addition, more than fifty community "fellowships," many in university towns, are loosely tied in various ways to parent conferences and official bodies.

Worship is an area where Mennonite and Amish practice is clearly distinguishable. The Amish continue the Anabaptist tradition of regarding churches as worldly, and use houses and barns for their services instead. The ministry is divided into three groups—bishops, preachers, and deacons—who are chosen by the small community of families they serve, and are self-supporting laity rather than ordained professionals. Two kinds of music, both in German, are utilized in the services—one a traditional, lengthy, slow-moving sort of the chant, the other quicker and more tuneful. Mennonite worship, on the other hand, takes place in churches and is not very different from that of the Methodists or other evangelical denominations.

A part of Mennonite history reflected in its various independent branches is the migration of a number of its people from Russia and the Ukraine in the late nineteenth century after the group had lost such privileges as an exemption from military service. These Mennonites followed the general pattern of agrarian emigrants of the time, and settled among the still-abundant lands of the American and Canadian prairies and plains, bringing with them their own interpretations of the tradition. A related group that settled in the same period and area was the Hutterites, or Hutterian Brethren, whose name derived from their founder, Jacob Hut[t]er (martyred 1536). Their beliefs and practices are similar to those of the more conservative of their fellow Anabaptist heirs, with one major exception. Where most Mennonites and Amish cooperate closely with other members of their communities in barn-raisings and other activities, actual property still remains privately owned. The Hutterites instead practice communal ownership of all goods, including modern farm equipment, which gives them an economic advantage over their more individualistic neighbors and often incurs the hostility of the latter. As of the late 1980s, there were more than 30,000 Hutterites divided among approximately

300 colonies (family-based settlements) in North America—roughly one-third of them in United States, primarily in the northern Great Plains, and the remainder in Canada.

Where the rise of Anabaptism had been the most significant manifestation of popular religious protest during the Reformation era, the Pietist movement that developed in the late seventeenth century was equally expressive of the religious ferment of that later era. By this time, the Evangelical (Lutheran) Church in the German-speaking states and the Reformed Church in the Netherlands had existed as established institutions for several generations. For the more devout, the result had been an institutional hardening of the arteries. The reaction among those in search of a more vital form of religious expression was not open revolt, but rather a quiet reshaping from within. Furthermore, the movement was not primarily popular in its beginnings. Just as many Anabaptist leaders had originally been Catholic priests, and were therefore more literate than most of their peasant followers, so were the first Pietists generally well-educated clergy who sensed a need for reform from within. Eminent among these was the Alsatian Lutheran Philipp Spener (1635–1705), whose *Pia Desideria* ("Pious Wishes," 1675) became a classic text of the movement.

The core of the Pietist impulse was a religion that spoke to the emotions as well as to the reason. Its method was not a lapse into anarchy and "enthusiasm," but rather a disciplined pursuit of spiritual growth within the context of *ecclesiolae*—that is, small groups of the devout who met among themselves for biblical study and prayer. Although the movement was not received with universal enthusiasm by the clergy of the day, it did not usually break with the established churches but rather served as an intensive supplement to the religious fare offered during the ordinary round of worship services. A particular and lasting impact of Pietism on churchly religious life was the creation of a new, devotional hymnody known best in English through the work of the British lyricists Isaac Watts and Charles Wesley.

Although the Pietist tradition had a broad impact on the Lutheran and Anglican traditions—the latter in the form of John Wesley's Methodism—its earliest impact on American religious life came through the sectarian movements to which it gave rise. One of these was the group of churches that had endured to the present under the name of the "Brethren." The earliest of these groups grew up in the German Palatinate in 1708 under the leadership of Alexander Mack, who had been influenced both by Pietism and by local Mennonites. Many of these early Brethren joined the widespread emigration to Pennsylvania then in progress, and established their first church in Germantown in 1723.

The Brethren are also known as "Dunkers" because of their practice of believer's baptism, usually by "trine," or triple, immersion. The early Brethren found a suitable home in Pennsylvania among their fellow German-speaking sectarians, with whom they shared a common ethos of pacifism and biblically based separation from the broader society. Distinctive to this tradition are several features of worship, based on their interpretation of New Testament practice and not often found outside the Pietist heritage. The central ritual is the *agape*, or "love feast," modeled on early Christian services. This includes foot-washing and the exchange of the "holy kiss" among Brethren of the same sex, and a communal meal with wine and unleavened bread.

As was the case among the heirs of the Anabaptist tradition, the Brethren in America were soon overtaken with the contention that inevitably leads to schism in a community without a strong central organization. As a result, the Brethren of today are divided among several independent groups that vary considerably in their openness to modern society and the apparatus of denominationalism. Many of these, needless to say, are very small. The largest, and most directly descended from the original Pennsylvania community, is the Church of the Brethren, with a membership of about 165,000 in the mid-1980s. Like the "mainstream" Mennonites, these Brethren sponsor colleges, missions, publications, and other denominational activities on a national scale. Its membership, and that of the numerous other smaller groups, is made up primarily of Americans of German descent, and is heavily concentrated in areas of eighteenth- and nineteenth-century German sectarian settlement: Pennsylvania, Maryland, Virginia, Ohio, and Indiana.

A Pietist group that has been considerably more influential than its small membership might indicate is the Moravians. The core of the movement was a group of followers of the Bohemian religious leader John Huss, who anticipated many of Luther's ideas and was burned as a heretic in 1415. Out of the ferment that he stirred arose the Bohemian Brethren, or *Unitas Fratrum* ('Unity of the Brethren"), who continued a twilight existence in central Europe throughout the next several centuries. The group was revitalized in the heyday of Pietism through the work of the German nobleman Nicholas Ludwig von Zinzendorf (1700–1760), who made his estate available as a home for the community.

These revivified Moravians, as they were now known from the location of Zinzendorf's *Herrnhut* ('the Lord's House"), exemplified the devotional ideals of Pietism to the extreme, and were tireless in attempting to spread their way of life and worship. Most notable among their practices was their devotion to the life and wounds of Jesus, which was expressed in a detailed, convoluted, emotional vocabulary of description and praise especially in hymns. (Music remains to the present day an important part of Moravian culture, and their trombone bands carried on flatbed trucks still mark the dawn of Easter in their communities.)

Also central to the early Moravian ideal was a semicommunal lifestyle, which was implemented both in Moravia and in their American settlements at Bethlehem, Pennsylvania (1741) and Salem, North Carolina (1753; now part of Winston-Salem. Both the Pennsylvania and North Carolina cities have preserved the original Moravian communal buildings nearly intact.) The colonists in these early settlements were divided into "choirs" based on age, sex, and marital status. Different groups (e.g., widows or young unmarried women) lived and worshipped together in their own buildings, which formed part of a broader complex of dormitories, stores, craftsworks, and places for worship, surrounded by orchards and farmlands.

As is the usual outcome of communitarian experiments that survive the first generation, however, the Moravians were soon influenced by the example of their less devout and more individualistic neighbors. They abandoned many of their communal practices, such as common property ownership and the "choir" system, and became one denomination among many. Their missions to native Americans in Ohio and Pennsylvania were notable for their humanity, but were ultimately unsuccessful. The community has perpetuated itself to the present day through descent rather than evangelization. The Moravian Church in America, as it is now known, has a membership of about 35,000, with its headquarters at Bethlehem, Pennsylvania. It also sponsors Moravian College in Bethlehem and Salem College in Winston-Salem.

Other German Pietist groups emigrated to the American colonies or arose among immigrants already arrived. Some, like the Schwenkfelders and the Churches of God, General Conference (Winebrennerians), maintain their independent existence, and claim a few thousand members each. Others, such as the monastic Ephrata community in Pennsylvania and the Rappites and Zoarites of Ohio, gradually disappeared. Still others, such as Church of the United Brethren in Christ, merged with larger, English-speaking denominations—in this case, the Methodists (after an intermediate merger with the Evangelical Alliance). Yet another possibility is exemplified by the Amana Colony in Iowa, which in 1932 separated its religious and economic dimensions, and transformed its earlier communitarian structure into a secular joint-stock company. Those that have survived the generations have usually taken one of two routes: the maintenance of a combination of religious and cultural (especially linguistic) identity through voluntary isolation, as with the Amish and Hutterites; or a gradual accommodation with all but a few crucial aspects of modern English-speaking American society, such as the Mennonites and the Brethren. Collectively, though, they have taken their place with the Quakers in maintaining their distinctive witness against war and violence, and have helped to define through a long series of court decisions the potentials, and limits, of religious freedom in America.

CHAPTER 20

Jews and Catholics in Colonial America

Through much of its history, Americans have understood this country as a Protestant nation, with other religious groups afforded legal tolerance but not a very enthusiastic acceptance. By the 1950s, Will Herberg could argue in his classic study *Protestant, Catholic, Jew* that membership in any one of these three communities had become a legitimate "style" of being American. For all their differences, Jews and Roman Catholics have shared a common experience as "outsiders" in America that has been overcome only in recent years. This experience has colonial roots, and warrants the juxtaposition of the two communities as examples of the introduction of non-Protestant elements into the early American experience of religious blending.

Although some converted Sephardim may have arrived in North America with Columbus himself, the story of the American Jewish community does not properly begin until the arrival of 23 Portuguese Jews from Recife, Brazil, in New Amsterdam in 1654. This small group of refugees was the nucleus of the Sephardic community that began to establish small Jewish settlements in the cities of the Atlantic seaboard during the remainder of the colonial era, and that constituted almost the totality of American Jewry until the beginnings of the Ashkenazic immigration in the late eighteenth and early nineteenth centuries.

Although Peter Stuyvesant did not care for these newcomers and attempted to expel them, the influence of Jewish shareholders in the Dutch West India Company reflected the role the Netherlands had assumed as a Jewish refuge and assured the continuing Jewish presence in New Amsterdam. From that time on, Jews in the colonies that would eventually coalesce into the United States suffered only the mildest disabilities compared with their European counterparts, and the commercial skills they had acquired in the Old World served them well in gaining acceptance in a nascent sea-based mercantile economy. Congregations were organized in New York (formerly New Amsterdam) in 1656; Newport, Rhode Island, 1677; Savannah, 1733; Philadelphia, 1745; and Charleston, 1750. The Sephardic variant of the traditional liturgy was observed in these lay-dominated communities; advice was sometimes sought from rabbinical leadership in London and Amsterdam on religious matters, since there were no rabbis in North America until the 1840s. The Sephardic community generally kept to itself, married within its own boundaries, and aroused little overt hostility from its dominant Gentile neighbors.

Although many colonial Jews faced a difficult choice of allegiance when the Revolution came, the large majority sided with the patriot cause and some, like the New York merchant Haym Solomon, played a crucial role in financing the revolutionary cause. Enfranchisement at the Federal level was guaranteed by the First Amendment, but many states proved laggard in extending full rights of citizenship to non-Christians. New York took the lead in its 1777 constitution but North Carolina, at the other extreme, did not follow suit till 1868.

If there may have been Jews on board Columbus's famed trio of ships, there is no doubt that the vast majority of his crew were Spanish Catholics. Whatever the claims of the Norse, the Welsh, and other European peoples who would like to think that their ancestors were the first to cross the Atlantic, the Spanish—led by their redoutable Italian navigator—were the first to establish a lasting and significant presence in the New World. Only a few years after Columbus opened up the New World for European settlement, the Spanish had divided this territory into spheres of influence with the Portuguese through papal mediation. The southern borderlands of what is now the United States marked the northern bounds of the viceroyalty of New Spain, with its capital in Mexico City and the large mass of its population south of the Rio Grande. The Spanish presence was not a long-term major factor in the political and cultural development of those regions until the twentieth century, and what religious impact resulted focused on the attempts of Spanish friars, especially Franciscans, to work with the Indians of the Southwest. The subsequent story of a new Hispanic presence—Mexican, Central American, Cuban, and Puerto Rican—will be taken up again in a later section.

As the Spanish settled the southern rim of North America during the colonial period, the French were similarly active to the north. The primary area of French Catholic settlement was in what is now the province of Quebec, where Jesuits, Sulpicians, Ursulines, and "Grey Nuns"—all of them fairly new religious orders—established churches, schools, hospitals, and Indian missions. French-speaking outposts were established in what is now the United States principally along the route of exploration of the Mississippi Valley. With few exceptions, however, this presence is now reflected mainly in place-names now pronounced in grotesquely Anglicized ways: Detroit, Dubuque, Versailles, St. Louis, New Orleans.

Two small areas of continuing French settlement did emerge, however, in northern New England and southern Louisiana. In 1755, the British expelled several thousand recalcitrant French settlers from Acadia (Nova Scotia), which had been ceded by France in 1713. Many of these Acadians, whose story was fictionalized by Henry Wadsworth Longfellow in his narrative poem *Evangeline*, made their way down to the bayou country of southern Louisiana, where their name became corrupted to *Cajun*. The rest of New France came under British dominion through the Treaty of Paris of 1763, which provided that the residents of Quebec would be guaranteed the maintenance of their traditional language, laws, and Catholic religion. The creation of a francophone (French-speaking) Catholic enclave in the midst of predominantly anglophone and Protestant Canada led to the French-Canadian church's development of a strategy of *survivance*—that is, the maintenance of the traditional religion and culture through voluntary isolation and perpetuation of the old ways of pre-Revolutionary rural France. As economic hardship encroached during the nineteenth and twentieth centuries, however, many of these *Quebecois* emigrated southward into the north of New England in search of employment. In both cases, the interpretation of Catholicism remained traditional and devotionally oriented; the French Catholic culture of New England, however, was much more strictly moralistic than that which developed in the warm land of *zydeco* music and jambalaya.

The other, less direct but more far-reaching impact of French traditions on American Catholicism was a consequence of the French Revolution's forcing large numbers of French clergy and other religious folk into exile in Ireland and America. In some cases the result was the temporary defusing of traditional Catholic-Protestant tensions, such as resulted during the tenure of the charming and cultivated Bishop Jean Lefebvre de Cheverus in Boston during the early 1800s. Many other French clergy found usefulness as faculty at institutions such as Maynooth seminary in Ireland and the new Mount Saint Mary's near Baltimore, established by Bishop John Carroll in 1791, the first institute for the training of clergy established in America. This and other seminaries were staffed by the Sulpician order, founded in France in 1642, which became known for specialization in clerical training, especially in the United States and Canada. Many of these *émigrés*, though staunchly orthodox, had been affected by the Augustinian emphases of the Jansenist movement of the seventeenth century, which was ultimately condemned as heretical in its more extreme forms. The ethos of suspicion of the life of the senses, and especially of sexuality, which it promoted spread far beyond its inner circle, and colored the character of French and, through the *émigrés*, Irish and Irish-American Catholicism as well. Many of the devotional practices of the "Baroque" era of the seventeenth and eighteenth centuries that later became popular in Ireland and America were also of French origin. These resulted from revelations in visions to the devout, usually nuns. Out of this intense religious culture came a number of religious orders that were to become active in nineteenth-century America, including the Ursulines, the Madames of the Sacred Heart, the Sisters of Notre Dame de Namur, and the Society of St. Vincent de Paul.

The English Catholic presence in the American colonies dated for practical purposes from the arrival on the shores of Maryland of the *Ark* and the *Dove* in 1634. The establishment of a New World colony in which English Catholics could find a suitable locale for settlement was brought about by the Calvert family, especially Cecilius Calvert (1606–1675), the second Baron of Baltimore. The Maryland colony was based on the principle of broad religious toleration, which was embodied in the "Act Concerning Religion" passed by Catholics and Protestants alike in 1649. In 1654, however, a Protestant faction took control and ended toleration, and later generations of the Calverts reverted to Anglicanism along with the colony itself.

The Catholic presence remained strong throughout the colonial era, through the presence of wealthy English Catholic families and Jesuit missionaries, who adapted themselves to the dominant southern ethos by becoming slave-holders. Public worship was prohibited, so Mass was usually said instead privately at the Jesuits' residences. One of the most prominent Maryland Catholic families was the Carrolls, who produced by the time of Independence two remarkable offspring. Charles Carroll of Carrollton was a wealthy landholder who was the only Catholic signer of the Declaration of Independence. His distant cousin, John Carroll (1736–1815), was to play a more direct role in the forming of the American Catholic community. Educated in Flanders, he entered the Jesuit order and helped to maintain its property and traditions during the period of its suppression by the papacy from 1773 till 1814.

With the coming of independence, the Vatican had to come to terms with the new political realities of North America, where Catholics in the British colonies had previously been under the aegis of the bishop of Quebec. Carroll was first appointed Vicar Apostolic for the new nation in 1784, then made the first Catholic bishop in the United States in 1789, with his see (i.e., place of residence and headquarters) in Baltimore. He was an enthusiastic supporter of the new American spirit of democracy and policy of church-state separation, and had himself been chosen by his fellow priests as their bishop in a rare example of Vatican-sponsored collegiality. Carroll became an archbishop in 1808 when four new dioceses (Boston, New York, Philadelphia, and Bardstown, Kentucky) were created. He spent the remainder of his career organizing governance structures for American Catholic life and promoting education, with the Sulpician-staffed Mount Saint Mary's Seminary (1791) and College (1808) taking place under his sponsorship. Carroll was also instrumental in the conversion of Elizabeth Bayley Seton, a New York Episcopalian of prominent family, to the Catholic Church. Seton, who would later be canonized as the first native-born American saint, was the founder of the first indigenous American religious order, the Sisters of Charity of Emmitsburg, Maryland, in 1809.

In the Old World, Jews had always lived in a precarious, symbiotic relationship with Christian or Muslim "host cultures," which could not be depended on in the long run. Catholics since the Reformation experienced the extremes of continued establishment and dominance in southern and parts of central Europe, and outlawry and persecution in much of the northwestern part of the Continent. In the Atlantic colonies, neither community numbered more than a few thousand, and neither consequently attracted a great deal of attention, hostile or otherwise. In the meantime, each became assimilated into a distinctively American culture. Sephardic Jews stopped speaking their ancestral Ladino, while life among English-speaking Catholics—many of them, like the Sephardim, quite affluent—differed little from that of their Anglican compeers.

This process of assimilation is illustrated graphically in the two most prominent houses of worship these cultures left behind them. The Touro Synagogue in Newport, Rhode Island, was commissioned by the Sephardic congregation as the first such structure in the colonies. It was designed in 1763 by Peter Harrison, often described as America's first professional architect, and renowned for works such as King's Chapel in Boston. The Touro Synagogue, which is well maintained today and open to visitors, looks at first glance like the home of a prosperous Newport merchant of the period. Its appearance is not discernibly Jewish or even religious; rather, it is domestic in scale and neoclassical in style. Inside, it contains the usual accoutrements for Orthodox worship—a *bema* or reading desk; an ark of the covenant; and seating divided by sex, with a gallery for women. Its message is that it represents a prosperous and sophisticated congregation desiring a tasteful and commodious place for worship, but not wishing to attract undue attention to its presence by anything that might seem indecorous or exotic.

Similarly, the first Roman Catholic cathedral in the United States was intended to signify an active endorsement of and participation in the life of the New Republic. After John Carroll had been named bishop, the prominent (non-Catholic) architect Benjamin Henry Latrobe offered him a choice of designs: an early version of the Gothic Revival and another in the Roman Revival style popularized by Thomas Jefferson. Significantly, Carroll opted for the latter, indicating his solidarity with the republican ideals with which it was associated in the public mind. Later Roman Catholic architecture in America would commonly be in style more specifically associated with its own heritage; here, though, was a happy combination of Roman and American symbolism. Although it no longer serves as a cathedral, Latrobe's and Carroll's handsomely domed Basilica of the Assumption (1804) still stands in Baltimore as a monument to the best of the period's taste as well as a reminder of the self-conception of English-speaking Roman Catholics before the onset of the great waves of immigration of the nineteenth century.

CHAPTER 21

Christian Missions to the North American Indians

Various expeditions of Norsemen may have landed in the northeastern parts of the North American coast during the Middle Ages, but the first significant European presence in the New World began with Columbus's first voyage in 1492. Although it took some time for these newcomers to sort out their cognitive confusions as to where they had actually arrived, the Spanish who followed in Columbus's wake lost little time in subduing and then colonizing almost the entirety of what we now refer to collectively as Latin America. The only significant exception to Spanish hegemony was the presence of the Portuguese, who established the right to a portion of the eastern coast of South America—Brazil—through a combination of papal bulls and the Treaty of Tordesillas, negotiated with the Spanish in 1494. The Spanish imperial government was organized into two viceroyalties, at Mexico City and Lima, during the 1530s. A bishop had already been established in Mexico by 1527, a result of the pope's grant to the Spanish Crown of the *real patronato,* or right of virtually complete patronage in appointing the officials of the Church in Spain and its rapidly growing overseas empire.

The evangelization of the natives was early identified as a major goal of the Spanish imperial venture, but this was not the primary mission of the *secular* clergy—those who served parishes and answered directly to a bishop as their immediate superior. Introducing the aboriginal peoples to the benefits of Christianity was initially the task of what have been called the "shock troops" of the Spanish Church—the religious orders, or *regular* clergy. (As discussed earlier, "regular" derives here from the Latin *regula* or "rule"—the set of precepts by which a religious community is expected to live.) The most important of these orders were the Augustinians, from whose ranks Martin Luther

was emerging in Germany at about the same time; the Franciscans and Dominicans, both of which had been founded in early thirteenth-century Europe as a
response to the need for an effective presence as preachers in the rapidly
growing late medieval cities; and the Jesuits, established in Spain in 1534 by
the ex-soldier Ignatius Loyola as a means of combating the incursions of
Protestantism at the beginning of the "Catholic (or Counter-) Reformation."

As the work of conversion was being undertaken, however, a major problem
had to be resolved as to the very nature of the aboriginal peoples. The European newcomers had no sure sense of who they actually were, and speculated
that they might be anyone from the Lost Tribes of Israel to the Welsh.
Learned debates raged over the basic question of whether they were even
human. This question was hardly academic, since the Spanish Crown entertained genuine reservations about some of the tactics of virtual extermination
being waged by the *conquistadores* against natives who did not immediately
succumb to their claims of dominion. The climax of this argument took place
as a full-dress debate at Valladolid in 1550, when the scholar Juan Ginés de
Sepúlveda argued before the Emperor Charles V that the American Indians
were brutish and less than fully human, and therefore subject to enslavement
according to Aristotle's theory of natural slavery. The opposite side was presented by Fray Bartolomé de las Casas, the Dominican "Apostle of the Indies."
Las Casas maintained that the culture of the Indians was hardly inferior to
that of the Spanish, and that they should be treated with the full respect due to
fellow humans. The result of the debate was inconclusive, but the general
tenor of imperial policy thereafter was to forbid the slaughter or actual enslavement of the Indians—injunctions frequently honored primarily in the
breach.

The attitudes of the missionaries entrusted with the conversion of the Indians varied considerably. Where the Franciscans were rather inflexible about
reconciling native beliefs and practices with those of Catholicism, the Jesuits of
both New Spain and New France were more accommodating in trying to
discover and exploit such correspondences. This could vary considerably, however, among individuals and contexts. Throughout Mexico, the Spanish attempted to superimpose the material presence of their religion on the remains
of the shrines of the Aztecs and their subject peoples. The Cathedral of
Mexico City was erected on the site of one of the principal temples of Monte-
zuma's imperial city, and the shrine of the Virgin of Guadalupe stands near
the ground sacred to the goddess Tonantzin. Indians were organized into
villages under the care of priests, and the rectilinear approach to town planning characteristic of the Spanish Renaissance gave rise to town squares bordered by a church and other public buildings.

The Spanish, in short, were imposing their own version of "cosmos" on
what they perceived as the "chaos" of the aboriginal habitations, a strategy that
also had the advantage of creating conveniently organized administrative
units and personnel. The Mexican missionaries labored valiantly to master
native languages and devise novel approaches to evangelization suited to the
situation. These included open-air churches, whose courtyards could accommodate far more people than a standard-sized enclosed structure, and dramas

in which Christian heroes inevitably defeated the Muslims or other evil forces. Although more benign than the *conquistadores,* the Spanish clergy regarded the Indians as perpetually dependent, and the order that they imposed on their charges was clearly paternalistic.

As New Spain began to be brought tightly under Spanish control, the secular clergy—the "army of occupation"—took control of the missions from the regulars. The latter were sent to the northern fringes of the Empire to deal with the natives who had thus far escaped the benefits of "civilization." Two major loci of missionary activity by the Franciscans during the middle and late colonial period were among the Indians of New Mexico and California. The stories of these two campaigns are worth rehearsing for the significantly different approaches to the missionary endeavor that they reveal within the same religious order.

The ancestors of the various peoples known collectively as the Pueblo of New Mexico had occupied what is now the American Southwest for some ten thousand years. At the time of the first permanent Spanish presence in 1598, these Pueblo—more accurately known as the Zuni, Hopi, and Acoma peoples—were united in a loose federation and led a stable, agricultural life centered on apartment-like multilevel dwellings. Their religious life was organized around voluntary societies of priests, which focused on the various significant aspects of earthly existence such as war, medicine, and hunting. Their most distinctive ritual was conducted in *kivas,* or underground ceremonial chambers in each town's plaza. These kivas represented the earth out of which the ancestors of the human race emerged at the beginning of the world. The priests played the role of masked *kacina* dancers, impersonating the divine figures who had taught the first humans how to live in their new above-ground cosmos.

With the first Spanish in New Mexico came Franciscan missionaries, who relied on their armed escorts for support in attempting to impose Christianity as forcibly as was necessary on the Pueblo. They made repeated raids on the kivas, destroying ceremonial apparatus wherever it could be found, and exerted little effort to master the local languages or to understand Pueblo culture. The friars moved frequently from settlement to settlement, and did not make much lasting contact with the local people, whom they set to work building their striking adobe churches. They had no interest in trying to translate the abstractions of European theology into the thought and language patterns of a radically different culture, and insisted that the natives accept the Christian religion and a European life-style as an inseparable package. Although some Indians accepted instruction in crafts and Catholicism from the priests, most kept an unbelligerent but skeptical distance.

The failure of the Franciscans to make any significant impact on Pueblo sensibilities became evident in 1680, after a prolonged drought seemed to the natives to disprove the efficacy of the new religion in sustaining even the basics of life. A revolt led by the Indian Popé temporarily drove out the Spanish, and the Pueblo's feelings toward the Franciscans were expressed by their killing twenty-one of the thirty-three missionaries stationed in the area. After the Spanish regained control in 1693, the Franciscans returned, but their influence over the natives was circumscribed considerably by the secular power.

Over the centuries, the Pueblo have succeeded more fully than most native peoples in preserving their traditional religious culture while adjusting to the inevitability of the white presence. One reason for this cultural survival may lie in the sophisticated organization of their voluntary societies, as opposed to the greater individualism among religious specialists in other native societies. Try as the Franciscans might to obliterate the traditional patterns, the native priests outwitted them and continued to celebrate their rites in secret. After the Franciscan power had been limited by the Spanish, the Pueblo learned to live in two worlds simultaneously through a sort of mental compartmentalization. The Pueblo accommodated themselves to political dominance successively by the Spanish, Mexicans, and Americans, and learned to adapt some of the more useful aspects of modern technology into their life-style and to master English as a second language. However, they persisted in maintaining their traditional rituals intact, and resisted blending Christian elements into a native base as many other peoples were to do. (This kind of blending of elements from two or more religious traditions is called *syncretism*.)

A very different mission campaign by Spanish-speaking Franciscans was launched in *alta* (northern) California in 1768 by Junípero Serra, one of the most remarkable and admired missionaries of all time. Together with his successor, Fermín Lasuén, and their fellow friars, Serra organized a chain of what would eventually become twenty-one mission stations spaced a day's journey (about 40 miles) from one another along *El Camino Real*—"the Royal Road"—from San Diego to San Francisco. (It is worth noting the place names—Saint James and Saint Francis—which have lost their religious connotations in current usage.) The California Indians were not nearly as complexly organized as the Pueblo, and lived a fairly simple life characterized by minimal clothing, brush-covered huts, and seminomadic food-gathering (especially of acorns). Their religious system was similarly lacking in complexity.

Serra and his companions approached these "Digger" or "Mission" Indians, as they were later called, with gifts of food and clothing, and avoided any coercion in trying to attract them to Christianity. In a reversal of the roles that had developed in New Mexico, the friars protected the natives from exploitation by the soldiers who had established military bases along the same route and provided the priests with protection. The friars invited the generally friendly natives to help them in the construction of the mission compounds, most of which survive to the present day. These compounds are of considerable interest architecturally, since they incorporate imperfectly remembered Spanish plans with local materials—primarily adobe—and native workmanship. The typical mission was organized around a rectangular *patio*, with a chapel as the focal point and cloisterlike arcades around the interior rim. Rooms were provided for priests' quarters—Serra's cell may still been seen at Carmel—and for craft workshops, cooking, storage, and accommodations for unmarried native women. Single men and married couples lived in adobe houses nearby.

The compounds were designed to be self-sustaining, and a profitable agriculture flourished around many of them. Under Franciscan tutelage the natives raised cattle, sheep, olives, grapes, and other produce, thus adopting a basically European life-style while being instructed in the rudiments of Christianity. Mission priests were expected to master the native language within a year of their arrival, but a common language incorporating elements of both Spanish and Indian dialects emerged as a sort of common *pidgin* tongue throughout all of the missions. What resulted can be described in the phrase of Erving Goffman as a "total institution," in which every aspect of the lives of the resident Indians was shaped by the program of mission life developed by the friars. The result was a benevolent paternalism, more European than indigenous in style, but representing a real cultural fusion nonetheless.

Even though the Indians were far more supportive of the California program than had been their counterparts in New Mexico—the largest mission had as many as four thousand in residence at its heyday—the endeavor of Serra and his compatriots to establish a permanent refuge for their charges proved to be only a "brief and shining moment" in the checkered history of North American missions. Secularization of the settlements began to take place under Mexican dominion in 1822, and the subsequent transfer of power to English-speaking Americans accelerated the process further. Mission land and property were sold off, and the buildings began to decay. The Indians dispersed into a disorganized wandering state, never to reassemble. A movement to restore the old compounds was begun in 1891, and some today are still utilized for Catholic services. The Indians they were built to serve, however, are forever gone as a people.

The California missions at their peak were probably the most comprehensive, sensitive, and, in the short run, successful of the attempts by European Catholics to convert Native Americans to their beliefs—and, almost inevitably, their life-style. (Serra, however, was criticized strongly by some Native American groups as having mistreated his Indian charges when he was beatified—the first stage on the road to canonization as a saint—by Pope John Paul II in 1988.) The attempts of the French at the other extreme of North America to conduct similar missions provide an interesting point of comparison. In New France, now known as Canada, the aboriginal peoples lived a more mobile and hunting-based existence than did many of their counterparts in the more temperate climes of the southern parts of the continent. Again, the religious orders rather than diocesan clergy were the agents of evangelization, and the Jesuits were particularly active among the Huron in what is now Ontario.

The Jesuits from early on had distinguished themselves from other Catholic missionaries through their willingness to accommodate their life-style and message to those of the peoples they were attempting to convert. Matteo Ricci, for example, assumed the role of Mandarin scholar during his controversial mission in China in the 1580s, and carefully avoided introducing any Catholic teachings that were irreconcilable with traditional Chinese culture. His later successors in Canada were of similarly innovative bent, but their work was seriously impeded both by internal resistance and external obstacles.

The religious life of the Huron was representative of that of the semi-nomadic native peoples of the north. Religion was not compartmentalized, and ritual or symbolic activity accompanied all important aspects of life. According to their cosmology, the world came into being after the goddess Aataentsic fell through a hole in the sky into the primeval water. The Great Tortoise and other animals came to her rescue, and brought up enough land to provide her with a cushion, which also served as the home for the human race. She gave birth to twin sons, one of whom became the"culture hero" for humanity. For the most part, however, supernatural power diffused throughout the world was much more significant for everyday life than were these rather remote divinities.

Jesuits began to work among the Hurons beginning in 1625, and set about to learn the language and immerse themselves in native culture. In the tradition of Ricci, they attempted to equate aspects of Catholic belief with traditional Huron ideas and practices. Their success, however, was limited by the gaps between the mental worlds of the Hurons and the French. The Huron language, for example, lacked abstract nouns, and traditional Catholic theology rested on abstractions such as "atonement." Monotheism made little sense to a people used to seeing supernatural power diffused throughout the natural world. In a society in which shamans were the only religious functionaries, with power based solely on producing tangible results, the more subtle notion of a priesthood ordained for the administration of sacraments did not go very far. Sin and eternal punishment similarly made no sense in the Huron cosmos, and a proper fear of hellfire was hard to drum up. Also, traditional Huron practices such as divorce and torture of prisoners were irreconcilable with the moral sense of the Jesuits.

The Jesuits had first gained access to and toleration by the Huron because of their connection with French traders and soldiers, who offered both worldly allures and protection. By 1648, however, this presence was insuffcient to defend the partially Christianized Hurons and their Jesuit mentors from the fury of their traditional enemies, the Iroquois. The latter launched an attack aimed at the total conquest of the Huron, and the Huron were powerless to resist effectively. In the ensuing battles, several Jesuits, including the now-sainted Jean de Brébeuf, fell into Iroquoian hands, at which they underwent the ferocious tortures traditionally reserved for prisoners of war. As Henry Bowden points out, however, a new element entered the drama that now took place. Brébeuf endured his torments in the stoic fashion of the Indian brave, refusing to ask for mercy under the most extreme duress. He earned the admiration of his captors (who proceeded to eat his heart), who admired him not for his Christian but rather his Indian virtues. Whether the Jesuits had converted the Hurons or vice versa is an open question.

As a result of this savage warfare, traditional Huron society was shattered, and the Jesuits who survived were successful in baptizing many of those who still lived. As in the case of Handsome Lake and the Seneca of upstate New York a century and a half later, social disintegration is often a prelude to dramatic religious change. (The story of Handsome Lake is recounted in a later chapter.) Some relocated Huron settlements have survived to the present, but have gradually been transformed by the incursion of modern society. As in the case of the Franciscan missions in California, the goal of an intermediate society—Christian but still distinctvively Indian—sought by the Jesuits was doomed to ultimate failure. The heroic legend of Brébeuf and his companion martyrs alone remains as an ambiguous testimony to their endeavors.

The missionary approach of Protestants during the colonial period was generally as inflexible as that of the most rigid Catholics. What missions were conducted during the seventeenth century were the work of a handful of Puritan clergy whose Calvinist faith did not easily lend itself to intercultural understanding. The god of the Puritans was not theoretically unwilling to include some natives among the small segment of humankind he had elected for eternal salvation. However, most Puritans simply did not have the inclination to expend very much effort on a people that seemed to them, if not actually hostile, at least an unlikely audience for the message of conversion grounded on intellectual assent to the highly propositional theology they taught. When the New Englanders did address themselves to their aboriginal predecessors, they insisted that the Indians accommodate to their own ways not only of believing but of living. Their success was not extraordinary.

The earliest of the New England Puritans to attempt a mission to the natives was Thomas Mayhew, Jr., who in 1642 began to evangelize the Algonkians on Martha's Vineyard in their own language. After his premature death, his work was carried on by both his father and his son, and later by two further generations of Mayhews. Although this family's work was successful in terms of continuity and the successful mastery of the native language exhibited by the Mayhews, its scope was strictly limited by its literally insular character.

Of broader reach were the endeavors of John Eliot in the Bay Colony, which began around the same time. Eliot produced a dictionary and grammar of the Massachuset tongue, and translated the New Testament and other Christian works as well. He converted considerable numbers of the Massachuset, and organized these "praying Indians" into "praying towns." These latter settlements, of which Natick was the most notable, were organized within a short distance of Boston. In their heyday later in the century they boasted a total population of about forty-one hundred, perhaps 10 percent of the local native population, whch had already been decimated by the English introduction of contagious diseases against which the natives possessed no immunity.

These towns, though shaped by Eliot's humane temper, nevertheless reflected the Puritan insistence that a Christian Indian must be as well a Europeanized Indian. The Massachusets who elected to live in them had to make a decisive choice to reject their entire life patterns, including their kinship ties. They also traded their seminomadic life-style, in which hunting and cultivation both provided food, for one of permanent stability of residence with an agricultural base. Vising Puritan ministers provided leadership, as did some natives who had been appointed to the status of elder or exhorter (i.e., deliverer of homilies). What might have grown into a fairly long-term settlement was disrupted by the outbreak of King Philip's War in 1675. This resulted in suspicious Puritans confining all Indians within reach, including Christian converts, in what amounted to concentration camps. Many died as a result, and the praying town experiment went into sharp decline and eventual dispersion.

A few scattered attempts during the eighteenth century met with similarly discouraging results. David Brainerd, whose brief career as an Indian missionary was immortalized by Jonathan Edwards as an exemplary life of heroic piety, converted practically no one. Eleazar Wheelock in Connecticut presided over a charity school that turned out one notable Indian preacher, Samson Occom, who was later ordained by the Presbyterians as a minister to his fellow Indians on Long Island. Occom broke with his mentor, however, after discovering that Wheelock's newly founded Dartmouth College, which had been intended for Indians, had become yet another academy for whites. The few Indians enrolled there had died or left in frustration with Wheelock's regimen, which was intended to break them of their traditional culture as rapidly as possible. (A few Indians had attended Harvard from time to time previously, and most died of the effects.) After leaving Long Island, where he had lived in wigwams and supported himself in various ways while conducting his missionary work, Occom concluded his career in Connecticut.

As the time of independence approached, other religious groups whose theologies and life-styles differed sharply from those of the Puritans began work among the Indians as well. David Zeisberger was a Moravian who worked extensively with peoples in Pennsylvania and then Ohio, where he helped establish three towns of Indians from a variety of tribes. These settlers were forced to migrate to Ontario when the Revolution came, and the better part of them were massacred by suspicious American frontiersmen when they returned to Ohio in 1782 to reclaim what remained of their possessions. The Society of Friends, or Quakers, another pacifist group, early gained a well-earned reputation for fair dealing with the natives through William Penn's early negotiations in the settlement of Philadelphia by his English followers. Quakers welcomed Indians to their meetings but generally did not actively seek to convert them. A group of Quakers working as a sort of "peace corps" among the Seneca in western New York, however, helped to plant some of the ideas that later became incorporated into the movement led by Handsome Lake, which is discussed at some length in a later chapter.

After the establishment of the new nation, federal policy toward the Indians alternated between rather half-hearted developmental assistance called "Civilization Funds," which were usually administered by the churches, and an aggressive policy of military subjugation and forcible removal. The latter was the fate of the Cherokee in Georgia, one of the "Civilized Tribes" forced by Andrew Jackson onto the "Trail of Tears" to Indian Territory (Oklahoma). The Protestant churches, which were the only ones at the time with the resources to attempt much in the way of mission work, channeled their efforts through the interdenominational American Board of Commissioners of Foreign Missions (ABCFM), one of the agencies of the informal "Benevolent Empire" that was attempting to spread evangelical Christianity through a nation in which no established church could legally exist.

The efforts of Protestant missionaries from the beginnings through the nineteenth century were not very productive, largely because of their insistence that Indians adopt not only Christianity as a religion but also the life-style that the missionaries believed to be inseparable from it. Robert F. Berkhofer, Jr., has demonstrated the primacy of Protestant virtues in the scheme of evangelization. Primary among these was sobriety, which was particularly important in the Native context since Indians seemed to lack the physiological capacity to partake of even small amounts of alcohol without becoming intoxicated. Other Protestant virtues such as cleanliness, punctuality, and stability of residence were not especially alien to the agriculturally inclined peoples, but were so to the hunting-based cultures of the Northeast and the Great Plains.

Similarly, private property ownership was a virtue only in the context of an agricultural or commercial society, and clashed sharply with the seminomadic attitude of land use only for immediate needs rather than private and exclusive ownership in perpetuity. White and Indian notions of law and order were also at odds; the personalized and traditional patterns of justice practiced by the Indians was not readily reconciled with the abstract, impersonal codes of the Anglo-Americans. Only Indians who had become demoralized over the prospects of continuing in their traditional patterns were likely to be receptive to a message predicated on such a thorough-going repudiation of their traditional values. A nature deprived of its supernatural resonances and divided neatly into privately owned farms and house-plots had little intrinsic appeal.

Despite occasional armed outbreaks such as that which resulted in the demise of General Custer at Little Big Horn in 1876, the inexorable movement of the American Indian after the Civil War was toward the government-supervised reservation. Under President Grant, the federal government again chose to share this supervisory work with the churches under what came to be known as the "Quaker Policy" of 1869. (The name referred to the origins of the idea among members of the Friends.) The Indian peoples were thereby divided up under the supervision of thirteen different denominations, with little regard to the previous history of work among particular peoples by each group. The Methodists were heavily favored under this scheme. Roman Catholics, who had been involved particularly in missions in the Northwest, came out on the short end, and organized their own mission board in 1874 as a countermeasure. The general policy of the government was first to isolate the Indians collectively on reservations, but the relentless pressure of whites for more land led to a new emphasis on promoting assimilation into the broader society and a concomitant treatment of Indians as individuals rather than members of groups. The Dawes Act of 1887 divided reservation lands among individual Indians, with much of the remainder being sold to whites. Not until John Collier, an anthropologist sympathetic to the preservation of traditional ways, was appointed as Commissioner of Indian Affairs in the 1930s did a major reversal take place. Since the New Deal years, federal policy has fluctuated considerably.

In the twentieth century, the newly organized Federal Council of Churches in 1908 took over the coordination of most Indian mission work among Protestants. Its successor, the National Council of Churches, eliminated any specific agency for the supervision of Indian missions, although individual denominations continued efforts. A poll cited by Henry Bowden taken in 1958 indicated that Catholics and more liberal Protestants tended to favor a mission strategy aiming at an accommodation between traditional ways and Christianity, while more evangelical Protestants were less hospitable to compromise.

The history of Catholic missionary work among the Lakota Sioux on the Rosebud and Pine Ridge reservations in South Dakota is a good example of the fortunes of Christian Indian missions during the past century. A regular Catholic presence became possible only in the 1880s, after the Sioux had been forced to abandon their seminomadic ways and settle down on reservations. With government aid, the Jesuits and Sisters of Saint Francis established boarding schools for native children. Despite the long Jesuit heritage of accommodations to traditional customs, however, this particular mission was deeply imbued with the common late-nineteenth-century philosophy of "developmentalism." As Harvey Markowitz has pointed out, the developmentalist theory held that native peoples represented an earlier, more primitive stage of development already passed through by Euro-Americans, whose duty was to pull their less-developed neighbors up to the modern standard as quickly as possible. The Catholic reservation schools therefore attempted to isolate Sioux children from their families, forbidding them to speak anything but English and cutting home visits down to a bare minimum. They also looked upon Sioux medicine men as dangerous heathen, and their religion as irredeemably pagan. Their impact on the Sioux was, not surprisingly, rather minimal.

Since Vatican II, however, the atmosphere of pluralism that has spread through the Catholic church more generally has influenced its "missiology"— philosophy of mission work—as well. Jesuits working on the same missions in the 1980s express radically different attitudes toward the Sioux people, and regard their traditions as deserving of respect rather than contempt. Some have gone so far as to participate in traditional Sioux practices such as vision quests and sweat lodge ceremonies. On the whole, however, these modern missionaries express discouragement over their relevance to the Sioux and over the tepid native response to their work. This experience may well be typical of the broader range of Christian mission experience among Native American peoples. Although many missionaries are far more sympathetic to these peoples and their traditions than their predecessors, they are almost powerless either to bring about a radical transformation in Indian consciousness or do more than mildly alleviate the collective deterioration of Indian life that has been taking place for two centuries. Like that of the most notable of their predecessors, Serra and Brébeuf, their work can at best be regarded as not entirely unsuccessful.

PART III

Religious Community Formation in the New Republic

INTRODUCTION

The decades between the Revolution and the Civil War were crucial in the formation of a new American society and culture. What Sidney Mead has called "the lively experiment" was free to unfold in a nation that had in its very Constitution guaranteed complete religious freedom, and that enjoyed what seemed at the time to be endless room for expansion. European visitors from Alexis de Tocqueville to Charles Dickens came in a never-ending stream to marvel at the fortunes and follies of their New World cousins. Natural wonders, utopian societies, frontier cities, black slaves, and even innovative prisons were among the novelties they noted and reported back to their news-hungry compatriots.

Religion was one of those cultural realms in which experimentation could and did take place ceaselessly. Without an established church, almost anything short of human sacrifice—or, more relevantly, polygamy—could be tried in the name of God's will. No religious group could count on anything but voluntary membership, but it did not seem difficult to attract new members to the most improbable sorts of religious, reform, and social movements, many of which combined features of all three. Primarily secular utopian experiments, such as Robert Owen's New Harmony or George Ripley's Brook Farm, did not usually last very long. Some, like "Mother" Ann Lee's Shakers and John Humphrey Noyes's Oneida, prospered for several decades, then fell into irreversible decline. Still others, like Joseph Smith and his Mormon followers, laid the foundations of an enduring new religious tradition.

For the more "mainstream" groups, the frontier presented new challenges. Social stratification was by no means absent in American religious alignments, and Presbyterians, Congregationalists, and Episcopalians continued to attract the prosperous and educated. The "growth industries" of contemporary Christianity, however, were the popular denominations—Baptists, Methodists, and Campbellites—who knew how to say what frontierspeople wanted to hear. But even these latter did not remain static. Just as American social classes have always been porous at the boundaries, denominations changed character with their constituents. As Methodists moved from frontier hamlets into middleclass urban neighborhoods, their circuit riders yielded to a settled clergy, and Gothic churches replaced outdoor camp-meetings. Religious revivals settled into the landscape, but changed character as well with the times.

These individual Protestant denominations, though, did not exhaust the religious energies of their members. Cutting across their organizational lines were the agencies of the "Benevolent Empire," a loosely related collection of evangelistic and reform societies led by both laity and clergy. In addition, a common evangelical religious culture developed during the earlier nineteenth century that could easily be shared by almost all who identified themselves as "Protestant." This culture was shaped by denominational and interdenominational agencies, and was spread through Sunday schools, colleges, books, periodicals, sermons, and hymns. If Americans shared a common culture during these years, its character was distinctively religious.

But not all Americans were white evangelical Protestants. Dissent manifested itself within the Protestant camp in the liberalism of the Unitarians and Universalists and in the liturgical preferences of many Lutherans and Episcopalians. Although blacks shared many of the religious premises of their white evangelical counterparts, they were often neither able nor willing to worship alongside them. Free blacks in the North formed their own churches, while their enslaved kindred developed a distinctive amalgam of Christian and African elements in their frequently surreptitious worship.

Beyond the bounds of Protestantism entirely were Jews and Roman Catholics, whose numbers were being rapidly expanded through immigration from Germany and Ireland. The Irish were confined by circumstance primarily to the eastern seaboard, while Germans of all religious stripes began to find new homes in the Midwest. Their story, together with that of later immigrants of their faiths from southern and eastern Europe, is dealt with in the following unit.

A. Toward Independence

CHAPTER 22

The Revolution and the Constitution

The question of just what caused the American Revolution is one of those convoluted problems that historians have wrestled with for generations with successive waves of insight but no definitive answer. In addition to specific political and economic grievances, such as taxation without representation, the momentum to make a definitive break with the mother country emerged from a transformation of consciousness. It was not enough simply to want to become independent *from* England; rather it was also necessary to be free *to become* Americans as well. During the seventeenth century, such an identity had not yet emerged. Colonists thought of themselves as members of a particular colony—Massachusetts Bay, Virginia, or Pennsylvania— and as English. Communication and travel were far more extensive between individual colonial ports and England than they were among the different colonies. An American identity that transcended regional loyalties was still in the future.

The Great Awakening was in some ways the first major event in *American* history—as opposed to the history of the British Empire. It is ironic that its catalyst was George Whitefield, an Englishman, but it is symbolic that he was buried in American soil. Although the roots of the Awakening may have lain deep in European Pietism, it was American colonists of all sorts and conditions who experienced the great revival, and few emerged from its fires unscathed. Far more than the French and Indian wars, which were essentially colonial affairs, a truly *national* event had taken place in which all Americans had been somehow implicated. In addition, the challenge of Whitefield and other itinerant evangelists to the various colonial establishments helped mold a new attitude toward authority, in which tradition became challenged by experience, and hierarchy by democracy.

The Awakening also helped prepare the way for the Revolution by nurturing

161

a national consciousness that made Americans aware of their commonality with one another, and familiarized them with intercolonial cooperation. In addition, it is possible to look upon the Revolution as a continuation of the Revival. Many Anglican clergy opposed both events, and Quakers and the German sects tried to stay neutral. Within the English-speaking Reformed churches—Congregational and Presbyterian—there was little hesitation among either New or Old Lights in lending their support to the coming conflict. Jonathan Mayhew especially among the liberals helped construct a rhetoric of defiance, while countless Puritan preachers took their turns in interpreting the struggle for independence as a religious act.

The basic argument promoted from many pulpits was this. Colonial preachers had already developed a theological framework for interpreting historical events on the premise that the Reformation in general, and the emergence of Reformed Christianity in Britain in particular, was the beginning of a divine plan for the transformation of the entire world. During the French and Indian wars, the French and the Papacy—France was a Catholic nation—were depicted in many sermons not just as secular enemies, but as agents of the Antichrist in an unfolding apocalyptic struggle. When the Revolution began to take shape, the framework remained steady while the characters changed. The Church of England had long been resented both as religiously corrupt and also as an instrument of political imperial control. The King of England became the embodiment of evil, while the French, who sided with the American cause, lost their sinister character. Furthermore, the old Puritan "jeremiad" tradition was invoked in the argument that the sufferings that Americans were undergoing at the hands of the British were a punishment for having strayed from the straight and narrow. If Americans repented and returned to the old ways, God would reward them by delivering them from tyranny. The Revolution, in short, was not just a war but also the occasion for a revival. Beyond that, it was part of the dramatic unfolding of God's millennial plan for transforming the world through an ongoing struggle between good and evil. The Americans were God's agent for good—assuming that they could get their proverbial act together.

On the other hand, it is dangerous to overemphasize the role that religious motives played in bringing about the Revolution. Although clerical zeal for liberty—Christian or political—ran high, the churches over which these clerics presided were generally unable to command the continuing allegiance of the generations following the Awakening, and church membership reached a low ebb during the Revolutionary era. The British Whig political thought that helped mold the ideological basis of the Revolution was rooted as much in secular as in religious sources, and Puritans, Anglicans and Deists had all contributed to the latter stream. As Nathan Hatch, George Marsden, and Mark Noll have pointed out in their cautionary work on viewing the emergent nation as a Christian society, even the redoubtable John Witherspoon, the Scottish divine who became president of Princeton, abandoned religious claims in the political theory he began to expound at that institution. It is also significant that Witherspoon was the mentor of James Madison, the Virginia

Anglican who contributed so much to the theory and practice of the separation of church and state first in Virginia and then in the Bill of Rights.

Illustrative of this interplay between sacred and secular is the emergence during and after the Revolution of a new kind of religious imagery around the nation itself and its leaders—a "civil religion." George Washington emerged as a cult figure, and was identified publicly with both Moses and Joshua as a divinely appointed agent of deliverance from bondage. Thomas Jefferson himself suggested that the official seal include a representation of Moses leading the children of Israel into freedom. Images from the Old Testament combined with those from the Roman Republic: Washington also became identified with Cincinnatus, the general who refused a kingship after victory and returned to his plow. The seal that still appears on our currency bears two Latin inscriptions: *Novus Ordo Seclorum* ("a new order of the ages") and *Annuit Coeptis* ("He has prospered our undertaking.")

What did the victory over the British and the constitution of a new republic mean? Clearly, two major sources of imagery converged: biblical and classical, sacred and secular. These same two strains also came together in resolving the question of what role organized religion was to play in this "first new nation." On the one hand, Jefferson, Franklin, and other representatives of the Enlightenment tradition feared that any government support for religion would lead to corruption of the state, as the entanglement of the Roman Catholic Church with the Bourbon monarchy indicated only too vividly. On the other, separatist spokesmen such as Isaac Backus of Massachusetts revived Roger Williams's old argument that such support would lead to a corruption of the church, as their experience with the New England "standing order" indicated only too clearly. From utterly different ideological perspectives, then, a solution different from what had been the norm in Europe and most of the colonies seemed very much in order.

Pennsylvania and Rhode Island had helped pave the way, with laws that had granted broad toleration for generations. The other Middle Colonies—New York, Delaware, and New Jersey—had at most limited establishment, and readily opted for pluralism when independence was at hand. Although a plan for the equal support by the state of all Protestant churches was debated in Virginia and briefly tried in South Carolina, the Southern states moved rapidly toward disestablishment and religious freedom, in part out of revulsion over the Tory allegiances of many Anglican clergy during the revolutionary struggle.

Virginia, which provided so much of the leadership in both the Revolution and the framing of the new nation, was the scene of one of the most complicated debates over what role religion should play in the emergent commonwealth. It was here that the Church of England had been most effectively established, and here as well that dissenting opposition to that establishment was highly vocal. Presbyterians were especially active in arguing for an end to state support of religion, out of fear of the harm that such support might wreak on the church—as, they argued, it so frequently had in the Old World.

The main proponents of disestablishment, however, were the Deist Jefferson and the more moderately "enlightened" Madison: the latter's "Memorial and Remonstrance" of 1785 helped secure passage of the former's "Statute for Religious Freedom" the following year. After a lengthy introductory section asserting that "Almighty God hath created the mind free" and enumerating the harm that results from attempting to coerce religious belief, Jefferson's act goes on to state

> Section II. We the General Assembly of Virginia do enact that no man shall be compelled to frequent or support any religious worship, place, or ministry whatsoever, nor shall be enforced, restrained, molested or burthened in his body or goods, or shall otherwise suffer, on account of his religious opinions or belief; but that all men shall be free to profess, and by argument to maintain, their opinions in matters of religion, and that the same shall in no wise diminish, enlarge, or affect their civil capacities.

The final provision goes on to warn future legislators that "the rights hereby asserted are of the natural rights of mankind, and that if any act shall be hereafter passed to repeal the present or to narrow its operations, such act shall be an infringement of natural right." The enactment of this sweeping declaration of religious freedom was part of a series of state actions from 1776 to 1802 in which payments to the established clergy were suspended, the Episcopal Church was deprived of its incorporated status, and its glebe (revenue-producing) lands were sold off as state property. It is noteworthy that Jefferson later regarded the Virginia statute as one of his three most significant accomplishments.

Although the actions of Virginia were highly influential, most were taken prior to the settlement of the question of relationship of church and state at the national level. This still had to be resolved at the Constitutional Convention in Philadelphia, where James Madison, one of the authors of *The Federalist*, again played a leading role. The practical consequences of de facto religious pluralism in the new states also pointed toward a formal acknowledgment of this situation as a norm. After all, even if it seemed wise for the federal government to support a religion, which one should it support? Too many mutually exclusive claimants were there to satisfy anyone. Furthermore, the pressure for limited central government and the maintenance of states' rights further militated against positive action at the federal level; had the national government attempted to interfere with the various courses individual states were pursuing with regard to religion, the result would doubtless have been rejected. It does not seem, in fact, that any of the delegates was inclined to argue for an establishment; the debates that preceded the Bill of Rights dealt only with questions of wording and of scope—that is, should their measure be binding on the states or simply on the national government, or should conscientious objection to participation in war be guaranteed? (The latter question somehow seems to have fallen by the wayside, though in later years the courts began to recognize such a right as implicit in the First Amendment.)

It is noteworthy in considering the Constitution that the only direct references to religion are negative: "No religious test shall ever be required as a qualification to any office or public trust under the United States" (Article VI); and the beginning of Article I of the Amendments, better known as the "Bill of Rights": "Congress shall make no law respecting an establishment of religion, or prohibiting the free exercise thereof." Although the Declaration of Independence invokes the deity several times, albeit in language that is scarcely traditionally Christian, the Constitution makes no such reference; rather, in Glenn Miller's words, "The document was one of the most secular in history."

The First Amendment was adopted in a newly forming nation in which religious establishment had already become severely weakened, and denominationalism a de facto reality. Moreover, the cultural hegemony enjoyed by Protestantism in its several varieties ensured that anything resembling absolute freedom of religion would be slow in coming. Nevertheless, the long-term impact of the First Amendment was revolutionary, and its implications are still being sorted out in the courts year by year. Instead of the religious *toleration* practiced in varying degrees in the colonies, religious *liberty* was now the nationally mandated norm. America was now a nation friendly but officially neutral toward the panoply of churches that it sheltered. Whether and how this neutrality could work itself out in practice is a major theme of the story of evangelical Protestantism in the nineteenth century.

B. White Evangelicalism

CHAPTER 23

The Second Great Awakening(s)

The winning of independence and the constitution of the new nation were both exhilarating and threatening for evangelicals. Most had supported the patriot cause, and rejoiced in yet another step being taken toward unfolding God's plan for the coming of the millennium here on earth. All of the evangelical denominations had experience in resisting tyranny—sometimes each other's—and all were prepared to join in the task of shaping the new democratic republic. Although some were more enthusiastic about democratic prospects than others, most agreed that the Kingdom of God was not simply going to arrive, but needed hard human work for it to be ushered in. Challenges abounded in religious freedom, pluralism, and disestablishment; the expansion of the frontier and the myriad of the unchurched who streamed out to inhabit the new lands opening up for pioneering and settlement; and the multiplication of enemies, real and imaginary, who had to be smoked out and vanquished by the sword of the Lord. The evangelicals, in short, had a full plate.

Who were these "evangelicals"? The word itself had a long history, going back to the "good news" of the Gospels and revived in Luther's *evangelische Kirche.** By the time of independence, "evangelical" as a designation for Anglo-American Protestants had taken on a distinct though broad meaning. It did not refer to a specific new tradition or single denomination, but rather included a wide variety of established and emergent groups—Congregationalists (formerly Puritans), Presbyterians, Methodists, and Baptists. In addition to describing most of the members of those groups, it included Low Church

---

* *Evangelical* came into English and other modern languages through Latin From the Greek words for "good" and "messenger." A compound form arose which meant "message of good news," which is rendered in English as *Gospel* (from the Anglo-Saxon "godspell"). *Angel,* which literally means "messenger," shares its etymology with "evangelical."

166

Episcopalians, who were gathering strength in Virginia and other parts of the South, and the Americanizing followers of Samuel S. Schmucker among Lutherans in Pennsylvania and Ohio. Various German-speaking sects and movements of frontier provenance, such as Alexander Campbell's "restorationists," also came under this umbrella.

All of these sorts and conditions of Protestants did not share a formal theology. Like Wesley and Whitefield, the archetypal revivalists, some were Arminians while others were Calvinists, and a new "middle way" between them was emerging in New Haven. What they did share was a set of three emphases, however much they might quarrel about other issues. First was a commitment to the Bible as the sole source of revelation and religious authority—the legacy of the Reformation. Second was an insistence on personal, emotional conversion as the hallmark of salvation—the fruit of the Great Awakening. Third was the "missionary imperative," the inexorable internal demand on the converted not to hide their lights under proverbial bushels, but to go out and share the good news with others who had not yet experienced its power. This could take the form of revival preaching, missionary work, personal witness, or participation in any of the number of benevolent societies founded to spread the Christian message and, beyond that, help to reshape society according to that message.

The first major problem confronting evangelicals after Independence was their legal status. During the colonial era, most of the New England and Southern colonies had some form of government support for organized religion. Even the Massachusetts Puritans, though, had been forced to share that support with other groups as they had become hemmed in by Separatist dissent on one side and Anglican interference on the other. The First Amendment to the new Constitution made it illegal from the start for the Federal government either to support or interfere with religion. This injunction did not apply to the states, though many of the latter rapidly followed the precedent of Virginia in refusing to sanction any sort of establishment.

Three of the old Puritan domains refused to follow suit: Connecticut, Massachusetts, and New Hampshire. Lyman Beecher (1775–1863), the staunch Connecticut Congregationalist revival preacher, described the situation in his *Autobiography:*

> The habit of legislation from the beginning had been to favor the Congregational order and provide for it. Congregationalism was the established religion. All others were dissenters, and complained of favoritism. The ambitious minority early began to make use of the minor sects on the grounds of invidious distinctions, thus making them restive. So the democracy, as it rose, included nearly all the minor sects, besides the Sabbath-breakers, rum-selling tippling folk, infidels, and ruff-scuff generally, and made a dead set at us of the standing order. [John Harvard Library ed., I, 251]

After this rather lurid characterization of his opposition, Beecher went on to describe both the complex religious scene and the rapid change in the political situation:

But throwing [Governor John] Treadwell over in 1811 broke the charm and divided the [Federalist] party; persons of third-rate ability, on our side, who wanted to be somebody, deserted; all the infidels of the state had long been leading on that side; the minor sects had swollen, and complained of having to get a certificate to pay their tax where they liked; our efforts to enforce reformation of morals by law made us unpopular; they attacked the clergy unceasingly, and myself in particular . . . with all sorts of misrepresentation, ridicule, and abuse; and finally, the Episcopalians, who had always been stanch Federalists, were disappointed of an appropriation for the Bishop's Fund, which they asked for, and went over to the Democrats. [Ibid., 251–252]

This combination of forces prevailed in 1818 to bring about disestablishment and the end of the complicated system of state support for various churches. Beecher was at first profoundly depressed, but soon changed his mind as to the implications of this radical act:

For several days I suffered what no tongue can tell *for the best thing that ever happened to the State of Connecticut.* It cut the churches loose from dependence on state support. It threw them wholly on their own resources and on God.

They say ministers have lost their influence; the fact is, they have gained. By voluntary efforts, societies, missions, and revivals, they exert a deeper influence than ever they could by queues, and shoe-buckles, and cocked hats, and gold-headed canes. [Ibid., 252]

New Hampshire yielded in 1819; Massachusetts held on till 1833, after a bitter court fight granted the new, liberal Unitarian party control over most of the church property that conservative Congregationalists had claimed. This "Dedham decision" of 1820 established the principle that all of the members of a geographical parish, rather than just the full members of the church proper, had legal control over the property. When the conservative faction realized that they had become the victims of their own system, they rapidly abandoned the principle, and eventually saw Massachusetts relinquish its dubious status as the last hold-out against disestablishment.

One result of this slow but steady process was the addition of two new words to the American religious vocabulary: *voluntaryism* and *denominationalism.* All organized religious life from now on had to be conducted on a voluntary basis. Informal social pressure might still exist, but no official governmental action could either support or hinder particular groups. No one church enjoyed any privileged status in the new nation or its constituent states; all, rather, stood equally on their own as *denominations,* sharing a common Christian heritage; differing from one another through particular emphases and practices *denominated* by their names; and alternately cooperating or competing as circumstances dictated. The burden was now on the churches to attract and retain members, and with them their support in energy, time, and money. As Lyman Beecher was ultimately constrained to observe, this turned out to be the best thing that ever happened—not only to the state of Connecticut, but to American Christianity itself.

The main engine of voluntaryism had already been set in place by the Great

Awakening: revivalism. Revivals became a staple of religious life for a broad cross-section of American Protestants, and after the Awakening of the 1740s manifested themselves in various, more restricted forms such as Whitefield's later tours, the "New Light Stir" in northern New England, and assorted outbursts throughout the Southern colonies. The Revolution diverted attention from religious life in the narrow sense, but itself took on the character of a revival for many of its clerical interpreters and well-wishers. After independence, the familiar postwar phenomenon of a brief decline in religious activity set in while Americans got their bearings and in many cases pulled up stakes and headed west or south.

Although formal church membership was low, Americans were too steeped in various traditions of piety to allow purely secular enthusiasms to prevail for long. By the 1790s, pressure was building up for a revival of religion both in New England and the southern frontier. What happened in both these regions, and subsequently in upstate New York and other parts of what was then the "West," has collectively been called the "Second Great Awakening." (Some scholars have identified at least seven such "awakenings" in American history, although only the first two are usually recognized.) The three major phases of this Second Awakening were so separated in space, time, and character that their unity is problematic. However, there is no doubt that the early decades of the nineteenth century were a period of extraordinary religious ferment, notable as much for its disparity as its intensity.

The first phase of this Awakening arose in New England, with its epicenter in Connecticut. The Congregationalist clergy in this most traditional of the sometime Puritan commonwealths was, as Beecher had described it, firmly committed to the established ways and allied with the most conservative political faction, the Federalists. Theologically, its most venturesome members were committed to the "New Divinity" developed by Jonathan Edwards and his followers: Joseph Bellamy, Nathanael Emmons, Samuel Hopkins, and Jonathan Edwards, Jr. These men attempted to continue the older Calvinist tradition while at the same time reconciling it with a New Light defense of the Awakening's revivals. Their thought is too diverse and highly technical to be summarized easily. Among their principal concerns were a stress on the moral character of God's government of the world, and a backing away from the doctrine of original sin toward an emphasis on the active role of individuals who actually do the sinning. Although these men regarded themselves as rigorous Calvinists, their thought was clearly pointing in a new direction.

The Second Awakening in Connecticut took place almost exclusively in its Congregational churches and at Yale College. Its early agents were the established clergy, most notably the parish minister Asahel Nettleton (1783–1844) and Timothy Dwight (1752–1817), the energetic president of Yale. Around 1797, they turned their energies to the task of conversion, and the results were highly gratifying. Dwight's preaching, which brought the revival to Yale in 1801, inspired a generation of students such as Lyman Beecher and his ally Nathaniel William Taylor. These two and a number of their contemporaries would together institutionalize the revival as a staple of religious life in New England and its extending sphere of influence for a generation. This Awakening stood firmly in the tradition of Jonathan Edwards rather than that of Tennent and Davenport. It was decorous, restrained, engineered by the established clergy, and very much under their control.

The same cannot be said of the "Great Revival" of what was then the Southwest, which is often regarded as the Awakening's second phase. After independence, sturdy Scotch-Irish pioneers were crossing the Cumberland Gap and spreading out into the new expanses of Tennessee, Kentucky, and southern Ohio. The ancestral Presbyterianism that they brought with them was not readily transplanted into a region where learned sermons and traditional polity made little sense. It was in this context that such men as James McGready, a Presbyterian from North Carolina who arrived in Logan County, Kentucky, in 1796, began to labor for a revival of the religious excitement that he and others had long desired.

Assisted by some Methodist friends from Carolina, McGready launched a new wave of revivals first at Red River and then at Gasper River, Kentucky, in 1800. These were followed by the even more dramatic outburst the following year at Cane Ridge, northeast of Lexington. Cane Ridge is still remembered as the greatest of the "Camp Meeting revivals"—a new form of indigenous frontier religious life. Here Presbyterians Barton W. Stone and Robert Finley were joined by Methodist and Baptist preachers in a revival that attracted tens of thousands of isolated, sensation-starved frontier people. These new immigrants were rapidly filling up the area, but found little organized social or religious life to relieve the dangers and privations they encountered daily.

The Cane Ridge Revival lasted a full week, and was by all accounts a spectacular success in terms of sheer numbers and enthusiasm. More took place at Cane Ridge, though, than its promoters had anticipated. In the midst of the excitement, many of the participants fell into neuromuscular seizures that were soon known as "exercises." These included "barking," "jerking," "falling," "dancing," "laughing," and other symptoms that might now be regarded as hysterical, but which were interpreted at the time as potent evidences of the power of the Spirit. On the other hand, the revival provided a chance to engage in more secular recreations, and skeptics observed that more souls were conceived than saved during the proceedings.

The camp meeting rapidly became a fixture of frontier life. At first it manifested itself in the semispontaneous, enthusiastic manner of Cane Ridge; later, it took on a more routinized form devised by the organizationally minded Methodists, who appropriated it as their own. Here was a form of religion generated by and uniquely expressive of the needs of the frontier. It was eagerly embraced by the popular denominations, such as Baptists and Methodists, who had a no-holds-barred approach to the challenge of evangelization. On the other hand, the active participation of Presbyterians was strong medicine for their East Coast counterparts who believed that traditional, decorous forms of worship and polity were divinely sanctioned.

Unstated but important themes of the Awakening in all its phases were community and authority. The Connecticut phase built on a society with a venerable history, but one in which authority had been called into question by the upheaval of the Revolution. Timothy Dwight and company thus carried on a movement of social as well as religious revitalization, together with a reassertion of establishment influence. On the Kentucky frontier, there was nothing to reestablish; community had to be built from the ground up, and the initial experience of community was chaotic and ecstatic. Authority was similarly non-existent, and the remote claims of eastern Presbyterians were hardly compelling. This early phase lasted only a few years, but while it did last contrasted dramatically with the sober rituals of the "land of steady habits."

The third major phase of the Second Great Awakening fell somewhere in between these extremes. Just as Virginians and Carolinians were pouring into the Southwest, so were countless Yankees from the rocky, unproductive farm-lands of New England following the path of the Erie Canal west across upstate New York from Albany to Buffalo. This "Yankee Exodus" continued west-ward, leaving a heritage of New England-like towns across northern Ohio and southern Michigan; skipping Indiana, which was settled by Southerners mov-ing northward; continuing across parts of Illinois, Wisconsin, Minnesota, and Iowa; and ultimately planting settlements in the Pacific Northwest and north-ern California. This demographic movement can be traced by looking at the spread of Congregational churches, which were usually built in the Greek Revival and "carpenter Gothic" styles popular at the time.

Upstate New York in the decades between independence and the Civil War soon became known as the "Burned Over District" for the intensity and vari-ety of the religious life that it generated. It was here that the Shakers created their distinctive communities, that John Humphrey Noyes and his followers sought perfection, and that Joseph Smith claimed to have encountered the angel Moroni, who made known to him a set of mysterious golden plates containing a new revelation. The followers of these new spiritual directions came from a wide variety of social and educational strata, but had in common a long familial nurture in New England piety. In this bustling environment they were free to seek new kinds of salvations as well as temporal fortunes. Lurking in the background, though, was the ancestral Puritanism that Charles Grandison Finney (1792–1875) set out to revive.

If there is any truth to Emerson's notion that each age generates its own characteristic "representative men," then Finney was certainly one of Emer-son's own era. Born in Connecticut, he was raised in upstate New York, and became first a schoolteacher and then a lawyer. After becoming converted, he abruptly forsook his law practice to take up "a retainer from the Lord Jesus Christ to plead his cause." Although lacking in formal theological education and a bit vague on certain doctrinal matters, Finney managed to inveigle a local presbytery to ordain him, and began a new life as a preacher.

Although sponsored by the Presbyterians, Finney's course was much too independent to be restricted by any denomination. He preached wherever he could, focusing on the Burned Over District he already knew well. Finney soon attracted attention through his employment of "New Measures Revival-ism," which was largely of his own devising. One of these new measures that raised many eyebrows was the "anxious bench," a seat placed near the revival-ist on which those who appeared to be on the brink of conversion could be placed and worked on intensively. Pressure for conversion was intensified by another measure, the "protracted meeting," which stretched on for hours at a time and often was continued on succeeding days. Women openly testifying at meetings and Finney's praying by name for his antagonists were still other innovations that were less than universally welcomed.

Among those who conspicuously withheld their approval for the new measures was Lyman Beecher, who confronted Finney at a dramatic meeting called at New Lebanon, New York, in July of 1827. Beecher at the time was serving a church in Boston, where he gained fame as a revivalist and vocal antagonist of both Unitarians and Catholics. Although Beecher vowed to fight Finney every step of the way east, Finney refused to compromise, and went on to conduct triumphal evangelistic tours in Boston and New York. What was really happening here was an example of what Sigmund Freud has called "the narcissism of minor differences." Beecher and Finney were so similar in approach to the question of evangelization that the flare-up between them was more an indication of closeness than distance. Beecher, that die-hard defender of establishment in Connecticut, would simply not yield the authority of the East to the upstart from the West. Ironically, Beecher was shortly thereafter called to be president of the new Lane Seminary in Cincinnati. He soon found himself in hot water, charged with heresy and hypocrisy by a local minister who found Beecher's views far too radical. Although Beecher was acquitted, the proceedings helped set in motion the split between Old and New School Presbyterians that took place in 1838, in part over revivalism.

Neither Finney nor Beecher was preaching primarily to the utterly unchurched, but rather seeking to revive religion and community among those who had left them behind. Finney went on to a career as professor of theology and later president of Oberlin College, located in the Western Reserve lands of Connecticut in northeastern Ohio. In addition to his *Memoirs* of 1876, he produced two notable works. One, a systematic theology, developed the ideas of holiness and perfection that he had absorbed from the Methodist tradition. The other, which is still kept in print by evangelical publishing houses, was far better known: the *Lectures on Revivals of Religion* of 1835. These *Lectures*, which were exactly that in their original form, constituted a how-to-do-it manual for would-be revivalists. In careful detail, Finney explained just how to go about organizing, promoting, and carrying out a revival campaign guaranteed to win souls. Finney was nothing if not practical, and was hardly concerned with holding onto trade secrets.

In his first lecture, Finney made it clear that a major theological shift had taken place from the time of the first Great Awakening. Jonathan Edwards had maintained that revivals were the work of God, and that preachers such as himself were simply God's instruments. Not so for Finney:

> *Religion is the work of man.* It is something for man to do. . . . A REVIVAL OF RELIGION IS NOT A MIRACLE. A miracle has been generally defined to be, a Divine interference, setting aside or suspending the laws of nature. All the laws of matter and mind remain in force. They are neither suspended nor set aside in a revival. . . . [A revival] is a purely philosophical result of the right use of the constituted means. [John Harvard Library ed., 9, 12, 13]

It is clear from Finney's words that the Calvinism of Edwards now lay far in the past. The emphasis here is clearly not on depravity and the bondage of the will by original sin; rather, it is on human ability to do what God wants. This is not to say that humans act autonomously; rather, it is to assert the presence of a God-given ability to exercise one's faculties to do the right by choice. Similarly, Lyman Beecher depended heavily for his theology on his old Yale comrade, Nathaniel William Taylor (1786–1858). "Taylorism," as his thought came to be known, advanced some of the directions taken by the "New Divinity" into a theological stance compatible with the activist spirit of revivalism. Instead of God's sovereignty, Taylor stressed the theme of God's "moral government" of the universe. Instead of stressing total depravity, Taylor pictured humanity as theoretically free to do good. In practical terms, all would sin and therefore need redemption; however, there was no metaphysical necessity lying behind this irresistible tendency. Although Taylor claimed to be faithful to the Calvinist tradition, he and Finney both were working out an essentially Arminian position consistent with the revivalist spirit. "Taylorism" also became known as the "New Haven theology," after Taylor's position as minister at that city's First Church and his professorship at Yale Divinity School.

Although the Second Great Awakening began in a revival of piety in New England, it is clear enough that its main arena was the expanding frontier. Revivalists were the shock troops of this initiative, and the revivals helped to secure beachheads—much like the role the religious orders played in the "spiritual conquest" of New Spain. The task for both old and new evangelical denominations then became the consolidation of the gains won by the vanguard of preachers. In this effort, Presbyterians and Congregationalists took a major step toward ecumenical cooperation through their "Plan of Union" of 1801. Engineered by Jonathan Edwards, Jr., this plan provided that no church of one denomination should be established within five miles of one of the other, that ministers of either denomination could be called by any of these churches, and various other stipulations for interdenominational cooperation. The Presbyterians were the major beneficiaries of the plan, since they were closer to the frontier and better able to mobilize their resources. The plan finally was abrogated in 1837, as one of the issues that precipitated the schism between Old and New School Presbyterians.

For the Methodists and Baptists, who had less of an established base from which to work, the task of evangelization and the establishment of order was more compressed. The exemplary Baptist figure was the "farmer-preacher," who felt a call to the ministry and preached to whomever he could gather to hear him on Sundays. Since Baptists traditionally resisted centralization, the movement spread primarily from these grassroots foundations. Methodists, however, loved organization, and "circuit riders" were their answer to the same set of challenges. Circuit riders were young men endowed with little education but enormous energy and dedication. Equipped with a horse and saddlebags filled with Bibles, hymnals, and the Methodist *Discipline,* they followed regularly assigned routes around the frontier, stopping to preach wherever an audience of a few could be found among scattered cabins, farmsteads, and hamlets. When possible, a small "class" of lay people would be gathered, who could continue the spiritual life on their own until the rider came round again. As settlement increased, these classes often grew into churches, and the circuit riders who had not yet died young from exhaustion yielded to a settled clergy. Peter Cartwright (1785–1872), one of the greatest of the breed, lamented in his classic *Autobiography* of 1856 the passing of this rugged frontier piety into what to him seemed a namby-pamby gentility.

The Second Great Awakening was clearly not a unified sequence of events as was the First, in which a direct cause-and-effect relationship could easily be traced. The discreet preaching of Nettleton and the barking and jerking of Cane Ridge were worlds apart, based on a common premise but executed in drastically different contexts. None of the loosely connected components of the Second Awakening can be simply described as revivals of religion, though. Each was firmly rooted in deeply felt social needs, reflected those needs, and helped bring about a transformation of community in a profound sense. Beecher and Finney, who emerged as giants in the Awakening's later phases, helped provide a continuity between East and West, Calvinism and Arminianism, civilization and frontier, old and new. As such, they were harbingers of a new social order, which started with revival, went on to reform, and ultimately shaped a culture that would endure for decades.

CHAPTER 24

Moral Reform, Antislavery, and Civil War

During the first Great Awakening, Edwards, Whitefield, and their fellow revivalists focused their efforts on the saving of individual souls. The revival influenced and was affected by society, but few were concerned with or even much aware of this. One of those long-range social effects was an undermining of the "parochial principle"—the notion that religion, geography, and politics shape and reinforce one another, and that one's religious allegiance is a function of where and under what authority one lives. Akin to this was the idea of freedom of religious choice, which ultimately had vast implications for the role of religion in the New Republic: America was the first country where one could elect a "community of memory"—in effect, where one could choose a past in the form of affiliation with a religious community. By the time of the Second Great Awakening, church membership was well on its way to becoming a voluntary matter. Revivals were needed again, to stir up the enthusiasm that would make voluntarily supported churches work.

During the colonial era, the institutions of society were in theory maintained through an alliance of church and state. The family, the church, and town or parish were the primary units of social organization, and it was through some combination of their work that children were educated, criminals punished, and the poor and disabled cared for. Relative at least to postcolonial times, society had an organic character, and everyone within its purview was simultaneously supported and supervised through its network of resources. The benefits of this arrangement were a psychological security of knowing one's place, and having someone to rely on in bad times. The negative side was an insistence on conformity and subordination; deviance, especially in the form of challenging society's norms, simply could not be tolerated.

With the disestablishment of the churches and the growing mobility and pluralism of the broader society, whatever reality had existed in this "ideal type" of an "organic society" came into serious jeopardy. The state churches were gone or rapidly going; people were no longer forced to dance to their tune, and became inclined to turn to the secular government for whatever needs they could not supply for themselves. For the likes of Lyman Beecher, this situation might have benefits; however, those benefits would not simply fall into American Protestant laps, but had to be actively cultivated if they were going to come about. The obvious conclusion was that revivalism simply as a means for soul-winning was necessary but not sufficient. To bring about a "Christian America"—Christian in practice, if not by statute—revivals had to be hitched to a new idea: reform.

Reform became the byword of early nineteenth-century America. Its roots lay in almost all of the major traditions of the colonial era. Quakers derived from their notion of the "inner light" the doctrine of the radical equality of all of humanity, which meant for them the promotion of peace, the active participation of women in society, the abolition of slavery, and humane treatment of the imprisoned and other unfortunate classes. Although Puritanism was never quite utopian, Winthrop's vision of the "city set upon a hill" had powerful implications for a vision of a society ordered according to God's wishes. The Enlightenment, which shaped the thought of the "Founding Fathers," took as one of its premises the notion that human progress was inevitable and illimitable if reason were the basis for social organization. Finally, John Wesley's Arminianism and his teaching that "entire sanctification" was within human reach provided yet another impetus to the broader idea that society could and should be changed for the better. For many evangelicals of the day, God's millennial kingdom emerged as an ultimate, achievable goal.

The Second Great Awakening was a high tide of reform as well as revival—the two simply would not be separated. Not only evangelicals took on the reform mantle—the activities of Unitarians, Quakers, and various utopians were all significant parts of the "Lively Experiment" of "Freedom's Ferment," and are discussed elsewhere. (Conversely, however, not all evangelicals, including many Lutherans and Old School Presbyterians, were especially keen on tinkering with existent social arrangements.) But just as the Awakening itself was complex and even contradictory in its various phases, so was reform.

The New England revivals that began in the 1790s and continued on for many years were rooted firmly in an established social and religious order. The defenders of this order felt a pressing need to reestablish its legitimacy against threats from Jeffersonian democracy and the perceived forces of "infidelity." In addition to rekindling individual religious enthusiasm through the revivals of Dwight and Nettleton, Lyman Beecher especially saw the need for a more general program of evangelical outreach to keep New England and the whole new nation from falling into the coils of sin and disorder. Beecher rapidly became involved in a whole array of reform endeavors that were springing up around him. Duelling, which had taken the life of Alexander Hamilton, was one evil against which he took up the (figurative) sword. Soon came campaigns against excessive drinking, the profanation of the Sabbath, and other signs that the new republic stood on the brink of moral chaos unless rescued by evangelical vigilance.

The result of this organized vigilance was a whole network of independent but interrelated societies that soon became known as "the Benevolent Empire." The societies usually were organized first at the local and state levels; by the 1820s, these had multiplied sufficiently that they began to coalesce into national organizations. Although most of their members were Congregationalists and Presbyterians, who were also collaborating in the Plan of Union, the societies themselves were interdenominational, and a fair number of Methodists and other evangelicals also became involved. Unlike the colonial period, in which the clergy and civil leadership were expected to take primary responsibility for religion and order, these societies were often led by laymen, though clergy such as Beecher were active participants. Also, as Beecher's career illustrates so well, many of the same men were active in a variety of organizations, thus creating an informal system of "interlocking directorates" binding the work of the "Empire" together. Crucial to the success of these societies was the lavish support of wealthy evangelical businessmen such as the brothers Arthur and Lewis Tappan. Finally, there was throughout this era a continual interaction between British and American evangelicals. Frequently, as in the beginnings of the Sunday School movement and the emancipation of slaves in the British West Indies, events in the parent country had major reverberations across the Atlantic.

As Robert Kelley has pointed out, the reform impulse also correlated significantly with the fortunes of the Whig party, which in turn was strongly related to regional, ethnic, and religious factors. As he observed in *The Cultural Pattern in American Politics*, "Wherever Yankee Whigs went in their westward migration, they carried with them a righteous and confident urge to use the secular government to create a morally unified society" (p. 166). From southern New England especially this cultural impulse spread along the paths of the "Yankee Exodus" across upstate New York, northern Pennsylvania and Ohio, southern Michigan, and on westward, and was conspicuous by its absence in such areas as the "Egypt" region of southern Illinois settled primarily by Southerners. Democrats, who generally opposed interference by the federal government in matters of religion and morality, found much of their support among outgroups who resented the pretensions to hegemony by the upwardly mobile, evangelical Protestants of English background who formed the core of

"Whiggery." Therefore, Irish and French Catholics, German Lutherans and Reformed, urban free-thinking intellectuals and—until the advent of large numbers of Irish Catholics altered the demographic balance—Scotch-Irish Presbyterians rallied in large numbers behind the banners of Jacksonianism. Similarly, in the South, slave-holders usually resented moralistic Yankee interference and supported the dominant Democratic party, while Whigs such as Kentucky's Henry Clay were strong in upland regions where slavery was of less economic importance.

The reform societies that constituted the Empire had a variety of intersecting and overlapping goals. One was the fostering of true religion, the basis of all genuine reform. This was the work of the American Bible Society (1816), which grew out of a network of state societies founded a few years earlier. The purpose was quite simply the printing and distribution of Bibles, especially among the unchurched, so that people could encounter the divine word directly. Closely related were the tract societies, which similarly merged into the American Tract Society in 1825. Tracts were brief pamphlets that presented an argument or appeal for religious truths or reform causes, such as temperance. Similarly, the American Sunday School Union (1824) built on the work of an earlier British prototype, which directed its efforts mainly toward fostering literacy among poor children. In America, the emphasis soon shifted toward direct evangelization, of both the unchurched and, eventually, the children of church-goers. One estimate has it that by 1836 the latter two organizations had distributed some seventy-three million pages of print.

The missionary impulse was another vital part of the Awakening. This was vividly exemplified in the "Haystack Prayer Meeting" of 1806, when a group of Williams College students was overtaken by a commitment to foreign missions while taking refuge from an outburst of rain. The American Board of Commissioners for Foreign Missions (1810), the American Home Mission Society (1826), and the General Convention of the Baptist Denomination in the United States of America for Foreign Missions (1814) represented some of the aspects of this movement, which sought the conversion of infidels at home and abroad. The Burma mission conducted under Baptist auspices by Adoniram Judson (1788–1850) and his succession of three wives was the inspiration for a flood of edifying literature, in which these intrepid souls were presented as Protestant saints. Despite the hardships endured by these and a myriad of other missionaries, especially in the Pacific, the Middle East, and Asia, American evangelicals were infused with enormous enthusiasm for the prospects of rapidly evangelizing the entire world—another harbinger that the millennium might be at hand.

The further objects of benevolence were legion. Societies arose to minister to sailors, rescue prostitutes, and reclaim drunkards. However vast and complex the Empire might become, though, some underlying premises always remained clear. Since the United States could and would not support religion directly, it was incumbent upon the evangelical churches to carry on their work though voluntary effort. This included both the conversion of individuals and the reform of institutions. Lobbying the government was not out of the question, as evidenced in the campaign of the General Union for Promoting the Observance of the Christian Sabbath to end Sunday mail delivery and other profanations of the Lord's day. The net result of this concentrated, coordinated campaign was to be the eventual achievement of a Christian America, where evangelicalism had won the day not so much by legal coercion as through moral suasion. When this had been achieved, the millennium might well have been ushered in—in part through human effort.

Although far more optimistic about human possibilities than their colonial predecessors, the promoters of the Benevolent Empire remained conservative when compared with their brethren further west. Alike as Finney and Beecher may have been in the general shape of their careers, there was still a significant difference in the thrust of their ideas and actions. Although Beecher had come closer and closer to an Arminian position, Finney outdid him in espousing perfectionism. No matter how aggressive in their posture toward reforming society in their own image, New Englanders such as Beecher generally retained a Puritan caution in their expectations as to how far society could, or should, be fundamentally altered.

Whether interpreted by Beecher or Finney, though, the reform impulse up until the mid-1830s was hardly intended to bring about any fundamental realignments in American society. The moral reforms advocated by the Benevolent Empire, such as temperance and Sabbatarianism, were clearly not attempts to bring about something new but rather to adapt something old to a very new context. That their advocates thought a vigorous campaign necessary reflected the rapidly changing social structure of Jacksonian America, in which one had to run faster than ever simply to stay in the same place.

Paul E. Johnson, in his study of the social background of Finney's revivals in Rochester, New York, in 1831 (*A Shopkeeper's Millennium*), concluded that the city in which these revivals had such an extraordinary effect—especially among the merchant classes—was in the midst of a profound transformation. Previously, employers had followed the colonial pattern of taking in many of their employees as boarders, sharing much of their everyday life with them— including a frequent tipple or two—and generally being in a position to supervise their behavior and bring them gently back into line if they deviated too much from informal societal norms. In the 1820s, however, employers and workers rapidly began to segregate themselves into separate communities, so that such "social control" was no longer possible or desired. The revivals had the incidental but important side effect of reuniting a merchant class that had become badly divided over religious and political issues, and creating a new cultural ethos in which conversion, followed by voluntary temperance and self-discipline, characterized management and the "right sort" of labor alike. Virtuous merchants now hired only temperance men for their help. Max Weber, who had postulated an "elective affinity" between the "Protestant ethic" and the "spirit of capitalism" in the Puritan era, would doubtless have felt vindicated by Johnson's findings.

That not all reformers were so committed to the interests of classes already entrusted with wealth and power is illustrated vividly in the unfolding drama over the "peculiar institution" of slavery, which exemplifies the stakes for which the game of reform could be played. Quakers—never, at least in theory, respecters of persons and status—were the earliest activists in the crusade against slavery. Anthony Benezet and John Woolman led the way in the eighteenth century among Friends in ending their own involvements in that sordid business. A considerable percentage of the membership of the earliest antislavery societies, not surprisingly, were Friends. (It is also worth noting that Friends tended to be Whigs in their political sympathies as the nineteenth century unfolded, indicating a sympathy with the mercantile and moral values of their evangelical contemporaries.)

The contribution of the Benevolent Empire to the movement took the form of the American Colonization Society (1816), which attempted to raise funds to purchase freedom for slaves and return them to Africa, where they established the Christian state of Liberia. Whatever the good wishes of the sponsors, who included Lyman Beecher, this was clearly a campaign not so much against slavery itself but rather of "Negro removal." Its premises were, implicitly, at best patronizing and at worst racist. Its success was limited. Ironically, the descendants of the original Liberian black colonists coalesced into an oppressive elite that was violently overthrown in the later twentieth century.

Actually, slavery appeared to many even in the South to be doomed to fall of its own economic weight, and antislavery sentiment was strong throughout the region in the early decades of the nineteenth century. It was a series of developments, including the invention of the cotton gin by the Connecticut Yankee Eli Whitney, that reversed directions and gave the institution a renewed vitality by about 1830. It was at this same time that a new spirit began to arise among slavery's opponents. William Lloyd Garrison (1805–1879), who had gained experience working with the Quaker abolitionist editor Benjamin Lundy, rapidly emerged as the irrepressible spokesman for a new idea: immediatism. In his *Liberator*, which he began to publish in Boston in 1831, Garrison took an uncompromising position not only on the evil of slavery but also on the necessity of abolishing it immediately. If the Constitution sanctioned slavery, then the Constitution was evil and must be discarded: It was, according to Garrison, "a covenant with death and an agreement with Hell."

Garrison thus served as the "point man" for radical abolitionism, and combined his concern with ending slavery with other "ultra-ist" causes. Chief among these were pacifism and the rights of women, concerns that up till then had been maintained steadily only by the Quakers. The Garrisonians first broke with the American Peace Society, which they did not consider radical enough in its acceptance of a government that was ultimately based on force. A more important division came in 1840 when the American Anti-Slavery Society split on the issue of whether it was proper for women to speak publicly to audiences not wholly composed of other women (as in the various Female Anti-Slavery Societies). The more conservatively inclined, including most of the clergy, withdrew from the Garrisonian-dominated group to form the American and Foreign Anti-Slavery Society, in which the role of women was more restricted. Whatever the implications for abolitionism, these events gave a clear boost to organized feminism. Antislavery and other reform societies presented some of the first occasions to women in the nineteenth century for acquiring political and organizational skills. These skill soon found expression at the historic Women's Rights Convention held in Seneca Falls, New York, in 1848 under the leadership of Elizabeth Cady Stanton and Lucretia Mott. (Mott was a Quaker who helped Stanton abandon her childhood Presbyterianism. Stanton did this so decisively that she later became friends with the agnostic Robert Ingersoll, and wrote in 1895 *The Woman's Bible*, a harsh critique of the portrayal of women in Scripture.)

The role of Garrison and his radical followers in helping or hindering abolition has been much debated; whatever the verdict, they certainly helped bring the issue to the forefront of public attention through their relentless activity. Another aspect of the "perfectionist" wing of the movement was focused in Ohio and led by Theodore Dwight Weld (1803–1895). Weld had been converted by Finney, and after a career as a revivalist and temperance advocate enrolled in 1832 at Lane Seminary in Cincinnati for more formal ministerial training. Weld rapidly converted most of the student body to abolitionist principles, and together they began to work with the Cincinnati black community. While Lane's president, Lyman Beecher, was back east raising funds, the Lane trustees ordered Weld and his followers to end their activism, which they refused to do.

As a consequence, the "Lane rebels" picked up stakes and left for Oberlin, where Finney was teaching theology and the sturdy abolitionist president Asà Mahan welcomed them. (Oberlin, founded in 1833 by New England Congregationalists, was known as a center for social radicalism, and was soon to become the first coeducational and interracial American college.) Weld went on to a career as an organizer and publicist for the antislavery cause, and his followers—the "Band of Seventy"—tirelessly and at great personal risk set about organizing antislavery societies in New York, Ohio, and their environs. The pressure that these groups were able to bring to bear on the federal government played a major role in turning around northern opinion on slavery.

No one factor was decisive in bringing about this shift. Northern opinion was swayed by moral revulsion against slavery, fear for white civil rights after the Dred Scott decision, dislike of the South, and attachment to the Union. Most Northerners probably shared to some degree the Southern argument that blacks were an inferior people needing paternal protection. However, the question of whether that protection was being provided received a resoundingly negative answer in Harriet Beecher Stowe's epoch-making *Uncle Tom's Cabin*, published as a book in 1852 after previously appearing in serial form. Stowe had lived in Cincinnati for many years with her father, Lyman Beecher, and had the opportunity to gather many first-hand impressions of slavery in bordering Kentucky. Stowe's heroes were the weak, the oppressed, and the peaceable: women, children, blacks, and Quakers. Notable among these heroes was Little Eva, a white slave-owner's child who dies in a wash of sentimentality. Most memorable, though, was Uncle Tom himself, whose death at the hands of the Vermont-born overseer Simon Legree transfigures him into a black Christ. Stowe ends the novel on an apocalyptic note:

> This is an age of the world when nations are trembling and convulsed. A mighty influence is abroad, surging and heaving the world, as with an earthquake. And

is America safe? Every nation that carries in its bosom great and unredressed injustice has in it the elements of this last convulsion.

Christians! every time that you pray that the kingdom of Christ may come, can you forget that prophecy associates in dread fellowship, the *day of vengeance* with the year of his redeemed? A day of grace is yet held out to us. Both North and South have been guilty before God; and the *Christian Church* has a heavy account to answer. Not by combining together, to protect injustice and cruelty, and making a common capital of sin, is this Union to be saved,—but by repentance, justice and mercy; for, not surer is the eternal law by which the millstone sinks in the ocean, than that stronger law by which injustice and cruelty shall bring on nations the wrath of Almighty God! [Signet Classic ed., 476–77]

The slavery issue took its toll on the organized Christianity that Stowe thus indicted. Biblical defenses of slavery, including God's curse on Noah's son Ham as the origin of the black race, began to be propounded by Southern divines and soon became common ideological currency in a region where religion was as ensconced as the "peculiar institution." Among the "liturgical churches"—Roman Catholic, Episcopalian, and Lutheran—antislavery sentiment was for varying reasons limited or regional, and no lasting schisms occurred. Congregationalists and Unitarians were scarce in the South, and so were barely affected organizationally. It was the three great national evangelical denominations—Baptist, Methodist, and Presbyterian—that were rent asunder by the growing debates. The Baptists were traditionally decentralized, so that the formation of the Southern Baptist Convention in 1845 created little turmoil. North and South went their own ways, and in the twentieth century grew so far apart that no reunion seems even remotely possible. Early Methodism had been steeped in John Wesley's antislavery teachings, and slave-holding was forbidden among early American Methodists. As the movement grew popular, though, it began to make its peace with the dominant mores of the South, so that slave-holding bishops began to appear by the 1830s. It was over this issue that the denomination finally split in 1844—a rift that was healed nearly a century later.

The situation among the Presbyterians was the most complicated. The trail of Lyman Beecher and other "liberals" in the 1830s was a sign that trouble was at hand, although the slavery issue was not yet a major factor. At stake was tradition versus innovation, and Beecher, for all his timidity on some questions, was clearly on the latter side in the denominational context. "Old School" Presbyterians gained the upper hand over the "New School" in the General Assembly of 1837, and two churches thus came into being. As slavery emerged as a decisive issue, both of these "Schools" were to split yet again. The New School, which had a firmer base in the North, divided in 1857 after taking a series of increasingly stronger antislavery positions. The Old School, always more conservative and Southern-based, held together until the war erupted in 1861. After the war, the various factions reformed on sectional lines, creating Northern and Southern Presbyterian churches that lasted until the merger of 1984.

Like most wars, the Civil War was viewed by many Americans as a religious event—or at least a political and military event with profound religious dimensions. Shortly before the war, a "third great awakening" had taken place in a series of urban revivals, or union prayer meetings, following the panic of 1857. Preachers from many denominations on both sides invoked divine sanction on the struggle. Many clergy, laity, and nuns served as chaplains or nurses, or in other humanitarian roles, such as those provided by the evangelical Christian Commission and the Unitarian-led Sanitary Commission—the predecessor of the Red Cross. It was on a visit to the nation's capital while working for the Sanitary Commission that Julia Ward Howe, a radical Unitarian from Boston, was inspired with an apocalyptic vision most out of keeping with her immediate theological convictions. The "Battle Hymn of the Republic," published in 1862, was immediately set to the tune of "John Brown's Body"—the antislavery martyr of Harper's Ferry—as an anthem of the Union army. Its rich biblical cadences not only stirred the war effort but provided it with a theological interpretation:

> He has sounded forth the trumpet that shall never call retreat;
> He is sifting out the hearts of men before his judgment seat;
> O be swift, my soul, to answer him; be jubilant, my feet!
> Our God is marching on.

Perhaps, in retrospect, the most interesting interpretation of the war's religious meaning came in President Lincoln's brief Second Inaugural Address of 1865. Such addresses have almost invariably contained some reference to God and his providential wishes for America, though usually not of a very imaginative sort. Lincoln himself came from a vaguely Baptist background; later in his career he attended services but maintained no regular church affiliation. Obviously, though, he was deeply steeped in Scripture, and demonstrated a remarkable talent for critical theology: He at one time characterized America as "this, His almost chosen people." Near the end of the war, he publicly offered these startlingly original and complex reflections on the drama in which he himself was a principal:

> Neither party expected for the war the magnitude or the duration which it has already attained. Neither anticipated that the *cause* of the conflict might cease with or even before the conflict itself should cease. Each looked for an easier triumph, and a result less fundamental and astounding. Both read the same Bible and pray to the same God, and each invokes His aid against the other. It may seem strange that any man should dare to ask a just God's assistance in wringing their bread from the sweat of other men's faces, but let us judge not, that we be not judged. The prayers of both could not be answered. That of neither has been answered fully. The Almighty has His own purposes. "Woe unto the world because of offenses; for it must needs be that offenses come, but woe to that man by whom the offense cometh." If we shall suppose that American slavery is one of those offenses which, in the providence of God, must needs come, but which, having continued through His appointed time, He now wills to remove, and that He gives to both North and South this terrible war as the woe due to those by whom the offense came, shall we discern therein any departure from those divine attributes which the believers in a living God always ascribe to

Him? Fondly do we hope, fervently do we pray, that this mighty scourge of war may speedily pass away. Yet, if God wills that it continue until all the wealth piled up by the bondsman's two hundred and fifty years of unrequited toil shall be sunk, and until every drop of blood drawn with the lash shall be paid by another drawn with the sword, as was said three thousand years ago, so still it must be said "the judgments of the Lord are true and righteous altogether."

CHAPTER 25

The Culture of Antebellum Evangelicalism

Revivalism and reform were two major components of a broader set of institutions, practices, literature, ideas, and viewpoints that together can be seen as a *culture*. This culture not only shaped the lives of evangelicals themselves, but became so pervasive in national life that all Americans had to come to terms with it in one way or another. Given the realities of religious pluralism and the need for cooperation, this culture could not be based on a hard core of agreed-upon theological assumptions, since evangelicals themselves had never reached such a consensus. In more diffuse form, though, they worked together from a common set of assumptions toward achieving the goal of creating a "Christian America" in which this culture would reign as normative.

Evangelical theology had two primary sources, Calvinism and Wesleyan Arminianism. Princeton emerged early in the century as a bastion of the former, and would later play a major role in forging the intellectual groundwork for a new movement, Fundamentalism. The rapidly growing Methodist denomination, of course, was the main repository of Wesley's thought. Beecher and Finney exemplify the middle ground toward which the two began to move. The "New Haven Theology," which claimed to continue the Calvinist tradition while in fact pulling out its predestinarian props, was vigorously promoted by Beecher among Congregationalists and Presbyterians. Finney in turn was equally vigorous in developing the implications of the "perfectionism" that arose from Wesley's idea of entire sanctification.

Meanwhile, in Hartford, the Congregationalist preacher Horace Bushnell was moving in yet another direction. Under the influence of the Romantic movement, Bushnell was working to undermine revivalism itself through downplaying the boundaries between the divine and the human and promoting the idea of "Christian nurture." The memory of Jonathan Edwards still commanded great prestige, but those who actively continued in his tradition grew fewer as the century wore on. Eventually, evangelical ranks would find themselves split first by those pulled in the direction of Liberalism, and then by others attracted by the hard line of opposing Fundamentalism.

For much of the century, though, evangelicals of a wide variety of particular theological persuasions—and even moderate Unitarians—agreed on the basic assumptions of the Scottish Common Sense philosophy that had been a major legacy of the Enlightenment. The Common Sense philosophy declared that God had created humans with the ability to perceive reality accurately through the senses; further, he had endowed them with an innate sense that enabled them to make accurate moral judgments. This philosophy placed a great deal of confidence in the human ability not only to know the truth but to do the good, a step decidedly away from the Calvinist notion of total depravity.

The Scottish philosophy became the staple of much of the curriculum at the colleges that were in a seemingly continual process of foundation throughout the century, many under evangelical sponsorship. At Brown, which had been established under Baptist auspices in the aftermath of the first Awakening, Francis Wayland (1796–1865) exemplified the crucial role that this system of ideas played in the curriculum. In his teaching, his preaching, and such popular textbooks as *The Elements of Moral Science* (1835), he helped to develop and propagate a unified view of the world echoed in countless pulpits and classrooms. By early in the century, it had become a standard part of the college curriculum for the president to teach a "capstone" course in moral philosophy for seniors. "Moral philosophy" included a great deal more than what might now be offered under the title of "ethics." It encompassed almost everything that would in the twentieth century be regarded as "social science": economics, political science, sociology, and ethnology. The approach, though, was hardly "scientific" in the modern sense; rather, it was highly prescriptive, and its practitioners attempted to interpret the entirety of human social activity under Common Sense evangelical guidelines. In Wayland's case especially, Protestant ethics were enlisted in the defense of the doctrine of the *laissez-faire* capitalism that another redoubtable Scot, Adam Smith, had introduced into the Anglo-American sphere a few decades earlier.

The college was thus an important part of the comprehensive educational system that was emerging during the antebellum decades under evangelical auspices. This is not to say that secular institutions, such as Jefferson's University of Virginia; bastions of theological liberalism, such as Harvard; Roman Catholic colleges, such as Georgetown, were not also doing well. Evangelicals, as their name implies, had a particular sense of mission in this regard, and colleges blossomed in their wake as they set about to win the West for Christianity. Higher education in Ohio, a major state in the early frontier era, still stands as a microcosm of this process:

- Marietta (Congregationalist, 1797)
- Kenyon (Episcopalian, 1824)
- Denison (Baptist, 1831)
- Oberlin (Congregationalist, 1833)
- Ohio Wesleyan (Methodist, 1841)
- Wittenberg (Lutheran, 1842)

- Baldwin-Wallace (Methodist, 1845)
- Otterbein (United Brethren, 1847)
- Heidelberg (Lutheran, 1850)
- Capital (Lutheran, 1850)
- Hiram (Disciples, 1850)
- Wooster (Presbyterian, 1866)

Miami University (1809), like Indiana University in Bloomington, illustrated a parallel pattern of receiving state support while in fact remaining under Presbyterian tutelage. Women's colleges, or "female seminaries," also flourished during this era, such as the Western College for Women (1853, later absorbed by Miami), and Lake Erie College (1856). Both began as daughter schools of Mt. Holyoke in Massachusetts, which was founded under Congregationalist auspices by Mary Lyon in 1837 as a bastion of evangelical piety. In addition to these three, which have survived in one form or another, many others were established that did not. In other states in which Northern evangelical influence was also strong, especially in the Old Northwest, the same pattern predominated. Southern culture, though also strongly evangelical, went in a different direction on education, which was confined largely to a few elite private colleges and an early system of state universities.

The Reformed tradition, especially in its New England Puritan form, had stressed literacy as an essential prerequisite for the systematic cultivation of piety. All of the laity were expected to be able to encounter Scripture directly, and the ability to read other forms of religious writings was a valuable side benefit. Well into the nineteenth century, a core of religious literature persisted that was supplemented but not superseded by later writings. Central was the King James, or Authorized, version of the Bible (1611), which became an icon of Protestant identity and was even thought to be specially inspired. Perennially popular as well were John Foxe's *Acts and Monuments* (or *Book of Martyrs,* 1554, 1563); John Bunyan's allegory of the individual's spiritual journey, *The Pilgrim's Progress* (1678); Richard Baxter's devotional classic, *The Saints' Everlasting Rest* (1650); and the eighteenth-century hymns of Isaac Watts and Charles Wesley. This Puritan-Pietist devotional tradition was continued in America in such works as Jonathan Edwards's edifying biography of his daughter's missionary fiancé, David Brainerd, whose premature death gave him a posthumous near-saintly stature in Edwards's account of 1749. This latter was widely reprinted, in such formats as the multivolume *Evangelical Home Library* of Anglo-American classics distributed by the American Tract Society. In addition to books, countless periodicals, benevolent society reports, tracts, and other publications made clear that the ability to read was central to active participation in this emergent culture.

Literacy, then, had religious as well as practical uses, and had to be taught systematically. By the nineteenth century, both evangelicals and liberals, such as Massachusetts's Secretary of Education Horace Mann, agreed on its value not only on these grounds, but also as a necessity for an informed electorate in a burgeoning democracy. Universal elementary education thus became a widespread goal, especially in the Northern states. Although this education was to be publicly supported, Protestants of most stripes agreed that the "common schools" could nevertheless serve as a conduit for nondenominational moral training. School boards thus commonly came to resemble local branches of the Benevolent Empire, with prominent evangelical laymen and clergy dominating their activity. Reading in class from the King James version of the Bible was a common practice, and many textbooks were very clear on the superiority of Protestant culture over that of Roman Catholics and non-Christians. Needless to say, Catholics were sufficiently indignant about these assumptions both to erect their own parallel system of parochial schools and also, eventually, to challenge evangelical domination of the common schools in court. A landmark decision was that of the Ohio Supreme Court in 1870 upholding the protest mounted by a coalition of Catholics, Jews, and freethinkers in Cincinnati against such use of the King James Bible. Other cultural forces soon joined with this legal hindrance to deflect public school curricula into more secular directions in the decades to come.

Among the classics of the didactic literature of this era were the series of graded readers edited by the Presbyterian divine and educator William Holmes McGuffey (1800–1873) with the help of his brother Alexander. These *Eclectic Readers* pervaded the Midwest and beyond well into the twentieth century, and sold in aggregate in excess of 122,000,000 copies. In addition to teaching reading, spelling, and pronunciation, the more advanced of these readers served as literary anthologies as well as not-so-subtle tools of moral edification. Although they did contain extracts from the King James Bible, no overt theology was included. Rather, many of the selections were exemplary stories demonstrating how respect for the Sabbath, temperance, punctuality, honesty, and other evangelical virtues were rewarded, often in very material terms. Conversely, vices, especially those of the young, were severely punished by divine intervention or human device. Not all of their contents were so explicitly didactic: Selections from the Unitarians Hawthorne and Longfellow were also included, and many readings reflected a romantic, even sentimental appreciation for rural life and nature. The net impact, though, was clearly moralistic, though scrupulously nondenominational.

In addition to the common school and the liberal arts college, other forms of education arose under evangelical purview during these years. In the colonial period, would-be clergy usually acquired their basic preparation at the collegiate level, then left to read divinity under the tutelage of a parish minister. By the early 1800s, such on-site training began to be displaced by the divinity school or seminary, devised to provide formal postgraduate education for the ministry among those denominations that valued such training—especially Congregationalists, Episcopalians, Presbyterians, and Roman Catholics. Colonial colleges such as Harvard and Yale established such schools respectively in 1811 and 1822. Harvard's liberalism had already spurred the founding of the more orthodox Andover Academy in Massachusetts in 1808. Presbyterians did likewise at Princeton Theological Seminary in 1812. Before too long, Methodists and then Baptists began to abandon their distrust of formal learning. Methodists especially became active in establishing a network of seminaries that would attain particular distinction in the twentieth century, especially in the South. After the Civil War, the proliferation of education beyond the collegiate level helped nurture a more research-oriented approach at some schools. Many of the best of these—Harvard, Yale, Union (New York), and the newly founded University of Chicago—distanced themselves from their earlier affiliations, and took on an interdenominational identity.

Although most evangelicals were content with the cultural fare offered by the public schools at the primary and secondary levels, they nevertheless desired a specifically religious supplement to this general academic and moral training. One answer lay in the Sunday School, which had its origins in British evangelical outreach to the poor in the late eighteenth century. The Sunday School was introduced in America at Philadelphia in 1790. It soon became oriented not so much toward providing the poor with a basic education, as had been the intent in Britain, as with the religious education of the children of the middle classes. In 1824 the American Sunday School Union joined the ranks of the Benevolent Empire. This Union soon produced a vast instructional literature, and a majority of antebellum American libraries began in Sunday Schools. Individual denominations soon founded their own educational bureaus, paralleling the break-off of mission societies and other agencies from interdenominational auspices as the Empire began to founder. After the Civil War, a nationally coordinated interchurch effort, featuring a standardized Uniform Lesson Plan taught across the entire country, gave the movement a new, national, and bureaucratic character on an unprecedented scale.

Central to evangelical culture, then, were literacy, learning, and the network of institutions designed to promote them. Theology was not yet restricted to research scholars at graduate-level institutions, but was intimately enmeshed in the work of college teachers and parish ministers. One important implication of the pervasive Common Sense philosophy was its stress on the availability to all of saving knowledge. Virtually every individual had the God-given faculties to arrive at truth. For most evangelicals, at least those no longer immersed in the raw culture of the frontier, the pursuit of this truth was aided by the network of churches, schools, religious publishing, and other institutions created to foster the quest. Common Sense and common schools went together. They were twin forces of evangelicalism in developing an ethos at once Christian and democratic—one, in short, that was highly appropriate for the citizenry of the new republic, in which church and state had a separate but cordial and cooperative relationship.

In addition to common and Sunday schools, the family home also received a new religious significance in the religious culture of the age. With the social, economic, and geographical changes of the mid-nineteenth century, middle class women found themselves for better or worse cut off from the workplace, and isolated with their children in their suburban homes. Although usually barred from the ranks of the clergy, women had always been staunch supporters of religion, and played any number of active roles ranging from the multidutied minister's wife to missionary, to Sunday-school teacher, to faithful attender at worship. With the advent of widespread middle-class status, a new "cult" of "domesticity" or "true womanhood" began to emerge by the 1830s among American Protestants that provided yet another linkage between women and the religious sphere.

As Colleen McDannel has demonstrated, the middle third of the nineteenth century witnessed a flourishing of the notion that the family home should be regarded as a Christian shrine, with the woman who presided over it a sort of secular priestess. The Gothic cottage, born of the Romantic movement in architecture, became popular among prosperous suburbanites not only for its picturesqueness but also for its associations with Christianity (even if in its medieval incarnation), and crosses sometimes appeared atop gables. (Lyman Beecher's redoubtable daughters, Catharine Beecher and Harriet Beecher Stowe, promoted houses of this sort in their *American Woman's Home* of 1869). Inside the house, samplers, bookmarks, Bibles, and even pincushions could be used to illustrate religious themes, often of the ornate and sentimental sort characteristic of the era. Although the *paterfamilias* would usually preside over family prayer, it was the mother who was primarily responsible for the maintenance and decoration of the home as well as the moral and religious nurture of the children. This sort of domestic piety, popularized in *Godey's Lady's Book* and innumerable other books and periodicals, had a profound influence on American Protestant piety, and manifested itself also in the devotionally oriented Catholic culture that began to spread widely in the century's latter decades.

Another aspect of evangelical culture in which the easy relationship between sacred and secular was evident was that of worship. A widespread consensus emerged during the early nineteenth century that the most appropriate architectural forms for the new nation were revivals of the styles of the ancient Greek and Roman republics. Just as George Washington was identified with Cincinnatus, so should the public buildings—banks, state and national capitols, and the like—be modeled on classical temples, with columns, domes, and other features evocative of democracy in antiquity. Interestingly, the nation's churches were among the most enthusiastic in joining this trend, and countless houses of Christian worship began to arise in the form of pagan temples. Evangelicals of all stripes participated in what was significantly known as an architectural *revival,* as did Jews and Christians of other traditions as well.

The form of worship varied considerably, ranging from the anything-goes spirit of the early camp meetings to the decorous services of New England Congregationalism. Revival preaching, of course, was widely accepted within the evangelical spectrum, and had been domesticated by Finney into a predictable routine. Revivals, however, could only be infrequent if they were to be effective. Worship in most evangelical churches followed a pattern developed in the colonial era. It consisted of prayer, which could best be described as "occasional"—composed for the occasion—rather than spontaneous; preaching, which could become highly dramatic; and singing. Isaac Watts and Charles Wesley had broken down early Puritan resistance to the use of hymns of human composition, as opposed to strictly scriptural psalms supposedly of divine authorship. An American hymnody began to augment British staples by the late eighteenth century. These hymn styles varied in nature according to region and tradition. In the South, for instance, "shape note" or "fasola" singing developed, with notes indicated by easily recognized, distinctive symbols. Finney's revivals drew on a somewhat more sophisticated native school based on the work of the prodigious Lowell Mason, together with Thomas Hastings and William Bradbury. Characteristic of this school was Hastings's music for Toplady's "Rock of Ages," a version of the lyrics of which contain a distinctively perfectionist sentiment:

> Be of sin the double cure,
> Save from wrath and make me pure.

In addition to such explicit reference to the Wesleyan doctrine of "entire sanctification," this version of "Rock of Ages" is also typical of the era's preference for devotional themes: "the water and the blood, from thy wounded side which flowed"; "In my hand no price I bring, Simply to Thy cross I cling." Many of these lyrics were actually composed in eighteenth-century England, and received new music and an enthusiastic reception in evangelical America.

Theology, literature, organizational and educational networks, revivals and more routine worship, church buildings, and hymnody were all important components of this culture, at once evangelical and republican, that was being fashioned during the decades between independence and the Civil War. To conclude this survey, we should note a few distinctive elements of the evangelical world view that prevailed at the time. In terms of place, there is little doubt that America itself occupied a preeminent position in the evangelical imagination. Literal and figurative peace had been made with England, and continual trans-Atlantic interaction reminded Americans of their British spiritual heritage. Nevertheless, since at least the time of Edwards, there was a growing conviction among Americans that it was their own country that was specially chosen by God for great things. It is no accident that one of the most enduring hymns of the "civil religion" was composed in 1832 by a young New England Baptist minister, Samuel F. Smith. "America" or, as it is better known, "My Country, 'tis of Thee," clearly celebrates the *American* landscape in its evocation of "thy rocks and rills, thy woods and templed hills" as God's presumed country.

God's special choice of America leads from space to time. When Jonathan Edwards had speculated that the millennium might well take place in America, he was preparing the conceptual groundwork for a view of time—or, more specifically, of history—that would become pervasive among antebellum Northern American evangelicals. This was the notion of "post-millennialism"—that is, the belief that the thousand-year kingdom described in the book of Revelation would unfold gradually, and be climaxed at the end of the millennium by the second coming of Jesus. The other version of this teaching—"premillennialism"—was a minority position at the time. Premillennialists believed instead that the thousand years of peace and prosperity could not begin until Jesus had made his second appearance. This would be accompanied by wars and cataclysms, and would throw the whole earth into convulsion. This latter position took a dim view of human possibilities in the present historical dispensation. It did enjoy occasional currency—for instance, among the followers of William Miller, who calculated that the Second Coming would take place in 1844. Postmillennialists, on the contrary, saw the United States gradually turning into a wondrous millennial kingdom, in part through concerted evangelical effort.

The ushering in of the thousand years, though, was not to come easily. History was not a smooth flow but a turbulent drama in which the forces of good and evil, of God and the Antichrist, were locked in mortal combat. Although the eventual outcome was sure, the precise course of events leading up to that end was revealed only in its unfolding. Already a tradition had developed among American preachers of interpreting historical events providentially, as part of this unfolding plan. The English Reformation, the coming of Protestantism to the New World, the wars against the French and Indians, and the Revolution had all revealed successively new aspects of the drama, and the Civil War now promised victory over yet another set of foes: slavery and the sinful, decadent slave-holders. As Julia Ward Howe proclaimed in the "Battle Hymn of the Republic," God was powerfully at work in our very midst.

Evil did not exist as an abstract force, but in very this-worldly personifications. The "slaveocracy" was its most current embodiment, and the contemporary literature of what David Brion Davis has called *counter-subversion* depicted with outraged relish the combination of sadistic and sexual gratification the "lords of the lash" derived from their helpless black charges. Although the French alliance during the Revolution temporarily brought about a rapprochement with Catholicism, the Irish immigration that reached a flood tide by the 1840s revived Catholicism as the most ancient and enduring denizen of the evangelical demonology. The subliterature of anti-Catholicism mythologically identified the Catholic Church and its Pope with the "Scarlet Woman" and the "Whore of Babylon" of the Book of Revelation—a representation of the Antichrist. Especially popular were bogus tales of nuns escaped from convents, where they had been held captive and sexually abused by priests. The all-time bestseller of this genre was Maria Monk's *The Awful Disclosures of the Hotel Dieu Nunnery of Montreal* of 1836. Ms. Monk, who had never been a nun, claimed that priests had regularly cohabited with the nuns of this Gothic institution; when children arose from these blasphemous unions, they were immediately baptized and then strangled and buried. Subsequent investigations in America and Canada of these and similar stories yielded no substantiation, though they never lacked a ready audience of eager believers. Maria Monk, whose mother attributed her vivid imagination to a pencil's having been stuck in her head, eventually died in prison after picking the pocket of one of her clients in a brothel.

Such stories continued not only to attract a wide readership but to help shape a climate of opinion and action. Lyman Beecher was a somewhat more respectable actor in this drama. His *Plea for the West* of 1835 was a fundraising effort on behalf of Lane Seminary. Beecher argued for such support on the grounds that Protestant bulwarks were needed in what was then the West to combat the growing Catholic menace. According to this line of argument, Beecher and others maintained that the Pope, through the Jesuit order, was attempting to subvert American democracy and possibly to prepare a future papal headquarters in the Mississippi Valley. To this end, Protestants must raise up a vigilant clergy to prevent the mass conversions that would undermine the Republic. Although Beecher was not directly responsible, his preaching in this vein in Boston helped prepare the climate that resulted in the burning of the Ursuline convent in Charlestown, Massachusetts, in 1834. Anti-Catholic riots later erupted in Philadelphia and New York, in part as a reaction to increasing Irish immigration and economic competition. By 1849 a political party, the Know-Nothings, had formed around an antiimmigrant, anti-Catholic platform. For a few years they scored some remarkable electoral victories, but rapidly faded as the "impending crisis" of the Civil War began to divert popular attention.

Evangelicals thus had a cosmic map: a sense of origin in the English Reformation; a promised land, in which the millennium was actively awaited; a destiny, to help usher in that millennium; and a demonology, which focused alternately on Catholic immigrants and slave-holders. Following the Civil War, the rise of the city would present new challenges, and the antipathy toward the non-Protestant and the foreign-born would if anything grow still stronger. And a familiar but newly potent demon loomed on the horizon—"demon rum."

C. Alternative Protestant Patterns

CHAPTER 26

Liturgical Protestantism: Lutherans and Episcopalians in Changing Worlds

Among the array of denominations that took shape under the terms of the American experiment, Lutherans and Episcopalians occupied an ambiguous position in the developing Protestant spectrum. Both had emerged in the vanguard of the Magisterial Reformation as state churches, so that democracy was hardly part of their formative experience. For Anglicans, the close relationship between the Church of England and the overseas regime against which the colonists—including many Anglicans—successfully revolted was a major factor in their problematic accommodation with the new order. For Lutherans, language—various German and Scandinavian tongues—and culture were more potent barriers to assimilation. For both, moreover, the relationship of their traditional, liturgically formal worship with the pressures of the emergent evangelical norm, which focused on revivalistic preaching, was also a source of considerable contention. The ways in which each tradition attempted to come to terms with these issues provide two interesting case studies in the problems of coming to terms with the American denominational pattern.

The first Lutherans to arrive in the American colonies came from Sweden, and settled in what were originally known as New Netherlands and New Sweden (which respectively corresponded with parts of present-day New York and Delaware). In the latter territory, the Lutheran Church was officially established, as it was in the homeland. The Dutch, however, prohibited public Lutheran worship until their hegemony yielded to that of the English, and the first Lutheran congregation was established in 1669. Growth was slow until the following century, when a larger-scale immigration from the German-speaking Rhineland brought thousands of Lutherans among other Germans to the hospitable colony founded by William Penn. It was thus Pennsylvania that became the center of colonial Lutheranism, and it was there that the German-born Henry Melchior Muhlenberg (1711–1787) organized the Pennsylvania Ministerium in 1748. This regional alliance of clergy represented the beginnings of organized Lutheranism in America, and was strongly influenced by the Pietist movement that came with the early ministers from Europe. Pietism, which had its origin at the University of Halle in Germany in the late seventeenth century, stressed personal devotion and spiritual cultivation over formal theology in the practice of the ministry, and conditioned early American Lutherans to be receptive to similar emphases in Anglo-American Methodism. The scarcity of clergy among the early Lutheran immigrants also contributed to the dilution of specifically Lutheran traditions.

The achievement of American independence, on which Lutherans took no formal or united stand, raised new questions for the identity of this heavily German-oriented community in the new nation similar to those confronted by Jews, Catholics, and others who were not English-speaking Protestants. Leadership in accommodating Lutheranism to American Protestant norms was provided by Samuel Simon Schmucker (1799–1873), who was instrumental in the early life of the General Synod (1820) and the Lutheran Seminary at Gettysburg (1826). Schmucker maintained that the best course for Lutherans in America was to become English-speaking and to conform their worship and piety to the practice of local Methodists, Presbyterians, and other evangelical Protestants. This program for "American" or "Eastern Lutherans," as his followers have been variously known, deemphasized formal liturgy and the importance of the sacraments, advocated strict Sabbath observance, promoted the cause of temperance, maintained Sunday Schools, supported missions, and sympathized with revival preaching. Schmucker's agenda was simultaneously to convert American Lutheranism into a denomination similar in ethos to its evangelical neighbors, and to provide an institutional framework for a loose union of the various Lutheran groups that already existed.

Schmucker's vigorous Americanizing met resistance among many Lutherans who had come under the influence of the "Old Lutheran" movement in Germany. This had emerged out of a resistance to Rationalism and to the enforced merger of the Lutheran and Reformed (i.e., of Calvinist heritage) churches brought about through Frederick William III's "Prussian Union" of 1817. The movement's American offshoot, which found a theological spokesman in Charles Porterfield Krauth (1823–1883), expressed itself institutionally through the General Council (1867) and a new seminary founded at Philadelphia in 1864. Originally it had appealed to doctrinally conservative Midwestern groups because of its vigorous adherence to the tenets of early Lutheran belief as outlined in the Augsburg Confession of 1530, which Schmucker had wanted to modify. Soon, though, it met resistance from that same quarter in its willingness to tolerate worship practices, such as open communion, that deviated from its avowed theological commitments. As a result, conservative groups in Ohio, Missouri, and other parts of the Midwest withdrew and organized a Synodical Conference in 1872, although even this alliance was doomed to failure because of the proverbial American Lutheran penchant for doctrinal in-fighting.

The General Council thus represented a middle though not a mediating ground in the nineteenth-century spectrum. Although theologically conservative in its stress on the objective truth of the doctrines formulated by Luther and his followers, it nevertheless was heavily English-speaking and accommodating to a wide range of practice. In contrast, the Lutheranism that was developing in the upper Midwest during and after the Civil War years had its origins in a mass immigration from northern Germany and the Scandinavian countries, often through whole communities leaving the Old World and resettling themselves as a bloc in the New. The availability of farmland in the unsettled stretches of Minnesota, Wisconsin, Iowa, and the Dakotas permitted a continuation of Old World language, customs, and religious practices in isolation from "Yankee" influence, so that the Americanizing forces promoted by Schmucker, which had resulted almost inevitably from enforced intermingling with English-speaking Protestants, were effortlessly resisted for decades.

The coming to the Midwest of Danes, Swedes, Norwegians, Finns, Icelanders, and Germans of all sorts resulted in unprecedented organizational confusion: sixty new Lutheran church bodies (usually called "synods") were organized between 1849 and 1875, though many did not last long. Geography, ethnicity, and doctrine all combined in various ways to produce this proliferation, and attempts at unity or even cooperation were not likely to encounter a favorable reception until the passage of generations, restrictions on immigration, and the anti-German hysteria that World War I brought about began to take their toll on differences based on Old World themes. The most durable result of the nineteenth-century Midwestern ethos of doctrinal combativeness and separatism was the Missouri Synod, founded primarily by Saxon immigrants in 1847, and led most notably by C. F. W. Walther (1811–1877). The Missouri Group had been a major force in the organization of the unsuccessful Synodical Conference, and continued into the twentieth century as a bastion of ultraconservative theology and partial cultural separatism (as manifested particularly in its comprehensive school system). On the other hand, its development of a congregationally based polity differentiated it from other Lutherans in both the Old and New Worlds, and indicated an American pragmatism even in this most traditional of denominations.

The American Lutheran experience during the formative decades of the eighteenth and nineteenth centuries paralleled that of many other immigrant groups from Continental Europe. Both Roman Catholics and Jews, for example, were disadvantaged in the New World by their lack of knowledge of the English language and American mores. Each also represented a religious community that incorporated a variety of cultural and linguistic diversity. However, the Lutherans *were*, after all, Protestants, which was at least generically the dominant religious persuasion in the new nation. One of their main dilemmas, however, was the choice that faced them as to *how* they were going to express this Protestantism: through the liturgical worship and cultural traditions of the Old World, or by adopting the methods and mores of American evangelicalism. Their ethnic diversity and lack of centralized leadership precluded a definitive solution. It was not until the twentieth century that the process of Americanization had proceeded far enough on all fronts for something approaching a common identity to emerge.

For American Anglicans, the impact of the Revolution and Independence was traumatic. Disestablishment rapidly took place at the state level, and the First Amendment to the Federal Constitution precluded any privileged status in the nation at large. Thus, they could no longer enjoy whatever benefits may have accrued from their established status in several of the colonies. To the left, many of the best lay minds were lost to Deism, the religious offshoot of the Enlightenment that scorned tradition and supernaturalism. On the right, the post-Revolutionary taint of disloyalty put what had now become one among many "denominations" under a cloud, especially in the North, since some half of its clergy remained loyal to tradition and the mother country, and many of them left for England or Canada.

The first major breakthrough in the establishment of ecclesiastical independence took place in 1784, when Samuel Seabury (1729–1796) of Connecticut became the first American Anglican bishop. The obstacles here had been formidable. On the one hand, the principle of the apostolic succession of bishops central to Anglican polity necessitated the laying-on of hands by at least three proper bishops in the consecration of a new one. On the other, bishops of the Church of England were required to swear allegiance to the English monarch as officers of a state church. Clearly, a citizen of the new nation could not take such an oath—even a curmudgeonly Tory like Seabury, who persisted in remaining in Connecticut after his politics had rendered him highly unpopular during the Revolutionary years.

The solution in this dilemma lay in a curious twist of church history. Following the overthrow of the House of Stuart in England's Glorious Revolution, a number of Scottish bishops refused to acknowledge the new dynasty and swear allegiance to it. These bishops and their handful of successors came to be called "non-juring," and the issue of oath-taking by candidates for consecration at their hands was thus moot. Seabury thus journeyed to Scotland after being turned down by the English, and paved the way for the apostolic succession, or "historic episcopate," to continue beyond the political confines of England and its established church. The latter, however, soon came to see the futility of continued resistance to the acknowledgment of American independence, and the next set of candidates in 1787 did not need to make the trek to Aberdeen. After two further consecrations under English auspices, a critical mass of an American episcopate was able to become self-perpetuating.

The remainder of the task of establishing an "infrastructure" took place at the Second General Convention in 1789. After some initial compromises, previously aloof Massachusetts and Connecticut sent delegates, and a truly national Protestant Episcopal Church in the United States of America came into being. Like the new nation itself, this church was bicameral in governance. Its polity at the national level consisted of a House of Bishops, in which the senior member took the title and function of Presiding Bishop; and a

House of Delegates, consisting of an equal number of elected members of both clergy and laity. The Convention's accomplishments also included the adoption of a code of canon (i.e., church) law and a version of the *Book of Common Prayer* adapted to American usage—for instance, in substituting prayers for the President for those for the English monarch.

Despite this impressive set of accomplishments, the newly reformed Protestant Episcopal Church proved unable or unwilling to join effectively in the competition for the allegiance of the multitudes of unchurched in the decades following independence. The revival spirit of the Second Great Awakening was uncongenial to most "Churchmen" (as Anglicans have often called themselves until recently), and the challenges of the evangelization of the frontier were not seized upon with great enthusiasm. Membership, therefore, remained very low for almost half a century, and the demoralization brought about by the exodus of clergy and the suspicions of lingering Toryism did not abate until the advent of a new generation of leadership in the 1810s and 20s.

Episcopal revival, when it came, followed two loosely coincident principles—theology and geography. The church in the Southern states found leadership in Virginia bishops Richard Channing Moore (1762–1841) and William Mead (1789–1862), and the seminary established in Alexandria supplied southern dioceses with clergy immersed in the "Low Church" or "evangelical" tradition that Moore espoused. Moore and other "Low Churchmen" regarded the Episcopal Church as fundamentally Protestant, different from the other evangelical denominations of the day not so much in doctrine as in polity and liturgy. As a consequence, Anglican worship in Virginia and many (though not all) of the Southern states commonly utilized the service of Morning Prayer for Sunday worship, with only a quarterly celebration of the Eucharist. Scriptural proclamation and preaching tended to be emphasized over the sacraments, and preaching was frequently oriented not so much toward instruction and edification but rather to the personal experience of conversion that was the common goal of evangelicals of all stripes.

The other focus of early nineteenth-century Episcopal strength was New York City, where Bishop John Henry Hobart (1775–1830) and the General Theological Seminary promoted a style of "churchmanship" dramatically at odds with that of Moore and Alexandria. The "High Church" movement in Anglicanism had its roots in the era of the early Stuart dynasty in England (1603–1640), and emphasized the Catholic (though not Roman) aspects of the Anglican heritage. Central to the High Church party was a theology that was at once historical and sacramental. The continuity of the life of the church was symbolized in the apostolic succession of bishops, and the integrity of doctrine and the sacraments had thus been maintained even during medieval times. Although Scripture and preaching were by no means rejected, emphasis instead was placed on the sacraments—the Eucharist and Baptism—as primary channels of divine grace. As in the Roman tradition, the church itself was recognized as sacramental in character—"the Body of Christ"—rather than simply a pragmatic necessity.

Forces external to the Episcopal Church reinforced both of these tendencies. The evangelical understanding of Anglicanism was not new to America, but had strong roots in eighteenth-century English piety, including John Wesley's Methodist movement. In the new nation, however, the Second Great Awakening in its various phases gave the evangelical cause considerable aid and comfort, and a number of Episcopal clergy were active in the agencies of the Benevolent Empire and parallel denominational structures aimed at the distribution of religious literature, moral reforms, and other common concerns of evangelicals of all denominations during the early decades of the nineteenth century. In the Tidewater South and a few of the early Western missions, to which Episcopalians were gradually beginning to turn, the evangelical party was in the ascendant, and was in many important ways more aligned with its Presbyterian and Congregationalist contemporaries than with its fellow "churchmen" to the north.

The great stimulus to the High Church party came during the 1830s and 1840s from the tumult that overtook the Church of England itself during those years. The beginning of the Oxford Movement as a distinct force in Anglicanism is usually dated from the publication of John Keble's sermon on "National Apostasy" in 1833. Keble was one of a group of Oxford dons concerned with the threat to the integrity of Anglican Christianity from an overly close dependence on the State, since the Church was (and still is) subject to King and Parliament in any number of questions of policy and governance. Keble and his colleagues, who included Richard Hurrell Froude, Edward B. Pusey, and John Henry Newman—later to become a Roman Catholic convert and ultimately a cardinal—had broader concerns. These were rooted in the older tradition of High Church Anglicanism, which they began to make known in a series of *Tracts for the Times,* ninety of which appeared between 1833 and 1841. In this series, these "Tractarians" set forth a thoroughly "Catholic" understanding of Anglican Christianity, stressing the sacramental function of the institutional church and its priesthood and hierarchy.

The manifestos of the Oxford Movement found a ready following in the Diocese of New York and the General Theological Seminary, which earlier under Bishop Hobart had maintained the High Church tradition in America. Throughout the decades to come, the lines were drawn for a viciously partisan division within the House of Bishops. Evangelicals expressed alarm over a small but significant defection of Anglo-Catholics to Roman Catholicism, including North Carolina Bishop Levi Silliman Ives (1797–1867). Over the years much of the theological and spiritual focus of the High Church party went beyond that of the Oxford Movement and became channeled into a preoccupation with highly elaborate, medievally inspired liturgical practices involving clerical vestments, processions, and the use of incense and bells during the Eucharistic service. Originally known as "Ritualism," this "Anglo-Catholicism" still manifests itself in a few, usually urban, parishes to this day, for instance, St. Mary the Virgin in New York City and the Church of the Advent in Boston. (Irreverent nicknames such as "Smells and Bells" are often attached to such churches by skeptics.)

These party lines were never absolutely correlated with geography—Tennessee, for example, was a High Church enclave in the South, and various Low Church clergy were to prove thorns in the sides of a number of New York bishops. As the Episcopal Church moved slowly westward, countervailing forces followed. Even in comparison with other "elite" denominations such as the Presbyterians, the "home missions" (i.e., in the United States itself) force was slow in developing. A popular saying had it that, in the settlement of the West, "the Baptists came on foot, the Methodists on horseback, and the Episcopalians in parlor cars." This saying, though, is belied by the vigor with which some Anglican pioneers undertook the task of frontier evangelization. The first major leader in this effort was Philander Chase (1775–1852), who converted to Anglicanism while a student at Dartmouth and set about aggressively to bring a distinctively Low Church brand of his adopted faith to the frontier. He had the distinction of founding two new dioceses (Ohio in 1818 and Illinois in 1835) as well as a church-sponsored college, Kenyon (which still flourishes) and Jubilee, in each. On the other hand Jackson Kemper, the first Missionary Bishop consecrated for service in the West in 1835, was of the High Church persuasion, reflecting an informal agreement that the Evangelical party would have foreign missions as its domain while its rivals would be entrusted with the task of evangelizing the American frontier. The upper Midwest soon became one of the bastions of the Anglo-Catholic movement, with the Nashotah House seminary (1840) providing an institutional basis for training clergy for service in the "Biretta Belt" (a nickname again indicating the High Church propensity for emulating Roman Catholic practices.) Missionary work on Indian reservations attracted some dedicated individuals such as Bishop William Hobart Hare, but Western growth of any sort was based more on the development of an indigenous white upper middle class than on sporadic and undersupported missionary endeavors.

In the South, the once-powerful position of the church as that of the upper classes was undermined both by the rapid growth of the Baptists and Methodists on the southern frontier and by the emergence of the Presbyterians as a rival for the allegiance of the elite. Nevertheless, many of the most powerful and respected leaders of the Confederacy—Robert E. Lee of Virginia and Jefferson Davis of Mississippi—were Episcopalians. One representative figure in the relationship between the Episcopal Church and the Old South was Leonidas Polk (1806–1864), a North Carolinian educated both at West Point and the seminary in Alexandria. In 1838 Polk was consecrated missionary bishop with responsibility for what was then the entire southwestern corner of the nation. His subsequent activities included unsuccessful management of a Louisiana sugar plantation and service as bishop of Louisiana. Most notably, Polk led the drive for the founding of the University of the South high on a mountaintop in Sewanee, Tennessee (1856–1860) as an indigenous means of education for a regional elite. After the war broke out, Polk was commissioned a general in the Confederate army and died in battle near Pine Mountain, Georgia.

During the decades leading up to the Civil War, individual Episcopalians both attacked and defended the institution of slavery, but the denomination as a whole never took an official stand on the issue. Some Southern blacks, especially in the older Tidewater area, belonged to the church—an estimate for the early nineteenth century is 35,000—but, as with whites, the less formal and more emotional worship of the Baptists and Methodists was far more attractive to the slave and free black population. When the war finally came, the Southern dioceses collectively withdrew from the national church and convened instead as the Protestant Episcopal Church in the Confederate States of America. This division lasted only for the war's duration, and the 1866 General Convention drew representatives from all of the dioceses of the reunited body. (The 1862 Convention was the only one from which Southern delegates were absent.)

The course of the Episcopal Church in the postbellum South continued to be conservative in tone, with segregation the norm in church life as elsewhere. A number of black colleges were founded under denominational sponsorship, some of which, such as St. Augustine's in Raleigh, North Carolina, are still in existence. Some blacks did enter the priesthood, and the Bishop Payne Divinity School was founded in Petersburg, Virginia, in 1887 to provide them with an education similar to but physically separate from that of the all-white parent institution in Alexandria. (The two finally merged in 1953). The church in general did not play a very active role in promoting desegregation until the 1950s, when the faculty at the School of Theology at Sewanee successfully forced positive action on racial integration in 1953 and blacks began to acquire full enfranchisement in the church as a whole.

The experience of the Episcopalians in the nineteenth century was, like that of all other religious traditions of European origin, one of continual adaptation. The Episcopal Church, with the Congregational, was the most reluctant to come to terms with the rapidly changing circumstances of a vibrant democracy with no established church, and it was even slower that the Congregationalists to respond to the inexorable fact of the frontier. The emergence of a new, urban frontier in the century's latter decades proved a more congenial challenge, and its manifold responses to social and cultural change—ranging from monasteries to institutional churches—restored its standing as a major presence in the American religious spectrum. By the end of the nineteenth century, it had emerged as perhaps *the* church of the American urban elite, a status—or stigma—that would last until well into the twentieth century.

CHAPTER 27

Religion in the Slave Community

African slaves began to arrive in the American colonies beginning in 1619 in Jamestown, Virginia. Specific statements about the religious life of these earliest Afro-Americans are difficult to make, given the sparsity of reliable evidence. Whatever may have happened to the traditions they brought with them, few were converted to Christianity, because of the reluctance of whites to permit their evangelization. The Southern colonies, where slavery flourished, were also largely outside the bounds of effective organized religion, so that clergy and missionaries were not widely distributed among the population in general, and many whites had no active religious life themselves. In the case of slaves, however, whites were further leery of spreading the Christian gospel for fear that black converts might acquire legal rights if baptized, and that notions of freedom suggested by various scriptural passages might give them dangerous ideas.

The eighteenth century brought about a number of developments that worked in the opposite direction. As slavery became more routinized, families began to develop among Afro-Americans. This provided a setting more conducive for the development of religious life than was usually possible for newly arrived, single, and unacculturated individuals. Colonial legislatures took measures to ensure that baptism did not guarantee liberation in any legal sense. The Church of England began to take a more serious interest in missionary work, as manifested in the founding of the Society for the Propagation of the Gospel in Foreign Parts in 1701. Its success, however, was less than complete, as its missionaries found work with whites easier and more productive than with slaves. Catholics in Louisiana and Maryland, including slave-holding Jesuits in the latter colony, were more conscientious than most in providing religious instructions for blacks.

The most important development in the eighteenth century for the shaping of Afro-American religious life was the Great Awakening of the 1740s. This first great American revival spread a new version of the Gospel among blacks and whites alike along the entire eastern seaboard, and stressed personal religious experience and conversion over theological learning and liturgical worship. The Awakening, which gave a great boost to the emergent Baptist and Methodist movements, also generated lay preachers with little formal education and no specific credentials other than their own claim to have been called by the Holy Spirit. This religious "enthusiasm" appealed greatly to the unlettered slaves, who identified with the kind of direct experience involved and who were now permitted to be exposed to Christian teachers by masters who themselves had been converted for the first time.

In the 1830s, the Methodist Charles Colcock Jones and others from several denominations launched an intensive campaign known as the "Mission" for the conversion of blacks on a larger scale. Since the not-so-hidden goal of much of this effort was to produce a more docile slave community, its lack of conspicuous success is perhaps not very surprising. The more authentic, indigenous Christianity that emerged among the slave communities in the century or so between the Awakening and the Civil War is frequently described as the "invisible institution," since the social and legal status of its clientele made all but the most minimal organization impossible. Baptist preachers and Methodist exhorters required little if any formal training. These two traditions therefore spread rapidly among black and white alike, although slave-holders generally exercised supervision over any black worship meetings. In a few cases, such as the Silver Bluff Baptist Church in South Carolina, independent black churches managed to emerge, but their autonomy was usually precarious and short-lived.

The religious lives of plantation blacks frequently exhibited a split quality, reflecting in public the desire of whites to utilize Christian teachings—especially certain texts of Paul enjoining slaves to obey their masters—to reinforce a spirit of obedience and docility in the services that they themselves attended or supervised. It was in private, however, that the "invisible institution" developed its particular character. When opportunities presented themselves, slaves would assemble surreptitiously wherever they might—for instance, in wooded areas known as "hush harbors" where worship could be conducted in secret. Sprituals, the unique musical expression of slave Christianity, sometimes conveyed coded messages, and "Steal Away to Jesus" was often a call to steal off quite literally for an impromptu service.

The kind of Christianity that developed along these lines was a folk religion that combined elements from both the African and European heritage in a unique social and cultural context that gave it an identity of its own. Black preachers enjoyed a special status within the slave community, based on charisma rather than any formal education or even literacy. Slaves were forbidden to learn to read, so that their knowledge of Scripture and Christian tradition was acquired entirely from hearing it preached. Folk preaching, which continues in modified form to this day, was formulaic, consisting of set phrases that could be inserted at various points in the narrative. It was also participatory, following a call-response pattern, possibly of African origin, in which the congregation would actively answer the preacher's words and injunctions. (This active participation still characterizes much black worship today.) Further, worship was not simply verbal, but also enacted. The "shout" or "ring-shout" was a familiar style of acting out the religious impulse. It consisted of a highly rhythmic counterclockwise shuffle-dance in which the whole body participates in the movement, again possibly echoing the rhythms of traditional African worship, which were beaten out on drums forbidden to American slaves.

One of the most enduring aspects of the tradition of slave Christianity is the "spiritual," a distinctive musical genre derived from the fusion of the Anglo-American style of hymnody founded by Isaac Watts with the distinctive rhythms and concerns of the slave community. (Southern white folk-hymns, such as those found in the "Sacred Harp" or "shape-note" tradition, have a similar origin, but reflect different cultural emphases.) Lyrics developed through oral adaptations of original Watts-style hymns became simplified and transformed to reflect black concerns, such as the pervasiveness of suffering and the longing for deliverance. Among the better known are "Go Down, Moses," "Joshua Fit de Battle of Jericho," "Roll, Jordan, Roll," "Were You There When They Crucified My Lord," and "Nobody Knows the Trouble I've Seen." Many of these titles reflect biblical themes, focusing especially on figures of deliverance: Moses and Joshua in the Old Testament, Jesus in the New. Musically, spirituals are usually in the African pentatonic or five-note scale, often with a "flatted seventh" that adds a note of melancholy. Spirituals have long outlasted slavery, having been adapted into modern choral settings and also providing the basis for later black Gospel music.

The actual meaning of the spirituals has been the subject of considerable debate in recent years. At one level, they express a yearning for deliverance from the woes of this world into a supernatural realm. More recently, they have been interpreted as more subversive of the social order, conveying a desire for a very this-worldly redemption involving escape to freedom in the northern states or Canada. Most probably, as Eugene Genovese has suggested, the distinction between the two was not as clear-cut as this dichotomy suggests. What they in fact express is an undifferentiated desire for deliverance, at times emphasizing the supernatural, at others the natural. Moses, Jesus, and Lincoln similarly were not always clearly distinguishable in the imagery of slave worship, but all represented figures of redemption at one level or another.

The broader question of the interpretation of slave religion was originally posed some years ago in a heated debate between the anthropologist Melville Herskovits and the black sociologist E. Franklin Frazier. Herskovits, who had started the debate in his *Myth of the Negro Past* (1958), had been concerned with refuting commonly held ideas about the inferiority of American blacks. He argued that African customs such as rituals involving rivers and certain burial practices had been carried over directly into Afro-American religion, for example, in the popularity of baptism by total immersion in the Baptist manner. Frazier took the position in such works as *The Negro Church in America* (1964) and *The Negro Family in the United States* (1966) that the numerical dominance of whites and the policy of systematically splitting up slaves of similar linguistic backgrounds had virtually obliterated all vestiges of African culture in North America.

Herskovits's position was strongly advocated by many militants during the 1960s, who felt that it enhanced black claims to respect on the basis of cultural continuity. More recent scholarship tends to side with Frazier's argument that it is very difficult to establish any direct continuities, such as are frequently apparent in the case of Latin American syncretistic cultures, between Afro-American and traditional African practices. This is not to say, however, that all continuity with Africa had been obliterated; rather, it manifested itself indirectly, for example, in the rhythms of the ring-shout and the call-response pattern of slave worship. The overt content of slave religion may have been derived from English-speaking Protestant Christianity, but the underlying pattern of nonverbal expression was quite clearly evocative of the African past. The result, however, was not simply a fusion of the two, but a *tertium quid*, a new synthesis invoking elements from each tradition but blending them with the unique concerns and experiences of the Afro-American slave community.

Although Afro-American slave religion was most often manifest in this synthesis of African patterns and evangelical Protestantism, especially in its Baptist and Methodist forms, it was not confined to this. Many slaves in Maryland and Louisiana were converted to Roman Catholicism, though they were barred from ordination to the priesthood till late in the nineteenth century. At the other end of the religious spectrum, New Orleans was the focus of the Voodoo

(Haitian *Vodun*) cult, one of the most direct descendants of African practices present in North America. As its practices spread throughout the South, however, they lost their explicit religious forms, and were practiced as "Hoodoo" or "rootwork" by "conjuremen," who enjoyed a following among both rural blacks and whites for their magical and curative powers. Slave Christianity tended toward a protean character, open to taking new shapes and elements because of its lack of formal organization. It thus could blend at the edges with this underground folk world of charms and curses that evoked the African world picture of a cosmos filled with diffuse power that could be harnessed, with the proper knowledge, for personal good or the harm of others. In this world, skill, fate, and luck challenged the Christian notions of good and evil, freedom and responsibility, grace and sin. The results were a twilight region of folklife: part Christian, part African, distinctly Afro-American.

D. "Freedom's Ferment": New Religious Movements

Unitarianism, Transcendentalism, and Universalism

Religious liberalism by its very definition is resistant to institutionalization. Openness to novelty and change is one of its major characteristics; it is not easily tied down by creeds, structures, and the apparatus that develops when a group establishes itself as a denomination. On the other hand, even a liberal religious impulse has to take on concrete social and intellectual form if it is to transcend the impulses of the moment, achieve a continuity of expression, and exert itself as an active influence in the broader community. Two parallel liberal movements emerged in the Revolutionary era that later were forced to take on denominational form, and that after nearly two centuries merged to form the Unitarian-Universalist Association. Of the two, Unitarianism has always overshadowed its "country cousin," Universalism—an illustration primarily of the differences that social class can make even when theological beliefs are remarkably similar.

American Unitarians have traditionally traced their religious roots to Reformation-era "free spirits" such as Servetus and Socinus and the movements they inspired in Transylvania, Poland, and other areas of central Europe. Another, more immediate source of influence was the emergence in England beginning in the seventeenth century of a small group of Christians who denied that God existed as three persons—a Trinity—and was instead solely one—hence the name "Unitarian." Later English Unitarians such as the renowned chemist Joseph Priestley found their way to America, and helped spread such ideas in this country in the post-Revolutionary era. English Unitarianism, however, was rooted in a philosophical materialism that did not find widespread acceptance in America, where a very different approach to the question of liberal religion had already begun to take shape.

One of the important results of the Great Awakening of the 1740s was the polarization of the Congregationalist clergy of New England into the revival's defenders, or "New Lights," such as Jonathan Edwards, as well as opponents, or "Old Lights," who were concentrated in the Boston area. Prominent among the latter were a trio of ministers—Charles Chauncy (1705–1787) and Jonathan Mayhew (1720–1766) of Boston, and Ebenezer Gay (1696–1787) of nearby Hingham. Working informally among themselves and like-minded allies, they developed a critique not only of the "enthusiastic" preaching of the revivalists but of traditional New England Calvinism as well. The most conspicuous teaching of the movement that thus took shape was the denial that God was a Trinity. More important was their equally determined assault on the Calvinist stress on the all-pervasive corrupting power of Original Sin and its corollary, God's predestining of all humanity for salvation or damnation. American Unitarianism was fundamentally an attack on Calvinist doctrine from the *Arminian* point of view—a theological outlook that stressed God's benevolence rather than his awesome power, and human potential rather than depravity.

The first open expression of Unitarian sentiments by a congregation took place at King's Chapel in Boston, an Anglican church that in 1785 adopted a version of the *Book of Common Prayer* from which references to the Trinity had been omitted. It was among the Puritan congregational churches, however, that the movement had special appeal. Although these early liberals wanted to avoid an open break with their more "orthodox" contemporaries, a number of the latter were sufficiently alarmed with the spread of these new ideas that they began to force the issue. One of the first skirmishes in this battle was over control of the Hollis Professorship of Divinity at Harvard, an institution crucial for shaping the future of the New England ministry. When the liberal faction prevailed, the battle lines were set for what would later be called the "First Unitarian Controversy."

This battle between liberal and orthodox Congregationalists took the form of a bitter pamphlet warfare led by Jedidiah Morse (1761–1826), a conservative clergyman who also had achieved renown as a geographer. The most eloquent spokesman for the liberals was William Ellery Channing (1780–1842), who in 1819 preached a memorable ordination sermon at Baltimore that set forth the liberal movement's emphases. Prominent among these were the unity of God, and his parental character; the single, human nature of Jesus; individual free will; and the moral and ethical character of the Christian religion. A few years later, in 1825, the liberal clergy of the Boston area met to form a loose alliance to promote their common interests. The result was the American Unitarian Association, the first formal institutional expression of this emergent branch of liberal Christianity.

Unitarianism had already triumphed in the Boston area, and eighty-eight of the hundred oldest churches of eastern Massachusetts aligned themselves with the liberal cause. The triumph was not to go unchallenged, since the perils of structure for liberalism were now appearing. The first important sign that the Unitarians were themselves hardening into an "orthodox" position was provoked by the address delivered to the graduating class of the Harvard Divinity School by Ralph Waldo Emerson (1803–1882) in 1838. Emerson had several years earlier renounced his ministry in Boston because he had difficulties with what he saw as too much of traditional Christianity within Unitarian belief and practice. His "Divinity School Address" came as something of a bombshell to the Unitarian community, for which Harvard and its Divinity School were the major educational vehicle.

The focus of this "Second Unitarian Controversy" was the question of the miracles attributed to Jesus in the Gospels. "Orthodox" Unitarians such as Harvard's Andrew Norton (1786–1853), who earned the nickname of the Unitarian "Pope," took the position that such miracles had been necessary to establish Jesus's authority as a divinely inspired teacher and prophet, even though he himself was not actually divine. Emerson refused to go even this far, and denounced such miracles as "monster" on the grounds that they contradicted his own belief that ultimate religious truth was eternal and potentially present everywhere; to constrict it with miracles and specific historical figures was to limit and thereby distort it beyond recognition.

Emerson was the most publicly successful of a band of Boston-area intellectuals who were attracted to one another through their collective interest in the "transcendental" philosophy that was filtering through to America from Germany through England during this "romantic" era of religious thought. These American "Transcendentalists" fiercely resisted being pigeonholed as an organized movement; still, their mutual enjoyment of one another's conversation, their collective dissatisfaction with even liberal "orthodoxy," and their involvement in various common endeavors makes it useful to consider them together as a short-lived but uncommonly influential force in American religious and cultural history.

Unitarian theology, like its more conservative evangelical counterparts, was firmly based on the affirmations of the Scottish Common Sense philosophy, which taught that all knowledge was accessible to humans through the senses. The central emphasis of Transcendentalism was on the human ability to enter into a deeper, more "original" relationship with the ultimate reality that underlies appearances, and that is present everywhere in nature. Human history, customs, and institutions, including organized religion, hindered rather than helped this quest, so that the burdens they imposed had to be cast off if a search for pure and authentic truth was to be pursued successfully.

Emerson's extremely popular essays and lectures, such as those on "Nature" and "Self-Reliance," emphasized the cultivation of this pursuit in the course of everyday life. More radical was Emerson's friend at Concord, Henry David Thoreau (1817–1862), whose *Walden* of 1854 was a chronicle of his attempt to slough off the baggage of civilization and live by himself at the shore of a rural pond in pursuit of an original and essential relationship with Nature. At the other extreme of Transcendentalist innovation was the Brook Farm community, established by George and Sophia Ripley in 1844 near West Roxbury,

Massachusetts. This experiment in communal living directed toward the cultivation of the higher faculties proved impractical and disbanded within a few years. In the long run, though, Brook Farm stood as an expression of faith that humanity need not be confined forever to the hopeless round imposed by materialistic urban and industrial civilization.

Although it resulted in some significant experiments in church organization, Transcendentalism was primarily a literary and intellectual movement. Its major organ was the *Dial,* an influential journal edited by Emerson and Margaret Fuller from 1840 to 1844. The massive output of this band of perhaps three dozen writers was part of a larger efflorescence of literary productivity that has been characterized variously as the "flowering of New England" or, more broadly, as part of the "American renaissance" of the pre-Civil War decades. At one end of this spectrum of writers was Nathaniel Hawthorne (1804–1864), who provided a profound reflection on his own Puritan heritage in *The Scarlet Letter* of 1850. Although Hawthorne had been raised in the Unitarian fold, his own writings reflected a preoccupation with the traditional themes of Calvinism, and he more than once provided biting critiques of what he saw as the follies of his Transcendental contemporaries (e.g., in *The Blithedale Romance* of 1852). Like his friend Herman Melville, Hawthorne was not an active participant in organized religious life, and preferred to reflect on eternal themes from his own detached and individualistic perspective.

More typical of the culture that Unitarianism nurtured was the work of the "Fireside Poets"—Henry Wadsworth Longfellow, James Russell Lowell, Oliver Wendell Holmes, Sr., and William Cullen Bryant. Their writings, which became extremely popular during the middle decades of the nineteenth century, reflected a greater optimism about human possibilities within more conventional bounds of society and thought. Also popular among the cultivated reading public was the *North American Review,* a literary journal founded in 1815 that dealt with a broad range of issues of the time and eventually left its Boston origins for a New York base. More generally, Unitarianism had become the accepted faith of the academic and professional classes of Boston and Cambridge, and taught what was becoming a rather comfortable faith in the possibilities of individual growth and social progress through the church, the schools, and other institutions of society.

Although some Unitarians, like Channing, eventually lent their voices to the growing protest against slavery, it was spokesmen outside the mainstream, such as Theodore Parker (1810–1860), who played the most significant roles in that struggle. Parker also aroused the wrath of the more conservative clergy with his address on "The Transient and Permanent in Christianity" in 1841, which mounted a critique of traditional religion that if anything was even more radical than Emerson's. Perhaps not surprisingly, Parker was ostracized by his fellow Unitarian clergy, and went on to take his congregation in an independent direction.

The questions that had been raised by the positions of Emerson and Parker continued to haunt the Unitarian movement, which was sorely divided between those who saw themselves as the exponents of a liberal but still explicitly

Christian faith, and others who did not want any restrictions placed on free religious inquiry. One expression of this tension was the formation in 1867 of the Free Religious Association by a small group of dissident New England ministers. More significant over the long run was a split that followed sectional lines. Unitarianism has always been based in eastern Massachusetts, where its adherents are said to believe in "the fatherhood of God, the brotherhood of Man, and the neighborhood of Boston." Nevertheless, the movement slowly and cautiously followed the frontier westward during the nineteenth century, and those who founded churches in the Midwest and beyond were frequently opposed to any creedal statements that defined Unitarians as Christians. It was from this western matrix that the association of Unitarianism with "humanism"—ethics and human values divorced from theology or even a belief in God—began to develop in the twentieth century.

Where Unitarianism had its American roots in a reaction against the Great Awakening, Universalism arose in the religious and cultural ferment that those revivals left as their heritage. It was especially in the northern, rural stretches of New England that were settled by Yankee in-migrants in the decades around the Revolution that a popular dissatisfaction with Puritanism began to stir. Universalism was from the beginning a faith not of the social elite but rather of ordinary people, neither blessed nor burdened with higher education, among whom a number of prophets of liberalism began to arise in the years in which the new nation was taking form.

The core of the Universalist message was that the entirety of humanity would ultimately be saved, a distinct repudiation of Calvinist predestination. Its theological sources were varied. Its exponents in America were influenced chiefly by the writings of the German George Klein-Nicolai, who wrote under the pseudonym Paul Siegvolck, and the Welsh Methodist James Relly. Two Americans in particular came under the spell of these new ideas about universal salvation, and began to spread its message far and wide. The first was John Murray (1741–1815), who was English-born but labored primarily in Gloucester and later Boston in Massachusetts. New England-born Elhanan Winchester (1751–1797) preached in the Philadelphia area, where his "Society of Universal Baptists" attracted the eminent scientist Benjamin Rush.

From these scattered beginnings, like-minded Universalist congregations began to overcome their aversion to organization in response to needs for legal standing. An early, nonbinding creedal statement was drawn up in Philadelphia in 1790, which was in part the work of Rush. Of more lasting impact was the so-called Winchester Profession of 1803, named after the New Hampshire town where it was composed, which emphasized that all of humanity would ultimately be restored through Jesus to a state of "holiness and happiness." A national spokesman also emerged in the person of Hosea Ballou (1771–1852), who began life as a Baptist farmer-preacher in New Hampshire, and eventually settled into a career as a Universalist minister and leader in Boston in 1817. In such works as his *Treatise on the Atonement* of 1805, Ballou articulated a systematic theological rationale for the Universalist movement, and aligned it more clearly with Unitarianism in his rejection of the Trinity.

By 1833, Universalists had developed a formal if rather loose denominational structure, which took the name of the Universalist Church of America. Like their Unitarian counterparts, the Universalists were firmly congregational in polity and were based in New England geographically. Unlike the urban Unitarians, however, Universalists were more likely to be located in the smaller towns of the Northeast and, eventually, throughout the South and other parts of the nation as well. In 1850, roughly 90 percent of the 246 Unitarian churches of the day were in New England; among Universalists, the figures were about 55 percent of 529. A century later, the figures were 145 of 357 for the Unitarians (40 percent), and a resounding 200 of 300 Universalist (66 percent). Membership peaked around the turn of the century at approximately 65,000, and remained stable until the merger of the two denominations in 1961.

The ethos of Universalism from the early days under Ballou's leadership until the time of the merger was probably more similar to that of the Northern Baptists than Unitarianism, although numerical growth was more similar to the latter than the former. Universalists moved from frontier farmer status to that of middle-class townsfolk, and turned their attention to the development of colleges such as Tufts and St. Lawrence—the two that have survived to the present—and accompanying theological schools. Universalists became involved in the message of Social Christianity toward the end of the nineteenth century, and to some extent in the Humanist movement in the twentieth. Like the Unitarians, they engaged periodically in ecumenical discussions of merger with several like-minded groups.

The natural and ultimately fruitful partner for such discussions was the Universalists' New England counterparts, the Unitarians. Thomas Starr King, who moved from a position as Universalist minister in Boston to being a Civil War-time Unitarian in California, observed that the real difference between the two groups was that the Universalists considered God too good to damn anyone, while the Unitarians considered themselves too good to be damned. After World War II, it became clear that neither group was destined for continued expansion, that the maintenance of parallel bureaucracies and institutions was a wasteful duplication of effort, and that the differences that had historically separated the two were far more sociological than theological. As a consequence, the Unitarian-Universalist Association was formed by mutual consent in 1961.

CHAPTER 29

New World Space and Time: Restorationist, Millennial, and Communitarian Movements

From the moment that Europeans first arrived on New World shores—or perhaps even from the time they began to imagine lands across the vast ocean—America has had a special role in the Western imagination. Giles Gunn has described this speculation on the ultimate significance of America as "New World Metaphysics"—the attempt to find transcendental meaning in the American experience of time and space. The Spanish quested after the fountain of youth and cities of gold, while their more austere English counterparts saw their sojourn in New England as a recapitulation of the biblical wilderness. In later colonial times, Jonathan Edwards became convinced that the Second Coming was likely to take place in the New World. The notion of God acting in American history and the imminence of the millennium began to inform American thought patterns over these decades, and to infuse what was becoming a national experience with an import beyond the merely political.

Two themes have especially dominated the quest for the meaning of America: limitless space and a new beginning in time. Although the trauma of depressions and world wars, Holocaust and Hiroshima, and potential ecological disaster has sobered Americans of the later twentieth century, these powerfully optimistic themes have never died out entirely in our culture. Certain times and places have been especially susceptible to the rise of cultural trends and new religious movements, in which these themes of the transcendence of ordinary time and space have become particularly potent. California, for example, has become legendary as a source of new and exotic social and religious expression from early Pentecostalism to the "New Age." The "New Light Stir" in New England during the Revolutionary era was an incubating ground for Shakers, Universalists, and Free Will Baptists. Periods of rapid social change and demographic movement seem especially apt times for religious innovation to flourish.

The Kentucky frontier in the decades following the Revolution was one of those places. English and Scotch-Irish pioneers eagerly followed Daniel Boone's lead through the Cumberland Gap westward across the mountains. The unprecedented excitement that took place at Cane Ridge and other sites of the "Great Revival" marked a protean phase of American religious history. The "Burned-Over District" of upstate New York in the 1820s and 1830s was another. The area made accessible by the Erie Canal, from Albany to Buffalo, was rapidly populated by emigrants from the rocky farm country and mountains of New England—the "Yankee Exodus"—seeking a better chance in life. Andrew Jackson's challenge to traditional notions of the relationship between government and society coincided with a rapidly changing economic order in which individualism was displacing kinship networks. Excitement over the nation's seemingly endless possibilities was balanced by apprehension over the loss of familiar patterns of life and work. If religious development in some way reflects cultural change, it would certainly have been reasonable to expect new religious movements in these volatile settings.

Although it is difficult to find *any* period of American history not characterized by rapid social change, the early decades of the nineteenth century and the area from the Hudson to the Mississippi are particularly fertile for our purposes. This was frontier country—the boundary between intensely settled land and that which was virtually uninhabited, at least by Europeans. As opposed to the later settlers of trans-Mississippi America, the in-migrants who flocked into New York, Ohio, and Kentucky came in large numbers and remained fairly close to their points of origin. Before long, this land was thickly settled and on the way to urbanization. It was this brief period of transition that was ripe for the excitements that seemed to be springing up continually. One theme that was common to a wide variety of highly disparate new religious movements of this era was the suspension of normal, historical time—what, in short, these settlers were experiencing in their own secular lives.

One of the moving spirits of the great revival of 1801 was Barton Warren Stone (1772–1844), a Presbyterian minister who had crossed the Alleghenies to take charge of the church at Cane Ridge in Bourbon County, Kentucky. In the aftermath of the Cane Ridge revival, Stone and several of his associates became estranged from the Presbyterians back East who frowned on what they saw as the excesses of the frontier spirit in religion. After they were expelled from the Kentucky Synod in 1803, they organized the short-lived Springfield Presbytery, which they dissolved the next year in a dramatic "Last Will and Testament." Thereafter they preferred to call themselves simply "Christians" rather than taking the name of a particular denomination of Christianity.

Another source of Presbyterian divisiveness was the ongoing quarrels among those still in Scotland and northern Ireland (Ulster) over the relationship of church and society that had resulted in the Seceder and Covenanter movements. From the former faction came Thomas Campbell, an Ulster minister who emigrated to Pennsylvania in 1807 and almost immediately got into trouble with his coreligionists there. Campbell was joined by his son Alexander (1788–1866) and formed a new group known as the "Christian Association," a name significantly similar to that chosen by Stone. Alexander soon took over the leadership of the emergent movement which for a while identified itself with the Baptist cause.

The moving ideas that underlay the Campbells' quest for a new Christianity, though, were really much closer to those of Barton Stone and other contemporaries such as Ohio's Walter Scott, who joined forces with Alexander in 1821. During the Christmas season of 1831–1832, representatives of the Campbell-Scott and Stone forces met in Lexington, Kentucky, and consummated a union of the two movements whose principles were so clearly harmonious. Campbell's "Disciples of Christ" and Stone's "Christians" were now joined in a new campaign to rid American Christianity of its confusing welter of denominations, and to restore instead the pristine, primitive church of New Testament times. Deliberately they avoided any restrictive denominational name, preferring to be known variously as "Christians," "Churches of Christ," or "Disciples of Christ." In the longer run, they inevitably succumbed to division and a measure of institutionalization. At the beginning, however, they were filled with optimism that they could transcend the factionalism of contemporary Protestant Christianity and return to Christian origins.

Key to this nascent Stone-Campbell tradition was the assurance that Scripture could be taken as an unambiguous roadmap for contemporary belief, practice, and organization. "Where the Scriptures speak, we speak; and where the Scriptures are silent, we are silent" was an early motto of Thomas Campbell that became authoritative for the whole movement. Their desire was to escape from "man-made" devices such as creeds and denominational structures, and literally restore the ways in which Jesus and his disciples lived and worshipped. After some initial disagreement among the merged factions, baptism by immersion also came to be a distinctive practice, on the New Testament model, as did congregational polity and the weekly administration of the Lord's Supper.

What differentiated these "restorationists" from the other popular denominations of the frontier, such as the Baptists and Methodists, was the rationalistic tone that characterized their approach to religion. Where others were highly emotional and experiential in their pursuit of salvation, the Stone-Campbell followers instead viewed Scripture as a text to be approached rationally, even legalistically. Despite the roots of part of the movement in the Great Revival, they came to reject dramatic conversion, and were much closer in spirit to the Scottish Common Sense empiricism espoused by John Witherspoon and the traditional Presbyterians of the East Coast. Alexander Campbell's renown as a public debater was one aspect of this confidence that truth could be arrived at through proper textual interpretation, and salvation through proper belief and action growing out of that interpretation. Consonant with this deliberate mood was an optimistic *postmillennialism* promoted by Alexander Campbell—the confidence that the millennial kingdom was gradually being ushered in through human discovery and application of God's law.

Like that of the Baptists, who also eschewed central organization, the Disciples/Christian message spread through South and West by the work of farmer-preachers and newspapers such as Alexander Campbell's *Millennial Harbinger*. Although they avoided formal denominational structures, the "Campbellites," as they have sometimes been called, founded schools, colleges, and a missionary society. A network of colleges and publications in the longer run emerged as a substitute for a centralized administrative apparatus in shaping an informal consensus of opinion, especially within the movement's conservative wing. Eventually, the division that emerged following the Civil War between the more liberal, urban "Disciples" and the stricter, rural "Churches of Christ" reached the breaking point, and resulted in the schisms that began to become visible early in the twentieth century.

Although caution must be used in making a sharp distinction between the two, the terms *premillennialism* and *postmillennialism* have become so common that they necessarily provide a starting point in looking at religious movements that take a radical view of historical time. The Stone-Campbell tradition in its earlier years has been called "postmillennial" that is, characterized by the belief that the thousand years of peace and harmony of earth allegedly foretold by the book of Revelation will be climaxed, rather than inaugurated, by the Second Coming (or advent) of Jesus. Postmillennialism, as evidenced in the title of Campbell's *Millennial Harbinger,* was not so much a strict theological tenet as a climate of opinion, of expectation, that was pervasive throughout nineteenth-century America. In its more secular forms, it was expressed in phrases such as *manifest destiny*—the divinely given right of America to expand its boundaries from coast to coast—and in the idea of "progress" that so dominated the Victorian imagination. ("Progress is our most important product," as Ronald Reagan reminded Americans weekly as host of television's "GE Theater.")

Premillennialism is the belief that the Second Coming of Jesus will come *prior* to the millennium, usually accompanied by great upheavals here on earth and an apocalpytic struggle between the forces of good and evil (see Revelation 20). The Civil War was frequently interpreted as this sort of apocalpytic struggle, as in Julia Ward Howe's stirring "Battle Hymn of the Republic" ("He is trampling out the vintage where the grapes of wrath are stored/He has loosed the fateful lightning of His terrible swift sword"). Beginning in the 1840s, though, the idea that Jesus was about to return, literally and soon, provided the inspiration for a series of religious American movements. That idea continues to this day, among fundamentalists of various denominations, as well as in distinctive sectarian groups such as the Jehovah's Witnesses.

William Miller (1782–1849) has achieved historical notoriety as one of the best-known and least successful millennial prophets in American history. Like many before and since, Miller approached the apocalpytic writings of Scripture, especially Daniel and Revelation, as containing a numerical code that could be cracked with the appropriate mathematical calculations. Using the widely accepted chronology of the seventeenth-century Irish Anglican Archbishop James Ussher, who had attempted to demonstrate that the world had been created in 4004 B.C., Miller calculated that the Second Coming was due in March 1843. Aided by the Restorationist publicist Joshua Himes, Miller began to attract a wide following during the early 1840s through his speaking tours and publications such as *The Midnight Cry.*

Jesus did not appear in March of 1843, nor, after Miller had made some recalculations, the following March. Finally, he fixed October 22, 1844 as the definitive time for the Second Coming. This non-event soon became known as the "Great Disappointment," and forced the many thousands who had believed in Miller's predictions to come to terms with the question. A gathering of those who remained faithful met the following year in Albany and set in motion an organizational plan to keep the movement alive. This did not prove very successful in the long run. Factions developed among the remaining adventists, but only one was destined for enduring success.

Ellen Gould Harmon White (1827–1915) was a follower of William Miller who married the adventist minister and writer James S. White. Of perpetually delicate health, Ellen G. White was also subject to visions, and claimed to have experienced some two thousand in the course of her lifetime. The milieu of folk religion of the rural northern New England in which she lived her early life was in many ways similar to that which had produced Joseph Smith and would later shape Mary Baker Eddy's "discovery" of Christian Science. Prominent in Ellen White's experience were Methodist camp meeting revivalism, which had led to her 1841 conversion; faith healing, which she continuously sought as a relief for her various distresses; dramatic visions of the supernatural realm, which critics attributed to mesmerism; and her involvement in the Millerite excitement of the early 1840s. Here was a religious culture that provided a rich mixture of dramatic symbols, and a troubled personality with the need for healing and the gift of leadership.

Around the prophetic leadership of Ellen White there began to coalesce a new movement that built upon the unfulfilled adventist message of William Miller, but that added a number of new emphases and refinements. This new adventism was based on a reinterpretation of Miller's prophecy developed by Hiram Edson, who had argued that Jesus had in fact cleansed the Temple, as was supposed to have taken place on his return, but that this had happened in heaven rather than on earth. The subsequent, earthly cleansing was yet to take place, and these postdisappointment adventists perhaps wisely refrained from being too specific about the date. To this reconceptualized millennial message was now added a reappraisal of the way in which the Sabbath was observed by Christians. White confirmed through one of her visions the arguments of a contemporary movement known as the Seventh-Day Baptists, who maintained that Saturday rather than Sunday—in the manner of the Jews—was the proper day for worship. This combination of teachings led to the name "Seventh-Day Adventist Church," which she and her followers adopted upon their organization into a distinct denomination in 1860.

Another theme that has continued to this day to be a major emphasis among Seventh-Day Adventists has been that of health and bodily purity. As the anthropologist Mary Douglas has pointed out, the integrity and wholeness of the human body often serves as a symbol for other sorts of wholeness, whether that of society or of the cosmos. From at least the time of Leviticus, Western religion has frequently incorporated this symbolism into its beliefs and practices. Further, a preoccupation with bodily health and wholeness emerged as an important theme in American culture during the middle and late nineteenth century. This may have been a reflection of the fragility of the rapidly changing society of the time and the anxieties it aroused. It also may have arisen from the rising expectations that science and technology were creating, and that the absurdly primitive medical knowledge and practice of the time were unable to fulfill. Yet another aspect, which was expressed forcefully again in the career of Mary Baker Eddy, was the problematic role of women at the time, and the frustrations that intelligent but poorly educated women such as Ellen White experienced and channeled into symbolic expression. None of these sorts of theories can ever be definitively "proven" or regarded as a final explanation of any particular religious behavior, but together they help to provide a context in which the rise of new movements such as Seventh-Day Adventism can be understood.

In any case, Ellen White on June 5, 1863 experienced a vision in which she learned that meat, alcohol, and tobacco were not to be consumed; that doctors and the drugs on which they relied were similarly to be avoided; and that her disciples were to rely for their health on air, sunshine, rest, exercise, and a proper diet. Masturbation, a means of sexual pollution, was also condemned. Some of these tenets had already appeared in her earlier teachings; further, as White's biographer, the historian of science Ronald Numbers, has demonstrated, many were commonplace amid the reformist enthusiasm of the day. Temperance, of course, had already become a popular evangelical cause. Sylvester Graham, whose name has survived in that of a popular cracker, originally developed this tasty product as part of a comprehensive scientific and philosophical scheme for promoting health and well-being at a time when the diet of many Americans was notoriously heavy and unsalubrious. Alternative medical systems to the unreliable "orthodox" practice of the times also flourished, as in the practices of homeopathy and hydropathy, and probably did at the least no more harm than their more socially respectable rivals.

This preoccupation with health and diet received some of its most explicitly religious expression in Seventh-Day Adventism. At the denomination's headquarters in Battle Creek, Michigan, where the Whites had earlier settled, considerable attention was turned to medical and dietary reform. Hydropathy—the use of water, both internally and externally, for the treatment of disease—was especially favored, and the Western Health Reform Institute opened in Battle Creek in 1866. White and her followers—most notably, John H. Kellogg—also turned their attention to developing a wholesome diet based on fruit, grain, and vegetables. Out of this developed the modern cold breakfast cereal, although it is doubtful that White and Kellogg would endorse products such as Froot-Loops or Count Chocula with the same enthusiasm bestowed on the early corn flake. A later rift between White and Kellogg resulted in the latter's expulsion, and the movement did not benefit from the enormous future profits of Kellogg's products. Over the years, however, the Adventists have remained true to their commitment to bodily wholeness. In addition to continuing to condemn the use of alcohol, tobacco, and unnecessary drugs (vegetarianism is optional), they maintain numerous medical centers and schools in America and abroad.

Closely related to the idea that a new era of time had begun was the notion that a new beginning in history could be achieved through the formation of an ideal community in space. The Puritans, though not utopians as such, certainly came to view New England as a providential opportunity for the creation—quite literally from the ground up—of as ideal a society as could be fashioned through human effort in a fallen world. German sectarian groups such as the Moravians experimented with a reorganization of society on semicommunitarian lines, though their effort had been abandoned by the time of independence. Other German Pietists experimented with communal living into the nineteenth century and even beyond, as in the cases of Ohio's Zoar and Iowa's Amana. At the other end of the theological spectrum, New England Transcendentalists had a go at communitarianism at Brook Farm, which later turned into an unsuccessful experiment in utopian socialism on the principles of Charles Fourier, and on a tiny scale at Bronson Alcott's Fruitlands. Beyond the confines of religion altogether was the secular, socialist community of New Harmony, established by the Englishman Robert Owen in Indiana in the 1820s. Even the Mormons tried communal ownership of property during their stay in Kirtland, Ohio, during the following decade, in the short-lived "United Order of Enoch."

Two of the longest-lived utopian communal ventures were founded explicitly on versions of the millennial theme: the Oneida Community, and those of the Shakers. Oneida was the inspiration of John Humphrey Noyes (1811–1886), a Vermonter who was educated for the ministry at Yale Divinity School. While still at Yale, Noyes got into trouble for maintaining that he had entered into a state of perfection, completely free from sin. Unlike the more traditional John Wesley, who also espoused a sort of perfectionism, Noyes maintained that sinlessness was possible because Jesus had in fact already come again in A.D. 70. Although this second advent had been spiritual, it made possible the attainment of perfection by all people, including Noyes.

Since Noyes could not hope for a career in the "orthodox" churches of the day, he decided to implement his ideas by founding a community of his own. An initial venture in Putney, Vermont, which he began in 1836, eventually came to an end because of the hostility of the neighbors to Noyes's extreme ideas in the realm of sexual relations. Noyes therefore moved the entire community to Oneida, New York—in the heart of the "Burned Over District"—in 1848. Noyes advocated the practice of "complex marriage," in which sexual partners were delegated through group mediation, and children were raised communally. When the latter were not desired, *coitus reservatus* was promoted as an effective preventative and discipline, and the pursuit of carefully regulated reproduction that resulted—a form of eugenics—was known as *stirpiculture*. Actually, these seemingly scandalous practices were an aspect of a common life that was tightly regulated through communal ownership of property and mutual criticism sessions. Life at Oneida may have been eccentric, but was hardly orgiastic.

The Oneida experiment was for a time a considerable success, and centered on the massive Mansion House at the heart of the community. Unlike many such communities, which foundered for lack of a firm economic basis, Oneida thrived through the manufacture and sale first of steel traps and then of silver-plated flatware (which continues to sell well). However, the religious perfectionism that had been the community's original inspiration had begun to flag even within Noyes's own lifetime. The community had never attempted any rigorous isolation from the external world, except for self-protection, and secular ideas and culture had always been welcome. As Noyes yielded control of the community to his son, Pierrepont, the religious trappings began to fall away, though much of the group—many of them Noyes's own descendants, courtesy of stirpiculture—elected to continue to live together semi-communally. Finally, by the 1930s, even the family aspects of Oneida had eroded, and control of the manufacturing enterprise passed into outside hands.

The other communal society based on millennial principles that enjoyed a long-term (though not indefinite) success was the United Society of Believers in Christ's Second Appearance, better known as "Shakers." The Shakers came into being through the life and work of "Mother" Ann Lee (1736–1784), an Englishwoman of the working class who had experienced considerable distress through the death of all of her children. In part, no doubt, as a result of her distressing and unproductive marriage, she became convinced that sexuality was the root of sin and evil. She also became associated with a group of ecstatic "Shaking Quakers" in England, and then began to have visions of her own. After she and her followers were harrassed in England, they emigrated to New York in 1774.

Although "Mother Ann" herself died within a decade of her arrival in America, her example and teachings inspired a movement that has survived, if only vestigially, into the late twentieth century. Shaker theology was unique in regarding Ann Lee as the second coming of Christ, in the form of Holy Mother Wisdom. Her teachings thus acquired an authority far greater than those, say, of Noyes. As with Oneida, however, the consequences of these new revelations involved a millennial perfectionism based on the regulation of sexuality and sex-roles. At the approximately two dozen Shaker communities functioning during the movement's heyday in the years before the Civil War, celibacy was the rule. Men and women lived, worked, and worshipped in close proximity, but all erotic contact was strictly prohibited. The communities perpetuated themselves through the conversion of outsiders and the rearing of adopted orphans, many of whom elected to remain upon reaching adulthood. In addition, communal life was based on a strict equality of the sexes, with two male and two female leaders in charge of each "family" (i.e., grouping within each settlement).

Although the fundamental impulse behind Shaker life was religious, the group has come to be known best for its aesthetics and craftsmanship. The handsome, simple-lined Shaker furniture that now commands premium prices on the antique market was not radically different from contemporary New England crafts, and neither were the symmetrical buildings the Shakers raised for living, working, and worship. The distinctiveness of these artifacts lay in the combination of devotion, skill, and desire for efficiency that inspired their design and execution. Brooms, washing machines, herbs, and the rows of pegs on every wall all reflected a desire to honor God through an ordered, industrious life. The Protestant ethic and "plain style" of the Puritans had combined with the celibate imperative of medieval monasticism to produce a uniquely Yankee religion.

The seemingly ubiquitous communal societies of early nineteenth century America attracted a never-ending stream of foreign observers, and the Shakers were no exception. The particular fascination they exerted for Americans and

Europeans alike was their worship, which was frequently open to the public. Shaker meetinghouses were their only buildings painted pure white, part of a color-coding scheme reflecting a correspondence here on earth with the heavenly sphere beyond. In the Puritan-Quaker tradition, the meetinghouse interior was plain and white, with no ornamentation. Spectators were seated on movable benches while the worshippers faced one another, men on one side, women on the other, and engaged in dancing and singing that often became ecstatic—hence the nickname "Shakers." Even here, though, this ecstacy, or *antistructure,* was expressed through rehearsed and stylized dancing rather than undisciplined, individualistic frenzy. Potentially chaotic emotion was thus channeled into the purposes of a higher order of social structure—what the anthropologist Victor Turner has called *communitas,* the absorption of the individual into a larger social whole.

The spiritual and social health of the Shaker communities depended on a strict external organization and a firmly internalized commitment of each believer to the demanding regimen that the life demanded. Although the communities welcomed visitors and generated considerable income through the sales of seeds and crafts to outsiders, their physical isolation reinforced their distinctiveness and helped maintain morale. Despite all of their means of reinforcing loyalty and discipline, however, the system on occasion showed signs of strain. One manifestation of this stress was the appearance in the 1830s and 1840s of "Mother Ann's Work," a phenomenon in which individual spirit possession threatened to undermine the collective emotional worship that reinforced rather than sundered community ties. It was during this period of shaky leadership as well that "spirit drawings," such as the popular "Tree of Life" motif that now appears frequently on posters and greeting cards, began to take place.

The heyday of the Shakers was the effervescent decades prior to the Civil War, when their numbers reached some six thousand, distributed over eighteen to twenty-four communities, depending on one's system of reckoning. With the changes in society that took place during the subsequent era of urbanization, new converts became scarcer, and natural reproduction was, of course, still nonexistent. Communities began to decline and were ultimately abandoned. During the late 1980s, two were still in existence—at Sabbathday Lake, Maine, and Canterbury, New Hampshire. At the latter, the handful of elderly members refused to recognize the legitimacy of the former, since the men who belonged to the Maine community had entered after the last males in the original succession had died. Tradition required that new converts confess their sins to a member of the same sex, which had been impossible in their case. In neither community, however, was there enough of a critical mass of membership to make chances of future survival appear very promising, and the New Hampshire group had simply decided to regard the venture as nearing its final end. In both cases, many outsiders have become involved as volunteers and interns, helping maintain the communities through tours, gift shop sales, and the like. A perilous balance is thus maintained among a few surviving Shakers, scholars, and volunteers trying to preserve their heritage, and the diffusion of that heritage into popular culture and commercial exploitation. The revival of the Shaker hymn "The Gift to Be Simple" by the folk-singer Judy Collins in the 1960s, and its metamorphosis into "Lord of the Dance" in the mainstream churches, are ambiguous signs of the tradition's penetration into the broader culture. The Shakers were the product of their times, and those times seem, for better or worse, to be over.

CHAPTER 30

New World Revelation: Joseph Smith and the Rise of the Mormons

The "Burned-Over District" of upstate New York was one of the classic sites of social ferment that provided an ideal matrix for the emergence of new religious movements. The career of Joseph Smith, Jr., reflected in a particularly intense way this volatile combination of social and cultural forces. Smith's family came from respectable old New England stock, but had not been overly blessed with worldly success. His father was skeptical and restless in religious matters, constantly exploring new alternatives and at times embracing the New England tradition of popular Deism. His mother identified more with the evangelical tradition launched by the Great Awakening and its aftershocks, and joined the Presbyterian Church after the family's move from the Vermont mountains to Palmyra, New York, in 1816. The family was also deeply involved with the rural tradition of folk magic, in which divining rods, astrology, and other mild forms of the occult promised access to knowledge and wealth not easily acquired through natural means.

Joseph, Jr., was raised in this uncertain world of shaky social status, religious experimentation, and magical investigation. From the beginnings, the details and significance of his later, remarkable career are inevitably colored by these origins and their possible meanings. Mormons (or, more properly, Latter-day Saints), continue to regard him as a divinely appointed prophet, and the events of his brief, vivid life as fraught with sacred meaning. Skeptics, such as the irrepressible Mark Twain, and former Mormons like the late historian Fawn Brodie, have seen him as at best an amiable fraud who managed to delude even himself into accepting his extravagant claims to latter-day revelation. Serious "Gentile" (i.e., non-Mormon) students of his life and the movement it launched have tried to avoid these extremes, interpreting his career as the coincidence of a remarkable personality with an unusually protean set of circumstances.

There seems little question that the younger Joseph Smith engaged as a boy in the traditional "white magic" practices such as divination and treasure-hunting that were part of his family folk heritage. The relationship of this innocent occultism with the unusual series of events that followed is more problematic, and probably not resolvable to everyone's satisfaction. The "sacred history" of Joseph Smith began at age 14 (1820), when a vision of "the Father and the Son" appeared to him and cautioned him against joining any of the competing denominations of the age. (Compare this with the desire to transcend "man-made creeds" that was motivating Thomas and Alexander Campbell at the same time.) Smith had now clearly ascended to a higher level of interaction with the supernatural: His career as a visionary and prophet had been launched.

Three years later, on September 21 and 22, 1823, Smith went into a trance in which the Angel Moroni appeared to him. Moroni had been the last survivor of an ancient American people descended from the Hebrews, who were ultimately destroyed by a rival tribe of similar origins. His father, Mormon, had entrusted him with his people's history, inscribed on golden tablets, the existence of which was now revealed to Joseph (as Mormons still refer to him). These plates were concealed nearby in the hill Cumorah. Together with them were two stones, the "Urim and Thummim," that constituted the means through which these plates might be translated from the "Reformed Egyptian" in which they were written. (The names are Hebrew words which originally designated stones used by high priests for casting lots.)

It was not until four years later that the plates themselves were given to Smith in another epiphany. From this critical moment in 1827, he now embarked on a full-time career as translator of these supernatural treasures, a task culminating in their publication in 1830. During these three years of toil, Smith was aided by Emma (née Hale), his new wife, and by other followers he had begun to attract. In 1829, Smith and Oliver Cowdery received together a new revelation announcing the restoration of the Aaronic priesthood of the ancient Hebrews, as well as baptism under a "new and everlasting covenant." As Jan Shipps has demonstrated, the nascent religion that would come to be known as Mormonism now had three central elements in place that qualified it as a potentially new and distinct religion, rather than simply as another denomination of Christianity. These elements were a *prophet*—namely, Smith himself; a *church*, called initially "The Church of Jesus Christ," in which restored Old Testament priesthoods such as the "Aaronic" would play a major role; and a *scripture*, the *Book of Mormon*.

The *Book of Mormon* is one of the most controversial works ever published in the United States. It is also widely disseminated, by Mormon missionaries and in Mormon-owned enterprises such as the Marriott Hotel chain, in each bedroom of which a copy can be found together with a Gideon Bible. In format it resembles closely a standard Bible, and is divided up into books, chapters, and verses. Its diction is very similar to that of the King James (Authorized) version of the Bible; the proper names that appear throughout are frequently identical or very similar to many of those in the Bible, and a considerable number of verses begin with the phrase "And it came to pass."

The story it tells is that of the Hebrew patriarch Lehi, who left Jerusalem just before the Babylonian conquest of 587 B.C. He and his family crossed the Atlantic and landed in the New World, where they began a new life together. His descendants divided into the Nephites and the Lamanites, who were often in conflict with one another. A break in this conflict came about with the appearance of the resurrected Jesus among these people. This event inaugurated a millennial-like reign of peace, though only for two hundred years. Conflict then erupted again, with the Lamanites destroying the Nephites. Moroni was the last survivor among the latter. As such, he added a concluding section to the account of this history written by his father, Mormon, and concealed the plates on which it was written in the hill Cumorah. It was only with the reappearance of his spirit to Joseph Smith several hundred years later that these remarkable documents would come to light as part of the divine plan of revelation. In the meantime, the surviving Lamanites, who lacked written records, lost all memory of their early history, and their descendants were encountered by later-arriving Europeans as American Indians. To this day, Mormons regard Native Americans as a people with a special religious significance, and have made particular efforts to enlighten them as to their true spiritual destiny.

Since the *Book of Mormon* is regarded as divine revelation by a considerable number of people, and as arrant imposture by many others, it is difficult to assess its character neutrally. Thomas F. O'Dea, the Catholic sociologist of religion, was the author of one of the most successful attempts at this perplexing task in his classic work, *The Mormons,* of 1957. As a scholarly outsider, O'Dea interpreted Smith's narrative skeptically but sympathetically as an "almost completely neglected primary source for the intellectual history of the common man." Behind the saga of the Nephites and the Lamanites could be found the social, political, and religious themes that preoccupied the inhabitants of the Burned-Over District in Smith's time: religious revivalism; Calvinist versus Arminian theology; virtue leading to prosperity, which then begets pride and sin; distrust of secret societies; egalitarian political sentiments; and other preoccupations of Jacksonian Americans. Whatever else it may be, the *Book of Mormon* can be read as a document of its times.

The publication of the *Book of Mormon* signified for Smith's followers a reopening of the canon (i.e., authoritative list of contents) of Scripture. Such was an act of religious radicalism only hinted at by the Quakers, who regarded the promptings of the Inner Light as continuing (but not written) revelation. Even the Shakers, who saw Mother Ann Lee as a redemptive figure, did not regard any new body of religious writings as authoritative. The most direct parallel in the history of Western religion is the Qu'ran, revealed many centuries before to the Prophet Muhammed, which stands together with Hebrew and Christian Scripture as the foundation of the religion of Islam. However, since the latter faith was virtually unknown in America during the 1820s, there is no reason to believe that Muhammed and the Qu'ran offered Smith any sort of model.

As noted by Jan Shipps, this prophet, scripture, and church betokened a new religion with an extremely complex relationship to the past, present, and future. Christianity had lost its original promise as the agency of redemption with the "Great Apostasy," which took place in the apostolic age itself and left a gap of centuries until the coming of a new prophet. Smith's new "Church of Jesus Christ" (later, "of Latter-day Saints") had been divinely established in "the last days" as a preparation for the Second Coming of Jesus. This was expected to take place soon—a reflection of the millennial enthusiasm characteristic of the age. The church's adoption of baptism by immersion and foot-washing, together with the institution of a new "Twelve Apostles," was indicative of its self-conception as a revival of primitive Christianity. Similarly, the divinely mandated restoration of first the Aaronic and later the Melchizedek priesthoods was an aspect of Smith's notion that his followers were quite literally reconstituting the ancient people of Israel. Further revelations over the next decade or so introduced new "ordinances" (rituals) not recorded in the Old or New Testaments, and added the *Doctrine and Covenants* and the *Pearl of Great Price* to the canon of latter-day scripture. "Mormonism" was to be all of these things—Israel and Apostles—and yet more.

Smith and his followers soon abandoned the Burned-Over District for Kirtland, Ohio, a town near Cleveland where the recent convert Sidney Rigdon and his congregation prepared the way for them. These new disciples had earlier embraced the message of Thomas and Alexander Campbell, who had called for the abolition of all creeds of human origin and a return to New Testament ways as the exclusive form of pure Christianity. This "restorationism" was also clearly part of Smith's message, and presumably was a major element in Rigdon's conversion. The move *en masse* to Kirtland in 1830–1831 was the first in a series of relocations by Smith and his followers, who now began to think of themselves in Hebrew fashion as engaging in a "Gathering"—a coming together as a distinct people. The westward moves they were to make during the next two decades reflected the pioneering spirit that was abroad in the land, but that here was acquiring a unique religious rationale.

At Kirtland, Smith and his followers for the first time set about creating a coherent community—not simply of belief and worship, but of the whole of their lives. Here they built their first temple, an eclectic combination of architectural elements with the frame of a New England meetinghouse. (The Kirtland Temple is still preserved as a museum.) This monumental structure, built by the community's pooling of resources and effort and sited high on a hill, provided a physical setting for the new rituals, or "ordinances," that were progressively being revealed to Smith. On the two main floors, for example, were two complete sets of pulpits facing one another at either end, which were designed for use by the newly restored Aaronic and Melchizedek priesthoods. The "patriarchal blessing," clearly based on the Old Testament, was introduced during the sojourn at Kirtland, as was—surreptitiously and controversially—polygamy. Another indication of the eclectic and sometimes exotic combination of elements that was contributing to the new religion was the display at Kirtland of Egyptian mummies and a papyrus scroll, which Smith translated as the *Book of Abraham* (later part of the *Pearl of Great Price*). Biblical, Ancient Near Eastern, and Masonic themes all were thus incorporated into

Mormonism through a process of *syncretism*—that is, borrowing from diverse sources to form a new whole.

The Mormons at Kirtland were thus becoming not just a new religion but a society, even a people, bound together by a common set of beliefs and practices that differentiated them from their Gentile neighbors. This goal of developing an entire culture grounded on religious values and symbols extended into the economic realm as well. While at Kirtland, Smith instituted the "United Order of Enoch," a system of communal property ownership with control in the hands of the church. Although this radical deviation from economic individualism did not last long, the principle of economic cooperation again proved valuable in the critical early years at the Great Salt Lake, and has persisted to the present day in the Mormon requirement of tithing and the provision of relief by the church rather than the secular government. In addition, Smith founded an "Antibanking Society"—called such in an attempt to circumvent requirements for a regular bank charter—that issued currency and engaged in other financial activities. Its collapse helped precipitate the Mormon departure from Kirtland in 1838.

During the Kirtland years, Mormon geographical horizons were expanding in several directions. On the one hand, missionaries were sent to northwestern Europe, particularly the British Isles and Scandinavia, where they were soon successful in recruiting converts willing to emigrate to America. On the other, Smith had launched a series of attempts at settlement in Missouri, where he believed that the Garden of Eden had originally been located. As in Kirtland, Gentile hostility contributed to the rapid failure of these ventures. However, these failures helped set expectations for further westward movement, and contributed to the growing belief that the history and destiny of America itself were an intimate part of a grand divine design now on the brink of fulfillment.

After the failure of the settlement at Far West, Missouri, in 1838, Smith and his followers moved back eastward to the town of Commerce, Illinois, on the banks of the Mississippi. They obtained a charter from the state granting semiautonomy, and Smith gave the city the new name of *Nauvoo*—"a beautiful plantation" in the "revised Hebrew" language to which Smith was privy. As were many of the new cities that were arising in America at the time, Nauvoo was carefully platted for planned growth on a rectangular grid. What differentiated it from others was Smith's intention to make it the symbolic and actual capital—the new Jerusalem—of the new Zion he envisioned in the American heartland. One of its two foci was the "Nauvoo House," which was to serve as Smith's residence and a hotel for visitors. The other, and more important, was the second of Mormonism's temples. The Nauvoo temple was an imposing neoclassical structure that incorporated explicitly the new set of visual symbols, such as suns and moons with human features, that Smith was working out to express his continuing revelations. Inside were the system of dual pulpits first used at Kirtland, as well as a massive pine tub, supported by twelve wooden oxen, for the newly introduced ritual of baptism of the dead. Nauvoo, in short, was the scene of the continuing development of Mormonism as both a religious and a social system.

Smith's identification with America as the new Jerusalem—the millennial kingdom—was further promoted with his announcement of his candidacy for the American presidency in 1844. (American secular titles such as "president" are mixed with traditional ecclesiastical titles such as "priest" and "bishop" in Mormon usage.) Smith also cracked down on an opposition newspaper that was being published in Nauvoo, and had its presses destroyed. What was perceived as the beginnings of a dictatorship aroused the already potent hostility of local Gentiles. The governor ordered Smith to surrender himself to face charges growing out of the incident. A mob burst into the jail at Carthage, Illinois, where Smith and his brother Hyrum were awaiting trial, and shot them and other leaders of the group to death.

The Mormons at Nauvoo now had a martyr but no leader. Contention over the succession to Smith's position led to the departure of Sidney Rigdon and other unsuccessful aspirants to the title, several of whom founded rival churches. Brigham Young (1801–1877), an early follower of Smith and a fellow Vermonter, had been president of the Twelve (Apostles) at the time of Smith's death, and was rapidly acclaimed as his de facto successor. Growing pressure from the Gentile community made it clear that a further—and final—move west was now called for. While working strenuously to complete the temple, the Mormons began preparations for one of America's epic *Volkerwanderungen*—the trek of a whole people, their numbers swelled by immigration, hundreds of miles over desolate territory to found a new Zion in the Utah desert.

It was Brigham Young who presided brilliantly over this "exodus," which added yet another opportunity for the Mormons to recapitulate the Hebrew experience. Beginning on February 4, 1846, the first contingent arrived at the Great Salt Lake—its ultimate resting place—by late July. In rapid succession a site for a temple was staked out, Young was confirmed as the new President as well as "Prophet, Seer, Revelator"—and, thereby, as Smith's full and official successor—and a provisional State of Deseret was established. (*Deseret* was a word from the *Book of Mormon* meaning "honeybee." A short-lived experiment with a Deseret alphabet, however, was unsuccessful, and Mormon culture has never generated more than a few such exotic terms.)

In 1850, this provisional state was recognized by the government as Utah Territory, and Brigham Young was appointed governor. The road to full statehood, however, was to be anything but straightforward. As the anthropologist Mark Leone has pointed out, the "Great Basin Kingdom" that Young and his followers established in the Utah desert was considerably more than another frontier outpost of American society. Rather, the Mormons were attempting to establish a "counterculture," which repudiated many of the values and practices that informed the lives of other Americans, and substitute alternatives that seemed radical in the context of Victorian America.

One deviation from standard American practice was the cooperative economic scheme that, under Young, literally made the desert blossom. To make the salt flats of Utah habitable, a massive and sophisticated system of irrigation had to be designed and constructed, a task clearly beyond the scope of any individual pioneers. The entire colonization of Utah and parts of adjoining states was centrally directed, with as little as possible left to chance. Land was distributed, infrastructure built and maintained, and need alleviated under the firm direction of the First Presidency at Salt Lake City. Utah thus rapidly became a *theocracy*—a government by divine will, as interpreted and implemented by the Prophet, Seer, and Revelator. Not since the Holy Commonwealths of seventeenth-century New England had America seen such a thoroughgoing attempt at governance according to God's plan. Probably never has it seen such a unified and successful attempt, at least for the "brief and shining moment" that the Deseret experiment was to survive.

Its survival was not really endangered by Young's unorthodox politics and economics, nor by his even less orthodox theology—manifested visually in the massive Salt Lake City Temple undertaken under his own supervision in 1847, and completed only after his death. The symbolic focus of Mormon "differentness" was the practice of polygamy, or plural marriage, that first came into the open at Salt Lake City. It was this oddly potent issue that would lead to decades of legal and political controversy, and even violence. When the controversy was finally resolved in 1890, the relationship of this gathered people and their kingdom with the rest of America would be irreversibly and radically transformed.

PART IV

The End of the Frontier and the Rise of the City

INTRODUCTION

The decades between the Civil War and World War I were a time of rapid growth and major demographic change. The issue of national unity had been definitively resolved, but the abolition of slavery only changed rather than settled the question of the status of blacks. Southern whites eventually rid themselves of hostile Northern tutelage, developed segregation to a veritable science, and worked variations upon the tradition of evangelicalism to produce an insular and distinctively Southern form of Protestantism. As Southern blacks began to flee their tenant farms for the promise of urban jobs precipitated by the "Great War," they began to work variations on their own evangelical traditions, and to generate remarkable new religious movements as well.

The movement of blacks to the great cities of the Northeast and the Great Lakes region was by no means the only facet of urbanization. In 1890, the Census Bureau announced that the great American frontier could now be regarded as closed; no more unclaimed arable land existed in sufficient quantity to attract new settlers. Meanwhile, technological change generated commercial and industrial employment in the burgeoning cities, and inventions such as the elevator and steel-frame construction gave those cities a new look and a new density. Their need for low-wage, low-skill workers was filled only later by Southern blacks. Before the arrival of these blacks in great numbers, the social and economic upheavals that were similarly transforming the face of Europe were pressing Italians, Greeks, Poles, Bohemians, Ukranians, and others from the less developed parts of that continent to seek their fortunes overseas. Most of these "new immigrants" found employment—brutal as it may have been—in the teeming cities, where they settled into ethnic neighborhoods. With amazing speed, they erected Roman Catholic and Eastern Orthodox churches and Orthodox Jewish synagogues to serve their needs and mark their presence. Americans of older stock and Protestant faith often recoiled in fear and amazement at this exotic transformation of their land.

The city was the frontier of the late nineteenth and early twentieth centuries in America. In Victorian Boston, Mary Baker Eddy turned her vision of Christian Science into an institution. In Chicago, Dwight L. Moody and Ira D. Sankey launched a new form of urban revivalism. In Detroit, New York, and Philadelphia arose the "black gods of the metropolis" that Arthur Fauset studied. Father Divine, Sweet Daddy Grace, W. D. Fard, and Elijah Muhammed were all prophets of new black religions that repudiated Christianity entirely. The black ghettoes of the great cities continued to be a frontier for blacks and more recently arrived minorities—Puerto Ricans, Mexicans, Central Americans, Cubans, Syrians, Lebanese, Vietnamese, and Laotians—as the twentieth century continued. It was among many of these people that the "storefront" church—usually Pentecostal, Holiness, or Fundamentalist—has continued to thrive.

It was these latter movements that would also prove crucial for the development of white Protestantism throughout the century. For decades, a liberal theology that transcended denominational lines gained a stronghold among many of the most influential pulpits and seminaries. Its offshoots—the Social Gospel and, later, Neo-Orthodoxy—added new elements of social concern to the liberal message, and continued to permeate elite circles of denominational leadership as the century progressed. Early on, however, a reaction began to set in, which had its roots at least as much in the cities of the North as in the rural hinterlands with which it became so strongly associated in the popular imagination. Elements of the old evangelical consensus now hardened into a Fundamentalism that was dead set against the liberal challenge. From another direction, the Holiness movement arose out of the older Wesleyan matrix to add a new element of experiential emphasis to the emergent conservative Protestant movement. Still another and even more potent force, Pentecostalism, rapidly emerged from Holiness, with nearly simultaneous origins in the Los Angeles ghetto, the Kansas heartland, and the Southern piedmont. It was here that the great national drama of the Scopes "Monkey Trial" would play itself out in the 1920s.

Urban expansion and rural reaction thus set in motion many of the forces that have dominated American religious life throughout the twentieth century. The American people were at once becoming more numerous, more ethnically diverse, and more geographically concentrated. Among some, the oldest religious traditions of the West—Roman Catholicism, Eastern Orthodoxy, and Orthodox Judaism—were experiencing a new vitality and dramatic expansion in the New World. For others, new religions were arising, with urban prophets appearing seemingly out of nowhere. Within what had been the evangelical "establishment" of American Protestantism, tensions erupted that proved uncontainable, and liberals and conservatives set in for a long, inconclusive struggle for cultural hegemony that is still unresolved as—after many twists, turns, and realignments—the twentieth century nears its end.

A. The Adjustments of Protestantism

Chapter 31

Victorian Evangelicals

Rarely has the name of one person captured so thoroughly the ethos of an era as that of Queen Victoria, in America as much as in England. The name conjures up the staid, censorious image of the Queen, in perpetual mourning of her lost Prince Albert, maintaining an aura of serene unamusement at the antics of her times. The Victorian decades in America saw a resurgence of many aspects of antebellum evangelicalism, especially its determination to form or reform the morals of a nation. Temperance in particular became the focus for this new Protestant crusade; the saloon and demon rum were the embodiment of moral evil. Carry Nation's hatchet and Anthony Comstock's blue laws came to symbolize a spirit of repression and censoriousness in which pleasure and sin were regarded as synonymous.

Or so, at least, the story goes—the story fashioned by the Baltimore *Sun*'s H. L. Mencken and other "debunkers" of latter-day "Puritanism" in the 1920s and beyond. It was in this school of journalism—and sometimes even scholarship—that the image of the American Puritan became conflated with that of the Victorian evangelical, and the more extreme representatives of the latter breed equated with the whole of a complex and often contradictory era. Whatever the excesses of some of its celebrities, Victorian America was anything but a sober, repressed, unchanging society when viewed as a totality. The decades between Reconstruction and the First World War were the most tumultuous in American history. Immigrants by the hundreds of thousands poured into the burgeoning industrial cities of the East and Midwest, transforming the country almost overnight from an agricultural to a predominantly urban society. Cities are almost by definition anything but decorous and orderly, and the exaggerated moralism of some Victorian reformers reflected the similarly exaggerated tumult of contemporary urban life.

230

Nor was moral reform the exclusive preoccupation of beleaguered defenders of the Old Order. Prohibition, which came to symbolize Victorian repressiveness to later generations, was in its day a *pro*gressive cause. It was actively promoted not only by Bishop James Cannon, Jr., and his Southern Methodist flock, but also by the leaders of the Social Gospel, ardent Progressives, and crusaders for women's suffrage. To understand this era in its complexity, we need to disburden ourselves of the legacy of caricature and reaction that has attached itself to these times, and try to see their sometimes surprising contours and alignments in their actuality.

The moral energies of the antislavery movement outlasted the Civil War for a few years, rallying themselves during the era of Reconstruction to assist in the task of aiding the "freedmen"—freed slaves—to adjust to their new circumstances. Just as the federal government under Ulysses Grant would turn much of the apparatus of Indian welfare over to the various Christian denominations, so was General Oliver Howard of the Freedman's Bureau more than willing to assist evangelical groups in the task of educating—and, if possible, converting—the former slaves. A wide variety of groups arose to take up this challenge, and the focus of home missions briefly turned south. The typical teacher of the freedmen was evangelical, Congregationalist, female, and from New England. Much was accomplished during these years in developing an educational infrastructure for southern blacks, ranging from elementary public schools to normal schools, to much of today's network of black colleges. The failure of Reconstruction, the passage of Jim Crow laws, the imposition of rigid patterns of segregation, and the accommodationist stance advocated by Booker T. Washington all prevailed over the ambitious visions of the abolitionists. Blacks throughout the country generally retreated into their own Baptist and Methodist denominations, and only slowly laid the foundations for what would decades later emerge as the Civil Rights movement. In the meantime, most white evangelicals turned their attention elsewhere.

The Victorian woman is typically represented as confined to a pedestal in restrictive clothing, and unnaturally preoccupied with the repression of sexuality. However, the impact of women on American culture in general and on religion in particular during these years is only now becoming clear to scholars. There is no question that a major change had been taking place for some decades in the American economic and social structure, with profound implications for sex roles. With the rise of a national economy and the displacement of small-scale commerce and manufacture, as well as agriculture, by increasingly complex enterprises, the role of middle-class women and children in economic life grew constricted. A series of parallel dichotomies became sharply etched in the American consciousness: male/female, work/home, power/purity, profane/sacred.

A middle-class mythology rapidly developed in which women were divinely entrusted with the sacred functions of the care of home and hearth and nurture of the family. Men, correspondingly, were expected to cope with the harsh, secular realities of the world of business and the professions. This division was further reinforced by changing patterns in land use. The development of the streetcar made it possible for middle-class families to live in residential suburbs far away from the clamor of commerce, while breadwinners could make the daily commute to serve Mammon. The poor of both sexes were still consigned to hard physical work, while the honor of the pedestal became more and more common for women of the wealthier classes—usually native-born, white, and Protestant.

The church was one area in which these boundaries became somewhat blurred. Throughout the century, the majority of churchgoers were women, and it was the time and effort of women that was the mainstay of much of church life and work. On the other hand, church leadership was almost exclusively a male province. Aside from the Friends, who for the most part rejected a formal ministry, it was the small, decentralized, liberal New England-based denominations—Congregationalists, Unitarians, Universalists—who took the lead in ordaining women. Similarly, women were barred from voting roles in most denominational bodies, and the schism within antebellum antislavery ranks over the question illustrates the pervasiveness of this pattern within voluntary societies as well. Women did found their own missionary, reform, and other benevolent societies, but were themselves divided as to whether they should be permitted to take a more active role in the governance of the broader organizations they themselves sustained.

On the other hand, the role of organized religion within American society was becoming confused in terms of the dichotomies that were shaping the way many churchgoers organized their perceptions of reality. If society could be divided up into dichotomous zones, what was the place of the church? The active role of the colonial and antebellum clergy had been straightforward: They were men who exercised a position of leadership not only in the churches but frequently in the wider society as well. Whatever Beecher and Finney may have been, their images were clearly masculine.

During the Victorian decades, however, this role for the clergy and the churches became blurred. One of the most influential religious figures of the era was its greatest evangelist, Dwight L. Moody (1837–1899). Moody's career is the embodiment of the American success story. Like Finney, he emerged from the matrix of New England evangelicalism into a secular career, as a shoe salesman in Boston. Seeking the main chance in Chicago, he experienced even greater success in the realm of soul-winning than in business, and became immersed in YMCA and other evangelistic work. Moody then teamed up with Ira D. Sankey, a talented musician and songwriter, and went on to adapt the well-established tradition of revivalism to the new urban context of late nineteenth-century America—after an initial, triumphant tour of the British Isles.

The Moody-Sankey revivals were in some ways the epitome of the new business civilization harnessed to the evangelical impulse. Before staging an interdenominational revival in a city, Moody insisted that a committee of clergy and laity make preliminary arrangements to ensure success. A vast "tabernacle" would be erected to accommodate the multitudes expected to "hit the sawdust trail"—that is, come forward to shake hands with the evangelist and thereby accept Jesus and his offer of salvation. Modern methods of advertising and publicity were lavishly employed, as were careful provisions made for financial management and physical arrangements. Among Moody's admirers and generous patrons were some of the wealthiest businessmen of the day, including George Armour, Cyrus McCormick, and John Wanamaker. Moody's presentation of the Christian message was thus very much in harmony with the masculine world of commerce and industry—and served the latter's interests in its lack of disturbing social and political implications.

It was Moody's message rather than his means that confused the issue as to where his revival campaigns fit into the culture matrix of his day. The god of Edwards and Beecher—and even of Julia Ward Howe—had been a masculine god, "trampling out the vintage where the grapes of wrath are stored." In *Uncle Tom's Cabin*, though, a shift of focus was clearly taking place. The agents of the divine were not aggressive clergymen, but rather "the meek and lowly"—little children and nonviolent, elderly slaves. Redemption came about not through the active mastery of the external environment and the aggressive conquest of sin, but through a passive, exemplary role exerted by the saintly. Stowe may not have been a formal theologian, but her powerful images affected far more readers than the learned disquisitions of scholars such as her husband Calvin.

Moody's preaching was not complex. Its theological content, in fact, was almost nonexistent, and could be reduced to the proposition that salvation was available for the asking. All that the sinner had to do was make a simple decision, symbolized in "hitting the sawdust trail." Instead of theological reflections, Moody's sermons were anecdotal—usually pathetic stories invoking premature death, longing for mother, and a gentle Jesus whose message of redemption was open to all. Judgment was largely gone, and mercy was everything. Sentimentality—the appeal to the heart, even in contradiction to the dictates of the head—had been raised to an ultimate principle in a way having little to do with Edwards's cult of the "affections." And sentimentality was the province of woman.

Nor was Moody the whole show. Sankey, too, played an active role in the success of the urban revivals, which were the first to use music on a systematic basis. Warming up the audience before Moody's appearance was one role of the music director; so was the provision of suitable accompaniment for later parts of the service, such as the "altar call." The latter event was the climax of a Moody-Sankey revival, in which the preacher would invite all present to hit the trail to indicate that they had made what Billy Graham would later call a "decision for Christ." Sankey and his contemporaries, such as the blind but enormously productive Fanny J. Crosby, devised a whole new genre of religious music for these occasions known as the "gospel hymn." (This should not be confused with black gospel music, which has a very different character.) The imagery of these songs could be powerfully visceral, as in "There is a fountain filled with blood, Drawn from Emmanuel's veins." Just as typical of the genre was the vintage altar call hymn of Will H. Thompson's:

> Softy and tenderly Jesus is calling,
> Calling for you and for me;
> See, on the portals He's waiting and watching,

Watching for you and for me.
Come home, come home,
Ye who are weary, come home.
Earnestly, tenderly, Jesus is calling—
Calling, "O Sinner, come home!"

Similarly, in Charlotte Elliott and William Bradbury's "Just As I Am"—still a popular altar call hymn—Jesus is the "lamb of God" whose blood was "shed for me." The Jesus through whom redemption comes is closer to Uncle Tom and Little Eva—the helpless sacrificial victim—than the God of Edwards, who dangled sinners over the fire like loathsome spiders.

Successful revivals conducted according to modern business methods, then, were very acceptable when the message they conveyed was relevant only to the hearth and not to the marketplace. In this vein, Ann Douglas has argued in her provocative study, *The Feminization of American Culture,* that middle-class women and Protestant clergy of the Victorian era found themselves in an implicit alliance in developing strategies to capitalize on their own powerlessness. Women, children, home and hearth, religion—and the ministry—all found themselves on the "sacred" side of the cultural divide, and were thus not expected to exert influence beyond their proper sphere. Douglas argues that a cult of powerlessness, expressed in sermons and popular sentimental fiction, emerged from this "holy alliance," in which claims to moral hegemony served as a rather poor substitute for genuine influence on society.

Not all Victorian women, though, were content with this trade-off. The reform crusades of the antebellum era, and antislavery in particular, had provided women with an opportunity to gain exposure to the world of politics and public life, however contricted their roles may have been in some cases. After slavery had ceased to be an issue, and the subsequent plight of black Americans had receded from public consciousness, the possibilities for sweeping moral reform took on new dimensions. From the early days of the Benevolent Empire, the cause of temperance had caught the imagination of many evangelicals. Alcohol had not always been a symbol of evil or pollution in the Protestant imagination; in fact, ordination celebrations in the eighteenth century sometimes ended as drunken carousals. Perhaps reflecting the demands of a new business culture, as against the laxer needs of traditional agrarian society, a revulsion began to set in against such indulgences beginning early in the nineteenth century. "Temperance" at first meant what it in fact denotes—moderation in the use of alcohol, and avoidance of hard liquor as opposed to beer and hard cider. This more balanced approach soon yielded to an absolutist position, and the temperate were only those who had "taken the pledge." By 1826, the American Temperance Society had been founded to promote this gospel of "teetotalism."

Opposition to the indiscriminate use of alcohol in the antebellum era was by no means a sign of fanaticism. According to W. J. Rorabaugh, male citizens of what he calls "The Alcoholic Republic" between 1790 and 1840 drank on the average a half a pint of hard liquor a day—presumably with some adverse consequences. Before long, temperance strategy shifted from the promotion of voluntary abstinence to legal coercion. In 1846, the "Maine Law," passed with the aid of abolitionist support, became the model for legislative prohibition of the manufacture and sale of intoxicants at the state level. Although it was soon emulated by other states, most of these laws were of brief duration, and it was not until the postwar period that temperance would again emerge as a major political force. This is not, however, to downplay its role in the antebellum era, when the cause attracted countless adherents among men and women, drunkards and paragons of sobriety, abolitionists and slave-holders, and any number of others regardless of rank and station. It was, in short, the quintessential American reform movement, which could link itself to anything from radical social transformation to revenge against the male sex, to the desire for personal respectability and success.

After slavery had disappeared from the national scene as an object of reforming zeal, temperance returned to prominence in the new social context of postwar urban America. The old argument, dramatized in such popular melodramas as T. S. Arthur's *Ten Nights in a Barroom* (1854), was the destructive effect of alcohol not only on individuals but on families as well. (Arthur had been strongly influenced by the Washingtonians, a secular temperance movement aimed not so much at committed evangelicals but at drunkards, Catholics, and other groups given little attention by the Benevolent Empire.) In the sentimental imagery of the day, the pathetic child vainly calling for her father at the door of the saloon captured the growing popular appeal of the movement. It was, in short, potentially a women's movement—uncontrolled drink cut right to the heart of women and children as well as the broader social fabric. And women began to organize.

The organization that captured the spirit of the age most fully was the Women's Christian Temperance Union. Founded in Cleveland in 1874, the WCTU began as a single-issue organization under the rather conservative leadership of its first president, Annie Wittenmyer. In 1879, Wittenmyer was defeated by the redoubtable Frances Willard (1839–1898), whose philosophy of "Do Everything" gave the Union both a more activist and more feminist dimension. Willard more than anyone illustrated the fusion of religious and political zeal that characterized Victorian reform as she showed that a woman could and would make herself heard. Significantly, this woman who dared to challenge both church and civil politics as a male preserve chose a white ribbon, for the purity of the home, and the slogan "Home Protection" as the Union's symbols. Her concerns included not just shutting down saloons but an activist drive for women's interests in the areas of labor, prisons, prostitution, drugs, health, welfare, racial issues, and virtually every area of society in which women were involved. Most controversially, this included the suffrage, for which Willard was an ardent campaigner, and on behalf of which a "Department of Franchise" was added to the WCTU's structure in 1882. Like Garrison before and Martin Luther King afterwards, Willard saw reform as holistic, and never feared compromising the central issue by taking aim at a host of other concerns affected by the underlying problems.

The WCTU was resoundingly successful in its campaign of propaganda and organization, but considerably less so in the realm of legislative and electoral politics. Willard's support for the Prohibition Party presumably helped it achieve some minor victories, and it may have influenced the outcome of the 1884 election. Third-party politics, however, has never been very successful in the American scheme of things, and Willard's later conversion to socialism deflected her potential impact further. By the 1890s, the WCTU had been overshadowed by a new group, the Anti-Saloon League, which was founded in Oberlin, Ohio, in 1893. The League was in many ways the legitimate successor to Theodore Dwight Weld and his "band" in its combination of evangelical fervor and grassroots lobbying. Unlike Willard's WCTU, it was strictly a single-issue movement, ready to support any candidate who pledged to vote "dry."

Just as the WCTU's name clearly revealed its identity, so did the League's. Today, "saloon" has become a quaint word used primarily by bars trying to evoke a "wild west" atmosphere. In the late nineteenth century, the term was particularly associated with an establishment that not only sold strong drink but also served as a meeting-place for the worst elements of society: prostitutes, crooked politicians, and immigrants. Together with the Catholic Church, the saloon had developed into a uniquely urban institution representing all of the social forces that stood against everything that rural evangelicals and urban Progressives had in common. The saloon helped perpetuate immigrant culture and reinforced Catholic mores; it robbed the workingman of his wages, sobriety, health, and usefulness to his family—and his employer; it served as a den for crime of all sorts; and it provided a convenient basis for corrupt urban machine politics. It was, in short, a symbol of everything that the "better" classes feared might undermine American morality and democratic culture.

The supporters of what was now shaping up as a drive for nationwide prohibition included, but were by no means confined to, evangelical churchpeople. Bishop James Cannon, Jr., the "Dry Messiah" of the Methodist Episcopal Church, South, was certainly an influential leader for that constituency. Cannon, though, was joined by such unlikely bedfellows as Archbishop John Ireland of St. Paul, Social Gospel spokesman Washington Gladden, and former President Theodore Roosevelt. The campaign dovetailed neatly with Progressive concerns for clean government and against trusts, including the liquor industry. At the core, though, were the League and the major evangelical denominations—Baptist, Presbyterian, and preeminently Methodist—who were persuaded that the imposition of a national prohibition on the manufacture and sale of alcoholic beverages would be a major step in ushering in the Kingdom of God and a Christian America. The crusade for Prohibition thus took on a character of what Joseph Gusfield has called a "symbolic crusade." Its ultimate message was a major victory for a Protestant culture accustomed to deference that was now beleaguered by the combined forces of the city, the immigrant, the political boss, an elite of new wealth, and the intellectual forces represented by Darwinism and the "new" biblical criticism.

The grassroots organizational work of the WCTU and the League were doubtless crucial to the movement's ultimate success, but it took a world war to win the final victory. Nativism—the fear of the foreign—had emerged as a potent aspect of the mythology of the prohibitionists; the saloon and its immigrant patrons were a symbol of the erosion of the fabric of traditional Protestant America. War with Germany, the nation that gave us both biblical critics and brewers of beer, mobilized nativism to the extent that the teaching of German was forbidden in some public schools and speaking it on the streets invited lynching. Catholics and Lutherans, who maintained the "Continental Sabbath" tradition of relaxation as well as worship on Sundays, who utilized wine in their communion services, who for the most part saw nothing wrong with the recreational use of alcohol in moderation, and who frequently were of German descent, were unenthusiastic, to say the least. Their objections were overrun by a public opinion that at times bordered on hysteria. The arguments for prohibition were further bolstered by the patriotic argument that the grain used in brewing and distilling was needed to support the troops.

In December 1917, the House passed the 18th Amendment, which was speedily ratified by all but two states. "The Noble Experiment" of national prohibition took effect on January 16, 1919. Interestingly, the 19th Amendment, guaranteeing women's suffrage, was ratified in August of the following year. As Edward R. Murrow later observed, it was now as illegal to take a drink as it was to deny a woman the vote. Frances Willard would have felt vindicated.

The victory, however, soon proved hollow. The 18th Amendment and its enforcing legislation, the Volstead Act, were widely ignored by upper and lower classes alike, however much the evangelical middle might remain committed. Organized crime, symbolized in Chicago's Al Capone, added a new and noxious dimension to the American urban scene, and owed its existence almost exclusively to the demand for illicit liquor. Public opinion more generally swung away from the crusading zeal that Prohibition represented. Evangelicalism in its new and extreme form of Fundamentalism was heaped with public scorn through the Scopes "Monkey" Trial of 1925, where Darwinian evolution was unsuccessfully attacked by William Jennings Bryan—the "beerless leader" who had served as Wilson's Secretary of State. Revivalism had been turned to vaudeville by Billy Sunday, who now found himself eclipsed by new, secular celebrities—Babe Ruth, Rudolph Valentino, Gertrude Ederle, and Charles Lindbergh. H. L. Mencken, the acerbic and agnostic journalist who had covered the Scopes trial for the Baltimore *Sun,* made relentless fun of the benighted denizens of what he called the "Bible Belt." Despite the efforts of the legendary enforcement agents Eliot Ness and Izzy and Moe, the victory of Prohibition had proven to be, indeed, largely symbolic.

The 20th Amendment, which repealed the 18th, was ratified in 1933, shortly after the election of Franklin Delano Roosevelt. The Catholic "wet" Democratic candidate, Alfred E. Smith, had been solidly defeated four years earlier in part through the opposition of Southern evangelicals and other supporters of Prohibition. Roosevelt, however, represented a new coalition. Himself an Episcopalian of patrician stock, he mobilized the support of Catholics, Jews, blacks, and other minorities—as well as traditional Democrats and those affected by the Depression. The New Deal thus marked the end of the laissez-faire economics that had been a staple of much of evanglical moral theology in the past, as well as the political dominance of the Protestant middle classes and evangelical moralism.

So thorough was the reversal of evangelical fortunes in the 1920s that this era is sometimes spoken of as the "Second Disestablishment"—a spiritual successor to the dislocation that Lyman Beecher had lamented in Connecticut a century earlier. Its symptoms were many. One heretofore unmentioned aspect of Victorian evangelicalism was its stress on world missions. This impulse was tinged with a sense of Anglo-American imperialism especially manifest in the war against Catholic Spain and the subsequent assimilation of the Philippines as a part of an American mini-empire. Following the successful fund drives to support the war effort, a vast campaign to promote home and foreign missions and bring about a general spiritual revival through a unified Protestant effort took shape as the Interchurch World Movement. Launched in 1920 in an outburst of optimism, it finally announced a goal of raising $1 billion. It didn't—and could not even raise enough to pay its debts. The era of interdenominational Protestant crusading had come to an end.

Part of the problem that underlay the ICWM's failure was the division of Protestantism into mutually hostile camps. Those who saw the emergence of evolutionary biology and "scientific" biblical criticism as healthy challenges to Christian self-understanding became known as "Liberals" or "Modernists," and gained a great influence on seminary faculties in particular. Others who saw these intellectual movements as radically corrosive of the traditions they represented coalesced into the "Fundamentalist" movement, with Modernism as the chief enemy within the ranks. Baptists and Presbyterians in the north were especially torn by the conflicts this split engendered, and heresy trials and internecine politics abounded until most Fundamentalists were forced to withdraw into their own groupings. Prohibition had been the last public issue on which Protestants of a variety of theological stripes had been able to unite; by the 1920s, the victory was proving hollow, and theological conflict had accelerated to such a degree that future united effort would never again be possible among the contending parties. The quest for a Christian America would resurface again in the 1970s and 1980s, but largely under Fundamentalist leadership.

Besides this internal division, the "second disestablishment" was precipitated by the rise of powerful external forces already hinted at—pluralism and secularism. Vast numbers of "new" immigrants from southern and eastern Europe had transformed the American urban scene, and had indirectly been the target of the Prohibitionists. Their entry into politics and the shift of population from a rural to an urban majority by 1920 helped make possible the Roosevelt coalition victory of 1932. From now on, Jews and Catholics were to play an active role in determining the course of American life. On the other hand, Billy Sunday's eclipse by sports and entertainment figures illustrated the power of secular mass culture—radio, tabloid newspapers, and film.

At another level, many social functions that had previously been dominated or strongly influenced by evangelical religion, education and social work in particular, were now coming under governmental or other secular aegis. Many women, for example, who might earlier have devoted their energies to the missions movement now could follow the example of Jane Addams at Chicago's Hull House and enter a career as a settlement worker. Social workers were now secular "professional altruists," as were teachers, nurses, administrators, and representatives of the other limited number of professions open to women.

The Victorian era had been one of ferment, change, and ultimate irony. Evangelicals had continued fervently in their quest for a Christian civilization, with America in its vanguard. Their numbers, however, had become so fraught with internal contradictions that their center could not hold for long. Questions of sexuality and sex roles preoccupied middle-class women and considerable numbers of men; some of the latter became so uneasy about their status that a cult of "muscular Christianity" ranged from elite prep schools to urban YMCAs. New extremes of wealth and poverty led many of the *nouveaux riches* into the arms of the Episcopal Church, strengthened the Roman Catholic presence, and gave rise to the Social Gospel among reform-minded Protestants. The immigrant influx revived nativist fears, enhanced the contrast between "us" and "them," and led to a demand for immigration restriction among the influential and the resurgence of the Ku Klux Klan in the 1920s among the disenfranchised. Temperance and then national prohibition became the panacea for these many, mingled anxieties. The result was a temporary triumph and an ultimate defeat. Much of the subsequent history of American Protestantism deals with the breakup of this uneasy evangelical alliance into "liberal," "conservative," and "mainstream" camps in a struggle that continues today.

CHAPTER 32

Protestant Liberalism and the Social Gospel

Although liberal religious thought had been in the air at least since the time of the Renaissance, it did not begin to take institutional form until the time of American independence. We have already discussed the problems of institutionalizing liberalism, since by definition it resists such confinement. The strains that were manifesting themselves within the Congregational churches and Harvard College by the year 1800, though, had grown so powerful and irreconcilable that a split seems in retrospect to have been inevitable. The American Unitarian Association had become a full-blown denominational entity by 1825, and its Universalist cousins had similarly taken steps toward institutional status by that time.

Among the sources of later Protestant liberalism in America, Unitarianism was a major influence. These liberal Congregationalists had already enunciated the themes of a benevolent deity, a humanity open to growth through religious nurture, and a stress on the ethical rather than the metaphysical. Transcendentalism was also an important intellectual precursor through its emphasis on the continuity among the divine, the human, and the natural. European Romantic thought, such as the ideas of the German theologian Friedrich Schleiermacher, also exerted a strong influence in America through a stress on continuity, process, and feeling rather than judgment, dogma, and abstraction.

One figure, however, among the evangelical denominations in antebellum America stands out especially as a harbinger of new lines of thought. This was Horace Bushnell (1802–1876), a Hartford Congregationalist minister whose writings helped create a whole new climate in American theology. As had his Transcendentalist contemporaries, Bushnell recognized that human language was by its nature imprecise and suggestive, like poetry, rather than expressive of hard-edged, unchanging facts. This approach to language and, more broadly, the whole of reality stood in sharp contrast with that of evangelical Protestantism as well as more conservative Unitarianism, which both subscribed to the Scottish Common Sense position that impressions received through the senses are accurate representations of external reality. Bushnell's approach undermined the traditional Christian assumption, both Catholic and Protestant, that essential truths about the nature of God and religion could be expressed in precise propositional form in creeds and other verbal statements of faith.

Bushnell's best-known work was *A Discourse on Christian Nurture* of 1847. Here Bushnell sought to undercut the evangelical assumption, which reached its strongest form in revivalism, that all Christians must experience an emotional conversion in order to be assured of salvation. The necessity for conversion was based on the radical influence of original sin, which had corrupted the human condition so thoroughly that a sharp break had to occur in an individual's life through the operation of divine grace. Even though the theology of contemporary evangelicals such as Lyman Beecher and Charles Finney had undercut the notion of human helplessness in bringing about such a conversion, most Protestants of the era nevertheless believed that an abrupt shift in direction had to take place in each life in order for the saving "new birth" to be effectual.

In attacking this fundamental premise, Bushnell posited a fundamental theme of subsequent liberalism in his denying the existence of sharp boundaries among the supernatural, natural, and individual worlds. The divine and human thus stood not in a contradictory but rather a complementary relationship, with God's grace permeating and redeeming the imperfect realm of creation. Similarly, redemption need not and should not be marked by an abrupt change in consciousness, but rather should come about gradually and imperceptibly in the development of a child through the influence of what Bushnell called "Christian nurture." This nurture was not confined to the church, but was also carried out in the divinely ordained realms of the home, the school, and society at large. Thus, instead of pointing to a precisely datable moment of conversion, properly reared Christians should never be able to remember a moment when they had not lived within the realms of the operations of grace.

The theme of gradual growth and change was central to much of the thought first of Romanticism and then of other aspects of nineteenth-century intellectual life. The most important manifestation of this emphasis for Protestantism was the new approach to biblical studies that had been developing in German universities during the earlier decades of the century. Sometimes known as the "higher criticism," this school regarded the Hebrew and Christian Scriptures not as a homogeneous, unified, divinely revealed pair of documents, but rather as a collection of religious texts that had been written, edited, and collected within their respective communities over many centuries. In some cases, such as Isaiah, biblical books that had been regarded as the work of a single divinely inspired scribe were now demonstrated through textual analysis to be the work of two or more hands. More dramatically the Pentateuch, which had traditionally been attributed to Moses, was now shown to be of extremely complex composition through the hands of the various redactors who had each given it a distinct emphasis representing their own concerns and those of their age and social setting.

Although the use of "form criticism" remains controversial in some circles even to the present day—and although biblical scholars who accept its basic premises are by no means in agreement on their conclusions—its implications were regarded by incipient liberals of the time as a promise rather than a threat. Liberals did not regard the idea that the Scriptures were of human authorship as an act of debunking; instead, they read this approach as an affirmation that God's message had not been revealed in static, propositional form but in a progressive, dynamic act of communication though human intermediaries. As the controversy over biblical criticism grew in the later decades of the century, controversies began to rage within the major denominations and their seminaries, and by the early twentieth century an organized reaction had emerged in the countermovement that took the name of Fundamentalism.

Related to the development of biblical criticism were the changes that were also taking place in the world of learning in general and the sciences in particular. Again, Germany took the lead in developing the seminar method of advanced instruction and the university as an institution for research on a rigorous, scientific model. Until the 1860s, Americans seeking doctorates in any field of investigation, including theology and biblical studies, were obliged to spend some time in Germany, where they could scarcely remain unaffected by the new scholarly ethos. When indigenous advanced degree programs in religious fields did emerge at Harvard, Yale, and the newly founded University of Chicago, they modeled themselves, much as did their secular counterparts, on the German prototype, and controversy frequently abounded. Notable among these was the heresy trial of Charles Augustus Briggs (1841–1913), a distinguished professor of Old Testament at New York's Union Theological Seminary. Even though Briggs was convicted by the Presbyterian General Assembly in 1893 of false teaching and deprived of his ministerial status, he retained his post at Union for many years and later became an Episcopal priest. In supporting Briggs, Union also demonstrated a commitment to another German concept, *Lehrfreiheit* (academic freedom), which was now rivaling the preservation of orthodox teaching as a value in all realms of higher education.

To conservatives, the findings of the sciences themselves could be as threatening as the application of their methods to religious research. The classic challenge came in 1859 when the English naturalist Charles Darwin first published *The Origin of Species*, followed by *The Descent of Man* in 1871. Although the Civil War diverted American attention from these developments for some time, Darwin's argument that all varieties of life came into being through a gradual process of natural selection rather than a specific act of divine creation eventually forced American Protestants to come to terms with this "Copernican revolution" in biological thought.

Not all Protestants agreed on the implications of Darwinism, however. Conservatives protested that the theory of evolution deprived humanity of its unique character and God of his special creative power. Further, it seemed to repudiate the literal accuracy of the opening chapters of Genesis, which were read by conservatives as an account of the distinctive, specific creation of humanity as opposed to other forms of animate life. On the moral plane, it reduced humanity to the level of beasts, engaged in a continual struggle for the "survival of the fittest."

Some thinkers, such as Yale's William Graham Sumner, welcomed the implications of Darwin's theories as a refreshing new model for the realm of human activity. Sumner, an Episcopal priest who had lost his religious faith and become a sociologist and social philosopher, coined the still-popular phrase "Social Darwinism." This characterized his view of the ideal society as one in which natural selection was left free to operate to reward human ingenuity and hard work, while condemning the "unfit" who did not merit social survival to a deserved oblivion. Social Darwinism, which carried with it a burden of philosophical determinism without the benefit of a personal god, came into favor among many political conservatives who saw in it a metaphysical justification for laissez-faire capitalism.

Protestant liberals tried to steer a mediating course between these extremes, and attempted to reconcile a belief in a benevolent, personal deity with an acceptance of evolution as a part of that deity's scheme for ultimate human betterment. The "higher criticism" of Scripture could thus be accepted optimistically, as a demonstration that God revealed himself progressively, and that a fuller knowledge of God was an indication of progress in the most comprehensive sense. This optimism was part of a broader mood of inevitable progress that was pervasive among much of Victorian America's intelligentsia. James Freeman Clarke, the Unitarian clergyman and scholar, captured this mood in his memorable phrase celebrating "the eternal progress of mankind, onward and upward, forever and ever."

Early Protestant Liberalism was thus characterized not so much by a specific, rigid creed as by a set of interests, emphases, and even moods. These included a stress on growth and development in all realms of existence, from divine revelation to the individual character; a confidence in benevolent divine guidance of these growth processes; a stress on the fundamental goodness of humanity, which could emerge through nurture in proper Christian institutions; a positive attitude toward secular learning, including the sciences, as an instrument of progress; and a tendency to downplay the boundaries distinguishing various realms of being, such as the sacred and the secular or the divine and the human. God did not stand against humanity and the rest of creation, but rather worked with and through them to achieve his ultimate purposes. Liberals disagreed among themselves on specific theological formulations, but, as liberals, tended to regard such disagreement as potentially fruitful rather than disruptive.

The vanguard of early Liberalism was not the seminary or the university but the pulpit. Victorian America was a golden age of preaching, and a galaxy of "Princes of the Pulpit" drew thousands of often newly prosperous urbanites to hear their optimistic rhetoric. These "princes" represented the spectrum of what had hitherto been primarily evangelical denominations, and frequently had handsome, capacious downtown churches erected by their congregations to enhance their stature. Especially prominent among this clerical elite were Phillips Brooks (Episcopalian), of Boston's Trinity Church; George Angier Gordon (Congregational), of New Old South across Copley Square from Trinity; and Henry Ward Beecher (Congregational), and his successor, Lyman Abbott, of Plymouth Church, Brooklyn. Many of these preachers were also prolific writers in an age when theology had not yet split into academic and popular fragments, and their essays and printed sermons found a wide readership among the American urban Protestant middle class.

The message of this generation of preachers, who flourished during the last quarter of the nineteenth century, as well as that of their successors such as Harry Emerson Fosdick of Manhattan's Riverside Church, has sometimes been characterized as "Evangelical Liberalism." Although they rejected much of the baggage of both Calvinism and revivalism, they nevertheless remained faithful to the traditional Protestant focus on the Bible and Jesus as sure paths to salvation. Their Bible might no longer be factually infallible, and their Jesus more of a friend and example than an atoning savior, but the familiar symbols were still central.

A closely related form of Liberalism that shared these premises but added some other crucial concepts was the Social Gospel that began to attract adherents in the midst of the massive transformations that American society was undergoing during these same decades. Where the Princes of the Pulpit tended to stress personal growth through adherence to a properly understood Christian Gospel, ministers such as Baptist Walter Rauschenbusch (1861–1918) brought Jesus's teachings to bear on a different aspect of human experience. Rauschenbusch began his ministerial career near the part of Manhattan known evocatively as "Hell's Kitchen." Here he came into first-hand contact with the squalor and violence of immigrant slum life that was beyond the experience of most native-born middle-class Protestants. Instead of blaming the immigrant poor for their own misery, Rauschenbush began to realize that other factors might be more responsible for their condition than their own depravity, and that Christianity had resources to illuminate both the causes and cures of contemporary social disorganization.

The core of Rauschenbusch's teaching was that the message of Jesus had not been directed solely to the salvation of individuals, but addressed the entire social dimension of human existence as well. The goal of Christianity was consequently the realization here on earth of the Kingdom of God, a biblical concept that had recently been emphasized by the German theologian Albrecht Ritschl. Later in Rauschenbusch's career, his earlier optimism became balanced by a stress on the objective reality of a Kingdom of Evil as well. In both cases, however, religious significance existed not simply in the soul of the individual believer but in the social realm in which all individuals are inextricably involved.

Rauschenbusch's ideas received a wide circulation through his lectures, his teaching at the Baptist seminary in Rochester, and such books as *Christianity and the Social Crisis* (1907) and *A Theology for the Social Gospel* (1917). However, his was by no means the only voice in the growing "Social Gospel" movement that was attracting more and more attention as urban poverty, crime, and labor unrest caught the reluctant attention of middle-class Americans. The other most important publicist of the movement was a Congregationalist minister who became involved in such issues at first hand in parishes in Springfield, Massachusetts, and Columbus, Ohio. Unlike Rauschenbusch, Washington Gladden (1836–1918) was not primarily a theologian, but rather an articulate activist clergyman who possessed a gift for theologically literate advocacy. Gladden, sometimes called "the father of the Social Gospel," was especially sympathetic with the emergent labor movement, and called for a spirit of cooperation to replace the growing antagonism between workers and capitalists. Gladden also was a strong supporter of interdenominational and interracial fellowship, was an early advocate of the cause of black rights, and regarded Jews and Catholics as potential allies rather than antagonists. Similar ideas were soon taken up by Catholic social thinkers such as Msgr. John A. Ryan, who used his position at Catholic University to advocate the "just wage" theory that echoed many ideas earlier developed by Gladden and other Protestant activists.

The Social Gospel movement, which Gladden and Rauschenbusch did so much to launch, articulate, and promote, rapidly found other channels as well. Just as the German model had influenced biblical studies, so did the emergent American research universities of the era apply the same "scientific" approach to the social realm. Where in earlier decades sociology, economics, and political science had been treated as topics within moral philosophy, the term *social sciences* now emerged to set them in a more empirical context. Many of the first American social scientists, however, were by no means content to regard these pursuits as morally neutral. Richard T. Ely, for example, was an Episcopalian layman who received a German doctorate in economics, taught at the University of Wisconsin and Johns Hopkins, and was instrumental in founding the American Economic Association in 1885. His study of economics was motivated by an ethical concern for what he saw as the destructive consequences of classical laissez-faire capitalism. W. D. P. Bliss, another Episcopalian, helped to put social work on a more scientific basis through his massive compilation of data in his *Encyclopedia of Social Reform* (1898). In the seminaries and universities, an alliance between theology and social science began to take shape in the new field of social ethics, which the Unitarian Francis Greenwood Peabody (author of *Jesus Christ and the Social Question* in 1900) introduced at Harvard and which was widely imitated elsewhere. Throughout the twentieth century, such courses have become standard parts of the curriculum at many seminaries, and a ministerial awareness of the complexity of the social realm and its problems is a major legacy of the Social Gospel among most "mainstream" Protestants and Catholics.

In addition to education and advocacy, the Social Gospel made its impact on American Protestantism in a variety of other ways. A distinctive innovation of the era was the "institutional church," of which the Episcopal St. George's and St. Bartholomew's in Manhattan were important prototypes. These were churches that focused not simply on congregational worship, but extended their professional staff, program, and physical plant to promote a wide variety of outreach endeavors for the broader community. These efforts did not exclude religious activity, but focused more on such basic matters as day-care, summer outings for poor urban children, and educational and training programs for the dispossessed of all ages. Because of this emphasis, they were closely related to the settlement house movement, pioneered by the more secular work of Jane Addams at Chicago's Hull House. Besides the institutional churches and other urban outreach programs, whole denominations responded by creating social service divisions in their emergent national bureaucracies. Beyond the denominational level, the ecumenical Federal Council of Churches of 1908 grew primarily out of a concern for a coordinated Protestant response to national social issues. Its Commission on Church and Social Service, led by Presbyterian Charles Stelzle, rapidly attracted attention with its investigation of the Bethlehem steel strike of 1910, which condemned such then-common practices as the 12-hour day and the 7-day week.

The Social Gospel was a central part of a broader late-nineteenth-century phenomemon known as "Social Christianity," but it did not exhaust that category. To the right should be mentioned such evangelical responses to social problems such as the YMCA/YWCA movement (with Catholic and Jewish counterparts), urban gospel missions, and the Salvation Army (with its schismatic offshoot, the Volunteers of America). All of these efforts recognized that new, sometimes even drastic responses were needed to reach the destitute, but all were premised on the evangelical assumption that the key to the redemption of the body was the prior salvation of the soul through conversion. In their early days in America, however, Salvation Army members often mounted a harsh attack against the excesses of capitalism and sympathized with radical secular reformers such as Eugene V. Debs.

In addition, it should be noted that advocates of Social Christianity were by no means homogeneous in their political and social inclinations. Gladden and Rauschenbusch, like the "mainstream" of the Social Gospel movement, could best be described as left-leaning reformers, who allied themselves with the progressive movement in American politics and who advocated a significant modification but not a radical upheaval in America's social and economic institutions. Bliss, who had been influenced by the Anglican socialists F. D.

Maurice and Charles Kingsley, openly aligned himself with a more radical approach to politics, and helped organize the first Christian Socialist Society in 1889. Congregationalist George Herron, who was later deposed from the ministry in part for his radical views, was an influential spokesman for an explicitly socialist perspective, and campaigned for Socialist presidential candidate Eugene V. Debs. Toward the other end of the spectrum, Congregationalist Josiah Strong was an impassioned advocate of Social Gospel reform principles, but manifested in his widely read *Our Country* (1885) a strong sense that American destiny was inextricably tied to the genius of the Anglo-Saxon race and the necessity of its triumph.

Although the Social Gospel at the time seemed to present a startling new paradigm for American Protestantism in its shift of emphasis from individual salvation to the Kingdom of God, later observers such as Martin Marty have noted the ambiguities that underlay the emphases of its leaders. The movement, for example, had little sympathy for the nascent feminist movement, and Vida Scudder of Wellesley was the only woman to play even a noticeable role in its development. Similarly, Rauschenbusch and his fellows had little sympathetic understanding of the aspirations of the black community and other minority groups, and accepted with little criticism the intellectual commonplace of the times that "Teutonic" peoples were inherently superior to others. Finally, as Marty notes, the movement was "vague on program, weak on detail, generally out of touch with laborers [and] inept at politics.* For all its inherent paternalism, however, the Social Gospel nevertheless introduced into the vocabulary of American Protestantism systematic concern with human suffering in the context of an unjust social order, a heritage that can be measured in the "outreach" committees and humanitarian endeavors of countless churches to this day.

Where the Social Gospel was based on a direct involvement of the Christian churches in the everyday experience of Americans, another variety of Protestant Liberalism took its stand on experience of a very different sort. Loosely known as "Modernists," religious thinkers at several major universities and interdenominational divinity schools turned to constructing a theology that was based not primarily on revelation or reason but directly on human religious experience. Harvard's William James (1842–1910), often called the founder of American psychology, helped lead the way in his *Varieties of Religious Experience* of 1902 to a scientific study of religious experience that had as its goal not the destruction of supernatural faith but rather an appreciation of the positive good that religion can effect among people from a purely this-worldly standpoint. James was also a founder of the distinctively American philosophical school known as "Pragmatism," which held that the truth of an idea lay not so much in its logical consistency but in its "cash value"—not its literal material worth, but rather its usefulness to real people in dealing with everyday life. Needless to say, James's approach, which stated that most religious experience generated "overbeliefs"—theological formulations that could not be empirically proven or disproven—promoted toler-

---

* *Modern American Religion* (1986), 290.

ance, but was hardly compatible with any tradition's claims to normative or exclusive truth.

James, however, was primarily a philosophical psychologist and not a theologian. A number of the latter emerged during the World War I era to apply James's leads to their specific purposes. Prominent among these "Modernists" were Yale's Douglas Clyde Macintosh, the University of Chicago's Shailer Mathews and Henry Nelson Wieman, and the school of "Christian Personalists" that developed around Boston University's Borden P. Bowne. Although their indiviudal formulations and their allegiance to traditional Christianity varied considerably, they were united in a common quest to put the analysis of religious truth on a firm empirical basis. Their systems, which were usually highly technical, affirmed that the universe was not starkly impersonal, but rather was infused with a dimension that was conducive to the evocation of the moral dimension in human life. With Wieman especially, however, this dimension bore little resemblance to the personal God familiar to most believers, and the long-term impact of the movement was considerably less direct than that of other varieties of Liberalism.

Liberalism in its various forms continued to find eloquent defenders throughout the 1920s, such as Harry Emerson Fosdick. Fosdick, a Baptist, came under attack in conservative circles, and eventually resigned his Presbyterian pulpit to accept a call to New York's interdenominational Riverside Church. Fosdick had aroused anger in his 1922 sermon, "Shall The Fundamentalists Win?" in which he took to task the coalescing conservative opposition to liberal positions that was rallying under the banner of Fundamentalism. But Fundamentalism, which suffered a major defeat in the realm of public opinion during the Scopes "Monkey" Trial of 1925, was not to play the most important role in bringing to an end liberalism's dominance over much of the life and thought of Protestant churches, seminaries, and denominational activity. Rather, the impact first of World War I and then of the Depression called into practical question for many Americans the resolute optimism that had characterized the spirit of liberalism in all of its forms. Among many erstwhile liberals, a new movement called Neo-Orthodoxy seemed attractive in its combination of certain major liberal premises such as biblical criticism, with a reappropriation of such traditional Christian emphases as the power of sin and the judgmental character of God.

Because of its protean character, however, liberalism did not simply disappear; rather, its more viable impulses were channeled into new directions. Again, such emphases as a critical approach to the interpretation of Scripture; a concern for the ethical dimensions of the Gospel in the social, political, and economic realms; a rejection of the demand for an emotional conversion and a corresponding emphasis on benevolent nurture in the faith, in part through the Sunday School movement; and a concomitant stress on the role of Christianity in promoting the development of a mature, responsible personality throughout life all remained staples of pulpit preaching, seminary and Christian education curricula, and denominational programming. Further, those denominations that in the twentieth century became known as "mainline"— Methodist, Presbyterian, and Episcopalian, among others—remained open to the advocacy of a wide variety of causes, both intellectual and social, for which liberalism in general and the Social Gospel in particular had prepared them. This was especially true in the 1960s and after, when the churches, their clergy, and many concerned laity became involved in the civil rights, antiwar, and other movements of the era. Although, later in the century, there is by no means a consensus on either theological or political matters in these denominations, the spirit of tolerance and the rejection of creedal tests that this pluralism betokens is in itself a sign that liberalism has been one of the most important constitutent forces in the shaping of contemporary American religious life.

CHAPTER 33

Episcopalian Renaissance

The Victorian Episcopal Church flourished especially in the established metropolitan areas of the northeast—most notably New York and Boston—as well as in newly thriving cities such as Chicago. These areas were in the vanguard of the social and economic changes that were rapidly transforming the nation into an urban, industrial, and polyglot society. On the one hand, many of the newly rich, and a number from backgrounds of more established wealth as well, were being attracted to a denomination that represented in visible form the allure of English customs and traditions. Unitarians in Boston and Quakers in Philadelphia both contributed converts, and New York City especially manifested the impact of the new wealth and enthusiasm in an outburst of church- and cathedral-building northward along Fifth Avenue and in other prestigious locales.

This situation evoked a number of institutional responses. For the wealthy families of the Northeast, a complex of "prep" schools modeled on the English church-related "public school" began to flourish, particularly in New England. These schools, for which Endicott Peabody's Groton (founded 1884) was among the best known, were frankly dedicated to the cultivation of a future elite nurtured on the "muscular Christianity" that had become popular in the England of the time. (Louis Auchincloss's effective novel, *The Rector of Justin* (1956), was based on Peabody's career, and is one of the few significant American novels with an Episcopalian theme.) The movement toward the church's playing an active role in secondary education was contemporary with another English import, the revival of both male and female Anglican monastic orders. The Society of Saint John the Evangelist, better known as the "Cowley Fathers," is one of the better known of these orders that still exists. The complex of schools sponsored by monastic orders that arose in conjunction with the

University of the South at Sewanee, Tennessee, are good examples of the interplay of the two impulses. (The novelist James Agee was a product of St. Andrew's at Sewanee, and his correspondence with his alma mater's Father Flye is a significant literary document.)

Where the demands of wealth created one kind of institution, its widespread and conspicuous absence brought forth others. One of the most important innovations of the era sponsored was the development of the "institutional church," a manifestation of "social Christianity" directed toward the alleviation of suffering and social disorder brought about by the deluge of "New Immigrants" engulfing New York and other major cities. The prototype of the institutional church was St. George's in Manhattan's once-fashionable Gramercy Park. Under the leadership of Irish-born William S. Rainsford (1850–1933), the parish resisted the temptation to follow its wealthy clientele uptown, and instead set about developing a comprehensive set of ministries to the poor: slum missions, trade school classes, fresh-air camps, and a wide variety of activities to involve all comers. Rainsford's mission was possible in large measure through the unwavering sponsorship of his Senior Warden (head lay official), J. P. Morgan—one of the "robber barons" whom another New York State Senior Warden, Franklin Delano Roosevelt, would later characterize as "malefactors of great wealth."

Other Episcopalian responses to the challenge of the "Social Gospel" were the founding of the Church Association for the Advancement of Labor (CAIL) in 1887, the work of which was continued in a more official denominational context by the Church League for Industrial Democracy (1919) and other agencies. Prominent among Episcopalian leaders for social justice in the context of the Christian Gospel were W. D. P. Bliss (1856–1926), a clergyman known for founding the Christian Socialist Church of the Carpenter in Boston (1890) and the compilation of the *Encyclopedia of Social Reform* (1898); Richard T. Ely (1854–1943), economist at Johns Hopkins University and later at the University of Wisconsin, who founded the American Institute of Christian Sociology and was cofounder of the American Economic Association and, with Bliss, the Christian Social Union; and Vida D. Scudder (1861–1954), who, while teaching English at Wellesley College, engaged in settlement and labor work, entered the semimonastic Companions of the Holy Cross, and wrote extensively on both the Middle Ages and the highly contemporary social reform ideas they inspired in her and her English predecessor, John Ruskin.

The other major challenge of the later Victorian age was on the intellectual front, in the impact of scientific and especially evolutionary thought on theology and biblical interpretation. One rather mild form of the religious liberalism that spread through the spectrum of denominations at the time was that of Phillips Brooks (1835–1893), known as one of the "Princes of the Pulpit" for his rhetorical performances at Trinity Church, Boston, and later briefly as Bishop of Massachusetts. His thought was not systematic or complex, but his spoken and published sermons were extremely popular in their stress on Christianity as a means of helping individuals realize their full innate possibilities. This stress on growth and potential rather than on depravity was a common theme in the liberalism of the day.

Brooks formed part of a new, loosely constituted "party" in both American and British Anglicanism known as the "Broad Church" movement. This movement, which hoped to transcend the internecine strife that had been generated by the factionalism of the nineteenth century, was anticipated in the career of William Augustus Muhlenberg (1796–1877), whose "Memorial" movement—stemming from his petition, or memorial, to the 1853 General Convention—urged the church to take the lead in transcending theological particularities and promoting Christian union. Although little concrete came from this ecumenical thrust, Muhlenberg, who characterized himself as an "Evangelical Catholic," helped pave the way for an outlook that would eventually smooth the road for later Episcopalian encounters with modern thought and society in a positive rather than defensive manner. The church's seminaries slowly embraced the new biblical criticism of the latter part of the century with little resistance, and the Fundamentalist movement that was to plague the Baptist and Presbyterian communities had little impact on a church that was never strongly given to precise theological formulations. One of the few casualties was Algernon Sydney Crapsey (1847–1927), an advocate of the Social Gospel in Rochester, New York, who was deposed from the ministry in 1906 on charges of his denying not the Bible's literal accuracy but rather that of the creeds of the early church.

What may be called the "Episcopalian Renaissance" of these (in Lewis Mumford's phrase) "Brown Decades" did not focus on theology, which was enhanced far more by contributions from heirs of the Reformed and Wesleyan traditions. With a few possible exceptions such as William Porcher DuBose (1836–1918) of the University of the South (Sewanee) and the twentieth-century process theologian Norman Pittenger, whose active career was spent chiefly in England, Episcopalians have not generally been leaders in American religious thought. Since the Anglican tradition has emphasized worship over doctrine, it should not be surprising to find that the most distinguished contribution of the Episcopal Church to the arts has been in the area of ecclesiastical architecture. Many colonial Anglican churches still survive along the Eastern seaboard, reflecting the Georgian (neoclassical) style dominant in England, and the wealth and social and political prominence of the church, especially in the earlier eighteenth century. Some of particular note include Bruton Parish Church, Williamsburg, Virginia (1711–1715); Old North (Christ) Church, Boston (1723), of Paul Revere fame; Trinity Church, Newport, Rhode Island (1725–1726); Christ Church, Philadelphia (1727); and St. Paul's Chapel, New York City (1764–1766), Manhattan's only surviving pre-Revolutionary building.

The architectural mode most closely associated with the Episcopal Church in America, which was to have a profound influence on American church building more broadly, was that of the Gothic Revival—part of a broader revival of appreciation for medieval culture manifested in the resurgence of monastic orders, boarding schools, social reform, and other aspects of "organic" community. Interest in medieval churches as the most appropriate prototypes for liturgical worship was encouraged by the Cambridge Camden Society in England, a development coordinate with the Oxford Movement in theology, and spread in the eastern United States by a similar group in New

York City. Richard Upjohn (1802–1878), an English emigrant, was most influential in adapting the Gothic to American purposes. In addition to Manhattan's monumental Trinity Church (1839–1846) at Broadway and Wall Street, Upjohn designed countless wooden small-town and rural churches around the country in the board-and-batten ("Carpenter Gothic") style that became an instant success among American Christians of all sorts and added an important new element to the religious landscape.

Later phases of American medievalism were contributed by Henry Vaughn, also an English-born Anglican who designed both Episcopal churches and "prep schools," and Henry Hobson Richardson, who employed the Romanesque mode in Boston's epoch-making Trinity Church (1872–1877), from the pulpit of which Phillips Brooks held forth. Together with the near-contemporary Boston Public Library and New Old South Church (Congregational), Trinity helped demarcate Boston's Copley Square as a quintessential public urban space for the Victorian era—a fitting platform for Brooks, the quintessential Victorian clergyman. Trinity served to display not only Brooks's preaching but also other arts that were undergoing a revival at the time—for example, the sculpture of Augustus St. Gaudens and the murals of John Lafarge. Clergy of other denominations, such as New York's literary Henry van Dyke at Brick Presbyterian, were also encouraging the visual and plastic arts as aids to worship in a land where centuries of dominance of the iconoclastic Puritan spirit had heretofore acted as a damper. The Episcopal Church, though, provided the most effective leadership, in part through the wealth and prestige at its command, but also through its long-standing emphasis on the sacramental role of the arts in liturgical worship.

One of the most influential American church architects, whose career spanned the later Victorian age and the early twentieth century, was Ralph Adams Cram (1863–1942), a New England Unitarian who converted to Anglicanism as a young man and became one of the tradition's foremost apologists as well. Cram's best-known design was that of the monumental (and still unfinished) Cathedral Church of Saint John the Divine (begun 1892) in New York City. Saint John's, however, was only the most spectacular of dozens of other churches, mostly Episcopal, that were conceived by Cram and his partners. In addition, Cram's voluminous writings attempted to provide a philosophical rationale for the role of Gothic in modern society, a role based on the alleged superiority of medieval culture and religion to that of the present.

The leadership of the Episcopal Church in promoting the arts did not last indefinitely. Resistance by other denominations to the uses of material and visual beauty had dissolved by the turn of the twentieth century, and the Gothic began to appear in such disparate churches as the Duke University Chapel (Methodist) and New York's Riverside Church (Baptist/interdenominational.) The graduated income tax, the Depression, and then World War II reduced the once-enormous resources available for church construction, and other liturgical denominations, especially the Lutheran and Roman Catholic, began to exert leadership in the design of architecture for worship.

Nevertheless, the association of the Episcopal Church with both the arts and social concern has by no means vanished. The Cathedral Church of St. John the Divine, for example, resumed in the 1980s its once-suspended building program to provide training in the crafts for neighborhood youth hired to work toward its completion, and sponsors regularly any number of events in the arts. (Madeleine L'Engle, a leading author of what might best be described as Anglican metaphysical fantasy, lives on the grounds as well.) In midtown Manhattan, controversy has also raged over the proposed sale of the property of St. Bartholomew's Church for high-rise commercial development, raising serious questions about the priorities of aesthetic witness versus funding for social programs. The challenge of the urban frontier for religion thus finds itself continuing in the Episcopal Church's ongoing course of self-appraisal.

CHAPTER 34

Reactions to Modernity: Fundamentalism, Holiness, Pentecostalism

Historians such as William G. McLoughlin have argued that American religious history can be read as a series of revivals. Some of these, like the two "great awakenings," have been explicitly religious in character, and also recognized by their participants as dramatic turning points in our collective religious life. Wars that have involved the whole nation in a protracted struggle—especially the traumatic Civil War, in which Americans killed and maimed one another and died on a scale unequalled before or since—have also been interpreted as religious awakenings, often by the clergy of the time.

Although rapid social change has been a constant in the American experience, particularly intensive periods of such change have been fertile incubators for religious excitement and innovation. The two great awakenings were good examples of such periods, and corresponded first with the emergence of a national consciousness and then with the settlement of the eastern reaches of the frontier. The simultaneous exhilaration and insecurity generated by these wide-ranging changes affecting such large numbers of Americans led to the generation of new, experientially oriented and doctrinally innovative movements, as well as reactions against them by those with stronger stakes in the status quo.

The period that ran roughly from the Civil War to the Depression was characterized by equally intense social change manifested in large-scale immigration, urbanization, and industrialization. In addition to the influx of immigrants from southern and eastern Europe into America's burgeoning industrial cities, countless other Americans, first white and then blacks as well, began a vast in-migration from the nation's farms and small towns into these same cities, always seeking "the main chance." The periodic economic upheavals of the era hit farmers especially hard, and the Populist movement filled much of the South and Midwest with deep suspicion of the ways of urban financial magnates whose machinations seemed to be putting a timeless way of rural life at risk. The foreigners who competed for the jobs generated by this new order themselves seemed a threat to the established ways in their exotic languages, religions, and cultures, and a new upsurge of nativism at both popular and elite levels also colored the political life of the times.

By the turn of the twentieth century, three broad-based new religious movements had emerged from this cultural ferment, which were to transform the character of American Protestantism dramatically during the following decades: Holiness, Fundamentalism, and Pentecostalism. Although all would eventually generate a number of independent denominations, each began more as a climate of opinion within a Protestant community that was finding itself profoundly divided over the challenges posed by evolutionary thought, biblical criticism, and theological "Modernism," as well as the inevitable pressures toward institutional routinization that came with the achievement of middle-class status.

The crucible in which the ingredients of this new evangelical realignment were forged was the Second Great Awakening. It was in this period that the two major theological strains of evangelicalism, the Reformed and the Wesleyan, entered into an ongoing working relationship in the contexts of such broader endeavors as revivalism and moral reform campaigns that often required cooperation as well as the more usual denominational competition. Cross-fertilization also took place in these years between popular outbursts of "enthusiasm" such as the Great Revival and the more sophisticated revivalist enterprises of such stalwarts as Lyman Beecher and Charles G. Finney.

It was Finney especially who during his lengthy career brought together a number of disparate elements that would prove exemplary for the future. Although ordained a Presbyterian, Finney was never very firmly grounded in Reformed theology, and in his later years became converted to a "perfectionist" position similar to that developed earlier by John Wesley. It was especially during his years in the 1830s as professor and president at Oberlin College that he and his colleague Asa Mahan became convinced that it was possible for Christians to become perfect followers of Jesus, thus attaining a spiritual state free from sin. Although they may have differed in detail from Wesley, this idea, expounded in the *Oberlin Evangelist,* was fundamentally identical with the notion of "entire sanctification" propounded by Methodism's founder.

In addition to moving toward a rapprochement between Reformed and Wesleyan ideals, Finney was also a "bridge" figure in the equivocal position he occupied within the domain of ecclesiastical structures. Although ordained, in spite of questionable preparation, by a major denomination, Finney functioned much more as an independent religious entrepreneur than as a traditional parish minister, and his "New Measures" reflected aptly his freedom from the constraints of tradition. His enthusiasm for reform causes such as antislavery also indicated that he was open to the application of religious ideas to a rapidly changing social order as well.

If Finney could have been Emerson's "representative man" for the antebellum era of evangelicalism, his postwar counterpart was certainly the redoubtable Dwight L. Moody. Moody could claim even less formal education than Finney, who had been trained as a lawyer, but was equally entrepreneurial as well as sensitive to the needs of another age of rapid social transformation. Further, like Finney, Moody did not operate under denominational aegis, but rather acquired the active support of the gamut of evangelical denominations for his urban revivals. Moody's prime constituency was not the unchurched, at whom his revivals were overtly aimed, but rather the displaced rural folk who made up much of the mass in-migration to the cities of Victorian America. In addition to the innovative techniques that he and his music leader, Ira D. Sankey, were continually devising, Moody was also receptive to a wide variety of new theological ideas that were developing in the ambit of Anglo-American evangelicalism. Among these were John Nelson Darby's dispensational premillennialism, a major doctrinal undergirding of the nascent Fundamentalist movement, and Keswick Holiness, an interdenominational variety of the perfectionism earlier espoused by Wesley and Finney.

Ideas, however, were subordinate to the anecdotal character and emotional appeal of Moody's presentations, which were aimed more at the heart than the head. Furthermore, Moody developed a widespread institutional network, based at the Moody Bible Institute in Chicago and the Northfield and Mount Hermon schools in western Massachusetts, through which his successors could mobilize rapidly in the cause of the new movements they were so well prepared to espouse.

It is important further to note that the Holiness and Fundamentalist movements, though frequently regarded as popular in character, had solidly middle-class social and intellectual origins. Holiness was nurtured in the highly respectable Manhattan parlor of Phoebe Palmer and similar domestic and ecclesiastical sites, while Fundamentalism had many of its roots in Moody's sentimental appeals to middle-class sensibilities and the respectably learned though extremely conservative ruminations of the Presbyterian divines at Princeton Theological Seminary. It was only in the social crucible of the latter days of the Victorian era and the dislocations attendant upon World War I that this potent mixture of forces coalesced into popular movements of extreme power and frequent volatility.

Of the three movements, Holiness was clearly the oldest, and emerged directly from the teachings of John Wesley. Although the attainment of Christian perfection was for Wesley a long-term process, it was nevertheless characterized by a discrete, instantaneous religious experience, known in Methodist lore as the "second blessing." This state of holiness pertained to the will of the believer, which was now free from voluntary sinful impulses and behavior, but was not necessarily permanent; continual discipline and vigilance were needed to sustain it.

Although American Methodists continued to subscribe to this distinctive feature of Wesley's teaching, the doctrine of "entire sanctification" was not always accorded a central place in the denomination's practice as its members began to attain middle-class status. Beginning in the 1830s, a coterie led by Phoebe Palmer of New York founded a "Tuesday Meeting for the Promotion of Holiness," which was premised on the centrality of the personal experience of entire sanctification. The Tuesday Meeting acquired a dedicated following among a gamut of evangelical leaders from a variety of denominations, including Bowdoin professor Thomas C. Upham, a Congregationalist; Asa Mahan, Finney's Oberlin colleague; Hannah Whithall Smith and David Updegraff, Quakers with evangelical leanings; and a variety of influential Presbyterians, Baptists, and, especially, Methodists. Palmer's *The Way of Holiness* (1843) and other books, journals, and spin-off meetings, numbering some 200 by the 1880s, helped spread this preoccupation with Holiness across the country. Although this interdenominational movement differed in details from Wesley's earlier theological formulations, it resembled his own movement in its origins not as a new church but rather as a religious climate of opinion promoted by a powerfully effective network of extraecclesiastical structures.

Holiness also proved similar to Wesley's original movement in the volatility that such an idea could bring to bear on the institutions it was designed to augment rather than challenge. Official Methodist tepidity on the slavery issue resulted in a number of schisms prior to the Civil War from impatient Northern factions, and it was not coincidental that the leaders of these movements were powerfully influenced by the Holiness impulse as well. Notable here was the Wesleyan Methodist Connection, founded by Orange Scott and Luther Lee in upstate New York in 1843, and characterized in Jean Miller Schmidt's phrase by "the conjunction of piety and radicalism." The Free Methodist Church, organized in 1860 in the same "Burned-Over District," sprang from a similar combination of motives.

Following the Civil War, the Holiness impulse began to assume new forms, which enhanced its efficacy as an informal institutional network especially within the broader Methodist ambit. A distinctive innovation was the Holiness camp meeting, which had its origins in the frontier gatherings that the Methodists had domesticated and routinized during the later antebellum decades. The lead in the further transformation of this institution was taken by John S. Inskip, a New York Methodist minister who had been converted to Holiness principles through his wife's example and who now directed his efforts to the movement's promotion. In June of 1867, Inskip convened a camp meeting at Vineland, New Jersey, from which emerged the National Camp Meeting Association for the Promotion of Holiness.

The Holiness camp meeting enjoyed extraordinary and rapid success through its fusing of a powerful religious impulse with the changing life-styles of the middle class. During the Victorian era, summer vacation resorts were now becoming financially accessible to members of this middle class, many of whom remained firm in their evangelical piety despite their newly enhanced social status. Summer camp meetings began to be held regularly at picturesque locales at Vineland, New Jersey; Wesleyan Grove on Martha's Vineyard off the Massachusetts coast; and other sites usually situated on an ocean or lake shore. Originally consisting of tents, many of these Holiness camp meetings soon upgraded to colorful wooden cottages for annual family use. In the center was a cleared area of several acres, in which elaborate wooden tabernacles for daily worship services were constructed. Architectural historian Ellen Weiss has described Wesleyan Grove as a "city in the woods"—a fusion of the rural camp meeting form with the "garden suburb" residential areas emerging rapidly on the outskirts of the cities of Victorian America. Owners of these cottages entered into formal associations with strict rules of conduct spelled out. The camp meetings also developed rituals and even a hymnody of their own, of which the ever-popular "Beulah Land" remains a good example.

Another phenomenon of the era with ties to both Holiness and Fundamentalism was the "Higher Life" movement, which was closely associated with the Keswick Conventions, held annually at St. John's Keswick Anglican parish beginning in 1875 after an initial gathering at Oxford. Like much of nineteenth-century evangelical activity, Higher Life was Anglo-American in scope, and British and American participants intermingled readily. American Holiness advocates from a variety of denominations participated actively. Following the Reformed rather than the Wesleyan theological formulation, the movement stressed a practical emphasis on the achievement of personal holiness in which sinfulness was suppressed rather than completely eradicated. This notion was popularized by Moody and Sankey in America in the slogan "power for service," an idea with a broad interdenominational appeal. At the same time, however, the Keswick movement has been linked with the planting of some of the seeds of nascent Fundamentalism in its premillennial teachings of Jesus's imminent return, and, in its emphasis on faith healing, a major theme of Pentecostalism as well.

By the 1870s, tension began to mount within American Methodism over the centrality of Holiness doctrines, and a number of the more committed Holiness advocates began to go their own way. Methodist bishops in both the northern and southern branches of the church denounced the growing independence of Holiness associations, and ferment at the grassroots level was sufficient for a new era of reorganization reminiscent of that of Methodism itself, when it broke with its Anglican ties a century earlier. Among the first groups to forge ahead on its own was the Church of God (Anderson, Indiana), founded by Daniel S. Warner in 1880. (Today it remains a leading Holiness denomination, with a membership in the mid-1980s of about 185,000.)

Although Warner's Church of God was typical of early Holiness schisms in its rejection of denominational identity, it, like the earlier antidenominational Campbellites, would ultimately coalesce into typical Protestant organizational status. Even more typical of the transition from sectarian "come-outer" beginnings to full denominational status are the Church of the Nazarene and the Wesleyan Churches, with membership of 516,000 and 110,000 in the mid-1980s, respectively. The origins of each lay in the decision of the charismatic leaders Phineas F. Bresee of Iowa and Martin Wells Knapp of Michigan to "come out" from the Methodist Episcopal Church and found Holiness-centered movements of their own. After a complicated series of mergers with like-minded groups, the two achieved a degree of institutional stability by the

1920s under the names of the Church of the Nazarene and the Pilgrim Holiness Church. The latter merged in 1968 with the like-minded Wesleyan Methodist Church of America to become The Wesleyan Church.

As opposed to the highly institutionalized Methodist Episcopal Church in both its northern and southern branches, these early Holiness movements were distinctly popular in leadership and outreach. Although they differed slightly in details of belief and organization, they were united in an emphasis on direct religious experience and a strict code of personal morality, including the by now standard evangelical bans on smoking, drinking, and various forms of "worldly" amusements. Although rigid in these matters, they also embodied some of the more radical social emphases of their heritage, such as according women a major role in church life. (One Holiness denomination, the Pillar of Fire, was founded by a woman, Alma White, in Denver in 1901.) Holiness churches were also active in the urban mission field, though varying in emphasis from advocacy of social reform to bringing the latter about through the conversion of individuals. The Salvation Army and its American split-off, the Volunteers of America, had their origins in the British Holiness movement and the work of "General" William Booth (1829–1912) and his family. Their colorful street-corner musical evangelism was brought to America in the 1880s. A disagreement with his father led to the formation of the Volunteers of America by Ballington Booth and his wife in 1896. His sister Evangeline Booth took over leadership of the Army proper in America during the following decade. The two groups have continued their parallel courses to the present, organized in military fashion with corresponding titles, emphasizing a simple Holiness theology and intensive outreach to those who have slipped through society's "safety net."

Another movement of middle-class Protestant origins that took on an astonishingly vital life of its own during these years was Fundamentalism. Basically, Fundamentalism represents a continuation of the major emphases of the Reformed strain of nineteenth-century Evangelicalism, with some distinctive doctrinal innovations and a combative nature honed in its origins as an adversary of the Protestant Liberalism that was rapidly gaining momentum late in the nineteenth century. From an interdenominational movement at the conservative end of the evangelical community, it rapidly acquired momentum as a force in the struggle that emerged by the the 1920s within the northern branches of the Baptist and Presbyterian denominations for theological dominance. When these attempts proved unsuccessful, the movement withdrew into alternative institutional channels until its dynamic reemergence as a national religious force in the 1970s and 80s.

Unlike the Holiness and Pentecostal movements, which stressed religious experience over the finer points of belief, early Fundamentalism demonstrated its Reformed roots in its emphasis on doctrine. Central to its emergent identity as the scourge of Liberalism was its insistence not only on the authority but also the "inerrancy" of the Bible in all points, including matters of history and natural science. The intellectual origins of this aspect of the movement lay squarely within the faculty of the Princeton Theological Seminary, which had long since gone its own way when the adjacent university had lost its Old School

Presbyterian identity earlier in the century. Rooted in the Common Sense philosophy expounded by their forerunner, John Witherspoon, latter-day Princeton conservatives such as Charles Hodge and, in the following generation, his son Archibald Alexander Hodge and Benjamin Warfield, provided an intellectual formulation for the new assault on advocates of the "higher criticism" being imported from Germany. This stressed that the "inspired Word [of God] . . . is without error" in its "original autographs"—that is, as it was originally "dictated" by God to the authors of Scripture, who were really scribes more than original writers. Scriptural inerrancy was one of the "five points" adopted by the General Assembly of the Presbyterian Church (northern branch) on several occasions between 1893 and 1910 as key doctrines.

These "points" would later become a widely accepted canon of Fundamentalist belief; they also included, with some variation, the Virgin Birth, which emphasized the miraculous origin of Jesus; the "Substitutionary Theory" of the Atonement, which gave the process of salvation a legalistic cast; the Resurrection of Jesus "with the same body" and the literal character of the miracles attributed to Jesus, both reflecting the Common Sense tendency to take a very concrete and literal approach to scriptural narrative.

In other versions of the basics of Fundamentalist doctrine, the imminent Second Coming of Jesus was added to or substituted for one these basics. This was the notion of "premillennialism," the belief that Jesus was about to appear again on earth in the near future to inaugurate the series of events that would culminate in the millennium. (Since in this scheme the Second Coming is to precede the millennium, rather than following it as other interpreters would have it, the idea has come to be known as *pre*millennialism.) This vivid eschatology had its roots in the world view of the earliest Christian community, and came to the forefront of belief at various intervals during the intervening centuries, including the Millerite movement of the 1840s. Since the time of Constantine, however, expectations of Jesus's imminent return had constituted only a sporadic feature of the belief system of most Christians, whether Catholic or Protestant.

The intellectual roots of modern premillennialism were formulated in England beginning in the 1820s in a wave of prophetic enthusiasm. John Nelson Darby (1800–1882) was a leader of a contemporary sect known as the Plymouth Brethren. (Also known as "Christian Brethren," they number some 80,000 in the United States today.) Darby formulated a method for interpreting the entirety of Scripture known as "dispensational premillennialism," in which the whole of salvation history from God's relation with Adam to the present and on to the end of time are divided into seven epochs known as "dispensations." Based mainly on the Books of Daniel and Revelation (perennial favorites for the prophetically inclined), Darby's scheme postulated that God was following different plans for two different peoples: one for Israel, his earthly people, and another for the (Christian) Church. When the Jews rejected Jesus as their Messiah, the Second Coming of Jesus, which was originally intended to follow rapidly upon his first, was postponed, and what Timothy P. Weber has called "a mysterious, prophetic time warp" or "great parenthesis" resulted.

In order for God's original plan to be fulfilled, the Darbyites postulated two supernaturalistic occurrences, which were expected to be imminent. First, the current and parenthetical dispensation—"the church age"—is nearing an end, as evidenced in widespread apostasy among the churches. (Each previous dispensation had also ended with a collective failure to fulfill God's demands.) Soon, however, those Christians who have remained faithful will be bodily translated into Heaven in an event known as the "Rapture." (Bumper stickers in recent years have proclaimed, "The Rapture—What a Way to Go!") After the saints have been thus cleared from the picture, a period of seven years known as "the Tribulation" will take place, in which those who have been left behind will undergo terrible ordeals during the reign of the Antichrist, a figure of cosmic evil. At the end of this period, in the midst of a great battle fought by the world's armies at Armageddon in northern Israel, Jesus and his saints will appear in glory to overthrow the Antichrist and inaugurate the millennial kingdom—a thousand years on earth of peace and prosperity. At the end of the thousand years, Satan will be briefly loosed and defeated, the dead will be resurrected and judged, and this world shall give way to "a new heaven and a new earth" (Revelation 21:1.)

One additional feature of this elaborate prophetic scheme is the role played in it by the Jewish people. During the Tribulation, many Jews will become converted to Christianity and suffer for it under the Antichrist. When Jesus returns, he will preside as the Messiah over a Jewish kingdom with a complete restoration of the Temple, its priesthood and sacrifices, and the whole panoply of observances of Israel during its heyday in the time of the Monarchy. Since the dispensationalist scheme is based on a belief that all of these events will take place in a very literal way, the restoration of an independent nation of Israel thus became a major item of faith. As the possibility of its fulfillment began to take on a new plausibility with the emergence of modern Zionism at the turn of the century and Britain's Balfour Declaration during World War I, Dispensationalists became reinforced in their beliefs through this seeming external confirmation of their predictions. Support for Israel has emerged in recent years as a major foreign policy commitment of latter-day Fundamentalists such as Jerry Falwell as a consequence.

As Fundamentalism began to grow into an organized movement, Dispensationalism no longer was the property of a few isolated sects, and moved into the mainstream of the new belief system that was being forged from an amalgam of the teachings of Darby with those of the Princeton theologians and the "Victorious Life" theme of the Keswick Movement. Dwight L. Moody again was a potent catalyst, and his Moody Bible Institute and its dozens of imitators soon provided a communications network through which these ideas attained a wide currency. A series of annual Niagara Bible Conferences, begun in 1876 and attended by an interdenominational assortment of sympathetic clergy and lay people, also popularized this core cluster of ideas. A further effective means of propagation was a series of twelve booklets of essays expounding the themes of Fundamentalism, written by a wide variety of scholarly advocates of the movement. Known, appropriately, as *The Fundamentals,* these booklets were distributed to a large audience at no cost through the beneficence of a pair of wealthy brothers from Los Angeles. Their advent was a turning point in Fundamentalism's emergence as a coherent movement rather than a loosely related collection of ideas, events, institutions, and spokespeople.

Where dispensationalism became a major doctrinal component for what we might (perhaps with some irony) call the "mainstream" Fundamentalism that flourished especially within the Baptist and Presbyterian folds, other forms of millennialism continued beyond the great Millerite excitement of the 1840s in more sectarian form. In addition to Seventh-Day Adventism, which has already been discussed, the Jehovah's Witnesses have been an enduring element in the American religious spectrum since their founding as the International Bible Students' Association by a Pittsburgh haberdasher, Charles Taze Russell, in 1872. Russell taught that Jesus had inaugurated a "Millennial Dawn" with his return in the "upper air" in 1874, and expected the millennial consummation of the worldly order in 1914. Russell himself moved the date up four years before his own death in 1916, and his successor, Judge J. R. Rutherford, continued to adjust it as the anticipated inauguration of a new world order failed to materialize.

Despite repeated "disconfirmations" the Witnesses, as they have called themselves since 1931, have continued to flourish, in part through their aggressive door-to-door evangelism and sales of *The Watchtower,* published at their Brooklyn headquarters. Their distinctive teachings, such as the restriction of full sainthood to 144,000 (Revelation 14:1–3) and their denial of a traditional interpretation of the Trinity, as well as "deviant" practices such as refusing blood transfusions (based on a unique reading of Psalm 16), have rendered them an archetypal example of a *sect* in modern society. Although they have been consistently attacked by conservative Christians as a "cult," their major societal difficulties have stemmed from their alleged lack of patriotism in refusing to serve in the military and to salute the flag. These refusals result from their sense of constituting a "theocracy" in which all members are ministers, and their concomitant rejection of the religious and political order of the broader world when that order goes against their beliefs.

The sometimes violent persecution this "deviant" behavior has incurred, especially in wartime, has only strengthened their sense of rightness, and has also broadened First Amendment protection for such stances through the 1943 Supreme Court decision *West Virginia State Board of Education* v. *Barnette.* (The courts have generally sustained their refusal of blood transfusions for adult believers, but not for children.) By the 1980s, Jehovah's Witnesses in the United States numbered about 700,000, having benefited from the general resurgence in conservative religion of the period. They are organized into about eight thousand local congregations that meet in "Kingdom Halls," with headquarters in Brooklyn.

A third movement of great power that had its roots in both the early Holiness and Fundamentalist movements was Pentecostalism. As its name implies, it was a movement of restoration, predicated on the belief that the gifts of the Holy Spirit bestowed on the Apostles on the day of Pentecost were now descending on contemporary Americans as the "latter rain" spoken of in the prophetic book of Joel (King James Version, 2:23; see also I

Corinthians 12 and 14 on the "gifts of the Spirit.") As Grant Wacker has pointed out, the world view of the early Pentecostals was radically ahistorical; they believed that a new Apostolic Age was bursting into the world, which was negating the significance of all history since the time of the first Apostles. Since they were not receptive to newer, historical approaches to biblical interpretation, they were inclined to believe that the Bible "dropped from heaven as a sacred meteor," and was therefore to be read with the same literalism that characterized the emerging Fundamentalist hermeneutic (i.e., method of interpretation). Not surprisingly, they also readily adopted the broad outlines of Dispensationalism, and eagerly awaited the Second Coming with their Fundamentalist contemporaries.

Although belief was important for Pentecostals, experience, was central. They accepted the basic premises of Holiness, but took them still further. Where Holiness advocates had equated the experience of entire sanctification with the "baptism of the Holy Spirit" (and often used the term *Pentecostal* in self-description), the new movement that emerged near the turn of the century out of the Holiness matrix insisted that this "baptism" was manifest in the experience of the gifts of the Spirit enumerated in I Corinthians. The most prominent of these gifts was the ability to speak in "tongues," as had the Apostles on the day of Pentecost itself. (Acts 2:3–4: "And they were all filled with the Holy Spirit and began to speak in other tongues.")

This phenomenon of speaking in tongues—*glossolalia*—which is central to Pentecostalism, has been the subject of considerable study and speculation, with no definitive conclusions as to its ultimate character. At one level, it appears to be a form of automatic motor behavior, possibly flowing from a trance-like state (although some claim that it can be induced deliberately during ordinary consciousness). The free flow of speech that results is linguistically distinctive, and is not readily confused with actual languages. In the movement's early days especially, however, many practitioners claimed that they and their fellow tongue-speakers had spoken actual foreign languages with which they had no previous familiarity. This phenomenon, known as *xenoglossia,* is still occasionally reported, but documentation is elusive. What is undeniable, however, is that Pentecostals *do* participate in a form of out-of-the-ordinary linguistic behavior to which they attribute vital religious significance.

Although glossolalia is one of the most distinctive aspects of Pentecostal practice, and is regarded by most believers as a necessary sign of Spirit baptism, it is not the only spiritual gift. Of great importance also is healing through religious faith, a phenomenon by no means confined to Pentecostals. (In recent years it has become a central concern for many "mainline" congregations.) Still others, such as the interpretation of tongues and prophesying, are less crucial though also recognized. The snake-handling groups found in a few Appalachian Pentecostal churches represent an extreme interpretation that, though widely publicized, is very uncommon.

Occasional glossolalia may have taken place in the Shaker communities of the earlier nineteenth century and among "enthusiastic" sectarians in Europe before that. These phenomena were scattered and evanescent, and the origins of modern Pentecostalism can be found in the volatile cultural matrix of the

American South, Midwest, and Far West at the turn of the century. Where both Holiness and Fundamentalism had their origins in the very respectable middle-class environments of the Wesleyan and Reformed traditions, Pentecostalism, with debts to both earlier movements, was much more clearly a popular movement in its beginnings. Like the Radical Reformation and the Great Awakening, its origins were multiple, with foci in Los Angeles, Kansas, and North Carolina, as well as a number of similar areas long familiar with revivalistic religion and often subject to troubling social change and conflict.

Although the origins of the movement remain shrouded in the realm of folklore, the movement's recorded history begins in Topeka, Kansas, at the turn of the present century. Here an erratic "come-outer" preacher named Charles Fox Parham founded a Bible institute where, according to a disputed tradition, "fire fell" among the students and faculty on New Year's Day in 1901. The tongue-speaking that then took place generated a brief flurry of revivalistic excitement in the region, which soon cooled down until Parham tried to revive it in 1903 through taking up a career as a faith-healer.

In 1905, a school for the promotion of this "Apostolic Faith" that Parham was conducting in Houston attracted the attention of an itinerant black Holiness preacher named William J. Seymour. The next year Seymour introduced Parham's teachings and practices into a black congregation which later moved to Azusa Street in Los Angeles—the "Midwest raised to flashpoint," as Reyner Banham has described that city. Soon he had a genuine phenomenon on his hands. Azusa Street lives in Pentecostal lore as the first real explosion of the Spirit. For three years, blacks, whites, Hispanics, Orientals, and the whole spectrum of Los Angeles's diverse population became involved in an ecstatic revival, much like the one at Cane Ridge only now with the gift of tongues as an added feature. The Azusa Street revival attracted attention from around the nation, and visitors left with a new message to take back to widely scattered parts of the South and Midwest in particular, where the ground had been well prepared by the Holiness enthusiasm of the preceding decades.

The early history of Pentecostalism resembles closely that of the Holiness movement from which it sprang. Founded by unpredictable leaders such as Parham and Seymour and characterized both by the radical "come-outer" sectarian spirit and intense religious enthusiasm, new groups arose, merged, feuded, split, and recombined over and over again before reaching institutional stability in the 1920s. The Church of God in Christ, today a large and primarily black denomination based in Memphis, was founded by two Holiness Baptist black preachers in Mississippi in 1897, who split a decade later over the issue of tongue-speaking. The Church of God (Cleveland, Tennessee) arose from a white Holiness group through the leadership of Ambrose Jessup Tomlinson, a volatile leader of Parham's stamp. Several schisms have led to a proliferation of churches tracing their lineage back to this founding, due in part to the volatility of later generations of Tomlinsons. The Church of God (Cleveland, Tennessee) has been numerically the most successful of these groups, with a membership of about half a million in the mid-1980s; the Church of God of Prophecy, the only other sizable branch, had about 75,000 members at that time.

These two earliest Pentecostal foundings are representative of the excitement and confusion of those early years, and were followed by a host of other new churches, some of which eventually grew into denominations of considerable size. Foremost among these today is the Assemblies of God, which grew out of a 1914 merger of like-minded groups in Texas, Alabama, Ohio, and Illinois who wanted to distance themselves from the Wesleyan character of much nascent Pentecostal belief and align themselves more clearly with the Reformed theological tradition. This they did by conflating the experiences of conversion and sanctification into a single event, followed by a discrete baptism by the Holy Spirit. By the 1980s the church had attracted a national constituency, with a membership of over two million. The Pentecostal Holiness Church arose from the merging in 1911 of a North Carolina Holiness group of that name with the Fire-Baptized Holiness Church of South Carolina. (The names of Pentecostal denominations vary from the highly routinized to the vividly evocative.) Foundings continued well into the 1920s, when the colorful Los Angeles evangelist Aimee Semple McPherson—"your sister in the King's glad service"—incorporated her Church of the Foursquare Gospel in 1927. (The name is derived from the symbolism of Ezekiel 1:4–28.)

Following these initial years of effervescence, these three upsurges of Protestant religiosity, at once conservative and radical, entered into a period of eclipse. They by no means disappeared, and continued to gather adherents especially in what H. L. Mencken dubbed the "Bible Belt" of the South and parts of the Midwest and Southwest. By this time they had acquired a reputation no longer as revitalization movements within the mainline of Protestantism, but rather as marginal religions, attracting the disinherited, both black and white, in the areas of the country least affected by the forces of modernization. The foibles of some of the early Pentecostal leaders and the occasionally bizarre claims made by the itinerant faith-healers of the middle decades of the century removed them from the center of national religious life until a new era of cultural shock in the 1960s and 1970s changed the American scene irrevocably and catapulted them into a new prominence.

The one movement among these three that actively strove to retain a role as a major force in the nation's religious life was Fundamentalism. Where Holiness and Pentecostal leadership arose from the come-outer margins of the denominations, that of Fundamentalism arose from the powerful right flanks of the Northern Baptists and Presbyterians. (The Southern churches were largely unaffected since Protestant Liberalism made few inroads in the region.) The Fundamentalist cause was disseminated in a number of highly effective ways: the colorful, aggressive evangelism of Billy Sunday and other, contentious followers along the "sawdust trail" blazed by Moody; the network of Bible schools modeled on Moody's institute, which generated a vast number of lay workers, teachers and evangelists; denominational groups, such as William Bell Riley's Baptist Bible Union; and a vast outpouring of books and periodicals. The movement was also promoted by a new generation of urban preachers who turned their churches into powerful centers of influence. Conservative successors to an earlier, liberal generation of "princes of the pulpit" included John Roach Straton of New York City's Calvary Baptist Church and

William Bell Riley, who presided for forty-five years at his First Baptist Church in Minneapolis. These urban preachers often acquired church memberships in the thousands, and were able to build enormous physical plants and employ the new medium of radio to broadcast their message and consolidate their influence. The congregational polity of the Baptists made it still easier for charismatic leaders of this stripe to acquire independent positions of religious power. The "superchurches" of the later twentieth century, often Southern or Independent Baptist in affiliation, and with membership running into the tens of thousands, are the direct heirs of this tradition.

By the 1920s, Liberals and Fundamentalists had polarized sufficiently to have generated an ongoing public struggle for the control of their denominations, especially the Baptists and Presbyterians. (Other primarily Northern groups, such as the Methodists and Episcopalians, were not seriously affected by the controversy, in part because of the Methodist "leakage" into the new Holiness and Pentecostal groups.) Moderates, however, were inclined to defend the rights of Liberals to freedom of theological expression, and the Fundamentalists were unsuccessful in attempting to impose their version of orthodoxy on their respective traditions. The results in some cases were schisms, such as the founding of the Orthodox Presbyterian Church in 1936 and the Bible Presbyterian Church the following year.

The symbolic event that marked the eclipse of religious conservatism from the 1920s until the 1970s was, of course, the Scopes Trial held in Dayton, Tennessee—not far from Cleveland—in 1925. The story of the small-town high school biology teacher, John Scopes, being tried for deliberately and publicly bringing about a test case on the Tennessee statute that forbade the teaching of evolution in the public schools has become part of the nation's folklore, and has been lightly fictionalized in the play "Inherit the Wind" (subsequently rendered in motion picture and television form as well). The trial took on the dimensions of a cosmic drama of confrontation, with the famous agnostic defender of unpopular causes Clarence Darrow as Scopes's attorney, and former Secretary of State and Democratic presidential candidate William Jennings Bryan aiding the defense as a spokesman for the Fundamentalist attack on Darwinian evolution as incompatible with a literal reading of the account of creation presented in the beginning chapters of Genesis. Comic relief was added by the sideshows this "media event" generated, such as the display of chimpanzees, as well as by the press coverage of the Baltimore *Sun*'s ace reporter, the acerbic and skeptical H. L. Mencken. (Mencken had gained notoriety through such coinages as the "Booboisie," the "Bible Belt," and the "Sahara of the Bozart"—i.e., beaux arts or fine arts—as characterizations of middle-class Babbitry, the Fundamentalist heartland, and the South respectively.)

Scopes's subsequent conviction was overturned by an appeals court on a technicality, though the law in question was not repealed until the 1950s. Regardless of the legal outcome, the hostile media attention generated by the trial had damaged the Fundamentalist cause badly, and it soon became relegated in the middle-class mind to the backwater status into which Pentecostalism and Holiness had already slipped. The eclipse of Fundamentalism, however, did not mean more than a temporary victory for its Liberal antagonists, since religion in general was sliding into what Robert T. Handy has called "the second disestablishment." The rampant secularism of 1920s urban culture and the ensuing turmoil of the Depression both contributed to the sense of irrelevance with which many Americans were inclined to regard organized religion. It was not until the 1950s that "religion in general" enjoyed a widespread new popularity. One of the most visible figures of that era was William Franklin "Billy" Graham, who helped launch the conservative resurgence that would emerge as a major characteristic of American religious life in the ensuing decades.

CHAPTER 35

Religion in the South

In the study of American culture, it is the South that has given particular importance to the question of *regionalism*. Other parts of the country still possess a certain amount of distinctiveness in their ethnic composition, voting habits, economic activity, religious makeup, and other components of regional variation. In terms of regional *culture*—or, perhaps more accurately, *subculture*—it is difficult to find any extended area of America, even New England, where ways of looking at and living in the world are as profoundly affected by the distinctive ethos of the region. California today has acquired some of this distinctiveness, based on its inhabitants' reputed contempt for tradition and openness to the future. In the South, the past, as historical reality and as cultural construct, continues to make heavy claims upon the present.

Geographically, the South is roughly coextensive with the eleven states that seceded in 1861 to form the Confederacy, in large part over the continued existence of slavery. One traditional point of demarcation was the Mason-Dixon line that resulted from a major survey of 1763–1767. More recently, cultural geographers have argued that the old U.S. Route 40, which cuts across Columbus and Dayton in Ohio, and parallels the newer I-70, is a more accurate dividing line. Most of Indiana, as well as parts of southern Illinois, Missouri, Oklahoma, and Texas are often regarded as basically southern in ambience; conversely, peninsular Florida, which was not developed until the twentieth century by "Yankees," has little distinctively Southern about it other than intense heat. Similarly, southern Louisiana, colonized by French-speaking Catholics, and the mountain South of the Appalachians and Ozarks constitute distinctive subcultural areas that can be included as parts of the broader South only with some qualifications.

Being Southern in a cultural as well as a geographical sense involves a number of social conditions and patterns of outlook. Although white Southerners often represent a mixture of national origins, the largest number trace their ancestry to the various components of Britain. Historians Forest Mc-Donald and Grady McWhiney have even argued that the Celtic strain has been culturally more influential that the Anglo-Saxon English in molding distinctively Southern attitudes toward, for example, warfare and violence. (It is worth noting that Scarlett O'Hara bore an Irish name.) In any case, the basic white ethnic stock that made up the core of American Southern society was predominantly English, Irish, Scottish, and Scotch-Irish. The emigration of the latter during the eighteenth century, at first to Pennsylvania and Virginia, then south and west into Kentucky, the Carolinas, and beyond, was a demographic factor of the greatest importance. The "New Immigration" of the later nineteenth century largely bypassed the South, which was neither sufficiently urbanized nor culturally receptive to such outsiders; even the growing cities of the "New South" failed to attract many who altered so dramatically the social complexion of the North.

The other major ethnic background of Southerners, of course, was African. The term *ethnic,* in fact, sounds slightly odd in this context, since the word *race* has been used so extensively to describe the cultural line between black and white. Anthropologists today shy away from the word *race,* since the physical reality of what it has usually been used to denote is so imprecise. For better or worse, however, American life in general and Southern life in particular has been inescapably intertwined with the notion that humans can be divided along a color line, on one side or the other of which each person must be classified. Distinctions based on physical as well as cultural characteristics are by no means unknown in other societies. However, even in Hawaii and Brazil, two cultures that can both be designated as "American," the coexistence of two or more racial groups has led to extensive intermarriage and a social system in which racial distinctions are real, but matters of gradation. In the United States, they are all or nothing; they are, so to speak, a matter of black or white.

Although racism has been endemic among white Americans since the beginnings of the nation, the situation in the South was compounded by its institutionalization in the form of chattel slavery. Black people were by their nature subject to enslavement by whites, and virtually all Africans prior to the Civil War entered America in that condition. Until the transformations brought about by the civil rights movement in the 1960s, even free blacks in the South lived under serious disabilities, whether sanctioned by law or simply by the weight of social custom, economic leverage, and the ever-present threat of violence. On the other hand, as Southerners have always been quick to point out, whites and blacks in the South have always lived in close social contact—not as equals, but often as intimates. This reality of genuine, if unequal, contact between the races has distinguished the character of the South from that of other parts of the country, where physical separation and economic inequality more than legal constraint has resulted in what social psychologist Joel Kovel has called "aversive racism."

In addition to the inescapable fact of a distinctive pattern of racial relations, the South has also generated a set of cultural attitudes that have reinforced its difference from the rest of the country. Sociologist John Shelton Reed has identified several such traits that he has claimed can be verified quantitatively. These include *localism*—that is, taking one's immediate social context rather than that of the broader society as one's point of reference and departure. Related to localism is a heightened importance placed on the role of the *family*, so that ties of kinship have traditionally taken precedence over those formed through various sorts of voluntary association. *Violence* has for centuries enjoyed a legitimacy in Southern culture that has shocked and baffled outsiders, as expressed in such forms as duelling, lynching, or even overly aggressive stock-car racing.

The final distinctively Southern emphasis Reed has identified is *religion*. Since at least the early nineteenth century, black and white Southerners have been more deeply and visibly committed to religion, especially several varieties of evangelical Protestantism, than residents of any other extended part of the nation. Religious commitment has coexisted, perhaps symbiotically, with other sorts of cultural expression, such as violence and racism, that outsiders have again found alternately perplexing and appalling. Southern religion has also reflected the fundamentally biethnic—British and Afro-American—character of Southern society in its relative homogeneity. As a consequence, nothing outside the evangelical spectrum has stood much of a chance for widespread popular acceptance except in those areas that are Southern only in a geographical sense, such as metropolitan Miami and New Orleans. Religion, in any case, is an intrinsic component of the culture of the American South, and the course it has taken there has shaped it in a way significantly different from the patterns even its evangelical cousins have taken elsewhere in the nation.

From the beginnings of the colonial era, the Church of England was brought to the South, first at Jamestown and then in the decades of plantation founding and development that ensued. Theoretically, at least, Anglicanism enjoyed the same status as an established religion that it did in England. As Donald G. Mathews has pointed out, however, the dispersed nature of Virginia society, the scarcity of qualified clergy, and the absence of a bishop militated against its functioning as a very effective presence. In the vacuum that ensued, the wealthy plantation aristocracy that dominated the civil realm took control of the sacred as well through their dominant role on the vestries, or lay governing boards, of the local churches.

This association of the Church of England with the plantation aristocracy did not in the long run serve it very well, since the unfolding American experiment was not conducive to the unquestioning acceptance of a stratified society based on the principle of deference of inferiors to superiors. Even before the Great Awakening began to challenge the prestige of religious establishments throughout the colonies, evangelical missionaries such as the Presbyterian Samuel Davies began to seek converts and to secure legal rights for religious dissent. The insurgence of Baptists that followed the Awakening added new dimensions of size and energy to this challenge to the established order, which involved a radical critique of Virginia's social and political structure as well as a rejection of Anglican belief and worship. As Rhys Isaac has pointed out, the close identification of the colonial version of the Church of England with the plantation aristocracy and what dissidents perceived as their rather relaxed morals was the subject of what amounted in the pre-Revolutionary decades to a thoroughgoing social and religious revolution.

In other parts of the colonial South and even in relatively civilized Virginia, however, the Anglican establishment was not the only target of evangelical protest, of which the Separate Baptists constituted the vanguard. As Bertram Wyatt-Brown has demonstrated, the colonial South prior to the Great Awakening was an extension of traditional English folk culture, governed by an ethos hardly touched by the values of either Anglican or evangelical Christianity. Privacy was scarcely thought of, magical practices mingled freely with what formal religion was known, and *honor* was the overriding cultural value. Anglicans and Baptists alike strove to impose order on what they thus perceived as social and moral chaos, though their visions of that order differed irreconcilably from one another.

The First Amendment and corresponding provisions in the constitutions of the several states brought an end to Anglican dominance and the harassment of dissenters, and the latter found the post-Revolutionary South ripe for their energies. The challenge was formidable, since the social critique mounted by the evangelicals was scarcely compatible with the institutions and values that characterized the dominant classes in the South. The first Baptists and Methodists were adamantly opposed to slave-holding, which they associated with aristocratic self-indulgence. As evangelicals gained more of a foothold on the social ladder, and as the South as a region became more and more irrevocably committed to the "peculiar institution," however, a dramatic shift in attitude was in the making.

By the 1840s, as the abolitionist movement began to gain strength in the North, Southern evangelical churches had largely made their peace with a social system that was itself undergoing change in response to external challenge and internal development. By now the Baptists and Methodists had become major religious forces, challenging the prestige and influence earlier accorded first to Anglicans—now the Protestant Episcopal Church—and then to Presbyterians. Clerical opposition to deeply rooted Southern practices such as the distilling of spirits (which proved an economical way of utilizing grain), duelling and other forms of ritualized violence, and slavery itself waned as evangelicals now were choosing to join what they could not beat. Clergy became active in defending slavery on biblical grounds—for instance, by reading God's curse on Noah's son Ham and his descendants as involving the black race (Genesis 9:25). Southern apologists such as George Fitzhugh also developed powerful moral critiques of the nascent industrial society of the North, which they claimed, with some plausibility, reduced nominally free factory workers to a social and economic status inferior to that of paternalistically protected slaves.

By the time of the Civil War, the Southern clergy had with virtual unanimity rallied to the cause of the Confederacy, and were instrumental in promoting morale among both troops and civilians through their religious justifications of their region's cause. Beginning with the Methodists and the Baptists in 1844 and 1845 respectively, the most powerful of the South's Protestant denominations began to break from their Northern counterparts and found alternative regional churches. The Old School-New School Presbyterian schism of 1837 had involved slavery as a peripheral issue, and both sides split further along explicitly regional lines as the war grew imminent. (The New School divided in 1856–1857, and the Old in 1861.) The Protestant Episcopal Church in the Confederate States of America lasted only for the duration of the war, and Roman Catholics, Lutherans, and other denominations without a firm stand on slavery or little Southern representation were relatively unaffected. The three major evangelical churches, however, were deeply scarred by these events: Methodists reunited in 1939, Presbyterians not till 1983, and Baptist reunion seems highly unlikely in the foreseeable future.

Although important differences of belief, worship, and social class continued to separate the Southern branches of these denominations following the Civil War, their common identification with their region's culture was far more important than any such divisions. The consensus that had developed on the slavery issue now continued with a slight adjustment in focus. One key notion helping shape the ethos of postbellum Southern Protestantism was the Presbyterian James Henley Thornwell's doctrine of the "spirituality of the church." By this, Thornwell meant that the concern of organized Christianity was with the salvation of the individual rather than with the social realm. The conservative political and cultural implications of this idea were profound, and mightily reinforced the social outlook that the dominant classes were in the process of formulating.

Although the "spirituality of the church" inhibited the Southern Presbyterian Church (PCUS) from taking public stands on social issues of any sort, Presbyterian attitudes did not differ substantially from that of most white Baptists and Methodists. Although the Social Gospel made some scattered inroads in the still largely rural South, the dominant cultural consensus favored the moral reform of the individual, preferably through religious conversion, rather than through religious social engineering. Prohibition was something of an exception, and Methodists such as Virginia's Bishop James Cannon, Jr., (1864–1944) energetically promoted its adoption and enforcement. Cannon's leadership in opposing the candidacy of the "wet" Roman Catholic Democrat Al Smith in 1928 further demonstrated the array of political commitments characteristic of Southern evangelicals prior to the 1960s. Apart from political activism, most evangelicals were also united in their endorsement of a strict code of personal moral behavior, which forbade smoking; alcoholic beverages; gambling; theater- and, later, movie-going; and even, especially among Pentecostals, the wearing of neckties for men and the use of cosmetics or bobbing one's hair among women. The contrast with the ongoing propensity in the same parts of society for "corn likker," cock-fighting, and other rural amusements indicates the extremity of the tensions that characterized much of Southern life, which cultural analyst W. J. Cash saw as rooted in the region's tradition of "orgiastic religion." The violence generated by this tension between repressiveness and exuberance has supplied much of the stuff of both popular and "high" cultural interpretations of that life, from Flannery O'Connor's grotesques to "Smokey and the Bandit."

Racial relations, of course, continued to play a major, even dominant role in

Southern life in the decades following the Civil War. Black worship was now freed from white supervision, and denominational organization began to flourish. In addition to joining the African Methodist Episcopal and AME Zion Churches, which were imports from the North, Southern blacks also organized the Colored (now Christian) Methodist Episcopal Church as an alternative to the segregated Methodist Episcopal Church, South. The National Baptist Convention, U.S.A., Inc., was organized in Atlanta in 1895, and later split twice into sizable factions. Black as well as white Baptists also gathered into many independent local congregations, as did the "sanctified" Holiness and Pentecostal churches that emerged around the turn of the century among both races—and, in the early days of Pentecostalism, sometimes took biracial forms. The distinctive character of Southern black religion is discussed more fully elsewhere; however, it certainly emerged from the same evangelical ethos that shaped much of the South's white Christianity, and the reciprocal influence of each on the other—for example, in patterns of worship, music, and personal experience—has begun to be appreciated only of late.

If black and white influenced one another in religion, they were held apart in other aspects of life by informal custom as well as, beginning in the 1880s, the "Jim Crow" laws that converted the South into a formally segregated society. Blacks were barred from sharing public facilities with whites and actively discouraged from voting, while many were effectively relegated to a condition of peonage through the practice of sharecropping. This color line was supported by most white churches as well, and the Ku Klux Klan re-emerged in the 1920s as a vigilante group dedicated to keeping blacks, as well as Catholics, Jews, and immigrants, in their alleged places. One interesting aspect of the social activism of the era was the formation of the Association of Southern Women for the Prevention of Lynching, by Jessie Daniel Ames in 1930, a crusade against one of the Klan's most notorious practices; this movement grew out of the work of the Woman's Department of the Commission on Interracial Cooperation.

However important a role social issues may have played in Southern religious life, the core of the region's religiosity has traditionally been intensely individualistic. As Samuel S. Hill has pointed out, the evangelical Protestantism that has been dominant since the days of the Great Revival at the beginning of the nineteenth century differs in some significant ways from its Northern counterparts. Central to its message is the devastating reality of sin and guilt, and a corresponding need for redemption through personal, often dramatic and sudden, conversion. Hill postulates that the burden of guilt Southerners have consciously or otherwise carried over the region's implication in slavery and racism may be a major constituent in this preoccupation with sin. The distinction between worship and revival services became blurred as a result on this focus on conversion, and revivalistic preaching aimed to bring about a change of heart has become a staple of Sunday morning life at many of the region's numerous churches.

During the post-Civil War decades, the level of church membership rose dramatically throughout the South. Baptists and Methodists benefited especially; Presbyterians and Episcopalians continued their role as high-status churches; and the Holiness and Pentecostal churches, as well as the Churches of Christ in the Campbellite/Restorationist tradition, began to acquire momentum after the turn of the century. As Hill also notes, church membership became during these years a virtual requirement for community acceptance and success. Religion and culture were thus more inextricably intertwined than in any other extended region in the country, with the possible exception of Mormon Utah.

In these same years, though, Southerners began as well to develop a parallel strain of religiosity that related to the Christian churches in roughly the same way the Buddhism and Shinto have coexisted in Japan. This "civil religion" that emerged from the experience of massive defeat during the Civil War has been dubbed "the Religion of the Lost Cause" by historian Charles Reagan Wilson. Growing out of a propensity during the war years to regard that epic conflict as a "baptism in blood," this postwar regional cult now built upon the earlier notion of the moral superiority of the South, which now had been purified by a fiery baptism. The cult that resulted expressed itself, among other ways, in the building of statues and other public monuments to the war's heroes, such as Robert E. Lee. (Richmond, Virginia, the capital of the Confederacy, particularly abounds in such statues.) Patriotic societies, veterans' groups reunions, sermons, orations, and other public activities helped to ritualize what amounted to a cultural religion, a latter-day version of which is still perpetuated by means ranging from visits to historical sites such as Chickamauga battlefield and Stone Mountain to bumper stickers reading "Forget, Hell."

Yet another aspect of the multifaceted character of Southern regional religion is the spectrum of popular and folk religion that still maintains a strong hold especially in rural areas, including the mountain subcultures of the Appalachians and Ozarks. The wide variety of Baptist churches, together with Holiness and Pentecostal groups, are dominant in shaping this aspect of religious culture much more than the more organized and urban United Methodist and Southern Baptist denominations. One aspect of a folk heritage that has endured to the present is manifest in the tradition of "shape-note" or "fasola" hymn singing, which originated early in the nineteenth century out of the necessity of providing a semiliterate people with a means of sight-reading. Instead of standard musical notation, triangles, squares, circles, and diamonds were used to indicate the notes to be sung. Spread widely through such works as *The Sacred Harp* of 1844, shape-note singing remains alive today through many parts of the rural South, though its appeal may be based increasingly on nostalgia. Many of the songs performed in this manner date back to the Wesleys of the eighteenth century and the American composer Lowell Mason of the early nineteenth, and include such perennial favorites as "Amazing Grace" and "Come Thou Fount of Every Blessing." The "gospel hymns" of the era of Fanny J. Crosby and Homer J. Rodeheaver have also remained popular, and male "gospel quartets," as well as women's trios, both black and white, frequently attain widespread regional reputations through traveling performances at many churches.

Another distinctive aspect of popular Southern religious life is the *homecoming*. Homecomings are basically reunions, which can be held by families, school classes, and other groups, but are frequently sponsored by churches. Church homecomings are held on their own grounds, which often have permanent picnic tables for the purpose, or at cemeteries or camp meeting grounds. They usually take place on the date of the church's founding, and involve the return to the community of the extended family members of the church's founders as well as those of current members to reminisce and socialize. Flowers placed on cemetery graves are often part of the ritual as well, and vast numbers can be seen on drives thorugh the rural South in the summer on Decoration Day. The homecoming illustrates vividly the intimate relationship that religion in the South has with other aspects of culture, especially its role as a point of reference for the identity and solidarity of an entire community, now in danger of being scattered through the forces of modernization. As Jack Temple Kirby has pointed out, participants in many of today's homecomings are urban dwellers returning briefly to their rural roots.

The religious life of the mountain South also has some characteristics that distinguish it from even the folk aspects of religion in other parts of the region. Unlike the Tidewater and Piedmont areas, many parts of the Appalachians and Ozarks have remained racially as well as ethnically homogeneous; since slavery was unprofitable in mountainous terrain, blacks seldom were brought to the region as slaves or, later, they came voluntarily. The isolation of these regions has also inhibited the modernizing forces of the "New South" movement that began to promote industrialization and urbanization in the late nineteenth century; rather, the outside world has been experienced most intensely in the form of exploitative coal companies engaged in strip mining.

The religious consequences of this cultural homogeneity and isolation are manifested in independent, individualistic, and highly expressive variations on the Baptist and Holiness-Pentecostal basic themes. Primitive, United, and Old Regular Baptists are three varieties of the former tradition that have found in Appalachia a far more congenial home than almost anywhere else. United by an adherence to one form or another of Calvinist theology, they reject activities such as missions or Sunday schools that their predestinarian beliefs render futile. Their worship is often traditional, featuring a capella shape-note singing and a preaching style that sounds more like a chant or whine than like ordinary spoken discourse. Yearly sacramental services feature the Lord's Supper and the ordinance of foot-washing, practiced by members of the same sex, which is also being revived in some parts of the country by liturgical churches. Pentecostals and Free-Will Baptists also abound, and mix such traditions as foot-washing with more "modern" innovations such as instrumental music and gospel singing.

Pentecostal and Holiness churches also abound in the mountains, and the area around Cleveland, Tennessee, which houses the headquarters of two branches of the Church of God, has sometimes been referred to as the "Burned-Over District" of these movements. It was rural Pentecostals who gave rise to such an extemely expressive form of public worship that they became known derisively by outsiders as "Holy Rollers." An extreme but very rare form of mountain Pentecostal practice that has attracted an exaggerated notoriety in the broader world is the previously mentioned phenomenon of "snake-handling." In a few churches, mainly in Appalachia, traditional Pentecostal worship forms such as glossolalia are intermingled with the introduction of live rattlesnakes into the midst of the worshipping assembly as a test of faith. This practice and related phenomena such as the "salvation cocktail"—a thimbleful of strychnine—are tests for the faithful of the literal accuracy of Mark 16:17–18 ("And these signs will accompany those who believe: in my name they will cast out demons; they will speak in new tongues; they will pick up serpents; and if they drink any deadly thing, it will not hurt them; they will lay their hands on the sick, and they will recover").

The South was irrevocably transformed by the civil rights movement and accompanying legislation of the 1960s. The color line could now no longer be maintained legally, and the integration of public high school and colleges supplied some of the most dramatic movements for the new "Lost Cause." In addition to Southern blacks, represented most eloquently by Martin Luther King, Jr., and civil rights workers from the North, a small but significant number of white Southern clergy banded together to form the Committee of Southern Churchmen in 1964 to promote the movement themselves. Will Campbell, a Baptist minister who has served both as Director of Religious Life at the University of Mississippi, and, in an effort at reconciliation, as a Ku Klux Klan chaplain, is a representative of this alternative consciousness in the recent South. His experiences have been memorably recorded in his autobiographical *Brother to a Dragonfly* (1977).

Irresistible forces toward change from outside have combined with internal social and economic development to produce a "New New South," as exemplified in such thriving, cosmopolitan urban centers as Atlanta and Charlotte. On the other hand, though, the South has undergone a simultaneous religious and political transformation, beginning in the 1960s, that has not been in either a liberal or a "Lost Cause" direction. With the exception of 1976, when the self-avowed evangelical Jimmy Carter carried his region in a successful bid for the Presidency, the once monolithically Democractic "Solid South" now tends to vote Republican in national elections and, less regularly, in Congressional, state, and local contests. (South Carolina Senator Strom Thurmond's conversion to Republicanism was a conspicuous sign of this shift.) Although racism is no longer a staple of what was once called the "Gothic politics" of the region, conservatism in economics, foreign policy, and "social issues" such as abortion and pornography now attract widespread popular support.

In the religious realm, urban areas in the South now attract a wide variety of religious congregations, from Unitarians to Hindus, reflecting an accelerating integration of such areas into the national culture. Rural areas continue to be heavily Churches of Christ, Baptist, Holiness-Pentecostal, and among the middle classes, Methodist in affiliation. A dramatic increase has taken place during the same years among Southern Baptists—now by far the largest American Protestant denomination, with over 13,000,000 members in the late 1980s—and their cousins, the Independent Baptists, such as Jerry Falwell of Lynchburg, Virginia. There are by no means churches of the "disinherited," as their rural and small-town counterparts have sometimes been characterized in the past. Rather, they can be viewed as churches of those in transition—

ascending, slowly or rapidly, the ladder of worldly success, often at the price of jarring cultural dislocations such as those occasioned by a move from town to city, or from the working class to the middle class.

At the same time that these churches have been growing numerically in the South, their constituencies have been expanding geographically into other parts of the country, especially the Midwest and West, where Southern Baptist congregations of considerable size can often be found today. Similarly, leading "televangelists" such as Independent Baptist Jerry Falwell, Pentecostal-turned-United-Methodist Oral Roberts, and Baptist/Pentecostal Pat Robertson became national rather than simply regional figures during the 1980s. At the same time, country music, which has incorporated much of the Gospel tradition into its repertoire, has become a national phenomenon, and figures such as Willie Nelson, Loretta Lynn, and Emmylou Harris have followings all across the nation and at all social levels. Just as the South has been inexorably transformed by an enforced or sought-out interaction with the rest of the nation, so now its distinctive culture and religion are becoming "export goods" as well.

B. Traditions in Transition: European Immigrants

Nineteenth-Century Catholicism: From Ethnic Pluralism to Institutional Unity

The relationship between religion and *ethnicity* in America has always been an extremely complex one. In some cases, as in Anglicanism until fairly recently, the relationship has been quite simple: most Episcopalians were of British, and particularly English, birth or descent. Lutherans have been diverse ethnically, but the European stocks that have been associated with that faith have been linked together to some extent through geographical (German, Scandinavian, Baltic) and linguistic (Germanic) proximity, though not identity. The Jewish people, scattered throughout the world and manifesting many cultural and linguistic variants, have been held together by a common historical and at least vestigial religious experience. In America, moreover, the experience of the "melting pot" often takes its toll after two or three generations, and the relationship between linguistic, cultural and historic experience on the one hand and religious identity on the other becomes increasingly problematic.

The story of the development of American Catholicism, especially to the time of World War I, is intimately bound up with the interaction of three kinds of forces. First, Rome has made its presence felt periodically, as both a unifying and a divisive power. Second, American culture, dominated first by evangelical Protestant and then by predominantly secular forces, has provided another context, sometimes welcoming, sometimes threatening, in which

American Catholics have had to work out a distinctive identity. Third, Catholics in America have represented the most diverse and pluralistic imaginable amalgam of ethnic identities. Irish, Polish, Lithuanian, French, Italian, Portuguese, and Hispanic immigrants have been overwhelmingly Catholic, although their interpretations of a common tradition have differed from one another in very important ways. But English and other British, Czechoslovak, Yugoslav, Hungarian, Middle Eastern, East and Southeast Asian, and Afro-American immigrants and/or their descendants have also adhered to the Catholic Church in significant numbers, simultaneously enriching and complicating the story still further. The story of American Catholicism during the nineteenth century can be understood best by looking first at the ethnic diversity that continuing immigration brought with it, and then at the impact of countervailing drives for uniformity and centralization that came to prevail against this diversity.

The majority of the handful of Catholic clergy and bishops in this early national period were native-born Americans of English descent and French *émigrés*. For the most part they were well educated and aristocratic in outlook, and sympathized with the aspirations of the new nation in which they were still too few to come under serious suspicions of being an alien and subversive presence. The complexion of the American Catholic community began to change rapidly in the 1820s, with the arrival of the first waves of the people who would rapidly come to dominate its life for decades to come.

The major spur to the immigration of Catholic Irish to America was the blight that induced the great potato famine. The "Great Hunger" that ensued devastated the Irish nation from the 1820s through the following two decades. Ireland had since the time of Oliver Cromwell in the 1650s been under the oppressive domination of the English, who regarded this Celtic people as simian-like barbarians and their Catholic faith as superstitious and treasonable. The transplantation of lowland Scottish Presbyterians through English encouragement sowed the seeds of future ethnic strife that has lasted to the present day, and the ownership of much of the Irish land by English absentees further exacerbated the plight of the native peoples. When the blight began to devastate Ireland's major subsistence staple, the potato crop, starvation and disease decimated the population. The English for once were eager to encourage the Catholic Irish—to emigrate.

The Irish who were able to leave came to America as best as they could, often as ballast in the holds of timber ships returning from the British Isles to Canada. These newcomers sought refuge in America as they were able, and the seaports of the northeast, especially Boston, provided the most convenient locales for settlement. Many of the Irish were poor and illiterate but English-speaking; their competition for available work at what seemed to the indigenous, Protestant working class as intolerably low wages created a resentment that was a major spur to outbreaks of *nativism*—hostility to the foreign-born. Early American nativism was inextricably bound up with anti-Catholicism, since the vast majority of these immigrants were Roman in their allegiance, and since popular Protestant mythology going back to the days of Queen Mary in England associated the Catholic Church and the Pope with the Devil and the Anti-Christ. Anti-Irish nativist riots broke out in Boston, New York, and Philadelphia beginning in the 1830s, and political movements such as the so-called Know-Nothing Party, which briefly gained some state and Congressional electoral victories in the 1850s, gave institutional expression to this anti-immigrant impulse.

Work on the railroad and canal systems that were providing America with a new infrastructure of transportation and communication provided many Irish with opportunities to earn a minimal living. Further, the nature of the work made it possible for them to venture further inland than their earliest circumstances had made possible. The best opportunity for upward mobility within the Irish-American community, however, was a career in the church. The priest had usually been the only member of Irish peasant communities who had the education necessary to serve as a communal spokesman, and an extraordinary prestige was accorded the religious life in Irish culture. In America, the chronic shortage of priests and sisters during the heyday of immigration—virtually the entire nineteenth century—forced a reliance on the recruitment of clergy abroad, and increased the pressure on Irish-American Catholics to encourage "vocations" to the religious life among their children. A vast number of Irish entered America during these years: A million were resident in 1850—one out of twenty-three Americans—and one and a half million more arrived between 1870 and 1900. From the ranks of these immigrants and their offspring came by far the largest part of the clergy and hierarchy that was to chart the path for American Catholicism well into the twentieth century.

The Irish-American Catholicism that thus became normative in America during the middle and later nineteenth century had a number of distinctive characteristics that set it apart both from the earlier religious cultures of the English and French and from that of the Germans and eastern and southern Europeans who were also beginning to arrive in significant numbers. In the first place, the institutional church and clergy enjoyed great prestige in the Irish-American community. Although this prestige was sometimes mixed with ambivalence and even resentment, there was seldom any question as to the final authority of the Church in matters of faith and morals. The role of the Church as a means of education and advancement for the children of a people who had been quickly transformed from a rural peasantry to an urban proletariat reinforced clerical prestige as well. The impact of the French on clerical education in Ireland and America shaped an ethos in which clerical celibacy, marital fecundity, and a general distrust of sexuality were prevailing values. Temperance was one value that Irish clergy shared with American evangelical Protestants, since alcohol was viewed as a far greater social and moral danger by Irish-Americans than most other Catholic communities. Finally, a "devotional revolution" took place in Ireland during the nineteenth century in which localized cults of saints were now displaced by universal pious practices, such as saying the rosary. This "revolution" was part of an attempt by both Rome and the Irish hierarchy to strengthen the institutional church. This piety gained rapid popularity in America as well during the later years of the century, as a heavily parish-oriented culture began to prevail.

The other Catholic people who began to arrive in America in significant numbers contemporaneously with the Irish were the Germans. The social and cultural orientation of these German-Americans was significantly different in many ways from that of the dominant Irish. In the first place, Germany, which did not achieve national unity until 1870, was a religiously divided society in which Catholics, Jews, freethinkers, and Protestants of a wide variety coexisted more or less amicably. (Bismarck's *Kulturkampf*—"cultural war"—against the Catholic Church later in the century would strain Germany's pluralism severely, though.) This was very different from the Irish context, in which allegiance to the Catholic faith was a major aspect of anti-English nationalistic sentiment. Second, most German Catholics who came to America, though seldom wealthy, were not as near destitution as the Irish frequently were. As a result, these newcomers were able to secure inexpensive farmland in the "German Triangle" bounded by Milwaukee, St. Louis, and Cincinnati that emerged during the middle of the nineteenth century. Whether settled as farmers or urban artisans, the Germans tended to keep to themselves, preferring that their children be reared in the midst of a German-speaking environment.

It was this desire to perpetuate the old ways in the New World that helped precipitate one of the major struggles for religious and cultural self-definition among America's Catholic peoples during the latter part of the century. German-speaking Catholics in both Europe and America were fearful that the program of Americanization favored by many Irish-American church leaders would lead not only to the loss of the old language and folkways (such as the *Biergarten*) but of the traditional religion as well. Anton Walburg, a Cincinnati priest, articulated this argument in 1889. In his *The Question of Nationality in its Relation to the Catholic Church in the United States*, Walburg argued that language, culture, and faith together formed the only effective bulwark against the inroads of American secularism and materialism. In 1886, Peter Abbelen, the vicar general of the heavily German Milwaukee archdiocese, presented a petition to the Pope arguing for parishes based on nationality rather than geography for similar reasons. A cognate argument was formulated in Germany and presented to Rome by Peter Paul Cahensly of the St. Raphael Society, which he had earlier organized to protect the interests of German emigrants and encourage missions to them. Cahensly argued in 1890 that vast losses to the church were occurring among German Catholics, and went even beyond Abbelen in arguing that a whole network of German-speaking institutions, including dioceses and seminaries, be established in America for the preservation of the faith. In fact, the German language was frequently used in churches, parochial schools, and other religious contexts among German-American Catholics, but its proponents were fearful that these temporary arrangements would not prevail in the face of concerted Irish-American hierarchical opposition.

Similar aspirations and fears characterized Polish-Americans, who constituted the largest and most articulate group of central and eastern European Catholics who were swelling the ranks of the "New Immigration" that had begun around 1870. The Polish experience in Europe had been in some ways closer to that of the Irish than of the Germans, since Poland had disappeared as a nation in the partitions of its territory among Prussia, Russia, and Austria-

Hungary at the end of the eighteenth century. A strong sense of nationalistic zeal thus combined with fervent Catholic allegiance in the American "Polonias"—Polish enclaves—that grew up in the industrial cities around the Great Lakes during the later nineteenth century. Also similar to Irish-American piety was Polish devotion to the Virgin of Czestochowa (ches-toe-HOE-vah), whose image took on nationalistic as well as spiritual connotations. Like the Germans, however, the Poles desired to perpetuate their faith, language, customs, and sense of traditional identity as a unity in the New World, and resisted with similar tenacity pressures toward assimilation.

The rallying-cry of Polish Catholics was *rownouprawnienie*, a call for parity of representation within the American hierarchy that was by this time almost totally dominated by the Irish. A partial victory was achieved in 1908 when Polish-American Paul Rhode was appointed Auxiliary Bishop of Chicago, whose Polish community had by this time become the largest in the world outside of Warsaw itself. Rhode's appointment was more of a symbolic than an actual victory; Poles and other Catholic "minority" groups, such as the similarly nationalistic Lithuanians, continued to enjoy only token representation at the higher levels until late in the present century. It was only in the 1960s and 1970s that archbishops with such names as Pilarczyk, (Polish, Cincinnati); Bernardin (North Italian, Cincinnati and Chicago); and Medeiros (Portuguese, Boston) began to appear in the higher reaches of American Catholicism's leadership.

One offshoot of the Polish struggle for parity of representation was the formation of the Polish National Catholic Church by Francis Hodur in Scranton, Pennsylvania, in 1897. Despite the ferocity with which many of these interethnic battles were conducted, it is remarkable that the PNCC was for all practical purposes the only even moderately successful schism from the Catholic Church in American history. In 1960, the last year for which statistics are available, it claimed 162 churches and about 280,000 members; by the late 1980s, its membership had probably dwindled to a small fraction of that figure.

Another component of the New Immigration with an experience significantly different from any so far discussed was that of the substantial number of Italians who were processed through Ellis Island with their counterparts from eastern and southern Europe during this "floodtide" of population movement. Although Italy had been the seat of Catholicism for centuries, it was by no means a culturally or, till 1870, a politically united nation. In cultural terms, the main division was between the north, which had for some centuries been the vanguard of economic development, learning, and sophistication—the land from which Popes had traditionally been chosen—and the southern part of the peninsula and Sicily, which continued to be enmired in a semifeudal economic and social structure that severely retarded the modernization process. The result of this cultural bifurcation was a suspicion of the institutional church, which was dominated by northern Italians, on the part of Silicians and other southerners, whose version of Catholicism was richly infused with folk elements such as the *festa*—a street festival honoring a local patron saint—and belief in the *malocchio* or "evil eye."

It was primarily the Sicilians, Neapolitans, and other southern Italians who chose to leave Italy for the United States and other New World destinations. Sometimes they embarked on temporary money-making forays, but often left Italy behind forever, rather than continue to endure the bleak future which the regional economy foreboded. Once in America, these Italians found themselves in a religious situation similar to the one they had left behind, with an unsympathetic Irish-American clergy in place of the north Italians. The result of this cultural clash was an alienation of many Italians from the institutional church. Some defections were brought about by aggressive Methodist and Baptist proselytizing, but a simple absence from the church except at "rites of passage"—marriages, baptisms, funerals—was more the norm. The old pattern of street *festa* recreated itself in neighborhoods with a heavily concentrated Italian population such as Boston's North End, South Philadelphia, and Italian Harlem in New York City. Also, the work of religious orders such as the Scalabrini Fathers and the Missionary Sisters of the Sacred Heart—the latter founded by Mother (now Saint) Frances Cabrini (1850–1918)—helped create an ethos more sympathetic to Italian customs.

Given this vast in-pouring of Catholic peoples into the United States during the nineteenth century, much of the attention of the institutional church was directed toward accommodating their needs. These needs were material as well as spiritual, so that much of the church's resources went not only into the conduct of worship but into the relief of the exigencies of everyday life as well. The assumption by the government of responsibility for the manifold needs of the population was not nearly as developed as it has since become. Priests and sisters therefore had to concern themselves extensively with education, medical care, emergency relief, and provision for the needs of society's many marginal members, such as the multitude of orphans created by periodic cholera epidemics. The shortage of indigenous clergy and religious women prompted frequent recruiting campaigns by bishops in Europe, where they sought both financial support and personnel. As a result, the clergy and sisters of the nineteenth-century American Catholic Church were nearly as polyglot as the laity, and it is not surprising that centralized controls of the church's manifold institutions remained fairly loose until some stability could be achieved.

The first organizational problem with which the American Church had to deal was the result of the new nation's refusal to sanction either religious establishment or persecution, as provided by the First Amendment. This created a situation unprecedented in the Catholic Church's experience, because it had become used to one or the other of these alternatives since the time of the Reformation. The Vatican's acquiescence in the election of the first American bishop directly by the clergy was a sign of tentative openness to the new situation, as was Bishop Carroll's involving his priests actively in the governance process.

Carroll's enthusiasm for democracy, however, was soon challenged by the emergence of the "trusteeism" question. This situation, in which parish property was owned and affairs managed by a group of elected laymen called "trustees," arose from a combination of reasons: the character of early state laws regarding church property, the scattered and unsupervised origins of the first Catholic parishes, the *congregational polity* that characterized the governance of many of the Protestant denominations, and the general ethos of democracy in the new nation. Still another complicating factor was the presence of a number of priests in these early decades who had left Europe—especially Ireland—because of the ill repute in which they stood with the hierarchy at home. The result was a number of instances of conflict between the early American hierarchy and individual parishes in Boston, New York, and Philadelphia. In the latter case, the Irish-born pastor William Hogan virtually waged war with his bishop for three years until his excommunication in 1822 and a subsequent papal condemnation of the whole arrangement. Eventually, a new legal arrangement in which each bishop was recognized as a *corporation sole* vested property rights directly in the church, and made such challenges to episcopal authority more difficult in the future. Together with nativism, trusteeism presented the antebellum Catholic Church in America with one of its first major challenges in adapting to a significantly new political arrangement and cultural ethos.

The middle decades of the nineteenth century were preoccupied mainly with the tasks of institution-building, the challenge of Irish and German immigration, and the fending off of nativist hostility. As the Civil War approached, American Catholics were divided over the issue of slavery, with both lay and clerical defenders of the "peculiar institution" emerging in the South. The lack of any doctrinal issue at stake and of any official Catholic teaching against slavery as such militated against the sorts of schisms that afflicted many Protestant denominations. Northern Catholics were hardly unanimous in their enthusiasm for the abolitionist cause, since many Irish saw the possibility of a larger free black community as a challenge to their own economic prospects. When the war came, however, most rallied to the cause of the Union, and the distinguished service of German and Irish units in battle, as well as the heroic role played by Catholic sisters as battlefield nurses, helped for the time being to allay nativist accusations of disloyalty. Sister Anthony O'Connell of Cincinnati's Sisters of Charity, "the angel of the battlefield," was representative of the role women frequently played not only under wartime stress but in the longer-term tasks of developing medical and educational facilities with minimal resources.

The postwar years saw the coming of the New Immigration on a scale even more massive than that of the old. Sheer numbers were exacerbated by the less ready adaptability of many of the later newcomers, whose linguistic and cultural differences from native Americans were far greater than those of the Irish and Germans. A major response of the institutional church was an increasing emphasis on church-sponsored education as a means both of assimilating the immigrants and their children, as well as insulating them from the threats presented by the Protestant- or secular-dominated "common" (i.e., public) schools. The Third Plenary Council of Baltimore, at which the American bishops convened in 1884, instructed all Catholic parishes to provide an elementary school as soon as possible, with construction of the school taking priority over the church edifice itself. The question of whether Catholic parochial education was to be polyglot, as it was in many predominantly German and Polish communities, or whether it was to further the assimilation process by promoting the universal use of English was one of the issues that were beginning to create some serious strains within the American church.

By the last decade of the nineteenth century, three distinct schools of thought had emerged within the American Catholic community on the question of what was to be the preferred attitude of the church toward American society. The most conservative faction, whose spokesmen were usually German-speakers such as Abbelen, Cahensly, and Walburg, was hostile to the whole notion of Americanization, and maintained that the faith could best be preserved as a unit together with the traditional languages and cultures of Europe. Catholic Americans would participate in the American economic and political systems, but insulate themselves from the broader society and culture. For them, America was welcome as a political and economic refuge, but the Protestant and secular elements in its culture were hostile to the nurture of the traditional faith as it had developed for centuries in the more hospitable climes of central Europe. Old World culture maintained on New World soil could combine the advantages of American prosperity and religious freedom with the traditional piety of Germany or Poland.

A second influential group, led by Irish-American Bishop Bernard McQuaid of Rochester and Archbishop Michael A. Corrigan of New York City, advocated a similar caution about overly extensive involvements in the social and educational networks of American society, but nevertheless maintained that Catholic solidarity could best be maintained by the uniform use of the English language. For them, the Catholic Church had a parental mission to shelter its family, many of whom were recent immigrants, from the spiritual as well as the material hazards of American life. The decentralization implicit in the German and Polish positions, however, worked against their vision of a centralized church that could emerge as a significant force in American life only through mastery of the social and political tools—for instance, the English language—necessary to survive and even provide an alternative to secularizing Protestant culture.

The third major faction among the American Catholic leadership became known as the "liberals," who were represented most forcefully by St. Paul's Archbishop John Ireland (1838–1918), "the consecrated blizzard of the Midwest." Ireland was backed by other Midwestern bishops such as John Keane of Dubuque and John Lancaster Spalding of Peoria, and had the behind-the-scenes support on many issues of the Archbishop of Baltimore, James Cardinal Gibbons (1834–1921), whose stature elevated him to the informal role of spokesman for the American Church. Ireland and his like-minded colleagues viewed American society as fundamentally benevolent, and saw its democratic ethos and policy of church-state separation not simply as tolerable options but as positive goods. Their inclinations, therefore, were to cooperate with other Americans in as many progressive endeavors as they could, as long as matters did not involve actual hostility toward the church or contradiction of fundamental Catholic teaching.

Among these causes were public education, which the liberals saw as fundamentally neutral and perfectly acceptable as long as it was supplemented by appropriate religious instruction under Catholic auspices. Release-time programs in which children were excused for a few hours a week to receive such instruction were experimented with in Faribault and Stillwater, Minnesota, under Ireland's aegis, as well as in Poughkeepsie, New York. The founding of the Catholic University of America in Washington, D.C., in 1884, with John Keane as rector, was another liberal enthusiasm opposed by the conservatives on the grounds of its potential for indoctrinating clergy in suspect teachings and attitudes. Ecumenical undertakings, shunned by the more cautious, were also a favorite liberal pursuit. Bishop Keane, for example, was delighted to deliver in 1890 the Dudleian Lecture at Harvard, which had been established during the colonial era for, among other things, "the detecting and convicting and exposing the idolatry of the Roman Church," together with other Catholic offenses. (Needless to say, Keane did not fulfill these objectives.) The active participation of some liberals in the World's Parliament of Religions in 1893, which they regarded as an opportunity to put the Catholic cause sympathetically before the world, was equally obnoxious to conservatives who saw such activities as an acknowledgment that Catholicism was no better than one religion among all of the rest of them. Finally, Cardinal Gibbons's success in persuading Rome not to condemn the Knights of Labor as a "secret society" also irritated those who saw labor unions in the same light as the secret anticlerical organizations such as the Freemasons who were out to subvert true religion and good order.

The unlikely event that brought these tensions to a head was the publication in France in 1897 of a translation of Walter Elliott's *Life of Father Hecker*, with an introduction by Archbishop Ireland and a preface by a like-minded French prelate. Isaac Hecker (1819–1888) was a German-American Methodist who, after a spiritual pilgrimage through the experimental communities of New England Transcendentalism, had converted to Catholicism and joined the German-based Redemptorists. Chafing under that order's Old World piety, Hecker left to found a new American group known as the Paulists, whose special mission was the evangelization of American Protestants. Hecker developed an apologetic that stressed the singular compatibility of Catholic and American values, which was promoted in his books as well as in the order's journal, *The Catholic World*. The activist pro-American bias of Hecker and his followers that was lauded so highly in Father Elliott's hagiographic account of Hecker's life alarmed French conservatives who happened upon it, and brought about their complaint to Rome that the whole affair smelled of heresy.

The result of the controversy that ensued over Elliott's work was the encyclical (papal letter) issued by Pope Leo XIII in 1899 with the title *Testem Benevolentiae* (i.e., a testament of good will). In it Leo, whose earlier *Rerum Novarum* had seemed to put him on the liberal side of contemporary issues, declared that the "Americanism" denounced by Elliott's accusers—a collection of highly technical theological propositions—was indeed unorthodox, and its teaching should be stopped if were being taught. Leo did not, however, assert that it was in fact being taught by anyone.

This omission prompted American liberals to declare that the whole matter involved only a "phantom heresy" that no one was really guilty of promulgating. Although the issues involved and the facts of the matter were extremely convoluted, the upshot of the affair was a victory for the Irish-American conservatives (i.e., Corrigan, McQuaid, and their sympathizers) in their probably correct reading of the encyclical as a Roman caution to American liberals to dampen their conspicuous enthusiasm for "new things." With the reinforcement of Pius X's *Pascendi Dominici Gregis* in 1907, which condemned theological "Modernism," the net effect of this papal attention to transoceanic matters was the effective end of Ireland and his colleagues as a dominant force in American Catholicism for the immediate future. (Ireland was never made a cardinal.) The early and middle decades of American Catholic life in the twentieth century were therefore to be characterized not by intellectual and social experimentation, but rather by a consolidation and expansion of a massive institutional presence, the groundwork of which had already been laid. It was only in midcentury that Catholic intellectuals would begin to vindicate Ireland with charges that their fellow American Catholics had developed a "ghetto" mentality that was insulating them from the good that contemporary society had to offer. The ultimate results of this new, critical attitude became manifest only after the upheavals of Vatican II.

CHAPTER 37

Eastern Christianity in America

The floodtide of the "New Immigration" that swelled the American population during the decades between the Civil War and World War I brought with it millions of new Americans who did not speak English and whose religion was none of the myriad varieties of Protestantism. The large majority of these culturally distinct newcomers were Jews and Roman Catholics. A significant minority, however, came from Greece, the Balkan States, and parts of what is now the Soviet Union and were Christian but neither Protestant nor Roman Catholic. Like other immigrants, they tended to form ethnic enclaves in the burgeoning cities of the East and Midwest, and to mark their neighborhoods with churches. These latter were conspicuous for their rounded or onion-shaped domes, which lent an exotic note to the architectural mixture that was then arising. Although the least familiar of the major religious traditions in America, the various types of Eastern Christianity that have taken root on these shores have added a distinctive and permanent ingredient to American religious pluralism.

Although a short-lived Greek colony was founded in New Smyrna, Florida, in 1768, the real beginnings of the Orthodox presence on the North American continent were the work of Russian explorers, military personnel, and especially missionaries in the nineteenth century. A diocese was established at New Archangel (Sitka) in Alaska in 1840, and the Russian Imperial Missionary Society, founded in 1870, helped support missions in Alaska and the adjoining islands until the 1917 revolution. In 1872 the diocese, which had undergone various jurisdictional reorganizations and had few Russians to serve after the acquisition of "Seward's Icebox" by the United States in 1867, was unofficially moved to San Francisco. (This move became formal in 1888.) This small Russian presence on the West Coast was rapidly overshadowed by the massive arrivals of Russian and other Orthodox on the East Coast, and in 1905 the *see* (Bishop's residence) was moved across the continent to New York City. Eastern Orthodoxy is thus the only major religious tradition in America to experience a movement of its center of gravity from west to east.

During the years following the Civil War, Eastern Orthodox immigrants from a variety of backgrounds began to settle in America, and generally worshiped at Russian-founded churches whether they themselves were of Greek, Syrian, or other ethnic extraction. The Russian leadership welcomed this expression of "pan-Orthodoxy," and was willing to appoint priests of other backgrounds to positions of responsibility—for example, the Syrian Raphael Hawaweeny became vicar-bishop of Brooklyn in 1904. However, Greeks and others preferred to worship in their own familiar languages and traditions, and the Orthodox community rapidly acquired the diversity—and with it, a measure of contention and confusion—that characterizes it to the present day.

The large-scale immigration of Eastern Christians to America was part of the broader movement of peoples that collectively constituted the "New Immigration" of the post–Civil War era. Many of the Orthodox who came to America seeking a better life were young single males who possessed little in the way of education or occupational skills. However, the rapid industrialization of the nation had ample need of unskilled labor, and these Central Europeans found ready, if ill-paid, employment in the anthracite fields of Pennsylvania and the industrial cities emerging into economic prominence around the lower Great Lakes. Greeks were less likely to perform heavy labor, and many found success as restaurateurs, confectioners, and stationers in Detroit, Chicago, and other "Greektowns" that sprang up in turn-of-the-century cities. Arabs, many of whom were Eastern-rite Christians, often began as itinerant peddlers on the Jewish model.

One religious anomaly that this massive immigration brought to a head was the arrival and rapid defection to Orthodoxy of thousands of Eastern-rite Roman Catholics known as *Uniates*. The "Unia" are a group of communities following rituals and customs more similar to Eastern than Western practice, who at various times entered into union with the Roman Church in exchange for a guarantee that their traditions would be respected. Upon arriving in America, however, these Uniates usually found that the American hierarchy, many of whom were hostile to the continuation of Old World customs, were unwilling to acknowledge the legitimacy of their clergy who, unlike Latin-rite

Western Catholic priests, were not required to be celibate and often had wives. After much delay, the Vatican backed the American hierarchy and declared that, though Eastern-rite liturgies and a certain measure of juridical independence might be maintained, Uniate clergy in America must be celibate. Even before this long-delayed resolution had come about, thousands of Carpatho-Russians (or Rusyns), Galicians, Ukranians, and other Uniates renounced their Roman allegiance and were welcomed into the Russian and, later, the Greek Orthodox folds.

Despite major organizational advances by the able Bishop Tikhon Bellavin (1865–1925) in the early years of the century, the impact of World War I and the subsequent upheavals that beset Russia and southeastern Europe had dramatic repercussions on Eastern-rite Christians in America, who as much as any ethnic and religious groups maintained close ties with their lands of origin. The Russian Revolution threw the status of Russian Orthodoxy in America into great confusion, and bitter and prolonged jurisdictional disputes plagued it and other Orthodox communities for decades. Among the Russians, the obvious question was whether continuing allegiance to Moscow was possible in a situation where an antireligious Communist regime now controlled the patriarchate. As a result, three distinct factions eventually emerged in the American scene that exist to the present day:

1. The *Orthodox Church in America* (OCA) is without question, with approximately a million followers, the dominant force in American Russian Orthodoxy. Although second to the Greek Orthodox in size, it is arguably the most important Eastern Orthodox community in the New World in terms of cultural and theological influence. Although the Metropolia, as it was previously known, was at odds with Moscow for decades over questions of jurisdiction, these issues were finally resolved in 1970 when the Metropolitan (i.e., Archbishop) in Moscow recognized the OCA as *autocephalous*—that is, an autonomous member of the Orthodox "family" of churches (literally, "self-headed"). The OCA has headquarters in Syosset, New York, and is divided into nine dioceses in America. It sponsors Saint Vladimir's Orthodox Theological Seminary in Crestwood, New York, which in the years after World War II became an academic home for such distinguished Orthodox theologians in exile as Alexander Schmemann and John Meyendorff.

2. The *Patriarchal Parishes of the Russian Orthodox Church in the United States and Canada* are a group of perhaps fifty thousand Orthodox in forty-plus churches in the United States (and others in Canada) who chose to maintain direct ties with Moscow even after the OCA had been recognized as autocephalous.

3. *The Russian Orthodox Church Outside of Russia* represents the wing of Russian Orthodoxy that has refused in any way to acknowledge the legitimacy of the post-Revolutionary Moscow leadership. It also has a membership in the range of fifty to sixty thousand, distributed among eighty-plus parishes, a few of which follow a Western rite. Like the other two Russian churches, it maintains national headquarters in metropolitan New York.

The largest of the Eastern churches in America is the *Greek Orthodox Archdiocese of North and South America,* with headquarters in New York City. Although Greek Orthodoxy in America was bitterly divided over the contest between monarchist and democratic factions that split the Greek homeland after World War I, unity was finally achieved under the leadership of Archbishop Athenagoras, who later was named Ecumenical Patriarch. Eight of the eleven dioceses that constitute the Archdiocese are in the United States, under the leadership of an Archbishop who represents the Ecumenical Patriarch in Istanbul (as Constantinople has been known for some time). It maintains the Hellenic College-Holy Cross School of Theology in Brookline, Massachusetts, and claims approximately two million members in 535 churches. As with most of the Orthodox churches, membership is drawn almost exclusively from the Greek-American community, which is concentrated in major urban centers with an especially large population in Chicago.

In addition to the Russian and Greek churches, American Orthodoxy is also represented by Albanian, Antiochian (Syrian-Lebanese), Bulgarian, Rumanian, Serbian, and Ukranian branches, some of which are further split by the sorts of issues that the Russians and Greeks had experienced, and some of which are under Russian or Greek jurisdiction. Although some misunderstandings and hostilities still persist—for instance, over the autocephaly of the OCA—all of these churches share an allegiance to what is known as "Chalcedonian" Orthodoxy, which affirms the validity of the first seven ecumenical councils and rejects Roman claims to primacy. These churches first entered into a cooperative relationship in their effort to gain recognition for Orthodox military chaplains during World War II, and have subsequently represented their collective tradition as America's "Fourth Faith" along with Judaism, Protestantism, and Roman Catholicism. Further recognition of "pan-Orthodoxy" has been manifest in the formation of the Standing Conference of Canonical Orthodox Bishops in the Americas in 1960, as has a broader ecumenical stance in the participation of several of the Orthodox churches in the originally Protestant National Council of Churches.

Eastern-rite Christianity in America, however, is not confined solely to the "Chalcedonian" church bodies. The Uniate traditions continue to be maintained under the jurisdiction of the Roman Catholic Church, despite their severe numerical losses at the turn of the century. In the mid-1980s they numbered about eight hundred thousand adherents divided into eleven constituencies, including the Melkite (Syrian), Maronite (Lebanese), Armenian, Ruthenian (Russian), and Ukranian. These five enjoy their own ordinaries (i.e., bishops, known as "exarchs" or "eparchs"), while the remainder are under the jurisdiction of Latin-rite bishops. Eastern-rite Roman Catholics are heavily concentrated in the areas of original settlement, especially Michigan, Ohio, New York, and Pennsylvania. A tour of the industrial and mining communities of these states will often reveal a whole panorama of small churches, many with Eastern-style onion domes, representing their various Orthodox and Uniate constituencies.

Finally, those Eastern Christians who rejected the Christological definition of Chalcedon and continued instead to adhere to the Monophysite interpretation of Jesus Christ's nature as solely divine have found representation in contemporary America as well. The largest of these "Non-Chalcedonian" or "Oriental Orthodox" is the Armenian Apostolic Church, which lists a membership of about four hundred fifty thousand. In the same family can be placed the Coptic Church and other small groups of Middle Eastern, North African, and Indian provenance for which membership figures are not too reliable.

Although the numbers of its adherents are considerable, and many have become thoroughly Americanized, Eastern Christianity still seems remote and exotic when compared with America's other "major" religious traditions. When Michael Dukakis, Governor of Massachusetts and a second-generation Greek-American, received the Democratic nomination for the presidency in 1988, reporters were puzzled by his curious status within his own church. Since Dukakis had married outside the faith—his wife, Kitty, is Jewish—he was automatically excommunicated, and has not been able to receive communion since his marriage. His identification with the Greek-American community nevertheless remained strong, and even the Archbishop helped bring him together with wealthy potential contributors to his candidacy.

That many Greek and other Orthodox Americans have become thoroughly assimilated into the mainstream of American society is reflected in the increasing use of English in Orthodox services. (The Antiochian Orthodox Christian Archdiocese, a merger of two earlier groups of Syrian origin, has been particularly active in promoting this sort of modernization.) However, many others of Orthodox background remain geographically and culturally isolated in urban neighborhoods and small mining and industrial towns, and their religious attitudes reflect the conservatism fostered by this isolation. Old World ties and a decentralized polity further inhibit a uniform pattern of assimilation, for better or worse. Orthodox Americans seem likely to continue for at least a generation or more to bridge collectively two worlds: one of exotic, Oriental strangeness, and the other of entrepreneurial Americanism.

CHAPTER 38

Ethnic Diversity and the Development of Jewish Denominationalism

From the later colonial period to the 1830s, Ashkenazic Jews from northwestern Europe had begun to arrive in small numbers and intermingle with their Sephardic predecessors. In the early decades of the nineteenth century, they had founded synagogues of their own in New York and Philadelphia. This gradual shift in ethnic background took a sudden dramatic turn in a new direction during the 1830s, when thousands and soon tens of thousands of German-speaking Ashkenazim began, with their Christian compatriots, to leave Bavaria and other German states for the New World.

These new immigrants lacked both the elite cultural background as well as the financial skills and resources of the Sephardim, and were forced to seek a new place for themselves in the rapidly expanding new nation. Frequently they set themselves up as peddlers, on foot or with horse-drawn wagons, and made the circuit of frontier settlements selling household items. Those who were particularly successful in this line often settled in small towns and established dry goods stores, some of which evolved into the major department stores of the twentieth century (e.g., Macy's). In many cases these merchants and their families constituted the only Jewish presence in large portions of the South and West. Although many stayed on for generations, others who were able liquidated their holdings and took up residence in more established Jewish communities such as those of New York and Cincinnati.

Communities of successful Ashkenazim had arisen in American cities from Atlanta to San Francisco by the Civil War era, establishing synagogues (now with rabbis), schools, mutual benefit and charitable societies, hospitals, cemeteries, and the other voluntary institutions that Americans of all sorts loved so well. When the Civil War arrived, Jews, like other Americans, tended to follow sectional allegiances, and Judah P. Benjamin of Louisiana held several cabinet posts in the Confederacy. It was during the Civil War, however, that one of the first public signs of anti-Semitism began to appear. Responding to accusations of war profiteering, General Grant issued in 1862 an executive order expelling all Jews from the military district of Tennessee. Although Jewish protests led to a reversal of this decree by President Lincoln, ancient motifs of Jewish disloyalty and covetousness had now played a distinct role in American public policy.

American Jewry in the years immediately following the Civil War tended to be urban, German-descended, English-speaking, public-school educated, commercially oriented, quite prosperous, and generously supportive of philanthropic causes, Jewish and otherwise. Their status in the American scene, however, was soon to be affected radically from two different directions: the vast influx of Eastern European Jews beginning in the 1880s, and the quiet but effective raising of barriers to Jewish participation in the higher reaches of Gentile society.

Just as a combination of social and economic upheavals earlier in the century had touched off the massive immigration of German-speakers of all sorts, including Jews, to the New World, so did a similar array of forces precipitate the even vaster rush of Eastern and Southern European peoples, most of them non-English-speaking and non-Protestant, to America from about 1880 until the World War I era. For Jews especially, economic distress was reinforced by violent persecution in the form of pogroms on Jewish settlements by czarist Cossacks. In consequence, hundreds of thousands of Yiddish-speaking Jews from Russia, Lithuania, Poland (or, rather, what once had been

Poland), the Ukraine, Hungary, and Rumania began to arrive in the "promised land" of America—usually New York City, to which most immigration was channeled after the creation of a federal processing center at Ellis Island in 1892. It was from here that hundreds of thousands of Jewish newcomers—"greenhorns"—found themselves thrust into the turmoil of Manhattan's Lower East Side, where Hester Street and other crowded tenement-lined avenues resonated with the Yiddish cries of pushcart vendors.

To keep these greenhorns from falling victim to exploiters, the already established and now largely English-speaking New York Jewish community began to organize efforts to help the newcomers orient themselves. Even though both groups were technically Ashkenazim, however, the prosperous second- and third-generation merchants who had frequently adopted the new Reform as their religious expression were generally dismayed by their newly arrived remote kinspeople. The German-American Jews looked askance at the prevalence of Yiddish, the abysmal poverty, and the traditional, "oriental" Orthodoxy or new socialist ideologies of these creatures of the "New Immigration." Although large numbers of the newcomers found employment in the garment workshops maintained by the older Jewish community, and welcomed the chance for Sabbath observance that working for fellow Jews usually made possible, the working-places were frequently no better than sweatshops, the hours long, the work tedious, and the pay wretched.

It was therefore in the context of one class of Jews protesting conditions imposed by another that much of America's first labor organization took place, with the Jewish immigrant cigar-roller Samuel Gompers playing a leading role in that struggle. Although the traditionally religious newcomers were less susceptible to such movements, the considerable numbers who had abandoned religion entirely proved enthusiastic converts to such new social causes. *Landsmanschaften,* or societies of immigrants from the same European city or province, played a major role in the social, political, and economic life of this dynamic Yiddish-speaking outburst of American Jewish life, which was destined to last for scarcely more than a generation.

The socioeconomic and cultural diversity that had come to characterize American Jewry by the late nineteenth century had religious implications as well. The division of American Jews into a number of organized, formally separate communities or "traditions" is an instance of the tendency of American religious groups to form into *denominations,* or independent organizations representing variations on a common theme. In their European experience, Jews had lived together in ghettos or shtetls; existed as isolated itinerants; formed movements, such as the Hasidic disciples of the Baal Shem Tov or the followers of the "messiah" Sabbatai Zevi; or assimilated in Gentile society. In none of these cases, however, had it been desirable or even legally possible to organize into discrete religious "camps," each with its own interpretations of Jewish thought, life, and worship, and each with its own formal organizational structure. In the broad sweep of the European experience, Jews were characterized by law as one separate people, and their communal life was defined by the implication of such laws. In America, however, constitutional separation of church and state on the one hand and the voluntary, denominational model provided by American Protestantism on the other were to shape the course that Judaism would take on these shores.

For the first two and a half centuries of its existence, Judaism in America did not know formal division. The synagogue was the fundamental unit of Jewish life from the beginning, and the half-dozen or so in the colonies were Sephardic in membership and ritual. These colonial-era synagogues were lay-dominated, with an occasional *hazzan* being the only professional in the universal absence of rabbis. By the end of the eighteenth century, sufficient Ashkenazim had arrived that splits began to occur in Sephardic-dominated congregations (e.g., B'nai Jeshurun separating from New York's Shearith Israel in 1825) or new Ashkenazic congregations founded (e.g., Rodeph Shalom in Philadelphia, 1795).

Ethnicity alone, however, was not to be the principle that prompted the division of American Judaism into clearly delineated "denominations." The influx of German-speaking Ashkenazim during the middle decades of the nineteenth century brought with it many Jews, including a number of rabbis, who had become imbued with the principles of Reform that had their origins in the Enlightened ideas of Moses Mendelssohn. The American Reform movement, led by Bohemian-born Isaac Mayer Wise (1819–1900), took the lead in developing an institutional infrastructure for Jewish life in America, including Hebrew Union College, America's first lasting Jewish seminary, which Wise founded in Cincinnati in 1875.

It was at the banquet held for Hebrew Union's first graduating class in 1883 that tensions between "traditional" and "progressive" American Jews reached a breaking point. As waiters began to serve the successive courses, observant Jews were shocked to see that much of the food was *trayf*: shrimp, crab meat, and frogs' legs. Although this unfortunate choice of provender was more likely a caterer's mistake rather than a deliberate affront, Wise refused to apologize for the offense against the kosher laws. From that time it became clear that Hebrew Union would not be a satisfactory school for other than Reform rabbis, and that the elements of the American Jewish community not comfortable with Reform's rejection of tradition would have to provide their own organizational structures.

Reform was the first of America's Jewish traditions to adapt itself to the American denominational pattern. It was in fact Reform that defined the issues that would precipitate the eventual institutionalization of Orthodoxy and the subsequent emergence of Conservatism as an alternative to both. Reform had its early origins in the thought and work of Moses Mendelssohn in eighteenth-century Germany, and began to express itself more concretely in the reform of worship in a number of early nineteenth-century German synagogues.

The emphasis among these Westernized, modernizing Jews was on "decorum" in worship, as opposed to what they saw as the "orientalism" and confusion of Orthodox services conducted in Hebrew, with the often illiterate congregation talking and milling about as they pleased. (These complaints would be echoed in America later in the century as assimilated German-American Jews contemplated the conduct of their Eastern European brethren with bemusement or contempt.) These reformers generally sought models in contemporary Protestant practice, and adapted such innovations as seating families together in pews rather than segregating the sexes, utilizing organs and choirs, and discontinuing the wearing of such traditional marks of male piety as the *yarmulke* (skull-cap) and prayer shawl. In addition, Hebrew was displaced as the language of worship by the vernacular—German or, later in America, English—which was also used in the delivery of another borrowing, the sermon.

It was such German-speaking Jews who began to carry the program of Reform with them as they settled in America in the early and middle decades of the nineteenth century, but its systematic implementation and the development of a philosophical rationale awaited the advent of German rabbis. Although early experiments with the reform of worship were introduced beginning in Charleston in the 1820s, it was the coming of first Max Lilienthal and then Isaac Mayer Wise to Cincinnati in the 1850s that provided the movement with its first organized leadership. It was Wise especially who used his base at Cincinnati's Bene Yeshurun systematically to create a denominational infrastructure for American Reform. His accomplishments included the founding of an English-language Jewish newspaper, *The American Israelite*, in 1853; the drafting of an early Reform prayerbook, the *Minhag America* of 1856; the founding of the first real Jewish denominational vehicle, the Union of American Hebrew Congregations, in 1873; and, perhaps his crowning achievement, the establishment of Hebrew Union College in 1875 (which later merged with the Jewish Institute of Religion).

It was after all of this apparatus was in place that Reform in America moved into its next phase, the creation of a systematic program of ideas that would give it more coherent identity than simply a modernization of worship. These ideas had their roots in nineteenth-century German "scientific" approaches to Judaism, and found their first significant American expression in the "Pittsburgh Platform" promulgated by nineteen rabbis in 1885. Altough the by now venerable Wise presided over this gathering, its moving spirit was Kaufmann Kohler (1843–1926), the son-in-law and disciple of Wise's more radical East Coast rival, David Einhorn. This brief statement was dramatic in the starkness with which it presented the central tenets of Reform as an ideology. These included the definition of Judaism as a "progressive religion, ever striving to be in accord with the postulates of reason" and not inextricably bound by the "primitive ideas" of biblical language and thought-patterns; a rejection both of the laws of *kashrut* and of Zionism; an empathetic identification of its own ideals with those of Christians and Muslims in a common quest for "the reign of truth and righteousness among men"; and a reaffirmation of the primarily ethical character of the Jewish mission.

The Reform commitment, then, was to design a program for a Judaism to be practiced normatively in diaspora—and, most particularly, in America. Although all three of the national Jewish denominational organizations accepted America and the English language, Reform was by far the most aggressive in promoting Americanization positively and, as a negative corollary, rejecting virtually all of the cultural, linguistic, and cultic apparatus of Jewish tradition. Emphasis throughout was on the reasonableness of Judaism, as reflected in the *Union Prayer Book* adopted in 1894, which was based on Einhorn's earlier version. Worship was in many ways hard to distinguish from that of liberal Protestants, which harmonized with the Reform program of emphasizing continuities with rather than differences from other religions. Similarly, the role of the rabbi changed from that of the traditional scholar of Torah and Talmud to something much more like that of the typical Protestant minister—preacher, counselor, and administrator.

Orthodoxy as a distinct branch of Judaism began to take shape in America with a meeting of twenty-six congregations in 1879, which attempted unsuccessfully to invite a distinguished European Talmudist to become their Chief Rabbi. The heavily Eastern European and localistic character of Orthodox communites in America worked against the process of organization, but success was eventually attained in 1898 with the formation of the Union of Orthodox Jewish Congregations of America. This group, though dedicated to a traditionalist emphasis on Torah and Talmud, alienated other Orthodox through their use of English rather than the Yiddish spoken by most recent immigrants. Their primary accomplishment was the regularization of kosher food preparation; their "U" symbol on food is still a reliable indication that the product conforms to the standards of *kashrut.*

Although Orthodox Jews have never been as uniformly committed to national organizational structures as their coreligionists, the beginnings represented in the UOJCA, together with the Union of Orthodox Rabbis, provided the groundwork for generating many of the structures that characterize most branches of American religious life. The first elementary *yeshiva,* or Hebrew school, was established in New York in 1886, followed by the Rabbi Isaac Elchanan Theological Seminary on the Lower East Side eleven years later. The two institutions merged in 1915 into the Rabbinical College of America. To this rabbinical foundation, Yeshiva College (later University) was added in 1928 to combine secular studies with traditional Jewish education. The founding of the Chicago Hebrew Theological College in 1922 provided a major Midwestern alternative for the training of Orthodox rabbis, and a considerable number of small schools of advanced Talmudic study exist as well. A network of Hebrew schools at all levels has proven the major source of supply for Orthodox rabbinical students during the twentieth century.

Orthodox Judaism, then, despite its lack of unity, is generally united around the precepts that traditional Jewish law remains binding on Jews even today in its multiplicity of prescriptions and prohibitions. The Torah, revealed by God to Moses, is the ultimate religious authority, and attempts to subject it to contemporary critical scrutiny meet with a chilly reception. Although it served at first primarily as a refuge for the most traditional, Yiddish-speaking members of the "New Immigration," its character has changed as the generation has died off, and its resurgence of popularity especially among younger Jews in the later twentieth century has been a remarkable development.

Conservative Judaism is the most distinctly American Jewish tradition, and originated in an attempt to provide an alternative to the polarization the Hebrew Union *trayf* banquet helped to bring about. Some have traced the movement's origins to the policies of various American rabbis in the earlier nineteenth century, such as Isaac Leeser and Sabato Morais at Philadelphia's Mikveh Israel. The founding of Jewish Theological Seminary in New York in 1886 by Morais helped to lay the infrastructure for this emergent "tradition," although the original intent was to provide a more Orthodox alternative to Wise's Hebrew Union. When the Union of Orthodox Rabbis excommunicated the new seminary in 1904 on the grounds of excessive flirtation with contemporary biblical criticism, however, it became clear that a *tertium quid,* or "middle way," between extreme liberalism and traditionalism was in the making almost in spite of itself.

Solomon Schecter (1847–1915), the president of JTS at the time of its censure by Orthodoxy, was the guiding spirit who gave form to Conservatism as a positive force within American Judaism. Formal status for the movement came with the founding of the United Synagogue of America in 1913. The Rabbinical Association of America provided another institutional vehicle, and supervised the publication of a Conservative prayerbook and the journal *Conservative Judaism.* A distinctive development within the Conservative movement was the *synagogue center,* a combination of house of worship with facilities for education, recreation, and other community activities (sometimes known irreverently as a "*shul* with a pool"). The first of these was founded in New York in 1916 by the redoubtable Mordecai Kaplan, founder of Reconstructionism, for the purpose of emphasizing the unity of Jewish life as a culture and tradition and not simply a "religion" in the narrow sense of the term.

This emphasis on Jewish life seen holistically in the context of a living, ongoing tradition is a major key to understanding the character of Conservative Judaism. Schecter himself expressed this idea in his phrase "Catholic Israel." By this he meant that the life of Judaism existed in the present as much as in the past. The current generation of Jews ought to help shape the character of Jewish life in the light of, but without being rigidly bound by, the precedents of Torah and Talmud. ("Positive historical Judaism" is another phrase used by early Conservatives to express this idea.)

A sense of historical perspective was also introduced by Schechter, whose German academic training in Jewish history imbued him with a sense of perspective not frequently found in rabbinical schools. Revelation, from this vantage point, was divinely inspired, but need not be taken literally—an approach that various Christian groups were also moving toward around the turn of the century. On the other hand, Conservatism recognized that being Jewish was more than simply a matter of proper belief and observance. A sense of participation in a millennia-old tradition, whose legacy could not simply be reduced to propositional form, was a major part of the Conservative outlook that emphasized Jewish culture and status as a distinctive people as well as ethics and ritual.

In terms of worship and ritual observance, Conservatism can best be seen as a flexible middle way between the paths of Reform and Orthodoxy. The prayerbook is in Hebrew, but sermons and other communications have always been in English. The maintenance of tradition in worship varies in detail from synagogue to synagogue, but in general the innovations of Reform have tended to prevail. In addition to synagogue worship, Conservatism has also emphasized home-centered rituals, and stresses the role of the family as a primary preserver and transmitter of Jewish tradition. Daily attendance at Hebrew school has also been part of the Conservative program.

Conservative Jews tend to keep kosher, but even this is by no means universal. Jewish law—*halacha*—is taken seriously but not literally, and innovation is possible to accommodate traditional dictates with contemporary exigencies. The decision in the 1980s by Conservative Jews to ordain women to the rabbinate is a good example of this flexibility that, needless to say, does not sit well with the Orthodox.

By the time of the First World War, American Judaism was well on its way in adjusting institutionally to its American circumstances by adopting the American pattern on denominationalism. One result of this was to give concrete expression to the real differences, both religious and cultural, that divided America's Jewry. Like many Roman Catholics, Eastern Orthodox, and Lutheran Christians, Orthodox Jews wanted to enjoy the political and economic benefits of life in the New World without surrendering their distinctive cultural heritage. Isaac Mayer Wise, like Samuel Simon Schmucker and Archbishop Ireland, enthusiastically led his Reform following into a wholesale adoption of American ways. The tension between the two approaches was mediated for many by the Conservative movement, an indigenous approach to a compromise between the two extremes. In the twentieth century, the emergence of Reconstructionism and the settlement of large numbers of Hasidic Jews in the New York City area would further enrich and complicate this pluralism.

Denominationalism, however, did more than simply express these emergent differences in attitudes toward tradition and modernity. The very process of institutionalization inexorably led American Jews into an encounter with modernity through being forced to differentiate themselves formally from one another. Further, the very process of establishing organizational structures, periodicals, seminaries, and the like was in itself a venture into Americanization. Some Orthodox Jews managed to resist this process through continuing a very decentralized, traditional style of worship and education, but many of their compatriots succumbed willy-nilly. America may have given them freedom to live as they liked, but it was also subtly prodding them to become something they had never imagined.

C. Old and New Frontiers

Native American New Religions

In earlier chapters, we have discussed the indigenous traditions of the Native American peoples and a variety of attempts by Euro-Americans to convert them to various interpretations of Christianity. In neither case have we been dealing with absolutes. Native traditions were fluid rather than constant, a fluidity abetted by intercultural contacts and by the nature of orally transmitted culture itself. Although many missionaries, both Catholic and Protestant, were unbending in the determination that their prospective converts give up their traditional beliefs and life patterns completely, others, such as the Jesuits and Quakers, were considerably more accommodating in their willingness to adapt Christian teaching to a non-Western cultural matrix. It should not be entirely surprising, then, to discover that during the past two centuries a number of movements have risen among Native Americans that have combined elements of both old and new religious cultures in their content.

One major category of new religious movement in North America has been what the anthropologist Anthony F. C. Wallace has called *revitalization* movements. The theme of revitalization—literally, of bringing back to life again, usually through a return to an older, purer state of being—is hardly confined to American Indians. The Protestant Reformation, for instance, was not originally conceived by Luther and Calvin as a radically new act, but rather as a return to the pure beginnings of the New Testament church after centuries of decline and corruption during the Middle Ages. Similarly, in Roman Catholicism, a whole series of monastic reform movements as well as ecumenical councils—for instance, Trent and Vatican II—have been interpreted by their advocates not as something new but rather as the restoration of something very old. "Secular" movements as diverse as romanticism and Nazism similarly have components of renewal through restoration, as do nineteenth-century

296

movements in American Christianity such as the Latter-day Saints and the Disciples of Christ. Revitalization or restoration, in short, are variants on the basic religious theme that Mircea Eliade has called "the Eternal Return."

Among Native Americans, revitalization movements usually embodied the related themes of the rejection of Euro-American religion and culture and the restoration of traditional Indian ways. Some early examples that also involved active resistance to white ways were the "conspiracy" of Pontiac in 1763 and the uprising orchestrated by Tecumseh at the time of the War in 1812. In each case, an armed campaign against Anglo-Americans was waged by a military leader abetted by a visionary adviser—the "Delaware Prophet" in Pontiac's case, and Tecumseh's brother Tenskwatawa. The visions of these seers added a supernatural legitimation and rationale to what might otherwise be interpreted as purely secular uprisings. However, as we have already noted repeatedly, natural and supernatural were never rigidly separated in the Native American world view, especially at crucial times in the life of an individual or a people.

Another feature characteristic of many such movements appeared for the first time in Tecumseh's case. Instead of the movement's being confined to one particular tribe or people, Tecumseh attempted the first pan-Indian alliance against the whites. Native Americans had previously not identified themselves as sharing a common identity with other Native peoples. Now a new sense was arising from prolonged contact and conflict with Euro-Americans that the Native peoples were more similar than different in their character and interests, and that it was to their advantage to pursue their common interests in coordination.

It was on the West Coast, toward which the Indians had been pushed continually during the course of the nineteenth century, that the most dramatic examples of this sort of movement took shape. One of the earlier versions resulted from the visions of the Wanapum shaman Smohalla ("the Dreamer") in Washington state beginning in the 1850s. Smohalla, who had been educated by Catholic missionaries, learned from his visionary experiences that the Indians had been the first humans to be created, and that Mother Earth, which the whites were now wounding with their metal ploughs, rightfully belonged to its original inhabitants who lived on the natural bounty of fish from the sea instead. Although Smohalla's movement was pacifistic, it was adopted by the neighboring Nez Percé led by Chief Joseph, who used its teachings as a rationale for armed, and ultimately unsuccessful, resistance against the whites who were pressuring them onto reservations. The movement continued well into the twentieth century after Smohalla's death, but only a handful of faithful outlasted its initial failure to produce any tangible positive results.

Similar to Smoholla's movement was the first Ghost Dance, which originated among the Paviotsos of Nevada and California in 1870. The moving spirit in the case was the prophet Wodziwub, who had a vision that was at once more far-reaching and more revealing of white influences than had been those of his predecessors. Where Smohalla's vision had taken the form of a reaction against white practices and a summons to return to traditional ways, Wodziwub saw his version of a restoration taking place in images explicitly supplied by Anglo-American culture. In this vision, the departed ancestors of the Indians of the day would return to life on a train. After this restoration, the earth would open up and swallow all of humanity; however, the followers of the Ghost Dance would then be resurrected, and would take over the property that had formerly been owned by the now-vanished whites. The sources of this vision are not clear, and some of its elements may have been derived from a stock of images circulating among the Western tribes which had also been incorporated into Smohalla's movement. However, it is clear that Western technology was now an element that had to be reckoned with, even in visions. Also, the motifs of the return of the dead, the restoration of the faithful in a land of peace and prosperity, and the obliteration of the wicked all parallel elements of traditional Christian eschatology (i.e., teachings about the end of the world), even though no direct connection may be at work here.

The early Ghost Dance spread among the Western peoples and took a variety of forms. Even Mormons became interested, since the message contained elements similar to some of Joseph Smith's prophecies. However, the movement was not militant, and began to dissipate when Wodziwub's visions were not fulfilled. Some of the major themes of the movement, however, were revived in 1889 through the prophecies of the Paiute Wovoka (or Jack Wilson), who was the son of an assistant to Wodziwub. In a visionary trip similar to his predecessor's, Wovoka visited a land that was filled with game and inhabited by all of the dead Indians of the past. While in this visionary land, he received instructions that the living Indians were to refrain from warfare and to perform the dance revealed to him. Those who kept these conditions would be reunited with the dead, and would live forever in health and prosperity in a world free of the whites.

Wovoka's movement spread rapidly among channels of intertribal communication that were now well established. Black Elk, for example, recounts how the Lakota Sioux dispatched envoys to learn of this new ritual once word of it had reached them. As the movement spread, it underwent local variations. The Sioux, who were among the most militant in their resistance to white encroachments and for whom the victory at Little Big Horn was still fresh, adopted the use of a "Ghost Shirt," which was supposed to provide its wearers with invulnerability against the whites. White opposition to the Dance and the general level of tensions among the Sioux culminated at Wounded Knee, South Dakota, in December of 1890, when a series of misunderstandings led to an outright massacre of some two hundred Sioux by Federal troops. From that time on, the Ghost Dance and similar movements fell into decline as their ineffectuality in bringing about a literal restoration of a happier past became manifest.

All of the movements discussed so far have demonstrated well the ability of Native American religious patterns to incorporate motifs from Anglo-American culture into visions promising a restoration of the old ways and the elimination of the hostile newcomers from the earth. Other movements have exhibited a similar *syncretism*—a grafting of elements from one religious tradition onto the stock of another—while advocating a new way of life based on an accommodation of the old ways to the new. One of the most interesting and successful of such *accommodationist* movements was that founded by the Seneca Handsome Lake around 1800. At this time, the Seneca of upstate New York had been profoundly demoralized by the effects of decades of military defeat, famine, disease, and exploitation by land speculators, all in consequence of prolonged contact with the whites. Alcoholism and witchcraft accusations, two common signs of social disintegration among Indians, were rife, and the Seneca were living in hovels Anthony Wallace has described as "slums in the wilderness."

In the midst of this squalor and confusion, Handsome Lake, who himself had fallen prey to poor health and drunkenness, began to experience a series of remarkable visions. Their way had been prepared by a number of sources: the Delaware Prophet; the role of visions in Seneca culture; and the presence of Quaker missionaries, who had provided a low-key witness through the establishment of a school and model farm. In his first vision, Handsome Lake encountered three angelic visitors, who called for the revival of the old Seneca customs and abstention from such destructive practices as alcohol abuse, witchcraft, magic, and abortion. In a subsequent vision a fourth angel appeared, who took Handsome Lake on a tour of Heaven and Hell, where he could see, as had Dante, how the faithful were rewarded and the wicked punished. While in Heaven he met and conversed with both George Washington and Jesus Christ, and learned how the latter had also been betrayed by the White Man.

These visions are clearly indicative of how much of the Christian world view and symbolic vocabulary had been absorbed by the Seneca at the time, in part through the quiet presence of the Quakers. The supernatural world that Handsome Lake had toured was clearly that of Christianity in its structure and general landscape, and bore little resemblance to the traditional native view of the world beyond. The message that Handsome Lake brought back to his fellow Seneca, which they rapidly adopted, was similarly syncretistic. The *Gaiwiio*, as it was called, was originally apocalyptic in character, and predicted the end of the present world within three generations. However, the spread of the message among the Seneca and the ups and downs of the reputation of Handsome Lake himself brought about a gradual change in emphasis from the cataclysmic to the ethical. The virtues and life-style that it stressed were basically those of Anglo-American Protestant Christianity, with perhaps a trace of Quaker influence: temperance, peace, settled agriculture, social unity, domestic harmony, the primacy of the nuclear family, and prohibitions on gambling, dancing, and alcohol.

The rapid adoption of the *Gaiwiio* and its continuation after Handsome Lake's death in 1815 to the present day are indicative of its appeal as a much-needed force for stabilization in a society that was disintegrating rapidly but was not ready to give up. Handsome Lake's message made sense out of a permanently divided world by providing a system of symbols that incorporated aspects of both sides of the division. On the one hand, traditional native patterns of seminomadic existence were no longer viable, and had to be abandoned for a more sedentary life-style. Many of the virtues of Protestant Christianity similarly had to be substituted for the older, more individualistic ways.

On the other hand, traditional elements such as the coming of new revelation through a shamanic vision persisted. The Seneca thus accommodated themselves to the new temporal dispensation, but still kept a certain physical, social, and religious distance from it. That they can still be found in and around Tonawanda, New York, is potent evidence of the power of the *Gaiwiio.*

The other accommodationist movement that has proven to be enduring and that has also attracted more public attention than any other form of Native American religious expression is the peyote religion or "cult." (*Cult* in this sense is used to refer to a ritual system rather than to contemporary movements focused on a strong, charismatic leader with a novel and demanding message.) The ritual use of peyote (*Lophophora williamsii*) has deep roots among many of the peoples of the Southwest and Mexico, but emerged in its modern form among the Mescalero Apache around 1870. From them it spread regionally among the Kiowa, Comanche, and Caddo, and ultimately among a wide variety of native peoples as far away as Wisconsin and British Columbia. The specific context of its spread as a *pan-Indian movement* was the failure of the Ghost Dance. The chain of events that culminated in Wounded Knee had simultaneously helped to create a climate of pan-Indian sentiment and a network of communication and cultural borrowing among a number of widely dispersed peoples, and had also demonstrated the lack of realism of movements based on a hope of violent cataclysmic upheaval. The Indians of the West were thus now prepared to accommodate themselves to the necessity of long-term nonviolent coexistence with the whites, and a new religion based on the ritual use of peyote provided an appropriate symbolic vehicle.

The focus of Peyotism is the ritual ingestion of a dried cactus resembling a button that contains nine alkaloids, of which mescaline is the most potent. The immediate reaction in the user is usually one of nausea, but eventually the bitterness recedes and a sense of euphoria accompanied by an altered state of consciousness and perception ensues. The result is a sense of personal relationship with the universe as a whole, which establishes a mood that can be developed and explored in the ritual context. This ritual is usually conducted in a tipi (teepee) around a fire and a crescent-shaped mound of earth. It begins on Saturday evening and runs till the following morning. A fixed part of the rite is set in English, but more spontaneous participation tends to be in native languages. The basic act is the eating of the peyote and subsequent meditation on the visions thereby produced. The goal of this contemplation is a contact of the individual with the power that permeates the cosmos—a diffuse sense of spiritual force characteristic of Native American tradition—and the use of this power to achieve an altered and more positive perspective on the problems of everyday life. A balance is thus maintained between individual and social observance, much as traditional Catholics say the Rosary during Mass. In this case, however, there is no priest to officiate, and each participant enters into a private journey while surrounded by others engaged in the same pursuit.

While the basic ceremony remains fairly standard among Peyotists, the context in which it is performed varies from group to group. Among the more assimilated, Christian symbols are identified with various aspects of the Peyote rite; among other groups, the experience itself is stressed in unmediated form, with little interest in a syncretistic blending of native and European approaches. The more assimilated branches of the religion also stress, as did Handsome Lake, a distinctive path of ethical conduct called the "Peyote Road." Like the Gaiwiio, this is an adaptation of Christian teachings to the Indian context, and stresses similar virtues such as care of family and avoidance of alcohol. Although organizational forms are as alien to the Peyote religion as to native religious practice in general, followers have had to enter into formal groups in order to attain exemption from state and federal laws that prohibit the use of drugs. John Collier was instrumental in helping achieve this organization while serving as Commissioner of Indian Affairs, and the present structure, the Native American Church, was organized in 1944. This institutional superstructure exists almost entirely to represent the group to the external world, and has virtually no impact on the actual character of Peyotism's beliefs and rituals.

The Peyote religion is the most enduring example of accommodation between the Christianity of Anglo-America and the traditions of the Native American peoples. While adapting some of the symbols, ethical values, and organizational forms of Western religion, it still maintains the flexibility, the individualism, and the sense of a cosmos filled with diffuse spiritual power that has always characterized Native religious attitudes. In its appeal to Indians of a wide variety of cultural backgrounds and geographical locales, it is an excellent example of the emergence of a "pan-Indian" consciousness that recognizes and builds on the similarities that unite all Native peoples in collective contrast with the dominant society of Euro-Americans. Finally, it provides a nonviolent means of perpetuating what has emerged as viable in the Native tradition in the context of the necessity of coexisting realistically with that dominant society, adapting from it that which has value, and rejecting the rest with reasonable freedom from external harassment. It is, in short, a paradigm of cultural accommodation—the ability to live in two conflicting worlds simultaneously, and to find the spiritual power to make that division endurable and, perhaps ultimately, a new world.

The political ferment of the 1960s resulted in a new interest and appreciation of native cultures, and a series of publications ranging from Carlos Castaneda's accounts of encounters with the Yaqui visionary Don Juan, to Vine Deloria, Jr.'s *God Is Red* (1973), which advocated a rejection of Christianity and a return to the traditional religious ways. Whether Castaneda's accounts, beginning with *The Teachings of Don Juan* (1968), were actual records of his experience or clever, ethnologically plausible inventions has been the subject of considerable scholarly debate. Their continual source of popular appeal lies in their sympathetic presentation of a drug-induced alternative to the linear world of mundane reality, which persists wherever the "counterculture" impulse of the 1960s endures. The political and social radicalism of Deloria and his contemporary, Dee Brown (*Bury My Heart at Wounded Knee,* 1971), has gone the way of most of the protest movements of the era, although many tribal peoples have continued, with mixed success, to pursue legal paths to securing their traditional rights.

Another Native American literary work, reissued in 1959, has attained what seems likely to be a permanent place in both popular and critical esteem. *Black Elk Speaks*, a hauntingly evocative autobiographical account of an Oglala Sioux shaman's life, has now achieved the wide readership it had been denied when first edited and published by the poet John Neihardt in 1932. Black Elk's narrative, as rendered by Neihardt, interweaves the linear history characteristic of the *Wasichus*—the Anglo-Americans—with his own visionary account of his life and the events surrounding it. Black Elk personally participated in Buffalo Bill's traveling Wild West show, including a trip to Europe and a meeting with Queen Victoria; the last stand of General George Armstrong Custer and his men in 1876 at Little Bighorn; the Ghost Dance of Wovoka and its spread eastward to the Lakotas; and the subsequent massacre of the Sioux at Wounded Knee in 1890. (Although it is not mentioned anywhere in either Black Elk's own words or Neihardt's commentary, Black Elk also served as a Roman Catholic catechist in his later years.) Black Elk does not see these events so much as items in a chronicle, but rather relates them in the context of the visions of the supernatural world that he experienced from early boyhood. In one of his most memorable images, he laments at the end of his life that his "nation's hoop is broken and scattered. There is no center any longer, and the sacred tree is dead."

CHAPTER 40

Black Nationalism and New Urban Religions

The revolutionary rhetoric of the Black Panthers in the late 1960s and early 1970s was by no means the first attempt by American blacks to call for an overthrow of American society or to abandon it entirely. The recovery of Afro-American history that the movements of the 1960s prompted focused new attention on a series of slave rebellions that had taken place in the early nineteenth century. Most notable of these was that led by Nat Turner in 1831 in Southampton County, Virginia. Turner's rebelliousness was nurtured by his sense of a divine calling. Although Turner and a number of his followers were killed in the course of the rebellion or hanged after their subsequent capture, sixty whites also died in the uprising, and the South was more than ever alert to the possibility that blacks could not be expected to remain docile.

The notion of black separatism also found expressions in the nineteenth century. Most black clergy opposed the American Colonization Society's program of relocating free blacks and later manumitted slaves in Africa, especially in Liberia, the African state founded in 1821 as a result of the Society's work. This approach to ending slavery was offensive to them, and they joined instead in the work of William Lloyd Garrison, Frederick Douglass, and other abolitionists. However, they generally supported those blacks who chose to return to Africa voluntarily to serve as Christian missionaries. Similarly, after the Civil War, the African Methodist Episcopal bishop Henry McNeal Turner (1834–1915) remained within the camp of Christianity, but urged blacks to arm for self-protection and later to abandon the United States and emigrate to Africa. Turner also called on blacks to imagine God as black, a theme that would resurface in both Christian and other black religious movements of the twentieth century. Not a great deal came of these and other attempts to establish a black Christian civilization in Africa, but a critique of American society and a rhetoric of separatism were clearly being forged.

It was not until the mass migrations of Southern blacks to Northern cities beginning early in the twentieth century that a new series of social and religious movements began to arise based on either a distinctively black Christianity or, more usually, a repudiation of Christianity altogether. The most influential of these nationalistic movements was led by a Jamaican named Marcus Garvey (1887–1940), who arrived in Harlem in 1916 and there introduced his Universal Negro Improvement Association (UNIA) into the United States. The UNIA had as its ultimate aim the creation of an entirely black society and culture that would eventually abandon the New World and restore American blacks to their ancestral home in Africa.

To accomplish this, Garvey and his followers created a broad network of symbols and organizations intended to unite American blacks into a unified social whole. This network included a motto, "One God! One Aim! One Destiny!"; a newspaper, *The Black World*; an African Legion and a corps of Black Cross Nurses, with appropriate uniforms; meetings, rituals, and a national anthem, "Ethiopia, Thou Land of Our Fathers." A religious dimension was provided in the African Orthodox Church headed by George Alexander McGuire, an Anglican priest from the West Indies who helped promote a new interpretation of Christianity with a black Jesus and Madonna and other Christian religious figures represented as literally black.

Garvey's movement also had an economic dimension, which proved its undoing. Central to this program was the founding of a Black Star steamship line, which was intended ultimately to provide a means for Garvey's followers to return to the African homeland. In-fighting, ineptness, and governmental hostility doomed the venture, and resulted in Garvey's conviction and imprisonment for mail fraud and eventual deportation during the 1920s. Like its radical precursors of the nineteenth century, the UNIA was not successful in its own terms, but again helped establish ideas and images that would continue to resurface in later contexts.

The conditions of life in the urban ghettos of the 1920s and especially the Depression era also led to new religious movements centered on charismatic figures who went beyond traditional Christianity by claiming divine inspiration or even divinity itself. Most notable among these was Father Divine (1877?–1965), who may (or may not) have been born George Baker in Georgia or South Carolina. Like other black urban "cult" founders, Baker/Divine maintained a certain aura of mystery about him, shrouding his origins in obscurity and changing his name and residence a number of times as his *persona* evolved. He can best be seen as a sort of protean or "trickster" figure, deliberately twitting his opponents and attracting followers through claims such as having been "combusted one day in 1900 on the corner of Seventh Avenue and 134th Street in Harlem."

After undergoing metamorphoses, Divine actually claimed to be god in an equivocal sort of way, and his followers coalesced into the Father Divine Peace Mission Movement. He first established a headquarters at Sayville, Long Island, where he and a number of followers were arrested in 1931 on charges of disturbing the peace. Three days after Divine was sentenced to jail, the judge who had pronounced sentence suddenly and unexpectedly died. Divine, whose conviction was later reversed on appeal, reportedly remarked, "I hated to do it."

From bases first on Long Island and later in Harlem and Philadelphia, the Peace Mission Movement attracted large numbers of both black and white followers with the abundant banquets and semicommunal life-style that it offered in the midst of widespread scarcity and want. Controversy surrounded almost every aspect of the Movement, from the sources of its extensive income to the white female "angels" who surrounded Divine as his secretaries. A large majority of his followers were female, many of them "seekers" who had experimented with a number of religious movements, including the "New Thought" that Divine himself found attractive, before finding their needs fulfilled in Divine's charisma. A major teaching of Divine was the nonexistence of racial differences, and white and black followers coexisted harmoniously.

The Peace Mission Movement had little theology, but rather was based on a life-style and allegiance to a unique individual's claims to divinity. The exact number of Divine's followers during the Movement's heyday is hard to reckon, but has been estimated at fifty thousand distributed among 160 centers in various cities. Although the Movement has continued to exist in Philadelphia since Divine's death, focused on the second "Mother Divine," it has recruited few new members without the founder's charismatic presence, and seems destined to eventual extinction, since celibacy is the norm.

One of Father Divine's rivals for the allegiance of Depression-era urbanites was Charles Emmanuel Grace (1881–1960), the founder of the United House of Prayer for All People in 1921 in New Bedford and Wareham, Massachusetts. Like Divine, he was a consummate showman and relished an abundance of life, in a Los Angeles mansion and a New Jersey estate. As "Sweet Daddy" Grace, he attracted followers primarily from the black "Sanctified" (Holiness and Pentecostal) churches. Although he was even more cautious than Father Divine in claiming divinity, his followers showed less hesitation. In addition to participating in worship services on the "Sanctified" pattern, they found relief from their sufferings in the curative powers of special Grace products including magazines, soaps, cold cream, toothpaste, and cookies. After Grace's death, the House of Prayer was reorganized as a Holiness church that claims (probably unrealistically) three million followers in sixty cities.

Still another approach to the question of black religious identity outside of the mainstream of black Christianity lay in an identification with non-Christian traditions that were seen as more authentically linked to the historic black experience. As illustrated in the Garveyite movement, Ethiopia held a particular fascination as a meeting-place of Africa and the Middle East, and news about the dark-skinned Falasha Jews of that country aroused great interest in the 1920s. Garvey's choirmaster, Arnold Josiah Ford, was one of several founders of black Jewish groups among American urban blacks that arose in the early decades of the twentieth century. These movements have had various relations to the mainstream of American Judaism, and some have claimed that only blacks can be authentic Jews. In addition, occasional blacks such as the entertainer Sammy Davis, Jr., have converted to historic Judaism, although their numbers have never been great.

More significant in the Afro-American religious experience has been the identification of American blacks with Islam. Although a few black slaves may have been Muslims, the story of the "Black Muslims" as an American phenomenon begins with the career of Timothy Drew (1886–1927), the founder of the Moorish-American Science Temple (among its several names) in Newark, New Jersey, in 1913. Under the name of Noble Drew Ali, the Prophet, he taught that blacks were really Asiatics and therefore Moors or Muslims. His teachings bore only a tenuous resemblance to traditional Islam, and acknowledged besides Muhammed the spiritual authority of the Buddha, Confucius, and Jesus, who was black. The movement, which had its own "Holy Koran," bearing no relation to the Qu'ran of Islam, survived Drew, who died under controversial circumstances in 1927. Reliable data on its present state are scarce, but temples exist in a number of cities in the North and upper South.

Another urban prophet whose life is shrouded in mystery was W. D. Fard (again, one of various names he used), who appeared in the black ghettoes of Detroit as an itinerant silk peddler around 1930. Fard simply disappeared in 1934, but not before he had established in Detroit a temple and a set of teachings. activities, and institutions that also linked Islam with antiwhite sentiment. His place as leader of this nascent movement was taken by Elijah Poole (1897–1975), who as Elijah Muhammed led this Nation of Islam into national prominence as a militant challenge both to white dominance and Afro-American Christianity during the 1960s.

Until his fall from grace in 1964, the most effective spokesman for these "Black Muslims" in the national forum was Malcolm Little (1925–1965). In his posthumous *The Autobiography of Malcolm X* (1965), he set forth his own pilgrimage through the worlds of the black ghettoes of the North as well as the message and sources of appeal of the Nation of Islam. Central to the movement was the story of Mr. Yakub, a rebellious scientist among what had originally been a superior black race that had dominated the earth. Through a series of experiments, Yakub created the white race as an inferior but evil enemy of the blacks, who became enslaved through this act of trickery. The future, however, offered a millennial hope in the prediction that this inverted order of things would end soon, the "white devil" would be exterminated, and the black people would return to their original position of authority.

Like many other Black Muslims, Malcolm Little first received this message while serving time in prison. He converted and, upon his release, rose rapidly in the Nation's ranks, becoming minister of the #7 Temple in Harlem. The Nation can best be understood as systematically attempting to raise American blacks out of the social and personal disorganization of ghetto life, and to instill instead a collective sense of pride and achievement through a puritanically disciplined life-style. This was implemented through a rejection of traditional "soul food" and all stimulants and intoxicants in favor of a nutritious regimen, marital fidelity, collective ownership of a variety of small businesses and farming enterprises, and as thoroughgoing a rejection and avoidance of white society as was possible. The "Fruit of Islam" formed a militant guard for the movement, and Muslims aggressively hawked the newspaper *Muhammed Speaks* on urban streetcorners during the 1960s. As was the case in many black movements, names were important carriers of meaning: when Malcolm Little joined the Nation, he repudiated his surname, which was seen as a heritage of slavery, and instead adopted an "X," signifying the traditional identity that had been lost when his ancestors had been forcibly alienated from their African past.

Clearly, the teachings of the Nation of Islam had as little to do with those of the original Muhammed as had those of Noble Drew Ali. A series of events led to a parting of the ways in 1964 between Malcolm X and his former mentor Elijah Muhammed. Malcolm, after a pilgrimage to Mecca, became convinced that traditional Sunni Islam offered a superior religious path based on racial inclusiveness rather than antagonism, and became a convert. In 1965 he was assassinated while speaking in New York City.

The Nation of Islam, however, did not continue indefinitely in the direction of racial separation. When Elijah Muhammed died in 1975, he was succeeded by his son Wallace Deen Muhammed, who rapidly espoused traditional Islam and changed the movement's name to the American Muslim Mission. Now welcoming members of other races, it was recognized by the World Muslim Council, and had a membership in the 1980s in the neighborhood of one hundred thousand. The old ways lived on, however, in the splinter movement led by Louis Farrakhan, who as Louis X had succeeded Malcolm X as minister of the Harlem temple in the older Nation. Farrakhan's group, also known as the Nation of Islam, attracted considerable attention during the 1984 presidential campaign through the anti-Jewish pronouncements of its leader, who also endorsed Jesse Jackson's presidential bid. Membership during the late 1980s probably stood in the five to ten thousand range.

A final group worthy of mention brings this account fill circle, with a return both to the West Indies and to Ethiopia as its sources. The Rastafarians attracted considerable attention on the broader American scene during the 1970s and 1980s for their association with a popular West Indian musical form called *reggae* and their ritual use of marijuana. This loosely organized movement originated in Jamaica in the wake of a prophecy of Marcus Garvey that a black king would be crowned in Africa in the near future, which would inaugurate a new era of liberation for blacks. When in 1930 Ras Tafari Makonnen was crowned emperor of Ethiopia and took the name Haile Selassie ("Power of the Holy Trinity"), several Jamaican ministers believed that Garvey's prophecy had been fulfilled, and began spreading the message through the island.

The Rastafarian movement that began to take shape through this preaching saw in Selassie, who had come as a messiah for black people, a descendant of King Solomon and the Queen of Sheba. The movement is thus a variety of Black Judaism, and believes that the Hebrews of old were in fact black. Although the movement is pacifist, young Jamaicans in America who have selectively adopted aspects of its lifestyle—the wearing of "dreadlocks" (tightly braided hair), the smoking of *ganga* (marijuana), and the *reggae* music of Bob Marley—have not always kept to the older path, and brought on the group a reputation for violence. In the United States, the Rastafarians have little organization or ideology, and exist more as a counterculture than as a religious movement.

Black nationalist movements in twentieth-century America have exhibited a protean character, absorbing and transforming elements from a number of religious, political, and cultural traditions, while adding their own novel myths and symbols to the mix. Like the "invisible institution" of slave religion and later organized forms of black Christianity, they have not been bound by Euro-American traditions; rather, like black musicians, they have improvised themes according to the needs of the hour. While many have proved ephemeral and some have taken suprisingly traditional new forms, their persistence illustrates the perennially problematic character of the experience of blacks in American society and their attempts to forge religious responses to that experience.

CHAPTER 41

Health, Wealth, and Metaphysics

One American character trait frequently noted by Alexis de Tocqueville and other observers from abroad has been a propensity to organize into voluntary groups. The prototype for this incessant organization has been as much religious as political. The panoply of denominations that took on a formal, legal structure after the coming of independence pressed religious life into organized form, as did the "Benevolent Empire," that loosely affiliated collection of voluntary societies devoted to advancing the cause of evangelicalism in a country in which religion could not be legally established. Benevolent, fraternal, and reform societies have proliferated ever since. Some, such as the Knights of Columbus, are explicitly religious. Others, such as Jerry Falwell's "Moral Majority" and a variety of antiabortion groups, have strong religious roots, though ostensibly being aimed at nonsectarian goals. Still others, such as ecological and animal rights movements, have no specific religious content, but are nevertheless based on deeply held moral convictions.

Religious and moral life, in short, do not begin and end with denominational boundaries. Many aspects of religious expression, such as revivalism, cut across organizational lines and emerge as forces of their own, alternately challenging and reinvigorating formal church life. Although a sizable majority of Americans belong to specific, mutually exclusive denominations, most nevertheless participate in one way or another in religious activities beyond the scope and control of those denominations. This may involve watching "televangelists," reading popular devotional books, or contributing to interdenominational causes. Even Roman Catholics, who prior to Vatican II stood firmly aloof from any religious participation not explicitly authorized by their leadership, now sometimes join with Fundamentalists in picketing abortion clinics or films offensive to their sensibilities.

Since the colonial era, however, there have been a number of Americans who have never been comfortable with membership in any formally organized religious body. For them, the religious life is an ongoing quest, and they have often been called "seekers" after the as yet undiscovered truth to which this quest will hopefully lead. Much of this questing takes place in their own minds and hearts, through reading and reflection. When the quest goes beyond this to the public forum, such seekers are usually reluctant to enter into any permanent commitments, but rather are content to ally on an ad hoc basis with fellow questers in the continuing pursuit of an elusive answer that lies beyond the boundaries of the visible and tangible. Such seekers also tend, in Robert Ellwood's phrase, to suffer from "status inconsistency"—alienated from or at least not well integrated into the society in which they find themselves forced to function because, for example, of a lack of formal education commensurate with their intellecutal abilities. Such people are often *autodidacts*—self-educated—and steer away from the conventional channels of learning and religious expression. By the standards of the dominant society, their philosophical and religious expression often seems highly eccentric. Institutions that arise in the course of their collective pursuit of truth, not surprisingly, are often evanescent—here one day and gone the next.

The organization, beliefs, and symbolism of Judaism and Christianity—the "classic" religions of the West—all express a rootedness in the social and material orders of this world. Belonging to a church or a synagogue usually entails a commitment to a community, and an acceptance of the necessity of seeking one's ultimate destiny in the context of a network of social relations and institutions. For Judaism, the family has been an especially potent locus of religious life, and blessedness in the Hebrew scriptures is often expressed in the begetting of an ample posterity. For Christians, the doctrine of the Incarnation is a powerful symbol of the rootedness of humanity in the realm of creation—this world—in which "the Word was made flesh and dwelt among us

(John 1:14)". The realms of matter and spirit, in short, are not radically alien from one another, but rather intersect.

Although most Americans have been at least informally aligned with some aspect of Christianity or Judaism, there has nevertheless existed from colonial times an alternate tradition that is fundamentally different from these distinctively Western religions. This tradition has manifested itself not usually in formal structures but in a bewildering variety of ever-changing forms at the edges of the mainstream of American religious life, sometimes aligning itself with that mainstream, but frequently going its own unobtrusive way at the sidelines.

Several terms can be used to describe aspects of this alternative tradition evocatively. One, popularized by the English novelist Aldous Huxley, is the *philosophia perennis*—the "perennial philosophy" found in the mystical traditions of both East and West. In Asia, Buddhism and Hinduism have been its dominant forms, while the Platonic, and especially neo-Platonic, philosophy has been its major Western expression. What these highly diverse traditions share is a repudiation of the Judeo-Christian affirmation that ultimate truth has broken through into the realm of earthly history, and can be personally experienced through participation in that history. As its name implies, the "perennial philosophy" rejects the historical realm as transient and illusory, devoid of enduring or ultimately significant reality.

The historian Sydney Ahlstrom coined another term—*harmonialism*—to describe this tradition from a slightly different angle. Harmonialism in its myriad of shifting forms is based on the premise that this-worldly phenomena are in correspondence with higher truths in other realms of being, which are the ultimate objects of our ongoing quest. The achievement of this truth is primarily intellectual, though it may be accompanied by the ecstacy of a mystical vision or by very this-worldly benefits, such as physical healing, psychological comfort, or even business success. What is sought after, fundamentally, is a state of harmony with the ultimate principles that underlie the universe. These principles themselves are impersonal but, when humans come into contact with them, they activate faculties that have profoundly personal repercussions.

A final relevant term for aspects of this tradition is *occultism*. The term *occult* has not been in favor in recent years, in part because of its similarity to *cult*, and possibly as well because of its somewhat dated flavor. (The "New Age" is a good-sounding phrase for much that once passed as occultism.) "Occult" basically refers to something hidden from the common view, which needs to be encountered through special investigations if its potential benefits are to be reaped. Under occultism especially have been lumped any number of activities and movements, from dowsing for water to astrology, to theosophy, to "pyramid power" and healing crystals. Although far removed from Buddhism and Neo-Platonism, their role in American religious life nevertheless shares some interesting features with these stately traditions of antiquity.

The America of the Second Great Awakening—roughly the period 1790 to 1830—was one of extraordinary social and religious effervescence. This was the time of rapid westward movement, and with it came a panoply of new religious movements: the Cane Ridge camp meeting, Finney's revivals in up-state New York, the rapid growth of the Shakers, and the Baptist and Method-ist movements. In the midst of this ferment, the young Joseph Smith emerged in Palmyra, New York, as a prophet of a new, distinctively American religion. Part of Mormonism's roots lay in the folk magic that Michael Quinn has shown to have been a pervasive part of Joesph Smith's cultural background: divining rods, digging for buried treasure, seer stones, and other practices employed for generations by humble people to connect with literal hidden treasures that lay below the earth and could enrich them once discovered. It is in this context that the angel Moroni's revealing to Smith the location of buried golden tablets and a stone for translating them makes cultural sense.

In addition to this popular tradition of folk magic, however, Smith began to align himself with another source of occult knowledge. Smith founded a Ma-sonic lodge at the Mormon settlement he established at Nauvoo, Illinois, and much of the esoteric symbolism he bestowed on the Nauvoo temple had Ma-sonic origins. Although its social status had lapsed considerably in the later twentieth century, Freemasonry was an elite movement in the early days of the Republic, and boasted Washington and Franklin among its devotees. (The sun/eye atop the pyramid on the reverse of the dollar bill is a Masonic symbol, and reflects the ambience out of which the nation's iconography emerged.) American Masonry, which began as early as 1730, traces its origins to the London Grand Lodge, founded in 1717. Early Masonry was a complex mix-ture of Renaissance occultism, Enlightenment rationalism, and, eventually, American fraternalism that claimed a direct continuity with the esoteric wis-dom of the stonemasons who had built Solomon's temple. In America, it served as a means of creating bonds among the aspiring professional classes dispersed across the country, and only later became associated with proces-sions of miniature dune buggies driven by balding men wearing odd hats.

In addition to the "Burned-Over District" of upstate New York, northern New England, the source of many of these transplanted "Yorkers," also contin-ued to be hospitable to a variety of popular movements with religious implica-tions during this fertile era. Some, like the Free-Will Baptists and Universal-ists, provided liberal alternatives to traditional Calvinism, and were explicitly both religious and Christian. Other movements, however, occupied the ill-defined "liminal" (transitional) territory between the sacred and the secular. Although not embodying themselves in any church or theology, they neverthe-less offered the promise of a personal wholeness that transcended the body, frequently by promising the attainment of harmony with forces hidden from the ordinary senses.

One current of "harmonialism" during this era that took explicitly religious form came from the popularization in America of the *Arcana Coelestia* and other writings of the Swedish scientist and mystic Emanuel Swedenborg (1688–1772). Swedenborg was a latter-day exponent of the Neo-Platonist tra-dition that had enjoyed a new popularity during the Renaissance era. At the core of this tradition was the belief that earthly phenomena were not ends in themselves, but rather corresponded to higher levels of truth in realms of reality that lay beyond the visible. His ideas were popularized at different levels by Ralph Waldo Emerson, who selected Swedenborg as one of his "representative men," and by Jonathan Chapman—"Johnny Appleseed"—who distributed both fruit trees and esoteric religion as he wandered the frontier. A Swedenborgian Society in America was organized in Baltimore in 1792, and today two different groups sharing the name "Church of the New Jerusalem" maintain the tradition in denominationalized form.

Another movement claiming contact with the unseen realms that surround the everday world was *Spiritualism,* whose chief publicist, Andrew Jackson Davis, was clearly influenced by Swedenborg. The craze for seances and communication with the departed that swept America in the 1840s was precipitated by the Fox sisters, three young women near Rochester, New York, who claimed in 1848 that they had established contact with the ghost of a murdered man who had previously lived in their house. Communication from the beyond took place through clicking noises, which the sisters eventually confessed were created by the cracking of their toe joints. Nevertheless, the will to believe that some people had the power of acting as *mediums*—intermediaries between the living and the dead—easily survived the Fox phenomenon, and flourished especially during the Victorian era in many a genteel parlor. Although much Spiritualism today, such as that utilizing the ubiquitous Ouija board, is rather light-hearted in character, dedicated groups such as those loosely allied in the National Spiritualist Association (founded 1893) take the phenomenon very seriously in a religious context.

A related though less clearly religious popular movement of the day was *Mesmerism,* named for its originator and popularizer, the Viennese physician Franz Anton Mesmer (1734?–1813). Through the use of magnets and other physical apparatus, Mesmer attempted to cure people of a variety of ailments that had proven insusceptible to more conventional remedies. From his empirical work, Mesmer generalized to a philosophical position that all disease was essentially the same, and resulted from the lack of equilibrium of "animal magnetism" in a person's body. His methods aimed at a restoration of this equilibrium through natural means, and achieved a craze-like popularity throughout much of Europe for some time. His followers began to emphasize the trance-like state that was induced as part of this curing process, and "mesmerism" thus became synonymous with a kind of hypnotism. From France the enthusiasm for this new kind of psychological manipulation spread to America, where it enjoyed a wide popularity beginning in the 1830s. As Robert C. Fuller has argued, this essentially secular cure for human ills laid much of the groundwork for both popular and academic psychology, as well as for any number of later movements based on psychological adjustment.

Following the Civil War, the rapid transformation of America from an agricultural to an urban-industrial society began to take its toll on city- and country-dwellers alike. Those who found themselves falling through the cracks of this nascent new social order often expressed their malaise in psychological and psychosomatic form. A representative work of the era was the pioneering neurologist George Beard's *American Nervousness* of 1881, which popularized the concepts of "neurasthenia" and "nervous exhaustion." Although the seeds of the science and profession of clinical psychology lay in this sort of approach, the decades before World War I were still a time of protean exploration of the implications of these insights.

William James, the Harvard scholar who gained a lasting reputation for his pioneering *Principles of Psychology* (1890), also continued in Emerson's footsteps as a sort of popular sage, and drew from his explorations in both religion and psychology to offer easily accessible wisdom on applying both to everyday life. His *Varieties of Religious Experience* (1902) remains a classic work in the psychology of religion, but is also eminently readable and down-to-earth in its concern with human needs and suffering. Similarly, a title such as *Talks to Teachers on Psychology; and to Students on Some of Life's Ideals* (1899) indicates James's sense of his role as a moral as well as intellectual guide for his unsettled contemporaries. It is noteworthy that his father, Henry James, Sr., was an active Swedenborgian, while his brother Henry has attained classic status as the author of psychologically profound fiction.

At another social level, the notion that a significant mental or spiritual reality lay concealed behind the facade of external appearances began to take root in the small towns of northern New England in the practice of one Phineas P. Quimby (1802–1866). Quimby, a Maine clockmaker, became impressed with mesmerism, and soon took up the practice himself. From here he moved in both theory and practice to a preoccupation with the mental causes of physical disorders, and acquired a considerable reputation regionally as a healer. In his manuscripts, which were not published till after his death, Quimby worked on providing his healing practice with a philosophical rationale, namely, that physical disease was caused by mental error—a fundamental misapprehension as to the nature of reality. These ideas finally saw print after being edited by Quimby's disciple and successor, Warren Felt Evans, a Methodist minister turned Swedenborgian.

Phineas Parkhurst Quimby would probably be little more than a footnote in American social history were it not for his influence on one of the most remarkable figures in American religious history: Mary Baker Eddy. Eddy (1821–1910), the founder of Christian Science, has probably evoked more scholarly controversy as to the character and meaning of her career than any American religious figure other than Joseph Smith. The literature on her is extensive, including Mark Twain's satirical *Christian Science* of 1907 (Twain had also ridiculed the Mormons), and Edwin F. Dakin's hostile, muckraking *Mrs. Eddy: The Biography of a Virginal Mind* (1929), as well as Robert Peel's scholarly and appreciative three-volume study of her life. The divergence that continues in contemporary interpretation can be profitably noted in a comparison of Sydney Ahlstrom's biographical sketch in *Notable American Women* (1971) and Stephen Gottschalk's essay on "Christian Science and Harmonialism" in the *Encyclopedia of the American Religious Experience* (1988). A particularly vexing, ongoing object of dispute is the role Quimby himself played in the development of Eddy's ideas: had Quimby moved beyond pragmatic healing techniques to a religious or at least metaphysical position, or did Eddy build so far beyond Quimby that they taught entirely different systems in their mature phases?

Mary Baker Eddy was raised on a farm near Bow, New Hampshire, in the very heart of the area where popular religious and healing movements had for many years been thriving. Her chronic poor health and nervous disposition were exacerbated by two marital disappointments—the first to George Washington Glover, a building contractor who died shortly after their union, and was buried with Masonic ceremonies. Her next alliance was with Daniel Patterson, an itinerant and not very reliable dentist who eventually abandoned her and from whom she was ultimately divorced. Physical and mental suffering, emotional disappointment, financial insecurity, and a disorienting series of changes of residence all thus conspired to make Eddy—the name she acquired upon her third marriage—an archetypal seeker after the relief and sense of personal wholeness that her native Congregationalism could not provide for her.

The rural and small-town culture of Mary Baker's New England exposed her over the years to the whole panoply of popular movements to which the region played host: Spiritualism, mesmerism, hydropathy (the "water cure"), and the like. None of these provided her with any significant relief until her path crossed that of the itinerant Mr. Quimby, now resident in Portland, Maine, in 1862. Quimby's "science of health" provided her with just what she needed in both theory and practice, and her own health and spirits improved rapidly and markedly. It was not till shortly after Quimby's death early in 1866, though, that she underwent her ultimately decisive experience. After being immobilized for several days following a fall on the ice, and possibly in danger of death, she was suddenly cured after reading Matthew 9:2—in which Jesus heals a paralytic—and "on the third day" arose from her bed.

This combination of physical healing and religious conversion galvanized this woman, who had been approaching a condition of helpless invalidism, into becoming a veritable dynamo of activity. Success, however, did not come easily. The next decade she spent peripatetically changing residences, drifting through what Sydney Ahlstrom has described as a nearly irrecoverable subculture of New England boardinghouses where popular movements proliferated and where the spiritually displaced continually, desperately, and with uncertain success sought relief. It was among and for just such a clientele that Mary Baker Eddy appeared as the prophet of a new, uniquely urban religion, which paradoxically had its roots in the religious culture of a vanishing hinterland. Like her New England-born contemporary Dwight L. Moody, she "discovered"—in her own word—a new approach to the spiritual life that met the needs of countless like-minded among the spiritually and socially dislocated.

Christian Science, which continues to this day in substantially the same form Eddy gave it, consists of an idea or set of ideas, a method, and an organization. The core idea is expounded in Eddy's central work, *Science and Health with Key to Scriptures* (1875, and many subsequent, revised editions). Her basic idea is central to all monistic systems of metaphysics: that physical matter is illusory and unreal. All that *is* real is Spirit, and salvation—or healing—lies in the realization of this truth and the working out of its full range of implications and applications. Disease, sin, and death are ultimately illusory and will vanish once the individual has assimilated this truth completely.

Eddy and her followers have always insisted on the *Christian* character of

Christian Science, although she would have been the first to admit—even to insist—that only she had been able to provide Christian revelation with an authoritative interpretation. She thus enjoyed a status in some ways similar to that of Joseph Smith among Mormons, as an inspired vehicle through which the fullness of revelation is now made accessible to all. Christian Science is of divine origin, and Eddy declared it to be a dimension of the Second Coming of Jesus. The *Key to Scriptures,* included in later editions of *Science and Health,* offers an exegesis of Genesis and Revelation along Swedenborgian lines, and is based on the premise that the Bible cannot be understood without a specially revealed key to its interpretation according to its "spiritual" sense.

The last portion of *Science and Health,* entitled "Fruitage," consists entirely of a distinctive aspect of Christian Science practice: testimonials to physical and psychological healings. Christian Science has always focused on healing as central to its message, and has rigorously forbidden its followers to employ conventional medical techniques in seeking healing. (This has over the years led to many lawsuits, especially concerning medical emergencies involving children. On the other hand Sydney Ahlstrom, not the most sympathetic of Eddy's interpreters, has observed that her greatest service was keeping people away from the many grotesquely incompetent doctors of her day.) Early in the movement's development, the title "pastor" was dropped in favor of "practitioner," emphasizing the practical focus of the church. In addition to practitioners, who devote full time to a healing ministry, the Church licenses teachers and readers. A pair of the latter, usually a man and a woman, are assigned to each church and read alternatively at Sunday services from the Bible and *Science and Health.* On Wednesdays, testimonial meetings on healings effected by Christian Science are also held.

The thought and practice of Christian Science are supported by an organization—the Church of Christ, Scientist—that was given definitive shape by Eddy herself, the movement's "Discoverer and Founder." After various attempts at teaching her ideas in Lynn, Massachusetts, she began to give the movement formal structure, and the Church of Christ (Scientist) was chartered by the state in 1879. Two years later, while still in Lynn, she also obtained a charter for the Massachusetts Metaphysical College. Following a series of bitter controversies with her disciples, which characterized much of her later career, she moved her establishment to Boston, which has remained to the present day the world headquarters of the Christian Science movement.

The mature Eddy unquestionably exerted a charismatic influence on her followers, but one that in the longer run could produce both intense loyalty and equally intense revulsion. She became convinced that her third husband, Asa Eddy, with whom she had enjoyed a happy relationship, had died not of the heart ailment attested to in an autopsy but rather as the result of "mental assassination" brought about by her jealous former disciples exerting "Malicious Animal Magnetism" on him. "M.A.M.," a term drawing on the vocabulary of mesmerism, later became an integral part of Christian Science teaching. Quarrels and even lawsuits involving former disciples were frequent in her later days, most of which were spent withdrawn from the public, and many branches of the "New Thought" movement had their origins in these rifts.

Despite continual leakage to incipient rival movements, Christian Science grew rapidly under Eddy's autocratic but compelling leadership, with 20 churches, 90 societies, 250 practitioners, and 33 teaching centers around the country by 1890, and a membership of about eighty-five thousand in 1906. (The Church does not release membership statistics; one estimate for the early 1970s gives four hundred seventy-five thousand in the United States and another about one hundred fifty thousand worldwide.) In 1886, the National Christian Science Association was founded, and then reorganized in 1889 to provide even firmer centralized control. The Church of Christ, Scientist, as it is now known, is governed by a self-perpetuating Board of Directors originally appointed by Eddy herself, which took charge of the Church's affairs after her death. The Mother Church, which forms the core of a headquarters complex near Copley Square in Boston, consists of two parts: an older, rather intimate Romanesque church (1895), and the grand neoclassical "Extension" (1906), which takes its place with such nearby public structures as Trinity and New Old South Churches and McKim, Mead, and White's grand Public Library. A more recent high-rise office structure and reflecting pool by I. M. Pei (built 1968–1973) extend the monumentality into a later twentieth-century idiom, and provide a physical plant for a cluster of church-sponsored activities such as the publication of the well-regarded *Christian Science Monitor,* a genuinely national newspaper.

The impressive scope of the appeal of both Christian Science and its New Thought competitors—many of them also led by women—on first a local and then a national scale was hardly accidental. Christian Science to this day remains foremost, or nearly so, among America's religious communities in terms of per capita wealth, as well as in the female and urban character of its constituency. A unique Christian Science institution is the "Reading Room," usually found in downtown shopping districts or suburban malls. Clean and well-lighted if somewhat austere, it offers passers-by an opportunity to sit down and examine a variety of the church's literature. The interaction here is impersonal, between the drop-in patron and the printed word.

Christian Science from the beginning shared the urban propriety and impersonality that these reading rooms perpetuate. The reverse side of Eddy's intense and problematic relationship with many of her early disciples was her later withdrawal into seclusion, regulating the Church from a distance but avoiding personal interaction with its adherents. Although Christian Science churches today—many of them designed on the monumental scale of the Mother Church—resemble other Christian denominations in holding regular worship services, they differ from most in their lack of communal activity, except for education programs. Christian Science as a group has been largely apolitical, has little involvement in philanthropic work, and lacks a sense of community, even at the local level. The emphasis is very much on the well-being of individuals, who are left to seek social life and community involvement on their own should they care to.

This individualistic emphasis has from the beginning marked both the breadth and the limitations of the appeal of the movement. Eddy's message had its greatest impact especially on Victorian women, of or at the margins of the middle classes, who were unsure of their role in a rapidly urbanizing society. As Donald Meyer has argued, Christian Science, as exemplified in the career of Eddy herself, represented a way for women to come to terms with the sense of powerlessness and futility many of them experienced, and frequently to set themselves up as allies, or rivals, of Eddy in spreading this new message of personal wholeness. This emphasis on female empowerment is especially well illustrated in Eddy's use of the term "Our Father-Mother God, all harmonious," in her paraphrase of the Lord's Prayer in *Science and Health,* and in the near-divine status accorded her by her followers. Her own prodigious success as a religious founder and organizer indicates that she especially was a women of enormous talent that could not find profitable outlet in conventional Victorian channels. This is not to detract from what may have been the authentic healing power of Christian Science, especially upon the "neurasthenics" diagnosed by Dr. Beard as the typical American invalids of their day, but rather to set the appeal of a radically new religious movement in the context of its time.

Christian Science remains unique in the American "harmonial" tradition in its strict and effective organization, its exclusive claims to truth, and its insistence on its explicitly Christian character. The impulses that its founder drew together clearly came from a variety of sources, and in turn almost immediately began to diffuse in many new directions. Religious healing took a number of forms, ranging from Pentecostalism, which grew out of a very different strain of popular religion, to the Emmanuel movement that emerged at the turn of the century in Boston among Episcopal clergy who collaborated with local physicians in their therapeutic and counseling endeavors. By the 1920s, courses in pastoral counseling with strong psychological components began to be added to the curricula of many seminaries as well.

A very different current in American religious life also found itself a home in the Victorian parlor and lecture hall, as did early Christian Science, and similarly drew on imagery of the attunement of the individual to impersonal metaphysical currents that lay behind the veil of the everyday world. The archetypal representative of Victorian occultism was Helena Petrovna Blavatsky (1831–1891), a Russian émigrée and spiritualist who formed a liaison with her long-time partner, Henry S. Olcott, in New York in the 1870s. Theosophy (i.e., divine wisdom), as explicated in such writings of Blavatsky as *Isis Unveiled* (1877) and *The Secret Doctrine* (1888), began as an exposition of the Western *philosophia perennis,* but began to look increasingly to Asia as Blavatsky traveled extensively in India, seeking contact with Hindu and Buddhist teachers. In its later versions, Blavatsky's teaching was based on the premise that all reality is ultimately one and grounded in Consciousness, and that individual souls must be successfully reincarnated through long cosmic cycles in order to approach their ultimate source. She claimed to have received her teachings through mysteriously appearing letters from "masters" or "mahatmas" who had attained high stages of enlightenment, which not surprisingly gave rise to charges of fraud and plagiarism.

After Blavatsky's death in 1891, the Theosophical Society split into rival fragments under the leadership of Annie Besant, Blavatsky's chosen successor, who established a headquarters in India, and William Q. Judge, who founded a separate group. The movement continues to this day to have a few thousand adherents in America, but the loose organization of Theosophy has never conduced to precise record-keeping.

A wide variety of other groups are also part of the American scene. Perhaps the best known are the Rosicrucians, who advertise widely in the popular press under the initials AMORC (Ancient and Mystical Order of the Rosae Crucis—"rosy cross"). This group, founded in 1915, maintains a complex that occupies an entire block in a residential neighborhood of San Jose, California. Its impressive Egyptian museum points up its claims to continue the ancient esoteric wisdom of that tradition. All such groups appeal more to a sense of individual study and development than to any group participation, and their sense of community tends to be rather abstract.

If faith-healing and occultism represent two dimensions of harmonialism taken to their extremes, New Thought is much more clearly related to Christian Science and what one might identify as the "center" of the tradition. "New Thought" is a generic term dating from the 1890s for a series of loosely related groups and movements that emerged in the wake of the success of Christian Science, often as split-offs from the latter following quarrels between Mary Baker Eddy and such disciples as Augusta Stetson, Emma Curtiss Hopkins, and Ursula Gestefeld. Unlike Eddy, these and a seeming myriad of other New Thought leaders have seldom been preoccupied with power and structure, but have attracted a fluid constituency not often interested in long-term institutional commitments and finding nurture within a whole continuum of teachings. Like Christian Science, most branches of New Thought teach that ultimate reality is singular, impersonal, and spiritual, and that human ills can be eliminated by a proper alignment of the individual consciousness with the vaster metaphysical reality of which it partakes. However, most followers of New Thought do not argue very strenuously for the Christian character of their movement; if they do, it is to claim that Christian symbols can be interpreted in a way compatible with broader cosmic truth.

One of the most successful manifestations of New Thought, and one that is also very explicitly Christian in its self-description, is the Unity School of Christianity. "Unity," as it is usually known, was founded by Charles and Myrtle Fillmore in 1889 in Kansas City. The Fillmores were typical Victorian-era "seekers," who had experimented with Christian Science, Theosophy, Rosicrucianism, Spiritualism, and Eastern religions before lighting upon a metaphysical mixture that cured them of their various ills, including financial. Unity, which combines an emphasis on Jesus as the Christ with the belief in reincarnation, maintains some three hundred centers across the country. Although Unity sponsors such traditional religious activity as preaching and baptism, its central work is conducted at long distance from Unity Village in Missouri, which receives hundreds of thousands of phone calls and letters annually requesting counseling and spiritual aid. Its message is also disseminated widely through books and radio and television programs.

In addition to Unity, New Thought is today represented by a probably uncountable number of groups sharing the sorts of principles that resulted in the founding of the International New Thought Alliance in 1915. New Thought groups are widely distributed over the entire United States and beyond, having spread originally from New England to Chicago and other parts of the Midwest and rapidly to California, whose protean and optimistic culture continues to encourage nontraditional religious and philosophical movements. Some of these, like Annie Rix Militz's "Home of Truth," counted numerous branches in their heyday, but eventually declined as their offshoots took on an independent character. Much of the ongoing New Thought impulse today has been incorporated into the similarly named "New Age" movement, which includes in the loosest possible fashion enthusiasts for, for example, channeling (long-dead individuals using those alive today as "channels" for communication), astrology, healing crystals, tarot cards and palmistry, meditation, near-death experiences, reincarnation, ecological mysticism, radical feminism, acupuncture, yoga, UFO cults, and so on *ad infinitum*. (*The New Age Catalogue*, compiled by the editors of *Body Mind Spirit Magazine* (1988), is a mine of information on this endless procession of enthusiasms, ranging from organized political movements to curious passing fads.) Instead of the church or even the parlor or lecture hall, however, the shopping-mall chain book outlet has become the principal link of distribution for New Age matter, which includes cassettes and videotapes as well as paperbound books.

A final offshoot of the harmonial impulse worth noting is the cult of self-help, which has taken both secular and religious forms in its distinctive twentieth-century career. Related to such other American enthusiasms as "do-it-yourself"—a motto appropriate for New Age phenomena as well—self-help emerged as a very this-worldly, individualistic strain of New Thought preoccupations in its belief that individuals can overcome their difficulties and achieve material success and physical and emotional health simply by thinking correctly. Emile Coué attracted wide audiences in the 1920s with his verbal formula, "Day by day, in every way, I am getting better and better," and Dale Carnegie's best-selling *How to Win Friends and Influence People* (1936) gave the notion that success was the direct result of positive thinking and self-projection one of its classic expressions.

"Positive thinking" began to be expressed in more religious terms as well, beginning in the success-oriented climate of the 1920s when postwar "normalcy," a bustling economy, and the influx of country folk to the grand cities of speakeasies and Art Deco skyscrapers promised fulfillment and gratification beyond one's wildest imaginings. Bruce Barton, a partner in the Batten, Barton, Durstine, and Osborne advertising agency, brought the spirit of that brand-new marketing enterprise to bear on Christianity. His widely circulated *The Man Nobody Knows* (1925) presented Jesus as the ultimate go-getter, putting together a highly effective team of promoters of his message from a selection of rather ordinary locals.

The ultimate correlation of religious belief and personal confidence leading to this-worldly success, of course, is that formulated by Norman Vincent Peale in his best-selling *The Power of Positive Thinking* (1952) and other, similar works. Peale had been a Methodist before becoming associated with the Reformed Church of America, the more liberal branch of the Dutch Reformed tradition in this country, through his call to Manhattan's Marble Collegiate Church in 1932—a position he held until his retirement in 1984. Peale's message, which has been widely disseminated first through the printed word in various forms and more recently through audio/visual materials, involves a kind of autosuggestion verging on self-hypnosis, whereby the subject acquires increasing self-confidence through repetition of affirming messages. As in Christian Science, testimonials also play a major part in Peale's literature; here, however, they are more likely to attest to business success than to physical healing.

Although Peale's career continued past his formal retirement, his clear successor in the field was another Dutch Reformed pastor, Robert Schuller of Garden Grove, California. Schuller early demonstrated his adaptability to changing social circumstances by preaching from the top of a drive-in theater's refreshment stand to a congregation who remained in the parking lot in their cars. The rapid success of his message, which is based on the idea of "possibility thinking," is manifest in his colossal "Crystal Cathedral," an ultra-modern glass-walled church on a gigantic scale designed by the prominent architect Philip Johnson. Completed in 1980 at a cost of $16.5 million, it stands on the site of the original drive-in complex—a mile or so from Disneyland in Anaheim—and provides for those in their cars as well. The Cathedral's plant also includes a bookstore, which features success-inspiring materials in a variety of genres and media, as well as a thirteen-story Tower of Hope office building. Schuller is best known to most Americans, though, through televised services, which are as exuberant as those of his fundamentalist "televangelist" counterparts though far more decorous in style. While Schuller remains within the Reformed tradition, he has been criticized by evangelicals for downplaying a traditional concern with sin and forgiveness in favor of a very this-worldly optimism.

Clearly, the differences that separate Christian Science, New Thought, the loose cluster of "New Age" enthusiasms, and Schuller's "possibility thinking" are significant. However, all of these movements share certain themes. None places a great deal of emphasis either on formal worship or on a sense of religious community. Each focuses instead on realizing the possibilities inherent in each individual, which have thus far been repressed through inadequate knowledge and negative thoughts. That individual realization, moreover, tends to manifest itself in very this-worldly forms, sometimes stressing physical health, at other times psychological integration or material success. Donald Meyer has argued that underlying these emphases and attitudes is a strategy for adapting to the exigencies of twentieth-century American life, in which success is achieved through acceptance of and conformity with the dominant social and economic system. Once one has aligned with this system correctly, the system then promises a never-ending supply of material and emotional abundance. While it is dangerous to affirm too uncritically any explanation that reduces religious experience to something else, the propensity of these movements toward either an apolitical or conservative stance regarding the social and economic orders lends plausibility to Meyer's observation—as do a few moments spent in one's living room in the company of the Reverends Schuller or Peale.

Part V

The Twentieth Century: Further Encounters with Modernity and Pluralism

INTRODUCTION

It is tempting to characterize *every* era of American history as one of rapid social and cultural change, but the decades following World War I seem particularly worthy of this description. With the 1920 census, demographers declared that the United States had become a nation with an urban majority. The dislocations brought about by the "Great War" and the ensuing disillusionment with internationalist idealism brought about a new sophistication and skepticism among some, and a strong reaction among others who feared the worst. The polarization within the Protestant community between Modernist and Fundamentalist had become unbridgeable, and the Scopes "Monkey" Trial of 1925 seemed to vindicate the former. A Protestant "mainline," theologically moderate and socially cautious, enjoyed an ascendancy that remained unchallenged until the turmoil of the 1960s and 1970s.

The Depression and World War II brought with them further shocks to middle-class complacency. Franklin Roosevelt's New Deal not only challenged the economic assumptions to which nineteenth-century evangelicalism had given divine legitimation, but also worked to include Catholics and Jews in its inner councils. The war also brought with it a knowledge of radical evil that took the faces of Auschwitz, Dresden, and Hiroshima. "After such knowledge," T. S. Eliot asked, "what forgiveness?"

The trauma of the war rapidly receded in the face of postwar economic recovery, accompanied by the flight of returned GIs to both the suburbs and college. Roman Catholics especially enjoyed new access to the delights of middle-class life, and the election of one of their number to the American Presidency in 1960 confirmed this acceptance. "Religion in general," as it was sometimes called, became widely appealing during the 1950s, and Billy Graham and Bishop Sheen both demonstrated the expanded variety of forms it could take in polite company. Both of these media celebrities were united as well in their militant opposition to Communism, which served as a symbol of cosmic evil for that generation.

The 1960s began on an upbeat note with the style of the Kennedys and the music of the Beatles promising a more lively cultural mixture in an era when youth seemed destined to dominate. Instead came violent death—for John and Robert Kennedy, John Lennon, Martin Luther King, Jr., and thousands of young Americans who found themselves entrapped in a hopeless war whose misery was relieved only by "dope." Before his death, though, Martin Luther King helped mobilize the anger and determination of millions of black Americans and their white allies to bring about an irreversible upheaval in the nation's social arrangements regarding race.

The promise of the civil rights movement triggered other drives toward liberation—among women, Hispanics, and homosexuals. Their militancy soon generated a reaction among many who feared that the newly "permissive" attitudes the nation seened to be taking toward sexual behavior and sex roles especially would rapidly undermine the moral fabric of the Republic. Jimmy Carter, America's first "born again" president, symbolized the enfranchisement of evangelicals; his subsequent defeat by Ronald Reagan, however, indicated that they sought a more vigorous implementation of their programs. The nation seemingly remained polarized between a secular professional culture and a new middle class that yearned to return to what it remembered as the old ways. By the late 1980s, neither had won a decisive victory.

CHAPTER 42

Neo-Orthodoxy and Ecumenism: The Foundations of "Mainline" Protestantism

The trauma of the Fundamentalist reaction to the rapidly entrenching Liberal movement in Protestantism in the early twentieth century put an end to what remained of the "Evangelical United Front" of nineteenth-century America. The Scopes Trial of 1925, though hardly resolving the legal questions raised by state laws constricting the teaching of contemporary science in public classrooms, dramatically illustrated the social and cultural rift that divided "cosmopolitan" from "provincial" America and that often used religious issues as its symbolic currency. Until the subsequent cultural trauma of the 1970s, American Protestants divided into a dominant cluster of denominations, united by shared premises about religion and culture and by a recognized social status, and a conservative opposition forced into the status of a resistance movement by its defeat on the battlegrounds both of the mass media and of the denominations themselves.

The "Princes of the Pulpit" of Victorian America—Henry Ward Beecher, Phillips Brooks, and their contemporaries—had laid the foundations for a "mainline" Protestantism that emerged triumphant in the Fundamentalist-Modernist controversy of the 1920s and persisted in its essentials for the next four decades as the arbiter of American religious life. Its constituency came primarily from native-born Protestants of northwestern European descent, who tended to be middle to upper-middle class in social status. Its organizational expression subsisted in seven denominations, or denominational clusters, that were more united than divided in their interpretations of a common Reformation heritage.

Of these groupings, Congregationalists, Episcopalians, and Presbyterians—the colonial "establishment"—were the most prestigious and influential. (This prestige they shared regionally with the theologically deviant Unitarians in the Boston area and the Friends in Philadelphia, although defections from both to the Episcopal Church were not uncommon.) Outside the Northeast, "mainline" status was also characteristic of four other denominations of humbler origins, whose constituents had nevertheless frequently acquired middle-class or even higher status in the smaller cities and towns of the South, the Midwest, and Far West: the Methodists, Baptists (Northern or American), Lutherans, and the Disciples of Christ.

Establishment Protestantism defined itself against several other clusters of socioreligious groups. Closest to them in religious and ethnic background were the conservative Protestants who controlled individual churches in the urban North but who were achieving far greater cultural influence in the South. Presbyterians and Methodists, together with a remnant of Episcopalians, still provided much Southern leadership, but their affiliation was with the much more conservative Southern branches of those denominations. Southern Baptists were slowly gaining strength, together with the Churches of Christ and a variety of Holiness and Pentecostal groups. In many cases, though, the latter cluster still could be characterized as "churches of the disinherited." (It is not accidental that H. Richard Niebuhr's influential *Social Sources of Denominationalism*, a pioneering demonstration of the correlation between religious affiliation and social class, which popularized the latter phrase, was first published in 1929.)

Sharing a common theological heritage with the Southern white Protestants but sharply differentiated by the "color line" were the black churches—Baptist, Methodist, and "Sanctified"—which exercised practically no influence outside their own constituencies. Like Catholic priests, black preachers did serve as mediators with the external community, and the prestige of secular black cultural forms, especially jazz, was clearly on the rise by the 1920s. It would be several more decades, however, till blacks began slowly to gain entree into the "establishment"—which, by the 1970s, had itself changed significantly in character.

The third "out group" against which establishment Protestantism could be defined consisted of Catholics, Jews, and other non-Protestants. The ranks of these "outsiders" had swollen to what many felt were alarming proportions through the "New Immigration" of the decades that bracketed the turn of the century. These ethnic groups were a much more serious challenge to the "East Coast Establishment"—as it would come to be known in later years—in a variety of ways. Catholics, especially those of Irish descent, were quick to develop their legendary political skills, and by the 1880s had begun to control political machines in a number of cities. Catholic episcopal and clerical leadership was also eager to influence public policy, especially in the realm of morals, and by the 1920s was attempting to regulate film content, the sale of contraceptives, and the like, though frequently in consonance with more conservative mainline Protestants.

Jews were too few in number to attain much political influence except locally, especially in parts of New York City and environs. However, the eagerness with which Jewish immigrants and their offspring pursued higher education began to put some stress on what for the older stock had become a comfortable system. As Jews gained the financial and educational credentials that would seemingly qualify them for entree into a strictly meritocratic social order, they began to discover that the American system was not based so strictly on the merit of achievement. Beginning in the late nineteenth century, Jews began to be turned away from country clubs, resort hotels, and other institutions that—as women in the later twentieth century have discovered—serve latent economic as well as overt social and recreational functions. In particular, Ivy League and similarly prestigious colleges began to enforce unannounced quotas on admission of otherwise qualified applicants to preserve a high percentage of WASP enrollment. (WASP, it might be noted—an acronym for "White Anglo-Saxon Protestant"—has of late become something of an ethnic slur, much like its coarser counterpart, "redneck.")

Genteelly in the North and more overtly and even violently in the South, Protestants moved to ensure their traditional role as molders and protectors of society. Covert anti-Semitism and anti-Catholicism in the Northeast was counterpointed by the rise of the Ku Klux Klan in the 1920s, led now by the lower fringes of the Southern middle classes. In addition to its traditional role, fashioned after the Civil War, of keeping blacks "in their place," the resurgent Klan turned its attention to harassing both native-born and immigrant Catholics and Jews as well as "damyankees" interfering in regional affairs. The Klan's influence also extended well into the North, especially Southern-oriented Indiana, where it was a dominant force in state politics during much of the decade. The drastic restriction of immigration by Congress during the twenties was a legislative manifestation of the same nativist impulse that seized much of the country, and contributed substantially to the defeat of Irish Catholic Al Smith in the 1928 presidential election.

It would be a mistake, however, to equate mainline Protestantism, even during these turbulent decades, with political reaction and social bigotry. The Social Gospel had its origins within this same social and religious milieu, and exerted a powerful progressive influence in the decades prior to World War I and after its "decline and revival" in the 1920s and 1930s, described by historian Paul Carter. Franklin Delano Roosevelt, for example, was the quintessential patrician of Dutch descent and Episcopal affiliation. Roosevelt came into power in the midst of a profound economic crisis that called the conventional wisdom of the "Establishment" into radical question, and with the support of a coalition of Catholic, Jewish, black, and other minority voters. His New Deal, which in many ways applied Social Gospel principles to the secular realm, was supported by many Catholic and Jewish intellectuals as harmonious with their own social ethics.

It was in part the crisis of the Depression that brought about a major shift in the theological underpinnings of establishment Protestantism during the 1930s. Both Liberalism and its close relative the Social Gospel could not weather the challenges of the World War and then the Depression without some serious adjustments to their optimistic appraisal of the human condition and the possibilities of indefinite social progress. In addition, the very accommodation with the secular culture that had been a leading characteristic of the Liberal movement was now working against its success, as the 1920s witnessed a flourishing of mass-media entertainments and diversions that no longer needed the legitimation that the clergy had been willing to provide it. Babe Ruth, Charles Lindbergh, and Rudolph Valentino drove the likes of both Harry Emerson Fosdick and Billy Sunday from center stage; it took a media spectacle as grand as the Scopes Trial to recapture for religion the spotlight even momentarily—and under the most doubtful of circumstances. In Robert Handy's words, the era from 1925 to 1935 underwent a "religious depression" from which Americans were jarred loose only by a social crisis of the first magnitude.

By 1935, even Harry Emerson Fosdick, who had championed the Liberal cause against the Fundamentalist challenge so eloquently a decade before, was now moved to ask in a widely distributed sermon whether it was not now necessary for Protestants to move "Beyond Modernism." What lay beyond Modernism was a powerful new theological movement whose name, Neo-Orthodoxy, suggested its content and its method—a tension between the traditional and the modern held together in a dialectical interaction.

Neo-Orthodoxy, which might equally well have been called "Neo-Liberalism" and which was never so much a formal school but rather a climate of theological opinion, had its most immediate origins in Continental Europe in the wake of the First World War's devastation. Its generally accepted founder was the Swiss Reformed thinker Karl Barth (1886–1968), whose multivolume *Church Dogmatics* has provided countless seminary students with a challenge comparable to that posed by one of Barth's major sources, Calvin's *Institutes*. Barth first captured the attention of his contemporaries with his *Römerbrief* of 1918, published in English in 1932 as *The Epistle to the Romans*. In this and his subsequent works, Barth rejected the conclusions to which German-language New Testament scholarship had been pointing. This tendency continually to refashion Jesus according to the wants and needs of the present day was extensively described by Albert Schweitzer in his classic *The Quest of the Historical Jesus* (1906). Sydney Ahlstrom, echoing the English Modernist George Tyrrell, characterized Schweitzer as having "found the scholars peering down the 2,000-year-long shaft of history and seeing their own bourgeois faces reflected from the bottom of the well." For Barth and his followers, the task instead was trying to rediscover "the strange world of the Bible," where the earliest Christians saw the world through eschatological categories far different from the optimistic assumptions of modern science and liberal theology.

The orthodoxy that was now being cast into new forms consisted for the most part of the ideas and writings of several of the classic figures of the Protestant traditions and their antecedents. Prominent among these were St. Augustine, Luther, Calvin, and the nineteenth-century Danish theologian Søren Kierkegaard (1813–1855.) Kierkegaard's copious writings such as *Fear and Trembling* (1843) began to be available through the English translations of Walter Lowrie beginning in 1939. His "dialectical" thought was intended to transcend metaphysics, doctrine, and the cultural captivity of much of European church life, and focus instead on the immediacy of the encounter of the individual with God—in a state of "fear and trembling." This existentialist motif became widely influential in Christian, Jewish, and secular philosophy in the twentieth century, and many of Kierkegaard's themes were taken up in Paul Tillich's (1886–1965) influential *The Courage To Be* (1952), *Dynamics of Faith* (1957), and other widely read works.

Unlike Tillich, though, Barth drew very directly on the Reformed (Calvinist) tradition for his most direct inspiration. Central to his thought were two complementary emphases developed first by Augustine and then again by Luther and Calvin: the potency of original sin and the absolute sovereignty of

God. For Barth, the realms of the human and the divine were utterly incommensurable, and came together only at the "tangent point" of the Incarnation, which made salvation possible. Despite Barth's heavy stress on human sinfulness and its consequences, however, he departed from his austere Reformed mentors in his rejection of predestination and his optimism about the ultimate salvation of all of humanity.

The forbidding character of much of Barth's writing precluded the widespread readership that his sometimes-friend, sometimes-anatagonist Paul Tillich was to receive. Many of Barth's ideas became influential in America as they resonated in the work of a remarkable pair of brothers, Reinhold (1892–1971) and H. Richard (1894–1962) Niebuhr. The two were sons of a German Evangelical pastor in St. Louis, where they attended Eden Theological Seminary—now part of the United Church of Christ—and from which they proceeded to graduate study at Yale. Reinhold began his career as a pastor in what was then the Evangelical and Reformed Church, in 1920s Detroit, where he had a chance to observe at first hand the inequities of the social order as manifested especially in race and labor relations. His early *Leaves from the Notebook of a Tamed Cynic* (1929) consists primarily of very personal theological reflections on these experiences, and reflects a combination of Barthian "theology of crisis" with a political critique of the American social and economic order that bordered on the radical.

After thirteen years in the parish, Reinhold followed the academic path already chosen by his brother, and began a long professorship in social ethics at the interdenominational Union Theological Seminary in New York City (where Paul Tillich also taught for a number of years before leaving for the University of Chicago and then Harvard). With Union as a base, Niebuhr rapidly gained national prominence as an "applied ethicist," leveling a profound criticism of American institutions in particular from his theological roots in the American Social Gospel and European Neo-Orthodoxy. Two of the most influential of his voluminous works are the two-volume *The Nature and Destiny of Man* (1941–1943), a systematic exposition of his theological position, and *Moral Man and Immoral Society* (1932), in which he explored the premise that human groups, such as nations, pursue an ethic based primarily on self-preservation, with little of the altruism found in at least occasional doses in individual consciences. Niebuhr was also instrumental in the founding of the magazine *Christianity and Crisis* (1941–), which brought to bear a somewhat sterner theological perspective on world events than in the long-established, more liberal, and at the time pacifist *Christian Century*. (The latter, still widely influential journal dates its present existence from its purchase in 1908 by Charles Clayton Morrison, a Disciples of Christ minister in Chicago.)

H. Richard Niebuhr spent over thirty years of his career teaching ethics, theology, and church history at Yale Divinity School. Sometimes characterized as a "theologian's theologian," H. Richard received less public attention than his more prolific brother, but arguably had an even greater long-range impact in academic circles. His earliest work, *The Social Sources of Denominationalism* (1929), has already been cited as a path-breaking analysis of American religious groupings in terms not of theology but rather such sociological categories as social class, race, region, and ethnicity. While taken largely for granted by later generations of scholars, Niebuhr's perspective was at the time radical, and drew on the thought of such German sociologists of religion as Max Weber and Ernst Troeltsch, as well as that of Karl Marx. The *Social Sources* was hardly a bloodless social-scientific exercise; instead, Niebuhr went well beyond the academic to level a scathing attack on American Christianity for what he bluntly called in his first chapter "the Ethical Failure of the Divided Church."

In his later work, Niebuhr refined his perspective into one more appreciative of the richness of the American theological tradition, as in his *Kingdom of God in America* (1937). In this work, he attuned himself with the movement under way among Harvard's literary historians, especially Perry Miller, to rehabilitate the reputation of the New England Puritans. The latter worthies, especially the more conspicuous Cotton Mather and Jonathan Edwards, had received rough treatment in the 1920s from the likes of H. L. Mencken and the historian Vernon Louis Parrington, who had caricatured them as antidemocratic bigots more like many repressive spokesmen for Victorian evangelicalism than their true selves. (Puritan studies flourished so abundantly during the next several decades that by 1970 one historian had observed that we now knew more about seventeenth-century Massachusetts than any sane person would want to.) Niebuhr's later works, such as *Radical Monotheism and Western Culture* (1960) and *The Responsible Self* (1963), were intended primarily for academic audiences, and helped shape the "contextual ethics" later developed by, for example, James Gustafson. No other Neo-Orthodox thinkers became nearly as widely known or influential as the Niebuhrs, but the primary emphases of the loosely constituted movement remained highly influential in many seminaries and pulpits until at least the 1960s.

Neo-Orthodoxy even became popular for a time in political circles, with prominent Kennedy-era figures such as George Kennan and Arthur M. Schlesinger, Jr., declaring their indebtedness to Reinhold Niebuhr's thought. The association of Presidents Nixon, Carter, and Reagan with various aspects of evangelicalism, however, displaced what influence Neo-Orthodoxy might have exerted in these quarters. In the seminaries, the "liberation theologies" of blacks, feminists, and Third World advocates, as well as newly influential work of Roman Catholic and evangelical thinkers, displaced the prominence of the older line of thought.

Still, the impact of Neo-Orthodoxy is hardly finished. Its staying power, if only in residual form, has subsisted in part in its refusal to reject the methods and findings of contemporary biblical criticism, as did its Fundamentalist contemporaries, but rather to rescue those findings from what both groups concurred were the excessive conclusions drawn from them by earlier Liberals. Another major strength of the movement was its sense of critical relativism. The doctrine of the sovereignty of God set limits on human possibilities, both moral and intellectual, and therefore precluded an overly easy identification of any creed, theology, or political position with the divine will. Reinhold Niebuhr expressed this stance memorably in *The Irony of American History* (1952), in which he argued that America's grand designs to lead the world have been repeatedly undermined by its inability to foresee the often ironic consequences of its prideful actions. On the one hand, this caution restricted the movement's influence somewhat; on the other, it shielded the movement from the faddish impermanence that befell the "Death of God" and "Situation Ethics" enthusiasms of the 1960s.

The theological basis of much of "mainline" Protestantism from the 1920s through the 1960s consisted of a mixture of themes from Liberalism, the Social Gospel, and the variations and critiques of these movements that Neo-Orthodoxy embodied. Many clergy were trained and much theological scholarship produced during these years, not only in denominational seminaries but in interdenominational divinity schools such as Harvard, Yale, Union (New York), and the University of Chicago. By the 1960s, consortia of theological schools began to develop in major academic centers such as Boston, New York, Atlanta, Chicago, and Berkeley, in which the seminaries of several traditions, including Roman Catholic, combined—often around the nucleus of a major university and/or interdenominational theological school—to share academic resources. In these ventures is manifest another major aspect of "mainline" religious life: *ecumenism.*

"Ecumenism" is derived from the Greek *oikoumene,* which indicates the whole inhabited world. The term "ecumenical" received widespread circulation during the 1960s, when the "ecumenical council" meeting at Rome—Vatican II—gave rise to "ecumenical discussions" between Roman Catholics and representatives of other religious traditions. The Council also fostered a broader "spirit of ecumenism" aimed at promoting interfaith understanding, cooperation, and even possible reunion among the "separated brethren." In the sense of common action or merger between similar Christian groups, though, ecumenism has been a particularly potent force in twentieth century "mainline" Protestant life and thought.

The need for an ecumenical movement within the Protestant community can ultimately be traced to the fragmentation of the churches during the Reformation era, but is rooted more particularly in the distinctively American phenomenon of *denominationalism.* Again, as H. Richard Niebuhr demonstrated so memorably, the divisions within American Protestantism have had as much to do with social factors such as race, region, ethnicity, and social class as with ostensible differences over belief, worship, and polity. Polity, however, has played a role in that churches without a strong, centralized governance structure—Baptists, Campbellites, and Lutherans, for instance—have been particularly subject to schism over various issues.

Although the frontier era was a time of fierce competition for the allegiance of the unchurched, it also promoted cooperation, as in the interrelated agencies of the "Benevolent Empire." The Plan of Union of 1801, in which Congregationalists and Presbyterians agreed to avoid duplication of effort in newly settled territory, was another major indication of the bonds that held together the evangelical denominations. Issues of race and region, however, brought about long-lasting rents within the Presbyterian, Methodist, and Baptist communities—which, in the latter case, have not healed and are not likely to. Immigration patterns also worked against unity among the Lutherans, who created a bewildering plethora of synods based on various combinations of doctrine, ethnicity, and geography. Among Congregationalists, issues of doctrine combined with cultural and social issues to produce the Unitarian controversy and the split-off of the latter community in 1825. Only the Episcopalians emerged from the century relatively unscathed, with a brief regional division during the Civil War and a small-scale schism in 1873 that gave rise to the Reformed Episcopal Church.

If the nineteenth century was characterized by division, the twentieth has witnessed much healing. At the most liberal end of the spectrum, the Unitarians and Universalists overcame a diversity of origins based primarily on social class to form the Unitarian Universalist Association in 1961. The Unitarians' one-time conservative adversaries, the Congregationalists, had also grown considerably more liberal over the years. In 1931, they united with the Christian Churches, a restorationist group related to the Campbell-Stone movement, to form the Congregational Christian Churches. Parallel to this union of English-speaking churches was the uniting of the (German) Reformed Church with the German Evangelical Synod of North America—itself the product of earlier mergers—into the Evangelical and Reformed Church (1934). Finally, these two church unions combined in 1957 to form today's United Church of Christ. (A smaller number of Congregational churches rejected the merger and remain independent.)

Methodists and Presbyterians both moved to repair the breaches that had involved other issues, but were precipitated by the issue of the morality of slave-holding. In 1939, the Methodist Episcopal Church; the Methodist Episcopal Church, South; and the Methodist Protestant Church, the heir of an 1830 division over the role of laity, combined to form the Methodist Church. In 1968, this amalgamated body joined with the Evangelical United Brethren, which itself was the result of two earlier mergers (1922 and 1946) of several Pietist groups of German and Wesleyan background. Until eclipsed of late by the Southern Baptists, the resultant United Methodist Church was for a time the largest single Protestant denomination. Similarly, the northern and southern branches of the Presbyterian Church merged in 1984 to form the Presbyterian Church (U.S.A.). Like the Methodists, the northern branch (UPCUSA) was the result of a number of several earlier mergers, which included the absorption of the Welsh Calvinistic Methodists in 1920.

The final series of mergers worth mentioning in this connection is that which led to the creation of the Evangelical Lutheran Church in America (ELCA) in 1988. Nineteenth-century Lutherans had been divided into dozens of distinct groupings based primarily on the arrival at various times and in various parts of the country—primarily Pennsylvania and the upper Midwest—of separate migrations of Germans and Scandinavians. By the early 1960s, two principal mergers had occurred to form the American Lutheran Church (ALC; primarily midwestern) and the Lutheran Church in America (LCA; more eastern). In 1976, a liberal spin-off from the ultraconservative Missouri Synod gave rise to the Association of Evangelical Lutheran Churches (AELC), which considered itself a holding operation, maintaining a temporarily distinct identity while awaiting, and helping to precipitate, a merger with the two larger merged groups. As the names of these more recent groups indicate—the ALC and

LCA, for instance, could scarcely be differentiated simply by name—the older sources of disunity had vanished in the wake of Americanization, and ecumenicity finally triumphed over residual particularism.

A final aspect of the ecumenical movement that deserves mention is the emergence of cooperative associations that have worked to transcend denominational differences in the interests of enhanced mutual understanding and cooperative endeavors. The "Benevolent Empire," the Plan of Union, and the broader-based American Evangelical Alliance of the nineteenth century all provided precedents for these endeavors. The immediate stimulus to a genuinely national association of churches came from the Social Gospel movement, and resulted in the creation of the Federal Council of Churches of Christ in America (FCC) in 1908. This new alliance, which included thirty-three denominations as members, immediately turned its attention to such contemporary social issues as the Bethlehem steel strike of 1910, on which it issued a caustic report on the exploitative practices of the steel industry. The FCC merged with other groups in 1950 into the newly created National Council of Churches of Christ in the U.S.A. (NCC), with offices at 475 Riverside Drive (the "God Box") in New York City. The NCC includes as members the "mainline" Protestant denominations, the major black Baptist and Methodist churches, most of the Eastern Orthodox churches, and a few smaller groups such as the Church of the Brethren. Its work focuses on areas of interdenominational cooperation such as evangelism, education, and ecumenism; in the area of social action as well as its liberal theological foundations, its work has frequently come under fire from conservatives within and outside its member churches.

Another source of interfaith cooperation at a still broader level was the missionary movement, which from the days of the Benevolent Empire had been a major concern of American Protestants. The Student Volunteer Movement for Foreign Missions had been organized in 1886 by America's most distinguished organizer of mission work, John R. Mott, at a conference convened by Dwight L. Moody. Together with representatives of the Young Men's Christian Association (YMCA)—another evangelical vehicle whose constituency transcended denominational lines—and of several northern European countries, Mott helped organize the World Student Christian Federation (WSCF) in 1895 at a meeting in Sweden. This new group took as its goal and slogan "the evangelization of the world in our generation," reflecting an optimism still possible among evangelicals and liberals alike in the calm before the First World War. Mott was also involved in the first world missionary conference held at Edinburgh, Scotland—an impetus that gave later rise to the International Missionary Council (IMC).

The IMC was one of the component organizations that would eventually combine to form the most global expression of Christian unity yet devised: the World Council of Churches (WCC), which was formally established in 1948 in Amsterdam. The WCC's other major sources were two international Christian movements that had both originated in the early twentieth century for parallel reasons. The Life and Work movement focused on applied social ethics in a turbulent world, and had its first conference at Stockholm in 1925. Similarly,

Faith and Order—concerned with the theological and political grounds of Christian cooperation—first met in 1927 in Lausanne, Switzerland, with representatives of 108 churches in attendance. Both of these movements continued to sponsor international conferences after they had become absorbed into what was in considerable part their own creation, the WCC.

The World Council of Churches in the mid-1980s consisted of 304 participating churches from 100 different countries. The members span the Protestant spectrum and also include many of the Eastern Orthodox communions. Prior to Vatican II, the Roman Catholic Church refused to take part in the activities of the WCC and its constituents. Although it has not formally joined, it now sends observers to WCC events and has created a permanent structure for dialogue. In addition, bilateral ecumenical dialogues between Roman Catholic theologians and representatives of most of the other major Christian traditions—especially Anglican and Eastern Orthodox—have become ongoing affairs, with a considerable degree of agreement already attained on key matters of belief (though not polity).

Interfaith dialogue among the Eastern Orthodox, Roman Catholic, and "mainline" Protestant groups now is a commonplace of American religious life. (Fundamentalists and many evangelicals, however, keep their distance.) Similarly, a considerable degree of reunion has taken place within the major denominational clusters, with the exception of the Baptists, who remain divided among the conservative Southern Baptist Convention, the "mainline" American Baptist Churches, the black National Baptist groups, and a plethora of smaller churches. On the other hand, even liberal and "mainline" Protestants have balked at the prospect of actual organic union with groups outside their own "families" whenever such proposals seem to become actual possibilities. Most recently, the Consultation on Church Union (COCU), launched by the Presbyterian leader Eugene Carson Blake in 1960, has largely remained in the realm of good wishes. Conceived as a plan for the close association, if not actual merger, of the principal "mainline" and black Methodist denominations, it continues to hold periodic meetings, but does not give promise of very concrete results in the foreseeable future. At the core of each major tradition seems to lie a conservatism that balks at its uniqueness becoming submerged in a broader synthesis. Perhaps Andrew Greeley was right in his hypothesis that denominational allegiance has replaced ethnic identity for many Americans, and that the need for some such particularistic identification remains unshakable.

CHAPTER 43

"Mainline" Protestantism in the Later Twentieth Century

Although the term *mainline* as applied to Protestantism is hardly technical, it still evokes a constellation of religious ideas, institutions, and movements specific enough to be very useful as an informal description. The following are some of the more important constitutents of that constellation:

1. The seven denominational clusters: American Baptist, Congregational (UCC), Disciples, Episcopal, Lutheran, Methodist, Presbyterian.
2. Social status of membership based in the middle and upper classes, implying a relatively high degree of income, education, prestige, and influence in the community.
3. Membership primarily of northwestern European ancestry, especially British, Dutch, Swiss, German, and Scandinavian.
4. National or at least interregional geographical distribution.
5. Worship varying in its degree of formality, but conducted in English; decorous in its avoidance of public displays of emotion; and sharing a common heritage of music and hymnody as well as architectural styles.
6. Use of a variety of biblical translations, such as the *Revised Standard Version* (1946, 1952), reflecting ecumenical scholarship.
7. Theology, reflected in preaching, strongly influenced by the Liberal, Social Gospel, and Neo-Orthodox movements.
8. Inclusiveness regarding theological, social, and political opinions among clergy and membership, with the balance differing somewhat from group to group (e.g., considerable evangelical sentiment among Presbyterians, Methodists, and Baptists, but little within the UCC).
9. Employment of an often complex denominational structure for the coordination of periodical and book publishing, the production and distribution of Christian education curricula and materials, missionary work and evangelism, political lobbying, and other activities.
10. Patronage, especially by the clergy, of nondenominational journals such as *Christianity and Crisis* and the *Christian Century*.
11. Frequent reliance on interdenominational divinity schools as well as denominational seminaries for clerical education.
12. Receptiveness to ecumenical activity, ranging from community worship services on special occasions to participation in the National Council of Churches, to organic mergers within the same tradition.

13. A relatively low sense of denominational commitment among many constituents, who are willing to change affiliations according to local circumstances.

14. Involvement in social issues regarded as having moral dimensions, ranging from Prohibition to gay rights.

15. Reliance primarily on public or secular private education, with religious instruction provided through active Sunday School programs.

16. More broadly, an acceptance of and support for the American government and social order, at least until the multiple crises of the 1960s.

17. Growing out of this, a participation in the cluster of patriotic activities and attitudes sometimes known as the "Civil Religion."

18. Official receptiveness to the inclusion of minority groups and the ordination of women.

19. Openness, if sometimes cautious, to new ideas in the scientific, social, and ethical realms.

20. A tension between a tendency to accept American society and culture as given and good—to be "at ease in Zion"—and a prophetic mandate for active engagement in social change and reform.

The 1960s were a major turning point for the fortunes of these churches. At the seminaries and among the denominational bureaucracies and leadership, strong support coalesced for the social movements of the era—civil rights, protest against the war in Vietnam, and acceptance of and access by women, gays, and other minorities to full opportunity in church and secular life. The ordination of women and, still more controversially, of gays to the ministry began to become divisive in some denominations. As the nation grew weary of turmoil and a more conservative mood began to prevail in the 1970s, however, discontent among the rank-and-file occupiers of local pews began to manifest itself in a variety of ways. Pressure from the grassroots to slow down or halt the rapid changes of the previous decade began to be felt at higher levels of governance. More dramatically, membership began to decline conspicuously.

As Wade Clark Roof and William McKinney point out in their important sociological study, *American Mainline Religion* (1987), this decline had a number of facets besides a widespread and growing social conservatism represented most conspicuously at the national level in the persona of Ronald Reagan. One important demographic factor was the declining birthrate among the members of these denominations, with a resultant increase in the average age of their membership. (In the most extreme case, almost half of United Methodists were over 50 years old in 1983—an increase from 40 percent to 49 percent from 1957.) This decline in family size correlates with high levels of income and education, and has affected Jews even more dramatically than "mainline" Protestants.

Other possible external sources of attrition lie in the two broad religious constellations flanking the "mainline" on either side of the ideological spectrum. On the one side, evangelical, pentecostal, and other conservative churches began to experience extremely high growth rates, drawing in part on alienated "mainliners" for recruits as well as enjoying a high birth rate among their membership. Where the "mainline" had once benefited from the appeal of its churches as badges of upward mobility, the new respectability of the conservative Protestant spectrum, as well as reduced social pressure for religious belonging as a prerequisite for community acceptability, now undercut this (perhaps doubtful) advantage. On the other, "mainline" socialization of the young had not proven strong enough to resist the pull of secularity, or the attraction of a "do-it-yourself" spiritual life offered by "New Age" religiosity. Although the pattern of the return to church life by youthful dropouts continued once they themselves had become parents, it was not strong enough to counteract the corrosive effects of these other trends. Table 43.1 demonstrates this pattern concretely.

TABLE 43.1   Membership Populations of Various Churches, 1960 and 1982

Denomination	Membership 1960	Membership 1982	Percentage Change
Disciples	1,801,821	1,156,458	−35.8
Episcopal	3,269,325	2,794,139	−14.5
Lutheran (LCA)	3,053,243	2,925,655	−4.1
Presbyterian (N&S)	4,161,860	3,157,372	−24.1
United Church of Christ	2,241,134	1,716,723	−23.4
United Methodist	10,641,310	9,405,164	−11.6
Compare with:			
Assemblies of God	508,602	1,119,686	+120.1
Church of God (Cleveland, TN)	170,261	463,992	+172.5
Southern Baptists	9,731,591	13,991,709	+ 43.7

Source: Jacquet, *Yearbook* 1986, 248–49. Note: Significance and accuracy of membership statistics vary considerably from group to group.

This is not to say that any of these denominations were in danger of dying out. Each still maintained a membership ranging from one to ten million, which are hardly paltry figures. By the last decade of the century, however, all were concerned both with their losses in numbers as well as with the diminished influence on national social issues that this decline portended.

So far we have been speaking of the "mainline" churches in collective terms. Underneath these useful generalizations, however, are a collection of highly particular religious communities, each with its own history, character, polity, membership, and characteristic emphases. Rather than write their collective obituary, it seems more appropriate to provide some sense of their still-vital individual stories. There are a number of plausible ways of grouping them—Roof and McKinney, for example, divide them into "liberal" (Episcopal, Presbyterian, UCC) and "moderate" (American Baptist, Disciples, Lutheran, Methodist). The following sequence is based instead on liturgy and polity, beginning with the "liturgical churches"—Lutheran and Episcopalian—which have as much in common in many ways with Roman Catholics as with fellow "Protestants"; continuing with the Methodists and Presbyterians, which have rather complex polities but less elaborate liturgies; and ending with those with the least formal structures, in the Free Church tradition— Congregationalists, Disciples, and American Baptists.

Where nineteenth-century Lutheranism in America had been characterized by fragmentation, the twentieth has been marked by movement instead toward a unity eased by the ongoing process of Americanization. The first major intra-Lutheran union was the creation of the United Lutheran Church in America through the 1918 merger of the two major "Eastern" groups, the General Synod and the General Council, with the United Synod of the South, which had split from the General Synod in 1862 over sectional issues. This new denomination was among the most Eastern-based and liberally inclined of the Lutheran denominations. It entered into a further merger in 1962 with the Augustana Lutheran Church (Swedish, 1860), the Suomi Synod (Finnish, 1890), and the American Evangelical Lutheran Church (Danish, various origins) to form the Lutheran Church in America (LCA), which later became one of the major components of the still more comprehensive union of the late 1980s.

The second major coalescence of Lutheran synods took place in the formation of the American Lutheran Church (ALC) in 1960. This merger consisted primarily of Midwestern synods of a variety of ethnic backgrounds: an earlier (1930) group of the same name, that had united the Buffalo, Ohio, and Iowa synods, all primarily German; the Evangelical Lutheran Church (Norwegian, 1917); the United Evangelical Lutheran Church (Danish, 1896); and, in 1963, the Lutheran Free Church (Danish, 1897). Most of these participating groups were the results of earlier mergers as well. The ALC traditionally had a primarily Midwestern constituency, with only a limited geographical overlap with the somewhat more liberal LCA.

Where the LCA and ALC stood for comprehensiveness, the third major Lutheran "family" of the twentieth century represented an unyielding firmness. The Missouri Synod had always stood for an uncompromising position on doctrine and practice, and some hints at a softening were dissipated with the ascendancy of J. A. O. Preus to its presidency in 1969. The Missouri Synod had never officially followed other Lutheran groups, especially the ULC/LCA, in accepting modern approaches to biblical interpretation, and this long-standing issue came to a head in the early 1970s at Concordia Seminary in St. Louis. Concordia was the premiere seminary of the Synod, and its faculty were considerably more open in their approach to theology and biblical studies than the denominational leadership—a situation not without parallel in other denominations. When the two parties were unable to agree on a solution, a large majority of the faculty left to found Christ Seminary, or "Seminex" ("Seminary in Exile"), which found a temporary home at nearby Jesuit-run St. Louis University. This move precipitated the formation of a temporary denomination, the Association of Evangelical Lutheran Churches, in 1976. The AELC drew its support primarily from dissidents on both coasts, and from the Synod's nongeographical but largely Midwestern English District.

The AELC was never intended as a permanent denominational structure, and rapidly took the initiative in bringing about discussions with the two other comprehensive and moderate American Lutheran groups. To the surprise of many, these discussions proved successful: They resulted in the formation of a new church including all three of these parties, known as the Evangelical Lutheran Church in America (ELCA). Final ratification of the merger took place at simultaneous meetings of the three groups in Chicago, Milwaukee, and Minneapolis—an indication of the geographical focus of their constituents—and went into effect on January 1, 1988. The extraordinary organizational complexity of American Lutheran denominational history thus was reduced to a remarkable simplicity by the late twentieth century, with the ELCA, the Missouri Synod, and the somewhat smaller and very conservative Wisconsin Evangelical Lutheran Synod accounting for all but about one hundred thousand Lutherans in America—that is, roughly 99 percent.

The increasing comprehensiveness and ecumenicity of the groups that now constitute the ELCA is indicative of a broader change in attitudes among many American Lutherans, especially their clergy. Historically, the close relationship between church and state in the German princedoms and Scandinavian countries where the Lutheran church had been established militated against extensive or critical involvement in the social order, and Luther himself supported the German princes strenuously against challenges to their legitimacy. In America, linguistic and geographical factors, together with the task of ministering to a large immigrant population, reinforced a predisposition among many of the later immigrants in particular to distance themselves from political and social affairs. The movement toward social involvement had its earlier leadership in the Eastern wing, where the evangelical drive toward social reform found a friendly audience among Samuel S. Schmucker and his followers. It was in this camp that first abolitionism and then temperance found Lutheran support, and also where Lutheran women first took an active role in social causes.

During the twentieth century, Lutherans divided over Prohibition, which ran against their traditional folkways in its inclusion of beer and wine among forbidden beverages. The impact of the world wars and the civil rights movement, however, combined with the growing acculturation of all Lutheran groups, has led to a greater receptivity to involvement in social causes, although by no means all AELC Lutherans could be classified as liberal or activist in their stance toward society. A major sign of change was the decision of both the ALC and the LCA in 1970 to ordain women, a constituency that still lacked even a vote in Missouri Synod congregational affairs until about the same time. The differences between the AELC and the Missouri Synod, in short, reflected broader divisions in American Protestantism in the later twentieth century. Despite some measure of inter-Lutheran cooperation, as in the development of a common *Book of Worship* in 1978, that division gave no signs of ending.

In worship, Lutherans have in recent years tended to identify themselves strongly with the other "liturgical churches" in their adherence to an elaborate, formal, traditional liturgy. Many congregations, accustomed for long to a simpler, more Protestant style of worship, have been reluctant to carry out the liturgy of the *Book of Worship* in its fullness. Hymnody and music more broadly are a strong component of worship, reflecting the heritage of Bach and Handel. With Episcopalians and Roman Catholics, Lutherans—even the tradition-minded Missouri Synod—have been in the forefront of architectural innovation. Here a major influence has been the work of the outstanding Minnesota-based architect and writer E. A. Sovik, who has advocated a discarding of the traditional longitudinal church shape in favor of an arrangement in which the altar-table is located centrally among the congregation.

Lutheran verbal culture has been dominated by religious writing; it is difficult to identify an American Lutheran literary tradition other than that represented in regional writings of the upper Midwest from Ole Rölvaag's *Giants in the Earth* to Garrison Keillor's *Lake Wobegon Days.* (The latter author, though not a Lutheran himself, acquired a considerable following during the 1980s in part through his humorously sympathetic depiction of Lutheran and Catholic church life in an imaginary small town in Minnesota.) Although the Lutheran theological tradition in Europe has produced some of the intellectual giants of modern Christianity, including Søren Kierkegaard, Albrecht Ritschl, Adolf Harnack, and Dietrich Bonhoeffer, American Lutheran thought has been concentrated more on historical work, as manifest in the studies of Arthur Carl Piepkorn, Martin E. Marty, and Jaroslav Pelikan. (The latter two are affiliated with interdenominational divinity schools.) Lutheran theologians such as Yale's George Lindbeck, however, have made major contributions to the ecumenical movement.

In demographic terms, Lutheran population continued to grow following the diminution of immigration after World War I, but primarily now through natural increase. Lutherans remain overwhelmingly of German or Scandinavian descent, and membership is predominantly by birth or marriage rather than conversion. The upper Midwest remains a Lutheran stronghold, with other pockets of influence stemming from colonial roots in New York and Pennsylvania, the Carolina Piedmont, and later settlements in the Pacific Northwest and parts of Texas and Southern California. Lutherans have traditionally been weakest in the Deep South and the Rocky Mountains. A sociological study conducted by Carl Reuss in 1980 indicated that Lutherans tended to be neither rich nor poor, to live in small cities or rural areas in the Midwest, and not to be involved in community activities other than those involving church, school, or service groups. Although their educational and income levels tend to be higher than average, their influence is predominantly local, and disproportionately few live near the centers of financial and political power.

By the time of the merger of three major Lutheran groups in the late 1980s, the membership of the respective constituencies was approximately as follows: ALC: 2,330,000; AELC: 110,000; and LCA: 2,900,000, for a total of about 5,340,000. In addition, the Missouri Synod claimed approximately 2,630,000 members; the Wisconsin Evangelical Synod, another conservative group, had about 410,000; and several small groups continued to exist autonomously. By the late 1980s, then, combined Lutheran membership was in the vicinity of eight and a half million.

The twentieth century was largely a quiet one for the Episcopal Church until the controversies of the 1960s and 1970s rendered it a major storm center. Denominational stances on public issues during the first half of the twentieth century were generally moderate, reflecting a constituency that was Anglophiliac (e.g., firmly committed to the British cause in World War I) and moderately Republican in its social and political outlook. (Franklin and Eleanor Roosevelt, however, provided an alternative model of the Episcopalian in public life during the 1930s and beyond.) Rapid growth, similar to that of the other "mainline" denominations, prevailed after World War II, but by the 1960s the denomination's association with upper-middle-class gentility began to undergo some major shocks. The church had already begun to take antisegregation measures during the 1950s, including moving the 1957 General Convention from Houston to Honolulu when the former city could not guarantee interracial accommodations. The most controversial action, however, was the 1967 General Convention's voting of $3 million for minority "empowerment," which in the context of antiwar and other liberal denominational positions led to considerable discontent and at times abrupt and dramatic declines in diocesan financial support. The falling-off of membership that subsequently began to afflict the Episcopal Church, like other "mainline" denominations, almost certainly reflected the distance between the political and social stances of the denominational leadership and the sentiments of the "grassroots."

The issues that have been most troubling to Episcopalians in the later twentieth century, however, have been internal questions about the ministry and the liturgy. One thorny problem for many denominations, including Episcopalians, has been the ordination of homosexuals. New York Bishop Paul Moore, Jr., created a stir when he ordained a self-designated, monogamous lesbian in 1977, but a subsequent motion of censure in the House of Bishops failed. In reaction, the General Convention of 1979 went on record against the ordination of practicing homosexuals and any others whose sexual relationships were carried out beyond traditional marital bonds.

The more acute issue concerning the ministry, however, was the ordination of women to the priesthood. Only one woman had even been admitted as a delegate to General Convention prior to 1970, but even by 1960 pressures from the rapidly developing feminist movement were militating toward a thorough reconsideration of the role of women in the church. The 1967 General Convention first authorized women to serve as lay deputies in succeeding conventions. The real turning point came in 1974 and 1975, when several groups of women were irregularly ordained, in some cases by retired bishops. Although these actions incurred the censure of the House of Bishops, the momentum for women's ordination had reached a point of irresistibility, and was approved finally by the 1976 General Convention assembled in Minneapolis. However, an "escape clause" was included that recognized the rights of individual bishops to refuse to ordain women on grounds of conscience—a right to dissent exercised by, among others, Presiding Bishop John M. Allin of Mississippi. Although women have since entered the priesthood in considerable numbers, they have frequently encountered the usual problems faced by female clergy of most denominations: reluctance of congregations to call them as rectors, and subsequent relegation to functioning as institutional chaplains and other roles lacking in full clerical authority.

The General Convention meeting in Detroit in 1988 anticipated that a woman would almost certainly be elected a bishop in the near future, and again provided an "escape clause" whereby congregations unwilling to accept the episcopal authority of a woman could import a male bishop on occasions such as confirmation when a bishop was required. The situation of women as clergy and bishops was further complicated by the reluctance of the Church of England to take similar steps, in part out of fear of endangering ecumenical conversations with Rome, and also in response to resistance in other parts of the Anglican Communion, especially in the Third World, to women clergy on cultural grounds. Despite these various sources of opposition, the Diocese of Massachusetts elected Barbara C. Harris, a black woman priest from Philadelphia, as suffragan (i.e., assistant) bishop on September 24, 1988, and she was subsequently consecrated on February 11, 1989. Her election touched off rumbles throughout not only the Episcopal Church but the entire Anglican world over the question of women and the Apostolic Succession.

One other blistering question echoed throughout the 1970s and 1980s, and together with the ordination of women led to vocal dissent, desertion from the ranks of the faithful, and even schism. Anglicans have periodically followed a variety of quests for spiritual fulfillment, including the "Renewal," or charismatic, movement of the 1960s. More dramatic were the bizarre ventures into spiritualism that led to the death in the Israeli desert of former California bishop James A. Pike (1913–1969), who had earlier been censured by his fellow bishops for his radical theological views. The traditional focus of Anglican piety, however, has been the public liturgy according to the rituals of the *Book of Common Prayer*. In 1967, the General Convention in Seattle authorized a reappraisal of the 1928 edition, which had preserved much of the language of versions dating back to the time of Cranmer. Various trial services were utilized during the 1970s, and a thoroughly revised version was adopted by the Convention in 1979. Traditionalists, who saw the older *Book*'s sixteenth century language as a great source of comfort and beauty, were outraged, and a society for a return to the older ways was organized to carry on a campaign to allow at least alternative use of the 1928 version, which can no longer be used officially in its entirety except with special episcopal permission.

In addition to protest, disgruntlement, and estrangement leading to withdrawal from active participation in church life, the twin innovations of women's ordination and *Prayer Book* revision helped precipitate what had previously been a rarity in the Episcopal Church: schism. The brief life of the Protestant Episcopal Church in the Confederate States of America during the Civil War years had no permanent institutional impact, and the only overt break in church ranks that had taken place prior to the 1960s had been the formation of the Reformed Episcopal Church by discontented evangelicals in 1873. (This group continues to exist, with a rather small constituency of about sixty-five hundred members and sixty-eight congregations.) The fallout of the "hot" issues of the 1960s and 1970s, however, led to the proliferation of a whole new set of traditionalist groups, including the Anglican Orthodox Church (1963), the American Episcopal Church (1968), the Old Episcopal Church (1972), the Anglican Episcopal Church of North America (1972), and the Anglican Church in North America (1977), which later became the Anglican Catholic Church. The relationships among these, which include schisms within schisms, are too complex to describe, but are typical of dissident movements without strong centralized control. Don S. Armentrout, the leading student of these movements, estimated in 1986 that the groups formed after 1976 (the year in which General Convention authorized women's ordination and gave preliminary approval to the revised *Prayer Book*) had a combined membership of about fifteen thousand, while those formed earlier had roughly the same number of adherents. The most severe losses to the Episcopal Church, though, have almost certainly come through a quiet dropping out into the realm of secularity rather than through losses to schismatic groups or other denominations.

In demographic terms, the Episcopal Church has always been national in scope but never vast in membership. Its traditional centers of geographical strength have been primarily in urban areas, especially in the Northeast, the Upper Midwest, and the Tidewater South, all of them concentrations of wealth and influence. There are many Episcopal parishes or missions (congregations unable to support themselves and receiving diocesan assistance) in smaller towns throughout the country; however, there are also many counties in the rural South, Midwest, and Far West with no Episcopal presence at all. In a few areas of the West, however, there is a numerical plurality or even majority of Episcopalians owing to nineteenth-century missionary work on Indian reservations.

According to virtually all sociological surveys, Episcopalians rank near or, usually, at the very top of American Christian denominations in income, educational level, occupational prestige, and other measures of social standing. However, a considerable number of traditionally Episcopalian families of wealth and influence are not active church members, while the church actively maintains and supports missions for poorer congregations. Although the image of the Episcopal Church as an "elite" or "establishment" denomination remains and in many ways continues to be based on social reality, the liberal social attitudes of the denomination as a whole stand in tension with some of the traditional stereotypes of that image.

Statistically, Episcopal Church affiliation remained very small until about 1840; increased continually and rapidly until the mid-1960s, when its overall strength stood at over 3.4 million; then began to experience the attrition that overtook other "mainline" denominations during the 1970s and 1980s. Statistics for 1983 indicate approximately 2.8 million baptized members and 1.9 million communicants. By the mid-1980s, the continual decline of the previous decade and a half had leveled off, and membership seemed stable. Other statistics for 1983 indicate a total of 7,387 churches and 13,342 clergy, of whom 7,695 were serving parishes.

Methodism, which originated as a devotional movement with a strong missionary outreach to the socially marginal, had by the twentieth century acquired a reputation as the most typically American of the "mainline" denominations. A Gallup Poll taken in 1967–1968 revealed that the Methodist Church was the religious group "most liked" by members of other denominations. It was also the largest single American religious group other than the Roman Catholic Church until its curve of declining membership intersected with the growth curve of the Southern Baptists in the late 1960s. At one time there were more Methodist churches in America than post offices; they can in fact still be found at assorted unlikely hamlets and crossroads in many parts of the country. Throughout most of its history, it has worked as a consensus church, exhibiting a moderation and a pragmatism that has been a major factor in its large and widely disseminated membership.

Today's United Methodist Church is the result of a series of mergers that reflect several variants on the Pietist-Wesleyan theme. The 1968 merger that created the UMC brought together The Methodist Church with the Evangelical United Brethren. The first group had been constituted through an earlier church union in 1939. That union had brought together the Methodist Episcopal Church and MEC South, which had split in 1844 over the permissibility of slave-holding by Methodist clergy, as well as the Methodist Protestant Church, which had split from the parent group in 1830 over demands for a more democratic polity. The Evangelical United Brethren were similarly the product of a merger, this one dating from 1946. The uniting groups here both represented the German-speaking Pietist tradition in America. The Church of the United Brethren in Christ had been founded in Maryland in 1800 by followers of two German immigrant preachers, Philip William Otterbein and Martin Boehm. (The movement had begun when Otterbein first met Boehm some years earlier and, on hearing him preach, exclaimed *"Wir sind Brüder"*— "We are brothers!") A similar movement grew around the Pennsylvania German Jacob Albright. "Albright's people," as his followers were originally known, banded together in 1816 to form *Die Evangelische Gemeinschaft*—later anglicized to The Evangelical Association. All shared the style of piety for which Wesley was noted, and subsequent Americanization eventually rendered superfluous the original divisions among these groups.

From its beginnings both in Britain and America, Methodism navigated between a nurture in the Anglican tradition and a willingness to adapt to new situations. Its distinctive polity illustrates this interplay between old and new. John Wesley's "classes" and the frontier circuit riders were early examples of this adaptability. Today's United Methodist Church, like most denominations, is organized at the national, regional, and local levels. (Organization aimed at practical results is a very Methodist characteristic.) *Conference* is the term used at each level:

1. The *General Conference* meets every four years, and makes policy for the denomination as a whole. It consists of about eight hundred delegates, including some from overseas churches belonging to the UMC, divided equally between clergy and laity. An extensive bureaucratic structure is organized into Commissions and Boards, which report to the General Conference. The denomination also operates an active publishing house and assists

a considerable number of colleges and other educational facilities. (The proliferation of colleges with "Wesleyan" as part of their name is testimony to the scope of Methodist involvement in higher education.) Missions, also a traditional area of Methodist emphasis, are directed at the national level as well. The *Discipline*, which dates back in its original form to John Wesley and contains the denomination's rules and standards, is revised periodically by the General Conference.

2. Five *Jurisdictional Conferences* operate on a regional basis, and are primarily charged with the election of bishops. A nongeographical "Central Jurisdiction" for blacks was abolished in the course of the formation of the UMC in the 1960s. Although many blacks participate in the Methodist tradition, the large majority belong to one of the three major black Methodist denominations—African Methodist Episcopal (AME), AME Zion, and Christian Methodist Church.

3. *Annual Conferences* are the rough equivalent of dioceses, but are defined in terms of constituent churches rather than geographical area as such. They are presided over by *bishops*. A bishop presides over an *area*, which may include more than one annual conference. In Methodist usage, bishops are not considered part of an apostolic succession. They receive life tenure in office upon election, but usually can remain for a maximum of eight years in any one area. In 1980 Marjorie Swank Matthews was elected United Methodism's first woman bishop, for the Wisconsin area. There were about forty-five active bishops in the UMC in the United States in the 1980s.

4. *District Conferences* are subdivisions of Annual Conferences, and are presided over by a distinctively Methodist officer, the *District Superintendent*. He or she is especially responsible for advising the bishop on the appointment of clergy and supervising their relationships with their churches.

5. The *Charge Conference* is organized around each local minister, who may serve more than one church in rural areas. The Ministry is divided into two orders: *deacons* and *elders*. Ordination to the latter rank, which usually takes place at Annual Conference, is a prerequisite for full Conference membership, which carries with it a guarantee of a ministerial assignment and life tenure. Women clergy, now quite numerous, did not receive full recognition as Annual Conference members until 1956, although they had been licensed to preach as early as 1866. Clergy couples, in which both mates have been ordained and share a ministry, had become quite common by the 1980s.

Methodist worship derives from the Anglican *Book of Common Prayer*, but its exact form varies considerably from church to church. Communion is most frequently celebrated quarterly, and a service for it similar to the Anglican is included in the hymnal for other Sundays, though many congregations prefer a more free-form style of worship. Methodist hymnody is eclectic, but at its core is the corpus of work of the incomparable Charles Wesley. Periodic attempts at purging the hymnal of "old-time" favorites, including both sentimental gospel hymns and militant Victorian works such as "Onward, Christian Soldiers," have usually not been very successful—an experience common to other denominations whose leadership may not realize the deep conservatism of ordinary churchgoers in matters of song. In the realm of architecture, the "Akron Plan," which features an interior arrangement in which large worship spaces could be quickly divided into smaller areas for Sunday School classes, was briefly popular around the turn of the century. No one style has ever prevailed, but the Gothic Revival, advocated tirelessly by Elbert M. Conover, the director of the MEC's Bureau of Architecture in the 1920s, was extremely popular for many decades.

Demographically, United Methodism is preeminently a national denomination. It is by far the largest of the "mainline" groups, with a membership of over nine million throughout the 1980s. Its traditional constituency has been solidly middle class, although a church of such size and scope—like the Roman Catholic—almost necessarily includes many representatives of virtually every region, social class, and ethnic group. Geographically, its center of strength has been described as the "south of the North and the north of the South." In the South, it has for well over a century constituted, with the Presbyterians and Baptists, one of the three dominant religious groups. Further statistics for 1983 include approximately thirty-eight thousand churches and thirty-seven thousand clergy.

For the Presbyterians as for the Methodists and Lutherans, the twentieth century has been a time of overcoming long-standing separations. Presbyterian divisions, as recounted earlier, lay in part in long-forgotten disputes in Scotland as well as in more pertinent arguments about theology (Old Side/New Side, frontier revivalism, Old School/New School, Fundamentalism) and slavery. The Fundamentalist controversy of the 1920s took its toll as heavily on Presbyteranism as on any denomination. J. Gresham Machen's Orthodox Presbyterian Church and the Bible Presbyterian Church remain today as small reminders of that dispute.

The largest division for many decades, however, resulted from the denomination's sundering by the Civil War. In the South, the Presbyterian Church in the United States (PCUS) was the primary institutional embodiment of an ongoing determination to maintain a militantly conservative stance on both theological and social issues. (The latter thrust was codified in theologian James Henley Thornwell's phrase, "the spirituality of the church.") In the North, the United Presbyterian Church in the U.S.A. (UPCUSA) was formed in 1958 through the merger of the erstwhile "Northern Presbyterians" (PCUSA) with the United Presbyterian Church in North America, a group mainly of Scottish origin. (The PCUSA had already absorbed most of the Cumberland Presbyterians and the Welsh Calvinistic Methodists in earlier unions.) In a joint meeting in Atlanta in 1983, North and South managed to overcome traditional differences to form the Presbyterian Church (U.S.A.) (PCUSA), which is today by far the dominant denominational expression of the Presbyterian/Reformed tradition in the United States.

Presbyterianism has traditionally distinguished itself most conspicuously from other members of the Reformed tradition (except the Dutch) through its polity—to which its very name calls attention. This polity is spelled out in the

PCUSA's *Book of Order*, which with the accompanying *Book of Confessions* makes up the denomination's constitution. (The *Book of Confessions* includes a number of historic documents such as the Westminster Confession, but its concluding "Confession of 1967" has little of Calvinism left in it.) On the other hand, contemporary Presbyterian polity does not differ that radically in practice from that of other denominations of national scope, such as the Methodists and Episcopalians, in its succession of increasingly more comprehensive units of governance. Specifically, these include the following in descending order.

At the national level, the *General Assembly* meets annually to legislate on matters of national significance. It consists of equal numbers of clerical and lay delegates elected by each presbytery, and is presided over by a Moderator, assisted by a Stated Clerk. As with most major denominations, a panoply of boards, agencies, and councils supervises national programs. Following what appears to be a broader trend, Presbyterian national headquarters relocated from New York City to Louisville, Kentucky, in 1988.

After the General Assembly come *synods*, regional bodies of somewhat less significance than in earlier days when travel and communication were less rapid. More important is the *presbytery*, roughly the equivalent of a diocese or annual conference in scope, but not headed by a bishop. Rather, like all other Presbyterian governing bodies, the presbytery consists of equal number of lay and clerical delegates from each of its constituent churches—or, more properly, the *sessions* that govern each local church. The presbytery functions rather as a collective bishop—ordaining clergy, settling disputes, and otherwise providing central authority and governance for its region.

In the local churches, clergy are known officially as "pastors" or "associate pastors." Although their functions are similar to those in other denominations, the Reformed tradition stresses preaching as a central concern, and "preaching tabs," which project from a clerical collar, are still at times worn with a robe while performing this task. In addition to the pastors, lay people are regularly elected to the offices of elders and deacons; it is from the ranks of the elders, who are technically ordained to their posts, that delegates to the presbytery are chosen. Governance of the individual church is primarily the responsibility of the session, which consists of pastors and elders together.

Presbyterian worship closely resembles that of other heirs of the Reformed tradition, such as Congregationalists and Baptists. It is liturgical in the sense that it usually follows an accustomed order, but that order is not as elaborate as in the "liturgical" churches—and, according to the *Book of Order*, "Public worship need not follow prescribed forms." Usual components include congregational and choral singing, the offertory, the Doxology ("Praise God from Whom all blessings flow . . . "), the Gloria Patri ("Glory be to God the Father . . . "), the prayer of confession, other prayers that come from the service book or are composed for the occasion, and, of course, the sermon. Communion ("the Lord's Supper") can be celebrated at varying intervals, from weekly to quarterly, with monthly observance—usually with grape juice taken from individual cups passed among the aisles—being most common. (This description of Sunday morning worship is applicable to many Methodist churches as well as the other three denominations yet to be described.) Several hymnals are employed, including the UCC's worship book, since none is mandated. Hymnody is for the most part similar to that of other "mainline" churches; a few hymns, such as several adaptations of the Psalms and later works such as Henry van Dyke's "Joyful, Joyful, We Adore Thee," are of specifically Presbyterian origin. Architectural styles vary, with Neo-Georgian a clear favorite especially in the South.

Historically, the Presbyterian Church has been national in scope (though for over a century divided regionally) and usually "elite" in clientele, with a membership not surprisingly heavy in British and especially Scottish descent. Although the membership, and especially the clergy, are sufficiently to the left of the political and theological spectrum for the denomination to be classified by some as "liberal," the Presbyterian church, like the Episcopal, has usually been regarded as one of the "status" churches in the many communities in which it is represented. A traditional Presbyterian emphasis has been on divine law and good order. In the past this emphasis has often been associated with a moral rigidity that has certainly diminished (if not entirely vanished) in more recent times. The membership of PCUSA at the time of the 1983 merger stood at about 3.2 million (of which roughly three-quarters came from the old UPCUSA) in twelve thousand churches, placing it third after the UMC and the ELCA among the "mainline" churches.

The close New England cousin of the PCUSA is the United Church of Christ (UCC), the result of the 1957 merger of the Congregational Christian Churches and the Evangelical and Reformed Church. Each of these branches was itself the result of an earlier union. In the first case, the dominant partner was clearly the Congregational Churches, the lineal descendants (after the departure of the even more liberal Unitarians) of the Puritan churches of colonial New England. In the latter case, the merger had taken place between two formerly German-speaking groups that, like their Catholic and Lutheran counterparts, had gradually become Americanized and desired union with their fellow heirs of the Reformed tradition. Two small split-off denominations were also formed at the time of 1957 merger by dissident Congregationalists.

The Congregational churches of the earlier nineteenth century were divided in sympathy among the new evangelicalism represented by Lyman Beecher, the "New Divinity" of Jonathan Edwards's followers, or still more traditional Calvinism. The open breach in 1825 with liberal Unitarians, who preferred to stay in fellowship with the more traditional clergy, was precipitated by pressure from militant conservatives such as Jedidiah Morse. Connecticut theologians Horace Bushnell and Lyman Beecher's confidante Nathaniel William Taylor began to provide an intellectual opening to the left, and by the Victorian era Liberalism and the Social Gospel found widespread support and leadership. The 1957 Statement of Faith adopted at the time of the union—as a "testimony rather than a test of faith"—is clearly Christian in content but just as clearly nondogmatic and even loosely poetic in form.

Today, the UCC is probably the most consistently liberal of the "mainline" groups on issues both of theology and individual and social ethics. Stances by the General Synod on public policy issues such as abortion, nuclear warfare, and gay rights are usually much to the liberal end of the spectrum. The UCC is consciously inclusive in its self-conception, and any number of caucuses of recognized interest groups, ranging from Hispanics to charismatics, are recognized by the denomination. Although policies on ordination are made locally, the ordination of homosexuals has not usually been controversial. Women have been ordained by Congregational churches since 1853, when Antoinette Brown became the first woman to enter formally the ranks of the clergy of a major denomination.

In polity, the UCC is, not surprisingly, highly faithful to the congregationalism that was first represented in this country by the Puritan churches, who had broken from the Church of England in part over this very issue. Final authority over all local governance questions, from finance to the engagement of clergy, resides firmly in the local congregation. Beyond congregational level, however, the governance structure more closely resembles that of Presbyterianism, with local *associations*, regional *conferences*, and a national *general synod* that meets biennially. This larger structure, however, has no authority over local churches, but formulates policy and coordinates activity for the denomination as a whole. In addition, a considerable network of boards, commissions, and other "instrumentalities" carries on the usual variety of denominational activities, including an active program of foreign missions.

Geographically, the UCC is, not surprisingly, strongest in those parts of the country where its constituent parts are most firmly rooted. On the Congregationalist side, this indicates New England as the major point of origin (with the footnote that many formerly Puritan churches in the Boston area are now part of the Unitarian-Universalist Association). From New England Congregationalists participated in the "Yankee Exodus" of the early nineteenth century, bringing New England religion and culture with them as they settled upstate New York, the lower Great Lakes area (e.g., northeastern Ohio), and across the continent to the Pacific Northwest and the San Francisco Bay. The other area of membership concentration lies in regions of heavy German immigration where the Evangelical and Reformed Church once found its constituency, such as Pennsylvania, Ohio, and Missouri. Lancaster Theological Seminary, in the heart of "Pennsylvania Dutch" country, now houses the denomination's archives, and Eden Seminary is honored in part as the site of the Niebuhr brothers' theological education. Denominational membership in the mid-1980s stood at about 1.7 million, spread among some sixty-four hundred churches and served by some ten thousand clergy. In the late 1980s, a movement was well under way to move the UCC's national headquarters from New York City to Cleveland.

The very name of the UCC indicates its receptivity to ecumenical discussion and merger. One of the denominations with which it has pursued such discussions most closely in recent years has been the Christian Churches (Disciples of Christ), the branch of the Restoration movement that has become most fully part of the "mainline." From the beginning, Alexander Campbell and other leaders of the movement were committed to an ecumenical policy, and saw their efforts as a way to transcend the differences dividing Christian communions by a return to Scripture as the sole guide for Christian belief and practice. This did not work out so well in practice, since the movement has since then experienced two major schisms. By 1906, a large group of more conservative and rural churches had parted company with their more urbanized counterparts, ostensibly over the permissibility of instrumental music in worship, to form the Churches of Christ. By 1952, another split had separated what are now known as the "Disciples" from a loose aggregate of more conservative congregations that refer to themselves as "Christian Churches and Churches of Christ." This latter group continues an early Campbellite theme by resisting formal denominationalization, and exists more as a loose fellowship of some twenty-three hundred like-minded independent congregations.

The second split in Restoration Movement ranks was occasioned by the Disciples's "restructuring" that culminated in 1968 and was made final in 1977. Although still firmly congregational, the Disciples now participate in a national denominational structure similar to that of the UCC, with a General Assembly and General Secretary providing coordination. The relationship of this leadership, based in Indianapolis, with the numerous denominational agencies, which are mostly in St. Louis, is sometimes described as "covenantal," without the formal hierarchical structure characteristic of, for example, the Methodists and Presbyterians. This noncoercive decentralization within the structures providing a broader unity is again very much in the Campbellite tradition. Periodicals also help bind the denomination together, as they do even more prominently in its more conservative counterpart, the Churches of Christ.

The Disciples have been particularly active in seeking ecumenical unity, and continue to pursue active conversations with the UCC without necessarily taking organic union as an ultimate goal. Disciples share a joint commission on the ministry with the UCC in New York state, and most clergy there hold joint standing in both groups. Cooperation between the two has also been achieved in such areas as foreign missions and church school curriculum. Conversations with other like-minded churches such as the American Baptists and participation in broader ecumenical endeavors such as COCU have been favorite Disciples' pursuits as well.

Although the Disciples stress their commonality with other Christians, their particular set of emphases and practices makes them distinctive. Worship services are in the Reformed pattern, and vary in elaborateness and formality with the character of the individual congregation. Little distinction is made between clergy and laity, and the latter can administer communion, which is celebrated weekly. Women have been recognized in the ministry since the nineteenth century. Like the Baptists, Disciples practice "believer's [i.e., adult] baptism," but do not insist on it as a prerequisite for members transferring from other traditions.

Demographically, the Disciples are primarily a middle-class denomination; this emergent status was most likely a significant but covert reason for the split-off of the Churches of Christ early in the century. Their geographical concentration lies in the middle vertical third of the nation: Texas, Oklahoma, Arkansas, Tennessee, Kentucky, Indiana, Ohio, and Missouri are all Disciples strongholds, as evidenced further by their administrative centers in Indianapolis and St. Louis. Conversely, Disciples congregations are less abundant in the Deep South, and very scarce in the Northeast, where the UCC and American Baptists provide regional alternatives. Membership in the 1980s was upwards of 1.1 million, distributed among about forty-three hundred churches and served by approximately sixty-eight hundred clergy.

The American Baptist Churches in the U.S.A. (ABC) were held together during the nineteenth century by the missionary and publication societies maintained collectively by a loose alliance of Baptist churches in the North. (Prior to the formation of the Southern Baptist Convention in 1845, Baptists from all regions had been involved in this alliance. The Baptists were the first major tradition to split definitively over the slavery issue.) In 1907 they coalesced into more strictly denominational form under the name of the Northern Baptist Convention, which later underwent two further name changes. (The shift from "Northern" to "American" in 1950 indicated a change in consciousness from regional to national status.)

It is noteworthy that the present name is plural in form, underscoring the traditional Baptist emphasis on decentralization and congregational autonomy, and the belief that the essence of the church resides in the local congregation. Paul M. Harrison, a prominent sociologist of religion and an American Baptist, has pointed out the implicit and unacknowledged tensions between the Baptists' insistence on local independence and the de facto power exerted by the national bureaucratic structures the denomination has created to coordinate the use of its collective resources. Delegates—several thousand in number—from potentially each of the sixty-three hundred local churches converge every two years for a national Biennial Convention, at which they are presented with requests for action by the various missionary and other agencies supported by the denomination as a whole. Local, state, and regional associations also provide means for coordinated activity, as does a national board that formulates policy between national meetings.

American Baptist churches consciously strive to play a mediating role between the liberal and conservative wings of the Protestant heritage, which results in comprehensiveness and, in the minds of some, identity confusion. Their theological heritage has been molded by both wings, as represented in the evangelical theologian Augustus Hopkins Strong (1836–1921) at Rochester Seminary; Walter Rauschenbusch (1861–1918), the theorist of the Social Gospel, who taught at the same institution for part of his career; the liberal Harry Emerson Fosdick (1878–1969) at New York City's Riverside Church; and Fosdick's Fundamentalist antagonist, William Bell Riley (1861–1947) of Minneapolis. Baptist ecumenism has been strong, but no organic mergers have yet resulted from negotiations with such kindred groups as the Disciples and the Brethren. Worship is very similar to that in other heirs of the Reformed tradition, with "old-time" gospel hymns playing a larger role than they would, perhaps, in most UCC churches. American Baptists recognize two "ordinances," baptism and communion. Baptism is, of course, of adults—"believers"—and by immersion, in a tradition dating back to the Radical Reformation.

American Baptist churches are predominantly middle class. As their original name indicates, they are concentrated in the northern part of the country, as well as in the Far West; however, the possibility of dual identification with other Baptist bodies has drawn a number of black congregations into joint affiliation, such as Martin Luther King's Ebenezer Baptist Church in Atlanta. Baptist diversity is also enhanced by its ethnic mix. This has benefited from both the "New Immigration" of the turn of the century, which brought in a number of Swedes, Italians, and other Europeans of diverse religious backgrounds, as well as the more recent Hispanic and Asian influx into the United States. Membership in the 1980s was in the vicinity of 1.6 million, with roughly fifty-eight hundred churches and seventy-four hundred clergy.

Such is the panorama of the "mainline" churches, whose fortunes have tended to wax and wane together. In the late twentieth century, their major institutional concern continued to be the leveling off—if no longer the absolute and even precipitous decline—in membership that had befallen most of them in the previous decades. For many, the causes of this decline lay not only in the competition offered by evangelical churches on the one hand and secularism on the other, but in what was perceived as a lack of spiritual vitality. The effervescence of individual spiritual experience and of community achieved in worship seemed to have yielded to the proliferation of bureaucratic structures and the special-purpose organizations that sociologist Robert Wuthnow has identified among the most important characteristics of what he has called the "restructuring" of American religion since World War II.

Another facet of this decline was a continuing unrest among the "grassroots" over the appropriateness of the national-level identification of several of these denominations with liberal positions on public issues. By the late 1980s, most of the "mainline" churches had tempered their positions on, for example, abortion, while continuing to advocate somewhat bolder stances on nuclear warfare and economic justice. In theory, issues of racial and sexual equality had been resolved, and conscious discrimination against women and racial minorities had become unthinkable. In practice, however, the sparse number of blacks in these denominations and the difficulty women clergy have encountered in being called to the larger churches indicate that the millennium has hardly yet been ushered in.

A final aspect of the common life of the "mainline" that deserves note concerns the realm of worship. During the same era that the Roman Catholic and Episcopal churches were moving toward a modernization of their somewhat archaic liturgies, many "mainstream" Protestants were converging with them in a renewed interest in more formal and traditional worship. The Gothic Revival style of architecture had spread widely among Methodists, Baptists, and Presbyterians in the early part of the century—until the Depression put a halt to most new construction—and arguably abetted this new inclination. The common body of hymnody of highly diverse origin—medieval, Lutheran, Reformed, Wesleyan, and Victorian—shared by all of these groups is another sign of convergence. More recently, most of these churches share a common lectionary, so that identical passages from scripture are read in thousands of churches of very different background or any given Sunday. Revision of liturgy, hymns, and even the Bible itself to omit gender-specific references, both to believers and to God, is another ongoing process that continues to generate often heated controversy. Although it is still not difficult to tell the difference between Baptist and Episcopal worship, the convergence in between is dramatic evidence of the continuing ecumenical thrust of the life of the Protestant "mainline."

CHAPTER 44

Conservative Protestantism: Culture and Politics

From the onset of the Depression through the years of World War II, conservative Protestantism fell into a period of cultural eclipse. Liberalism and Neo-Orthodoxy were clearly the theologies that dominated the seminaries and pulpits and the "mainline" denominations, and aggressive conservatism was viewed outside the South as a mark of ignorance and poor taste. At their most respectable, Fundamentalism and conservative evangelicalism were represented in the career of J. Gresham Machen (1881–1937), a professor of New Testament at Princeton Theological Seminary who abandoned that institution in 1929 in frustration over its drifting away from the Fundamentalist interpretation of orthodoxy, and went to teach at the newly founded Westminster Theological Seminary in Philadelphia. He was soon thereafter expelled from the northern Presbyterian Church for his role in a controversy over foreign missions, and helped found a schismatic denomination, the Presbyterian Church of America, in 1936 (which three years later took on the name of the Orthodox Presbyterian Church after another schism involving millennialism. It survives today with a membership of about eighteen thousand in the mid-1980s.) The General Association of Regular Baptists (1932) and the Conservative Baptist Association of America (1947) were similar split-offs within the northern Baptist community.

For most Americans outside its cultural orbit, the term *Fundamentalist* was likely to evoke an image not of Machen-style doctrinal conservatism but rather the Bible-thumping, tent evangelism associated with Billy Sunday, whose "sawdust trail" had relegated him to the smaller cities and towns of the South in the declining years of his tempestuous career. Faith-healers of doubtful authenticity similarly worked the circuit of the sleepy towns of Oklahoma, Arkansas, and Tennessee, claiming miracles that enthralled their audiences but met with skepticism and derision in the wider world. Sinclair Lewis's Elmer Gantry, a genial fraud probably based on Sunday, joined Babbitt and Main Street in the collection of images the 1920s had provided "sophisticated" Americans for dismissing the small-town life and the right wing of Protestantism as shallow and contemptible.

Where the Holiness and Pentecostal denominations withdrew almost completely from the broader arena of American religious life to form self-contained, largely regional subcultures of their own, much of the Fundamentalist community continued to define itself negatively in terms of mainline Protestantism and American culture more broadly. The National Association of Evangelicals, founded in 1942, represented a more ecumenical attempt to bring together conservatives of various stripes, but clearly constituted an alternative to the Federal (later National) Council of Churches. On the right, it was flanked by Carl McIntire's more radically separatist American Council of Christian Churches (1941), which insisted on members' keeping a strict distance from denominations tolerating Liberalism.

By the 1940s, conservatives were beginning to align along issues of this sort; during the next decade, the journal *Christianity Today,* edited by accommodative evangelicals such as Carl F. H. Henry, emerged as a rallying point for "Neo-Evangelicals" who repudiated the intransigence of more militant Fundamentalists such as McIntire. Since conservative Protestantism crossed and often repudiated denominational boundaries, it has from its beginnings lacked a clarity of institutional definition, as witnessed in its constituents' ongoing experimentation with nomenclature. (There is no clear line separating "evangelicals" and "Fundamentalists"; the latter, however, tend to be more aggressive in their postures—of late, in the political as well as the religious realm—and to emphasize biblical literalism and premillennialism.) Another consequence of its lack of firm institutionalization has been its inability to settle doctrinal disputes definitively; instead, such disputes have frequently led to internecine warfare between contending leaders and their factions, which has often resulted in lasting and unresolvable bitterness. (George Marsden's account of the history of Fuller Theological Seminary provides an interesting case study and analysis of this phenomenon.)

During these years of internal reassessment, conservative Protestantism rapidly emerged into the national spotlight through the career of William Franklin "Billy" Graham. Born in North Carolina in 1918 into an extremely conservative Presbyterian family, Graham was shaped by what William G. McLoughlin has identified as the Bible-centered subculture of between-the-wars Fundamentalism nurtured in summer camps and Bible schools and colleges. Graham prepared for what would be a stunning career as an evangelist in such hard-core Fundamentalist institutions as Bob Jones College—then located in that latter-day "burned-over" hotbed, Cleveland, Tennessee—as well as at Wheaton College, a more moderate evangelical institution. Ordained as a Baptist minister, Graham began his career as a worker for the Youth for Christ movement, and from that base moved into revival preaching. His entrance into the national spotlight came about through the widespread media coverage that his Los Angeles "crusade" of 1949 attracted—possibly through William Randolph

Hearst's legendary telegram commanding "Puff [i.e., promote] Graham." From that time on, Graham's crusades, first in tents and later in giant coliseums, became regular features of the American landscape, and the "decision for Christ" indicated by hitting what had once been a literal sawdust trail and shaking Graham's hand took its place in the vocabulary of the popular evangelical tradition.

Graham's subsequent career is representative of many of the profound changes that took place within the conservative Protestant camp from World War II to the 1980s. His early preaching was heatedly animated in tone and premillennial in content. Graham capitalized on American fears in the postwar years that the world was headed for nuclear annihilation, and the impending threat of "the Bomb" gave his apocalyptic message a new resonance. Handsome, clean-cut, and earnest, Graham soon acquired national celebrity status through his crusades and a radio program, "The Hour of Decision," in much the same way that his Roman Catholic contemporary Bishop Fulton J. Sheen became a national figure. Graham and Sheen both demonstrated how a skillful spokesman for a minority tradition could exploit the mass media to help bring his religious community into the mainstream of American life, gaining sympathy and acceptance if not massive conversions.

Like Sheen, Graham was also associated during the 1950s with militant anti-Communism, a cause that further enhanced the "American" image of each. By the end of the decade Graham had become the head of a virtual empire of communications, publishing, and preaching in his Minneapolis-based Billy Graham Evangelistic Association (established in 1950). His public prominence made his friendship highly desired by national politicians, and Dwight Eisenhower and his successors were all pleased to receive Graham's patronage. As a sort of informal national chaplain, Graham was perceived to be "friends" with Presidents Kennedy and Johnson, but was clearly more comfortable with the conservative Richard Nixon.

The Watergate debacle of the 1970s, however, taught Graham a potent lesson about the dangers to his credibility in becoming too closely associated with politicians whose careers might take unexpectedly disastrous turnings. Since that time, Graham has emerged as an elder statesman of conservative Protestantism, expanding his sphere of influence while simultaneously moderating his message. In the 1970s and 1980s he began to hold crusades in previously unthinkable locales such as the Notre Dame campus, Moscow, and various Soviet-bloc countries. Regularly rated in opinion polls as the most influential figure in American Protestantism, his message can now be best described as a moderate, ecumenical evangelicalism rather than the red-hot Fundamentalism with which he began his career.

The turmoil of the 1960s had a great impact on conservative Protestantism as well as on the broader society. The crisis in the South over segregation brought about by the civil rights movement generated considerable resistance, which took religious form in the establishment of numerous "Christian academies" as white-only alternatives to the integrating public schools. Bob Jones University, a bastion of aggressive Fundamentalism since 1926 and presided over by Bob Jones III since 1971, took an aggressive stance maintaining racial segregation, and was denied tax-exempt status by the federal government for its defiance of public policy.

On the other hand, many Neo-Evangelicals, especially of the younger generation, began to argue that liberal ideas of social justice were compatible with a traditionalist theology. More radically, "Jesus People," such as the Living Word Fellowship near San Francisco, adopted the communitarian life-style of the nearby hippies of Haight-Ashbury as a means of adapting evangelical teachings and values to the culture of the time. Still another path for younger people was taken by such militantly evangelistic groups as Bill Bright's Campus Crusade for Christ, which aggressively seeks out converts on college campuses. (InterVarsity Christian Fellowship, a more academically oriented evangelical campus group of British origin, had already been on the American scene since 1941.)

Accommodation to a more conventionally middle-class life-style also began to emerge in such 1970s phenomena as a "Christian Yellow Pages," which promoted evangelical patronage of businesses owned by the like-minded, and Christian book stores, which specialized in paperbacks and audiovisual materials promoting conservative Christianity. (The term *Christian* in these contexts became equated solely with its evangelical form.) Marabel Morgan's bestselling *The Total Woman* (1973) was a good example of this new drive to reconcile evangelicalism with mainstream culture in its simultaneous espousal of a traditionalist role for women with such sexually provocative techniques as greeting one's husband at the door wearing only "black mesh stockings, high heels and an apron." (One unsuspecting spouse's reaction was to exclaim "Praise the Lord!": Morgan, 119–20.)

On a different tack, what may be the largest-selling nonfiction work of all time other than the Bible itself is Hal Lindsay's *The Late Great Planet Earth* (1970). Lindsay here added a flair for drama to the tradition of dispensational premillennialism, and produced a scenario in which the sequence of events supposedly foretold in the Book of Revelation are acted out in the contemporary Middle East, with the United States and the Soviet Union as principal contenders. Lindsay's association of Fundamentalist theology with the political realm helped pave the way conceptually for the dramatic turn that conservative Protestantism was to take during the 1970s in its relation to the political order.

The entry of conservatives into politics on a large scale was symbolized by the victory of Jimmy Carter in the presidential election of 1976—a year celebrated by *Time* and *Newsweek* as "the year of the evangelical." Carter, a moderate Democrat and Southern Baptist who had previously served as governor of Georgia, was a self-proclaimed "born-again Christian," and the ensuing publicity as to his religious convictions helped push conservative Protestantism into the public spotlight in a generally positive fashion. (The antics of Carter's brother Billy also nurtured a sort of "redneck chic" manifested as well in the growing popularity of country music and television programs such as "The Dukes of Hazzard." Their sister, Ruth Carter Stapleton, was also well known as a faith-healer.) In response, Carter's opponent Gerald Ford, an Episcopalian, felt prompted to declare himself to have been "born again" as well. In any case, evangelicalism had now become respectable and even fashionable in a way reminiscent of the Irish Catholic John Kennedy's electoral victory sixteen years previously.

Carter's subsequent defeat four years later at the hands of Ronald Reagan was a tangible indication that a major transformation had taken place in the realm of American religion and politics in the last years of the 1970s. Reagan, whose religious background lay in the Disciples tradition but whose actual church affiliations were rather dim, had first acquired prominence as governor of California during the 1960s at a time when political conservatism was making a new impact on the American scene. Although Fundamentalist leaders such as Carl McIntire had for years been involved in militant anti-Communist activities, the candidacy of Arizona Senator Barry Goldwater, an Episcopalian of Jewish antecedents, in the 1964 presidential election marked the entrance of secular conservatism into the national scene. Although Goldwater was soundly defeated, his ally Reagan was simultaneously launching himself on a political career that would involve a new alliance between social and economic conservatives and Fundamentalists newly willing to abandon their traditional aloofness from compromising alliances. Goldwater's and Reagan's bases in the "Sun Belt" also betokened a new geopolitical shift in the nation, in which the South, the traditional seat of religious conservatism, was enjoying a prosperity and demographic resurgence in conjunction with its neighbors to the southwest.

The New Religious Right that emerged in the later 1970s and promoted Reagan's candidacy drew on a variety of ideas and tactics to lead conservative Protestants into a vigorously engaged style of political involvement. First, the tradition of church/state separation that had prevailed in the Free Church/Baptist tradition since the days of Roger Williams was quietly abandoned in favor of an activist stance by these churches on social and political issues. Second, conservative Christians demonstrated an eagerness and aptitude for taking advantage of the technological and logistical mechanisms of contemporary politics such as direct-mail solicitation, computerized data banks, and, especially, television. Fundraising and legislative lobbying through mail campaigns rapidly became major components of the New Religious Right's repertoire of tactics. Their alienation from modernity was thus objectively at an end, at least in regard to their appropriation of "high tech" media for their purposes. Third, an ideology that transcended denominational lines rapidly developed to explain what many conservatives perceived as the decadence of contemporary society and to provide a "social agenda" in the political realm to reverse these tendencies. Here again, their accustomed position as outsiders railing against modern society began to yield to a new and activist role in the political order while maintaining a continual barrage of criticism toward that order.

The ideology that was thereafter promoted by Jerry Falwell's Moral Majority, Inc., (later changed to the Freedom Foundation) and other New Religious Right vehicles such as the Religious Roundtable and the Christian Voice resembled very closely that advocated by Roman Catholic spokesmen during the later "ghetto era" of the 1940s and 1950s. In the international realm, anti-

Communism took on veritably mythical dimensions, as exemplified in Ronald Reagan's characterization of the Soviet Union as an "evil empire." (This phrase was reminiscent of Stephen Spielberg's popular "Star Wars" film trilogy, which had self-consciously incorporated many mythical themes.) Domestic "witch-hunting" of suspected subversives, though, never reached the dimensions of Senator McCarthy's crusade of the 1950s, and only ultra-far-right politicians such as North Carolina Senator Jesse Helms rattled this particular cage very frequently. International items such as opposition to American ratification of the treaty returning the Panama Canal to Panama, however, periodically emerged as items on the New Religious Right's agenda.

Usually more pressing were domestic issues, in which "Secular Humanism" emerged as a bugbear comparable in symbolic portentiousness to the "International Communist Conspiracy." "Secular Humanism," personified in New Religious Right rhetoric as an organized movement, was in reality more of a general trend in the society toward edging the supernatural out of the realm of public discourse. Crucial here was the role of the public schools, which conservatives feared were being corrupted by the Supreme Court ban (*Engel* v. *Vitale*, 1962) on school prayer. A prominent item on the "social agenda" of the 1980s, which received support from the Reagan Administration but has never been successful legislatively, was a "School Prayer Amendment" to the Constitution that would supersede the High Court's interpretation of the First Amendment in this case. Other conservatives, following the Roman Catholic example, opted for a parallel system of private religious oriented "Christian" schools, and have lobbied—again, unsuccessfully—for federal aid for such enterprises.

Closely related to the school prayer question was that perennial bone of contention, the teaching of evolution in the public school biology curriculum. During the 1970s, a number of state legislatures, primarily in the South, passed various laws not outlawing the teaching of evolution but rather mandating that an alternative, conservative Christian interpretation of human origins known as "creationism" or "creation science" be taught as well. The issue came to a head in 1982, when an Arkansas law requiring such teaching of creationism was overturned by a Federal court judge on the grounds that it violated First Amendment guarantees of church/state separation. This decision in what became popularly known as "Scopes II" was reinforced by a 1987 Supreme Court ruling that struck down a similar Louisiana statute.

In addition to the schools, the "social agenda" also focused extensively on the realm of sexual morality and its public regulation, a theme that had earlier been raised frequently by Roman Catholics and now drew many conservative Catholics into political alliances that three decades earlier would have been unthinkable. A key issue here was the Supreme Court's *Roe* v. *Wade* decision of 1973, which legalized abortion, and which social conservatives now worked to overturn. Picketing or disruption of abortion clinics, opposition to Planned Parenthood on the grounds that it promoted abortion, and other protest activities attracted support from conservatives from a wide variety of religious backgrounds.

Opposition to gay rights, which had become an open and usually controversial cause since the 1970s, was another aspect of conservative reaction to what was often portrayed as a nationwide cult of permissiveness and consequent collapse of moral fiber, which the dislocations of the counterculture of the 1960s and the Watergate debacle of the 1970s had fostered. "Secular humanism" here again became a focus for opprobrium in allegations that it had penetrated the prayerless public school curricula and substituted "values clarification" for instruction in moral absolutes. Finally, rapid changes in the culture in the realm of sex roles as well as sexuality manifested themselves in the quest for an Equal Rights Amendment to the Constitution, which in the 1970s passed both houses of Congress but failed to secure the requisite approval of three-quarters of the state legislatures. The maintenance of traditional male-female relationships and patriarchal nuclear family patterns was dear to the conservative cause, which had lobbied heavily against ERA passage.

By the later 1980s, it appeared that the "social agenda" had been more successful in its negative than its positive goals. The defeat of the ERA was quite possibly the New Religious Right's most conspicuous achievement. The Reagan Administration had continually espoused most of its other causes, but had not been successful—or very energetic—in promoting them in Congress. Simultaneously, organizations such as the Moral Majority began to lose popular support, due in part to the harsh character of their rhetoric as well as the disrepute into which "televangelism" more generally was falling at the time. Reagan had appointed one vocal premillennialist, James Watt, to be his Secretary of the Interior, but Watt was eventually forced to resign in the face of widespread protest against his environmental policies. Although Reagan's successor, Episcopalian George Bush, was widely endorsed by conservative religious groups, and engaged in campaign activities such as attacking the American Civil Liberties Union for its "permissiveness," the New Religious Right played little visible role in the 1988 presidential campaign.

The series of scandals labeled by the media as "Preachergate" or "Pearly Gate" during the mid-1980s marked the end of an important phase in the conservative resurgence of these decades. Media ministries of one sort or another had appeared in America since the introduction of radio in the 1920s, although Roman Catholic Father Charles Coughlin and Bishop Fulton J. Sheen had been the most successful clerical exploiters of radio and television in the earlier days of those media. The major prototype for latter-day "televangelism" was Charles E. Fuller's "The Old Fashioned Revival Hour," which was broadcast nationwide from Long Beach, California, on the Mutual radio network beginning in 1937. (Fuller was later instrumental in the establishment of Fuller Theological Seminary in California, to which he gave his name as well as substantial financial backing.)

Where earlier radio and television preachers had generally been scorned by larger audiences for the crudity of their appeal—as encapsulated in their catchphrase, "Keep those cards and letters coming in"—the television preachers of the new "Electronic Church" were far more sophisticated in their tactics. By the late 1970s, Independent Baptist Jerry Falwell, Assemblies of God ministers Jimmy Swaggart and Jim Bakker, charismatic Southern Baptist Pat Robertson, and Reformed Church of America Robert Schuller had all emerged as national celebrities who had attracted vast audiences through their smoothly produced television offerings. Their styles varied considerably. Swaggart, for example, was an "old-time religion" preacher who sang and screamed and moved about antically on the stage in a manner reminiscent of his cousin, Jerry Lee Lewis. Jim Bakker (BAY-ker) and his wife, Tammy, conducted their PTL ("Praise the Lord" or "People that Love") Club as a sort of evangelical talk and variety show, a format also employed by Pat Robertson. Schuller was the furthest of the group from the evangelical norm, and emphasized a message of worldly success from his Crystal Cathedral.

By 1987, however, the "Electronic Church" seemed about to come apart at the seams. Robertson had resigned from the ministry and his "700 Club" to pursue, unsuccessfully, the 1988 Republican presidential nomination, and had attracted negative attention through such extravagant claims as having diverted a hurricane from the path of his Christian Broadcasting Network headquarters in Virginia Beach. Jim Bakker was forced to resign as head of the PTL Club in the wake of both sexual peccadilloes in his past as well as serious irregularities in PTL's finances. The extravagant life-style led by Bakker and his wife (who had promoted, among other things, a line of cosmetics on their show), aroused considerable criticism for their worldliness as well as satire in the form of Ray Stevens's country music single, "Would Jesus Wear a Rolex on His Television Show?" Jimmy Swaggart was soon thereafter suspended by the Assemblies of God after revelations became public about his association with a Louisiana prostitute, while Robert Schuller and that perennial media personage Oral Roberts both received unfavorable publicity over financial questions. Scandal among celebrity clergy was nothing new, as the adultery trial of Henry Ward Beecher and the escapades of Aimee Semple McPherson had indicated decades earlier. To the televangelists' followers, however, the shock was considerable.

The media ministries of Swaggart, Bakker, and company involved vast sums of money, raised by continual solicitations on their television programs as well as through the mail. In addition to the programs themselves, many of these evangelists also developed large-scale auxiliary enterprises that in turn demanded large-scale support. Oral Roberts, for example, had begun his career in the demimonde of itinerant faith-healing, while his older contemporary A. A. Allen was casting out demons and William Branham raised the dead (including a defunct fish). After a successful career as a faith-healer, Roberts left behind his tent and the Pentecostal Holiness Church, affiliated with the United Methodists, and embarked on an "upscale" career as the host of a religiously focused variety program on television. He went on to found the Pentecostally oriented Oral Roberts University in Tulsa, together with the adjoining City of Faith medical center whose financial problems led Roberts to declare that God might "call him home" if his supporters did not produce sufficient funds to rescue the operation. (They did.) Falwell's Liberty University near his Liberty Baptist Church in Lynchburg, Virginia; Robertson's Christian Broadcasting Network, CBN University, Freedom Council, and other allied organizations; and the Bakker's Heritage Village, a Disneyland-like vacation resort in South Carolina, all evidence the entrepreneurial inclinations of successful televangelists.

A large scale of operation can also be seen in the "superchurches" that have emerged, especially among Southern and Independent Baptists in the extended South (including, e.g., Oklahoma and Indiana). Churches such as W. A. Criswell's First Baptist in Dallas often have memberships in the range of ten to twenty thousand, with a vast array of sponsored activities, including the radio programs that Fundamentalists such as William Bell Riley first began to sponsor in the 1920s. Independent Baptist churches such as Falwell's Liberty Baptist in Lynchburg have especially been a "growth phenomenon" of the 1970s and 1980s. The two groups differ mainly in polity—Independent Baptists have no formal ties with any other churches, while Southern Baptists participate in annual conventions that maintain, among other commonly sponsored enterprises, theological seminaries. In addition to rapid growth—membership in the Southern Baptist Convention exceeded 14 million by the late 1980s—the two communities have emerged as institutional bulwarks of aggressive Fundamentalism and conservative political causes. The SBC, however, has been torn between a slight Fundamentalist majority that gained ascendancy in the mid-1980s and a large moderate minority that has resisted, for example, the new drive to impose Fundamentalist orthodoxy on the denomination's seminary faculties.

Although Independent and Southern Baptists have enjoyed rapid growth and exerted considerable leadership among resurgent Fundamentalism, the spectrum of conservative Protestantism by no means ends with them. Pentecostalism has also enjoyed rapid growth, as evidenced in the dramatic membership increases enjoyed by such denominations as the Assemblies of God and the Church of God in Christ. The latter, which is predominantly black, also emphasizes the fact that conservatives still remain institutionally and culturally divided along racial lines. Fundamentalism, with its theological roots in the Reformed tradition, also differs doctrinally and experientially from the Wesleyan-descended Holiness and Pentecostal communities, though cooperation in "para-church" endeavors such as the Moral Majority and the "bridge" role of charismatic-oriented Southern Baptist Pat Robertson have diminished some of these historic differences in recent years. In addition to politically oriented groups such as the Moral Majority, extra-ecclesiastical agencies such as Demos Shakarian's Full Gospel Business Men's Fellowship International have also been instrumental in promoting these religious movements—Pentecostalism, in the case of the FGBMFI. Very different conservative traditions are also maintained by sizable groups such as the Lutheran Church, Missouri Synod, and the Churches of Christ, which separated in 1906 from the more urban and liberal Disciples of Christ. (Respective membership figures in the mid-1980s were roughly 2.6 million and 1.1 million.) In addition, many Mormons, Roman Catholics, and even Orthodox Jews shared some of the cultural emphases that characterize conservative Protestants, and have cooperated with them in political lobbying activities.

Internal diversity within the evangelical community is considerable, and cannot be cataloged in all its detail. A final note, however, should be made on the emergence in recent years of an intellectually oriented academic cadre among conservative Protestants, which has some of its origins in the group—

including Harold Lindsell and Carl F. H. Henry—that launched *Christianity Today* in 1956 as an intellectually respectable conservative alternative to *The Christian Century*. (Billy Graham, interestingly, played a major role in the journal's founding, and hoped that it would serve as a moderate evangelical alternative to the militant antiintellectualism of radical separatists such as Carl McIntire.) Institutions such as Fuller Theological Seminary in California (now the largest independent theological seminary in the world) and Wheaton College in Illinois have also emerged in recent years to a level of academic maturity comparable with that of their older Roman Catholic counterparts such as Notre Dame and Georgetown (not, however, without provoking attacks from the separatist right wing of Fundamentalism). Further, a number of younger scholars, identifying themselves as evangelicals and based at major research institutions such as Yale, North Carolina, and even Notre Dame, have begun to produce a scholarship of the highest quality on the histories of their own movements. As their counterparts in the churches continue to create conservative history, these scholars are poised to interpret it.

The conservative upsurge of the 1970s and 1980s has had a number of implications for American religious life. At one level, it reflects the swing of the pendulum away from a period of extreme social stress and cultural confusion—namely, the era of the civil rights movement, the Vietnam War, the counterculture, and Watergate. Another dimension lies in the relationship of religion to social mobility. As Frances Fitzgerald reported in her account of Jerry Falwell's Liberty Baptist Church, in her *Cities on a Hill,* Falwell's constituency lies not with the "disinherited"—the stereotypical Fundamentalists and Pentecostals of the Depression era—but in young people in the process of ascending into the lower and middle reaches of the middle class. The appeal of conservative religion for this large rising group lay in its sense of assurance that absolutes existed within a world in dizzying transition—in Grant Wacker's phrase, a social cohort "searching for Norman Rockwell." Parallels with the American Catholic community, which underwent a similar transition in status from working class to middle and upper-middle class a generation earlier, are again instructive.

The rapid rise of a complex religious culture that combines a conservative theological and social outlook with financial power and political activism will certainly continue to influence the shape of American society into the indefinite future. As already noted in passing, however, the enthusiastic appropriation by religious conservatives of modern techniques of communication and political lobbying are indicative of a major transformation of their earlier posture of alienated outsiders to a group on the brink of full participation in modern life. In addition, the emergence of complex bureaucratic structures within the "superchurches" and the conservative denominations may result before long in the same problems of impersonality and alienation that resulted in membership loss from the "mainline" churches into the conservative ranks. How distinct this subculture will remain from "mainline" Protestantism as its constituents continue to become more sophisticated and acculturated— "at ease in Zion"—thus remains to be seen.

CHAPTER 45

Traditions and Structures in the American Jewish Community

By the end of World War I, the institutional foundations had been thoroughly established for an American Judaism that was definitively divided into denominations, sharing a common tradition but irreparably split over differences on how to interpret and implement the dictates of that tradition. As indicated by the radically secular socialist element among New York's immigrant Jewish proletariat at the turn of the century, by no means all American Jews were religious. But for the many who remained so, a choice was necessary—first among the three major "denominations" or "traditions," and later among still other choices that the twentieth century presented.

The fourth and by far the smallest of the Jewish denominations is Reconstructionism, an outgrowth of the Conservative movement and inextricably bound up with the thought and work of Mordecai Kaplan (1881–1983). Kaplan, a professor at the Jewish Theological Seminary, was active throughout his long career in a variety of causes aimed at promoting the ideal expressed in the title of his most influential work, *Judaism as a Civilization* (1935). Kaplan's ideas combined several important concepts: that God is not personal, that the Jews are not a chosen people, and that Judaism is best understood as a complex of culture and tradition. The Reconstructionist emphasis on Jewish culture was a logical extension of some of the basic premises of Conservatism, but the deemphasis on a personal God was a radical break with tradition.

The Reconstructionist movement was not originally intended to form the basis of a new denomination, but rather to promote an emphasis within the Conservative community. The original synagogue-center that Kaplan helped found in New York in 1915 was the first institutional expression of this emphasis, and provided a means of promoting Jewish culture in a nonsupernaturalist context. In 1940 the Jewish Reconstructionist Foundation was established, which published the journal *The Reconstructionist* and promoted the *havurot* movement—that is, small fellowships within synagogue congregations for focused pursuits of Jewish studies and causes. A Reconstructionist Press was established in 1945, and published a controversial prayer book that same year. The Reconstructionist Rabbinic Fellowship was organized in 1950, followed by the Reconstructionist Federation of Congregations in 1955, which in 1961 added the words "and Fellowships" to indicate the inclusion of this particular vehicle for disseminating the movement's ideas. Finally, in 1968 the Reconstructionist Rabbinical College opened in Philadelphia.

Reconstructionism had thus traveled the road from a movement into a full-fledged tradition, though by far the smallest of America's Jewish traditions—about sixty thousand in the late 1980s. By the latter time, however, the tradition was beginning to modify its early deemphasis on the supernatural by including references to biblical miracles and the Messianic age in its newly revised prayer book. Most Reconstructionist Jews, however, understand these previously omitted themes as symbolic or mythical rather than factual in character. In addition, the inclusion of the Matriarchs with the Patriarchs in the new prayer book was an indication that movement was not entirely in a traditionalist direction.

Although they do not constitute a formal denomination, the *Hasidim* concentrated in metropolitan New York present one of the most picturesque and also controversial aspects of Jewish life. The Hasidic movement began in eighteenth-century Poland among the followers of Israel ben Eliezer, the Baal Shem Tov ("Master of the Good Name") or, for short, *Besht*. The Besht's message was shaped in a mysticism expressed in ecstatic singing and dance and a life of down-to-earth, extremely traditional Jewish piety. The Hasidic movement spread rapidly through the Jewish communities of Central Europe, and then, following World War II, to the United States. Of the roughly quarter-million Hasidim in the world today, some 80 percent live in America, and about half of those in Brooklyn.

The Hasidic communities of Crown Heights, Williamsburg, Rockland County, and other enclaves in greater New York practice a "total immersion" style of Orthodox (i.e., traditional) Judaism in which all other considerations are subordinated to the imperative of leading as pure a religious life as possible. One keynote of Hasidic practice is the sanctification of everyday life, even in its minutest details. Hasidic neighborhoods possess all of the material needs for strict observance: synagogues, religious schools, Hebrew bookstores, kosher restaurants and butcher-shops, and at least one *mikva*, or ritual bathhouse where Jewish women cleanse themselves before their wedding and after menstruation and childbirth. Women, whose marriages are arranged, play traditional family roles, are encouraged to have many children, and are strictly segregated from men during services. Hasidim of both sexes, however, eschew the life of the secular world as much as possible, and are easily recognizable by their distinct style of dress. Men wear beards (though not necessarily sidelocks), fur-rimmed hats, and long black coats, all characteristic of shtetl life in the Old World. Women shave their natural hair and wear wigs instead, on the grounds that their sexual provocativeness is thereby diminished.

The Hasidim in America are divided into a number of separate, sometimes violently antagonistic communities reflecting Old World divisions as well as contrasting attitudes to contemporary issues such as Zionism. The Lubavicher are probably the best known, in part because of their greater openness to outsiders and their zeal in evangelizing young Jews on secular college campuses. (Group names are derived from Hasidic "courts" in Europe or occasionally America where *rebbes*, or charismatic leaders, first attracted the community's core.) Their bitter enemies are the anti-Zionist Satmar, who in 1976 moved from Williamsburg to Monroe, New York, where they established a suburban complex of houses and apartments geared to Hasidic needs (e.g., twin sinks and stoves for ultra-kosher cooking). The *New York Times* periodically carries features on the conflicts not only of Hasidic groups with one another, but between Hasidim and their neighbors over such issues as Hasidic boys refusing to ride school buses driven by women.

Hasidism is the least centralized of the branches of Judaism, since each community, or court, looks to its *rebbe* (a variant of rabbi) for personal direction. Education at all levels is separate from that provided by other Jews as well as secular society. Some groups maintain small rabbinical seminaries, and the Skvirer of Rockland County, New York, help support a significant number of their young men while they engage in full-time Talmudic study.

Reconstructionism and Hasidism represent almost polar alternatives, each illustrating the diversity of interpretations possible within the broader Jewish tradition. Neither, however, has ever attained great numerical strength. The large majority of American Jews who express their heritage in religious terms have continued to divide themselves among the three major denominations or traditions—Orthodox, Reform, and Conservative—in a ratio of roughly 3:3:4. (Precise statistics, especially for Orthodox Judaism, are very hard to come by.) During the twentieth century, however, each of these traditions has seen some significant changes.

Although Reform enjoyed great popularity in its early years, its appeal to American Jewry, and even to many of its own followers, began to come into serious question as the events of the twentieth century cast doubts upon the optimistic rationalism of its early proponents. The Depression, the Holocaust, and the reestablishment of the State of Israel all raised new questions about the agenda expressed in the Pittsburgh Platform. Demography also had its impact, as the ranks of the latter generations of Reform rabbis arose from Jews of East European rather than German stock.

As a result of these pressures, post-World War II Reform began to exhibit some significant differences from its earlier character. As did most other American Jews, Reform Jews became enthusiastic supporters of Israel, and some, like Rabbis Stephen S. Wise of New York and Abba Hillel Silver of Cleveland, became prominent advocates of the Zionist cause. Hebrew began to find its way back into the liturgy, as did the voluntary practice of other Jewish traditions and observances. As early as 1937 the Central Conference of American Rabbis, the Reform counterpart of similar groups formed by the other Jewish denominations, drafted a new set of "Guiding Principles" that superseded the Pittsburgh document. This "Columbus Platform," as it came to be called, stressed Jewish particularity, as opposed to the universal aspects of Judaism emphasized by earlier Reform, and the importance of Sabbath and holiday observation, including the use of Hebrew. A later statement adopted in 1976 in San Francisco made clear the impact that the Holocaust and Israel had on Reform consciousness. Despite these shifts in priorities in a more traditional direction, however, all of these successive platforms have reaffirmed the Reform commitment to social justice and ethics, that is, Prophetic Judaism.

Conservative Judaism has continued to serve as a mediating force in the Jewish community, preferring to follow tradition but not averse to even dramatic breaches of long-standing custom when such a breach appears warranted by contemporary needs. One of the most striking examples of this is the Conservative decision to follow the example of Reform Jews in ordaining women to the rabbinate, of which Amy Eilberg became the first in 1985—following the example of Sally Preisand, ordained in the Reform tradition in 1972. Women rabbis of whatever tradition, however, have faced the same obstacles to full employment as have those ordained in the various Christian traditions, and frequently are called to chaplaincies rather than synagogues.

Although Conservatism, which modified the strict literalism of Orthodoxy in scriptural interpretation and ritual observance in a variety of ways, achieved numerical predominance in the twentieth century, the questions about Jewish identity raised by the Holocaust together with an influx of European Jews following World War II have given Orthodoxy a new vitality in America during the past few decades. In 1984, in fact, the *New York Times Magazine* carried a feature story about its revived appeal for highly Americanized business, professional, and academic people who have lately been drawn back to the traditional observance of their ancestors.*

In addition to the denominations, American Jewish life has taken institutional form in a wide variety of other ways. One of the first groups to take as its goal the service of the American Jewish community as a whole was B'nai B'rth (b'-NAY brith, "Sons of the Covenant"), which began in 1845 as an Ashkenazic fraternal organization but soon branched out into broader endeavors. Two of its best-known activities are its Anti-Defamation League, which investigates and publicizes instances of anti-Jewish activity, and its Hillel Foundations on secular college campuses for the promotion of Jewish religion and culture. Similar work in civil and human rights is carried out by the American Jewish Committee (1906) and the American Jewish Congress (1918), which also publishes the journal *Judaism*. *Hadassah* ("myrtle") was founded in 1912 by the redoubtable Henrietta Szold as a women's Zionist organization concerned particularly with the promotion of health in Palestine/Israel. The United Jewish Appeal (1934) has also been a major force in raising funds for the support of Israel. Perhaps the largest of these agencies is the Council of Jewish Federations (1932), which coordinates the work of 194 local federations and other agencies, and manages a half-billion dollar annual budget. For many secular Jews, support of the Federation is a primary means of identification with the broader Jewish community and tradition.

This list could be extended almost indefinitely to include any number of other Jewish activities and organizations, including such marginal ones as the Hineni Ministries, or "Jews for Jesus," founded in 1973 by aggressively evangelistic Jewish converts to Christianity. This panoply of institutions is indicative

* Natalie Gittelson, "American Jews Rediscover Orthodoxy," *New York Times Magazine*, September 30, 1984, 41, 60–61, 63–65, 71.

both of the appeal of the American style of voluntary organization to the needs and temperaments of American Jewry as well as the multiplicity and complexity of answers to the question of what it means to be a Jew in America. Religious options range from various forms of Hasidism on the right to Reconstructionism at the other extreme. Even then, membership in one of the four "denominations" can entail a great deal more than worship, as indicated by the panoply of educational, cultural, and recreational activities sponsored by many synagogues. And, though the synagogue has from the beginning served as the focus of American Jewish life, the emergence of such causes and organizations as those coordinated by the Federation is indicative of possibilities for identification and participation for those unwilling to make a particular affirmation.

CHAPTER 46

Jewish Identity and Jewish Culture in Twentieth-Century America

To be Jewish in twentieth-century America involves making choices—more so, perhaps, than for any other major religious group. Even among religious Jews, to live as a Jew is to participate to a greater or lesser degree in a subtle network of social and cultural patterns that are rooted partly in the long historical experience of the Jewish people, and partly among particularly American circumstances. To understand more fully the complexity involved in making such choices, we need first to review the social transformation of the American Jewish community after the great influx of Eastern European Ashkenazim during the years of the "New Immigration" had come to a halt.

While the assimilated and established earlier wave of Ashkenazim was engaged in coming to terms on one hand with these Yiddish-speaking newcomers, they were also experiencing opposite pressures from their Gentile counterparts. The era of the "New Immigration" was also that of the emergence of a new "upper crust" of American urban society precipitated by the amassing of vast new fortunes by the "robber barons." This elite was symbolized in the famous list of "The 400" New York families who constituted a closed social clique in which Jews, no matter how wealthy or cultivated, were unwelcome. During succeeding decades, social institutions such as urban and country clubs, resort hotels, and the more prestigious Eastern colleges began either to bar Jews entirely or, as in the case of the "Ivy League" schools, to impose tacit but very definite quotas on the number of Jewish applicants who could be admitted.

These policies, which did not begin to come under serious public scrutiny until the close of World War II (e.g., in the film "Gentlemen's Agreement"), precipitated the creation of a parallel set of institutions catering primarily to Jews. American Jews had from early in the nineteenth century banded together for a combination of religious, fraternal, and philanthropic purposes, and external pressures now advanced the process still further. (Stephen Birmingham has amusingly chronicled the emergence of a "Jewish 400" in his popular *Our Crowd* and similar, later developments among Jews of Eastern European descent in *The Rest of Us.*) The ultimate result was a network of institutions such as Grossinger's and other resorts in the Catskills's "Borscht Belt," country clubs catering respectively to German and Eastern European Jews, Jewish debutante parties, and the like.

In the economic sphere, a similar process was at work through which Jews, together with others not of British descent and Protestant affiliation, found entree into the higher reaches of the larger corporations and law firms difficult or impossible. Jewish fortunes were rather made in firms founded and maintained by Jews themselves, such as the clothiers Hart Schaffner and Marx, or the brokerage house of Lehman Brothers Kuhn Loeb. Entry into academic and professional life was facilitated by traditionally free tuition at New York's City College, which emerged for thousands of immigrants and their children as a symbol of secular salvation in this new "promised land," supported by a strong work ethic and the prestige that Talmudic learning had enjoyed in the Old World. Medicine, dentistry, and psychiatry attracted many young Jews, and the numerous universities of the New York area provided opportunities in teaching and scholarship.

American Jews, especially those born in America of Old World parents, thus found themselves in a problematic situation. On the one hand, they were still perceived by many Gentiles as the perennial outsiders, simultaneously strange and familiar. Like other ethnic groups especially of eastern Mediterranean origin, they were superbly adapted by culture and experience for success in a commercially oriented society where education, enterprise, and adaptability all conduced toward material reward. However, they were often barred from access to the highest levels of acceptance—into business and law firms, prestigious colleges, and resorts and social clubs. In a few brand new areas of American life, such as motion pictures, they were able to enter at the proverbial ground floor and give that industry a distinctive culture of its own. Whether creating or reacting, however, American Jews of the early to middle twentieth century took part in shaping a distinctive social and cultural realm of their own, drawing in part on tradition and in part on contemporary experience for its ingredients. To seek the roots of a distinctively Jewish-American culture, we have to retrace our steps many centuries to reconsider the historical experience of the Jewish people after the final downfall of ancient Israel.

Jewish culture is a rich and complicated subject, reflecting the long and intricate history of the Jewish people. Its ultimate roots are in the Hebrew Bible and the Talmud, which are obviously religious in character, but also reflect the intertwining of religious motifs and regulations in the minutest details of everyday life. From the beginnings, Jewish culture was not primarily a matter of detached theological speculation, but one that permeated the lives of ordinary Jews and gave shape to the very stuff of their existence.

With the onset of the long process of Diaspora, a separation began to take place in this wholeness that had been possible when the Hebrew people had lived with one another in their own land and under their own governance. The Septuagint, for instance, reflects the Hellenization of Jewish culture in the translation of scripture from Hebrew into the previously alien Greek. The Sephardim and the Ashkenazim had to come to terms with the dominance of Muslims and Christians, respectively, and the cultures they developed reflected an accommodation of Hebrew tradition with Gentile ways. Again, language reflects this process of accommodation. The Sephardim in Iberia developed a speech called *Ladino,* based on Castilian Spanish but with an admixture of words from Hebrew and other Mediterranean languages. More important for the American Jewish experience, the Ashkenazim gradually came to speak *Yiddish,* a Germanic language, like Ladino modified with additions from Hebrew, but drawing from the various Slavic languages of the host cultures—Polish, Russian, Czech—as well. In both cases, these distinctively Jewish languages served as a vernacular tongue for everyday affairs, while Hebrew, pronounced somewhat differently in each case, continued to be the language of worship and learning.

The question of Yiddish is a useful way of posing the question of the meaning of Jewish culture in America. Sephardic Jews were quick to adapt to American ways, and Ladino did not survive long in the New World environment. Although some of the early Ashkenazim in America spoke Yiddish, the later, larger contingents from the German states were among the most assimilated of American Jews; they spoke German, and soon learned English as well. It was not until the influx of hundreds of thousands of Eastern European Jews in the later nineteenth century that the question of language became seriously problematic in the Jewish community. German-American Jews looked askance at the newcomers' Yiddish, which could not claim, like Hebrew, a religious justification. Yiddish was clearly a mark of ethnic, or cultural, identity, rather than of religion. Even the organized Orthodox community shared with Reform a desire to Americanize these newcomers by teaching them English as rapidly as possible. The use of Hebrew in ritual may have been debatable, but the vernacular was not.

As Irving Howe has demonstrated in his popular *World of Our Fathers,* the Yiddish language was the core of the Jewish-American culture that flourished briefly but ardently in Manhattan's Lower East Side during the decades around the turn of the century. Yiddish was the language of coffee-house debates, poems, popular drama, innumerable newspapers, the *landsman-schaften,* and everyday conversations in the home and on the street. It was spoken by learned rabbis and labor organizers alike. It expressed, in short, the identity of the Eastern European Jews as a people and a culture rather than as a religion. The separability of these concepts—people, culture, religion—has been a perennial topic of debate among religious and secular Jews alike.

As the Jewish immigrants and their offspring in New York and elsewhere began rapidly to assimilate into American society, Yiddish started to disappear as a living language. By the latter part of the century, only the *Jewish Daily Forward* survived as a Yiddish-language newspaper, and it was mostly among the elderly that the language continued to be a means of casual communication. The American Yiddish archives, YIVO, has had to campaign vigorously for the preservation of Yiddish-language publications in recent years, since little is now published in Yiddish and much of the output of the past has met the fate of ephemera regarded by later generations as having doubtful value. Except for the elderly and for recent immigrants, the language of American Jews has thus universally become American English.

American English, however, like the English language more generally, is a complex amalgam of elements from the widest variety of sources—including Yiddish. Leo Rosten, the author of the delightful *The Joys of Yiddish,* identifies a distinct variety of speech known as "Yinglish"—that is, a variety of English vernacular in which Yiddish words, phrases, constructions, and intonations play a prominent role. "Yinglish" is spoken not only by some Jewish-Americans, particularly those nurtured in predominantly Jewish neighborhoods, but by others as well—for example, those participating in the "show biz" cultures of New York City and Hollywood. Yiddish words that have entered the American vocabulary are especially those that characterize distinctive personality types or social roles: the *gonif,* or crook; the *yenta,* or gossip; the *kibitzer,* who offers unsolicited comments; the *schnorrer,* or beggar; the *schlemiel,* or clumsy unfortunate. Although these are character types that were once familiar in the now-vanished shtetl, their universality has rendered Yiddish a happy medium with which to render them in "Yinglish." In addition to words, phrases such as "alright already," "so I lied," and "Nazi-Schmatzi" use English words in Yiddish constructions or rhythms to indicate exasperation, sarcasm, or other desired special emphases.

In addition to language, food is another fundamental component of everyday life that has given Jewish-American culture a special flavor. Dishes such as corned beef and pastrami, matzoh balls, gefilte fish, and latkes (potato pancakes) have multiple origins: in the laws of *kashrut,* in special holiday foods such as those used in the Seder, and in borrowings from the host cultures of central Europe. Restaurants and delicatessens in Jewish neighborhoods feature these and similar dishes, and many supermarkets have special sections of kosher foods. In addition to products that carry the "U" sign indicating approval as kosher, there is another label—"kosher style"—indicating only that the item is prepared in a traditional way, but does not carry rabbinical approval. Jewish-American cuisine, then, has both religious and secular origins, and may be consumed in conformity with traditional dietary prescriptions or simply as an exercise in secular enjoyment.

The emergence of a distinctive Jewish-American culture in the twentieth century has also generated an expression and reaction in what we might call "high culture," that is, literature and the arts that aim at more than simple entertainment. The moral and emotional ambiguities of the immigrant drive for material success were evoked in the now-classic novel *The Rise of David Levinsky* (1917). The author of this poignant work was Abraham Cahan, an immigrant labor organizer who later edited the *Jewish Daily Forward*. The plays of Clifford Odets and Elmer Rice reflected the social concerns implicit in Cahan's work. Henry Roth's *Call It Sleep* (1934) and Michael Gold's *Jews Without Money* (1930) also drew on the immigrant experience for their subject matter, as did some of Bernard Malamud's earlier works such as *The Assistant* (1957) and *The Magic Barrel* (1958). The postwar transition of much of the Jewish community from immigrant slum to prosperous suburb received scathing attention in Philip Roth's *Goodbye Columbus* (1959) and *Portnoy's Complaint* (1969), which dealt satirically and even scatologically with such stereotypes of American Jewish culture as the "Jewish-American Princess" and the "Jewish Mother." At a somewhat lower level of literary aspiration, popular novels such as Leon Uris's *Exodus* (1958) and Herman Wouk's *Marjorie Morningstar* (1955) dealt respectively with the independence of Israel and the ambiguities of assimilation and the quest of success among American Jews.

The work of three recent Jewish-American winners of the Nobel Prize also illustrates aspects of what has sometimes been called a Jewish-American literary renaissance, displacing the role the South had previously enjoyed as a cultural source of powerful fiction. Elie Wiesel, born in Rumania in 1928, is a survivor of Auschwitz who later immigrated to America and has written some of the most significant fictional interpretations of the experience of the Holocaust. Where Wiesel composes in French, Isaac Bashevis Singer's writings are first written in Yiddish—like those of his predecessor, Sholem Aleichem—and then translated into English and frequently printed in such literary outlets as *The New Yorker*. Singer, who was born in Poland in 1904, takes as his world the pre-Holocaust culture of Central Europe's ghettoes and shtetls. His themes are drawn from everyday experience; the mystical world of the Hasidim and the *Kabbalah*, or system of esoteric and occult interpretation of Scripture; and the realm of Jewish folklore, populated with strange and wonderful figures like the *dybbuk*, or evil spirit, and the *golem*, or artificial human.

In contrast with both Wiesel and Singer, the novels of the third Jewish Nobelist, Saul Bellow, are set very much in twentieth-century America, especially Bellow's Chicago. (Bellow was born in Canada in 1915.) His characters, from *The Adventures of Augie March* (1953) to *Henderson the Rain King* (1958) to *Herzog* (1964), are usually Jewish, but the religious dimension of their lives, if any, is not a primary concern. Beginning with the situation of the Jew in America, Bellow expands into more universal questions of human meaning in the twentieth century urban context. Thus, he represents a transition into the realm of a number of other distinguished contemporary American writers who, though of Jewish origin, do not deal explicitly for the most part with distinctively Jewish subject matter—for instance, Norman Mailer, J. D. Salinger, Arthur Miller, and E. L. Doctorow. Rather, their work reflects a Jewish perspective in a broader sense, namely, that of the "marginal man" seeking meaning in modern secular life and developing—or failing to develop— personal or political responses in a postreligious world where the traditional rootless, alienated situation of the Jew has become normative for humanity in general.

On the latter theme, American Jews have reacted to their society with ambivalence. On the one hand, America has provided a refuge for millions of Jewish as well as other immigrants, offering economic opportunity in addition to freedom from overt persecution. On the other hand, the disparities between the land where the streets were allegedly paved with gold and the actualities of American life have prompted two typically Jewish responses: satirical critique and political protest. Early in the twentieth century many second- and third-generation Jews, like other minority-group members, found the emergent world of popular and mass entertainment an area in which institutional practices were too fluid for them to be automatically excluded. Although Jews more typically became sports commentators than sports heroes, the possibilities of show business seemed ready-made for their talents. First on the "Borscht Belt" of the Jewish resorts in the Catskills and in the vaudeville houses of New York, then on radio, film, and television, Americans Jews became intimately involved in entertainment, and especially in comedy.

Comic styles have ranged greatly, including the long-suffering, penny-pinching *persona* of Jack Benny; the antic vulgarity of Milton Berle; the sophisticated monologues of Shelley Berman; and the bitter, iconoclastic social commentary of Mort Sahl. The films of the Marx Brothers, in which Groucho, Chico, and Harpo wrought havoc with the conventions and pretensions of proper Gentile society, perhaps best encapsulate the possibilities of this kind of social critique. On the other side, reflecting a corresponding Jewish-American strain of ironic self-criticism, is Woody Allen's self-description of being "Jewish, with an explanation" (as in the plea of "Guilty, with an explanation.")

The line separating theater and politics is a fine one, and is also illustrative of some of the ambiguities of Jewish-American identity. No Jewish candidate has yet emerged as a serious candidate for the presidency. (Barry Goldwater, the 1964 Republican nominee, is an Episcopalian of Jewish descent, and Kitty Dukakis, the wife of the 1988 Democratic nominee, is Jewish.) A few Jews representing states with large Jewish constituencies, such as New York, have achieved distinction in Congress—for instance, Senator Jacob Javits. Although lobbying efforts by Jewish groups have been instrumental in securing American support for Israel, American Jews have more generally been supportive of political and social movements rooted in the ancient prophetic tradition of advocacy of social justice. Jews, for example, have been disproportionately influential not only in the B'nai B'rth Anti-Defamation League but in secular organizations such as the NAACP and the American Civil Liberties Union—as well as, traditionally, the Democratic Party.

Jews in both Europe and America have also played a leading role in more radical causes, beginning with Karl Marx himself. Jewish immigrants such as Samuel Gompers and Abraham Cahan were active as leaders in the early days of the American labor movement, and many Jews involved themselves in socialist causes. More controversial was the heavily Jewish membership of the American Communist Party in its heyday, before revelations about Stalin's purges and the anti-Jewish character of Soviet Communism induced serious afterthoughts in many. In a less political vein, the "Beat" culture of the 1950s found expression in the poems of Allen Ginsberg, including his "Kaddish." Later, during the "counterculture" era of the 1960s, the Jewish-American Abbie Hoffman (d. 1989) and Jerry Rubin played central roles in the formation of the "Yippie" Party, and were arraigned as part of the "Chicago Seven" following the militant protests against the Democratic National Convention in Chicago in 1968. Many other young Jews were active in various phases of the antiwar movement and such radical organization as SDS (Students for a Democratic Society). More recently, a number of "New York Jewish intellectuals" such as Norman Podhoretz have aligned themselves with the Neo-Conservative political movement of the 1980s, and secular Jewish journals of opinion such as *Commentary* have reflected this drift.

One explanation for the prominence of Jews in a wide variety of contemporary secular movements is based on the hypothesis of a simultaneous need by many Jews to divorce themselves from traditional Jewish particularism while continuing to maintain the tradition of prophetic witness. According to this theory, Marxian Communism, Freudian psychoanalysis, and a variety of other political and ideological movements are seen as an attempt to resolve the illusions and injustices of society by resort not to religion but rather to some other, nontheistic but nevertheless ultimate explanatory principle. To embrace such a cause is thus a means of being simultaneously Jewish and non-Jewish— an escape from the burden of a problematic religious heritage and ethnic identity while nevertheless carrying out the prophetic mission of Judaism. While such an approach inevitably oversimplifies, it does present some interesting insight into certain aspects of the secular dimension of contemporary Jewish culture.*

In the realm of education, Jews again have excelled in academic pursuits far out of proportion to statistical expectations. The roots of this may lie in part in a "success ethic" and also in the prestige that religious learning was accorded in the Old World. In America, that kind of learning has been displaced by the secular, and many American Jews have utilized nonreligious educational institutions extensively. The public school system and the tuition-free City College of New York both became vehicles for the "melting pot" and the process of upward social and economic mobility that characterized the second generation of the Eastern European immigrants. Although most American religious groups vied with one another during the nineteenth and earlier twentieth centuries in the establishment of colleges, Jews generally held back and preferred public and nondenominational private schools instead. One exception is the network of institutions maintained by the Hasidim and to a lesser extent by the Orthodox, of which Yeshiva University is the focus for the latter. The other exception is Brandeis University, established as a secular Jewish institution in 1948, and one of the few major private American universities to be founded since World War II.

For most American Jews, the pursuit of Jewish learning takes place in addition to rather than in place of secular schooling. All of the Jewish denomina-

---

* Kurt Lewin, quoted in Neusner, *American Judaism*, 98–99.

tions have sponsored educational programs for younger people, though with different strategies. Reform Jews have generally utilized instruction on weekends, while Conservative and Orthodox congregations have also sponsored day schools. Jewish community centers and synagogue-centers have also included extensive adult education in their programs. Only the Hasidim and some of the Orthodox have attempted to erect an entire educational system parallel to and apart from the American social mainstream.

In the realm of theological education, the leading Jewish seminaries—Hebrew Union College, Jewish Theological Seminary, and Yeshiva—have provided the bases not only for rabbinical education but also for research in Jewish studies in America. As with other American religious groups, most theology as well as other religious scholarship has emerged from the seminary context, augmented by the work of Jewish academics on secular university faculties. Prior to World War II, Jewish theology was mainly conducted in the context of the emergent denominational communities. Orthodox scholars generally pursued traditional Talmudic studies. Early Reform spokesmen such as Isaac Mayer Wise, David Einhorn, and Kaufman Kohler expressed themselves in that movement's early manifestoes and other writings. They advocated in particular the notion that Judaism's mission was universal, and that America rather than Palestine was the place to promote the call to spread monotheism in cooperation with liberal Christians. Conservatives such as Solomon Schecter began to articulate a more distinctive and particularistic path for Jews rooted in the preservation of Jewish traditions. Mordecai Kaplan, the founder of the Reconstructionist movement, began with the matrix of Conservatism but went on to substitute for the traditionally personal God of Judaism the phrase "God-idea," thus transforming God into a force arising out of the collective social experience of the Jewish people.

The experience of the Holocaust and the reemergence of Israel, however, led to a distinctive shift of emphasis in Jewish thought in America and elsewhere. The most urgent question was now that of *theodicy:* If there is a God, how and why does that God permit evil in the world? At one extreme, Richard Rubenstein denied in his work *After Auschwitz* (1968) that there was a God, thus joining ranks with the "Death of God" movement then popular in radical Christian theological circles. Rubenstein did not call for an end to Judaism, however, but rather argued that solidarity among the Jewish people, even without a theistic basis, was now more necessary than ever.

The more dominant note in contemporary Jewish thought was not so radical, but emerged out of the broader intellectual movement known as Existentialism. This approach was clear in the title of what has probably been the most broadly influential work of modern Jewish writing, Martin Buber's *I and Thou,* which takes as its starting point the personal encounter between God and the individual. Where Buber's popularity has been even greater among Christians than Jews given the universality of his message, his German contemporary Franz Rosenzweig rooted a similar approach more directly in traditional Jewish categories of God, Torah, and Israel. Variations on the theme of individual response to divine commandment in the context of Jewish tradition and community can be found in the work of twentieth-century American Jewish thinkers such as Eugene Borowitz, Emil Fackenheim, Will Herberg, and Abraham Joshua Heschel as well. Heschel (1907–1972), a professor first at Hebrew Union College and then at Jewish Theological Seminary, gained special influence through his active participation in the civil rights movement and other social causes.

Creativity in the American Jewish experience has manifested itself primarily in the realm of verbal expression, but has not been entirely lacking in the other arts. That it has not always taken primarily religious form is clear from the preeminence of Jews as violin virtuosi, but in the context of secular performance. The religious arts have focused on worship, where there has not been a strong distinctively Jewish tradition. Jewish-American liturgical music, for example, has been derived from a combination of Jewish and Gentile sources, and has not been notable. Its main distinction has been in liturgical pieces specially commissioned from secular Jewish composers such as Leonard Bernstein, Ernst Bloch, Arnold Schoenberg, and Kurt Weill. Folk music derived from both European and Middle Eastern sources, such as that popularized by recently revived *klezmer* bands, has gained a wide audience, and folk or folk-like songs such as "Hava Nagila" are now well known among Jews and Gentiles alike. Folk elements have also been incorporated into the paintings of Marc Chagall and the stories of Isaac Bashevis Singer.

As a consequence of the Diaspora, a distinctive style of Jewish religious architecture never developed in the Old World, and synagogues were usually designed in the styles of Christian or Muslim host cultures. America's first Jewish house of worship was the Touro Synagogue in Newport, Rhode Island (1763), designed by the prominent architect Peter Harrison in the neoclassical style. Nineteenth-century synagogues similarly utilized contemporary modes such as the Greek Revival, the Romanesque, and the Gothic. The desire for a more distinctively Jewish expression in the era of Romantic revivalism led to such structures as Cincinnati's B'ene Yeshurun (1866), which incorporated the intricate design elements of the Venetian Gothic with minaret-like towers evoking the Islamic tradition. This, interestingly, was the setting for Reform worship led by Isaac Mayer Wise. Even more exotic were the bulbous domes that graced the towers of New York's Central Synagogue (1872) and other "Jewish-Victorian" structures. The later twentieth century has seen dramatic experiments in new architectural idioms, such as Norman Brunelli's tent-like B'nai Jehudah in Kansas City (1958 and 1969). Modern synagogues sometimes feature striking sculptural renditions of biblical motifs as well.

A commentary on the character of Jewish culture in contemporary America should finally include a few words on the demographical and geographical patterns of the distribution of the American Jewish community. The approximately 5.3 million American Jews in the mid-1980s constituted the largest Jewish population of any nation in the world, equalling the combined total of its two nearest competitors, Israel and the Soviet Union. The New York City metropolitan area represented by far the largest concentration, with an estimated Jewish population of roughly 1.25 million (1983). Chicago, Los Angeles, Miami, Philadelphia, and Washington, D.C., together with northern

New Jersey, are other areas of heavy Jewish residence, though almost every major metropolitan area in America has a significant Jewish community.

Although Jews continue to be overwhelmingly urban or suburban in their residential preferences, their original concentrations in the cities of the Northeast and Great Lakes area have been modified by dispersion throughout the Sunbelt states of the South and West, following the broader national trend. In 1983, roughly 54 percent lived in the Northeast, 12 percent in the North Central zone, $17\frac{1}{2}$ percent in the South, and $16\frac{1}{2}$ percent in the West. Patterns of residential segregation, partially through self-selection and partly as a result of discrimination, persist in many places, and "Jewish neighborhoods" can be identified not only in older urban areas but in newer suburbs as well. A distinctive instance of special settlement is Miami Beach, to which Jewish retirees from New York City began to flock in the 1930s and where the Art Deco hotel district represents a unique ethnic and architectural enclave in American society.

This brief survey of American Jewish culture should make clear the complexity of the issue. Its sources are multiple, from folklife as well as the heights of contemporary thought, from Europe and the Middle East, all blended in the American crucible. One can attempt to differentiate "high" and "low" (or everyday) culture, religious and secular culture, or the amalgamation of various strata in such movements as Reconstructionism. For analytic as well as ideological purposes, it is possible to speak of the religion of Judaism; of Jewish culture(s); and of Jewish nationality or peoplehood, rooted in history and endogamy—all as separate and separable categories. Much of American Jewish dialogue has focused on the relationship of these aspects of the Jewish experience, and the plurality of answers to the question of American Jewish identity indicates that this dialogue is likely to continue with vigor.

CHAPTER 47

Vatican II and the End of the Catholic "Ghetto"

The decades that followed Leo XIII's encyclical *Testem Benevolentiae* were a period of physical expansion and intellectual retrenchment in the American Catholic Church, in which the attitudes of the English-speaking conservatives were to dominate. Hopes for the perpetuation of foreign-language ethnic parishes were soon dashed by episcopal policy, which frequently resulted in the assignment of English-speaking pastors to German or other ethnic parishes. Further, the onslaught of World War I brought about a nearly hysterical public revulsion against all things German. The war itself and the restrictive legislation passed by Congress during the 1920s slowed Catholic immigration considerably, and the passage of the years also promoted the process of Americanization as new generations were brought up speaking English as their first language and having it reinforced in parochial as well as public schools. The expansion of Catholic education at the secondary as well as the primary level by the 1920s also had the indirect result of promoting further standardization by bringing into being centralized high schools, diocesan school boards, and certification programs for teaching sisters.

This drive toward centralization and standardization was typical of institutional American Catholicism as a whole during the decades between World War I and Vatican II. This was the era of the "builder bishop," exemplified in such figures as Cardinals George Mundelein (1872–1939) of Chicago and Francis Spellman (1889–1967) of New York. These princely figures reigned over their sees with unchallenged authority; presided over ambitious building programs of churches, schools, and hospitals; and served as nationally recognized spokesmen on the "Catholic position" on public issues. Among these positions were calls for American intervention or a pro-Catholic neutrality abroad where Catholic interests were threatened, such as the Mexican Revolution and the Spanish Civil War; government aid to parochial schools, which were still promoted as an alternative to the secularism of the public system; opposition to Prohibition, which was interpreted as implicitly anti-Catholic in its incompatibility with European folkways and sacramental use of wine; censorship of films, many of which were said to promote immorality; and vigorous opposition to artificial contraception. After World War II, both Pope Pius XII and Cardinal Spellman emerged as incarnations of militant anti-Communism as much of eastern and central Europe fell under Soviet dominance, with a corresponding persecution of Catholic leaders such as Hungary's Cardinal Josef Mindszenty. American Catholic opinion on the wisdom of Joseph McCarthy's anti-Communist tactics during the 1950s varied considerably, though Cardinal Spellman's endorsement of the Catholic junior senator from Wisconsin created the impression of a more monolithic support from his own church than was really the case.

Throughout this era the public stance of the institutional Catholic Church was remarkably uniform—only a few lay-edited journals such as *Commonweal* and *The Catholic Worker* publicly dissented on the issue of American neutrality in the Spanish Civil War, which would aid the pro-Catholic cause of Francisco Franco, and which became a touchstone of loyalty within the Catholic leadership. On political issues which primarily involved economics, however, Catholic sentiment was considerably less conservative than that suggested by these other positions on matters of public morals and international affairs. Leo XIII's encyclical *Rerum Novarum,* which promulgated the idea of the "just wage" and took a generally progressive stance on other issues involving the rights of working people, provided the groundwork for an influential movement in the American church exemplified in the career of Monsignor John A. Ryan (1869–1945), the "Bishops' Program of Social Reconstruction" of 1919, and the National Catholic Welfare Conference. Ryan and other Catholic clergy were also employed in labor mediation and other social programs during the administration of Franklin Roosevelt. Roosevelt had come to power in part through the support of Catholic working people, and in turn appointed unprecedented numbers of Catholics to the cabinet, the judiciary, and other branches of the federal government.

Other, more extreme political options also began to be promulgated by articulate Catholics during the 1930s and beyond. Charles Coughlin (1891–1979) gained national attention as the "radio priest," broadcasting from his Shrine of the Little Flower in Royal Oak, Michigan, and publishing his views in his periodical *Social Justice*. Coughlin began during the Depression era as a supporter of the New Deal, but soon turned against Roosevelt and toward a not-too-covertly anti-Jewish populist program similar to that of Louisiana's Huey Long. Coughlin helped form a new Union Party to oppose Roosevelt in 1936, but its complete failure and subsequent pressure from his bishop forced him into political retirement by the end of the decade.

At the other end of the political spectrum was the Catholic Worker movement, formed by the ex-Communist Catholic convert Dorothy Day (1897–1980) and her French anarchist friend, Peter Maurin. Inspired by a philosophy of Christian personalism, which made the integrity of each human being the central object of religious concern, Day and her compatriots set about the propagation of a critique of the American capitalist economic order in their tabloid, *The Catholic Worker*. Another major feature of the Workers' program was the "houses of hospitality" they established in many large cities, where volunteers provided food and shelter for the down-and-out. The Worker movement, which has survived its founders, taught that the American system erred in its dehumanization of the poor, and tried to provide positive Christian alternatives to the facelessness of the contemporary social order. Although Day's ideas were in many ways radical, her doctrinal orthodoxy and care not to offend ecclesiastical leadership saved the movement from episcopal interference or censure.

This strain of Catholic radicalism received a new lease on life during the 1960s, when the civil rights movement and the Vietnam War engaged many Catholics in new forms of political activism. Particularly prominent in this era were the brothers Daniel and Philip Berrigan, respectively a Jesuit and Josephite priest. Both were subsequently imprisoned for their roles in a variety of antiwar protests, including the destruction of draft files at Baltimore and Catonsville, Maryland. Catholic opinion on Vietnam was by no means homogeneous, however, as Cardinal Spellman continued his public anti-Communist stance in support of American involvement in Southeast Asia.

Catholic support for World War II had been much less controversial, and the "last good war" helped to promote the integration of many "ethnic" Catholics into the mainstream of American life through the inevitable mixing of peoples brought about by military service and the emphasis of wartime propaganda on the "melting pot" motif. Following the war, thousands upon thousands of Catholic veterans benefited from the provisions of the "G.I. Bill" of 1944, which made higher education a reality for unparalleled numbers of young men and which also promoted the expansion of educational facilities, including those sponsored by the Catholic Church, on a vast scale. The effects of the postwar exodus to the suburbs, where previously separate ethnic groups now mingled easily in parishes with no history of national or linguistic particularity, also furthered the process of assimilation and homogenization. Television also contributed to the progress of these latter social forces. The Catholic Church's public image was especially enhanced by the "Life Is Worth Living" series, the video vehicle for the extraordinarily mediagenic Bishop Fulton J. Sheen (1895–1979).

The early 1960s were dominated in American Catholic public life by the "two men named John": John F. Kennedy and Pope John XXIII. Previously, only one Catholic had ever received the nomination of a major party for the American presidency. Al Smith, the Irish-American governor of New York who ran unsuccessfully as a Democrat against Herbert Hoover in 1928, was defeated in part through organized anti-Catholic efforts, but also because of his urban and ethnic image, his anti-Prohibition stance, and the futility of any Democrat's trying to oppose the high tide of Republican prosperity prior to the Great Crash of 1929. Kennedy was also an Irish-American with ties to a big-city ethnic political machine—his grandfather "Honeyfitz" Fitzgerald had been mayor of Boston during the 1920s—but his Harvard pedigree and personal charm helped him overcome prejudice and eke out a narrow victory over Richard Nixon in 1960 despite attempts by anti-Catholics to use the religious issue against him. Kennedy's assassination in 1963 elevated him to the status of virtual popular sainthood; since his breakthrough, the Catholic affiliations of political figures such as his brothers Robert and Edward, as well as Edmund Muskie, Alexander Haig, Sargent Shriver, Mario Cuomo, and Thomas P. "Tip" O'Neill has seldom been problematic.

During the 1984 presidential election, however, Democratic vice-presidential candidate Geraldine Ferraro, an Italian-American Catholic Congresswoman from New York's borough of Queens, became engaged in a public controversy with New York Archbishop John O'Connor over her refusal to oppose government-funded abortions. Many conservative Catholics had by this time abandoned their traditional association with the Democratic party. Instead, they supported the "social agenda" of Ronald Reagan, which called for a strong public stand against abortion, pornography, and other sexually related issues. This alliance of Catholics with militant Protestant evangelicals such as Jerry Falwell and Pat Robertson represented a dramatic change from the hostility between the two camps that had characterized American religious politics in the past.

The impact of Vatican II—"Pope John's Revolution"—on the American Catholic community was even more profound. Its thoroughgoing program of reappraising traditional thought and practice created a mood of great hope and expectation among many Americans, as well as a profound sense of disorientation for others—at times the same people. The abandonment of the Latin Mass and experimentation with new liturgical forms, including the use of folk music, was the most visible change. It contributed to the loss of a sense of certainty, which was exacerbated by the widespread disregard of

Paul VI's condemnation of artificial contraception. On the right, the Traditionalist Movement led in the United States by Father Gommar A. De Pauw led a number of parishes into near-schism in their rejection of the vernacular liturgy.

At the other end of the political spectrum, both lay and religious women became more and more vocal in their protest against the exclusion of their sex from positions of authority and participation in the life of the church. Controversies on this subject ranged from the use of "altar girls" at Mass to the ultimate question of the ordination of women to the priesthood, which in the late 1980s still seemed only a remote possibility. In the meantime women, even though unordainable, continued to enroll in Catholic seminaries, with growing numbers of women providing instruction in theological subjects. Roman Catholics such as Rosemary Radford Ruether had by the 1980s attained prominence as advocates of increasingly radical critiques of "patriarchal," male-dominated church life and thought, and devised new rituals such as those of the "Women–Church" movement to express a distinctively feminist perspective in liturgy as well as belief. Mary Daly, based at Boston College, went even further in renouncing her Catholic identity while continuing to teach at a Jesuit institution. Her later work, such as *Pure Lust* (1984), was based in part on the old European traditions of witchcraft which antedated Christianity. Others, such as Indiana University's Mary Jo Weaver, remained clearly within the Catholic fold while vigorously advocating the enhanced role of women in the church from a historically grounded theological perspective. Still another manifestation of ferment in the postconciliar church was less easily classified on a "left" to "right" spectrum. This was the *charismatic* movement that affected the Catholic community as well as many "mainline" Protestant denominations beginning in the 1960s. This "Catholic Pentecostalism" was based on the premise that ordinary believers could receive such "gifts" of the Holy Spirit as speaking in tongues (*glossolalia*) and spiritual healing. Beginning on college campuses—Duquesne, Notre Dame, the University of Michigan—it spread throughout many parishes, and frequently resulted in stresses between its proponents and skeptics. On the other hand, such practices were not contrary to official church teaching, and were never condemned. By the 1980s the charismatic movement had subsided somewhat, but continued as a significant current in church life.

Ethnic pluralism has also been a continuing source of change and challenge in twentieth-century American Catholicism, though the cast of characters has changed almost completely from that of the the era of of "New Immigration." Immigration from Europe was delayed substantially by the outbreak of World War I and curbed drastically afterwards by a series of laws passed by Congress during the nativistic 1920s that placed severe limits on the numbers of immigrants allowed yearly from regions other than predominantly non-Catholic northwestern Europe. Emergent regions of the world were rather to provide much of the new American stock of the present century. The influx of significant numbers of Spanish-speaking Catholics into the United States did not commence until the end of the nineteenth century, when Mexican *braceros* or "wetbacks" began to seek work in American agriculture. The acquisition of

Puerto Rico as an American territory in the aftermath of the war with Spain in 1898 added another potential source of Hispanic population, resulting in massive immigration to the mainland, especially New York City, following World War II. Then, following Fidel Castro's overthrow of the Batista regime in 1959, a new exodus of middle-class Cuban Catholics began, this time settling mainly in Miami and South Florida. French-speaking Haitians, again mainly Catholic, followed in the 1980s, as did refugees from the strife-torn countries of Central America. In both of the latter cases, controversial immigration policies made easy settlement in the United States difficult, and Catholic and other church groups began to devise such counterstrategies as the "sanctuary" movement—the sheltering of illegal refugees by church people—to deal with the newcomers' needs.

Even though all of these Spanish-speaking groups were overwhelmingly Catholic by background, the form their religious life assumed once they were settled in the United States varied considerably. Mexican-Americans, who concentrated in the area from Texas to Southern California (with northern outposts in Chicago and Detroit), brought with them a Catholicism heavily tinged with folk religion. The elements of the latter included a devotion to the Virgin of Guadalupe, the patron saint of Mexico, who reputedly appeared to the Indian Juan Diego near Mexico City in 1531. Images of the Virgin appear all throughout Mexico and the American Southwest—in churches, in living-room shrines, on automobile dashboards. Although this devotion is quite orthodox, the central role it plays in regional religious life renders Mexican-American Catholicism highly distinct. Religious folk-life also includes a reliance on local healers, or *curanderos,* typical of other folk religions, as well as beliefs in a wide variety of miracles and supernatural events not formally recognized by the institutional church. The cultural distance between a primarily Irish-American hierarchy and a Spanish-speaking laity has also proven problematic in terms of bringing Mexican-Americans firmly under official ecclesiastical guidance. One sign of convergence of cultures, however, has been the role of César Chávez in bringing the spiritual and political resources of the Catholic Left to bear in organizing and otherwise witnessing on behalf of farm workers in California and the Southwest.

Other Hispanic Catholic groups have had different experiences. Puerto Ricans, for example, have tended to aggregate in "ghetto" areas of New York City and environs such as Spanish Harlem and the South Bronx. The absence of a strong institutional Spanish-speaking Catholic presence, combined with the zealous work of conservative Protestant missionaries, has resulted in the proliferation of Spanish-speaking Pentecostal store-front churches in these communities. (It was estimated in 1989 that 20 percent of Hispanic Catholics in the United States had converted to conservative Protestantism.) Cubans settling in Dade County, on the other hand, have come primarily from middle-class backgrounds, and their religious and political attitudes have been correspondingly traditional. Central Americans have not settled sufficiently into American life yet to have produced a distinct style, but the relevance of "Liberation Theology" to their situation is notable.

In addition to Spanish-speaking and Haitian immigrants, new groups of

Catholics arrived as a result of various worldwide political upheavals later in the twentieth century, particularly after the modification of the quota system by Congress in 1965. Catholic communities arose in many cities composed of Hungarian refugees following the abortive 1956 uprising against the Communist government; Cubans fleeing Castro's socialist regime in 1959 and afterwards; and many from southeast Asia, Central America, and the Middle East seeking refuge from the chronic political instability of those regions.

To round out this portrait of ethnic diversity, conflict, and comprehension, a final word needs to be said about the Catholic presence among two other significant minority communities in America. Although the vast majority of churchgoing blacks are affiliated with the Baptist, Methodist, and Holiness-Pentecostal traditions, a successful Catholic outreach to Afro-Americans did take place in two areas where a Catholic presence had existed since colonial days—Maryland and southern Louisiana. Other significant work was carried on by Katherine Drexel (1858–1955), the wealthy Philadelphian who founded the Sisters of the Blessed Sacrament to promote home missionary work among blacks and Native Americans, as well as a few predominantly black religious orders such as the Oblate Sisters of Providence. Most dioceses and religious orders were unenthusiastic about black candidates for the priesthood until fairly recently; however, James Augustine Healy, one of three brothers of Afro-Irish origin who entered the priesthood, served as Bishop of Portland, Maine, from 1875 to 1900. Work by Katherine Drexel's Sisters, the Bureau of Catholic Indian Missions (established 1874), and other attempts among Native Americans was similarly inconclusive. On the whole, Catholic efforts to evangelize Native and Afro-Americans have not been very successful, although the reappraisals necessitated by the upsurges of ethnic and racial consciousness during the 1960s have begun to lead to some serious evaluations of this situation.

Liturgical and theological experimentation, new forms of charismatic religious experience, and ethnic diversity all converged from the 1960s onward to promote a spirit of pluralism and effervescence within the American Catholic community, which included nearly one of every four Americans by this time. Other forces, however, worked in the direction of consolidation and retrenchment. The pontificate of John Paul II resulted in the same tensions in the American church as in Western Europe and Latin America, as the new pope attempted to reassert an authority that had been relaxed, deliberately or otherwise, by his predecessors.

In America, signs of this new attitude were reflected in the character of episcopal appointments—for example, of the conservative John O'Connor and Bernard Law to the crucial sees of New York and Boston, respectively. In addition, the Vatican in 1986 intervened directly into the life of the American church by suspending the teaching privileges of Charles Curran, a controversial professor of ethics at the Catholic University of America. Curran's stances on a number of issues, including abortion, euthanasia, and homosexuality, were regarded as moderate by many American Catholics, but seemed to Rome to deviate too far and too publicly from traditional Catholic teachings. During the same year the Vatican also deprived Archbishop Raymond Hunthausen of

Seattle of some of his authority and delegated supervision of such sensitive matters as marriage annulments and the employment of former priests to an auxiliary bishop. Further examples of a "crackdown" in the 1980s were a whole series of attempts to discipline religious women who were involved in a variety of ways in activities that seemed to compromise the unbending opposition to abortion that had emerged in this decade as a test of Catholic rigor on matters of private and public morality.

The situation of the Catholic Church in America as the new century approaches is one of considerable ferment and uncertainty. Liberal Catholics are firmly at odds with the Vatican and a significant portion of the American hierarchy in their use of artificial contraception, their rejection of traditional stances on sexual morality, and their advocacy of a fuller role for women in the life of the institutional church. Conservatives find themselves more comfortable in many ways with their Protestant counterparts who share their concerns with the maintenance of traditional authority, their anti-Communist stance on international affairs, and their firm stands on such matters of public morality as abortion, homosexuality, and pornography.

Complicating the picture even further is a shortage of clergy and sisters that began in the wake of the Council, as many priests and sisters left the religious life. The seminaries, which had been filled to overflowing with candidates for the priesthood during the 1950s, now stand nearly empty, and many have had to be closed because of underutilization. Those that enjoy reasonable enrollments are the beneficiaries of the lay women who now seek theological education, some out of a desire for ordination not available to them. Most dioceses are formulating contingency plans for the continuing life of parishes for which priests will not be available. New models of staffing are accentuated in these plans, involving the sharing of the time of priests and the increased active participation of the laity and religious women in parish governance and various forms of ministry. This has come about in part out of sheer necessity, but also from an enhanced sense of the responsibilities of the laity in the church that Vatican II had articulated.

Whether seemingly radical solutions to the problems of the day—such as the ordination of married men or, more daringly, women—will come to pass still remains to be seen. As one tongue-in-cheek scenario has it, at the Third Vatican Council, the bishops will bring their wives; at the Fourth, they will bring their husbands.

CHAPTER 48

Roman Catholic Education, Thought, and Culture

The history of the Roman Catholic community in America as it has emerged in preceding chapters can be divided into a number of distinct phases. The colonial period saw only scattered English-speaking settlements, characterized by a high degree of sophistication but very small numbers. The influence of these early English and French Catholics was soon diluted by the massive immigration from Ireland, Germany, and central and eastern Europe, which flooded the church with logistical problems and demands on its resources. As these began to succumb to organization, the conflicts over the question of Americanization were resolved in favor of a cautious middle road between the extremes of ethnic nationalism and extreme assimilation. This pattern dominated American Catholic life until the era of Vatican II, which brought to a head movements for change that had been slowly emerging for some time. The liberalization that Vatican II launched, however, soon ran into resistance from more conservative papal leadership, and precipitated a struggle over issues of authority, especially among American Catholics, that remain unresolved to this day.

The development of a distinctively Catholic culture in the United States follows the contours of this broader history. On the one hand, American Catholics, especially those speaking English, have participated in the dominant culture shaped primarily by its British roots. Many other Catholics of a wide variety of ethnic and linguistic backgrounds have attempted to maintain alternative patterns, usually of Continental European origin, with greater or lesser success. Although some interesting beginnings of a distinctively American Catholic school of thought took shape in the mid-nineteenth century, it was not until the mid-twentieth that the American Catholic community had achieved sufficient maturity and independence to take on a significant identity of its own—after the Catholic community as a whole was well on the way to thorough acceptance and assimilation. Throughout this process of cultural development, a systematic and thoroughgoing drive toward providing education at all levels created an institutional infrastructure through which cultural life could find nurture and expression.

During the colonial period, Catholic efforts in education, thought, and the arts were severely restricted by low numbers, especially in the English-speaking Maryland-Pennsylvania area. The mission complexes built under the direction of the Spanish friars in the Southwest aimed at providing the Indians with some rudimentary secular and religious education, and also featured striking architectural design and artistic achievement. In the chain of California missions built under the direction of Junípero Serra and Fermín Lasuén, native materials and workmanship fused with imperfectly remembered Iberian patterns to produce forceful if rough mission chapels and accompanying decorative arts. The stark, thick-walled mission churches of New Mexico and their more European Baroque counterparts in Texas (e.g., the Alamo) provide an indication of the variety within this range of vernacular frontier building. In Maryland, on the contrary, Catholic life was entirely the province of the English settlers, with no serious attempts at Indian evangelization. The first Catholic school was opened in 1640, but all overt Catholic activity had to be conducted in private from the establishment of Anglicanism in 1692 until independence. Some German-speaking Jesuit schools were founded in Pennsylvania during the eighteenth century, but these efforts were small and scattered.

John Carroll, the first Roman Catholic bishop in the United States, was also the first significant English-speaking American Catholic figure on a variety of fronts besides the organizational dimensions of his career. It was under Carroll's aegis that the first comprehensive set of Catholic educational institutions was begun in the new nation. In 1791, the French Sulpicians began the first seminary, Mount St. Mary's, and Georgetown Academy also opened its doors. In addition, Elizabeth Bayley Seton's newly founded Sisters of Charity established a school in Emmitsburg, Maryland, in 1810. Carroll also manifested in his numerous writings the influence of many currents of the same Enlightenment that had molded the shape of American institutions, and vigorously defended the spirit of American democracy in the ecclesiastical as well as the civil order.

This same spirit manifested itself when the prominent architect Benjamin Henry Latrobe presented Carroll with two alternate designs for the new cathedral at Baltimore. Instead of choosing the Gothic, whose historical resonances were those of the medieval Catholic tradition, Carroll instead opted for a domed Roman Revival plan that seemed to him more in harmony with the classically inspired ideals of the new republic. The resultant Basilica of the Assumption (its present name), erected in Baltimore in 1804, remains as one of the architectural gems of the early National period, though it is no longer used as a cathedral. As Jay Dolan has noted, Carroll also fostered a "plain style" in Catholic observance that focused on Sunday liturgy and private, individual piety, a style reflected in the stark character of Catholic church design and ornament in the antebellum era.

The middle decades of the nineteenth century were dominated by the needs of rapid expansion to accommodate the floodtide of Catholic immigration, and creative "high" cultural expression did not generally flourish. Education was undertaken on a rather ad hoc basis, with religious orders such as the Jesuits and Ursulines taking a good deal of the initiative for the founding and staffing of schools at all levels. The impetus for a more systematic approach to Catholic education came in large measure from the external pressures of nativism. In 1834, for example, the first Catholic school in the Boston area, which had been established by the Ursuline Sisters in 1820 and which educated many non-Catholic young women, was burned by a mob enraged by anti-Catholic propaganda claiming that the Catholic Church was inimical to American democracy. At a subtler level, the "common" or public schools in most American cities were supervised by boards dominated by evangelical Protestants who thought that a necessary component of education was the inculcation of a nondenominational but still Protestant version of Christianity, as disseminated in McGuffey's *Readers* and symbolized by the use of the King James rather than the Catholic Douay version of the Bible.

A series of court cases during the middle decades of the nineteenth century succeeded in removing many of these overt manifestations of Protestantism from the public classroom, but the secularized alternative was scarcely more acceptable from the Catholic viewpoint. The edict of the Third Plenary Council of Baltimore in 1884 mandating parochial elementary schools for all parishes marked the beginning of the American Catholic movement to create systematically a set of educational institutions parallel to those provided by secular society. This centralized program of educational development gradually displaced the previous pattern of schools—frequently called "academies"—maintained by religious orders, which often charged tuition and were thus out of the reach of most immigrant and working-class Catholics.

The drive toward centralization and standardization within education and the professions in the culture as a whole also promoted this tendency. The first diocesan school board was created in New York in 1886, and the Catholic Educational Association came into being in 1904. Teaching sisters were required in the twentieth century to conform to state norms for certification, which again promoted both higher standards and standardization. These trends also tended to subordinate the autonomy of religious orders, especially those of women, to episcopal control.

Nineteenth-century Catholic thought and culture did not have a matrix very conducive for development in the flood of practical concerns that dominated the church's attention. Two notable exceptions, Orestes A. Brownson (1803–1876) and Isaac Hecker (1819–1888), proved this rule through their entrance into the church as converts. Both had been involved in the ferment of Jacksonian politics and Transcendentalist religious thought and social experimentation, but neither found the wide variety of options he explored satisfying until conversion to Catholicism brought relative peace. Brownson was a prolific journalistic editor and writer, and made the *Boston*—later *Brownson's*—*Quarterly Review* the vehicle for his voluminous polemics on virtually every topic imaginable. Brownson sought in the thought of contemporary European writers such as Victor Cousin, Pierre Leroux, and Vincenzo Gioberti the basis for a philosophy in which the problem of the isolation of the individual was overcome by involvement in a broader social context. The ultimate version of this context for him was the Catholic Church, which overcame the perennial Protestant (and Transcendentalist) dilemma of excessive individualism.

Hecker, who became the founder of the Paulist order, took as his mission the apologetic presentation of the Catholic faith to other Americans, and argued that the genius of American institutions and character was more compatible with Catholicism than any other religious system. Neither was very influential within the Catholic community or overly successful in making other converts, but each attained an originality of thought that, perhaps because of its novelty, was uncharacteristic of the Catholic intellectual life of the era. It was Hecker's Paulists especially who, through their emphasis on the Holy Spirit, provided an alternative to the emphasis on authority and devotion that came to dominate American Catholic culture by the early twentieth century.

More characteristic of Catholic writing during the later nineteenth and earlier twentieth centuries was a massive outpouring of various genres intended for widespread consumption and edification, including diocesan newspapers, devotional manuals, prayer books, popular novels, and children's literature. These efforts were based on an expanding Catholic reading public and the emergence of a number of Catholic publishers, of which P. J. Kenedy, Bruce, Benziger, and Sheed & Ward were the best known. Journalism was generally of the episcopal house-organ sort, although an important exception was the *Boston Pilot* while under the editorship of John Boyle O'Reilly from 1870 to 1890.

As Ann Taves has pointed out, a convergence of technological, economic, and sociological factors brought about something resembling mass-market publishing within the Catholic community by the 1840s. The staples of this new printed culture reflected the "devotional revolution" that had transformed both European—especially Irish—and then American Catholicism in the middle decades of the nineteenth century. Frequent collective observance at the parish level of public exercises such as novenas (nine successive days of prayer) and the exposition of the Blessed Sacrament began to rival and even displace the celebration of the Mass as the focal point of Catholic religious life. Organizations known as confraternities and sodalities began to multiply in response to popular demand for these devotions, and clergy—especially itinerant "mission" preachers—and bishops were enthusiastic in encouraging their proliferation. Fostered by popular literature, the Catholic school curriculum, household religious objects, and the ornate interior decoration of churches built during these years, devotionalism molded a cosmos for Catholics in which the supernatural, as manifested in Jesus, Mary, and the company of saints, took on a vivid reality in the midst of mundane life.

The locus for this para-liturgical activity was the *parish*, which, as Jay Dolan has pointed out, by the late nineteenth century had assumed a new importance in American Catholic life. One stimulus to this change was the "new immigration," which brought to the nation's emergent cities a flood of physically and cognitively displaced persons who sought a firm point of reference in the social chaos confronting them. Public devotions were only one of a host of parochial activities that rapidly generated networks of local organizations for carrying out social, charitable, educational, literary, athletic, and any number of other collective enterprises that simultaneously served the needs of parishioners and also reinforced the role of the church as the focus of its members' lives. In the decades around the turn of the century, many parishes were dominated by particular ethnic groups, so that their activities were often recreations of the religious cultures of Polish, Italian, or Mexican villages. As ethnicity began to fade, both through assimilation and episcopal policy, the parish organizational networks continued, together with the Catholic educational system, to be potent vehicles for socialization and the maintenance of group loyalty. It was not till the 1960s that a convergence of new social and theological forces began to erode, or at least significantly transform, this powerful role of the parish in American Catholic life.

The transformation of the character of the parish from ethnic particularism to the social expression of a common American Catholic culture took place at different rates, but the 1920s represented something of a watershed. In the days of heavy immigration, many urban parishes especially were dominated by non-English-speaking immigrants for whom the parish and its staff were significant agents in mediating between an older world that had grown economically untenable and therefore irrecoverable, and a new world that was filled with apparent promise but in its initial appearance was hostile and forbidding. Together with the saloon, the urban political machine, and other less respectable agencies, the Catholic parish provided a milieu where the old celebrations of saints' days could be conducted in the familiar language, and where pressing material problems could be alleviated through kinship networks, fraternal societies, and in many cases the intervention of priests and sisters in helping cope with any number of unfamiliar and often desperate situations.

Life for the second and third generations of American Catholics, though not always easy, was usually less desperate. Parochial culture in the years following World War I, which had helped put a damper on all things foreign, was shaped by American-born bishops and clergy, usually of Irish descent, more than by the foreign-born priests and nuns and their immigrant clientele who had molded an earlier era of Catholic life. The emphasis on devotional piety and ecclesiastical authority developed in the nineteenth century was now continued in a more extensive and centralized institutional network in which Catholic schools played a rapidly growing role. Emphasizing the dangers of Protestant and secular society, this new, English-speaking "ghetto" culture provided an insular but reassuring environment as Catholics tentatively moved into the middle-class mainstream. Garry Wills, the historian and columnist, evoked its distinctive ethos in his bittersweet memoir of "growing up Catholic," *Bare Ruined Choirs,* in 1972:

> We grew up different. There were some places we went, and others did not—into the confessional box, for instance. There were other places we never went, though others could—we were told, from youth, to stay out of non-Catholic churches.
>
> The habits of childhood are tenacious, and Catholicism was first experienced by us as a vast set of intermeshed childhood habits—prayers offered, heads ducked in unison, crossings, chants, christenings, grace at meals; beads, altar, incense, candles; nuns in the classroom alternately too sweet and too severe, priests garbed black on the street and brilliant at the altar; churches lit and darkened, clothed and stripped, to the rhythm of liturgical recurrences; the crib in winter, purple Februaries, and lilies in the spring; confession as intimidation

and comfort (comfort, if nothing else, that the intimidation was survived), communion as revery and discomfort; faith as a creed, and the creed as catechism, Latin responses, salvation by rote, all things going to a rhythm, memorized, old things always returning, eternal in that sense, no matter how transitory. [15–16]

One cost of this sense of changelessness—what Wills goes on to call the "dirty little secret" of pre-Vatican II Catholicism—was an imposed uniformity of thought and practice. The quashing of the impact of contemporary European thought signaled by the papal encyclicals *Testem Benevolentiae* in 1899 and *Pascendi Dominici Gregis* in 1907 put an end to some mildly venturesome intellectual activity at the Catholic University of America, the seminary at Dunwoodie, New York, and the University of Notre Dame. At the latter, which like most Catholic colleges remained basically a secondary-level boarding institution until well into the twentieth century, Father John Zahm's 1896 work *Evolution and Dogma* was suppressed by Rome in 1898 when he tried to incorporate evolutionary thought into a Catholic framework.

The intellectual and cultural life of American Catholics during the first half of the twentieth century has frequently been characterized by Catholic critics as that of a religious "ghetto," shielded by internal and external pressure from active contact with the broader world. This criticism is not without some substance, since the emergence of a strong centralized domestic hierarchy and the defensive stance of Rome did not promote intellectual adventuresomeness. Seminaries flourished at a variety of levels: minor seminaries for high school age prospects for the priesthood, major seminaries for more direct preparation for ordination at the collegiate level, and those maintained by religious orders as an alternative to seminaries under diocesan sponsorship. Most, however, offered a curriculum that stressed character and spiritual formation, physical exercise, and a theology derived from textbooks expounding derivative versions of the system of St. Thomas Aquinas, whose thought was made normative by papal decree in 1913.

Curriculum at the primary and secondary levels was similar to that offered in the public schools, but with systematic instruction in religion and with texts reflecting a distinctive Catholic outlook in controversial areas. Bishop Richard Gilmour of Cleveland, for example, created a popular series of readers in the late nineteenth century that were basically Catholic versions of those of the Presbyterian William Holmes McGuffey. During the 1940s, the "Faith and Freedom" series originating from Catholic University stressed much the same values, especially patriotism, characteristic of the nation at large, but emphasized Catholic themes and achievements where appropriate. Catholic book clubs and radio programs arose to present alternatives in the various media, as did a wide variety of periodicals, such as *Our Sunday Visitor*, that paralleled the dominant popular culture. Where a Catholic alternative was not readily available, such as in the realm of film, pressures for governmental censorship and self-control by Catholics—the "Legion of Decency" pledge—were relied upon.

Exceptions to this general rule of uniformity did gradually appear throughout the decades between *Testem Benevolentiae* and Vatican II, however. The Jesuit order began publication of the weekly *America*, a journal of religion, culture, and politics, in 1909, and a group of laymen led by Michael Williams founded the similar but somewhat more liberal and independent *Commonweal* in 1924. Most significant authors of Catholic background during this period, such as Eugene O'Neill, F. Scott Fitzgerald, and Theodore Dreiser, no longer practiced their familial faith, and the depth of the Catholic religious identity of the converts Ernest Hemingway and Robert Lowell was questionable. The Catholic presence in literature was more evident in American appreciation of the work of English and Continental Catholic authors such as Evelyn Waugh, Graham Greene, François Mauriac, and Sigrid Undset, and occasionally in the sensitive depiction of Catholic themes by non-Roman Catholics such as T. S. Eliot, Henry Adams, and Willa Cather.

It was not until the 1950s and 1960s that genuinely distinguished Catholic fiction began to appear in the work of the Southern writers Flannery O'Connor and Walker Percy and the Midwestern satirist J. F. Powers. The cultural impact of Vatican II was ambiguous. After its impact began to be felt, any number of writers of American, and especially Irish-American, Catholic background reflected on their experiences in their fiction. While it has not always been clear how committed they have remained to institutional Catholicism, the impact of Catholic culture on their work has been unmistakable.

In the more strictly intellectual sphere, American Jesuits, already prominent in their education enterprises and their journal *America,* began to distinguish themselves especially in aspects of theology and ethics impinging upon the public and political spheres. Gustav Weigel, S.J. (1906–1964), for example, helped pave the way for serious ecumenical outreach to other Christians. His *American Dialogue,* written in collaboration with Presbyterian theologian Robert McAfee Brown in 1960, was a pioneering work of mutual exchange. John La Farge, S.J. (1880–1963), promoted papal social teaching in his work at *America,* and anticipated later civil rights involvements through the Catholic Interracial Council of New York (founded 1934).

Perhaps the most eminent of these Jesuits, for whom *America* and the seminary in Woodstock, Maryland, provided intellectual foci, was John Courtney Murray, S.J. (1904–1967). In *We Hold These Truths* of 1960, Murray argued that American principles of religious liberty were consistent with traditional Catholic teachings. Although his earlier writings encountered some suspicion in official circles at first, his work as Cardinal Spellman's *peritus* (expert theological advisor) at Vatican II was instrumental in the tradition-breaking "Declaration of Religious Liberty" promulgated by the Council in 1963.

Ferment was at work in other ways in Catholic circles during the 1950s and 1960s. Through the work of Notre Dame's Theodore Hesburgh, C.S.C., and other educational leaders, a small group of Catholic institutions—Notre Dame, Georgetown, Boston College, Holy Cross, Fordham, and a few others—began to modify their traditional emphasis on orthodoxy and sports with a new emphasis on intellectual inquiry and scholarly research—the goals for which Catholic University had been founded several decades before, but which had never been very fully realized in that context.

A major rallying point in this movement was John Tracy Ellis's "American Catholics and the Intellectual Life," published in *Thought* in 1955. Ellis, a priest and one of America's leading Catholic historians, took his coreligionists to task for the antiintellectualism of the Catholic "ghetto" culture that had developed in America, and called for a new ethos in which active intellectual inquiry would be nurtured. This summons to maturity became fulfilled in considerable measure in the decades to come, thanks in large part to the change in atmosphere brought about by Vatican II. The reassertion of papal authority in the 1980s by John Paul II, however, began to put some of these gains at risk as controversial thinkers such as Charles Curran, the Catholic University ethicist, began to come under fire for nonconformity with official teaching.

At the primary and secondary levels, Catholic education also began to undergo some major transformations beginning in the 1960s. Under the impetus of the Third Council of Baltimore's decree, the infrastructure of parochial education had expanded rapidly for several decades. Catholic school attendance increased from about four hundred thousand in 1880 to 1.7 million in 1920, and tripled again by the early 1960s. By the time of Vatican II, however, and perhaps even a few years before, this long-term trend began to shift. The entrance of more and more Catholics into the middle classes brought about a drop in birth rate, and the increasing acceptance by Catholics of American social mores made the public schools a more attractive and less expensive alternative. The rapid drop in the availability of low-paid teaching sisters in the later 1960s necessitated a rethinking of the most effective use of diminished resources.

Still another factor was the abandonment of many inner-city parishes in the relentless movement during that era toward the suburbs; the announcement of the closing of dozens of such parishes by Archbishop Szoka in Detroit in 1988 touched off widespread controversy, especially among the black Catholics who formed their major constituency. Many parochial schools now lacked their traditional demographic base as a result; on the other hand, however, many upwardly mobile black families, only a few of whom were Catholic, saw the discipline and generally high standards of the Catholic schools as a preferable alternative to the public system for their children. Desegregation had come slowly but steadily within the American church since the end of World War II—at times in the face of massive resistance, as in traditionally Catholic southern Louisiana—but it had come, and a new social mission thus presented itself for Catholic education.

One way to provide a retrospective on the development of American Catholic thought and culture is to examine some ways in which Catholics viewed the Christian past. A good part of nineteenth century thought was conspicuous by the absence of systematic speculation of this sort. The church's personnel were absorbed in the exigencies of the present, and too little of a scholarly community existed to pay much attention to earlier ages. Churches for the most part were designed in the common styles of the day, which were derived from the work of the Anglican Christopher Wren. The first attempts at monumental Catholic architecture were often the work of Protestant architects, such as Latrobe's Baltimore Cathedral and St. Patrick's Cathedral (1858–1879) in New York City, designed by the Episcopalian James Renwick, Jr.

An enhanced historical consciousness began to emerge toward the end of the nineteenth century as Catholic resources increased substantially. The Irish-born Patrick Keely executed Boston's Holy Cross Cathedral in the popular Gothic style in 1875, and probably designed over six hundred Catholic churches, most of them in similar modes, throughout the entire eastern United States. This focus on the Middle Ages as the "strong time" of Catholic history was reflected in the more sophisticated Gothic Revival architecture of Maginnis & Walsh and Allen & Collens in the early twentieth century, as well as in the often-reprinted *The Thirteenth, Greatest of Centuries* by James J. Walsh (1907). On an international level, the revival of Gregorian Chant, the papal declaration making the theology of Thomas Aquinas normative, the creation of a Papal Institute of Medieval Studies, and the emergence of a strong school of neo-Thomist thinkers such as Etienne Gilson and Jacques Maritain as the twentieth century progressed also betokened a preoccupation with the Middle Ages as a source of contemporary inspiration. A historiography of American Catholicism of professional calibre also began to emerge in the work of John Gilmary Shea (1824–1892) and Peter Guilday (1884–1947). In both cases, however, their solid documentary work seldom transcended the level of informèd chronicle—a marked contrast with the sophisticated interpretive viewpoints of Notre Dame historians Jay Dolan and Philip Gleason in the 1970s and 1980s.

A new historical point of reference began to emerge in 1937 with the founding of the Catholic Biblical Association of America, which two years later commenced publication of the *Catholic Biblical Quarterly*. (*The Catholic Historical Review* had already come into being in 1915.) Catholic scholarship was by this time beginning to emerge from the damper put on contemporary biblical scholarship by earlier papal condemnations of Modernism, and a new wind blowing from Rome was signaled by the encyclical *Divino Afflante Spiritu*, issued by Pius XII in 1943 and encouraging modern "scientific" approaches to biblical research. By the 1960s American Catholic biblical scholars began to exert leadership within their professional circles, and men such as Roland Murphy, O. Carm.; Joseph Fitzmeyer, S.J.; and Raymond Brown, S.S., came to be regarded as among the leading lights in their fields.

More critical attitudes towards the Catholic past and its relationship to the American heritage were also emerging in the work of John Tracy Ellis and John Courtney Murray mentioned earlier. The combination of these new intellectual currents, together with the work of the Liturgical Movement and new forces in theology, helped to provide the intellectual undergirdings for Vatican II, whose "constitutions" reflected a much more thorough grounding in Scripture, viewed historically, than had ever been the case in modern times. This shift of point of reference from the medieval to the biblical period, together with a newly critical sense of the institutional past and present as a whole, helped shape the entire course of reforms brought about by the Council. Conspicuous among these was the abandonment of medieval revival styles in architecture in favor of new geometrical shapes, especially rounded forms, that enhanced the sense of congregational participation in the celebration of the sacraments, as well as a new emphasis on Scripture and vernacular worship. The medievalism of earlier American Catholicism thus yielded on a variety of fronts to an enhanced appreciation of the age of Christian origins on the one hand and a new receptivity to the culture of the present—and the future—on the other.

CHAPTER 49

Black Christianity: "Eyes on the Prize"

Whether in slavery or relative freedom, black life in America has mainly been lived at the edge of society, restricted in its development by enslavement, discrimination, and poverty. The religious experience of many Afro-Americans has thus been highly adaptive, combining elements of traditional African culture, American Christianity, and a free-form imagination that has resulted in a wide variety of expressions ranging from the ring-shouts of the slave community to the miracle-working of Father Divine, to the militancy of Malcolm X. The overwhelming majority of American blacks who have acquired formal religious affiliation, however, have been Protestant Christian, especially within the Baptist, Methodist, and "Sanctified" or "Spirit Baptized" (Holiness and Pentecostal) traditions. To bring the story of Afro-American religion up to the present requires a focus on black Christianity, which began to take on institutionalized form around the beginnings of the nineteenth century among the free blacks of the cities of the Northeast.

Although the lot of free blacks in nineteenth-century America was considerably more favorable than that of their enslaved counterparts, they were far from being universally regarded as the equals of whites in North or South. The churches were no exception. One of the classic stories illustrating this situation was the reception of Richard Allen (1760–1831) and his black colleagues when they attempted to participate fully in worship at St. George's Methodist Church in Philadelphia in November 1787. (This, at least, is the date traditionally given; these events may in fact have taken place in the early 1790s.) Although Allen, a Methodist preacher, and other members of the free black community had contributed extensively to the church's remodeling, they were barred by white ushers from assuming the places they had chosen, and were physically removed when they demurred. Perhaps not surprisingly, they collectively withdrew from the church, and Allen was launched on a path that would soon lead to the formation of a network of black churches that paralleled the white denominations in which they could not find acceptance.

Allen founded the Bethel African Methodist Episcopal Church in Philadelphia in 1794, the lengthy name indicating both its Methodist identity ("Methodist Episcopal" was the name of the parent body at the time) and its conscious affirmation of the African origins of its congregation. A convention of black Methodists in 1816, tired of fighting white trustees for control of their own church property, organized an independent denomination, the African Methodist Episcopal (AME) Church, and elected Allen their first bishop. An affiliation developed with a group of black Methodists in New York led by James Varick (1750?–1827), but tensions between the leaders resulted in the New York group's founding a separate though very similar denomination in 1821 that eventually adopted the name African Methodist Episcopal Zion (AMEZ) Church. The two groups attracted considerable membership in both North and South, and engaged in many of the same sorts of denominational activities that characterized their white counterparts, such as publishing and education. Wilberforce University (1856) and the adjoining Payne Theological Seminary in Ohio were two of the more enduring results of the AME educational effort.

Various other black Methodist bodies have also arisen, the largest of which is the Christian (previously Colored) Methodist Episcopal Church. This was founded in 1870 by Southern blacks who no longer chose to belong to the Methodist Episcopal Church, South, which had earlier split from its Northern counterpart over the slavery issue. A considerable number of blacks continued to belong to the latter, usually in segregated annual conferences (the Methodist equivalent of a diocese), which at the time of the reunion of the Northern and Southern branches (1939) were consolidated into a Central Jurisdiction. (This and other segregated branches of Methodism were dissolved, beginning in 1964, in the context of the coming together of the United Methodist Church.) Comparative statistics for the three major independent groups are shown in Table 49.1.

Table 49.1   Membership Populations of Three Black
Methodist Churches, 1896 and 1980s

	1896	*Early 1980s*
AME	452,725	2,210,000
AMEZ	349,788	1,134,179
Colored/Christian	129,383	718,922

Sources: Ahlstrom & Jacquet.

The other major Protestant tradition to attract large numbers of free blacks was the Baptist. Like the Methodists, they stressed self-discipline, the need for an emotional personal conversion, and highly expressive worship. Unlike the Methodists, who benefited from a tight organization, Baptists of both races enjoyed the advantage of congregational independence and maximal flexibility. Throughout the nineteenth century, this independence stood in the way of any extensive denominational organization. Regional groupings began to emerge by the 1830s, with the Providence Baptist Association in Ohio the first in 1836. It was finally in 1895 that the National Baptist Convention was founded in Atlanta as a coalescence of several related earlier groups that had arisen to deal with education, missions, and other traditional denominational needs. As Baptists are wont to do, however, the Convention split in 1915 over internal political issues into the National Baptist Convention of America and the National Baptist Convention of the U.S.A., Inc. A further schism in the latter group in 1961 gave rise to the Progressive National Baptist Convention, Inc. The most recent statistics available for these three groups are NBCA—2,668,799 (1956); NBCUSA Inc.—5,500,000 (1958); and PNBC—521,692 (1967).*

The third major family of black Christian churches is made up of those groups that had their origins in the Holiness and Pentecostal ferment of the late nineteenth century. The Holiness movement arose from Methodism, and emphasized the experience of "entire sanctification," through which the believer becomes free from the lingering effects of original sin. Pentecostalism builds on the foundations of Holiness, but stresses the reception of the "gifts of the Holy Spirit," of which speaking in tongues and healing through faith are among the most conspicuous. In the early days of Pentecostalism especially, the boundaries between the races counted for little in the effervescence created by the sense of having the Holy Spirit in the midst of the believers. The most important early center of black Pentecostalism was the Azusa Street Mission in Los Angeles, where in 1906 William J. Seymour, a black Holiness preacher, became the focus of a powerful interracial Pentecostal revival that lasted for three years.

After these heady beginnings, the usual forces of schism, routinization, and segregation overtook what became known as the "Sanctified" black churches, and a number of denominations began to take on organizational form. Notable among these was the Church of God in Christ, which was organized as a Holiness church in Memphis by Charles Harrison Mason and Charles Price Jones, Sr., in 1895. After Mason and other of the movement's leaders had become converted to the Pentecostal way on a visit to Azusa Street, the two founders parted company over the issue: Mason and the original denomination followed the Pentecostal path, while Jones and his Holiness group withdrew in 1907 and soon established the Church of Christ (Holiness) U.S.A. Other schisms plagued the latter group, which still exists but has dwindled to a very small membership. On the other hand, the Church of God in Christ remains based in Memphis, has been extremely active in overseas evangelism, and in 1982 claimed over 3.7 million members. There are a considerable number of smaller Holiness and Pentecostal denominations, most rather small in size, and innumerable independent churches, many of which meet in storefronts in urban neighborhoods.

Worship in black churches shares many of the theological and liturgical premises of the broader Methodist, Baptist, Holiness, and Pentecostal tradi-

---

* Note that the figures for the NBCUSA Inc. antedate the later split. The inclusion of other black Baptist organizations and independent churches would increase these estimates somewhat.

tions in which they participate, but few black services are exactly like those of their white counterparts. Social class plays some role here, with middle-class, especially Methodist, black churches tending toward more restraint and decorum in their style. Much of the distinctiveness of black Christian worship has roots in patterns developed in the era of slavery, some of them most likely echoing earlier African sources. These include preaching, which is often based on a narrative held together by formulaic phrases that make it possible virtually to chant a biblical story by inserting set verbal units to maintain cadences and provide brief respites when memory temporarily falters. Narrative and moral exhortation are much more common in black preaching than doctrinal instruction, which has never been emphasized. In addition, the congregation interacts enthusiastically with the preacher, responding with "amens" and other interjections in keeping with the rhythms of the sermon. Open emotional expression is a common feature, especially in "Sanctified" worship.

A direct derivative of the slave tradition of "spirituals" is the gospel music of the late nineteenth and twentieth centuries. This style was originally made popular with black and white audiences alike by the Jubilee Singers of Fisk University in Nashville, beginning in the 1870s. Although their versions of black spirituals were heavily modified to conform with middle-class Victorian taste, they greatly aided the cause of black education and helped to legitimate a distinctively black musical tradition.

The more immediate origins of the modern black Gospel tradition lie in the 1920s, when jazz and the blues were attracting wide attention as highly sophisticated and somewhat daring secular musical styles with distinctly black origins. Thomas A. Dorsey, who gave the movement its first coherent shape, was born in 1899 in rural Georgia, the son of a rural Baptist preacher. By moving to Chicago, Dorsey joined in the exodus of Southern blacks moving to the cities of the North that was already under way. He first made a name as a blues musician, then joined a Baptist church, experienced a conversion, and turned his attention to religious music. Dorsey's compositions, such as "Precious Lord, Take My Hand" and "Peace In the Valley," found an enthusiastic audience among whites as well, but their emphasis on the distinctively black experience of hope amidst suffering made it clear that here was a music significantly different from the Gospel songs of white evangelicals such as Fanny Crosby and Ira D. Sankey.

Black Gospel had its origins at a time when popular music in the modern sense was being made possible by the expansion of the recording industry and radio, and its distinctive rhythms spread rapidly through the record companies that served primarily black audiences, who were known as the "race market." Black Gospel thus had a double character, incorporated as part of the worship of black congregations but also enjoyed as popular music via records and radio. (Interestingly, recorded "sermons with singing" such as J. M. Gates's "Black Diamond Express to Hell" and A. W. Nix's "Death's Black Train Is Coming," were best-sellers in the 1920s, outselling Bessie Smith by quite a bit.) Some Gospel singers such as Mahalia Jackson attained star status, and Gospel groups such as the Drinkard Sisters and the Soul Stirrers provided the early musical experience for popular secular artists such as Dionne Warwick and Sam Cooke, respectively. Much of the "Motown Sound" of the 1960s and after, as exemplified in popular groups such as the Temptations and the Four Tops, was firmly rooted in the Gospel tradition, and one of the best-selling records of the late 1960s was the Gospel recording "O Happy Day" by the Eddie Hawkins Singers. The relationship between secular and sacred in Afro-American culture is often a problematic one: Sometimes the two are starkly opposed, as in the case of 1920s blues and Gospel; at others, the lines separating them are nearly invisible.

The development of Gospel music is very closely tied in with broader events that deeply affected the black community in America and its religious expression. Fisk University, which gave black music its first national exposure, was one of a number of colleges founded in the post-Civil War era by the American Missionary Association. Many of these have continued to provide higher education for many black professionals and clergy to the present day. (Other black colleges founded during the Reconstruction era through collaboration of the Freedmen's Bureau with the AMA or denominational bodies include Howard University in Washington, D.C.; Morehouse College in Atlanta; Talladega in Alabama; and Tougaloo in Mississippi.) Jim Crow laws enforcing new patterns of segregation, economic hard times, and the reduction of many Southern blacks to virtual serfdom through the sharecropping system combined with new economic opportunities stimulated by the war economy of the 1910s to lead thousands of blacks into the great cities of the North—an exodus that had already begun late in the nineteenth century. Harlem, Chicago, and Detroit joined New Orleans, Atlanta, and Memphis as centers of black cultural life, which expressed itself most vividly in music and religion. The traditional woes of Afro-Americans were then compounded by the Depression of the 1930s, which hit both rural and urban blacks particularly hard, given the precarious situation in which most lived.

One of the few centers of stability within this constant situation of social marginality and economic insecurity was the church. Among more prosperous congregations, large-scale urban structures were often built in the Victorian eclectic (primarily Romanesque) style of the late nineteenth and early twentieth centuries. Frequently older churches outgrown by white congregations moving to more fashionable quarters were taken over by black Methodists and Baptists, and the poorer "Sanctified" groups frequently made do with storefronts or small rural wooden churches. The interior arrangements were usually similar to other Baptist and Methodist churches of the period, with curved rows of "opera-style" seats and a large frontal platform with room for a preacher and a colorfully robed choir.

The preacher occupied an especially prominent role in the black community, since he was one of its few members who, if not formally educated, at least had sufficient experience in public speaking, organization, and other social and political skills useful not only in mediating differences within the black community but in representing that community in the broader society as well. Large urban churches provided a ready-made political base for those who sought to cross the "color line" into national politics, as exemplified in the congressional career of Adam Clayton Powell, Jr., pastor of Harlem's Abyssinian Baptist Church. Martin Luther King, Jr. (1929–1968), was similarly descended from a family of black Baptist ministers, and utilized his position first in Montgomery and then Atlanta as a platform for his leadership in the civil rights movement. More recently, Jesse Jackson of Chicago has gained attention as the founder of the "Rainbow Coalition" for interracial social justice and as a candidate for the Democratic nomination for the presidency, the first black to ever mount a serious campaign for America's highest office in a major political party.

The civil rights movement that began with the Montgomery, Alabama, bus boycott of 1955–1956 was the culmination of many themes in the Afro-American experience. Black clergy had long played a leading role in early civil rights organizations such as the National Association for the Advancement of Colored People (NAACP, 1910), and had often made their churches available as meeting-places for such groups. The Southern Christian Leadership Conference (SCLC), founded in Atlanta in 1957 with King as the first president, was a new organization consisting primarily of Southern black clergy dedicated to pursuing the traditional interests of the black community in the political realm under clerical leadership.

Another source of continuity lay in the motif of liberation, which had been a staple of black preaching and religious thought since slavery days. This quest for freedom found particularly memorable expression in the rolling cadences of Martin Luther King's "I Have A Dream" address delivered from the Lincoln Memorial on August 28, 1963, during the "March on Washington for Jobs and Freedom," one of the culminating events of the movement. King's rhetoric had an Old Testament quality to it. Following in the tradition of the Hebrew prophets, he made it clear that the black Christian quest for deliverance was not simply confined to longings for a better world in the hereafter, but was based on a demand for social justice in the here-and-now. "We Shall Overcome," which became the universal anthem of the movement, further echoed the traditional rhythms of the black spiritual.

Even before the movement had achieved some important victories in a series of laws passed by Congress, especially the Civil Rights Act of 1964, it was becoming clear that the influence of Christianity on the black movement was problematic. King, who held a doctorate in theology from Boston University, was very much committed to the black Baptist tradition, but was also deeply influenced by such non-Christian thinkers as Henry David Thoreau and Mohandas Gandhi. These ideas combined with a traditional emphasis on love for one's enemies in the philosophy of nonviolent resistance that was exhibited in the campaign of sit-ins and peaceful demonstrations that dominated the early civil rights movement. More traditional groups such as the NAACP and SCLC, however, were soon augmented and to some degree rivaled by militant secular organizations such as the Student Non-Violent Coordinating Committee (SNCC) and the older Congress of Racial Equality (CORE), which organized "freedom rides" from the Northern states to help mobilize change in the South. Among the leaders of the former group was Stokely Carmichael, one of a new breed of black militants who found the pace of actual social change too slow, and who were ready to challenge the older leadership to espouse more aggressive tactics to secure their goals.

Until his assassination in 1968 in Memphis, where he had come to support a municipal workers' strike, King himself had broadened his critique of American institutions to include an attack on American involvement in the war in Vietnam. The implications of what had begun as a reform movement were becoming radical, leading to an indictment of American institutions on the one hand and a transformation of consciousness on the other. A new vocabulary was coming into being, indicative of the inadequacy of earlier language to deal with the issues involved. *Negro*, which had long been the socially acceptable term for "colored" Americans, now yielded to *black* and *Afro-American* as preferred designations. (By the late 1980s, some black leaders were advocating the adoption of *African-American* as the most descriptive and emotionally resonant term.) *Soul*, a traditional religious term, now acquired a new significance as expressive of the deeply felt longings, experience, and spiritual character of American blacks, and appeared in such forms as *soul food, soul music,* and *soul brother*.

A related new phrase that indicated a dramatic change in the aspirations of many Afro-Americans was *Black Power*. The title of a 1967 book by Stokely Carmichael and Charles V. Hamilton, it became the focus for a new emphasis among many black leaders on the need to take aggressive measures to ensure that blacks enjoyed not only abstract legal rights but also the specific political and economic power that could alone guarantee their genuine equality with other Americans. One strategy to this end was the "selective patronage" campaign led by an alliance of black Philadelphia ministers, who helped achieve greater black employment by urging their congregations to boycott businesses that did not cooperate with their aims. A more startling manifestation of this new militancy was the proclamation of the "Black Manifesto" by James Forman in the midst of a service in progress at Manhattan's liberal Riverside Church in 1969. The manifesto was an indictment of American society and especially its white religious groups for their obliviousness to injustices done to the black community, and demanded of them extensive financial "reparations" to begin to rectify the economic imbalance between the races. Although the effects were clearly not as far-reaching as Forman and other militants had hoped for, the message delivered was one of impatience with gradual change and a reliance on directly confrontational tactics.

The impact of this militancy also made itself felt in the realm of black religious thought. One of the more radical expressions of the desire to reconcile Christianity with the new black consciousness was the Detroit minister Albert Cleage's *The Black Messiah* of 1969, which argued that Jesus had quite literally been black in physical appearance. A more systematic articulator of these concerns was Union Theological Seminary's James Cone, whose *Black Theology and Black Power* of 1969 set forth the argument that the goal of the Christian Gospel was the liberation of the poor and powerless. Although Cone relied heavily on European theologians in his early work, he later shifted his emphasis to exploring more fully the resources of the Afro-American tradition, as in his book *The Spirituals and the Blues* of 1972.

Still more militant factions of the black community identified both with the Marxism that had informed some of Forman's rhetoric and the new consciousness that was emerging throughout the nonwhite Third World. Radical secular ideologies were espoused by the Black Panthers as well as the erratic Symbionese Liberation Army, which came to a violent end in California in 1974. After the dust had settled from the wake of these movements and the unsystematic violence that had erupted in many urban black ghetto neighborhoods in the late 1960s and early 1970s, however, the national mood began to turn in different directions. The force of the radical movements dissipated, and the moderate successors of King such as Fred Shuttlesworth and Ralph Abernathy were unable to sustain the momentum of the earlier movement. Much of black religious life, especially in the "Sanctified" churches, went on more or less as usual. Nevertheless, a new level of consciousness and expectation had been introduced into the black community, religious and secular, that could never be reversed. Black caucuses had formed in such primarily white denominations as the Roman Catholic and Episcopal Churches that continued to articulate black needs and perspectives to the broader Christian community, though most blacks retained their traditional denominational affiliations. Jesse Jackson continued in the 1980s the role of the black minister as political leader; declaring himself a candidate for the Democratic presidential nomination in both 1984 and 1988, he made an impressive though ultimately unsuccessful showing in the latter race against Michael Dukakis. Radicalism had retreated dramatically, if it had not died entirely. What seemed to lie ahead was an undramatic but unrelenting campaign on the part of the black churches to continue their struggle to achieve the elusive goal of equality, while worshiping in the same styles they had brought with them out of slavery over a century before.

CHAPTER 50

Mormons and the "Mainstream"

The history of the Latter-day Saints in Utah underwent an abrupt and decisive shift in 1890, with President Wilford Woodruff's *Manifesto* bringing to an end the distinctive practice of polygamy or plural marriage. Heretofore, the Mormons had lived apart, distancing themselves from the larger American society by physical separation, doctrinal peculiarity, economic semicommunitarianism, theocratic leadership, and—most notoriously for "Gentiles"—the practice of plural marriage. This distinctiveness had proved invaluable in rallying the morale, determination, and willingness to subordinate the will of the individual to the good of the group necessary to make the Western deserts into veritable gardens. Its main function was to remind all that the Mormons were not like the Gentiles: They had an identity, a mission, and a destiny all their own.

The price this distinctiveness exacted in a continual tightening of the screws by the federal government eventually proved too costly. A series of congressional acts, with escalating enforcement by federal marshals, proved almost impossible to resist in the long run, and the 1890 *Manifesto* was a signal that the Saints were now willing to adjust their self-interpretation to bring it sufficiently into conformity with that of the dominant society to ensure survival. Not all Mormons accepted President Woodruff's revelation as binding, though, and splinter groups of polygamists survive in remote towns of Utah and other parts of the Southwest, as well as in Mexico, to the present day. (Violence over polygamy-related issues still occurs periodically; for instance, a policeman was killed and a polygamist leader injured in a siege and shoot-out in Marion, Utah, in January of 1988.)

The ending of polygamy was both a symbol and a precondition of a new age in which Mormons would become much more thoroughly integrated into national life, although in a highly distinctive fashion. Mormons have remained a dominant force in the political and social life of Utah, where they still constitute roughly 80 percent of the population, and in parts of contiguous states; however, they have also diffused throughout the nation—as witnessed in their spectacular temple near Washington, D.C.—and, through vigorous evangelism, in many parts of the Third World as well. Where religion and government had once been inextricably intertwined, the Church of Jesus Christ of Latter-day Saints now became a denomination, albeit a highly demanding one, while the government of Utah now follows the broader American pattern—but with Mormons prominent in its affairs. Instead of participating in a semicollective economy, Mormons now are among the most vocal advocates of individualistic capitalism in the nation, while the LDS Church continues to have extensive investments in the private sector, and provides relief for Mormons down on their luck.

Mormonism has thus adapted to its incorporation into American society not by abandoning its earlier practices and values (except in extreme cases such as polygamy), but by creating a network of beliefs, values, and structures capable of maintaining their identity as a distinctive *people* in the face of the pressures of religious competition as well as secularization. They have done so in part by abandoning their earlier critical posture toward America at large, and instead embracing certain aspects of American culture as religiously normative. The anthropologist Mark Leone probably overstated his case when he argued that Mormons have done such a turn-about on capitalism that they have changed from a "counter-culture" to a "colonial" people without a clear identity of their own. However, he is certainly perceptive in noting that, whatever continuities may exist in the underlying social reality, the overt Mormon *posture* toward American society has executed a highly dramatic about-face in the course of the past century or so.

Like other branches of Christianity, with which Mormons identify despite the distinctiveness of their attitude toward revelation, the Latter-day Saints have developed a distinctive theology, a pattern of worship, and an organizational structure. For many, in practice, the latter is the most important of the three, since Mormon life is structured around a pattern of seemingly ceaseless activity. This activity, generated and sustained in large part by the group's structures, further contributes to a pattern of life that is intense and distinctive enough to be called a *culture*—or, perhaps, more accurately, a subculture, partaking of and yet curiously distinct from the patterns of life of other middle-class white Americans. To understand the reality of twentieth-century Mormonism, it is useful to examine belief, worship, structure, and, finally culture.

The Mormon belief system is inextricably tied in to the unique revelation that its founder and prophet, Joseph Smith, claimed to have derived through the good offices of the angel Moroni. The authenticity of the *Book of Mormon* and of Joseph Smith's prophetic role are cardinal points of faith, which also serve to distinguish Mormon from Gentile in a clean-cut fashion. Out of this revelation and subsequent interpretations of it, however, has arisen a distinctive body of religious beliefs at once closely related to that of most Christians, but possessing some features virtually unknown elsewhere.

The most important general feature of the Mormon belief system is its lack of a sense of transcendence. There is no sharp line drawn between the realms of the natural and the supernatural, but rather a difference in quality (and visibility). The elements of the universe are uncreated, eternal, and *material*. There is certainly a personal God, but one who lacks the distinctively transcendent character of the traditional Christian God. The God of the Mormons, though invisible, is part of the world of time and space, and is continually engaged in a process of development and self-creation. Jesus Christ, who plays a role in the dispensation of salvation in many ways similar to that for traditional Christians, is the first-born of this God; Adam, one of God's earliest "spirit children," assisted Jesus in the creation of the world.

Humans, the offspring of Adam, are not really that different from God. Like him, they are uncreated and eternal. Like him, they are capable of change and development, both in this world and the world yet to come. Further, in the Mormon interpretation, human nature is not flawed by original sin; sin is real, but is the direct responsibility of each individual who commits it. Humanity thus enjoys extraordinary freedom to fashion itself into something quite literally divine. Humans are like what God once was, and from which God made himself into what he now is. To pursue this path of becoming godlike, however, humans are in need of the redemption made possible by the saving act of Jesus Christ who, on his future coming to earth, will enlist his "latter-day saints" in the task of recreating the world.

Life in this world, however, is neither the beginning nor the ultimate end of human existence. All humans enjoyed a preexistence in the supernatural world, which they voluntarily left to come to earth to grow further in knowledge. Depending on their choices and progress in this life, they will continue to progress after physical death. Although a few will be damned, the great majority of humanity will enjoy a future existence at one of three levels of increasing felicity: the Telestial, the Terrestrial, and the Celestial. Life there will be an exalted version of that experienced in this world, with pain and suffering gone; for the particularly worthy, it will involve reunion with one's earthly family. Mormons, of course, will have the advantage in the pursuit of bliss in the afterlife because they alone have been privy to the fullness of truth in this existence; similarly, they are also in greater jeopardy of damnation because of this privileged status.

The elaborate structure of the Church of Jesus Christ of Latter-day Saints is designed to assist the Saints in the pursuit of salvation through a lifelong involvement in the Mormon community. First, it should be noted that the paths followed by men and women are substantially different. Patriarchal imagery from the Hebrew scriptures informed Joseph Smith's vision from the beginning. Mormons have never aspired as a group to a vision of identical status for the sexes, maintaining rather that men and women have separate but equal roles. Women, of course, participate actively in public worship and in the Women's Relief Society, but cannot aspire to the priestly roles that are reserved exclusively for their fathers, brothers, husbands, and sons.

The priesthoods established by Joseph Smith—or, as he would have it, *re*established—are two: the *Aaronic* and the *Melchizedek*. The first consists of a series of three levels—Deacon, Teacher, and Priest—which boys begin at age 12 and progress through until reaching 18 or 19. At the latter age, they are recognized as adults through initiation into the status of Elder, the first stage of the Melchizedek order. As elders, at 19 years of age, they spend two years, supported by themselves, as missionaries in the United States or abroad. (The spectacle of pairs of neatly groomed, conservatively dressed young men ringing doorbells and testifying to their faith is a familiar one for many American Gentiles.) The rank of High Priest is that to which Bishops and other holders of higher office are ordained on the basis of performing a particular role, and not simply age. A Quorum of the Seventy also deals with missionary endeavors at an advanced level.

The basic unit of Mormon organization is the *ward*, roughly the equivalent of a parish, and typically including about seven hundred members. The ward is presided over by a bishop—like all priests, a layman engaged in a secular occupation as well—and provides the structure for weekly worship, Sunday School classes for all ages, meetings of the various priesthoods, and other social, educational, and charitable activity. The basic unit of worship is the sacrament meeting, which is held weekly at the ward chapel, usually a rather ordinary building with appropriate facilities for assemblies and classes. Worship typically consists of informal talks by members of the congregation, hymn-singing, and the administration of the sacrament in the form of bread and water. On the first Sunday of each month a Fast and Testimony Sunday is observed, for which worshipers maintain a complete abstinence from food for twenty–four hours and then offer personal testimonies at the sacrament meeting.

Besides supervising worship and other aspects of ward life, bishops also exercise the important "gate-keeping" function of certifying whether their congregants are worthy of admission to temple ordinances. The temple, which as an institution dates back to the early days at Kirtland and Nauvoo, is a distinctive Mormon institution where equally distinctive rituals are regularly carried out. As the Mormon population has dispersed so widely from its center in Utah, new temples are in an almost continual process of construction, and exist throughout not only the United States but much of the rest of the world as well. Unlike ward chapels, they are architecturally elaborate and frequently visually striking, evoking Gothic cathedrals, fantastic palaces, or Aztec temples in their eclectic, monumental designs.

The rituals performed at Mormon temples are known as *ordinances,* participation in which is restricted exclusively to worthy believers, and the details of which are carefully guarded from outsiders. The ordinances, which seem to derive in part from those of the Freemasonry in which Joseph Smith and other early Mormons participated, are said to have been revealed directly to Smith, and do not have direct analogues in Judaism or Christianity. Prominent among them is the baptism for the dead, which is performed vicariously in the immersion of a living person. Such baptism permits the enjoyment of the company of a large family extended through the generations in the afterlife, which is central to the Mormon vision of blessedness. To further this process, the Latter-day Saints maintain a vast genealogical library in Salt Lake City, and older people especially are encouraged to spend their time in tracing their ancestors for retroactive initiation into the fold. These holdings are the result of an extensive worldwide microcopying of demographic records, and are a treasure-trove for secular researchers as well.

Two other important ordinances are carried out in Mormon temples as well. *Endowment* ceremonies are rites of initiation undergone by young adults before setting off on missionary work or marriage. Those participating wear special garments and engage in ritual bathing, during which their important organs are anointed with oil. They witness a dramatic reenactment of cosmic history, are instructed in the Plan of Salvation, and are given secret biblical names. *Sealing* ceremonies bind a man and woman together for "time and eternity," and children may be sealed into this everlasting relationship as well. (Divorce is frowned upon by Mormons, but Utah's divorce rate is fairly high nevertheless.)

At the higher levels of governance, *stakes* are administrative units that include ten to twelve wards, for a total of about five thousand people. (Their full name, which indicates their significance, is "Stake of Zion.") Stakes are presided over by a Stake Presidency of three, part of a High Council of fifteen. The highest leadership of the Church resides with the *General Authorities,* who are based in Salt Lake City. Prominent among these are the Council of Twelve Apostles and the First Presidency, which consists of the President and two counsellors. The First President is more than a powerful bureaucrat; as the successor of Joseph Smith, he inherits the latter's titles of "Prophet, Seer and Revelator," and may become the vehicle for communicating ongoing revelation on important matters (such as, in 1890, plural marriage). The eldest of the Twelve Apostles automatically assumes the office of First President upon its vacancy, so that the highest leadership may take on the aspect of a gerontocracy at times. Like all members of the priesthoods, the General Authorities are not specially trained for their roles, and are usually successful businessmen. (Ezra Taft Benson, Secretary of Agriculture under Dwight Eisenhower, served as First President beginning in 1985.) Since all males are expected to play leadership roles and belong to the several ranks of the priesthoods, there are no seminaries, and theology is largely the product of each individual's reflections on revelation and experience. Religious instruction for children, youth, and adults is offered each Sunday, however, as part of the ward's activities.

In addition to these formal structures of belief, worship, and authority, Mormons participate in a culture closely linked to but still transcending all of these formal components. Like the Hebrews, upon which much of their collective identity is modeled, Mormons may be viewed not simply as a religious denomination, however distinctive its identity, but also as a *people*. Central to this notion of "peoplehood" is the Mormon notion of the *gathering*—the sorting-out of the followers of Joseph Smith from the Gentiles. Mormon teenagers are given a "Patriarchal Blessing," which lets them know from which part of the House of Israel they are descended. In short, the Mormons in the present age represent in a very real way a reconstitution of the nation of Israel, in a spiritual if not a genetically literal sense. (The recruitment of the early Mormons primarily from Americans of northwestern European descent and Europeans of similar provenance has in fact given many Mormons a common gene pool, reinforced by generations of intermarriage. Continual evangelization, especially in the Third World, had diluted this homogeneity in recent years, however.)

Although Mormons are now dispersed throughout the nation and the world, the original land of settlement in the Great Salt Basin retains a powerful significance. Salt Lake City is not only the administrative but also in many ways the symbolic and spiritual center for most Latter-day Saints as well. Temple Square, where Brigham Young's great temple and other structures are located, serves as a sort of *axis mundi*—a "center of the world"—much as Jerusalem and, more broadly, Israel function for the Jewish people. Particularly interesting is the Seagull Monument in Salt Lake City, commemorating the deliverance of the earliest Utah settlers from famine when crickets devouring the crops were unexpectedly consumed by a flock of seagulls. (The parallel with the children of Israel feeding on heaven-sent manna during their years in the wilderness is striking, as are other features of the Mormon "Exodus.") Other shrines commemorating major events in the life of Joseph Smith, such as the site of his birthplace in Vermont, are also maintained by the LDS Church as shrines, and a colorful historical pageant is enacted each summer in Palmyra, New York.

The life of the Mormon people is thus rooted in a shared history, which even recent converts share vicariously and adopt as their own. Other parallels with the Hebrew people are instructive in understanding the Mormon way of life and self-understanding as a people, and are by no means accidental. A parallel to the Hebrew *kashrut* laws on clean and unclean foods is derived from the "Word of Wisdom," section 89 of the *Doctrine and Covenants* (which is composed of further revelations to Joseph Smith). Mormons are thereby enjoined from using tobacco, alcohol and "hot drinks" (caffeinated beverages including, today, many soft drinks), and to be moderate in the consumption of meat. These probably reflect the evangelical ethos of Smith's day—John Wesley gave his Methodist followers very similar dietary advice—as well as the exigencies of frontier life. The Mormon custom of keeping a year's supply of food always at hand, which is no longer universally honored in its literal sense, reflects a similar prudence in dealing with frontier hardships, and may take on eschatological overtones for some as a preparation for the "last days."

Other aspects of Mormon culture also reflect the stresses and isolation of the frontier years. Many towns in Utah were built along patterns prescribed by Brigham Young, and the older houses constitute a distinctive vernacular style. A body of folk songs, many dealing with the hardships endured during the trek to Utah and later adversities, persist, as does a distinctive Mormon hymnody. (The Mormon Tabernacle Choir, of course, is an ongoing source of national publicity and good will, and performs from a wide musical repertory.) The frontier years also generated a folklore, in which stories of providential deliverances (such as that commemorated in the seagull monument) and legends about Smith and Young join with versions of standard folklore motifs such as the story of the three Nephites. In this latter story from one to three strangers mysteriously appear to aid Mormons in distress, and then vanish. It later turns out that these strangers were Nephites, the good people of pre-Columbian days whose story is told in the *Book of Mormon*. In other forms, the tale still makes its anonymous rounds—most recently in modern America as "the phantom hitchhiker."

As the prohibitions on intoxicants and stimulants indicate, cleanliness and health are primary components of the Mormon value system—part of what has sometimes been called their "Work, Health, Education, Recreation" complex. Hard work, usually now in white-collar and professional occupations; education, such as that provided by Brigham Young University and other Mormon-sponsored institutions; a stress on the recreational value of sports; and a general emphasis on "clean living" are all characteristic Mormon virtues, echoing the earlier American religious cultures of Puritanism and nineteenth-century evangelicalism.

Combined with these virtues is a social and political conservatism that continues to make Mormonism controversial among other Americans. Mormons tend to vote Republican, and Utah's delegates to Congress are usually firmly within the conservative wing of the Republican Party. Until 1978, black males were barred from the priesthoods, until a revelation similar to that which had ended plural marriage brought about a change in policy. (The pressures generated by the civil rights movement, as well as the difficulties of evangelism in Latin American countries with much more interracial mixture than is common in the United States, may both have played a role in this reversal.) Mormon attitudes toward the role of women remain very conservative. Large families are encouraged, and Mormon evangelism stresses heavily the attractiveness of stable, traditional family. Although a feminist movement has been making itself felt in recent years within the more liberal wing of the Mormon community, considerable media attention focused in 1979 on Sonia Johnson, who was excommunicated for overly vocal public support of the Equal Rights Amendment.

Two other events of the 1980s that received widespread media coverage are indicative of tensions within the Mormon community. In 1987 Mark W. Hofmann, a rare book dealer, pleaded guilty to two counts of murder that he had committed in the course of negotiating the sale of a series of forged documents on Mormon origins to prominent members of the LDS community. Apart from the gory details of the bombings involved, the central issue at stake here is the emphasis that Mormons place on the precise authenticity of the community's origins in the events narrated by Joseph Smith. In particular, Mormon leaders were concerned with documents providing alternate accounts of Smith's discovery of the golden plates, which emphasized the folk-magical character of these events as well as the possible unreliability of Smith's narrative. Fortunately for traditionalist Mormons, the documents, which spoke among other things of a "white salamander," proved to be skillful forgeries by Hofmann.

Illustrative not of history but rather of the Mormon role in contemporary politics was the controversy over the administration and subsequent impeachment and removal from office of Arizona Governor Evan Mecham, a Mormon, in 1988. Mecham aroused considerable opposition over a number of remarks on racial and sexual subjects (including a militant aversion to homosexuality), as well as his repeal of the state's observance of the birthday of Martin Luther King, Jr. Although his impeachment took place as the result of alleged financial irregularities on his part, some of his Mormon defenders were firmly convinced that he had been divinely chosen to be governor, and that attacks on him were attacks on the LDS community as well.

Strains within the LDS community are clearly real, as is continuing opposition from without. The principal external foes of the Mormons had at one time been mainly evangelical Protestants exercised both about polygamy and the deviance of Mormon belief from what they held to be the Christian norm. More recently, however, conservative Protestants and Mormons have converged on traditionalist attitudes on social and political issues, while political and religious liberals have become increasingly critical about Mormon conservatism. This shift in alliances forms an interesting parallel to the cooperation of conservative Catholics with Fundamentalists on the abortion issue.

Conflict within the Mormon ranks—real but muted today—is hardly something new. The persistence of a "fundamentalist" minority demonstrates the schismatic potential of such a radical change in direction as that which occurred in 1890. Although these groups are small and decentralized, and for obvious reasons prefer to avoid publicity, their continuing existence demonstrates the pluralism that has characterized the Mormon tradition since the time of Joseph Smith. The largest rift in the tradition in fact dates back to Smith's death and the temporary vacuum in leadership in which it resulted. The majority of Smith's followers quickly accepted Brigham Young as their leader, and followed him across the Plains to Utah. A number of small splinter groups also emerged, such as that led by James Jesse Strang, who briefly headed a theocratic community of Mormon dissidents on Beaver Island, Michigan, from 1845 till his murder in 1856.

Although the "Strangites" still survive vestigially, most of Strang's followers left after his death to join what today is still the principal organized alternative to the "Utah Mormons." The "Missouri Mormons," as they are sometimes known, constitute the Reorganized Church of Jesus Christ of Latter Day Saints (RLDS), with a national headquarters at Independence, Missouri. This group was organized by Smith's wife and several other early Mormons who had rejected Young's leadership, and who eventually persuaded the Prophet's son, Joseph Smith III, to assume the group's presidency, which he did in 1859. One of its principal differences from "Utah Mormonism" is its principle of leadership, through which the presidency automatically devolves upon Smith's descendants. Although it affirms the authenticity of Smith's revelations, the RLDS have never accepted more distinctive later Mormon practices such as polygamy, "blood atonement" (the killing of murderers, which sometimes took place in Young's day), and the various temple ordinances. The RLDS church is much more liberal in social attitudes than its larger counterpart: It ordains women to the priesthood, has never drawn lines based on race, and is open to ecumenical relations with other Christian groups. Its membership in the mid-1980s stood at about one hundred ninety-two thousand, compared with the much larger (3.6 million) numbers of its Utah counterpart.

Mormonism has been called the most American of religions, and has at times been treated as subversively un-American. It is clearly a community of apparent paradoxes: while its teachings strike most traditional Christians as extremely deviant, its social attitudes have brought it into increasing visibility as the American cultural and religious mood drifted rightwards in the 1970s and 1980s. Although appearing to compromise on issues such as plural marriage and, later, racial segregation, it has nevertheless continued on a conservative course that both aligns it with and estranges it from major sectors of American society. Its growing "normality" has led to higher levels of acceptability, while its aggressive evangelism and high birth rate have resulted in continuing dramatic growth. Whether its cultural "success" will lead to further erosion of its distinctiveness and the relegation of its distinctive beliefs to vestigially symbolic status remains to be seen.

CHAPTER 51

Liberalism, Radicalism, and Secularism

Religious liberalism in the twentieth century, as in the past, has acted more as a moving spirit than as an organizing principle. With the exception of a few extremely conservative denominations, such as the Assemblies of God, it has influenced almost every major religious group in America from Mormons to Methodists. Its fortunes have varied: Forced underground by papal encyclicals at the turn of the century, the liberal spirit in American Catholicism did not receive widespread legitimation until the upheavals of Vatican II in the 1960s. On the other hand, the pervasive influence of liberal theology and its descendant, Neo-Orthodoxy, on "mainline" Protestantism remained strong till the 1970s, when a new, national wave of cultural conservatism called its premises into question and led to a significant decline in the strength and influence of those denominations in which it had previously flourished.

Liberal religion in nineteenth-century America had found its firmest institutional base in Unitarianism. As Unitarians emerged into the present century, though, they found their leadership challenged from a number of directions. Agnosticism had become socially acceptable, at least among the educated classes, and such distinguished figures from prominent Unitarian families as Henry Adams and Charles Eliot Norton made no pretense of keeping up any formal religious affiliation or espousing any belief system. At the other end, many of the ideas that Unitarians had developed decades earlier, such as a stress on the benevolence of God, the potential for human happiness through moral growth, and the compatibility of religious faith with contemporary science and philosophy, were now disseminated widely through other Christian denominations under the generic name of "liberal Protestantism" or "modernism." A humanist movement began to assume organized form, resulting in the publication of such provocative documents as the "Humanist Manifesto" of 1933. Finally, the Depression and uncertain leadership impaired the denomination's ability to mount an effective witness for its principles—assuming that its members could agree upon what the latter might be.

The revival of Unitarianism in the middle decades of the twentieth century was based on administrative reorganization, a renewed commitment to inclusiveness, a reassertion of traditional social concerns, a willingness to experiment with new forms of local structure and ultimately a consummation of a long-term interest in merging with like-minded groups. One tactic for recruitment of new members was the Lay Fellowship Plan launched in 1948. Traditionally, most Unitarians were either natives of New England or else resident in cities or academic communities where churches had been founded by emigrant Yankees and attracted others who were sympathetic with liberal principles. The Fellowship movement was based on the idea that, where potential recruits were scattered and few, they might be better attracted by a small, informal group meeting in private homes or rented quarters without having to make a commitment to build a church and support a minister. The movement was advertised in newspapers throughout the nation. It resulted in the founding of a considerable number of fellowship groups, some of which eventually grew into churches and others of which remained small and informal. In contrast to the more traditional worship patterns that continued to be popular in New England and in urban churches, fellowships tended to resemble discussion groups more than church services, sometimes with recorded classical music used to establish an atmosphere conducive to ethical reflection and debate. Unitarian churches until recently followed the styles of their eras;

more recently, though, many are avant garde in their symbolism, such as Louis Kahn's design in Rochester meant to evoke a question mark.

In 1961, the American Unitarian Association merged with the Universalist Church of America to form a new denomination, the Unitarian Universalist Association. This merger followed decades of discussions, and brought together into one body the two oldest and most successful institutional embodiments of the liberal religious impulse in America. The new denomination exhibits the New England origins of both traditions in maintaining its headquarters at 25 Beacon Street in Boston, in the shadow of the State House. It publishes a monthly journal, the *World,* and also supports the Beacon Press, which has for several decades taken the lead in publishing books with a liberal, sometimes highly controversial, perspective. Since "UUs," as they refer to themselves, have always disliked rigid boundaries, their publications are not restricted to denominational authors or issues, but reflect a broad range of contemporary religious, social, and intellectual perspectives.

As appropriate to its tradition, Unitarian-Universalists of the later twentieth century are typically involved in the social issues of the day. Many nineteenth-century feminist leaders, such as Elizabeth Cady Stanton, Susan B. Anthony, and Lucy Stone, had been Unitarians, and both Unitarians and Universalists had been among the first denominations to ordain women to the ministry. Although Unitarian involvement in the antislavery movement had been ambivalent, twentieth-century UUs were notably active in the civil rights movement of the 1960s, although only a handful of the membership and clergy are black. Unitarian-Universalists have been especially vocal in the 1980s in championing gay rights, including the ordination of gay men and lesbian women, as well as other liberal causes of the day such as the protection of the environment. The UUA's statement of "Principles and Purposes," expressed as a covenant affirmation, includes the following:

> The inherent worth and dignity of every person.
> Justice, equity, and compassion in human relations.
> The goal of world community with peace, liberty, and justice for all.
> Respect for the interdependent web of existence of which we are a part.

The statement goes on to list sources of the UU tradition, which include "direct experience of . . . transcending mystery and wonder," "words and deeds of prophetic women and men," "wisdom from the world's religions," "Jewish and Christian teachings," and "Humanist teachings" (from the 1984/1985 by-laws).

Today's UUA is a small denomination, with a membership of approximately one hundred eighty thousand distributed among some one thousand churches and fellowships in 1986. Approximately 80 percent of the membership is through voluntary affiliation rather than birth; the latter is most important in New England. Membership is concentrated in the northeastern quadrant of the nation, with churches and fellowships elsewhere usually found in urban areas, college and university communities, and "high tech" centers such as Oak Ridge, Tennessee. Education and income levels of members are high. Polity is congregational, continuing the tradition of its New England roots. Similar to the Quakers, Unitarian-Universalists do not seriously contemplate becoming a major denomination in size. Rather, they constitute a small elite who see themselves as evangelists not for their group itself but rather for the causes it espouses. Advancement of social and spiritual ends, not the triumph of organizational means, is the ultimate goal.

The liberal spirit has also found itself institutionalized—insofar as that may be possible—in other forms. The Ethical Culture Society, discussed more fully below, goes even beyond Unitarian-Universalism in its rejection of traditional theism, but has never gained a widespread following. Quakers (Friends), especially the Philadelphia Yearly Meeting, have historically allied themselves with liberal or even radical social stances, but their distinctive theology has distanced them from the more rationalistic approaches of Unitarian-Universalism and Ethical Culture. Among the "mainline" Protestant denominations, the United Church of Christ stands out as the most clearly liberal in both theology and social and political positions. Ironically, its historical roots are in large part in the conservative Congregationalist churches from which the early Unitarians were forced to separate in 1825. The Episcopal and Presbyterian (PCUSA) churches are also identified by some as liberal, but the range of outlook found among their memberships makes such a label seem more doubtfully accurate.

Liberal religionists have often been perceived by their more conservative compatriots as not only unsound in belief but as scarcely distinguishable from nonbelievers. As Martin Marty has pointed out, the role of the "unbeliever" or "infidel" has often been a construct, a straw man, devised by conservative believers as a way of arousing alarm and renewed zeal among the faithful. As such, it is analogous to the phenomenon that David Brion Davis has called "countersubversion" in American history. By this, Davis means those crusades that flourished especially in the early nineteenth century against a number of groups that were labeled as deviant and therefore dangerous to the Republic. Among these were Roman Catholics, Masons, Mormons, and Southern slaveholders, all of whom were accused at one time or another of a combination of sexual immorality and political subversion—charges spread through lurid, inflammatory literature that might be called the moral equivalent of pornography. Identifying deviants, even if their deviance has to be invented from the whole cloth, is a way of establishing or reinforcing one's own identity when the latter is called into doubt by rapid social change.

This is not to say, however, that there have not been self-proclaimed "infidels" in American history. During the Revolutionary era, Tom Paine and Ethan Allen, both with substantial reputations as patriots, published tracts that repudiated traditional Christianity. Allen, known as the leader of the "Green Mountain Boys," mounted a rather amateurish attack in his *Reason the Only Oracle of Man* (1785). Paine had been an especially effective propagandist for the American cause through his pamphlets "Common Sense" and "The American Crisis"; later, his *Age of Reason* (1794–1796) presented an equally eloquent but less effectual argument for Deism, combined with an attack on the effects of institutional religion. Although Paine tried his hand at organizing a "Theophilanthropist" society, he attracted few followers.

The early republic, which Alice Felt Tyler identified as the great era of "Freedom's Ferment" in the realm of religious and social experimentation, was characterized simultaneously by the rapid growth of evangelical Protestantism in the "Second Great Awakening" as well as a bewildering diversity of alternatives such as the Mormons, Shakers, and other sectarian groups. Unbelief provided a convenient target for militant evangelicals such as Timothy Dwight, the president of Yale, and Lyman Beecher, one of evangelicalism's leading orators, propagandists, and organizers. Dwight, for example, helped launch a phase of the Second Awakening at Yale through his cry of alarm over undergraduates calling one another "Voltaire," "Rousseau," and other names of French Enlightenment leaders. Deist Thomas Jefferson became for the New England Federalist-Congregationalist establishment a symbol of the evils of unbridled democracy. More sophisticated attacks on traditional religion than the affectations of young Yalies came from such utopian socialist thinkers as Robert Dale Owen and Fanny Wright. Their experiments were generally short-lived; however, the dozens of communitarian societies that were founded in the early nineteenth century attracted an inordinate amount of attention, especially from the never-ending stream of bemused foreign visitors to American shores.

Meanwhile, the majority of Americans never joined any religious group in a formal way. This did not mean that they were hostile or skeptical; it indicated rather that, in a fluid society with free religious choice, there was not enough tradition or other pressure to make church membership an urgent matter, except perhaps during flurries of revivalism. During the earlier nineteenth century, such widespread lack of affiliation was characteristic of ordinary people, who seldom articulated their preferences publicly.

After the Civil War, attacks on traditional religion played a small but important role in the public realm of debate. Colonel Robert Ingersoll drew fame on the lecture circuits with such attacks, while simultaneously playing a leading role in Republican party politics. Mark Twain, probably the best-loved author of his time, satirized not only "deviant" religious groups such as Mormons and Christian Scientists, but also questioned traditional religion itself in such brooding later works as *The Mysterious Stranger* (1916). Moreover, a subtle change began to pervade the more articulate strata of society. The cumulative impact first of Enlightenment rationalism and skepticism and then of Darwinist naturalism certainly played a role in this process, as did the erosion of dogma in much Christian thought.

While many Protestants expressed this change in religious sensibility through espousing one or another variety of liberalism, others quietly dropped out of the ranks of believers altogether. *Agnosticism,* a term coined by the English Victorian skeptic Thomas Henry Huxley, now entered the American vocabulary to describe those who did not deny the existence of a personal god, but who rather did not think that the question could be resolved by human minds. The "cult" of science as a virtual alternative to religion became widespread in many academic and professional circles. Another poignant example of this process of "dropping out" is narrated in *The Education of Henry Adams* (1907), the autobiographical account of the personal and intellectual odyssey of the scion of New England's leading family.

The clash between Fundamentalism and Modernism in the 1920s evoked further "elitist" attacks on religion, such as the journalist H. L. Mencken's ridicule of the Bible Belt and its unenlightenened denizens. (Mencken covered the Scopes Trial for the Baltimore *Sun* in 1925). Such stridency, however, was less common than the gradual shift of mood among many of the leaders of thought and culture away from religious questions altogether. For many academics, professional writers, and other shapers of opinion, a more or less conscious secularism became the norm.

As society itself grew more pluralistic, court decisions began to constrict the expression of religious themes in public arenas. This judicial caution combined with a fear by politicians and advertisers of offending popular opinion to lead to a banishment of religion from much of the public sphere: the schools, the political arena, and the mass media. By the 1970s, a backlash against this gradual development took shape in the form of aggressive Fundamentalist attacks on "secular humanism," the generic term that gained popularity as a label for these accumulated social forces.

"Humanism" in the sense of a conscious rejection of a personal god and a corresponding exaltation of human moral capacities has remote roots in the Renaissance, clearer sources in the Enlightenment, and a genuine though modest history of institutional expression in America. The Free Religious Association, founded in 1866 by dissident Unitarians who objected to their denomination's explicitly Christian identity, was an early though short-lived attempt in this direction. More enduring has been its offshoot, Ethical Culture, which in 1983 had about four thousand members spread among twenty-two local groups. Ethical Culture came into being in 1876 through the work of Felix Adler (1851–1933), a Reform rabbi who had served as the second president of the Free Religious Association. Similar in spirit to humanistic Unitarianism, Ethical Culture stresses human moral responsibility and potential, and provides an organized forum for discussion and education for families who are not comfortable with traditional religion.

The term *Humanism* has gained currency through the "Humanist Manifesto," first issued in 1933 and signed by the philosopher John Dewey and other intellectual and liberal religious leaders (including several Unitarians), and reissued in 1973 as the "Humanist Manifesto II." An American Humanist Association was organized in 1941; with headquarters at Yellow Springs, Ohio (home of Antioch College), it continues to publish *The Humanist,* and maintains a small membership. Allied with organized humanism in a very limited way are a number of organizations that are vocal defenders of civil liberties, and are continually alert to what they regard as violations of the proper boundaries separating church and state. These include the American Civil Liberties Union; Norman Lear's People for the American Way, which was founded specifically to counteract the "Social Agenda" of the Moral Majority and other New Religious Rights groups; and various Jewish organizations sensitive to claims that America is basically a "Christian nation." In addition, a few very small groups of organized atheists, such as the flamboyant Madalyn Murray O'Hair's "American Atheists, Inc.," periodically attract publicity through their combination of philosophical unbelief and legal challenges in church-state separation cases.

It is difficult to assess the impact on American life of this combination of organized movements that might be collectively identified as "secularist"— that is, working against the involvement of organized religion in the political and social realms. The ACLU and kindred groups have the most document-able force, and have made a genuine impact in their advocacy in courts and legislatures on behalf of church-state separation. The claim of Fundamental-ists that "Secular Humanism" as an organized, conscious force has been suc-cessful in eroding the fabric of American society is much harder to demon-strate, since it is difficult to find very many people who identify themselves as "secular humanists," organized or otherwise. What seems to be happening here is a resurfacing of the theme of "counter-subversion": an attempt to blame long-term undesirable social trends such as pluralism and secularism to achieve their wicked ends. (The phrases "atheistic Communism" and "interna-tional Communist conspiracy" that were current in the 1950s McCarthyite stir are indicative of the same preoccupations.)

If secular humanism is a bugbear of the political and religious right, this is not to say that secularism and secularity are illusory. What distinguishes such secularists from the very small number of organized "secular humanists" is the former's passive rather than active rejection of traditional, theistic religion. Such secularists are not united in any campaign to combat or destroy religion; they simply are not very interested in the whole issue, and express this lack of interest mainly by distancing themselves from any organized religious activity.

Intellectually, the 1960s provided a rationale for a distancing from tradi-tional, organized religion significantly different in kind from earlier skepti-cism and "infidelity." A classic text of that era was Harvey Cox's *The Secular City* (1965), which argued that authentic biblical Christianity was not to be found so much in the churches as in the midst of social change and conflict in contemporary urban America. Part of the theological underpinnings for Cox and other like-minded writers of the period came from Dietrich Bon-hoeffer's *Letters and Papers from Prison* (published 1953). Bonhoeffer, who had been exectued in 1945 for resistance to the Third Reich, argued in this last and posthumous work for what he called a "religionless Christianity" in which God's will for humanity should be interpreted in secular rather than supernaturalistic terms. Various interpretations of this line of argument also helped shape the short-lived "Death of God" movement popularized by theo-logians such as Thomas J. J. Altizer and Gabriel Vahanian. Although the recipient of much media attention, the "Death of God" did not enjoy a long life nor exert a great deal of influence on subsequent speculation. A further variation on the theme of "radical theology" was embodied in Richard Ruben-stein's *After Auschwitz* (1966), a Jewish reflection on the significance of the Holocaust that concluded with a denial of the existence of a God who could permit such atrocities.

At least as disturbing to readers who were most likely to encounter such ideas through the cover story on *Time* or in one-minute segments on network evening news was the "radical turn" in ethical thought that was occurring simultaneously. The civil rights movement, which by the mid-1960s had achieved many of its initial goals, held a broad appeal outside the South because of its deep roots in earlier American thought and experience, and the biblical themes and cadences brought to bear on its behalf by Martin Luther King. The same was not true of the protest movement against the Vietnam War. Its more extreme adherents' burning of draft cards and desecration of flags evoked for the historically minded the more radical tradition of Garrisonian abolitionism, and raised considerable alarm and anger among the newly self-conscious "hardhats" and other conservative segments of society. (William Lloyd Garrison had denounced the Constitution as "a covenant with Death and an agreement with Hell.")

These challenges to racism and war helped generate for many young people a broader challenge to the structures and values of American middle-class culture. Theodore Roszak fixed a label on this loosely organized but culturally powerful impulse in his popular *The Making of a Counter Culture* (1969), significantly subtitled "Reflections on the Technocratic Society and Its Youthful Opposition." For Roszak, the components of this new movement of opposition to prevailing norms and life-styles included neo-Marxist and post-Freudian cultural criticism (as exemplified in the thought of Herbert Marcuse and Norman O. Brown); a fascination with Asian religions, especially Zen and Tibetan Buddhism; and the pervasive use of drugs, particularly LSD, as a way to escape the trammels of everyday consciousness. The popularity of Carlos Castaneda's *The Teachings of Don Juan* (1969) among young people also reflected a simultaneous fascination with alternative worlds of consciousness, drugs, and unmodernized cultures.

In the more private sphere, the conservatively minded also found cause for distress in the "New Morality" advocated in such works as Joseph Fletcher's *Situation Ethics* (1966). The core of this new approach to personal, and especially sexual, responsibility lay in the rejection of traditional arguments that both divine and natural law laid down certain inflexible rules with regard to human conduct. According to the "New Morality"—which tended to lose any nuances it may have originally possessed as it became dispersed through the media—the only guide for personal decision-making was the question of whether one's actions were likely to foster love. Traditional cautions about premarital sex were the most conspicuous victim of this new attitude, and the impact on campus mores was especially striking. Buttressed by a more general revolt of the young against traditional authority, as expressed in the fascination of the youthful "counterculture" for consciousness-altering drugs, the "sexual revolution" was launched on its inexorable course.

Themes raised both by the civil rights movement and the "new morality" combined in another set of causes. Feminism was hardly a newcomer to the American scene, but the impulse toward the equality of women had become submerged in the quest for suburban "normalcy" that had dominated the 1950s. Sparked by Betty Friedan's *The Feminine Mystique* (1963), many women began to question, sometimes radically, the assumptions about their proper social, economic, and sexual roles that seemed implicit in the American society of the day. This new women's movement rapidly became embroiled in questions about philosophy and tactics: whether its aim should focus on correcting traditional economic equalities and other concerns of women who were working in the marketplace by choice or necessity, or whether it should challenge more basic societal assumptions about sexuality and sex roles. By the late 1980s, the question was far from resolved.

Other "liberation" movements, many accompanied by theological and ethical reflections in the seminaries and among denominational leaders, followed in the wake of the black and women's movements. Gay men and lesbian women rapidly began to "come out of the closet," avow their sexual identities publicly, and protest against the opprobrium and discrimination that had traditionally been their lot. Hispanics and Native Americans also began to find articulate advocates for their grievances. On the other hand, a backlash began to take shape among *ethnics*, a term now usually reserved for Americans, often of the second to the fourth generation in this country, descended from the stock of the "New Immigration" of the turn of the century. Primarily of the lower middle classes, these Italian-, Polish- and other "hyphenated" Americans found a voice for their conservative concerns in Michael Novak's *The Rise of the Unmeltable Ethnics* (1972). Novak, who had begun his academic career as a liberal lay Roman Catholic voice, executed an abrupt turn to the right in his sociopolitical outlook, and helped form the cadre of "neoconservatives" who would later articulate the intellectual groundwork of Ronald Reagan Republicanism.

Many younger people who were influenced by some combination of these movements in the 1960s and early 1970s began as a result to question the need for traditional religious practice and institutions. Although not necessarily irreligious, they tended to "drop out" of their parents' churches and synagogues, and did not automatically reenter as they matured. This trend away from organized religion that reemerged among a significant segment of the population at this time has historical roots both in the particular nature of the American republic and in broader, "macro-social" forces pervasive in the Western world during the past century and a half. Changes from a predominantly localistic, village-oriented, agricultural society to an impersonal, specialized, urban industrial order have inevitably undermined the bonds that held people together and promoted participation in churches inclusive of entire communities by definition within their membership.

In the United States, cultural and religious pluralism received legal validation through the First Amendment. Social pressures in many more traditional communities often made church membership prudent for those desiring acceptance and success, but no legal means could henceforward be brought to compel participation. The revivalism that so pervaded nineteenth-century Protestant life was in part a reaction to the ease with which American citizens could avoid religious involvement through a simple passive act of choice (or refusal to choose actively.).

By the late twentieth century, this "passive secularism" had emerged as a major, though invisible, force in American religious life. As Wade Clark Roof and William McKinney have demonstrated in their influential *American Mainline Religion* (1987), a major source of attrition from the "mainline" (liberal and moderate) Protestant denominations has not been loss to other churches, but rather the widespread practice of simply "dropping out." Closely related is the phenomenon described by Robert Bellah and his associates in their *Habits of the Heart* (1985). In one of the interviews upon which this study of contemporary American social values was based, they encountered a young woman named Sheila who described her own religious position as "Sheilaism." By this she meant that she had no need of traditional, organized religious groups; rather, she was content to fashion her own, highly individualistic system of beliefs for herself. In short, "Sheilaism" is a vividly specific example of religion in the modern world not disappearing but rather become so highly personalized that it has entirely detached itself from the sense of community that traditionally characterized the religious life.

At the end of this investigation, there remains a paradox: that American society has simultaneously grown both more secular and more religious. A significant majority of Americans in the late twentieth century belong to organized religious groups, and attend worship at least occasionally. When those who are not affiliated with any religious group but who claim to believe in God are added to this already large number, the total is overwhelmingly large. (In 1988, the Gallup Poll found that some 85 percent claimed to believe in the divinity of Jesus Christ.) The percentages of affiliation are much higher than in the early nineteenth century during the heyday of revivalism. On the other hand, the reality of religious pluralism, the impact of the marketplace and the mass media, and the dilemmas of dealing with beliefs and values in the context of universal public education have all led to the banishment of specific religious symbols and discourse from the public arena. "America" as a sentimental idea may involve the notion of divine sanction, but the "United States" as a functioning society has become pervasively secular. How to resolve the emotional and practical tensions that result from this contrast remains an unsolved issue on the public agenda.

CHAPTER 52

Asian Traditions and New Religions

The American encounter with the Far East has been one of the most problematic issues in the development of this nation from a string of British colonies to a microcosm of the entire world. Jewish, Catholic, and Eastern Orthodox immigrants have all seemed ominously foreign, and encountered hostility before their descendants had become thoroughly assimilated. Afro-Americans, of course, still have to deal with a long heritage of racism, but have lived in America for so long and in such numbers that they are an integral part of the domestic scene. Asians, however, are still something of a novelty, evoking two contrasting reactions from many Americans. On the one hand, the Chinatowns of New York, San Francisco, and other large cities remain exotic and alien, and simultaneously attract and repel the casual Euro-American visitor. On the other, aggressive postwar Japanese entrepreneurship has made Americans confront a social and economic system at once similar to and different from their own. The ambivalence with which we contemplate their finely engineered and competitively priced stereos, VCRs, and automobiles from Sony, Yamaha, and Mitsubishi is another example of the way in which we still are trying to come to terms with the "inscrutable" dimensions of Eastern cultures. It is this perception of radical "otherness" associated with Asia that gives the story of Asian religions in America an extra dimension no longer associated with faiths of European origin.

American encounters with the Orient can be divided into several phases. Until the late nineteenth century, Asians were rare in the United States, and knowledge of their cultures was restricted to a scholarship that was beginning to circulate among an intellectual elite beginning with the New England Transcendentalists in the 1830s. The need for inexpensive labor as the railroad network linking the East and West Coasts was coming to fruition brought over three hundred thousand Chinese, mainly unskilled workers, to this country as part of a larger emigration fleeing political and economic change at home. Other Chinese labor was invested in agriculture, mining, and manufacturing, especially throughout the rapidly developing state of California. A series of Chinese exclusion acts passed by Congress beginning in 1882 resulted in a rapid reduction of the Chinese community in America, which declined from one hundred seven thousand in 1890 to a low of sixty-one thousand in 1920.

A similar pattern characterized Japanese immigration, primarily to the West Coast, with a decline in the number of newcomers from over one hundred thousand during the years 1901-1907 to slightly more than six thousand from 1925 to 1940. The forced resettlement of some one hundred ten thousand Japanese Americans, of whom nearly two-thirds were American citizens, in "relocation" camps during World War II marked the culmination of anti-Oriental sentiment, which attained a virulence unmatched in American treatment of any other people identified as an enemy. (War-era propaganda against Germany lacked the racist dimensions of that directed against the "Japs.")

The postwar era was marked by two opposing tendencies in American attitudes toward the Orient. On the one hand, the familiarity that Americans gained with native Asians first during the occupation of a defeated Japan, and then through the stationing of combat and support troops in Korea and Vietnam, led to first-hand familiarity with the cultures of East Asia and considerable intermarriage. The resurgence of the Japanese economy and increasing commercial relations with other Asian countries also stimulated cultural interchange. (For example, the "chop suey joints" of an earlier day, which purveyed wok-fried combinations of foods unknown in China, began to yield around 1970 to sophisticated restaurants specializing in Szechuan, Hunan, and other authentic regional Chinese cuisines.)

On the other hand, hostile encounters with North Korean, Communist

Chinese, and Vietcong troops did little to create a positive image of Orientals among American servicemen and their supporters. (The same might be said of Japanese economic competition.) However, liberalized immigration laws since World War II have resulted in dramatic increases in Asian immigration, including refugees from Vietnam, Laos, and Cambodia as well as highly skilled professionals from the Indian subcontinent. By the 1980s, Korean fruit-markets, Pakistani physicians, and Japanese sushi bars had all become familiar features of the urban American scene.

In terms of religion, the Asian impact on America can be divided into three broad categories that are by no means mutually exclusive. First, there are what we might call "ethnic religions," those practiced by Asian immigrants themselves (and, to a lesser extent, by their descendants) and adapted to American circumstances. Second come what have been called "export religions," versions of Asian traditions that have become popular primarily among intellectuals and better-educated Americans in part through aggressive missionary activity by Asians themselves. A subdivision of this latter category might be included as well under a third heading of "cults" or, more neutrally, "new religions." Although the latter category also includes groups such as Scientology, which might be classified as "neo-harmonial," a number of others, such as the Unification Church and the Divine Light Mission, have Asian roots of one sort or another. (Scientology, founded by science-fiction writer L. Ron Hubbard in 1954, is nontheistic, and combines elements of depth pyschology with a belief in reincarnation. Its primary activity, called "auditing" with the aid of devices known as "E-meters," is aimed at helping individuals attain a state known as "clear." The expensive and intimate character of this process, together with questionable intelligence-gathering tactics employed by the group's leadership, led to extensive difficulties with government at various levels in America and abroad in the 1970s. Hubbard, who died in 1986, spent much of his controversial later years in isolation at sea or in southern California.)

Prior to the later twentieth-century immigration of business and professional people, the large majority of Asian settlers in this country were laborers and artisans who brought with them the traditional popular religions of China and Japan especially. These religions have been described, in the anthropologist Robert Redfield's phrase, as "little traditions": local and popular interpretations of the "great traditions" of Hinduism and Buddhism, or latter-day adaptations of older popular strains such as Japanese Shinto and Chinese Taoism (DOW-ism). Since these traditions were brought over in piecemeal fashion, and since the American style of denominational organization was not a feature of traditional Asian religions, these ethnic religions have been decentralized, highly varied, and prone to *syncretism*—that is borrowing elements from other traditions to form new strains. Further, where monasticism is an important feature of both the Hindu and Buddhist traditions in Asia, those faiths have been carried on in America primarily by lay people. For these latter, both philosophical reflection and meditative withdrawal from the world have not been practical options, so that their practice has focused more on the performance of public and household rituals than on difficult and prolonged contemplative practices.

If we look at these traditions individually, we should first note that the designation of *Islam* as an "Eastern" religion is problematic, even though its practitioners are most commonly found in the Middle East, the Indian subcontinent, and Southeast Asia. Rather, it is definitely a "religion of the book"—emphatically monotheistic—and shares the Hebrew and Christian scriptures with its two major Western relations. (Conversely, the Middle Eastern origins of the two latter faiths have led some to ask whether they might not be considered "Eastern" religions as well.) Islam is not just a belief system but a way of life intended for both individuals and entire societies, based on the holy book, the *Qur'an* (sometimes westernized as the "Koran"), which was revealed through the prophet Muhammed (A.D. 570?–632). After the Prophet's death, his followers became divided over the issue of the succession of leadership. The majority group, known as Sunni Muslims, believe that caliphs, or political and military leaders beginning with Muhammed's associated Abu Bakr, are the rightful successors. The minority view, held by the Shi'i (Shi'ites, Shi'ite Muslims) rather believe that the succession was intended by Muhammed to continue through the bloodline of his cousin and son-in-law 'Ali. The latter group has attracted considerable attention in recent years through its fundamentalist views calling for a strict enforcement of Muslim law by the state. (The radical group "Islamic Jihad" takes its name from the Muslim word for "holy war," which has been practiced by Muslims periodically to extend Muslim political hegemony.) The role of radical Shi'ites in the overthrow of the regime of Shah Reza Pahlavi in Iran and their subsequent holding of American hostages has made them, to say the least, controversial.

American Muslims have come from a wide variety of national and ethnic backbrounds. Like their Greek, Italian, and Syrian Christian neighbors from the Mediterranean basin, Muslims from Syria-Lebanon first began to emigrate to the industrial cities of the North—particularly the Detroit area in the 1920s, when Henry Ford's new assembly lines promised alluring wages. After World War II, these primarily Arabic Muslims began to be joined by co-religionists from the Balkans (Albania and parts of Yugoslavia), Iran, Egypt, and Pakistan (the eastern part of which later became Bangladesh). By the late 1980s, their numbers in the United States and Canada had reached the neighborhood of 3 million, putting them within sight of overtaking the Jewish community as numerically second only to Christians. A large majority of Muslims resident in North America are urban, with particularly sizable concentrations in New York, Los Angeles, Chicago, Detroit, Houston, Washington, D.C., and Toronto. (Although New York City still holds its place as a *cosmopolis*—world-city—and blender of newly arriving immigrants, Los Angeles has come to rival it in recent years in these roles.)

Like their other Asian counterparts, American Muslims have practiced their religion in a very decentralized fashion, although organizations such as the Islamic Society of North America provide some coordination. Professional clergy are not needed for proper worship, although full-time *imams* in larger population centers do preside over *mosques*—places for public worship, often designed in traditional Muslim style—or "Islamic centers," which provide broader cultural and educational programs. The observation of the "Five

Pillars of Islam" by American Muslims varies considerably since, for example, interruptions of the work day for prayer facing Mecca is often difficult. Many, however, observe the Ramadan fast, and American affluence facilitates the traditional pilgrimage to Mecca, Muhammed's birthplace.

Although the Muslim religion has become divided into sects or factions, such as the Shi'ites and Sunnis, it nevertheless has a clear core of scripture, belief, worship, and practice that give it a unity conductive to common observance throughout the world. This centralized character is notably lacking in other "ethnic" religions practiced by Asians in this country. Hinduism, for example, has never existed anywhere in an organized and uniform fashion, but has evolved in India for centuries around a common set of texts (the Vedas and Upanishads); ideas (e.g., reincarnation and *karma*, the principle of retribution that follows individuals through successive incarnations); and the discipline of *yoga* in a wide variety of forms, including the physical exercises (*hatha yoga*) more familiar to Westerners through exercise classes than as formal meditation.

Hinduism in America is observed as an ethnic religion in America primarily by immigrants from India—about four hundred thousand in 1980—and their families. (Residential patterns are similar to those of American Muslims.) Religious activity is family- and home-centered, although Hindu temples have begun to arise in many urban areas—Chicago, Pittsburgh, and New York for instance—with substantial Indian populations. Women especially are likely to practice some daily meditation, often through the use of *mantras* (sets of syllables whose sound value promotes meditation). On major religious festivals, and sometimes for "rites of passage" such as births, American Hindus may conduct or participate in *pujas*—rituals involving the offering of gifts such as flowers and fruit—before images of a god at a household shrine or a public temple. At the latter, which are not always accessible for American Hindus, professional priests preside over *pujas*, often with support from temples back in India.

For both Chinese and Japanese resident in America, religious life may reflect a combination of traditions adapted to an American setting. To begin with, a fair number of East and Southeast Asian-Americans are Christians, whose forebears were converted by French Catholic missionaries in what was once known as "Indochina" (Vietnam, Laos, and Cambodia), or American Protestants, especially Presbyterians, in China and Korea in particular. For those who are not Christian or members of such "new religions" as Nichiren Shoshu or the Unification Church, though, religious identity may be divided between various manifestations of Buddhism on the one hand and indigenous religions such as Japanese Shinto on the other.

Among both Chinese and Japanese, "Pure Land" Buddhism in its various forms is one of the most popular traditions, in both sense of the term *popular*. Forms involving extended meditation, such as Zen, are more likely to be followed by an elite and by Western converts. Pure Land Buddhism had its origins in fifth- and sixth-century China, and represents a move to make the forbiddingly austere Buddhist tradition more vividly graspable. It is a devotional cult focusing on the Buddha Amitabha (Amida, in Japan), who, after many lives of heroic self-perfection, became a Buddha whose power created a Western Paradise and whose grace makes it possible for followers to join him there after a final death in the world's present degenerate age. This could be accomplished rather easily through repetition of the Buddha Amitabha's name. This vision of a concrete afterlife is more like the popular Christian notion of Heaven than the more rarefied state of *nirvana* sought after by traditional Buddhists. The only very far-reaching attempt to give American ethnic Buddhism organized form is the Buddhist Churches of America (1899), which is national in scope and Pure Land in orientation. Although reliable statistics on American Buddhism are hard to come by, the Buddhist Churches list in the mid-1980s a membership of about one hundred thousand distributed among one hundred churches served by one hundred fifteen clergy.

In addition to Buddhism, many Chinese also are followers of versions of the nation's traditional religions, Confucianism and Taoism. The former, named after the sage Confucius (571–479 B.C.), is based on patterns for ordering the entirety of life to give it sacred significance. Taoism, known by Americans primarily through the *I Ching* (Yi Jing), or "Book of Changes," began as a philosophical system emphasizing harmony with nature rather than, as the Confucians would have it, primarily with society. Religious practice at the popular level drew freely on all three traditions—Buddhist, Confucian, and Taoist—for its elements, and concerned itself not so much with abstract systems but with the sacred character of particular places, activities, and people—especially ancestors. The "joss houses" (from Spanish *dios*, "God") that arose in America's Chinatowns served believers in a variety of these religious idioms, which did not retain a great deal of distinctiveness in the abstract. Although Buddhist "churches," which have adopted a Western nomenclature and organizational form, are not insignificant, much Chinese traditional religion in America constitutes, in Carlyle Haaland's phrase, an "invisible institution" whose rituals are conducted in private.

In Japan, the coexistence of very different religious traditions without contradiction in the life of the individual has its clearest expression in the simultaneous appeal of both Buddhism in its various forms and *Shinto*. Similar to many aspects of Chinese popular and "civil" religion, Shinto is the collective name for the myths, symbols, and rituals with which the Japanese endow everyday life with sacred meaning. Its dimensions range from the cult of the Emperor, who is thought to rule in direct succession from Amaterasu-O-Mikami, the sun goddess, to household and village shrines where seasonal and life-cycle festivals are observed. In the United States, "Imperial Shinto" came in for hard times through its association with Japanese militarism during World War II. Although a small number of Japanese-Americans on Hawaii and the mainland are affiliated with various sectarian forms of Shinto, such as Tenrikyo ("Religion of Heavenly Wisdom"), the religious impulse that Shinto embodies is manifested more typically in seasonal festivals, the cultivation of gardens, and the maintenance in the home of alcoves of *kami* —the sacred power that Shinto shrines delineate.

The first major impact of Eastern religions in their more philosophical dimensions among Americans began in the 1830s, when Emerson, Thoreau, and other New England Transcendentalists began to familiarize themselves with the Hindu scriptures that were slowly becoming available in English translations. In his poem "Brahma," Emerson articulated an interpretation of the cosmos and human destiny very distinct from that of his Unitarian and Calvinist contemporaries, and one that implied a severe criticism of the materialistic civilization those creeds fostered. ("If the red slayer thinks he slays/Or if the slain thinks he is slain,/They know not well the subtle ways/I keep, and pass, and turn again.") Some decades later, Henry Adams expressed an even more pessimistic appraisal of Western possibilities in his "Buddha and Brahma."

Although Oriental scholarship at America's emergent research universities expanded domestic knowledge of Asian traditions, the turning point for Eastern religions in America came with the World's Parliament of Religions. This latter gathering, which met in conjunction with the World's Columbian Exposition in Chicago, was convened in 1893 to promote understanding among the world's religious faiths. The Parliament thus provided an opportunity for spokesmen of a wide variety of traditions scarcely known to most Americans to represent themselves publicly. It was here that Swami Vivekananda found a base for acquainting Americans with the Hindu tradition and subsequently founding the Vedanta Society, which today has twelve locations in San Francisco, New York, and other major cities.

Vedanta, as interpreted by Vivekananda, struck a minor but real chord among Victorian Americans who were simultaneously intrigued by the claims of Christian Science, New Thought, Theosophy, Spiritualism, and other manifestations of "harmonialism" that were enjoying a wide popularity in the parlors and lecture halls of the period. Vedanta was rooted in the Upanishads, and presented the traditional Hindu teaching that the task of the individual is to free the *atman*—one's individual manifestation of the *Brahman*, or ultimate reality—from the web of illusion in which it is caught. Vedanta stresses meditation, and exercises an intellectual, individual appeal very different from the popular "ethnic" versions of the Hindu tradition. Vivekananda also added a syncretistic dimension to the gospel he preached to Americans by recognizing such figures as Jesus and the Buddha as *avatars*—earthly manifestations or incarnations—of perfect realization of the Brahman. The English writers Aldous Huxley and Christopher Isherwood were associated with the Vedanta Society, which enjoyed a considerable cultural cachet. Other early versions of "export" Hinduism at the elite level were promoted by Swami Paramahansa Yogananda and his Self-Realization Fellowship (1925) and Jeddu Krishnamurti, who was promoted by the American occult community in the 1920s as a world savior until becoming an independent teacher of hatha yoga.

Elite Buddhism in America has usually taken the form of *Zen* (Japanese, from Chinese *Chan*, "meditation"). Zen is a particularly austere form of Buddhism that minimizes dependence on scriptures, images, and other externals in favor of concentrated meditation. This was often aided by the contemplation of *koans*, paradoxical riddles such as "What is the sound of one hand clapping?" In addition, Zen has also emphasized such arts as gardening, tea ceremonies and even athletics, as revealed in the title of Eugen Herrigel's popular exposition (*Zen and the Art of Archery*, 1953). (Robert Pirsig's widely read *Zen and the Art of Motorcycle Maintenance*, 1974, has been a continuing campus favorite indicative of the popularization of Zen in American culture in recent years.) Zen was introduced to America through the presence of Soyen Shaku at the World's Parliament of Religions, who sent disciples to America following his second visit and lecture tour in 1905. The most influential of these was D. T. Suzuki, who tirelessly spread his message through lectures and books that are still widely read and respected as expositions of Zen.

Since Suzuki's time, Zen has become both indigenized and transmuted in this country. Its appeal to first the "Beat Generation" writers and their successors, the hippies and other denizens of the 1960s "counterculture," gave it wide currency though in somewhat misleading forms. (Both Jack Kerouac, author of *On the Road* and *The Dharma Bums,* and Alan Watts, who popularized Zen in numerous expositions, have drawn heavy criticism from scholars for their alleged oversimplifications and misinterpretations.) The appeal of Zen and other Eastern religions to the popular consciousness-transforming psychology of the "Human Potential" movement of the 1960s and beyond has also raised serious questions as to how accurately the tradition has been represented. On the other hand, a more authentic indigenized Zen has been promoted by the San Francisco Zen Center (1961), led by an American *roshi* (master) after the death of its Japanese founder. It has become especially well known beyond the rather small circle of American Zen practitioners through Edward Espe Brown's *Tassajara Cooking* (1973) and other works that teach a vegetarian cuisine in the Zen tradition. More recently, the appeal of Zen has been displaced somewhat by a widespread interest in Tibetan Buddhism, a colorful and ritualistic form of the tradition that employs both the mantra and the *mandala*—a psychocosmic diagram at once of the universe and the inner spaces of the mind, made up of circles and rectangles—as aids to mystical contemplation.

Although the American pursuit of such "export faiths" as Vedanta and Zen has certainly taken on faddish dimensions from time to time, they have never been the objects of the fear and loathing that other new religious groups, many of Asian origin, have inspired in this country. By the early 1970s, the term *cult* had become revivified as a blanket pejorative description for a broad range of small religious groups that many Americans found alien and threatening. The term, which derives from the Latin *cultus* ("worship") and ultimately from the same root as "cultivation" and "agriculture," is used neutrally in religious studies as a term for devotion to special objects of reverence, for instance, in the cult of the Virgin Mary. In popular usage, however, the term *cult* usually designates a sectarian group that deviates significantly, and perhaps ominously, from the "mainstream" of accepted Christian belief and practice. In the fairly recent past, such indigenous groups as Unitarians, Christian Scientists, Seventh-Day Adventists, Jehovah's Witnesses, and Mormons have been singled out as "cults," especially in Fundamentalist literature. In more recent usage, charismatic leadership, a communal and highly regimented lifestyle, isolation from the rest of the world, and teachings that deviate radically from the mainstream are usually part of most people's nonacademic definition of the term.

The countercultural ferment of the late 1960s and early 1970s led to a whole new ethos among America's middle-class young people. This ethos proved highly conducive to the formation of new religious groups that seemed, at least to concerned parents and clergy, to deviate even more alarmingly from accepted norms. Some of these groups were combinations of conservative Protestant theology with countercultural aspects, often involving communitarian life-styles. Such groups of "Jesus People" as David Berg's "Children of God" occasionally took on some of the characteristics of "cults" that had been distilling through these years into a typology of alarm. On the whole, however, most groups that were within the Christian tradition tended to diffuse themselves into the broader conservative upsurge that was gaining strength through the 1970s, though even here the single-minded conversion of college-age young people to aggressive Fundamentalist movements such as the Navigators and the Campus Crusade for Christ prompted dismayed "mainline" parents to wonder whether something insidious might not be afoot.

In contemporary usage, a cult involves the presence of a charismatic leader capable of the psychological manipulation of his or her followers into blindly carrying out the leader's will. The archetype of this sort of leader was James Warren "Jim" Jones (1931–1978), a faith-healer from Indiana who gained a considerable following in San Francisco that he organized into the "Peoples [sic] Temple." Beginning as a combination of apocalyptic fundamentalism and political organization for social services, the Peoples Temple rapidly developed a distinctive blend of eccentric Marxist ideology and extreme religious claims made by Jones as to his own divine or prophetic character. (The Symbionese Liberation Army, which held Patty Hearst captive for several months during the early 1970s, and the "family" of Charles Manson later jailed for ritual murders are other examples of "cults" in which ideology substituted for religion as a core organizing principle. The Peoples Temple seems to have been a borderline case in this regard.)

In 1977, Jones and many of his followers left California in the wake of impending political and legal scandal to found a commune in Jonestown, Guyana, on the northern coast of South America. The murder of an American congressman who had come to Jonestown to investigate allegations of abuse made by relatives of the communitarians raised the community's level of apprehension to the crisis level, and Jones himself seems to have become acutely paranoid. As news spread throughout the United States, he organized his followers into one of the most grotesque events of modern times. On November 18, 1978, he and 911 others died in a mass suicide, mainly effected through the voluntary or, in the case of many of the hundreds of children involved, forced drinking of a soft drink laced with cyanide. Not surprisingly, Jones has since been regarded as the epitome of the demented cult leader capable of leading his followers into anything whatever.

Another highly controversial feature of these new cults was embodied in the accusation that they "brainwashed" young people into membership when the youths were not in a psychological state capable of offering any resistance. ("Brainwashing," or intensive, coercive resocialization into a new sense of personal identity defined in terms of group allegiance, entered the American vocabulary in the wake of accounts by American P.O.W.'s during the Korean War having received such treatment from their Communist captors.) Charges of brainwashing arose especially from accounts published of the extreme tractics of deceptive recruitment and intensive indoctrination allegedly practiced by members of the Unification Church's commune at Booneville, California.

Widespread fear that the practice was commonplace among new religious groups led to deploying the counterstrategy of "deprogramming," publicized largely through the work of Ted Patrick, who for a while made a career of the practice before running into prohibitive legal difficulties. Deprogramming involved the forced abduction of individual members of controversial religious groups, usually through deception, and isolating them for an extended period while placing intensive psychological pressure upon them to abandon the group and return to their former way of life. The practice of deprogramming raised difficult legal questions about its compatibility with First Amendment guarantees, even as it aroused the sympathies of many who believed that families should retain access even to adult children who had chosen to isolate themselves from their kindred. After a number of court cases had cast doubt on the practice's legality, and Patrick and other deprogrammers had spent time in jail, deprogramming—together with the groups that had engendered it—began to fade from public view.

If the Peoples Temple represented the extreme to which new religious movements might go, the Unification Church is a classic instance of the continuing controversy that cults—or "new religions," to use a more neutral term—can arouse. If founding and leadership by a charismatic leader is a cult characteristic, the role of Sun Myung Moon, a Korean businessman who organized the movement in Korea in 1954, certainly qualifies the Church. In the movement's theology, which is expounded in the *Divine Principle* (1977), Moon outlined a reinterpretation of Christianity, reminiscent in some ways of early Christian Gnosticism as well as of Mormonism, which introduced ideas extremely alien to most "mainstream" Christians. In the beginning, God had intended that Adam and Eve would beget a perfect family. Eve's seduction by "Lucifer" ruined this hope, and successive divinely chosen figures have been appointed to restore the pure family relationship originally intended. One of these, Jesus, was spiritually successful in this program, but died before he could go on to restore physically the perfect family.

It is only in the present day that this long-frustrated fulfillment is now taking place. Sun Myung Moon and his wife are referred to by Moon's followers as "Our True Parents," and the entire movement is viewed as constituting the beginnings of the newly restored perfect family. One characteristic of Unification life-style that has aroused the ire of more conventional Americans has been the practice of arranged group marriages presided over by Moon, in which unmarried followers are united with mates, often of different cultural backgrounds and whom they have not previously known, in mass ceremonies. Together with charges of alienation of converts from their biological families, in some cases through alleged "brainwashing," this sort of practice has been central to the designation of the Unification Church as a cult and the widespread hostility and suspicion it has aroused.

Although the Unification Church is much more unconventional than the Mormons by today's standards, accusations against the two groups at different eras are instructive. During the nineteenth century, Mormons were widely accused not only of radical religious innovation (hardly a crime), but also of sexual irregularity (polygamy), separation from the mainstream of society, and of hostile, even violent actions directed against dissenters as well as external enemies. Today, Mormons are disliked by liberals especially because of their church's extensive economic holdings and the tendency of the group to vote heavily for extremely conservative political candidates. Similarly, the Unification Church has considerable wealth, obtained in part through the sale of artificial flowers at airport terminals and other public places by neophyte converts. These proceeds are often used lavishly in public-relations ventures to influence skeptical clergy and religion scholars to think better of them. The Church also has heavy investments in a wide variety of secular enterprises, ranging from fishing fleets to the very conservative *Washington Times,* which were the occasion of Moon's conviction in 1982 and subsequent imprisonment for tax fraud. The conservative tenor of the movement's politics is based in part on a messianic interpretation of American destiny as a bulwark against Communism, a teaching interestingly comparable to early Mormon views of this country's divinely guided historical mission.

The Unification Church, which probably numbers between five and ten thousand American members (out of a considerably larger worldwide total), may thus be viewed as a nonlethal "cult" par excellence, which has managed to survive and even thrive on the hostility, culminating in Moon's imprisonment, that it has experienced. What will happen after Moon's death, and after the children of the original adherents reach maturity, will be an interesting test of its staying power: whether it can withstand the process of "routinization of charisma" that must invariably be faced by a new religion's second generation.

Although the Unification Church has its origins in Asia, it is clearly a highly Westernized "new religion" that owes more to Christianity for its inspiration than any of that continent's traditional religions. At the other extreme might come the new religions of Japan—"the rush hour of the gods," in H. Neill McFarland's title—which are novel but distinctively Asian. Most influential in America has been Nichiren Shoshu or Sokka Gakkai, the "Value Creation Society." Rooted in the militant Nichiren Buddhism of medieval Japan, a variant of the Pure Land movement, Sokka Gakkai has attained some political impact in Japan in its aggressive program to convert the nation into a "Buddhaland." Its authoritarian posture and rather heavy-handed evangelistic tactics called *shakubuku* ("smash and flatten") have gained it a number of American converts as well as detractors, but it has not maintained a very high profile in this country in recent years.

As illustrated in the teachings of its "missionary" exponents since the days of the World's Parliament of Religions, the Hindu tradition has undergone continuous adaptations in the varied ways it has been presented to and adopted by Americans. One of its mildest contemporary forms is Transcendental Meditation, or TM, introduced in this country in 1959 by the Maharishi Mahesh Yogi and publicized by the patronage of, among others, the Beatles. Transcendental Meditation does not claim to be a religious movement; rather, it calls itself "the science of creative intelligence." As such, TM is an adaptation of yogic meditation techniques, especially the repetition of a personalized *mantra*, to the more secular "harmonial" goals of stress reduction and the achievement of personal composure. Although it has taken on some of the trappings of an institution, with a colorful guru as founder and the campus of failed Parsons College in Iowa as the headquarters of "Maharishi University," it bears more affinity to the less intensive side of the "Human Potential Movement" of the New Age than to various "cultic" groups.

Closer in style to the Unification Church as well as to the popular devotional *bhakti* yoga of the Hindu tradition have been other groups that have riled middle-class parents of American converts and on occasion mobilized the deprogrammers. The Divine Light Mission, for example, was introduced to America in 1970 by the erratic young Guru Maharaj Ji (mah-hah-RAHJ-ji), who claimed to be a *satguru* or "perfect master" of this age just as his father had earlier been. Physical techniques for inducing a very sensuous religious experience, such as pressing on the eyeballs until flashes of light appear, are a major part of the Mission's practice. Mararaj Ji's public prank-playing, and subsequent abandonment of such early essential teachings as a vegetarian diet, led to a power struggle within his family and his mother's withdrawing support in favor of his brother. The movement's communitarian life-style, supported by restaurants and other enterprises as well as the surrender of worldly goods by converts, seemed to many outsiders to be very like that of a cult. An active membership of ten thousand claimed in 1977 has probably diminished since then.

A better-known version of devotional Hinduism given a new guise is presented in ISKCON: the International Society for Krishna Consciousness, whose followers are better known as "Hare Krishnas" after their continuous chanting (which was also incorporated into the popular mock-countercultural musical *Hair.*) Brought to America by the late A. C. Bhaktivedanta Swami Prabhupada in 1965, ISKCON is derived from the *bhakti yoga* movement founded by the sixteenth-century Bengali Caitanya.

Central to this movement, which has much in common with various "ethnic" versions of Hinduism, is devotion to the god Krishna, who is here presented as the supreme personality of the godhead. In addition to the continual chanting of "Hare Krishna Hare Rama," which invokes Krishna (also known as Rama) and his consort, food offerings (*prasada*) and other features of *puja*, including the use of fire, are part of the routine of the movement's devotees. The latter live communally in many American cities as well as rural retreats such as the elaborate compound known as New Vrindaban, billed as "America's Taj Mahal" and located at the end of a harrowing mountain road a few miles off Interstate 70 near Wheeling, West Virginia. (The latter is visited as an authentic Hindu temple by many ethnic Indians as well as group members.)

The saffron robes, shaved heads, and continual chanting of devotees as they solicit donations and converts at airport terminals, shopping malls, and other public places have made the "Hare Krishnas" widely known as well as disliked by those put off by exotic evangelists. Their communal life-style also alienated many relatives of devotees, who charged that their children had been alienated from their families by isolation and brainwashing. Although the movement had begun to fade from view by the late 1980s, the 1986 drug-related murder conviction of one of the New Vrindaban commune's members did not enhance the group's public image.

The Divine Light Mission and ISKCON reached their heyday in the late 1970s, when public alarm over cults was at its peak, and they were only two among many movements vying for youthful converts and raising public alarm over the safety of the nation's vulnerable adolescents and young adults. In the 1980s, after the initial hue and cry had subsided, yet another movement of Hindu origins came into the public view in a spectacular trajectory of well-reported rise and subsequent meteoric decline and demise. Its leader, known as the Bhagwan Shree Rajneesh, denied that his movement was a religion; actually, it combined elements of the Hindu tradition with a heavy dose of Human Potential Movement practices, some of which bore a superficial resemblance to the "harmonial" aspects of Hinduism.

As such, the Bhagwan, first at his *ashram* (Hindu mediational community) in India and then at his self-styled "commune" (a deliberately chosen Westernism) in Oregon, attracted a clientele that can only be described as "Yuppie" (young urban professional) in sociological composition. Rajneesh openly embraced a playful and sexually permissive approach to communal life, and he and his followers enjoyed a hard-working but affluent life-style based on an explicit teaching that financial insecurity and enlightenment did not go well together. Most conspicuous was the Bhagwan's fleet of Rolls Royces, which numbered about eighty-five in their heyday. Frances Fitzgerald's account of the community in her *Cities on a Hill* (1986) captures vividly the mixture of exoticism yet very familiarly American elements that characterized life at Rajneeshpuram.

The Bhagwan's commune seemed at first only mildly eccentric to many Americans who had been accustomed to their own domestic "rush hour of the gods" of the 1960s and 1970s. It began to attract first local and then national attention, however, when it became overtly aggressive and even hostile in its attempts to take over the nearby town of Antelope, Oregon. Antelope had been a small ranching community in a remote part of the state, and the presence of an exotic commune was in itself rather upsetting to the traditionally minded local residents. After tensions with the government at all levels from the local to the federal increased, the entire experiment suddenly disbanded in a flurry of revelations of the Bhagwan's arrest and deportation for immigration fraud—he had arranged numerous false marriages to allow followers to enter the country illegally—as well as the conviction of his sometime-lieutenant, Ma Anand Sheela, on charges of having poisoned the Bhagwan and various other of her "enemies" together with a variety of crimes including the dynamiting of municipal offices.

The impact of Asian traditions on American religious culture, especially since the mid-1960s, can be read as a recapitulation of many of the themes that have characterized American religious history from our national beginnings. Frances Fitzgerald, following William G. McLoughlin, argues in the epilogue to her *Cities on a Hill* that the 1960s were in many ways analogous to the Second Great Awakening, especially the successive waves of religious and reform excitements that swept over the "Burned-Over District" of upstate New York from the 1820s to the 1840s. The weakening of traditional family bonds; the breaking-away of young people enfranchised with votes, education, and discretionary income in abundance; explosive geographical and social mobility; the bursting into national prominence first of black and then feminist, gay, Chicano, and other movements of political liberation; and the rapid escalation of an unpopular war all provided the protean social setting in which large-scale disorder and experimental attempts at reintegration could be expected in abundance.

The influx of new Asian immigrants, prompted in part by the catastrophic denouement of the American military presence in Vietnam and environs, is in many ways a recapitulation of older immigration patterns, with predictable variations on established themes. The success-orientation of many Asians and their children has been noted repeatedly, and viewed by some neonativists as nearly as threatening as Japanese economic competition from abroad. This theme is particularly reminiscent of Gentile American reactions to the industrious Jewish immigrants of the turn of the century. A major difference, however, is that of the future of "ethnic" Asian religions. Some have already undergone adaptation, as in the adoption of Christian organizational structures and terminology by the Buddhist Churches of America. Whether the second and third generations convert to Christianity, opt for the secularism that has been more and more characteristic of the professional classes, maintain their traditions, or devise some new, syncretistic alternatives remains uncertain.

The "export" religions from Asia that have achieved unprecedented popularity since the 1960s in many ways continue the harmonial tradition of the nineteenth century. At one level, they have had a highly selective impact, in isolation from the context of their broader tradition. The best example here is the black Baptist minister Martin Luther King, Jr.'s, appropriation of Mohandas Gandhi's teaching of *ahimsa,* or constructive nonviolence, as a keystone of his civil rights strategy. Hatha yoga and Transcendental Meditation require only a selective commitment. As such, they are consonant both with the "do-it-yourself," marginally secular character of earlier harmonialism as well as the "Human Potential Movement" or "Growth Movement" legitimated by the "Third Force" "Humanistic Psychology" of Carl Rogers, Abraham Maslow, and other therapeutic innovators of the 1960s and 1970s. The stress in all of these movements, later subsumed under the generic "New Age" label, is a breaking away from traditional social and intellectual structures to find freedom and self-realization in an expanded and liberated consciousness. At the extreme, a small number of disciplined and dedicated American devotees of Zen totally live their new commitment on an ongoing basis—analogous, perhaps, to Thomas Merton's celebrated conversion to Roman Catholicism and entry into a Trappist monastery in the 1940s.

Finally, in the case of "new religions," the continuity of the pejorative use of the term *cult* since the nineteenth century is a witness to an ongoing process of religious ferment. Mormons, as already noted, experienced even greater organized hostility and opposition in their formative years than did any new religion of the present age. Although much of the early wave of new religious activity seemed ominous, the burst of energy that led to the founding and initial success of these movements seems to have dissipated, drained off in part by the success of conservative Christian groups as well as a natural process of cultural entropy. In the dramatic and horrific case of the Peoples Temple, the movement quite literally self-destructed, as did, in a mercifully less dramatic way, Rajneeshpuram. The Unification Church seems destined to survive indefinitely, but its quest for respectability and influence points toward a lowering of the social and symbolic barriers that had earlier insulated its followers from the broader community. For better or worse, American society seems both loose and coherent enough to tolerate a continuing ferment of religious creativity, some of it trailing off into oblivion, while other parts go on to become routinized members of an ever-increasing family of denominational bedfellows.*

CHAPTER 53

Toward 2001: America's Religious Odyssey at the End of the Twentieth Century

Once the study of America's religious history transcended the stage of denominational chronicle and self-celebration, its students have been preoccupied not only with finding out what happened, but also with what it meant. William Warren Sweet, writing during the decades between the World Wars, harnessed Frederick Jackson Turner's "frontier thesis" to the realm of religion, and argued that the continual adaptation of our religious institutions to the freedoms and exigencies of frontier life was crucial in the formation of a distinctive American tradition. Sidney Mead, writing in the 1960s, turned instead to the Enlightenment as a key to understanding, and maintained that

---

* Because of the scope of this work, a full exposition of the basics of the religions of Asia dealt with in this chapter has unfortunately not been possible. For background in more depth, the reader is referred to Niels C. Nielsen, Jr. et al., *Religions of the World* (New York: St. Martin's, 1983).

the attitudes of the Founding Fathers toward such issues as the relationship of church and state were even more critical. Sydney Ahlstrom, whose magisterial *Religious History of the American People* appeared in 1972, instead saw Puritanism as central. He insisted on the colonial New England origins of so many distinctive features of American religious thought and culture to the extent that Mead was moved to express his skepticism in a critical review entitled "By Puritans Possessed."

All of them were right in what they included, if not in what they left out. The First Amendment, deeply rooted in Enlightenment thought, lies at the very heart of the American system of religious liberty and denominationalism. Puritanism molded not simply the premises of evangelical Protestantism, which dominated American religious life throughout the nineteenth century and beyond, but also shaped the "American character" through the work ethic, a stress on literacy, and the notion of an entire people in covenant with God. And, on the frontier, the Puritan emphasis on conversion and the Bible combined with the denominational competitiveness engendered by the Bill of Rights to produce a pragmatic, optimistic, revivalistic, reform-minded evangelicalism impatient with Calvinist determinism and theological niceties in general.

Ahlstrom evocatively defined what he called "the Great Puritan Epoch" as extending from the reign of Elizabeth I, under whom the Puritan movement began, to the time of Jacqueline Kennedy, whose husband was the first Roman Catholic to be elected President of the United States. The Post-Puritan age that lay beyond, however, remained *terra incognita*. As the Christian era approaches the end of its second millennium, the terms *secularism, pluralism,* and *voluntaryism* have taken on a new significance as clues to understanding where we may be heading. Prophecy is a risky business, which we had probably best avoid; however, a retrospective look at how the past led to the present and a topographic analysis of what lies about us at the moment may be more within our effective reach.

One key concept to understanding the transition from the past to the present is the process of *Americanization*. Such a term is full of complex and even contradictory meanings, but its relevance is virtually self-evident nevertheless. To become American means more than to effect a geographical relocation to the horizontal midsection of the North American continent, or even to become a citizen of the United States. In its fuller sense, it means becoming acculturated, adopting a distinctively American way of living and looking at the world as one's own. For better or worse, even "Native Americans"—the continent's aboriginal inhabitants—have been forced to come to terms with a new culture very different from those they had known for centuries. Although a wide variety of subcultures continue to exist and even thrive in this country, there is little question that a "mainstream" endures that has always compelled other, less powerful currents to take it into account.

Some aspects of that mainstream have remained fairly constant over the centuries that have elapsed since the settlements at Jamestown and Plymouth. Most conspicuously, English is the de facto language of American public life, and the growth of a sizable Hispanic population has prompted ballot initiatives to make it so *de jure* as well. English common law, land settlement patterns, even—perish the thought—English cooking have had major roles as starting points for distinctly American developments. In addition to adopting the English language as part of the process of acculturation, other religious traditions in America have had to come to terms with the cultural and social power exercised by the cluster of denominations of British origin—Episcopalian, Presbyterian, Congregationalist, Methodist, Baptist, and Quaker—that for decades set the terms of religious debate in this country. Roman Catholics, Lutherans, and Jews all went through major struggles in the nineteenth century over the degree to which they would become Americanized, and the struggle of democratically inclined American Catholics with a more traditionalist Rome remains a major issue as the turn of the millennium nears.

The chief external matrix in which Americanization has worked out its varied ways has been *denominationalism,* which grew simultaneously out of de facto pluralism, Free Church suspicion of establishments, and an Enlightenment distrust of institutional religion. Like it or not, traditions such as Roman Catholicism and Judaism, which had very different legal situations in the Old World, were eventually compelled to adjust to the American pattern of standing on their own, with neither hope of government aid nor fear of harassment of officialdom. However, as R. Laurence Moore has argued, this process has not been strictly linear; rather, initially "nonmainstream" groups such as Roman Catholics, Mormons, and Fundamentalists have gone through phases of distancing themselves from the broader culture and adopting an attitude of partial separation and aggressive critique of the "mainstream." In the longer run, however, the attainment of middle-class status and broader education has generally led to an accommodation and a lowering of boundaries.

Another broad dynamic of religious change that can be detected over long periods is the dialectic between institutionalized and popular religion. The emergence of the Holiness and Pentecostal movements out of Methodism in the nineteenth century is a good example; similarly, the "Electronic Church" and its relationship to an increasingly routinized, middle-class Pentecostalism is an instructive sequel. Since the days of George Whitefield, revivalism has provided an unbroken line of continuity in this distinctively American extra-ecclesiastical phenomenon. Although it is futile to seek precise cause-and-effect sequences, there has been a rough correlation over the centuries between rapid social change in particularly volatile areas—for example, northern New England, upstate New York, central Tennessee, and southern California—and the outbreak of "enthusiastic" religious movements that have emphasized personal experience and supernaturalistic occurrences over and against the more institutional, doctrinal, and ethical thrusts of the established denominations. The process has generated a broad gamut of innovation, ranging from Joseph Smith to Jimmy Swaggart, and is likely to continue as long as social change thrusts groups of people into situations of cognitive confusion and tension.

Yet another persistent dynamic is the interplay of organized religious communities with that elusive phenomenon of "civil religion." This phrase was introduced into the vocabulary of both scholarly and everyday discourse when it was popularized by the sociologist Robert Bellah in an influential essay of

1967. Since then, there has been a vigorous debate among scholars as to its character, value, and even its very existence. Bellah himself initially defined it as a set of scriptures, such as the Declaration of Independence; sacred places, such as the Washington and Lincoln monuments in Washington, D.C.; and hymns, such as the "Battle Hymn of the Republic," that all converge into an actual cult of the United States.

After Bellah had given the idea its initial delineation, other scholars such as Conrad Cherry went on to illustrate its dynamic, historical nature, and its deep indebtedness to the Jewish and Christian traditions in its underlying sense of God acting providentially in history on America's behalf. Catherine Albanese went on to depict its contours during the Revolution, and Charles Reagan Wilson described its appropriation in the South in the form of the "religion of the lost cause." Bellah himself, in *The Broken Covenant* of 1975, launched a powerful critique of the nation's betrayal of what he saw as its positive premises. Amorphous as the concept itself may be, there is little question that America's religious communities have alternately fostered and criticized the nation's tendency toward, if not collective self-worship, at least an inclination to give its history a theological significance not derived from any one specific religious tradition.

There is no doubt that some of these processes have pushed America's religious communities toward a certain uniformity, as illustrated in the effective dominance of the English language and the widespread development of standardized denominational structures for the administration of organizations with national constituencies. On the other hand, as the recurrent upsurge of popular religious movements shows, the result has been neither stasis nor homogeneity. As the phenomenon of ecumenism in America demonstrates, union among religious groups has been extensive, but stops at a certain point. Andrew Greeley has observed that religious identity has displaced ethnicity as a means through which Americans can differentiate themselves from others, a process for which humans have a seemingly unquenchable need no matter what the extent of sophistication or modernization. To a considerable degree, however, denominational lines no longer reflect the real cleavages that separate the broader units—what we might call the "cognitive communities"—of religion in America.

Drawing the lines of these communities is a subtle matter, since they lack the clear-cut definition that denominational boundaries provide. Further, they tend to overlap, like a series of Venn diagrams, so that individuals might feel allegiance to several different such communities whose lines are drawn at different levels. Will Herberg's triad of "Protestant, Catholic, Jew" is still evocative, despite the deep rifts within each of those traditions and the internal structural differentiation that has taken place within the first and the third. "Protestant," however, has become an increasingly amorphous designation; attempts to break down its components into categories such as "liberal," "mainline," "conservative," and "evangelical" persist among its observers. Within Christianity more broadly, the implications of the convergence of patterns of worship within the "liturgical traditions"—Eastern Orthodox, Roman Catholic, Anglican, and Lutheran—need to be noted, as does the similar convergence among conservative Protestants from very different theological traditions—Fundamentalist, Holiness, Pentecostal, and Restorationist—on any number of issues.

More broadly, we can attempt an overview of the American religious scene as the year 2000 approaches by a somewhat arbitrary but useful division of most Americans into four broad "cognitive communities." We need, of course, to be careful about reifying these "ideal types" into anything more substantial than conceptual aids, and to keep in mind the continual interplay of these constructs with denominational structures and the other categories described above. Reality is dynamic and elusive; scholarship is the necessary but inevitably incomplete quest to pin it down.

At one end of our typological spectrum lies a community of indeterminate size characterized by what we might call "passive supernaturalism." These are groups, whether sects, independent congregations, or constituencies within broader religious groups, that have little interest in the social order, but rather focus on religion as a source of personal experience and a relief from the seemingly unbearable pressures of worldly life. The impact of both liberal and conservative activist ideals have made such religious life less likely to be found in its pure form, as it may have been, for example, in classic Pentecostalism. Nevertheless, it likely persists among the least modernized and enfranchised segments of American society—recent immigrants, Hispanics, poor blacks, Appalachians—in both Roman Catholic and conservative Protestant forms, as well as in non-Western or syncretistic guises.

Second, it is clear that the most rapidly expanding of these communities has been what we might call "activist traditionalism." The emergence of the New Religious Right during the 1970s and 1980s has been the most conspicuous manifestation of this alliance, which has its most immediate roots in nineteenth-century evangelical Protestantism. Included here are a variety of believers, predominantly Christian, who share an aggressive commitment to maintain a traditional moral order within the broader society through means ranging from individual evangelism to nationally orchestrated political lobbying. The tactics of Jerry Falwell's Moral Majority, which deliberately appealed not just to evangelicals but to a broader range of the conservatively inclined, is emblematic of the coalescence of this new constituency in recent years. It includes not only conservative Protestants of a variety of stripes—Southern and Independent Baptists, Fundamentalists and conservative evangelicals in other denominations, Holiness and Pentecostal church members, Missouri Synod Lutherans, and members of the Churches of Christ—but also traditionally inclined Catholics, most Mormons, and even some Orthodox Jews. While they may differ broadly in matters of belief and worship, they are united by a common moral vision and commitment to public, political strategies for achieving it.

If our first category includes those who are cut off or alienated from active participation in the social order, our second attracts several groups whose relationship to contemporary society is problematic. One constituency consists of an older stratum of American society—enterpreneurs and managers, usually on a small scale and living in smaller communities—who are uneasy about a newer class of professionals, often involved in the rapidly growing information and communication sector, whose values and life-styles are often very different from their own. Another group is amply represented in congregations such as Jerry Falwell's, who are in an uneasy state of transition into the middle class from less affluent and sophisticated backgrounds. Still a third constituency, small but powerful, are many of the newly rich Sunbelt-dwellers, who have been highly successful in wrenching control of the Republican Party from their "Eastern Establishment" rivals, and who as active laity exert considerable power in the Mormon, Southern Baptist, and other conservative denominations.

Moving further left, we come to a third, more amorphous category that we might, borrowing from contemporary political parlance, label "moderate to liberal churchgoers." These are the people, largely middle to upper-middle class, who belong to the "liberal" Protestant denominations—Episcopalian, Congregationalist (UCC), Unitarian-Universalist—as well as, to a somewhat lesser extent, their more "middle-of-the-road" counterparts—Methodist, Presbyterian, American Baptists, and Disciples. (A considerable number of the latter might fall into the previous category as well.) In addition, many Reform and Conservative Jews and a considerable number of Roman Catholics can be found here as well. These are people who feel well integrated into the social order, but share an ethical critique of many of its institutions in the wake especially of the civil rights movement and subsequent efforts at liberal social reform.

Finally, there has emerged in recent years a growing number of affluent and educated Americans for whom institutionalized religion is simply not significant. Some of these *secularists,* as we might call them, may participate to a greater or lesser extent in the "do-it-yourself" spectrum of "New Age" religious options, while others simply read the *New York Times* on Sunday mornings. Their world view tends to be mildly conservative to reformist, cosmopolitan, and secular. It is within this class, many of whom are involved in the new socioeconomic stratum generated by the upsurge of the information and communications professions, that the "secular humanism" so loathed by "activist traditionalists" can be found. This ideology, however, is not likely to be formulated very clearly, but rather emerges from a diffuse climate of opinion shared by this cohort.

These categories hardly exhaust the entirety of the American population, nor are they mutually exclusive. Many people might be positioned midway between any two groups in the order listed, but not often easily between any other two. What those in any given group share is the ability to understand readily the assumptions of one another, even when they may disagree on particulars of doctrine or political strategy. They constitute, in short, what we have called "cognitive communities"—communities of shared, or sharable, discourse, even when the premises of that discourse may not be consciously articulated. The major exception here is the first category, which consists of an indefinite number of subcommunities who are no more likely to be able to communicate readily with one another than with members of the other, larger communites described here.

Lest these formulations seem too relentlessly sociological, we might conclude with still another attempt to help focus the character of the contemporary American religious spectrum. Three major themes run through the history of American religion, and remain vital in the present day. These themes, which are by no means confined to America, reflect deep and abiding concerns of the human spirit: *experience, authority,* and *justice*. All have to do with the quest for ultimacy that lies at the heart of religion. How each is expressed, however, tells us a great deal about the particular cultural matrix in which it is manifested. The fact that the expression of these themes in America today is multiple and contradictory tells us something of value in itself about the contemporary scene.

Experience in religion involves a *felt* and not simply perceived or mediated contact with the realm of the supernatural. Many people, especially in conditions of emotional stress or cognitive confusion, yearn for a sense of ultimacy that they can experience with their whole beings. The spread of glossolalia and other "gifts of the Spirit" from the realm of Pentecostalism into the charismatic movement in the Roman Catholic, Episcopal, and other churches to whom this sort of experience has in the past quite foreign is one example of the upsurge of this impulse in recent times. Visions of the Virgin Mary at Medjugorje in Yugoslavia, which have attracted the attention of and even pilgrimages by many Americans, is another manifestation of this hunger for direct contact with the source of ultimate meaning and existence, which most religious groups have to learn to routinize and control if they are going to go about their everyday business without excessive disruption.

Authority is another fundamental desire in religion that continually stirs up routine, and is a potent source of religious change. Reaction against authority perceived to be stultifying is a hallmark of every major religious innovation in history; the Protestant Reformation, the Wesleyan movement, Reform Judaism, and Vatican II all represent major attempts to shake up settled patterns, disturb comfortable assumptions, and rethink the basis of the institutions that have grown up to channel the exercise of faith. Reassertion of eroded or abandoned authority has been especially significant in the years since 1970, which followed the tumult of revolts against authority in the preceding decade. The emergence of the New Religious Right and the restraining grip on innovation imposed on the American Catholic Church by Pope John Paul II are powerful examples of this tendency.

Finally, the quest for *justice* remains a central theme in American religion. The nineteenth century especially was a time of crusading zeal for moral reform, as was the civil rights movement of the 1960s. The objects and means of this quest, however, are hardly agreed upon by contemporary Americans. The abortion issue, which has provoked considerable heat since the emergence of the feminist movement in the late 1960s, is a particularly good example of this ambiguity. Those in the "activist traditionalist" camp regard the rights of the unborn as paramount, and believe that abortion is a moral wrong of the highest order. At the opposite extreme, secularists and some religious liberals believe that imposing the birth of an unwanted child on an unwilling mother is a coercive denial of justice to the woman. Others, including many liberal Catholics, regard abortion as a moral wrong, but believe that public policy should not be based on individual sentiments that have not evoked a social consensus. Recent statements by Roman Catholic bishops on economic injustice brought about by unrestrained capitalism have similarly evoked protests from conservative Catholics who argue that the welfare of the many is best promoted by the unfettered economic activity of the few.

There can be little doubt that American religious life today is the result of a convergence of social and intellectual processes with roots in particular American circumstances, such as the frontier and religious pluralism, as well as broader trends in the Western experience, such as the hegemony of Christianity and the inexorable process of modernization. Ongoing dynamic change and pluralism continually reinforced by immigration appear likely to continue as major parts of the American religious dynamic, as does the ongoing generation of new movements—at times from the right, at others from the left—as means of protest and release for those not at ease in the New World Zion.

In the early 1970s, Sydney Ahlstrom tried impressively to weave the long and intricate story of America's religious life together through the unifying theme of the cultural power of Puritanism. He realized, however, that the "Great Puritan epoch" was ending even as he wrote, and that a new pluralism, including the previously inconsequential strain of secularism, was now at hand. From the vantage point of an additional decade and a half, it seems futile to draw together all the processes and components that make up the American religious experience of today through a unitary explanation. Most Americans continue to profess a belief in God, and to attend worship—usually Christian of some variety—at least occasionally. As the 1988 presidential campaign demonstrated, symbols of "civil religion" such as the flag still evoke powerful responses.

Still, it is hard to point to religion any longer as the mainspring of American culture, since its manifestations are so diffuse and contradictory. The future direction of this pluralistic religiosity seems both dynamic and volatile, as the unexpected twists and turns of the past several decades have indicated. The power to shape the future, however, no longer seems to reside primarily in any one of the four cognitive communities among which most Americans seem to be distributed. Conservatives will continue to aspire to power, secularists will denounce or simply ignore them, and liberals will try to find a way of reconciling freedom and justice. The results are not predictable, but are not likely to take the form of a new consensus. Perhaps they can best be anticipated as a continuation, in Sidney Mead's memorable phrase, of America's "lively experiment," the essence of which lies not in its content but rather in the processes through which that content is continually expanding, changing, and multiplying.

Bibliography

The following is a comprehensive but hardly exhaustive selection from the vast scholarship in the study of American religion, which has proliferated especially during the past two decades. Instead of corresponding directly to each chapter in the text, it is organized according to clusters of topics, paralleling in many cases the scheme outlined in the "Topical Guide to Chapters." Most sections include references to Charles H. Lippy and Peter W. Williams, eds., *Encyclopedia of the American Religious Experience* (3 vols.; New York, 1988) (hereafter *EARE*); the pages cited pertain to specific chapters, each of which includes lengthy bibliographical sections in which readers will find more extensive citations to work of the mid-1980s.

This bibliography combines selected works of various sorts: classic studies of particular topics; recent scholarship of high quality; bibliographies, anthologies, and reference works; scholarly works alluded to in the narrative and/or works on which portions of the narrative are based; and works on topics such as music (including a few recordings), architecture, or popular culture, which are not usually cited in other bibliographies. Most subtitles have been omitted in the interest of brevity and are included only when necessary to identify a work's contents. Primary works cited in the narrative are not usually included; data on current editions can best be located in *Books in Print* and *Paperbound Books in Print*.

The bibliography is organized as follows:

A. American Religion: Surveys and Overviews

B. American Religion: Reference Works and Collections

C. Church, State, Society, and Civil Religion

D. Religion and American Culture

E. Native American Religions

F. African-American Religions

G. Judaism

H. Eastern Christianity

I. Roman Catholicism

J. Protestantism and the Reformation Era

K. Luther and the Lutheran Tradition

L. Anglicanism and the Episcopal Church

M. The Reformed Tradition
   1. Calvin and Calvinism
   2. The Reformed Faith in Britain

In some cases, most notably concerning women and American religion, I have chosen to integrate titles into the whole rather than to establish a separate category.

A. AMERICAN RELIGION: SURVEYS AND OVERVIEWS

Ahlstrom, Sydney E.. *A Religious History of the American People.* New Haven, Conn., 1972.
Albanese, Catherine L. *America, Religions and Religion.* Belmont, Calif., 1981, 1992.
Gaustad, Edwin Scott. *A Religious History of America.* Rev. ed. San Francisco, 1990.

Handy, Robert T. *A History of the Churches in the United States and Canada.* Oxford, 1976.

Hudson, Winthrop S., and John Corrigan. *Religion in America.* 5th ed. New York, 1992.

Lippy, Charles H. *Being Religious, American Style.* Westport, Conn., 1994.

Marty, Martin E. *Pilgrims in Their Own Land: 500 Years of Religion in America.* Boston, 1984.

————, ed. *Modern American Protestantism and Its World: Historical Articles on Protestantism and American Life.* 14 vols. Bethesda, Md., 1992-93. Each volume is a collection of articles on a specific topic, such as "Women and Women's Issues" or "Protestantism and Social Christianity."

Mead, Sidney E. *The Lively Experiment.* New York, 1963.

Moore, R. Laurence. *Religious Outsiders and the Making of Americans.* New York, 1986.

Noll, Mark A. *A History of Christianity in the United States and Canada.* Grand Rapids, Mich., 1992.

Williams, Peter W. *Popular Religion in America.* 2d ed. Urbana, 1989.

Wind, James P., and James W. Lewis, eds. *American Congregations.* 2 vols. Chicago, 1994.

B. AMERICAN RELIGION: REFERENCE WORKS AND COLLECTIONS

Bass, Dorothy C., and Sandra Hughes Boyd, eds. *Women in American Religious History: An Annotated Bibliography and Guide to the Sources.* Boston, 1987.

Bowden, Henry Warner. *Church History in an Age of Uncertainty: Historiographical Patterns in the United States, 1906-1990.* Carbondale, Ill., 1991.

————. *Dictionary of American Religious Biography.* 2d ed. Westport, Conn., 1993.

————. "The Historiography of American Religion." *EARE* 1:3-16.

Burr, Nelson R. *Religion in American Life.* New York, 1971. Annotated bibliography.

Gaustad, Edwin Scott. *A Documentary History of Religion in America.* 2 vols. Grand Rapids, Mich., 1982, 1983.

————. "Geography and Demography of American Religion." *EARE* 1:71-84.

————. *Historical Atlas of Religion in America.* Rev. ed. New York, 1976.

Halvorson, Peter L., and William M. Newman. *Atlas of Religious Change in America.* Washington D.C., 1978.

Jacquet, Constant H., Jr., ed. *Yearbook of the American and Canadian Churches.* Nashville. Annual.

Lippy, Charles H., ed. *Religious Periodicals of the United States: Academic and Scholarly Journals.* New York, 1986.

————. *Twentieth-Century Shapers of American Popular Religion.* New York, 1989.

Lippy, Charles H., and Peter W. Williams, eds. *Encyclopedia of the American Religious Experience.* 3 vols. New York, 1988.

Mead, Frank S. *Handbook of Denominations in the United States.* Nashville. Published every fifth year.

Melton, J. Gordon. *The Encyclopedia of American Religions.* 3d ed. Detroit, 1989, and supplements.

Piepkorn, Arthur C. *The Religious Bodies of the United States and Canada.* 4 vols. New York, 1977, 1978, 1979.

Ruether, Rosemary Radford, and Rosemary Skinner Keller, eds. *Women and Religion in America.* 3 vols. San Francisco, 1981, 1983, 1986.

Smith, H. Shelton, et al., eds. *American Christianity: An Historical Interpretation with Representative Documents.* 2 vols. New York, 1960.

C. CHURCH, STATE, SOCIETY, AND CIVIL RELIGION

Albanese, Catherine L. *Sons of the Fathers: The Civil Religion of the American Revolution.* Philadelphia, 1976.

Bellah, Robert. *American Civil Religion in Time of Trial.* 2d ed. Chicago, 1992.

Bellah, Robert, et al. *Habits of the Heart.* Berkeley, 1985.

Bonomi, Patricia U. *Under the Cope of Heaven: Religion, Society and Politics in Colonial America.* New York, 1986.

Carter, Stephen L. *The Culture of Disbelief.* New York, 1993.

Cherry, Conrad, ed. *God's New Israel.* Englewood Cliffs, N.J., 1971.

Davidson, James West. *The Logic of Millennial Thought: Eighteenth-Century New England.* New Haven, 1977.

Fuechtmann, Thomas G. *Steeples and Stacks: Religion and Steel Crisis in Youngstown.* Cambridge, 1989.

Gaustad, Edwin S. *Faith of Our Fathers: Religion and the New Nation.* San Francisco, 1987.

Hammond, Phillip E. *Religion and Personal Autonomy: The Third Disestablishment in America.* Columbia, S.C., 1992.

Handy, Robert T. *Undermined Establishment: Church-State Relations in America.* Princeton, 1991.

Hatch, Nathan O. *The Sacred Cause of Liberty: Republican Thought and the Millennium in Revolutionary New England.* New Haven, 1977.

Hatch, Nathan O., and George M. Marsden. *The Search for Christian America.* Westchester, Ill., 1983.

Hoffman, Ronald, and Peter J. Albert, eds. *Religion in a Revolutionary Age.* Charlottesville, Va., 1994.

Jones, Donald G. "Civil and Public Religion." *EARE* 3:1393-1408.

Marty, Martin E. *Religion and Republic.* Boston, 1987.

Miller, Glenn. "Church and State." *EARE* 3:1369-93.

Miller, Robert T., and Ronald B. Flowers. *Toward Benevolent Neutrality: Church, State, and the Supreme Court.* Waco, Tex., 1987.

Morgan, Edmund S. "The Puritan Ethic and the American Revolution." *William and Mary Quarterly,* 3d ser., 24, no. 1 (Jan. 1967): 3-43.

Niebuhr, H. Richard. *The Social Sources of Denominationalism.* Cleveland, 1957. Originally pub. 1929.

Noll, Mark A. *Religion and American Politics.* New York, 1990.

Pahl, Jon. *Paradox Lost: Free Will and Political Liberty in American Culture, 1630-1760.* Baltimore, 1992.

Richey, E. Russell, and Donald G. Jones, eds. *American Civil Religion.* New York, 1974.

Stokes, Anson Phelps, and Leo Pfeffer. *Church and State in the United States.* New York, 1964.

Swanson, Wayne R. *The Christ Child Goes to Court.* Philadelphia, 1990.

Wills, Garry. *Under God: Religion and American Politics.* New York, 1990.

Wilson, John. *Public Religion in American Culture.* Philadelphia, 1979.

———. *Religion in American Society.* Englewood Cliffs, N.J., 1978.

———. "Sociological Study of American Religion." *EARE* 1:17-30.

Wilson, John F., ed. *Church and State in America: A Bibliographical Guide: the Civil War to the Present Day.* New York, 1987.

Wilson, John F., and Donald L. Drakeman, eds. *Church and State in American History.* 2d ed. Boston, 1987.

Wuthnow, Robert. *The Restructuring of American Religion: Society and Faith since World War II.* Princeton, 1988.

———. *The Struggle for America's Soul: Evangelicals, Liberals, and Secularism.* Grand Rapids, Mich., 1989.

D. RELIGION AND AMERICAN CULTURE

Albanese, Catherine. *Nature Religion in America.* Chicago, 1990.

Fuller, Robert C. *Alternative Medicine and American Religious Life.* New York, 1989.

Goethals, Gregor T. *The Electronic Golden Calf: Images, Religion, and the Making of Meaning.* Cambridge, Mass., 1990.

Lane, Belden C. *Landscapes of the Sacred.* New York, 1988.

Linenthal, Edward Tabor. *Sacred Ground: Americans and Their Battlefields.* Urbana, 1991.

Marsden, George M., and Bradley J. Longfield, eds. *The Secularization of the Academy.* New York, 1992.

May, John R. *Image and Likeness: Religious Visions in American Film Classics.* New York, 1992.

McDannell, Colleen. *Material Christianity: Religion and Popular Culture in America.* New Haven, 1995.

Moore, R. Laurence. *Selling God: American Religion in the Marketplace of Culture.* New York, 1994.

Morgan, David. *Icons of American Protestantism: The Art of Warner Sallman.* New Haven, 1996.

Nissenbaum, Stephen. *The Battle for Christmas.* New York, 1996.

Oberg, Barbara B., and Harry S. Stout, eds. *Benjamin Franklin, Jonathan Edwards, and the Representation of American Culture.* New York, 1993.

Schmidt, Leigh Eric. *Consumer Rites: The Buying and Selling of American Holidays.* Princeton, 1995.

Sears, John F. *Sacred Places: American Tourist Attractions in the Nineteenth Century.* New York, 1989.

Silk, Mark. *Unsecular Media: Making News of Religion in America.* Urbana, 1995.

Sweet, Leonard I., ed. *Communication and Change in American Religious History.* Grand Rapids, Mich., 1993.

Williams, Peter W. *Houses of God: Region, Religion, and Architecture in the United States.* Urbana, 1997.

Wuthnow, Robert, et al. *Faith and Philanthropy in America.* San Francisco, 1990.

E. NATIVE AMERICAN RELIGIONS

Berkhofer, Robert F., Jr. *Salvation and the Savage.* New York, 1976.

Bowden, Henry Warner. *American Indians and Christian Missions.* Chicago, 1981.

Capps, Walter H., ed. *Seeing with a Native Eye.* New York, 1976.

DeMallie, Raymond J., and Douglas R. Parks, eds. *Sioux Indian Religion.* Norman, Okla., 1987.

Devens, Carol. *Countering Colonization: Native American Women and Great Lakes Missions, 1630-1900.* Berkeley, 1992.

Eliade, Mircea. *Shamanism: Archaic Techniques of Ecstasy.* Princeton, 1972.

Elzey, Wayne. "Meso-American Religions." *EARE* 1:119-36.

Gill, Sam D. *Native American Religions.* Belmont, Calif., 1982.

——. "Native American Religions." *EARE* 1:137-52.

Hanke, Lewis. *Aristotle and the American Indians.* Bloomington, Ind., 1959.

Hultkrantz, Ake. *The Religions of the American Indians.* Berkeley, 1979.

LaBarre, Weston. *The Peyote Cult.* New York, 1969.

Loftin, John D. *Religion and Hopi Life in the Twentieth Century.* Bloomington, Ind., 1991.

Martin, Joel W. *Sacred Revolt: The Muskogees' Struggle for a New World.* Boston, 1991.

McLoughlin, William G. *Cherokee Renascence in the New Republic.* Princeton, 1986.

——. *The Cherokees and Christianity, 1794-1870.* Athens, Ga., 1994.

——. *Cherokees and Missionaries, 1789-1839.* New Haven, 1984.

Nabokov, Peter, and Robert Easton. *Native American Architecture.* New York, 1988.

Ortiz, Alfonso. *The Tewa World.* Chicago, 1969.

Radin, Paul. *The Trickster.* New York, 1972.

Roscoe, Will. *The Zuni Man-Woman.* Albuquerque, N.M., 1991.

Smith, Theresa S. *The Island of the Anishnaabeg: Thunderers and Water Monsters in the Traditional Ojibwe Life-World.* Moscow, Idaho, 1995.

Sullivan, Lawrence E., ed. *Native American Religions: North American.* New York, 1987.

Szasz, Margaret Connell. *Indian Education in the American Colonies, 1607-1783.* Albuquerque, N.M., 1988.

Underhill, Ruth M. *Red Man's Religion.* Chicago, 1965.

Wallace, Anthony F. C. *The Death and Rebirth of the Seneca.* New York, 1970.

Washburn, Wilcomb E. *The Indian in America.* New York, 1975.

Waters, Frank. *Book of the Hopi.* New York, 1963.

———. *Masked Gods: Navaho and Pueblo Ceremonialism.* Athens, Ohio, 1950.

Wilson, Bryan R. *Magic and the Millennium.* London, 1973.

F. AFRICAN-AMERICAN RELIGIONS

Andrews, William L. *Sisters of the Spirit: Three Black Women's Autobiographies of the Nineteenth Century.* Bloomington, Ind., 1986.

Angell, Stephen Ward. *Bishop Henry McNeal Turner and African-American Religion in the South.* Knoxville, Tenn., 1992.

Baer, Hans A., and Merrill Singer. *African-American Religion in the Twentieth Century.* Knoxville, Tenn., 1992.

Barrett, Leonard E. "The African Heritage in Caribbean and North American Religions." *EARE* 1:171-86.

Booth, Newell S., Jr., ed. *African Religions: A Symposium.* New York, 1977.

Branch, Taylor. *Parting the Waters: America in the King Years, 1954-63.* New York, 1988.

Brotz, Howard M. *The Black Jews of Harlem.* New York, 1964.

Broughton, Viv. *Black Gospel.* Poole, Dorset, U.K., 1985.

Brown, Karen McCarthy. *Mama Lola: A Vodou Priestess in Brooklyn.* Berkeley, 1991.

Burkett, Randall K. *Garveyism as a Religious Movement.* Metuchen, N.J., 1978.

Campbell, James T. *Songs of Zion: The African Methodist Episcopal Church in the United States and South Africa.* New York, 1995.

Cone, James H. "Black Religious Thought." *EARE* 2:1173-88.

———. *Martin & Malcolm & America.* Maryknoll, N.Y., 1992.

Davis, Cyprian, O.S.B. *The History of Black Catholics in the United States.* New York, 1990.

Davis, Gerald L. *I Got the Word in Me and I Can Sing It, You Know: A Study of the Performed African-American Sermon.* Philadelphia, 1987.

Dyson, Michael Eric. *Making Malcolm: The Myth and Meaning of Malcolm X.* New York, 1995.

Essien-Udom, E. E. *Black Nationalism.* Chicago, 1962.

Fauset, Arthur Huff. *Black Gods of the Metropolis.* Philadelphia, 1944.

Franklin, Reverend C. L. *Give Me This Mountain: Life History and Selected Sermons.* Edited by Jeff Todd Titon. Urbana, 1989.

Frazier, E. Franklin. *The Negro Church in America,* and C. Eric Lincoln, *The Black Church since Frazier.* Published as one volume. New York, 1963 and 1974.

Genovese, Eugene D. *Roll, Jordan, Roll.* New York, 1972.

Harris, Michael W. "African American Religious History in the 1980s: A Critical Review." *Religious Studies Review* 20, no. 4 (Oct. 1994): 263-75.

———. *The Rise of Gospel Blues: The Music of Thomas Andrew Dorsey in the Urban Church.* New York, 1992.

Herskovits, Melville J. *The Myth of the Negro Past.* Boston, 1958.

Higginbotham, Evelyn Brooks. *Righteous Discontent: The Women's Movement in the Black Baptist Church, 1880-1920.* Cambridge, Mass., 1993.

Hodges, Graham Russell, ed. *Black Itinerants of the Gospel.* Madison, Wis., 1993.

Johnson, Paul E., ed. *African-American Christianity.* Berkeley, 1994.

Johnston, Clifton H. *God Struck Me Dead: Religious Conversion Experiences and Autobiographies of Ex-Slaves.* Philadelphia: Pilgrim, 1969.

Lawson, E. Thomas. *Religions of Africa.* San Francisco, 1984.

Levine, Lawrence W. *Black Culture and Black Consciousness.* New York, 1977.

Lincoln, C. Eric. *The Black Muslims in America.* Boston, 1961.

Lincoln, C. Eric, and Lawrence H. Mamiya. "Black Militant and Separatist Movements." *EARE* 2:755-74.

Lischer, Richard. *The Preacher King: Martin Luther King, Jr., and the Word that Moved America.* New York, 1995.

Luker, Ralph E. *The Social Gospel in Black and White: American Racial Reform, 1885-1912.* Chapel Hill, N.C., 1991.

McCloud, Aminah Beverly. *African American Islam.* New York, 1995.

Montgomery, William E. *Under Their Own Vine and Fig Tree: The African-American Church in the South, 1865-1900.* Baton Rouge, La., 1993.

Murphy, Joseph M. *Santeria.* Boston, 1988.

———. *Working the Spirit: Ceremonies of the African Diaspora.* Boston, 1994.

Oliver, Paul. *Songsters and Saints: Vocal Traditions on Race Records.* New York, 1984. Also 2-vol. record set with same title issued by Matchbox (Badminton, Glos., U.K., 1984, distributed in United States by Down Home Music, El Cerrito, Calif.).

Pitts, Walter F., Jr. *Old Ship of Zion: The Afro-Baptist Ritual in the African Diaspora.* New York, 1993.

Raboteau, Albert J. "Black Christianity." *EARE* 1:635-48.

———. *A Fire in the Bones: Reflections on African-American Religious History.* Boston, 1995.

———. *Slave Religion.* New York, 1978.

Raboteau, Albert J., and Timothy Fulop, eds. *African-American Religion.* New York, 1997.

Rankin, Tom. *Sacred Space: Photographs from the Mississippi Delta.* Jackson, Miss., 1993.

Ray, Benjamin C. *African Religion.* Englewood Cliffs, N.J., 1976.

Reagon, Bernice Johnson, ed. *We'll Understand It Better By and By: Pioneering African American Gospel Composers.* Washington D.C., 1992.

Rosenberg, Bruce A. *The Art of the American Folk Preacher.* New York, 1970.

Sanders, Cheryl J. *Saints in Exile: The Holiness-Pentecostal Experience in African American Religion and Culture.* New York, 1996.

Sernett, Milton C. *African American Religious Studies.* Durham, N.C., 1989.

———. *Afro-American Religious History: A Documentary Witness.* Durham, N.C., 1985.

Spencer, Jon Michael. *Protest and Praise: Sacred Music of Black Religion.* Minneapolis, 1990.

Watts, Jill. *God, Harlem U.S.A.: The Father Divine Story.* Berkeley, 1992.

Weisbrot, Robert. *Father Divine and the Struggle for Racial Equality.* Urbana, 1983.

Williams, Ethel L., and Clifton L. Brown, comps. *Afro-American Religious Studies: A Comprehensive Bibliography with Locations in American Libraries.* Metuchen, N.J., 1972.

G. JUDAISM

American Jewish Committee. *American Jewish Yearbook.* New York. Annual.

Anderson, Bernhard W. *Understanding the Old Testament.* 4th ed. Englewood Cliffs, N.J., 1986.

Birmingham, Stephen. *Our Crowd: The Great Jewish Families of New York.* New York, 1967.

Blau, Joseph L. *Judaism in America.* Chicago, 1976.

Braunstein, Susan L., and Jenna Weissman Joselit, eds. *Getting Comfortable in New York: The American Jewish Home, 1880-1920.* New York, 1990. Museum exhibit catalog.

Chafets, Ze'ev. *Members of the Tribe: On the Road in Jewish America.* Toronto, 1988.

Davidman, Lynn. *Tradition in a Rootless World: Women Turn to Orthodox Judaism.* Berkeley, 1991.

Encyclopaedia Judaica. 16 vols. Jerusalem, 1972.

Fishman, Sylvia Barack. *A Breath of Life: Feminism in the American Jewish Community.* New York, 1993.

Gerber, David A., ed. *Anti-Semitism in American History.* Urbana, 1986.

Glazer, Nathan. *American Judaism.* Rev. ed. Chicago, 1972.

Goldy, Robert L. *The Emergence of Jewish Theology in America.* Bloomington, Ind., 1990.

Greene, Melissa Fay. *The Temple Bombing.* Reading, Mass., 1996.

Grossman, Susan. *Daughters of the King: Women and the Synagogue.* Philadelphia, 1992.

Harris, Lis. *Holy Days: The World of a Hasidic Family.* New York, 1985.

Howe, Irving. *World of Our Fathers.* New York, 1976.

The Jewish Experience in America: A Historical Bibliography. Santa Barbara, 1982.

Joselit, Jenna Weissman. *New York's Jewish Jews: The Orthodox Community in the Interwar Years.* Bloomington, Ind., 1990.

———. *The Wonders of America: Reinventing Jewish Culture, 1880-1950.* New York, 1994.

Karff, Samuel E. "Judaism." In *Religions of the World,* edited by Niels C. Nielson, Jr., et al., part 6. New York, 1983.

Karp, Abraham J. "The Emergence of an American Judaism." *EARE* 1:273-90.

———, ed. *The Jewish Experience in America.* 5 vols. Waltham, Mass., 1969. Documents.

Karp, Deborah B., and Abraham J. Karp. "Jewish Thought and Literature." *EARE* 2:1015-38.

Knox, Israel. *Rabbi in America: The Story of Isaac M. Wise.* Boston, 1957.

Korros, Alexandra Shecket, and Jonathan D. Sarna. *American Synagogue History: A Bibliography and State-of-the-Field Survey.* New York, 1988.

Kraut, Benny. *German-Jewish Orthodoxy in an Immigrant Synagogue.* New York, 1988.

Levine, Hillel. *The Death of an American Jewish Community.* New York, 1992.

Marcus, Jacob Rader. *The Colonial American Jew, 1492-1776.* 3 vols. Detroit, 1970. Documents.

———. *United States Jewry, 1776-1985.* 4 vols. Detroit, 1989-93.

Medding, Peter Y. *A New Jewry? America since the Second World War.* New York, 1992.

Mintz, Jerome. *Hasidic People: A Place in the New World.* Cambridge, Mass., 1992.

Moore, Deborah Dash. "Social History of American Judaism." *EARE* 1:291-310.

———. *To the Golden Cities: Pursuing the Jewish Dream in Miami and L.A.* New York, 1994.

Neusner, Jacob, *American Judaism: Adventure in Modernity.* Englewood Cliffs, N.J., 1972.

———. "Judaism in Contemporary America." *EARE* 1:311-14.

———. *The Way of Torah, An Introduction to Judaism.* 4th ed. Belmont, Calif., 1988.

Papo, Joseph. *Sephardim in Twentieth-Century America.* San Jose, Calif., 1987.

Postal, Bernard, and Lionel Koppman. *American Jewish Landmarks.* 4 vols. New York, 1977, 1979, 1984, 1986.

Raphael, Marc Lee. *Profiles in American Judaism.* San Francisco, 1984.

———, ed. *What Is American About American Jewish History?* Williamsburg, Va., 1993.

Rischin, Moses. *The Promised City: New York's Jews, 1870-1914.* Cambridge, Mass., 1962.

———, ed. *The Jews of North America.* Detroit, 1987.

Rosten, Leo. *The Joys of Yiddish.* New York, 1968.

Roth, Cecil. *A History of the Jews.* Rev. ed. New York, 1970.

Schappes, Morris U., ed. *A Documentary History of the Jews in the United States, 1654-1875.* New York, 1971.

Schoener, Allon. *The American Jewish Album.* New York, 1983.

Silverstein, Alan. *Alternatives to Assimilation: The Response of Reform Judaism to American Culture, 1840-1930.* Hanover, N.H., 1994.

Sklare, Marshall. *Conservative Judaism.* New York, 1955.

Slobin, Mark. *Chosen Voices: The Story of the American Cantorate.* Urbana, 1989.

Strassfeld, Michael. *The Jewish Holidays: A Guide and Commentary.* New York, 1985.

Trepp, Leo. *Judaism, Development and Life*. 3d ed. Belmont, Calif., 1982.

Wenger, Beth. *New York Jews and the Great Depression*. New Haven, 1996.

Wertheimer, Jack. *A People Divided: Judaism in Contemporary America*. New York, 1993.

———, ed. *The American Synagogue: A Sanctuary Transformed*. Cambridge, 1987.

Whitfield, Stephen J. *American Space, Jewish Time*. Hamden, Conn., 1988.

Wischnitzer, Rachel. *Synagogue Architecture in the United States*. Philadelphia, 1955.

Woocher, Jonathan S. *Sacred Survival: The Civil Religion of American Jews*. Bloomington, Ind., 1986.

Zborowski, Mark, and Elizabeth Herzog. *Life Is with People: The Culture of the Shtetl*. New York, 1962.

H. EASTERN CHRISTIANITY

Benz, Ernst. *The Eastern Orthodox Church*. Garden City, N.Y., 1963.

Chadwick, Henry. *The Early Church*. Harmondsworth, Middlesex, U.K., 1967.

Dyrud, Keith P., Michael Novak, and Rudolph J. Vecoli, eds. *The Other Catholics*. New York, 1978.

Fitzgerald, Thomas E. *The Orthodox Church*. Westport, Conn., 1995.

Galavaris, George. *The Icon in the Life of the Church*. Leiden, 1981.

Garrett, Paul D. "Eastern Christianity." *EARE* 1:325-44.

Geanakoplos, Deno John. *Byzantine East and Latin West*. New York, 1966.

Hardwick, Susan Wiley. *Russian Refuge: Religion, Migration, and Settlement on the North American Pacific Rim*. Chicago, 1993.

Kopan, Andrew T. "Greek Survival in Chicago: The Role of Ethnic Education, 1890-1980." In *Ethnic Chicago*, edited by Melvin G. Holli and Peter D'A. Jones, pp. 80-139. Grand Rapids, Mich., 1981.

Meyendorff, John. *The Orthodox Church*. New York, 1962.

Oleksa, Michael, ed. *Alaskan Missionary Spirituality*. Mahwah, N.J., 1987.

Pelikan, Jaroslav J. *The Spirit of Eastern Christendom (600-1700)*. Chicago, 1974.

Saloutos, Theodore. *The Greeks in the United States*. Cambridge, Mass., 1964.

Schmemann, Alexander. *The Historical Road of Eastern Orthodoxy*. New York, 1963.

Tarasar, Constance J., ed. *Orthodox America, 1794-1976*. Syosset, N.Y., 1975.

Ware, Timothy. *The Orthodox Church*. Baltimore, 1964.

I. ROMAN CATHOLICISM

Abbott, Walter M., S.J., ed. *The Documents of Vatican II*. New York, 1966.

Abell, Aaron I. *American Catholicism and Social Action*. Notre Dame, Ind., 1960.

Abramson, Harold J. *Ethnic Diversity in Catholic America*. New York, 1973.

Appleby, R. Scott. *"Church and Age Unite!" The Modernist Impulse in American Catholicism*. Notre Dame, Ind., 1992.

Avella, Steven M. *This Confident Church: Catholic Leadership and Life in Chicago, 1940-1965*. Notre Dame, Ind., 1992.

Barry, Colman J., O.S.B. *The Catholic Church and German Americans*. Milwaukee, 1953.

———, ed. *Readings in Church History*. 3 vols. Westminster, Md., 1965-66

Billington, Ray Allen. *The Protestant Crusade, 1800-1860*. Chicago, 1964.

Bokenkotter, Thomas. *A Concise History of the Catholic Church*. Garden City, N.Y., 1979.

———. *Essential Catholicism*. Garden City, N.Y., 1986.

Brown, Alden V. *The Grail Movement and American Catholicism, 1940-1975*. Notre Dame, Ind., 1989.

Campbell, Debra. "Catholicism from Independence to World War I." *EARE* 1:357-74.

Canedo, Lino Gomez, O.F.M. "Religion in the Spanish Empire." *EARE* 1:187-200.

Carey, Patrick W., ed. *American Catholic Religious Thought.* New York, 1987.

Catholic Almanac. Huntington, Ind. Annual.

Choquette, J. E. Robert. "French Catholicism in the New World." *EARE* 1:223-38.

Cogley, John. *Catholic America.* Garden City, N.Y., 1973.

Crosby, Donald F., S.J. *God, Church, and Flag: Senator Joseph R. McCarthy and the Catholic Church, 1950-1957.* Chapel Hill, N.C., 1978.

Cross, Robert D. *The Emergence of Liberal Catholicism in America.* Cambridge, Mass., 1967.

Curran, Robert Emmett. "American Catholic Thought." *EARE* 2:997-1014.

Davis, Cyprian, O.S.B. *The History of Black Catholics in the United States.* New York, 1990.

Dolan, Jay P. *The American Catholic Experience.* Garden City, N.Y., 1985.

————. *Catholic Revivalism.* Notre Dame, Ind., 1978.

————. *The Immigrant Church.* Baltimore, 1975.

————, ed. *The American Catholic Parish.* 2 vols. Mahwah, N.J., 1987.

Dolan, Jay P., and Allan Figueroa Deck, S.J., eds. *Hispanic Catholic Culture in the U.S.* Notre Dame, Ind., 1994.

Dolan, Jay P., and Jaime R. Vidal, eds. *Puerto Rican and Cuban Catholics in the U.S., 1900-1965.* Notre Dame, Ind., 1994.

Ebaugh, Helen Rose Fuchs. *Women in the Vanishing Cloister.* New Brunswick, N.J., 1993.

Ellis, John Tracy. *American Catholicism.* Rev. ed. Chicago, 1969.

————, ed. *Documents of American Catholic History.* 2 vols. Chicago, 1967.

Ellis, John Tracy, and Robert Trisco. *A Guide to American Catholic History.* 2d ed. Santa Barbara, Calif., 1982.

Fisher, James Terence. *The Catholic Counterculture in America, 1933-1962.* Chapel Hill, N.C., 1989.

Fogarty, Gerald P., S.J., ed. *Patterns of Episcopal Leadership.* New York, 1989.

Gleason, Philip. "A Browser's Guide to American Catholicism." *Theology Today* 38, no. 3 (Oct. 1981): 373-88.

————. *Keeping the Faith: American Catholicism, Past and Present.* Notre Dame, Ind., 1987.

————, ed. *Catholicism in America.* New York, 1970.

Gray, Francine duPlessix. *Divine Disobedience: Profiles in Catholic Radicalism.* New York, 1971.

Greeley, Andrew. *The American Catholic: A Social Portrait.* New York, 1977.

————. *That Most Distressful Nation: The Taming of the American Irish.* Chicago, 1972.

Greeley, Andrew, and Peter H. Rossi. *The Education of Catholic Americans.* Chicago, 1966.

Greene, Victor. *For God and Country: The Rise of Polish and Lithuanian Ethnic Consciousness in America.* Madison, Wis., 1975.

Hales, E. E. Y. *The Catholic Church in the Modern World.* Garden City, N.Y., 1960.

Halsey, William M. *The Survival of American Innocence.* Notre Dame, Ind., 1980.

Handlin, Oscar. *Boston's Immigrants.* New York, 1968.

Hassan, Bernard. *The American Catholic Catalog.* San Francisco, 1980.

Hennessey, James, S.J. *American Catholics.* New York, 1981

————. "Catholicism in the English Colonies." *EARE* 1:345-56.

Kane, Paula M. *Separatism and Subculture: Boston Catholicism, 1900-1920.* Chapel Hill, N.C., 1994.

Kantowicz, Edward T. *Corporation Sole: Cardinal Mundelein and Chicago Catholicism.* Notre Dame, Ind., 1983.

Kennelly, Karen, C.S.J., ed. *American Catholic Women.* New York, 1989.

Madsen, William. *The Mexican-Americans of South Texas.* 2d ed. New York, 1973.

McBrien, Richard P. *Catholicism.* 2 vols. Minneapolis, 1980.

McGuire, Meredith B. *Pentecostal Catholics.* Philadelphia, 1982.

McKenzie, John L. *The Roman Catholic Church.* Garden City, N.Y., 1971.

Morris, Charles R. *American Catholic.* New York, 1997.

New Catholic Encyclopedia. 16 vols. New York, 1967.

O'Brien, David J. *Isaac Hecker.* Mahwah, N.J., 1992.

Ochs, Stephen J. *Desegregating the Altar: The Josephites and the Struggle for Black Priests, 1871-1960.* Baton Rouge, La., 1990.

O'Connell, Marvin R. *Critics on Trial: An Introduction to the Catholic Modernist Crisis.* Washington, D.C., 1994.

———. *John Ireland and the American Catholic Church.* St. Paul, Minn., 1988.

The Official Catholic Directory. New York. Annual.

Orsi, Robert Anthony. *The Madonna of 115th Street: Faith and Community in Italian Harlem, 1880-1950.* New Haven, 1985.

———. *Thank You, St. Jude: Women's Devotion to the Patron Saint of Hopeless Causes.* New Haven, 1996.

O'Toole, James M. *Militant and Triumphant: William Henry O'Connell and the Catholic Church in Boston, 1859-1944.* Notre Dame, Ind., 1992.

Piehl, Mel. *Breaking Bread: The Catholic Worker and the Origin of Catholic Radicalism in America.* Philadelphia, 1982.

Reese, Thomas J., S.J. *Archbishop.* San Francisco, 1989.

Sanders, Cheryl Jean. *Saints in Exile: The Holiness-Pentecostal Experience in African American Religion and Culture.* New York, 1996.

Sparr, Arnold. *To Promote, Defend, and Redeem: The Catholic Literary Revival and the Cultural Transformation of American Catholicism, 1920-1960.* New York, 1990.

Steele, Thomas J., S.J. *Santos and Saints: Folk Art of Hispanic New Mexico.* Santa Fe, N.M., 1994.

Taves, Ann. *The Household of Faith: Roman Catholic Devotions in Mid-Nineteenth Century America.* Notre Dame, Ind., 1986.

Vollmar, Edward R., S.J. *The Catholic Church in America: An Historical Bibliography, Second Edition.* New York, 1963.

Weaver, Mary Jo. *New Catholic Women.* San Francisco, 1985.

———. "The Roman Catholic Heritage." *EARE* 1:153-70.

Weaver, Mary Jo, and R. Scott Appleby, eds. *Being Right: Conservative Catholics in America.* Bloomington, Ind., 1995.

Williams, Peter W. "Catholicism since World War I." *EARE* 1:375-90.

Wills, Garry. *Bare Ruined Choirs.* Garden City, N.Y., 1972.

Wrobel, Paul. *Our Way: Family, Parish, and Neighborhood in a Polish-American Community.* Notre Dame, Ind., 1979.

Zimdars-Swartz, Sandra L., *Encountering Mary: From La Salette to Medjugorje.* Princeton, 1991.

J. PROTESTANTISM AND THE REFORMATION ERA

Bainton, Roland H. *The Reformation of the Sixteenth Century.* Boston, 1952.

Chadwick, Owen. *The Reformation.* Baltimore, 1963.

Dillenberger, John, and Claude Welch. *Protestant Christianity.* New York, 1988.

Hillerbrand, Hans J., ed. *The Protestant Reformation.* New York, 1968.

Ozment, Steven. *Protestants.* New York, 1992.

Spitz, Lewis W. *The Protestant Reformation, 1517-1559.* New York, 1985.

Weber, Max. *The Protestant Ethic and the Spirit of Capitalism.* New York, c. 1958.

K. LUTHER AND THE LUTHERAN TRADITION

Bainton, Roland H. *Here I Stand: A Life of Martin Luther.* Nashville, 1950.

Bodensieck, Julius, ed. *The Encyclopedia of the Lutheran Church.* 3 vols. Minneapolis, 1965.

Coburn, Carol K. *Life at Four Corners: Religion, Gender, and Education in a German-Lutheran Community, 1868-1945.* Lawrence, Kans., 1992.

Dillenberger, John, ed. *Martin Luther: Selections from His Writings*. Garden City, N.Y., 1961.

Erikson, Erik H. *Young Man Luther*. New York, 1958.

Haile, H. G. *Luther: An Experiment in Biography*. Garden City, N.Y., 1980.

Inter-Lutheran Commission on Worship. *Lutheran Book of Worship*. Minneapolis, 1978.

Jordahl, Leigh D. "American Lutheranism: Ethos, Style, and Polity." In *The Lutheran Church in North American Life*, edited by John E. Groh and Robert H. Smith, pp. 34-55. St. Louis, 1979.

Klein, Christa R. "Lutheranism." *EARE* 1:431-50.

Kuenning, Paul P. *The Rise and Fall of American Lutheran Pietism*. Macon, Ga., 1988.

Lagerquist, L. DeAne. *In America the Men Milk the Cows: Factors of Gender, Ethnicity, and Religion in the Americanization of Norwegian-American Women*. Chicago, 1991.

Lueker, Erwin L., ed. *Lutheran Cyclopedia*. St. Louis, 1954.

Nelson, E. Clifford, ed. *The Lutherans in North America*. Philadelphia, 1975.

Nichol, Todd W. *All These Lutherans*. Minneapolis, 1986.

Pelikan, Jaroslav J. *Bach among the Theologians*. Philadelphia, 1986.

———. "The Lutheran Heritage." *EARE* 1:419-30.

Pelikan, Jaroslav J., and Helmut T. Lehmann, eds. *Luther's Works*. 53 vols. St. Louis, 1958– .

Reuss, Carl F. *Profiles of Lutherans in the U.S.A.* Minneapolis, 1982.

Tappert, Theodore G., ed. *The Book of Concord*. Philadelphia, 1959.

Thorkelson, William. *Lutherans in the U.S.A.* Minneapolis, 1978.

L. ANGLICANISM AND THE EPISCOPAL CHURCH

Albright, Raymond W. *A History of the Protestant Episcopal Church*. New York, 1964.

Armentrout, Don S. "Episcopal Splinter Groups: Schisms in the Episcopal Church, 1963-1985." *Historical Magazine of the Protestant Episcopal Church* 55, no. 4 (Dec. 1986): 295-320.

Bray, Gerald. *Documents of the English Reformation*. Minneapolis, 1994.

Bridenbaugh, Carl. *Mitre and Sceptre*. London, 1967.

Butler, Diana Hochstedt. *Standing against the Whirlwind: Evangelical Episcopalians in Nineteenth-Century America*. New York, 1995.

Chorley, E. Clowes. *Men and Movements in the American Episcopal Church*. New York, 1946.

Davies, Horton. *Worship and Theology in England*. 5 vols. Princeton, 1961-75.

DeMille, George E. *The Catholic Movement in the American Episcopal Church*. Philadelphia, 1950.

Dickens, A. G. *The English Reformation*. New York, 1978.

Donovan, Mary Sudman. *A Different Call: Women's Ministries in the Episcopal Church, 1850-1920*. Wilton, Conn., 1986.

The Episcopal Church Annual. Wilton, Conn.

Evans, G. R., and J. Robert Wright, eds. *The Anglican Tradition: A Handbook of Sources*. Minneapolis, 1991.

Guelzo, Allen C. *For the Union of Evangelical Christendom: The Irony of the Reformed Episcopalians*. University Park, Pa., 1994.

Holmes, David L. "The Anglican Tradition and the Episcopal Church." *EARE* 1:391-418.

———. *A Brief History of the Episcopal Church*. Valley Forge, Pa., 1993.

Isaac, Rhys. *The Transformation of Virginia, 1740-1790*. Chapel Hill, N.C., 1982.

Loveland, Clara O. *The Critical Years: The Reconstruction of the Anglican Church in the United States of America, 1780-1789*. Greenwich, Conn., 1956.

Manross, William Wilson. *A History of the American Episcopal Church*. New York, 1935.

Mullin, Robert Bruce. *Episcopal Vision/American Reality*. New Haven, 1986.

Neill, Stephen. *Anglicanism*. 4th ed. New York, 1978.

Prelinger, Catherine M. *Episcopal Women*. New York, 1994.

Sachs, William L. *The Transformation of Anglicanism.* Cambridge, 1993.

Steiner, Bruce. *Samuel Seabury.* Athens, Ohio, 1971.

Sumner, David E. *The Episcopal Church's History, 1945-1985.* Wilton, Conn., 1987.

Upton, Dell. *Holy Things and Profane: Anglican Parish Churches in Colonial Virginia.* Cambridge, Mass., 1986.

Wall, John N., Jr. *A New Dictionary for Episcopalians.* Minneapolis, 1985.

Woolverton, John F. *Colonial Anglicanism in North America.* Detroit, 1984.

———. *The Education of Phillips Brooks.* Urbana, 1995.

M. THE REFORMED TRADITION

1. Calvin and Calvinism

Bouwsma, William J. *John Calvin.* New York, 1988.

Dillenberger, John, ed. *John Calvin, Selections from His Writings.* Garden City, N.Y., 1971.

McNeill, John T. *The History and Character of Calvinism.* New York, 1954.

———, ed. *Calvin: Institutes of the Christian Religion I and II.* Philadelphia, 1977.

Stroup, George W., ed. *Reformed Reader: A Sourcebook in Christian Theology.* Louisville, Ky., 1993.

Tipson, Baird. "The Calvinist Heritage." *EARE* 1:451-66.

Wendel, François. *Calvin.* London, 1963.

2. The Reformed Faith in Britain

Delbanco, Andrew. *The Puritan Ordeal.* Cambridge, Mass., 1989.

George, Charles H. and Katherine. *The Protestant Mind of the English Reformation, 1570-1640.* Princeton, 1961.

Haller, William. *The Rise of Puritanism.* New York, 1938.

Hill, Christopher. *Society and Puritanism in Pre-Revolutionary England.* New York, c. 1964 and 1967.

Hoopes, James. *Consciousness in New England.* Baltimore, 1989.

Knappen, M. M. *Tudor Puritanism.* Chicago, 1939.

Little, David. *Religion, Order and Law: A Study in Pre-Revolutionary England.* New York, 1969.

New, John F. H. *Anglican and Puritan.* Stanford, Calif., 1964.

Ridley, Jasper. *John Knox.* New York, 1968.

Simpson, Alan. *Puritanism in Old and New England.* Chicago, 1955.

Walzer, Michael. *The Revolution of the Saints.* Cambridge, Mass., 1965.

Wilson, John F. *Pulpit in Parliament: Puritanism during the English Civil War Years, 1640-1648.* Princeton, 1969.

3. New England Puritanism

Note: In the late 1960s, one scholar remarked that we now know more about seventeenth-century New England than any sane person would want to. Since the late 1940s, scholarship on American Puritanism has burgeoned. The following are only some of the most important works of a vast body of writing on the topic.

Benes, Peter, ed. *New England Meeting House and Church: 1630-1850.* Boston, 1979.

Bercovitch, Sacvan. *The Puritan Origins of the American Self.* New Haven, 1975.

Boyer, Paul, and Stephen Nissenbaum. *Salem Possessed.* Cambridge, Mass., 1974.

Bozeman, Theodore Dwight. *To Live Ancient Lives: The Primitivist Dimension in Puritanism.* Chapel Hill, N.C., 1988.

Bremer, Francis J. *The Puritan Experiment.* New York, 1976.

Donnelly, Marian Card. *The New England Meeting Houses of the Seventeenth Century.* Middletown, Conn., 1968.

Fairbanks, Jonathan L. *New England Begins.* 3 vols. Boston, 1982.

Foster, Stephen. *The Long Argument: English Puritanism and the Shaping of New England Culture.* Chapel Hill, N.C., 1991.

Gaustad, Edwin Scott. *Liberty of Conscience: Roger Williams in America.* Grand Rapids, Mich., 1991.

Hall, David D. *The Faithful Shepherd: A History of the New England Ministry in the Seventeenth Century.* Chapel Hill, N.C., 1972.

———, ed. *The Antinomian Controversy, 1636-1638: A Documentary History.* Durham, N.C., 1990.

———. *Witch-Hunting in Seventeenth-Century New England: A Documentary History.* Boston, 1991.

———. *Worlds of Wonder, Days of Judgment: Popular Religious Belief in Early New England.* New York, 1989.

Hall, Michael G. *The Last American Puritan: The Life of Increase Mather, 1639-1723.* Middletown, Conn., 1988.

Hambrick-Stowe, Charles E. *The Practice of Piety: Puritan Devotional Disciplines in Seventeenth-Century New England.* Chapel Hill, N.C., 1982.

Heimert, Alan, and Andrew Delbanco, eds. *The Puritans in America: A Narrative Anthology.* Cambridge, Mass., 1985.

Holifield, E. Brooks. *The Covenant Sealed: The Development of Puritan Sacramental Theology in Old and New England, 1570-1720.* New Haven, 1974.

Karlsen, Carol F. *The Devil in the Shape of a Woman: Witchcraft in Colonial New England.* New York, 1987.

Knight, Janice. *Orthodoxies in Massachusetts: Rereading American Puritanism.* Cambridge, Mass., 1994.

McGiffert, Michael, ed. *Puritanism and the American Experience.* Reading, Mass., 1969.

Middlekauff, Robert. *The Mathers.* New York, 1971.

Miller, Perry. *Errand into the Wilderness.* Cambridge, Mass., 1956.

———. *The New England Mind: From Colony to Province.* Cambridge, Mass., 1962.

———. *The New England Mind: The Seventeenth Century.* Cambridge, Mass., 1963.

———. *Orthodoxy in Massachusetts, 1630-1650.* New York, 1970; reprint of 1933 ed.

Miller, Perry, and Thomas H. Johnson, eds. *The Puritans: A Sourcebook of Their Writings.* 2 vols. New York, 1963.

Morgan, Edmund S. *The Puritan Dilemma: The Story of John Winthrop.* Boston, 1958.

———. *The Puritan Family.* New York, 1966.

———. *Visible Saints.* New York, 1963.

Pettit, Norman. *The Heart Prepared: Grace and Conversion in Puritan Spiritual Life.* 2d ed. Middletown, Conn., 1989.

Porterfield, Amanda. *Female Piety in Puritan New England.* New York, 1992.

Stannard, David E. *The Puritan Way of Death.* New York, 1977.

Stoever, William K. B. *'A Faire and Easie Way to Heaven': Covenant Theology and Antinomianism in Early Massachusetts.* Middletown, Conn., 1978.

Stout, Harry S. *The New England Soul: Preaching and Religious Culture in Colonial New England.* New York, 1986.

Tipson, Baird. "New England Puritanism." *EARE* 1:467-80.

Walker, Williston. *The Creeds and Platforms of Congregationalism.* Boston, 1960; reprint of 1893 ed.

Youngs, J. William T. *The Congregationalists.* New York, 1990.

4. Presbyterianism

Balmer, Randall, and John R. Fitzmier. *The Presbyterians.* Westport, Conn., 1993.

Bruggink, Donald J., and Carl H. Droppers. *Christ and Architecture: Building Presbyterian/Reformed Churches.* Grand Rapids, Mich., 1965.

Coalter, Milton J., John·M. Mulder, and Louis B. Weeks, eds. *The Mainstream Protestant "Decline": The Presbyterian Pattern.* Louisville, Ky., 1990.

———. *The Organizational Revolution: Presbyterians and American Denominationalism.* Louisville, Ky., 1992.

———. *The Re-Forming Tradition: Presbyterians and Mainstream Protestantism.* Louisville, Ky., 1992.

Fisk, William Lyons. *The Scottish High Church Tradition in America.* Lanham, Md., 1995.

Leyburn, James G. *The Scotch-Irish: A Social History.* Chapel Hill, N.C., 1962.

Longfield, Bradley J. *The Presbyterian Controversy.* New York, 1991.

Melton, Julius. *Presbyterian Worship in America.* Richmond, Va., 1967.

Noll, Mark A. *Princeton and the Republic, 1768-1822.* Princeton, 1989.

Schmidt, Leigh Eric. *Holy Fairs: Scottish Communions and American Revivals in the Early Modern Period.* Princeton, 1989.

Slosser, Gaius Jackson, ed. *They Seek a Country.* New York, 1955.

Smylie, James H. *American Presbyterians: A Pictorial History.* Philadelphia, 1985. (*Journal of Presbyterian History* 63.)

Trinerud, Lionel. *The Forming of an American Tradition.* Philadelphia, 1959.

Weeks, Louis. "Presbyterianism." *EARE* 1:499-510.

[See also section R, subsections 1-8, and section S.]

5. Congregationalism and the Puritan Tradition

Cayton, Mary Kupiec. "Congregationalism from Independence to the Present." *EARE* 1:481-98.

Goddard, Carolyn E., ed. *On the Trail of the UCC: A Historical Atlas of the United Church of Christ.* New York, 1981.

Howe, Daniel Walker. "The Impact of Puritanism on American Culture." *EARE* 2:1057-74.

Phillips, Joseph W. *Jedidiah Morse and American Congregationalism.* New Brunswick, N.J., 1983.

Rohr, John von. *The Shaping of American Congregationalism, 1620-1957.* Cleveland, 1992.

Scott, Donald W. *From Office to Profession: The New England Ministry, 1750-1850.* Philadelphia, 1978.

Stoever, William K. B. "The Calvinist Theological Tradition." *EARE* 1:1039-56.

[See also section R, subsections 1-8, and section S.]

6. Other Reformed Churches

Balmer, Randall H. *A Perfect Babel of Confusion: Dutch Religion and English Culture in the Middle Colonies.* New York, 1989.

Bratt, James D. *Dutch Calvinism in Modern America.* Grand Rapids, Mich., 1984.

Bruins, Elton J. *The Americanization of a Congregation: A History of the Third Reformed Church of Holland, Michigan.* Grand Rapids, Mich., 1970.

Butler, Jon. *The Huguenots in America.* Cambridge, Mass., 1983.

Coalter, Milton J., and John M. Mulder. "Dutch and German Reformed Churches." *EARE* 1:511-24.

De Klerk, Peter, and Richard R. De Ridder, eds. *Perspectives on the Christian Reformed Church.* Grand Rapids, Mich., 1983.

DeJong, Gerald F. *The Dutch Reformed Church in the American Colonies.* Grand Rapids, Mich., 1978.

Hoeksema, Gertrude. *A Watered Garden: A Brief History of the Protestant Reformed Churches in America.* Grand Rapids, Mich., 1992.

Kroes, Rob. *The Persistence of Ethnicity: Dutch Calvinist Pioneers in Amsterdam, Montana*. Urbana, 1992.

Nichols, James Hastings, ed. *The Mercersburg Theology*. New York, 1966.

Penzel, Klaus. *Philip Schaff*. Macon, Ga., 1991.

Schneider, Carl Howard. *The German Church on the American Frontier*. St. Louis, 1939.

Swieringa, Robert P. *They Came to Stay: Essays on Dutch Immigration and Settlement in America*. New Brunswick, N.J., 1984.

VandenBrege, Peter N. *Historical Directory of the Reformed Church in America, 1628-1978*. Grand Rapids, Mich., 1978.

N. THE FREE CHURCH (BAPTIST) TRADITION

Brackney, William Henry. *The Baptists*. Westport, Conn., 1988.

Ernst, Eldon G. "The Baptists." *EARE* 1:555-577.

Leonard, Bill. *God's Last and Only Hope: The Fragmentation of the Southern Baptist Convention*. Grand Rapids, Mich., 1990.

———. "Independent Baptists: From Sectarian Minority to `Moral Majority.'" *Church History* 56, no. 4 (Dec. 1987): 504-17.

McLoughlin, William G. *Isaac Backus and the American Pietist Tradition*. Boston, 1967.

———. *New England Dissent, 1630-1833*. 2 vols. Cambridge, Mass., 1971.

———. *Soul Liberty: The Baptists' Struggle in New England, 1630-1833*. Hanover, N.H., 1991.

Wardin, Albert W., Jr. *Baptist Atlas*. Nashville, 1980.

[See also section R, especially subsection 6, "The South and Appalachia," and section S.]

O. THE PEACE CHURCHES

1. The Society of Friends (Quakers)

Baltzell, E. Digby. *Puritan Boston and Quaker Philadelphia*. Boston, 1979.

Barbour, Hugh, and J. William Frost, eds. *The Quakers*. New York, 1988.

Endy, Melvin B., Jr. "The Society of Friends." *EARE* 1:595-614.

———. *William Penn and Early Quakerism*. Princeton, 1973.

Frost, J. William, and John M. Moore, eds. *Seeking the Light: Essays in Quaker History* . . . Philadelphia, 1986.

Hamm, Thomas D. *The Transformation of American Quakerism*. Bloomington, Ind., 1988.

Ingle, H. Larry. *Quakers in Conflict: The Hicksite Reformation*. Knoxville, Tenn., 1986.

Russell, Elbert. *The History of Quakerism*. New York, 1942.

Steere, Douglas V. *Quaker Spirituality: Selected Writings*. New York, 1984.

Tolles, Frederick B. *Meeting House and Counting House*. Chapel Hill, N.C., 1948.

2. Anabaptists and Pietists

Bender, Harold S., and Henry C. Smith, eds. *The Mennonite Encyclopedia*. 4 vols. Hillsboro, Kans., 1955-59.

Bowman, Carl E. *Brethren Society: The Cultural Transformation of a "Peculiar People."* Baltimore, 1995.

Gollin, Gillian Lindt. *Moravians in Two Worlds*. New York, 1967.

Hostetler, Beulah Stauffer. *American Mennonites and Protestant Movements*. Scottsdale, Pa., 1987.

Hostetler, John A. *Amish Society*. Baltimore, 1963, 1968.

Juhnke, James C. *Vision, Doctrine, War: Mennonite Identity and Organization in America, 1890-1930*. Scottsdale, Pa., 1989.

Kraybill, Donald B. *The Riddle of Amish Culture*. Baltimore, Md., 1989.

Longenecker, Stephen L. *Pietism and Tolerance: Pennsylvania German Religion, 1700-1850.* Metuchen, N.J., 1994.
Smaby, Beverly Priot. *The Transformation of Moravian Bethlehem.* Philadelphia, 1988.
Stoeffler, F. Ernest, ed. *Continental Pietism and Early American Christianity.* Grand Rapids, Mich., 1976.
Thorp, Daniel B. *The Moravian Community in Colonial North Carolina.* Knoxville, Tenn., 1989.
Wentz, Richard E. *Pennsylvania Dutch: Folk Spirituality.* New York, 1993.
Williams, George H. *The Radical Reformation.* Philadelphia, 1962.
Yoder, Don. "Sects and Religious Movements of German Origin." *EARE* 1:615-34.

P. METHODISM

Allen, Charles L. *Meet the Methodists.* Nashville, 1986.
Bucke, Emory Stevens, ed. *The History of American Methodism.* 3 vols. New York, 1964.
Davies, Horton. *Worship and Theology in England.* Vol. 3. Princeton, 1961.
Halevy, Elie. *The Birth of Methodism in England.* Chicago, 1971.
Harmon, Nolan B. *Encyclopedia of World Methodism.* 2 vols. Nashville, 1974.
Norwood, Frederick A. *The Story of American Methodism.* Nashville, 1974.
Outler, Albert C., ed. *John Wesley.* New York, 1965.
Schneider, A. Gregory. *The Way of the Cross Leads Home: The Domestication of American Methodism.* Bloomington, Ind., 1993.
Semmel, Bernard. *The Methodist Revolution.* New York, 1973.
Tuell, Jack M. *The Organization of the United Methodist Church.* Nashville, 1982.
Wallace, Charles I., Jr. "Wesleyan Heritage." *EARE* 1:525-38.
Yrigoyen, Charles, Jr. "United Methodism." *EARE* 1:539-54.
[See also section R, subsections 1-8.]

Q. RELIGIOUS LIBERALISM

1. Enlightenment and European Background

Aldridge, Alfred Owen. *Benjamin Franklin and Nature's God.* Durham, N.C., 1967.
Bailyn, Bernard. *The Ideological Origins of the American Revolution.* Cambridge, Mass., 1967.
Bainton, Roland H. *Hunted Heretic: The Life and Death of Michael Servetus.* Boston, 1953.
———. *The Reformation of the Sixteenth Century.* Boston, 1952. See especially chapter 7, "The Free Spirits."
Becker, Carl L. *The Heavenly City of the Eighteenth-Century Philosophers.* New Haven, 1952.
Boorstin, Daniel J. *The Lost World of Thomas Jefferson.* New York, 1948; Boston, 1960.
Corrigan, John A. "The Enlightenment." *EARE* 2:1089-1102.
———. *The Hidden Balance.* Cambridge, 1987.
———. *The Prism of Piety: Catholick Congregational Clergy at the Beginning of the Enlightenment.* New York, 1991.
Cragg, G. R. *The Church and the Age of Reason.* New York, 1961.
Gay, Peter. *The Enlightenment.* 2 vols. New York, 1966, 1969.
Kloos, John M., Jr. *A Sense of Deity: The Republican Spirituality of Dr. Benjamin Rush.* Brooklyn, N.Y., 1991.
Koch, Adrienne, ed. *The American Enlightenment.* New York, 1965.
May, Henry F. *The Divided Heart: Essays on Protestantism and the Enlightenment in America.* New York, 1991.
———. *The Enlightenment in America.* New York, 1976.

2. Unitarianism, Transcendentalism, and Universalism

Ahlstrom, Sydney E., and Jonathan S. Carey, eds. *An American Reformation: A Documentary History of Unitarian Christianity.* Middletown, Conn., 1985.

Albanese, Catherine L. *The Spirituality of the American Transcendentalists.* Macon, Ga., 1988.

———. "Transcendentalism." *EARE* 2:1117-28.

Cassara, Ernest, ed. *Universalism in America: A Documentary History.* Boston, 1971.

Cayton, Mary Kupiec. *Emerson's Emergence.* Chapel Hill, N.C., 1989.

Frothingham, Octavius Brooks. *Transcendentalism in New England.* New York, 1959; reprint of 1876 ed.

Harris, Mark W., ed. *Unitarian Universalist Association Directory.* Boston. Annual.

Howe, Daniel Walker. *The Unitarian Conscience.* Cambridge, Mass., 1970.

Hutchison, William R. *The Transcendentalist Ministers.* New Haven, 1959.

Marini, Stephen M. *Radical Sects of Revolutionary New England.* Cambridge, Mass., 1982.

Miller, Perry, ed. *The Transcendentalists.* Cambridge, Mass., 1950.

Miller, Russell E. *The Larger Hope.* 2 vols. Boston, 1979, 1985. (History of Universalism.)

Robinson, David. *The Unitarians and the Universalists.* Westport, Conn., 1985.

Rose, Anne C. *Transcendentalism as a Social Movement, 1830-1850.* New Haven, 1981.

Wilbur, Earl Morse. *A History of Unitarianism: Socinianism and Its Antecedents.* Boston, 1977; reprint of c. 1942 ed.

———. *A History of Unitarianism in Transylvania, England and America.* Boston, 1978; reprint of c. 1945 ed.

Williams, George Hunston. *American Universalism.* Rev. ed. Boston, 1976.

Williams, Peter W. "Unitarianism and Universalism." *EARE* 1:579-94.

Wright, Conrad. *The Beginnings of Unitarianism in America.* Boston, 1966.

———. *The Liberal Christians.* Boston, 1970.

———. *Three Prophets of Religious Liberalism.* Boston, 1961.

———, ed. *A Stream of Light: A Sesquicentennial History of American Unitarianism.* Boston, 1975.

Wright, Conrad Edick, ed. *American Unitarianism, 1805-1865.* Boston, 1989.

3. Protestant Liberalism, Urbanization, and the Social Gospel

Abell, Aaron I. *The Urban Impact on American Protestantism, 1865-1900.* Cambridge, Mass., 1943; reprint Hamden, Conn., 1962.

Averill, Lloyd J. *American Theology in the Liberal Tradition.* Philadelphia, 1967.

Cauthen, Kenneth. *The Impact of American Religious Liberalism.* New York, 1962.

Christiano, Kevin J. *Religious Diversity and Social Change: American Cities, 1890-1906.* New York, 1987.

Curtis, Susan. *A Consuming Faith: The Social Gospel and Modern American Culture.* Baltimore, 1991.

Dorn, Jacob H. *Washington Gladden, Prophet of the Social Gospel.* Columbus, Ohio, c. 1966, 1967.

Handy, Robert T., ed. *The Social Gospel in America.* New York, 1966.

Hopkins, C. Howard. *The Rise of the Social Gospel in American Protestantism, 1865-1915.* New Haven, Conn., 1940, 1967.

Hutchison, William R. *The Modernist Impulse in American Protestantism.* Cambridge, Mass., 1976.

King, William McGuire. "Liberalism." *EARE* 2:1129-46.

Lippy, Charles H. "Social Christianity." *EARE* 2:917-32.

Massa, Mark A., S.J. *Charles Augustus Briggs and the Crisis of Historical Criticism.* Minneapolis, 1990.

May, Henry F. *Protestant Churches and Industrial America.* New York, 1949.

Minus, Paul M. *Walter Rauschenbusch*. New York, 1988.

White, Ronald C., Jr. *Liberty and Justice for All: Racial Reform and the Social Gospel (1877-1925)*. San Francisco, 1990.

White, Ronald C., Jr., and C. Howard Hopkins. *The Social Gospel*. Philadelphia, 1976.

4. Secularism and Free Thought

Kraut, Benny. *From Reform Judaism to Ethical Culture*. Cincinnati, 1979.

Krauthammer, Charles. "The Humanist Phantom." *New Republic,* July 25, 1981, 20-25.

Marty, Martin E. "Free Thought and Ethical Movements." *EARE* 2:731-40.

——. *The Infidel: Freethought and American Religion*. Cleveland, 1961.

Persons, Stow. *Free Religion: An American Faith*. New Haven, 1947.

Turner, James. *Without God, Without Creed*. Baltimore, 1985.

Walters, Kerry S. *The American Deists*. Lawrence, Kans., 1992.

R. CONSERVATIVE PROTESTANTISM

1. The Great Awakening and Its Aftermath

Bushman, Richard L., ed. *The Great Awakening: Documents on the Revival of Religion, 1740-1745*. New York, 1970.

Butler, Jon. *Awash in a Sea of Faith: Christianizing the American People*. Cambridge, Mass., 1990.

Cherry, Conrad. *The Theology of Jonathan Edwards*. Bloomington, Ind., 1990.

Coalter, Milton J., Jr. *Gilbert Tennent, Son of Thunder*. New Ewer, 1986.

Conforti, Joseph A. *Jonathan Edwards, Religious Tradition, and American Culture*. Chapel Hill, N.C., 1995.

Crawford, Michael J. *Seasons of Grace: Colonial New England's Revival Tradition in Its British Context*. New York, 1991.

Edwards, Jonathan. The Works of Jonathan Edwards Series. Various titles and editors. New Haven, Conn., 1957–. Continuing series.

Faust, Clarence H., and Thomas H. Johnson, eds. *Jonathan Edwards*. New York, 1962.

Gaustad, Edwin Scott. *The Great Awakening in New England*. New York, 1957.

Goen, Clarence C. *Revivalism and Separatism in New England, 1740-1800*. New Haven, 1962.

Hall, Timothy D. *Contested Boundaries: Itinerancy and the Reshaping of the Colonial American Religious World*. Durham, N.C., 1994.

Heimert, Alan, and Perry Miller, eds. *The Great Awakening*. Indianapolis, 1967.

Juster, Susan. *Disorderly Women: Sexual Politics and Evangelicalism in Revolutionary New England*. Ithaca, N.Y., 1994.

Lambert, Frank. *"Pedlar in Divinity": George Whitefield and the Transatlantic Revivals, 1737-1770*. Princeton, 1994.

Lovejoy, David O. *Religious Enthusiasm and the Great Awakening*. Englewood Cliffs, N.J., 1969.

Marini, Stephen A. "The Great Awakening." *EARE* 2:775-98.

Miller, Perry. *Jonathan Edwards*. Cleveland, 1959; reprint of 1949 ed.

Pointer, Richard W. *Protestant Pluralism and the New York Experience*. Bloomington, Ind., 1988.

Stout, Harry S. *The Divine Dramatist: George Whitefield and the Rise of Modern Evangelicalism*. Grand Rapids, Mich., 1991.

Valeri, Mark. *Law and Providence in Joseph Bellamy's New England*. New York, 1994.

Ward, W. R. *The Protestant Evangelical Awakening*. Cambridge, 1992.

2. Nineteenth-Century Evangelicalism

Bristol, Sherlock. *The Pioneer Preacher: Incidents of Interest, and Experiences of the Author's Life*. Edited by Dewey D. Wallace, Jr. Urbana, 1989.

Conkin, Paul. *The Uneasy Center: Reformed Christianity in Antebellum America*. Chapel Hill, N.C., 1995.

Hackett, David G. *The Rude Hand of Innovation: Religion and Social Order in Albany, New York, 1652-1836*. New York, 1991.

Handy, Robert T. *A Christian America*. 2d ed. New York, 1984.

Hanley, Mark Y. *Beyond a Christian Commonwealth: The Protestant Quarrel with the American Republic, 1830-1860*. Chapel Hill, N.C., 1994.

Hatch, Nathan. *The Democratization of American Christianity*. New Haven, Conn., 1989.

Johnson, Curtis D. *Islands of Holiness: Rural Religion in Upstate New York, 1790-1860*. Ithaca, N.Y., 1989.

Marty, Martin E. *Protestantism in the United States: Righteous Empire*. 2d ed. New York, 1986.

McLoughlin, William G., ed. *The American Evangelicals, 1800-1900*. New York, 1968.

Rabinowitz, Richard. *The Spiritual Self in Everyday Life*. Boston, 1989.

Smith, John E., Harry S. Stout, and Kenneth P. Minkema, eds. *A Jonathan Edwards Reader*. New Haven, 1995.

Sweet, Leonard I. "Nineteenth-Century Evangelicalism." *EARE* 2:875-900.

———, ed. *The Evangelical Tradition in America*. Macon, Ga., 1984. Contains extensive bibliographical essay.

Taves, Ann, ed. *Religion and Domestic Violence in New England*. Bloomington, Ind., 1989.

3. Revivalism

Blumhofer, Edith L., and Randall Balmer, eds. *Modern Christian Revivals*. Urbana, 1993.

Brown, Kenneth O. *Holy Ground: A Study of the American Camp Meeting*. New York, 1992.

Carwardine, Richard. *Transatlantic Revivalism*. Westport, Conn., 1978.

Dorsett, Lyle W. *Billy Sunday and the Redemption of Urban America*. Grand Rapids, Mich., 1991.

Hardman, Keith. *Charles Grandison Finney, 1792-1875*. Syracuse, N.Y., 1987.

Henry, Stuart C. "Revivalism." *EARE* 2:799-812.

Kling, David W. *A Field of Divine Wonders: The New Divinity and Village Revivals in Northwestern Connecticut, 1792-1822*. University Park, Pa., 1993.

McLoughlin, William G. *Modern Revivalism*. New York, 1959.

———. *Revivals, Awakenings, and Reform*. Chicago, 1978.

Robertson, Darrel M. *The Chicago Revival, 1876*. Metuchen, N.J., 1989.

Weisberger, Bernard A. *They Gathered at the River*. Boston, 1958.

[See also subsections 1, above, and 4, below.]

4. The Second Great Awakening(s)

Birdsall, Richard D. "The Second Great Awakening and the New England Social Order." *Church History* 39, no. 3 (Sept. 1970): 345-64.

Boles, John B. *The Great Revival, 1787-1805*. Lexington, Ky., 1972.

Cross, Barbara M., ed. *The Autobiography of Lyman Beecher*. 2 vols. Cambridge, Mass., 1961.

Cross, Whitney R. *The Burned-over District*. Ithaca, N.Y., 1950.

Johnson, Paul E., and Sean Wilentz. *The Kingdom of Matthias*. New York, 1994.

Keller, Charles Roy. *The Second Great Awakening in Connecticut*. New Haven, Conn., 1942.

McLoughlin, William G., ed. *Lectures on Revivals in Religion by Charles G. Finney*. Cambridge, Mass., 1960.

Mead, Sidney E. *Nathaniel William Taylor, 1786-1858: A Connecticut Liberal*. Chicago, 1942.

[See also subsection 3, above.]

5. Reform, Antislavery, and Civil War

Note: The literature on antebellum reform in general and antislavery in particular is vast.

The following is only a sampling of some important scholarly studies of these topics.

Abzug, Robert. *Cosmos Crumbling*. New York, 1994.

Bodo, John R. *The Protestant Clergy and Public Issues, 1812-1848*. Princeton, 1954.

Carwardine, Richard J. *Evangelicals and Politics in Antebellum America*. New Haven, 1993.

Cayton, Mary K. "Social Reform from the Colonial Period through the Civil War." *EARE* 3:1429-40.

Cherry, Conrad, ed. *God's New Israel*. Englewood Cliffs, N.J., 1971. See especially part 2, "Civil War and National Destiny."

Davis, David Brion. "Some Themes of Countersubversion." In *The Fear of Conspiracy*, edited by Davis, pp. 9-22. Ithaca, N.Y., 1971.

Filler, Louis. *The Crusade against Slavery, 1830-1860*. New York, 1960.

Foster, Charles I. *An Errand of Mercy: The Evangelical United Front, 1790-1837*. Chapel Hill, N.C., 1960.

Griffin, Clifford S. *Their Brothers' Keepers*. New Brunswick, N.J., 1960.

Johnson. Paul E. *A Shopkeeper's Millennium: Society and Revivals in Rochester, New York, 1815-1837*. New York, c. 1978.

Kelley, Robert. *The Cultural Pattern in American Politics*. New York, 1979.

Merrill, Walter M. *Against Wind and Tide: A Biography of William Lloyd Garrison*. Cambridge, Mass., 1963.

Mintz, Steven. *Moralists and Modernizers*. Baltimore, 1995.

Perry, Lewis. *Radical Abolitionism*. Ithaca, N.Y., 1973.

Rothman, David J. *The Discovery of the Asylum*. Boston, 1971.

Smith, Timothy L. *Revivalism and Social Reform*. Nashville, 1957.

Tyler, Alice Felt. *Freedom's Ferment*. Minneapolis, 1944.

Walters, Ronald G. *American Reformers, 1815-1860*. New York, 1978.

Wolf, William J. *The Religion of Abraham Lincoln*. New York, 1963; originally published as *The Almost Chosen People*.

Wyatt-Brown, Bertram. *Lewis Tappan and the Evangelical War against Slavery*. Cleveland, 1969.

6. The South and Appalachia

Alabama Sacred Harp Convention. *White Spirituals from the Sacred Harp*. Notes by Alan Lomax. New World Records. New York, 1977.

Bailey, Kenneth K. *Southern White Protestantism in the Twentieth Century*. New York, 1964.

Barnes, William Wright. *The Southern Baptist Convention, 1845-1953*. Nashville, 1954.

Burton, Thomas. *Serpent Handling Believers*. Knoxville, Tenn., 1993.

Calhoon, Robert M. *Evangelicals and Conservatives in the Early South, 1740-1861*. Columbia, S.C., 1988.

Dorgan, Howard. *Giving Glory to God in Appalachia: Worship Practices of Six Baptist Subdenominations*. Knoxville, Tenn., 1987

————. *The Old Regular Baptists of Central Appalachia*. Knoxville, Tenn, 1989.

Eighmy, John Lee. *Churches in Cultural Captivity: A History of the Social Attitudes of Southern Baptists*. Knoxville, 1972.

Farmer, James Oscar, Jr. *The Metaphysical Confederacy: James Henley Thornwell and the Synthesis of Southern Values*. Macon, Ga., 1986.

Goen, C. C. *Broken Churches, Broken Nation: Denominational Schisms and the Coming of the American Civil War*. Macon, Ga., 1985.

Harrell, David Edwin, Jr., ed. *Varieties of Southern Evangelicalism*. Macon, Ga., 1981.

Heriot, M. Jean. *Blessed Assurance: Belief, Actions and the Experience of Salvation in a Carolina Baptist Church*. Knoxville, Tenn., 1994.

Hill, Samuel S. "The South." *EARE* 3:1493-1508.

————. *Southern Churches in Crisis*. Boston, 1968.

————, ed. *Encyclopedia of Religion in the South*. Macon, Ga., 1984.

————. *On Jordan's Stormy Banks*. Macon, Ga., 1983.

————. *Religion and the Solid South*. Nashville, 1972.

————. *Varieties of Southern Religious Experience*. Baton Rouge, La., 1988.

Hood, Fred J. *Reformed America: The Middle and Southern States, 1783-1837*. University, Ala., 1980.

Kimbrough, David L. *Taking Up Serpents: Snake Handlers of Eastern Kentucky*. Chapel Hill, N.C., 1995.

Lippy, Charles H. *Bibliography of Religion in the South*. Macon, Ga., 1983.

Mathews, Donald G. *Religion in the Old South*. Chicago, 1977.

Miller, Randall M. *Catholics in the Old South*. Macon, Ga., 1983.

Neville, Gwen Kennedy. *Kinship and Pilgrimage: Rituals of Reunion in American Protestant Culture*. New York, 1987.

Ownby, Ted. *Subduing Satan: Religion, Recreation, and Manhood in the Rural South, 1865-1920*. Chapel Hill, N.C., 1990.

Patterson, Beverly Bush. *The Sound of the Dove: Singing in Appalachian Primitive Baptist Churches*. Urbana, 1995.

Peacock, James L., and Ruel W. Tyson, Jr. *Pilgrims of Paradox: Calvinism and Experience among the Primitive Baptists of the Blue Ridge*. Washington, D.C., 1989.

Proctor, Samuel, and Louis Schmeir. *Jews of the South*. Macon, Ga., 1982.

Spain, Rufus B. *At Ease in Zion: A Social History of Southern Baptists, 1865-1900*. Nashville, c. 1961, 1967.

Thompson, James J., Jr. *Tried as by Fire: Southern Baptists and the Religious Controversies of the 1920s*. Macon, Ga., 1982.

Titon, Jeff Todd. *Powerhouse for God: Speech, Chant and Song in an Appalachian Baptist Church*. Austin, Tex., 1988. Also recordings published under same title by University of North Carolina Press, Chapel Hill, 1982.

Tyson, Ruel W., Jr., James L. Peacock, and Daniel W. Patterson, eds. *Diversities of Gifts: Field Studies in Southern Religion*. Urbana, 1988.

Wilson, Charles Reagan. *Baptized in Blood: The Religion of the Lost Cause, 1865-1920*. Athens, Ga., 1980.

————, ed. *Cultural Perspectives on the American South. Volume 5: Religion*. New York, 1991.

————. *Religion in the South*. Jackson, Miss., 1985.

Wyatt-Brown, Bertram. "Religion and the 'Civilizing Process' in the Early American South." In *Evangelicalism and American Politics*, edited by Mark Noll and Joel Carpenter. New York, 1989.

[See also section N.]

7. Nineteenth-Century Protestant Education, Thought, and Culture

Boylan, Anne M. *Sunday School*. New Haven 1988.

Caskey, Marie. *Chariot of Fire: Religion and the Beecher Family*. New Haven, 1978.

Elson, Ruth Miller. *Guardians of Tradition: American Schoolbooks of the Nineteenth Century*. Lincoln, Neb., 1964.

Gorn, Elliott J., ed. *A McGuffey Reader*. Boston, 1997.

Hewitt, Glenn A. *Regeneration and Morality: A Study of Charles Finney, Charles Hodge, John W. Nevin, and Horace Bushnell*. Brooklyn, N.Y., 1991.

Hill, Patricia R. "The Missionary Enterprise." *EARE* 3:1683-96.

Marsden, George M. *The Evangelical Mind and the New School Presbyterian Experience*. New Haven, 1970.

McDannell, Colleen. *The Christian Home in Victorian America, 1840-1900*. Bloomington, Ind., 1986.

Miyakawa, T. Scott. *Protestants and Pioneers*. Chicago, 1964.

Moorhead, James. *American Apocalypse: Yankee Protestants and the Civil War, 1860-1869*. New Haven, 1978.

Mulder, John M. *Woodrow Wilson: The Years of Preparation*. Princeton, 1978.

Rudolph, Frederick. *The American College and University*. New York, 1962.

Smith, H. Shelton. *Changing Conceptions of Original Sin*. New York, 1955.

Wosh, Peter J. *Spreading the Word: The Bible Business in Nineteenth-Century America*. Ithaca, N.Y., 1994.

Wright, Louis B. *Culture on the Moving Frontier*. Bloomington, Ind., 1955.

8. Foreign Missions

Boyd, Nancy. *Emissaries: The Overseas Work of the American YWCA, 1895-1970*. New York, 1986.

Carpenter, Joel A., and Wilbert R. Shenk, eds. *Earthen Vessels: American Evangelicals and Foreign Missions, 1880-1980*. Grand Rapids, Mich., 1990.

Clymer, Kenton J. *Protestant Missionaries in the Philippines, 1898-1916*. Urbana, 1986.

Hutchison, William R. *Errand to the World: American Protestant Thought and Foreign Missions*. Chicago, 1987.

Ruoff, E. G., ed. *Death Throes of a Dynasty: Letters and Diaries of Charles and Bessie Ewing, Missionaries to China*. Kent, Ohio, 1990.

Walker, Randi. *Protestantism in the Sangre de Cristos, 1850-1920*. Albuquerque, N.M., 1991.

Zwiep, Mary. *Pilgrim Path: The First Company of Women Missionaries in Hawaii*. Madison, Wis., 1991.

9. The Victorian Era

Braude, Ann. *Radical Spirits: Spiritualism and Women's Rights in Nineteenth-Century America*. Boston, 1989.

Brighten the Corner Where You Are: Black and White Urban Hymnody. New World Records. New York, 1978.

Carter, Paul A. *The Spiritual Crisis of the Gilded Age*. DeKalb, Ill., 1971.

Douglas, Ann. *The Feminization of American Culture*. New York, 1977.

Findlay, James F., Jr. *Dwight L. Moody*. Chicago, 1969.

Gusfield, Joseph R. *Symbolic Crusade: Status Politics and the American Temperance Movement*. 2d ed. Urbana, 1986.

Kerr, K. Austin. *Organized for Prohibition: A New History of the Anti-Saloon League*. New Haven, 1985.

Mayer, John A. "Social Reform after the Civil War to the Great Depression." *EARE* 3:1441-61.

Rorabaugh, W. J. *The Alcoholic Republic*. New York, 1979.

Rose, Anne C. *Victorian America and the Civil War*. New York, 1992.

Sinclair, Andrew. *Era of Excess: A Social History of the Prohibition Movement*. New York, 1964.

Sizer, Sandra S. *Gospel Hymns and Social Religion*. Philadelphia, 1978.

Timberlake, James H. *Prohibition and the Progressive Movement, 1900-1920*. Cambridge, Mass., 1963.

10. Fundamentalism

Ammerman, Nancy Tatom. *Bible Believers: Fundamentalists in the Modern World*. New Brunswick, N.J., 1987.

Bendroth, Margaret Lamberts. *Fundamentalism and Gender, 1875 to the Present*. New Haven, 1993.

Brereton, Virginia Lieson. *Training God's Army: The American Bible School, 1880-1940*. Bloomington, Ind., 1990.

DeBerg, Betty A. *Ungodly Women: Gender and the First Wave of American Fundamentalism.* Minneapolis, 1990.

Hart, D. G. *Defending the Faith: J. Gresham Machen and the Crisis of Conservative Protestantism in Modern America.* Baltimore, 1994.

Kraus, C. Norman. *Dispensationalism in America.* Richmond, Va., 1958.

Marsden, George M. "Fundamentalism." *EARE* 2:947-62.

———. *Fundamentalism and American Culture.* New York, 1980.

———. *Reforming Fundamentalism: Fuller Seminary and the New Evangelicalism.* Grand Rapids, Mich., 1987.

Marty, Martin E., and R. Scott Appleby, eds. *Accounting for Fundamentalisms.* Chicago, 1994.

Russell, C. Allyn. *Voices of American Fundamentalism.* Philadelphia, 1976.

Sandeen, Ernest. *The Roots of Fundamentalism.* Chicago, 1970.

Trollinger, William Vance, Jr. *God's Empire: William Bell Riley and Midwestern Fundamentalism.* Madison, Wis., 1990.

Weber, Timothy P. *Living in the Shadow of the Second Coming: American Premillennialism, 1875-1925.* Enlarged ed. Chicago, 1987.

[See also section N.]

11. Holiness

Brasher, J. Lawrence. *The Sanctified South: John Lakin Brasher and the Holiness Movement.* Urbana, 1994.

Jones, Charles Edwin. *Perfectionist Persuasion: The Holiness Movement and American Methodism, 1867-1936.* Methuen, N.J., 1974.

Murdoch, Norman H. *Origins of the Salvation Army.* Knoxville, Tenn., 1994.

Oden, Thomas C., ed. *Phoebe Palmer: Selected Writings.* New York, 1988.

Raser, Harold E. *Phoebe Palmer.* Lewiston, N.Y., 1987.

Schmidt, Jean Miller. "Holiness and Perfection." *EARE* 2:813-30.

Smith, Timothy L. *Called unto Holiness.* Kansas City, Mo., 1962.

Stanley, Susan Cunningham. *Feminist Pillar of Fire: The Life of Alma White.* Cleveland, 1993.

Weiss, Ellen. *City in the Woods: The Life and Design of an American Camp Meeting on Martha's Vineyard.* New York, 1987.

12. Pentecostalism

Anderson, Robert Mapes. *Vision of the Disinherited: The Making of American Pentecostalism.* New York, 1979.

Blumhofer, Edith L. *Aimee Semple McPherson.* Grand Rapids, Mich., 1993.

———. *Restoring the Faith: The Assemblies of God, Pentecostalism, and American Culture.* Urbana, 1993.

Burgess, Stanley M., and Gary B. McGee, eds. *Dictionary of Pentecostal and Charismatic Movements.* Grand Rapids, Mich., 1988.

Crews, Mickey. *The Church of God: A Social History.* Knoxville, Tenn., 1990.

Dayton, Donald W. *Theological Roots of Pentecostalism.* Methuen, N.J., 1987.

Goff, James R., Jr. *Fields White unto Harvest: Charles F. Parham and the Missionary Origins of Pentecostalism.* Fayetteville, Ark., 1988.

Harrell, David Edwin, Jr. *All Things Are Possible: The Healing and Charismatic Revivals in Modern America.* Bloomington, Ind., 1975.

Jones, Charles Edwin. *A Guide to the Study of the Pentecostal Movement.* 2 vols. Methuen, N.J., 1983.

Synan, Vincent. *The Holiness-Pentecostal Movement in America.* Grand Rapids, Mich., 1971.

Wacker, Grant. "The Functions of Faith in Primitive Pentecostalism." *Harvard Theological Review* 77, nos. 3-4 (1984): 353-75.

———. "Pentecostalism." *EARE* 2:933-46.

13. Later-Twentieth-Century Developments

Balmer, Randall. *Mine Eyes Have Seen the Glory: A Journey into the Evangelical Subculture in America.* 2d ed. New York, 1993.

Bruce, Steve. *Pray TV: Televangelism in America.* New York, 1990.

Capps, Walter H. *The New Religious Right.* Columbia, S.C., 1990.

Elzey, Wayne. "Popular Culture." *EARE* 3:1727-42.

Fitzgerald, Frances. "Liberty Baptist." In Fitzgerald, *Cities on a Hill,* pp. 121-202. New York, c. 1981, 1983, 1986.

Frady, Marshall. *Billy Graham.* Boston, 1979.

Frankl, Razelle. *Televangelism: The Marketing of Popular Religion.* Carbondale, Ill., 1987.

Harrell, David Edwin, Jr. *Oral Roberts.* San Francisco, 1985.

———. *Pat Robertson.* San Francisco, 1987.

Hunter, James Davison. *American Evangelicalism.* New Brunswick, N.J., 1983.

Liebman, Robert C., and Robert Wuthnow, eds. *The New Christian Right.* New York, 1983.

Lienisch, Michael. *Redeeming America: Piety and Politics in the New Christian Right.* Chapel Hill, N.C., 1993.

Martin, William. "Mass Communications." *EARE* 3:1711-26.

———. *A Prophet with Honor: The Billy Graham Story.* New York, 1991.

———. *With God on Our Side: The Rise of the Religious Right in America.* New York, 1996.

Numbers, Ronald L. *The Creationists.* New York, 1992.

Quebedeaux, Richard. "Conservative and Charismatic Developments of the Later Twentieth Century." *EARE* 2:963-76.

Wacker, Grant. "Searching for Norman Rockwell: Popular Evangelicalism in Contemporary America." In *The Evangelical Tradition in America,* edited by Leonard I. Sweet, pp. 289-315. Macon, Ga., 1984.

Wagner, Melinda Bollar. *God's Schools.* New Brunswick, N.J., 1990.

Watt, David Harrington. *A Transforming Faith: Explorations of Twentieth-Century American Evangelicalism.* New Brunswick, N.J., 1991.

Wilcox, Clyde. *God's Warriors: The Christian Right in Twentieth Century America.* Baltimore, 1992.

14. Overviews and Bibliography

Blumhofer, Edith L., and Joel A. Carpenter, eds. *Twentieth-Century Evangelicalism: A Guide to the Sources.* New York, 1990.

Boyer, Paul. *When Time Shall Be No More: Prophecy Belief in Modern American Culture.* Cambridge, Mass., 1992.

Brereton, Virginia Lieson. *From Sin to Salvation: Stories of Women's Conversions, 1800 to the Present.* Bloomington, Ind., 1991.

Dayton, Donald W., and Robert K. Johnston, eds. *The Variety of American Evangelicalism.* Downers Grove, Ill., 1991.

Magnuson, Norris A., and William G. Travis. *American Evangelicalism: An Annotated Bibliography.* West Cornwall, Conn., 1990.

Marsden, George M. *Understanding Fundamentalism and Evangelicalism.* Grand Rapids, Mich., 1991.

Peshkin, Alan. *God's Choice: The Total World of a Fundamentalist Christian School.* Chicago, 1986.

Schuster, Robert D., James Stambaugh, and Ferne Weimer, comps. *Researching Modern Evangelicalism: A Guide to the Holdings of the Billy Graham Center.* Westport, Conn., 1990.

S. *"MAINLINE" PROTESTANTISM AND THE TWENTIETH-CENTURY SCENE*

Balmer, Randall. *Grant Us Courage: Travels along the Mainline of American Protestantism.* New York, 1996.

Baltzell, E. Digby. *The Protestant Establishment.* New York, 1964.

Brown, Charles C. *Niebuhr and His Age.* Philadelphia, 1992.

Bucher, Glenn R., and L. Gordon Tait. "Social Reform since the Great Depression." *EARE* 3:1441-62.

Carroll, Jackson, and Wade Clark Roof, eds. *Beyond Establishment: Protestant Identity in a Post-Protestant Age.* Louisville, Ky., 1993.

Crow, Paul A., Jr. "The Ecumenical Movement." *EARE* 2:977-96.

Ferm, Deane William. "Religious Thought since World War II." *EARE* 2:1159-72.

Fox, Richard. *Reinhold Niebuhr.* New York, 1985.

Gallup, George, Jr., and Jim Castelli. *The People's Religion: American Faith in the 90s.* New York, 1989.

Handy, Robert T. *A History of Union Theological Seminary in New York.* New York, 1987.

Hudnut-Beumler, James. *Looking for God in the Suburbs: The Religion of the American Dream and its Critics, 1945-1965.* New Brunswick, N.J., 1994.

Hutchison, William R., ed. *Between the Times: The Travail of the Protestant Establishment in America, 1900-1960.* New York, 1989.

Lotz, David W. *Altered Landscapes: Christianity in America, 1935-1985.* Grand Rapids, Mich., 1989.

Marty, Martin E. *Modern American Religion.* Vol. 1: *The Irony of It All: 1893-1919.* Chicago, 1986; vol. 2: *The Noise of Conflict: 1919-1941.* Chicago, 1991; vol. 3: *Under God, Indivisible: 1941-1960.* Chicago, 1996.

———. *Religion and Republic.* Boston, 1987.

———, ed. *Where the Spirit Leads: American Denominations Today.* Atlanta, 1980.

Michaelsen, Robert S., and Wade Clark Roof. *Liberal Protestantism: Realities and Possibilities.* New York, 1986.

Roof, Wade Clark, and William McKinney. *American Mainline Religion.* New Brunswick, N.J., and London, 1987.

Voskuil, Dennis N. "Neo-Orthodoxy." *EARE* 2:1147-58.

Wuthnow, Robert. *The Restructuring of American Religion.* Princeton, 1988.

T. *THE AMERICAN WEST*

Banker, Mark T. *Presbyterian Missions and Cultural Interaction in the Far Southwest, 1850-1950.* Urbana, 1993.

Engh, Michael E. *Frontier Faiths: Church, Temple, and Synagogue in Los Angeles, 1846-1888.* Albuquerque, N.M., 1992.

Frankiel, Sandra Sizer. *California's Spiritual Frontiers.* Berkeley, 1988.

Griffith, James S. *Beliefs and Holy Places: A Spiritual Geography of the Pimería Alta.* Tucson, 1992.

Guarneri, Carl, and David Alvarez, eds. *Religion and Society in the American West.* Lanham, Md., 1987.

Luchetti, Cathy. *Under God's Spell: Frontier Evangelists, 1722-1915.* New York, 1989.

Maffly-Kipp, Laurie F. *Religion and Society in Frontier California.* New Haven, Conn. 1994

Pascoe, Peggy. *Relations of Rescue: The Search for Female Moral Authority in the American West, 1874-1939.* New York, 1990.

Steele, Thomas J. *Santos and Saints: The Religious Folk Art of Hispanic New Mexico.* Santa Fe, 1994.

Szasz, Ferenc M. *The Protestant Clergy in the Great Plains and the Mountain West, 1865-1915.* Albuquerque, N.M., 1988.

Treib, Marc. *Sanctuaries of Spanish New Mexico.* Berkeley, 1993.

Tucker, Cynthia Grant. *Prophetic Sisterhood: Liberal Women Ministers of the Frontier, 1880-1930.* Boston, 1990.

Weigle, Marta. *Brothers of Light, Brothers of Blood: The Penitentes of the Southwest.* Santa Fe, N.M., 1989.

U. ASIAN RELIGIONS AND ISLAM

Booth, Newell S., Jr. "Islam in North America." *EARE* 2:723-30.

Fenton, John Y. "Hinduism." *EARE* 2:683-98.

———. *Transplanting Religious Traditions: Asian Indians in America.* New York, 1988.

Fenton, John Y., et al. *Religions of Asia.* 2d ed. New York, 1988.

Fields, Rick. *How the Swans Came to the Lake: A Narrative History of Buddhism in America.* Boulder, Colo., 1981.

Haaland, C. Carlyle. "Shinto and Indigenous Chinese Religion." *EARE* 2:699-710.

Haddad, Yvonne Yazbeck, ed. *The Muslims of America.* New York, 1991.

Haddad, Yvonne Yazbeck, and Jane Idleman Smith, eds. *Mission America: Five Islamic Sectarian Communities in North America.* Gainesville, Fla., 1993.

———. *Muslim Communities in North America.* Albany, N.Y., 1994.

Jackson, Carl T. *Vedanta for the West.* Bloomington, Ind., 1994.

Layman, Emma McCoy. *Buddhism in America.* Chicago, 1976.

McCloud, Aminah Beverly. *African American Islam.* New York, 1995.

Prebish, Charles S. *American Buddhism.* North Scituate, Mass., 1979.

———. "Buddhism." *EARE* 2:669-82.

Tweed, Thomas. *The American Encounter with Buddhism, 1844-1912.* Bloomington, Ind., 1992.

Waugh, Earle H., Baha Abu-Laban, and Regula B. Quereshi, eds. *The Muslim Community in North America.* Edmonton, Alberta, 1983.

Williams, Raymond Brady. *Religions of Immigrants from India and Pakistan.* Cambridge, 1988.

[See also Melton, section B, and section W.]

V. MORMONISM AND OTHER INDIGENOUS RELIGIOUS GROUPS

1. Mormonism (Latter-day Saints)

Note: The University of Illinois Press publishes an extensive series of historical studies of the LDS tradition, selections from which are listed below.

Arrington, Leonard J. *Brigham Young.* New York, 1985.

Arrington, Leonard J., and Davis Bitton. *The Mormon Experience.* New York, 1979.

Arrington, Leonard J., Feramorz Y. Fox, and Dean L. May. *Building the City of God: Community and Cooperation among the Mormons.* 2d ed. Urbana, 1992.

Barlow, Philip L. *Mormons and the Bible.* New York, 1991.

Brodie, Fawn M. *No Man Knows My History: The Life of Joseph Smith.* New York, 1971.

Brooke, John L. *The Refiner's Fire: The Making of Mormon Cosmology, 1644-1844.* New York, 1994.

Bushman, Richard L. *Joseph Smith and the Beginnings of Mormonism.* Urbana, 1984.

Cornwall, Marie, Tim B. Heaton, and Lawrence A. Young, eds. *Contemporary Mormonism: Social Science Perspectives.* Urbana, 1994.

Hanks, Maxine. *Women and Authority: Re-Emerging Mormon Feminism.* Salt Lake City, 1992.

Hardy, B. Carmon. *Solemn Covenant: The Mormon Polygamous Passage.* Urbana, 1992.

Leone, Mark P. *Roots of Modern Mormonism.* Cambridge, Mass., 1979.

Lieberson, Goddard, producer. *The Mormon Pioneers.* Columbia Records Legacy Collection. New York, 1965.

Madsen, Carol Cornwall. *In Their Own Words: Women and the Story of Nauvoo.* Salt Lake City, 1994.

O'Dea, Thomas F. *The Mormons.* Chicago, 1957.

Paul, Erich Robert. *Science, Religion, and Mormon Cosmology.* Urbana, 1992.

Quinn, Michael D. *Early Mormonism and the Magic World View.* Salt Lake City, 1987.

———. *The Mormon Hierarchy: Origins of Power.* Salt Lake City, 1994.

Shipps, Jan. "The Latter-day Saints." *EARE* 1:649-68.

———. *Mormonism.* Urbana, 1985.

Taber, Susan Buhler. *Mormon Lives: A Year in the Elkton Ward.* Urbana, 1993.

Van Wagoner, Richard S. *Mormon Polygamy.* Salt Lake City, 1989.

Whittaker, David J. *Mormon Americana: A Guide to Sources and Collections in the United States.* Provo, Utah, 1995.

2. Christian Science and "Harmonialism"

Ahlstrom, Sydney E. "Mary Baker Eddy." In *Notable American Women,* edited by Edward T. James et al., 1:551-61. Cambridge, Mass., 1971.

Braden, Charles. *Spirits in Rebellion.* Dallas, 1963.

Ellwood, Robert S. "Occult Movements in America." *EARE* 2:711-22.

Fuller, Robert C. *Mesmerism and the American Cure of Souls.* Philadelphia, 1982.

George, Carol V. R. *God's Salesman: Norman Vincent Peale and the Power of Positive Thinking.* New York, 1993.

Gomes, Michael. *Theosophy in the Nineteenth Century: An Annotated Bibliography.* New York, 1994.

Gottschalk, Stephen. "Christian Science and Harmonialism." *EARE* 2:901-16.

———. *The Emergence of Christian Science in American Religious Life.* Berkeley, 1973.

Judah, J. Stillson. *The History and Philosophy of the Metaphysical Movements in America.* Philadelphia, 1967.

Meyer, Donald. *The Positive Thinkers.* Middletown, Conn., 1988.

Moore, R. Laurence. *In Search of White Crows: Spiritualism, Parapsychology, and American Culture.* New York, 1977.

Parker, Gail Thain. *Mind Cure in New England.* Hanover, N.H., 1973.

Peel, Robert. *Christian Science.* New York, 1958.

———. *Mary Baker Eddy.* 3 vols. New York, 1966, 1971, 1977.

Wessinger, Catherine, ed. *Women's Leadership in Marginal Religions.* Urbana, 1993.

3. Adventism

Bull, Malcolm, and Keith Lockhart. *Seeking a Sanctuary: Seventh-day Adventism and the American Dream.* New York, 1989.

Doan, Ruth Alden. *The Miller Heresy, Millennialism, and American Culture.* Philadelphia, 1987.

Gaustad, Edwin S., ed. *The Rise of Adventism.* New York, 1974.

Harrison, Barbara Grizzuti. *Visions of Glory: A History and Memory of the Jehovah's Witnesses.* New York, 1978.

Knight, George R. *Millennial Fever and the End of the World.* Boise, Idaho, 1993.

Land, Gary. *Adventism in America.* Grand Rapids, Mich., 1986.

Lippy, Charles H. "Millennialism and Adventism." *EARE* 2:831-44.

Moorhead, James H. "Searching for the Millennium in America." *Princeton Seminary Bulletin,* new ser., 8, no. 2 (1987): 17-33.

Numbers, Ronald L. *Prophetess of Health: A Study of Ellen G. White.* New York, 1976.

Numbers, Ronald L., and Jonathan M. Butler, eds. *The Disappointed: Miller and Millenarianism in the Nineteenth Century.* Bloomington, Ind., 1987.

Penton, M. James. *Apocalypse Delayed: The Story of the Jehovah's Witnesses.* Toronto, 1985.

Rogerson, Alan. *Millions Now Living Will Never Die: A Study of Jehovah's Witnesses.* London, 1969.

Rowe, David L. *Thunder and Trumpets: Millerites and Dissenting Religion in Upstate New York, 1800-1850.* Atlanta, Ga., 1985.

[See also section C and section R, subsection 9.]

4. Restorationism

Harrell, David Edwin, Jr. *Quest for a Christian America: The Disciples of Christ and American Society to 1866.* Nashville, 1966.

———. "Restorationism and the Stone-Campbell Tradition." *EARE* 2:845-58.

———. *The Social Sources of Division in the Disciples of Christ, 1856-1900.* Nashville, 1973.

Hughes, Richard T., ed. *The American Quest for the Primitive Church.* Urbana, 1988.

Hughes, Richard T., and C. Leonard Allen, eds. *Illusions of Innocence: Protestant Primitivism in America, 1630-1875.* Chicago, 1988.

McAllister, Lester G., and William E. Tucker. *Journey in Faith: A History of the Christian Church (Disciples of Christ).* St. Louis, 1975.

Tristano, Richard M. *The Origins of the Restoration Movement.* Atlanta, Ga., 1988.

Williams, D. Newell. *A Case Study of Mainstream Protestantism: The Disciples' Relation to American Culture, 1880-1989.* Grand Rapids, Mich., 1991.

5. Communitarian Societies

Andrews, Edward Deming. *The People Called Shakers.* New York, 1963. (See also numerous other titles by Andrews.)

Carden, Maren Lockwood. *Oneida.* Baltimore, 1969.

Fogarty, Robert S. *All Things New: American Communes and Utopian Movements, 1860-1914.* Chicago, 1990.

Foster, Lawrence. *Religion and Sexuality: Three American Communal Experiments of the Nineteenth Century.* New York, 1981.

———. *Women, Family, and Utopia: Communal Experiments of the Shakers, the Oneida Community, and the Mormons.* Syracuse, N.Y., 1991.

Hayden, Dolores. *Seven American Utopias.* Cambridge, Mass., 1976.

Humez, Jean M., ed. *Mother's First-Born Daughters: Early Shaker Writings on Women and Religion.* Bloomington, Ind., 1993.

Kanter, Rosabeth Moss. *Commitment and Community.* Cambridge, Mass., 1972.

Lippy, Charles H. "Communitarianism." *EARE* 2:858-74.

Patterson, Daniel. *The Shaker Spiritual.* Princeton, 1979.

Promey, Sally M. *Spiritual Spectacles: Vision and Image in Mid-Nineteenth-Century Shakerism.* Bloomington, Ind., 1993.

Terri, Salli, arranger. *Music of the Shakers.* Pleiades Records. Carbondale, Ill., n.d.

Thomas, Robert David. *The Man Who Would Be Perfect: John Humphrey Noyes and the Utopian Impulse.* Philadelphia, 1977.

W. "CULTS," NEW RELIGIONS, AND THE NEW AGE

Adler, Margot. *Drawing Down the Moon: Witches, Druids, Goddess-Worshippers, and Other Pagans in America Today.* Boston, 1986.

Editors of *Body Mind Spirit.* *The New Age Catalogue.* Magazine. New York, 1988.

Bromley, David G., and Larry D. Shinn, eds. *Krishna Consciousness in the West.* Lewisburg, Pa., 1989.

Brown, Michael F. *The Channeling Zone.* Cambridge, Mass., 1997.

Chidester, David. *Salvation and Suicide: An Interpretation of Jim Jones, the Peoples Temple, and Jonestown.* Bloomington, Ind., 1988.

Chryssides, George D. *The Advent of Sun Myung Moon.* New York, 1991.

Daner, Francine Jeanne. *The American Children of Krsna.* New York, 1976.

Downton, James V., Jr. *Sacred Journeys: The Conversion of Young Americans to Divine Light Mission.* New York, 1979. .

Ellwood, Robert S. *Alternative Altars.* Chicago, 1979.

————. *The Eagle and the Rising Sun: Americans and the New Religions of Japan.* Philadelphia, 1974.

————. *Eastern Spirituality in America.* New York, 1987.

————. *The 60s Spiritual Awakening.* New Brunswick, N.J., 1994.

Ellwood, Robert S., and Harry B. Partin. *Religious and Spiritual Groups in Modern America.* 2d ed. Englewood Cliffs, N.J., 1988.

Fitzgerald, Frances. "Rajneeshpuram." In Fitzgerald, *Cities on a Hill,* pp. 247-82. New York, c. 1981, 1983, 1986.

Hall, John R. *Gone from the Promised Land: Jonestown in American Cultural History.* New Brunswick, N.J., 1987.

Judah, J. Stillson. *Hare Krishna and the Counterculture.* New York, 1974.

Lewis, James R., and J. Gordon Melton, eds. *Perspectives on the New Age.* Albany, N.Y., 1992.

Mickler, Michael. *The Unification Church in America: A Bibliography and Research Guide.* New York, 1987.

Palmer, Susan Jean. *Moon Sisters, Krishna Mothers, Rajneesh Lovers: Women's Roles in New Religions.* Syracuse, N.Y., 1994.

Robbins, Thomas, and Dick Anthony. "'Cults' in the Late Twentieth Century." *EARE* 2:741-54.

Roszak, Theodore. *The Making of a Counter Culture.* Garden City, N.Y., 1969.

Shupe, Anson D., and David G. Bromley. *The New Vigilantes.* Beverly Hills, 1980.

Tipton, Steven M. *Getting Saved from the Sixties.* Berkeley, 1982.

Zaretsky, Irving, and Mark Leone, eds. *Religious Movements in Contemporary America.* Princeton, 1974.

Index